Implementing Excellence in Diversity, Equity, and Inclusion

A Handbook for Academic Libraries

Edited by

Corliss Lee and Brian Lym

with Tatiana Bryant, Jonathan Cain,
and Kenneth Schlesinger

Association of College
and Research Libraries
*A division of the American
Library Association*

Chicago, Illinois 2022

The paper used in this publication meets the minimum requirements of American National Standard for Information Sciences–Permanence of Paper for Printed Library Materials, ANSI Z39.48-1992. ∞

Library of Congress Control Number: 2022930903

Dedication

This book is dedicated to one of our contributors, Latanya Jenkins, who passed away in April 2021. We hope that this book honors her scholarship and her contributions to academic librarianship.

Contents

SECTION I: RECRUITMENT, RETENTION AND PROMOTION

SECTION VI: ASSESSMENT

Foreword

Perhaps not since the civil rights era has such keen attention been paid to issues related to diversity, equity, inclusion (DEI), accessibility, belonging, and engagement. This attention—at least since May of 2020—has surfaced with an unprecedented urgency in a wide range of professional sectors and in society at large. In the library and information science (LIS) field, while many professional conferences were being forced to transition to online/virtual formats, a number focused on DEI-related themes in programming, while others have added evaluation rubrics concerning the degree to which program and paper proposals address those topics. Several special, DEI-focused issues of prestigious journals have been published or are in process at the time of release of this monograph. And, although the thematic focus on much of the materials and discussion has been on racial equity—especially since the murder of George Floyd in May of 2020— recent social and political movements have provided significant opportunity for "airtime" across a wide range of issues and priorities. In fact, leaders, scholars, practitioners and others who track the literature and discourse across the range of topics may wonder why yet another collection of essays on DEI-related topics is needed. What is the value of yet more research at the point of intersection of LIS and diversity, especially when the corpus is so rich? Haven't the topics seen treatment to a point of universal understanding, if not saturation in published literature, conference presentations, and other dissemination venues? If topics such as racial or gender equity have surfaced in even high-profile political races, might that be an indicator of a universal familiarity with and expertise about the range of topics?

Perhaps what the confluence of the global pandemic with the world-wide racial awakening has done is afforded the opportunity for even experts in diversity, equity, and inclusion to rethink their perspectives, their assumptions, and their interpretations of social and political realities and phenomena. This has occurred to the extent that terms and phrases such as "systemic racism," "intersectionality," and "non-binary gender (and other) identity" are referenced in the daily news broadcasts as well as debated by pundits, social scientists, and everyday citizens. The presumption here, of course, is that there exists a universal understanding of how these terms are defined, what their implications are for social interactions and social systems, and most importantly what their impacts may be on communities affected by the issues such as minoritized or racialized individuals, as well as those not. But is that presumption correct? An even informal scan of news outlets across the political spectrum would lead one to great confusion regarding the very definitions of terms and phrases such as "critical race theory," as well as assessments as to veracity and value that these and other theories and analyses bring to contemporary life. Further, many of these terms and related discussions, at least in the media, have led to political and social polarities that may be unprecedented. So then, again, what value does yet another monograph of this nature bring to the discourse? Will the contents herein bring new perspectives to the conversation that could transform one's thinking, or provide behavioral or organization development models that can lead to substantive and enduring change for institutions willing to follow similar paths?

To answer this question, one can reflect on the writing of two giants in the fields of organization development and diversity, Judith Katz and Frederick Miller. In their seminal article "The Path from Exclusive Club to Inclusive Organization," the authors offer an analogy for organizational diversity based on chemical principles in metallurgy, where materials such as iron are made stronger and more malleable with alloys of carbon and nickel.[1] In other words, the addition and melding of diverse metals makes the native/original metal stronger, more durable, and more useful to the enterprise. In this same way, the diversity of perspectives presented within this publication will build on the reader's existing knowledge to bring nuances and alternative approaches to these enduring, seemingly intractable challenges within the LIS profession and within society. Of course, it is unreasonable to expect that readers will agree with every interpretation of data or every analysis presented. Adult learning is maximized, and this content will be best leveraged when one takes the time and effort to examine where data presented conflicts with the knowledge that one may have about a topic, thus challenging assumptions that may be long-held, or based on observations that may have been colored by other biases or prejudices. It takes courage and generosity to do so, but the result may be profound.

As you engage with this publication and the multiple topics presented—some familiar, some new—I invite you to approach the numerous essays with a mind open to growth and renewed understanding but recognizing that a certain amount of skepticism can be healthy. Although readers of this publication are likely to be members of the same choir and dedicated to the same quality of artistry and meaning-making, we must remember that even accomplished choirs must study and rehearse. They must explore the nuances of the score and understand the complexity of how their vocal lines harmonize (and sometimes create dissonance) with other vocal or instrumental parts. Choir members must acknowledge when their vocal lines are providing the melody to the composition or when their part is complementary as harmony. Choir members must study and tend to the intricacies of dynamics; knowing when sound must be strong and forceful and when they must taper to the quietest pianissimo. And, of course, each choir member must acknowledge and perform the beats and measures of rest; that is, moments when they must remain silent, while still providing the supportive energy needed to fully realize (i.e., perform) the musical composition. Unlike a musical composition, however, the path to creating a more just and equitable profession and society does not conclude at the double bars at the end of the score. The work continues and must change as new perspectives, empirical data, and analyses bring new meaning and hope to the work. Although the contemporary landscape might feel, to many, as particularly challenging, we must maintain a sense of hope that these perspectives and efforts will bring substantive and enduring change to academic libraries and to the communities in which we live.

—Mark A. Puente

Associate Dean for Organizational Development, Inclusion, and Diversity
Purdue University Libraries and School of Information Studies

Notes

1. Katz, Judith and Frederick Miller. "The Path from Exclusive Club to Inclusive Organization: A Developmental Process," The Kaleel Jamison Consulting Group, 2007. Accessed December 21, 2021, https://www.mcds.org/uploaded/Campus_and_Community/CC365/The_Path_from_Exclusive_Club_to_Inclusive_Organization.pdf.

Bibliography

Katz, Judith and Frederick Miller. "The Path from Exclusive Club to Inclusive Organization: A Developmental Process." The Kaleel Jamison Consulting Group, 2007. Accessed December 21, 2021. https://www.mcds.org/uploaded/Campus_and_Community/CC365/The_Path_from_Exclusive_Club_to_Inclusive_Organization.pdf.

Preface

We started this book project in early 2019, which seems about a century ago. We recruited coeditors, sent out a call for proposals, evaluated and selected proposals, and started receiving drafts of chapters.

And then the world fell apart. A global pandemic with a stunning death toll, the police killings of George Floyd and other unarmed Black Americans, and a bitterly contested election with our very system of democracy hanging in the balance were only some of the horrors we faced in 2020. Everything changed—but in fact the pandemic showed us that nothing had changed at all—systemic inequities in income, health care, worker security, housing, food, education, and indeed all aspects of life were only worsened by the pandemic, but they had been there all along.

Most colleges and universities and their libraries were shut down, doing their best to educate and support students remotely, though it required redesigning a lot of what we do on the fly. Higher education was in crisis. Carving out the time to work on the book was more difficult than ever. Among our coeditors and contributing authors, there were changes to job descriptions, new jobs, illnesses, sick relatives, and, tragically, one death.

Our desire to contribute to real change regarding diversity, equity, and inclusion (DEI) in the world of academic libraries—the purpose of the book—was stronger than ever. We had set out to gather practical examples of projects that academic librarians could undertake now. Our conviction that our original framework would be useful was shaken at times—in the face of everything going on, would anything we could do really make a difference?

As we read and reread contributed chapters, we were deeply moved by the determination, creativity, and commitment to social justice demonstrated by the authors. Some were able to harness the energy from a campus crisis or a national reckoning to start the process of change in their libraries. Others took advantage of collegial networks or created new networks. Many sought to reeducate themselves and their colleagues. And some took hold of everyday library activities and tried to change them in the service of equity for library workers and users.

It was not until we heard Tressie McMillan Cottom deliver the ACRL 2021 opening keynote address that we realized there was a name for what we were doing: "pragmatic hope—'having a set of beliefs and ideas and knowing from the outset that you are going to fall short of them,' but figuring out how to try anyway…. 'Pragmatic hope is about translating those big ideas—human-centered, ethical, fair, just—what does that look like on Tuesday at 5?'"[1]

Many library workers are committed to transforming libraries into change agents for social justice. Every library is in a different place when it comes to equity, some further along than others, which means that each library and library worker has a different set of tools available to them. Some of us are dreaming of wide-scale change, and some of us are hoping for small wins. We hope this book offers ideas for both.

Note

1. Tressie McMillan Cottom, quoted in Lisa Peet, "Keynoter Tressie McMillan Cottom Talks Human-Centered Data Rights and Pragmatic Hope | ACRL 2021," *Library Journal*, April 14, 2021, https://www.libraryjournal.com/?detailStory=Keynoter-Tressie-McMillan-Cottom-Talks-Human-Centered-Data-Rights-and-Pragmatic-Hope-ACRL-2021

Bibliography

Peet, Lisa. "Keynoter Tressie McMillan Cottom Talks Human-Centered Data Rights and Pragmatic Hope | ACRL 2021." *Library Journal*, April 14, 2021. https://www.libraryjournal.com/?detailStory=Keynoter-Tressie-McMillan-Cottom-Talks-Human-Centered-Data-Rights-and-Pragmatic-Hope-ACRL-2021.

Acknowledgments

We thank our coeditors—Tatiana Bryant, Jonathan Cain, and Kenneth Schlesinger—for their insight, close reading, and advice, and we must thank Jonathan for suggesting the concept of a handbook. We are indebted to Erin Nevius of ACRL for her extraordinary patience, wisdom, and kindness in guiding first-time editors through this challenging process during a surrealistically difficult time.

We thank all of our contributors for somehow balancing their regular work, their DEI work, and the onslaught of our suggested edits, all at the same time.

We also thank all of the library workers and authors who have been doing work in this area for years; we are definitely standing on the shoulders of giants!

We acknowledge, with sadness, the impact of COVID-19 on library workers and library patrons everywhere.

Corliss: I must thank all of my colleagues at the UC Berkeley Library, past and present, who have taught me so much about library work, especially my warm and supportive colleagues in the Instruction Services Division. Without Brian Lym, my longtime friend and coeditor, I might not have found the library field at all, and without Ellen Meltzer, my first boss, I might not still be at Berkeley. Thanks also to my husband, Hal Jordy, who lived with this project as long as I did and learned not to ask about deadlines.

> UC Berkeley sits on the territory of Huichin, the ancestral and unceded land of the Chochenyo Ohlone, the successors of the historic and sovereign Verona Band of Alameda County. This land was and continues to be of great importance to the Ohlone people. We recognize that every member of the Berkeley community has benefited, and continues to benefit, from the use and occupation of this land since the institution's founding in 1868. Consistent with our values of community and diversity, we have a responsibility to acknowledge and make visible the university's relationship to Native peoples.

By offering this Land Acknowledgement, we affirm Indigenous sovereignty and will work to hold the University of California, Berkeley, more accountable to the needs of American Indian and Indigenous peoples.

—*Borrowed with thanks from the UC Berkeley Native American Student Development Office*

Brian: I deeply acknowledge the very diverse librarians and library staff who have mentored me throughout my career. This book is a tribute to their generosity and encouragement, which have sustained my commitment to academic librarianship as my life's calling. I especially recognize the mentorship of the late Norma Kobzina, UC Berkeley Library, and the late Cynthia Clark, Adelphi University Libraries.

Introduction

With *Implementing Excellence in Diversity, Equity, and Inclusion: A Handbook for Academic Libraries*, we intend to capture emerging practices that demonstrate ways academic libraries and librarians can work to create more equitable and representative institutions. The collection of chapters here comprises practical guidance for academic libraries seeking approaches to improving workforce diversity, equity, and inclusion (DEI).

A leading premise of this book is that implementation of DEI initiatives in libraries is dependent on leveraging existing resources available within their parent institutions. Our original framework for organizing was based on the American Association of College and Universities (AACU) model for implementing DEI initiatives in higher education.[1] This institution-wide approach posits that the implementation of inclusive excellence must consider organizational structures and behavior, which must be understood within a five-dimensional framework: systemic (campus relationships with the external environment), bureaucratic/structural (formal structures within a campus), collegial (faculty), political (power dynamics), and symbolic (use of symbolic strategies). However, the chapters of this book are evidence of a more nuanced model for understanding how and why diversity, equity, and inclusion efforts succeed for academic libraries and the institutional changes that are necessary.

Work within Existing University Structures

Academic libraries have indeed leveraged and deployed their institutions' resources to effect DEI improvements in their workforce through a range of measures—from recruitment and hiring, mentoring, and professional development to large scale strategic planning for organizational change and assessment.

Some libraries have leveraged existing institutional structures to work toward implementing systemic solutions while responding to the activism of the university community. Renna Redd, Alydia Sims, and Tara Weekes, in "Framework for Change: Utilizing a University-wide Diversity Strategic Planning Process for an Academic Library," describe how Clemson University Libraries' diversity strategic plan was mandated by the university administration and shaped by the university's strategic plan. The Clemson initiative was particularly urgent, given racially motivated incidents at the university that prompted campus community protests and the recognition that fundamental systemic changes had to be implemented in the library to support diversity, equity, and inclusion. Saira Raza, Melissa Hackman, Hannah Rutledge, Jina DuVernay, Nik Dragovic, and Erica Bruchko's chapter, "The Making of Emory Libraries' Diversity, Equity, and Inclusion Committee: A Case Study," outlines how Emory Libraries' DEI initiative, led by a committee charged with implementing a wide-ranging plan addressing diversity, equity, and inclusion in the libraries' programs, policies, hiring, workforce training, communications, space planning, and assessment, drew from the resources of other offices at the university focused on diversity, equity, and inclusion. Emory's initiative, like that at Clemson, responded to demands by the Black students at Emory University for racial justice.

Canadian librarians have responded to a national call to action with ambitious and substantive programs. In "Journeying to Accountability: Labor and Responses of Settler Knowledge Institutions to Indigenous Communities and Issues," Oy Lein "Jace" Harrison, Jamie Lee Morin, Desmond Wong, and May Chan profile the University of Toronto Library's wide-ranging program to deeply engage and educate staff about First Nations issues, a program informed and guided by the university's Elders and Indigenous Student Services. The UTL initiative, driven by mandates of the Truth and Reconciliation Commission of Canada (TRC) to redress cultural genocide of Indigenous communities that occurred through the Indian Residential School System, included cultural competency training, relationship building with Indigenous community members, redressing metadata practices, an environmental scan of Canadian library policy and practices related to Indigenous populations, and development of an Indigenous Library Services tool kit. Similarly, Camille Callison and Lyle Ford's chapter, "An Introductory Indigenous Cultural Competency Training Program in the Academic Environment," underscores the primary role of the University of Manitoba's Indigenous Elders and Cultural Advisor and the Indigenous Student Centre director in development of a training module aimed to educate library staff about an Indigenous worldview and enable staff to form relationships with the UM Indigenous community. UMI's effort was also prompted by the Truth and Reconciliation Commission of Canada, especially with respect to the TRC's specific mandate that all government employees be educated about the history of Aboriginal peoples.

Some chapters highlight collaborations between libraries and campus entities to their mutual benefit. In "A Journey to Hiring with Heart: A Case Study on Implementing Leading Practices in Inclusive Hiring" at Grand Valley State University, Annie Bélanger, Sarah Beaubien, Scott Ayotte, and Abigail Smathers describe how the library's executive team collaborated with the campus's Division of Equity and Inclusion to create an inclusive hiring process, which then was formally adopted and implemented library-wide. Latanya N. Jenkins and Elizabeth L. Sweet at Temple University profile their library's radical compassion and cultural humility workshops for library staff in "Embracing a Culture of Humility, Diversity, and Inclusion: A Case Study of an Academic Library's Radical Compassion Programming." These workshops were informed and shaped by campus-wide training sponsored by the faculty senate Committee on the Status of Faculty of Color and the Academic Center for Research in Diversity.

Creating New Processes and Structures for the Library and Institution

Other chapters illustrate that—in the absence of clear and well-defined formal institutional structures—academic librarians have made grassroots efforts to create processes and structures for DEI initiatives where none existed within their library or institution. In turn, some of these grassroots actions triggered or reinforced and strengthened nascent DEI efforts in external offices in wider institutions. Relevant chapters here include those focused on recruitment, training, and professional development. With regard to recruitment, Amy Tureen's "Transitioning from Passive to Active Diversity Recruitment Strategies: A Case Study" documents a groundswell movement starting with an individual librarian who spearheaded a retooling of the University of Nevada, Las Vegas, University Libraries' recruitment process, which was eventually codified and adopted by University Libraries administration. With regard to grassroots efforts leading to institutionalized workforce training, Melanie Bopp's contribution, "Your Workforce Is More Than You Think: Looking at Diversity and Inclusion with Student Workers," outlines how those responsible for Northeastern University Library's student hiring and training approached the university's Office of Division and Inclusion for assistance with developing a student workforce program. The Office of Division and Inclusion, in response, promoted the library's diversity training for student workers to other departments of the university. In "Mentoring and Diversity," Barbara Lewis, Matt Torrence, Tomaro Taylor, and Meghan Cook document how a volunteer committee of library faculty and staff at the University of South Florida, Tampa Campus, formed and created the blueprint for a libraries-wide mentoring program incorporating diversity goals for all levels of employees. Katherine Kapsidelis and Elizabeth Galoozis, in their chapter "Introducing Cultural Competency in Libraries: A Case Study in Grassroots Professional Development," describe how an ad hoc group within the University of Southern California Libraries responded to a high-level call from the university and library administration for diversity and inclusion in the libraries and developed an internal training program for all library employees from the ground up. These examples show how individual libraries and librarians themselves initiated DEI workforce improvements and, in so doing, facilitated development of library-wide or institution-wide changes.

Promotion, Professional Development, and Representation

Also included are emerging methods and approaches for promotion and professional development. Kimberley Bugg's research on advancement of librarians of color from mid-level into library dean roles, summarized in "Bare Witness: Library Leaders of Color Tell Their Stories of Advancing into Senior Leadership Positions," points to specific recommendations that organizations can implement to support promotion of librarians of color into executive leadership. Michelle Villagran's chapter, "Cultural Intelligence in Academic Libraries," explains the concept of cultural intelligence and asserts that it should be a focus of professional development in academic libraries for diversity training.

Not all communities are individually represented in this book, but two chapters remind us to complicate our understanding of identity and what it means to have a diverse workforce. Sally Stieglitz makes the case that academic libraries should recognize employment discrimination against older women applying for full-time academic librarian positions in "Gendered Ageism as a Barrier to Tenure-Track Librarianship." Kenneth Litwak's contribution, "Desperately Seeking Librarians with a Disability," explores the apparent lack of full-time academic librarians with visible disabilities and suggests through survey research that ableism is a discriminatory factor in hiring of academic librarians.

Internal and External Politics and Communication

The other primary factors in the AACU model for implementing DEI change pertain broadly to institutional factors related to collegial networks, politics, and communications. Our chapters include evidence of both internal and external collegial and social-political dynamics that can affect success of DEI implementation in academic libraries. In "Bridging the Gap between Residencies and Retention: A Case Study of the University of North Carolina at Greensboro's Diversity Resident Librarian Program and the Inception of the Library Diversity Institute," LaTesha Velez underscores the value of UNC Greensboro's development in collaboration with the ACRL Diversity Alliance of a cohort model for improving the experience of diversity residents at individual libraries, as well as fostering a professional network for the cohort members. Shannon Jones, Kelsa Bartley, Melissa DeSantis, Ryan Harris, Don Jason, and Dede Rios outline how Medical Library Association resources were deployed to foster dialogue and awareness of implicit bias among librarians at multiple institutions in their contribution, "Braving Our Blind Spots: Using a Virtual Book Discussion Group to Continue Conversations on Implicit Bias in Libraries." V. Dozier, Sandra Enimil, and Adebola Fabiku's chapter, "Critical Analysis of ARL Member Institutions' Diversity Statements," considers the way ARL libraries communicate their commitment to diversity.

Assessment and Accountability

Besides all these contributions related specifically to the AACU five-dimensional framework for implementing DEI excellence, the final section of our book focuses on overall assessment of diversity, equity, and inclusion initiatives in academic libraries. As emphasized in the AACU model, it is through the lens of assessment that the framework for implementing DEI change in libraries can be examined. However, unlike the general performance scorecard assessment presented in the AACU model, our contributions pertaining to assessment are specific to academic libraries. In "Assessing DEI Efforts in Academic Libraries: More Than a Body Count," Kawanna Bright describes the continuing development of a DEI assessment instrument she designed to holistically measure academic libraries' DEI efforts. The chapter is also a preview of a soon-to-be- released finalized DEI assessment resource based on her original pilot. Toni Anaya and Charlene Maxey Harris's summative chapter, "Diversity, Equity and Inclusion Plans and Programs in ARL Libraries," comparatively analyzes the outcomes of two surveys conducted in 2010 and in 2017 on diversity plans and programs in ARL librar- ies. The authors underscore how ARL libraries' DEI efforts are increasingly a response to larger social justice and political movements, especially in the 2020s.

In the end, the original framework for this book merits reconsideration. Academic librarians often make use of systemic, bureaucratic, political, collegial, and symbolic dimensions of organizational behavior to achieve their diversity, equity, and inclusion goals, but many of the authors included in this book find themselves pushing back at the systems they are employing in ways small and large. This is most obvious in section V, on Organizational Change, in which authors are leveraging their organizational structures in order to change them from within. The chapters on cultural competency, cultural humility, cultural intelligence, and implicit bias training all seek to fundamentally change our concepts of ourselves and others. The chapters focusing on hiring, retention, and promotion remind us that, although the library field has failed to diversify its ranks decades after establishing this as a goal, we must continue to try to hire, retain, and promote the change we want to see in the world regardless of existing structures and systems, and to improve those structures and systems for the future.

Note

1.   Damon A. Williams, Joseph B. Berger, and Shederick A. McClendon, *Toward a Model of Inclusive Excellence and Change in Postsecondary Institutions* (Washington, DC: Associa- tion of American Colleges and Universities, 2005), https://www.aacu.org/sites/default/files/ files/mei/williams_et_al.pdf.

Bibliography

Williams, Damon A., Joseph B. Berger, and Shederick A. McClendon. *Toward a Model of Inclusive Excellence and Change in Postsecondary Institutions*. Washington, DC: Association of American Colleges and Universities, 2005. https://www.aacu.org/sites/default/files/files/mei/williams_et_al.pdf.

SECTION I
Recruitment, Retention and Promotion

CHAPTER 1

Transitioning from Passive to Active Diversity Recruitment Strategies

A Case Study

Amy Tureen

The *2017 ALA Demographic Study* reveals that a significant majority of credentialed librarians, 86.7 percent, identify as white, with only 13.3 percent of the profession identifying as any racial or ethnic minority.[1] The numbers are even more stark in the area of disability status, with only 3.7 percent of credentialed respondents in the same survey identifying as having "limited" physical ability.[2] While significant time, research, and funding support has been dedicated to increasing diversity within the profession both before and after the release of "Diversity Counts" and its updates,[3] a great deal of the available research on the topic emphasizes major initiatives, funding opportunities, or scholarship programs designed to address the perceived "pipeline problem."[4] Less attention has been paid to the efforts of individual institutions, particularly efforts spearheaded by individuals who do not occupy upper-level administrative positions. This chapter will address initiatives at a single institution to increase the recruitment of

diverse candidates between 2017 and 2019. Most of the initiatives described originated from individuals in middle management or nonmanagement roles, illustrating that while moving an organization forward in the area of diversity recruitment requires intentionality, it does not necessarily require organizational leaders to spearhead change.

This case study explicitly examines changes to recruitment efforts over a two-year period. In doing so, the author is aware that this chapter may be perceived by some as an exercise in diversification only and acknowledges Clara Chu's 1999 assertion that "representation alone cannot solve the problem of white privilege in LIS any more than (self-) congratulatory visions of inclusive multiculturalism can defeat historical legacies and institutional manifestations of racial discrimination."[5] Given this, the author is keen to note that this chapter serves only as a record of how their home institution proactively sought to increase the presence of diverse candidates within its applicant pools and the organic nature in which changes were envisioned, recommended, and enacted within the specific context of recruitment. It is not intended to imply that the presence of diverse individuals indicates that a state of equality has been achieved or that recruitment can be permanently uncoupled from concerns associated with retention, equity, or true inclusion.

University of Nevada, Las Vegas, and the UNLV University Libraries

Established in 1957, the University of Nevada, Las Vegas, is a large metropolitan research university located only 1.7 miles away from the world-famous Las Vegas Strip. Recently designated R-1, it serves approximately 30,000 students[6] and has been identified as both the best college in Nevada for LGBTQ students and among the most diverse colleges in the nation,[7] with 61.1 percent of students identifying as racial or ethnic minorities.[8] Additionally, UNLV has been designated both a Hispanic-Serving Institution and an Asian American and Native American Pacific Islander Serving Institution. UNLV employs 1,190 tenured and tenure-track faculty,[9] but this population is less racially and ethnically diverse than the students that it serves.

The UNLV University Libraries consists of one main library and four branch libraries spread across both the Maryland Parkway campus (main campus) and the growing Shadow Lane Campus (medical campus) on the city's north end. In addition to numerous student employees, the University Libraries employs 135 individuals in tenure-track academic faculty, non-tenure-track administrative faculty, and classified professional roles.[10] While more ethnically and racially diverse than the national averages defined in "Diversity Counts," the employee pool of the UNLV University Libraries is still majority white and fails to fully reflect the diversity of the student body that it serves.

Enhancing Existing Passive Recruitment Tools—Refining Job Ads and Qualifications

In fall of 2017 Amy Tureen (head, Library Liaison Program) was charged with drafting advertisement material for an upcoming music and dance librarian vacancy in her department. Because she was new to the organization, Tureen was provided with text from past vacancies and instructed to adapt the content as she saw fit. In addition to providing the expected updates to portions of the job ads that detailed the assigned position responsibilities, Tureen elected to update and enhance language in the pre-populated Commitment to Diversity subsection appended to all UNLV University Libraries advertisements. Tureen reviewed similar statements found at other intuitions both within the Greater Wester Library Alliance (GWLA), of which the UNLV University Libraries is a member,[11] as well as key Canadian institutions such as the University of Toronto, the University of Calgary, the University of Alberta, the University of British Columbia, and the University of Victoria, which Tureen identified as being particularly progressive in their diversity statement construction.[12] Based on this comparison, Tureen adapted the Commitment to Diversity boilerplate statement to note that the UNLV Libraries "especially welcomes applications from women, persons of color, persons with disabilities, persons of minority sexual orientation or gender identity, and others who contribute to diversification."[13] In that same music and dance librarian advertisement, Tureen also included a preferred qualification that was new to UNLV Libraries advertisements. The new qualification called for "competence and sensitivity in working at a university in which students, faculty, and staff are broadly diverse with regard to many facets of identity, including but not limited to gender, ethnicity, nationality, sexual orientation, and religion."[14]

Subsequent searches conducted by Tureen, Amanda Melilli (head, Teacher Development and Resources Library), Melissa Bowles-Terry (head, Educational Indicatives), and Mellanye Lackey (director, Health Sciences Library) resulted in an organic, undirected replication and refinement of Tureen's new language. By January of 2019 nearly all advertisements for vacancies in the UNLV University Libraries replicated the new Commitment to Diversity language. Meanwhile, the competence and sensitivity requirement had been updated from its 2017 structure to call for "competence and sensitivity in working at a university in which students, faculty, and staff are highly diverse with regard to many facets of identity, including but not limited to gender, ethnicity, nationality, sexual orientation, *income, level of educational attainment,* and religion [emphasis added]."[15] Additionally, the qualification rapidly transitioned first from the "preferred qualifications" category to the "required qualifications" category and then rapidly ascended the list of required qualifications. So valued was the capacity to behave with competence and sensitivity in a diverse environment that in some cases it took primacy over even the ALA-accredited MLIS requirement that is universal to all UNLV University Libraries faculty postings. Anecdotal evidence indicates that these changes were valued by applicants, many of whom reflected positively on the inclusiveness of the language used in UNLV University Libraries job ads. The employee-driven changes, as well as applicants' positive feedback, were ultimately noted and codified by the UNLV University Libraries' Leadership Team, which formalized the changes of Tureen, Melilli, Bowles-Terry, Lackey, and others in a new and more inclusive job advertisement template that was finalized in mid-2019.[16]

During this same period, advertisements for the UNLV University Libraries began to feature significantly slimmed-down lists of required qualifications. This transition to being more conservative when quantifying the skill sets an incoming employee would be required to have upon arrival was largely driven by nonsupervisors, who used the mandatory faculty advertisement review process to question why some skills could not be learned on the job and advocated for job ads that would encourage a broader pool of applicants to apply. While the final text of all job ads remained in the hands of individual supervisors, comparisons of advertisement text before and after faculty review show that either refinement of qualifications overall or a transition of previously "required" qualifications to "preferred" qualifications occurred in the majority of advertisements.

From Passive to Active Hiring Practices—Getting Ahead of Potential Employee Concerns and Advertisement Locations

One of the most lamented challenges of recruitment at the University of Nevada, Las Vegas, is the belief that candidate preconceptions about or bias against the city of Las Vegas prevent people from applying. Turn-away data for job postings does not exist, much less turn-away data the reveals a candidate's personal reasons for declining to apply, but the fear of Las Vegas's reputation as "Sin City" still looms large among recruitment officers and search committees. Demonstrating within the confines of a one-to-two-page job announcement that Las Vegas consists of more than the 4.2 miles of casinos known colloquially as "The Strip" presents even more challenges. In 2018 Amy Tureen and Lateka Grays (hospitality and career services librarian) sought to address this challenge by developing a LibGuide focused on Las Vegas amenities and services beyond The Strip.

The "Living in Las Vegas" guide, as it was eventually titled, was originally intended to be shared with on-campus candidates for vacancies solely within the Library Liaison Program. It identified fourteen areas of potential interest to candidates who were considering relocation and provided both general information and links to further resources. Areas of focus included community engagement and volunteerism (see figure 1.1), Department of Motor Vehicles (DMV) resources, education, entertainment, fitness, food and beverage, government, hair care and grooming, health care, history, the Las Vegas Convention and Visitors Authority (LVCVA), local libraries, local news sources, and area neighborhoods.[17] In addition to providing significant resources that articulated life and leisure opportunities that did not center around gambling and resort hotels, Tureen and Grays also sought to identify resources that might be of interest to candidates from minority backgrounds and that gestured toward the diversity of the Las Vegas citizenry. These resources included everything from affinity organizations in the community (LGBTQ Center of Southern Nevada, Las Vegas Indian Center, Jewish Community Center of Southern Nevada, etc.) and on campus (Women's Council, Council of African-American Professionals, UNLV Latina/o Faculty Alliance, etc.), to salons that employed stylists familiar

FIGURE 1.1

The Community Engagement and Volunteerism page from the "Living in Las Vegas" LibGuide

with the unique needs of ethnic hair types or markets catering to the culinary needs to specific cultural communities.[18] While Tureen and Grays serve as the guide's principal authors, they incorporated a feedback process that enabled their colleagues to provide recommendations of further resources for inclusion in the guide.

As with the changes to text and diction in both the Commitment to Diversity statement and the associated competency requirements, the use of the "Living in Las Vegas" guide expanded organically from its original intended use and deployment. Upon becoming aware of the existence of the guide, other department heads requested permission to share the document with their on-campus candidates. After several requests, Tureen and Grays realized that with minimal adaptations, the guide could be shared universally. They extended this offer to Kim Kaplan (director, libraries human resources), who consented to include a link to the guide in the shared job announcement template. Concurrently, but not in collaboration with Tureen and Grays or each other, Mellanye Lackey and Jason Vaughan (division director, library technologies) were seeking to add copy to advertisements for their units that better communicated the livability of Las Vegas and reduce the emphasis on services associated with The Strip. Their text sought to instead emphasize Las Vegas's function as a culinary destination, the hub of a growing professional sports empire, and a place surrounded by national and state parks with year-round outdoor activity opportunities. The efforts of Vaughan and Lackey were combined with Tureen and Gray's guide to establish new benefits and amenities language:

> The Libraries provide generous support for individual professional development, and residents of Nevada enjoy no state income tax. Home to many major annual conventions, Las Vegas is one of the best-connected cities in America and the nearest major city to several of the nation's richest natural treasures. In addition to the world-renowned Las Vegas Strip providing a variety of culinary and entertainment opportunities, Las Vegas is home to five professional athletic organizations and continues to expand local cultural opportunities, including the internationally recognized Smith Center for the Performing Arts.
>
> To learn more about living in Las Vegas visit our guide at https://guides.library.unlv.edu/lasvegas/welcome.[19]

This new wording was formalized in the 2019 job advertisement template and now appears near the conclusion of all UNLV University Libraries job announcements.

With the job advertisement template changing and growing under the influence of multiple hands, it was unsurprising that attention swiftly turned to the topic of job advertisement placement. As with other elements of the search process, search committees and supervisors at the UNLV University Libraries have the benefit of significant latitude when identifying job advertisement placement opportunities. By default, all advertisements for faculty positions within the UNLV University Libraries are posted by human resources personnel on job lists maintained by HigherEdJobs.com, the Association of Research Libraries (ARL), the Nevada Library Association (NLA), the Greater Western Library Alliance (GWLA), the Mountain Plains Library Association (MPLA), REFORMA, the Black Caucus of the American Library Association (BCALA), and the Chinese American Librarians Association (CALA).[20] Search committees can also request that paid ads be posted to relevant specialized job listings as appropriate, such the Music Library Association, the Medical Library Association, the Special Libraries Association, and so on.[21] Additionally, all employees are encouraged to share notifications of job postings with likely candidates or through any professional e-mail discussion lists they may be members of.

Between 2017 and 2019 multiple UNLV University Libraries employees explored additional alternative approaches to increasing awareness of current job openings. Brittany Paloma Fiedler (teaching and learning librarian), Chelsea Heinbach (teaching and learning librarian), and Amy Tureen explored the use of Twitter to push advertisements using the library employment–related hashtags #libraryjobs #LISjobs, and #libjobs (see figure 1.2).

Amy Tureen
@ATureen

Come join my team at UNLV (most diverse university for undergraduates, per U.S. News & World Report) as our new Sciences Librarian! Tenure track, $65-68K, MLIS required by date of appointment (new & soon-to-be grads welcome!) higheredjobs.com/institution/de… #libraryjobs #LISjob #libjobs

11:21 AM · Aug 26, 2019 · Twitter Web App

ılı View Tweet activity

29 Retweets   **41** Likes

FIGURE 1.2
Posting on Twitter promoting a job opening at UNLV University Libraries

Some search committees also opted to make use of a tool developed by Twitter user @craftyhilary that provided swift access to ALA-accredited library school job lists and relevant contact people.[22] Using this tool, search committees at the UNLV University Libraries were able to, for the first time, make direct and intentional contact with recent and soon-to-be grads at intuitions across the US and Canada. This in turn bolstered support for transitioning the default requirement for candidates to have a completed ALA-accredited degree in hand at time of application to requiring a completed ALA-accredited degree by date of hire.

Efforts were also made to establish an approach to job announcement sharing that was less passive and went beyond the simple broadcasting of information. Fiedler began leveraging her role as an ALA Emerging Leader, Spectrum Scholar, and REFORMA member to craft job announcements on both Twitter and via e-mail discussion lists that invited interested parties to contact her to discuss her experiences as a person of color (POC) in the employ of both the University of Nevada, Las Vegas, and the UNLV University Libraries. Her actions articulated a need for the organization to consider the unique concerns diverse candidates may have and to potentially build opportunities for candidates to address those concerns early in the application process. Uncertainty arose, however, regarding how to develop such a system that did not necessitate diverse employees engaging in unpaid diversity, equity, and inclusion–related labor (emotional or otherwise), particularly labor that their non-diverse colleagues would not, and perhaps could not, be asked to do. As of publication, this question has yet to be answered and remains a topic of ongoing thoughtful consideration within the organization.

Proactive Hiring—Candidate Cultivation, Task Forces, and Next Steps

Employees of the UNLV University Libraries were quick to latch on to the idea that the recruitment of new employees, particularly those who prioritized diversity in workplace, must extend beyond the passive broadcasting of new openings and hiring opportunities. Moreover, they were aware that savvy would-be employees were increasingly at risk of regarding terms like *diversity*, *equity*, and *inclusion* as standard buzzwords within job descriptions and position announcements that did little to reflect an organization's true commitments. The UNLV

University Libraries would need to demonstrate its commitment to these values while engaging not only in active hiring processes but, indeed, in *proactive* hiring processes. This would necessitate identifying potential future hires who shared diversity, equity, and inclusion values and actively inviting them to participate in appropriate searches as they came open.

Diversity-focused conferences such as the Joint Conference of Librarians of Color 2018, IDEAL/Advancing Inclusion, Diversity, Equity, and Accessibility in Libraries and Archives 2019, and People of Color in Library and Information Science (POCinLIS) provided robust opportunities to identify library professionals who valued increasing diversity within the profession. So too did presentations, posters, and discussion sessions focused on diversity topics at larger, less narrowly themed conferences such as ALA Annual, ACRL, or ALA Midwinter. As before, efforts to utilize these spaces as combined conference locations and recruitment grounds initially began as individual efforts. Individual employees and conference attendees would identify potential candidates and share current openings or known future openings, exchange business cards, and follow up post-conference with job ad specifics, application deadlines, and updates to proposed search time lines. This model was effective but required individuals to either be well versed in all current openings or to prioritize vacancies in their home departments or divisions. To better ensure all UNLV University Libraries openings were represented regardless of the presence of an employee-advocate, a universal employment opportunities card (see figures 1.3 and 1.4) was developed and made available to all employees.

Double-sided, colorful, portable, and universal, the recruitment cards shifted some of the responsibility for follow-up onto the potential candidate, as well as facilitated more general recruitment to the organization at large, rather than in connection with specific roles. The cards also provided a physical memento of the recruitment interaction, something not offered with alternatives such as "I'm Hiring" badges or buttons that identify potential employers but render the recruitment pitch somewhat ephemeral.

UNLV University Libraries search teams and supervisors overseeing vacancies have also experimented with direct invitations to candidates either cultivated by themselves at a conference or recommended by others within the organization. Full transparency is recommended when inviting a candidate to apply directly, including clearly identifying the individual who has recommended the candidate. This provides the potential candidate with an easily identifiable contact from whom to

FIGURE 1.3
Employment opportunities card: front

FIGURE 1.4
Employment opportunities card: back

solicit more information, including personalized information regarding why the recommender felt the candidate may be a good fit for the position and organization. In addition to providing an obvious information pathway to the candidate, this approach may offset an imbalance of unpaid recruitment work that might otherwise fall to one or a small number of employees willing to answer questions.

In May of 2019 the UNLV University Libraries Leadership Team, responding to the growing upswell of individuals seeking to improve diversity recruitment and search processes on an ad hoc basis, charged the Equity and Inclusion Committee to launch three Diverse Recruitment Task Forces. In an article articulating the origin and work of the Equity and Inclusion Committee, Brittany Paloma Fiedler, Rosan Mitola, and James Cheng defined the purpose of each individual task force as follows:

- Task Force 1 was asked to conduct a literature review of current practices for hiring faculty and staff from underrepresented groups in academic libraries.

- Task Force 2 was asked to review current hiring policies and practices at UNLV and in the University Libraries.

- Task Force 3 was asked to gather data and information from recent University Libraries search committees and hires.[23]

Collectively, however, the task forces worked to capture the myriad approaches and uncelebrated processes individuals had enacted to further the recruitment of diverse personnel at the UNLV University Libraries. Further, these task forces sought to identify ways in which those individual processes could potentially be systematized to better ensure that all searches prioritized diverse recruitment strategies and approaches in the same way. These efforts were intended to enhance equity across all searches as well as to lessen the burden of unpaid labor that was disproportionately affecting those most dedicated to the cause.

As of early 2020, the combined report reflecting the findings of all three task forces is still under ongoing review by the Library Leadership Team. Those most interested in continuing to increase the diversity of the UNLV University Libraries employee pool are eagerly awaiting administrative response to the extensive list of proposed changes to existing recruitment policies. Many proposed changes emphasized not only relatively simple-to-enact process changes (e.g., a uniform requirement to share interview questions in advance, the insertion of candidate meetings with the Equity and Inclusion Committee or selected affinity groups, the establishment of an antibias monitor on all search committees, etc.) but also cost-heavy policy shifts to support the ongoing diversity, equity, and inclusion work of current and future employees. Some proposed policy changes included guaranteed additional funding beyond employees' annual professionalization budgets to select diversity-oriented conferences, a commitment for the UNLV University Libraries to serve as an official sponsor or host for diversity-oriented conferences, and a process by which the labor of employees heavily involved with diverse recruiting can be acknowledged financially.

These recommendations and those like them reflect the growing desire for the UNLV University Libraries to more generously acknowledge the work of individuals who promote organizational priorities. These recommendations should not be viewed, however, as an indication that the previously successful model of organic change is at an end. Rather, the process is cyclical. Much as changes to the competence and sensitivity qualification were edited, retooled, and replicated by individuals before being formalized into expected practice by human resources and leadership, so too some of the active and proactive processes developed by individuals are transitioning into a phase wherein they could potentially be established as organization-wide norms with the full weight of administrative expectation behind them. Codification of this previous work will then free its developers to identify a new area of focus for iterative improvement and allowing the cycle to continue indefinitely.

Tips for Employees of All Levels to Promote Diverse Hiring Practices

As is evident by the work of the employees of the UNLV University Libraries, envisioning and enacting change in organizational approaches to enhancing diversity recruitment processes do not need to live only with those empowered to establish an administrative mandate. Rather, this vital work is incumbent on employees of all levels regardless of their formal organizational power to enact change. Potential first steps for employees at a variety of levels are suggested below.

Actions for Employees without Hiring Responsibilities

- Participate in any available review process for job advertisements. Make suggestions for changes that help develop advertisements that are more inclusive and reflect your organization's diversity-related goals and values

- Take an active part in sharing information about current openings in your organization; share advertisements on your social media feeds and with e-mail discussion lists you are active in.
- Invite individuals whose work you admire to apply for open positions at your organization. Alternatively, forward recommendations for specific potential candidates to search committees or supervisors with current or upcoming openings.
- Offer to answer questions candidates may have about the organization despite not serving on the search committee. These conversations should be confidential and can be held outside of the confines of an on-campus interview.
- Request that your employer provide resources such as handouts or "we're hiring" buttons and information regarding current and upcoming searches to employees attending conferences so that you can participate in proactive recruitment.

Actions for Employees with Hiring Responsibilities

- Regularly review job advertisements for language that invites minoritized communities to apply and provides an accurate reflection of the equity, diversity, and inclusion values of your organization. Terminology changes rapidly, so commit to reviewing boilerplate advertisement text at least twice a year.
- Require search committees in your assigned areas to commit to best practices that reduce bias and seek to give candidates an equal footing. This can include using rubrics, distributing questions to candidates in advance, making use of a neutral third-part bias observer during search committee meetings, and so on.
- Commit to asking candidates about how they will support diversity and inclusion efforts at your institution if hired. Commit to asking versions of this question more than once and at all stages of the interview process to underline the importance of these values within your organization.

- Stay up to date on the best practices for hiring and decreasing implicit bias during the search process. As an employee with hiring responsibilities, it is your obligation to keep up to date on this topic and craft search processes that provide candidates with a fair and equitable search experience.
- Ensure that draft job advertisements in your area are open to comment and review by all employees. Take provided feedback seriously and adjust tone, word choice, and stated qualifications.

Actions for Employees with Administrative Authority

- Make increasing diversity a priority in both your organization's goal statements and planned budget expenditures. Provide funding for necessary cultural humility training, sponsor or host diversity-focused conferences, and underwrite travel and registration fees associated with diversity-focused conferences and learning opportunities.
- Honor the unpaid labor of employees who work beyond their assigned job duties in support of equity, diversity, and inclusion goals. If policies permit, pay people for their labor. If additional pay or funding is not available, publicly acknowledge their work. Consider recommending these individuals for awards so that their labor is not rendered invisible.
- Establish a committee focused on equity, diversity, and inclusion work. Meet with this committee regularly to discuss concerns, proposals, and so on. Active engagement with this committee and its work will communicate that diversity work is taken seriously by the very highest levels of administration.
- Participate in the candidate search process at all stages. This includes providing feedback to draft job ads, attending candidate presentations and Q&A sessions, and providing candidate feedback. Ask questions about how candidates will support diversity and inclusion initiatives and what goals in these areas are particularly important to them.
- Make yourself available to answer candidate questions, including very direct questions. Know how you will answer if a candidate asks specifically how you support minoritized candidates as well as what you hope to do in the future to support marginalized employees.

Notes

1. Kathy Rosa and Kelsey Henke, *2017 ALA Demographic Study* (Chicago: American Library Association, 2017), https://www.ala.org/tools/sites/ala.org.tools/files/content/Draft%20 of%20Member%20Demographics%20Survey%2001-11-2017.pdf.
2. Rosa and Henke, *2017 ALA Demographic Study*.
3. American Library Association, "Diversity Counts," last updated 2012, https://www.ala.org/ aboutala/offices/diversity/diversitycounts/divcounts.
4. Agnes K. Bradshaw, "Strengthening the Pipeline—Talent Management for Libraries: A Human Resources Perspective," in *Where Are All the Librarians of Color?* ed. Rebecca Hankins and Miguel Juarez (Sacramento, CA: Library Juice Press, 2015), 97–131.
5. Clara Chu, "Transformative Information Services: Uprooting Race Politics" (paper presented at the Black Caucus of the American Library Association Conference, Las Vegas, NV, July 19–22, 1999).
6. University of Nevada, Las Vegas, "Fall 2019 Official Enrollment Report—Final," accessed January 20, 2020, https://ir.unlv.edu/IAP/Files/Final%20NSHE%20Enrollment%20 Report%20-%20Fall%202019.aspx (page discontinued).
7. University of Nevada, Las Vegas, "UNLV Named Best College in Nevada for LGTBQ Students!" News Center, January 18, 2018, https://www.unlv.edu/about/highlights/best-ne-vada-lgbtq; University of Nevada, Las Vegas, "U.S. News & World Report: UNLV Most Diverse Campus in the Nation," News Center, September 12, 2017, https://www.unlv.edu/ news/release/us-news-world-report-unlv-most-diverse-campus-nation.
8. *US News and World Report*, "Campus Ethnic Diversity: National Universities," accessed December 14, 2019, https://www.usnews.com/best-colleges/rankings/national-universities/ campus-ethnic-diversity.
9. University of Nevada, Las Vegas, "Employee Counts," accessed December 14, 2019, https:// www.unlv.edu/hr/employee-info/employee-counts.
10. University of Nevada, Las Vegas, "Library Organization Chart," last updated November 14, 2019, https://www.library.unlv.edu/sites/default/files/inline-images/libraryorgc-hart2019-11-15.pdf.
11. Greater Western Library Alliance, "Member Institutions," accessed December 14, 2019, https://www.gwla.org/about-gwla/members.
12. Amy Tureen, "You Have to Work for It: Transitioning from Passive to Active Diversity Recruitment" (presentation at IDEAL: Advancing Inclusion, Diversity, Equity, and Accessi-bility in Libraries and Archives, Columbus, OH, August 7, 2019), https://digitalscholarship. unlv.edu/libfacpresentation/186.
13. Brittany Paloma Fiedler, Rosan Mitola, and James Cheng, "Responding to Hate: How National and Local Incidents Sparked Action at the UNLV University Libraries," *Reference Services Review* 48, no. 1 (2020): 71, https://doi.org/10.1108/RSR-09-2019-0071.
14. UNLV University Libraries, "Sciences Librarian, UNLV University Libraries [R0117863]," HigherEdJobs, accessed December 12, 2019, https://www.higheredjobs.com/faculty/ details.cfm?JobCode=177076329.
15. UNLV University Libraries, "Social Sciences & Interdisciplinary Studies Librarian, UNLV University Libraries [R0114723]," HigherEdJobs, accessed December 12, 2019, https:// www.higheredjobs.com/faculty/details.cfm?JobCode=176937052.
16. Fiedler, Mitola, and Cheng, "Responding to Hate."
17. UNLV University Libraries, "Living in Las Vegas: Welcome," accessed October 30, 2018, https://guides.library.unlv.edu/lasvegas/welcome.
18. UNLV University Libraries, "Living in Las Vegas."

19. UNLV University Libraries, "Social Sciences & Interdisciplinary Studies Librarian."
20. UNLV University Libraries, "Search Guidelines & Process Overview for Academic, Administrative, and Visiting Faculty" (internal document, May 16, 2019), electronic file.
21. UNLV University Libraries, "Search Guidelines.
22. Hilary Kraus (@craftyhilary), "Posting Jobs via iSchools," Google Sheet, last updated October 22, 2019, https://docs.google.com/spreadsheets/d/1bTejD6F3ACpL-zZi8i7q_l7L5tThs2N0LhzpZ-0bE7A/edit#gid=0.
23. Fiedler, Mitola, and Cheng, "Responding to Hate," 71.

Bibliography

American Library Association. "Diversity Counts." Last updated 2012. http://www.ala.org/aboutala/offices/diversity/diversitycounts/divcounts.

Bradshaw, Agnes K. "Strengthening the Pipeline—Talent Management for Libraries: A Human Resources Perspective." In *Where Are All the Librarians of Color?* Edited by Rebecca Hankins and Miguel Juarez, 97–131. Sacramento, CA: Library Juice Press, 2015.

Chu, Clara. "Transformative Information Services: Uprooting Race Politics." Paper presented at the Black Caucus of the American Library Association Conference, Las Vegas, NV, July 19–22, 1999.

Fiedler, Brittany Paloma, Rosan Mitola, and James Cheng. "Responding to Hate: How National and Local Incidents Sparked Action at the UNLV University Libraries." *Reference Services Review* 48, no. 1 (2020): 63–90. https://doi.org/10.1108/RSR-09-2019-0071

Greater Western Library Alliance. "Member Institutions." Accessed December 14, 2019. https://www.gwla.org/about-gwla/members.

Kraus, Hilary. "Posting Jobs via iSchools." Google Sheet. Last updated October 22, 2019. https://docs.google.com/spreadsheets/d/1bTejD6F3ACpL-zZi8i7q_l7L5tThs2N0LhzpZ-0bE7A/edit#gid=0.

Rosa, Kathy, and Kelsey Henke. *2017 ALA Demographic Study.* Chicago: American Library Association, 2017. https://www.ala.org/tools/sites/ala.org.tools/files/content/Draft%20of%20Member%20Demographics%20Survey%2001-11-2017.pdf.

Tureen, Amy. "You Have to Work for It: Transitioning from Passive to Active Diversity Recruitment." Presentation at IDEAL: Advancing Inclusion, Diversity, Equity, and Accessibility in Libraries and Archives, Columbus, OH, August 7, 2019. https://digitalscholarship.unlv.edu/libfacpresentation/186.

University of Nevada, Las Vegas. "Employee Counts." Accessed December 14, 2019. https://www.unlv.edu/hr/employee-info/employee-counts.

———. "Fall 2019 Official Enrollment Report—Final." Accessed January 20, 2020. https://ir.unlv.edu/IAP/Files/Final%20NSHE%20Enrollment%20Report%20-%20Fall%202019.aspx (page discontinued).

———. "Library Organization Chart." Last updated November 15, 2019. https://www.library.unlv.edu/sites/default/files/inline-images/libraryorgchart2019-11-15.pdf.

——— "UNLV Named Best College in Nevada for LGTBQ Students!" News Center, January 18, 2018. https://www.unlv.edu/about/highlights/best-nevada-lgbtq.

———. "U.S. News & World Report: UNLV Most Diverse Campus in the Nation." News Center, September 12, 2017. https://www.unlv.edu/news/release/us-news-world-report-unlv-most-diverse-campus-nation.

UNLV University Libraries. "Living in Las Vegas: Welcome." Accessed October 30, 2018. https://guides.library.unlv.edu/lasvegas/welcome.

———. "Sciences Librarian, UNLV University Libraries [R0117863]." HigherEd-Jobs. Accessed December 12, 2019. https://www.higheredjobs.com/faculty/details.cfm?JobCode=177076329.

———. "Search Guidelines & Process Overview for Academic, Administrative, and Visiting Faculty." Internal document, May 16, 2019, electronic file.

———. "Social Sciences & Interdisciplinary Studies Librarian, UNLV University Libraries, [R0114723]." HigherEdJobs. Accessed December 12, 2019. https://www.higheredjobs.com/faculty/details.cfm?JobCode=176937052.

US News and World Report. "Campus Ethnic Diversity: National Universities." Accessed December 14, 2019. https://www.usnews.com/best-colleges/rankings/national-universities/campus-ethnic-diversity.

CHAPTER 2

A Journey to Hiring with Heart

A Case Study on Implementing Leading Practices in Inclusive Hiring

Annie Bélanger, Sarah Beaubien, Scott Ayotte, and Abigail Smathers

Introduction

Have you ever wondered if the interview process could be a kinder, more accessible, candidate-focused experience, which is meant to develop connections? Our library professional values and core principles are meant to inform our practice as librarians and library professionals. How would it work if we took those values and working principles into the realm of recruitment and hiring? The authors sought to examine and improve the hiring process and candidate experience.

In 2017, Grand Valley State University Libraries set out to do the work of critically examining the existing hiring processes, designing an inclusive recruitment planning system, and implementing a new structure in order to ensure empathy for applicants going through the process. In order to take a closer look at the libraries' own recruitment and hiring practices, the libraries' executive team collaborated with the director of affirmative action, a member of the campus's

29

Division of Inclusion and Equity. This partnership led to a series of changes, which in turn led to a more positive experience for candidates while advancing the libraries' organizational outcome of an active practice of inclusion, diversity, equity, and accessibility. Ultimately, the authors developed and documented a set of inclusive recruitment and high-empathy hiring practices centered on the principles of equity and accessibility. These practices have been tested in administrative, faculty, and staff searches since then.

Examining the process used to review the hiring and recruitment process life cycle, the authors will lay out a practical approach that may be adapted to conduct a similar reflective and transformational process within other organizations. They will explore how to bring respect, empathy, kindness, transparency, and active bias mindfulness to every stage of the hiring life cycle. In particular, the authors considered the intersection of diversity, lifelong learning, user-centered practice, empathy, and respect. They made a commitment to transform the recruitment processes from a grueling challenge where only the worthy may be left standing to a learning opportunity for all. They committed to bring the compassion and empathy that libraries regularly demonstrate to users to the candidate experience.

The authors believe in social responsibility to the profession and to society. They sought to support candidates' discovery of what kind of librarian and library professional they would desire to be. They sought to do this through the professional modeling of a strong, confident library where informed risk taking occurs and inclusion is woven right into the hiring processes. By centering the needs of the candidates as interview processes are prepared, they sought to challenge habits and biases to ensure the libraries were using only components that would truly inform hiring decisions and support the provision of constructive, formative feedback to the candidates by rooting these processes in empathy and respect.

Grounded in an understanding of leading recruitment practices as well as an understanding of the profession's opportunities and challenges, the authors offer pragmatic approaches to move from the theory of inclusive hiring to implementation. They will review tips and questions to consider at each stage of the hiring life cycle, from language bias in position announcements to methods for developing interview questions.

Additionally, the authors will articulate some of the foundational work required to ensure a successful integration of inclusive hiring outcomes into the broader organizational culture. They will consider the dialogues and questions that must be answered about a work culture to ensure that the emotional labor and equity work are not isolated to historically underrepresented professionals. They believe that leadership must be an integral part of shepherding these crucial conversations on inclusion, diversity, equity, and accessibility in order to set clear expectations and support the growth needed for an engaged, inclusive workplace.

Making the Case for High-Empathy, Inclusive Approaches to Hiring

In 1999, the American Libraries Association (ALA) affirmed diversity as a core value of the profession.[1] Many efforts have been created since to advance diversity and inclusion in the profession. Yet the profession remains predominantly white and cis-gendered.[2] This reality is even starker in academic libraries. Those with nondominant identities face hurdles in attaining positions in academic libraries, in retaining them, and ultimately in thriving in them.[3]

Fourteen years after ALA's commitment was made, little progress was seen by Morales and colleagues, who called for "active and collective commitment to diversify the profession and, ultimately, pursue social justice in the broader world."[4] The library profession must move beyond the concept of diversity to embrace equity, accessibility, and inclusion. It cannot be driven by one-off diversity initiatives. "Well-intentioned attempts to create a more inclusive campus may unwittingly reinforce practices that support exclusion and inequity,"[5] particularly when these fail to address power and privilege.

In the last decade, Grand Valley State University Libraries became known for their work toward reducing library anxiety, deep engagement with user experience, and the creation of peer-to-peer services. The efforts also came in part from their use of strengths-based management approaches for over a decade. The combination of these parallel efforts encouraged an entrepreneurial culture, where informed risk is an ongoing expectation.

During this period, the libraries also worked toward a culture of belonging and empowerment. This meant that there were ongoing efforts to increase inclusivity in the libraries. Approaches included engaging with university inclusion and diversity training, discussing the nature of inclusion, creating a libraries-based task force to further explore inclusion and diversity, and supporting the development of university inclusion advocates within their faculty and staff.[6]

The libraries sponsored diversity-related events for users, but these were not tied to a program of systemic change. Inclusion was beginning to be understood as everyone's responsibility, but it had not yet become a formalized expectation of those who worked in the libraries. Inclusion also did not explicitly include the concepts of equity and accessibility; the expanded meaning came later as the inclusion task force cocreated its future as a working committee. Moreover, good faith efforts to transform recruitment and retention practices failed to create a more diverse workforce.

In 2017, Grand Valley State University Libraries started the process of critically examining their hiring practices. The process began by asking, "How would it look if we took those values and our core workplace principles into the realm of recruitment? How might it change our hiring practices? What if we bring the compassion that we have for our users and colleagues to our candidates?"[7] The authors believed that an empathy-first approach combined with leading hiring practices would lower barriers for candidates during the process.[8] In line with the cultural evolution that placed cognitive empathy as one of its cornerstones, cognitive empathy served as the basis for inclusive approaches. At minimum, an empathy-first approach would create a high-quality candidate experience.

Grand Valley State University Libraries worked closely with the Division of Inclusion and Equity's director of affirmative action to challenge habitual approaches to hiring. Through the director, the libraries began to plan for the entirety of the employee life cycle (ELC). In order to have a candidate-centered, inclusive approach, they sought to develop cognitive empathy for those being considered for positions at each stage of the ELC.

The employee life cycle (see figure 2.1) is a model utilized in organizational development and talent acquisition functions. It's used to visualize how an individual engages with their employer. The ELC establishes six critical stages or engagement points an employee goes through: (1) attraction, (2) recruitment, (3) onboarding, (4) development, (5) retention, and (6) separation.[9] The ELC helps employers create a focus on the outcome of a highly engaged and retained employee. For the purposes of this chapter, the authors will focus on the first five stages. Below, the ELC will be further articulated, as well as how inclusion efforts fit into these early stages, a portion of ELC known as full life cycle recruiting.[10]

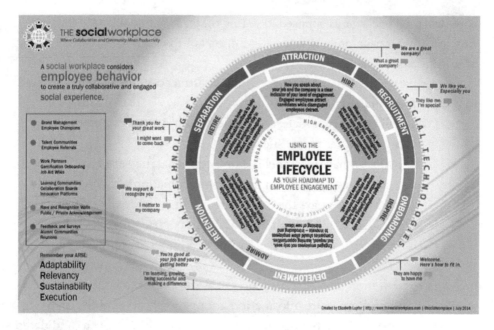

FIGURE 2.1

Diagram of the employee life cycle (Source: Elizabeth Lupfer, "The Social Workplace Employee Lifecycle," image, Social Workplace, July 2014, last updated August 2017, http://thesocialworkplace.com/thesocialworkplaceemployeelifecycle2014b-140805182512-phpapp02-2/.)

Attraction and Recruitment Stages

At the *attraction* stage, the focus is the potential candidates' perception of the employer and its regional surroundings. Having a clear understanding of the target demographic an organization wishes to attract is paramount in order to build and manage its identity. Here, the authors do not posit that a false identity should be created; rather, organizations should ensure that the story of who they are as employers should be told. Employers must understand what future employees are drawn to and highlight where those areas align, while also ensuring that candidates are well-informed.

As pertains to inclusion, organizations should consider the attraction factors that will be most important to historically underrepresented candidates. At the same time, organizations should consider what factors will be obstacles if they remain unsaid. For example, an organization should be explicit about the compensation package, as opposed to stating that it is "commensurate with experience." This transparency is especially important to candidates with a history of low income.

As organizations plan to start a search and to attract candidates, they will need to answer these questions:

- What will attract candidates to this field? To this type of library?
- Is the organization's career site visible?
  - o If so, does it have a compelling or intentional message about inclusion and equity? About employment information?
  - o If not, are there ways the organization can enhance the information?
- Is social media used? If so, are the hashtags current and relevant?
- Does the organization leverage positive testimonials from colleagues or students?

As an organization plans for attraction, it is important to consider how job applicants will find out more information about the library and the organization. This is most likely via the website. As a site is considered from a candidate's perspective, the questions "Who are these visitors?" and "How are they finding you?" should be answered. Here are some ways to enhance awareness:

- Run website analytics on both the online career page and the organization's website.
- Pay special attention to the ways in which job applicants see postings.
  - o Where are these visitors geographically?
  - o Which websites directed them to the organization?
  - o Which websites were the best and worst sources for referrals to an organization's career page?
- Structure job applications to allow applicants to list what resources led them to the organization. This is especially helpful if the organization subscribes to online job posting services and sites.
  - o Did these resources generate any candidates who were interviewed or hired?
  - o Applicant tracking systems are treasure troves when it comes to applicant and employee data. If possible, solicit source information from candidates when they apply. Something as simple as "How did you learn about this opportunity?" followed by a list of sourcing avenues provided can reveal much about the effectiveness of recruitment sources.

At the *recruitment* stage, the focus is about evaluating the candidates who are applying for positions at the organization. The goals here are (1) quality of hire and (2) diversity of applicants and hires. It is important that success be defined ahead of the search: is it hiring anyone, the most experienced, or the most likely to succeed?

Adopting a data-driven approach is key to ensuring inclusive talent acquisition. Data can help identify problems or point to areas of improvement. Creating evaluation criteria ahead of review is critical to ensuring that all members of a search committee have shared understanding of the needs and what success for a candidate in the interview process could be. Doing this also helps to manage bias by ensuring that *fit,* defined as fitting in, does not become the decision criterion because it leads to hiring those with similar characteristics, reinforcing implicit bias.[11] Rather, the ability to do well at work should be considered, and the alignment with core organization values should be considered to support future success.[12]

Onboarding Stage

Research supports that the first ninety days of a new employee's job are the most critical when accounting for longevity, engagement, and retention.[13] People tend to still feel like outsiders especially during the first few weeks in a new organization or new department. At the *onboarding* stage, organizations will focus their efforts on ensuring new hires are introduced to the organization in a manner that creates a sense of belonging, provides transparency, and ensures support from the onset. This phase is typically the most critical because a successful onboarding process can help individuals connect to the organization's purpose. The goal is to move from being an outsider (exclusion) to being an insider (inclusion).

The first few weeks of starting a new position come with many challenges, questions, and uncertainties. "Will I do well here? Will I be able to fit in and make friends? Will I be truly accepted here for who I am?" are all very common concerns that any new employee will have. By making explicit the implicit, onboarding supports understanding of the culture, expectations, and how to grow and succeed as a professional. Being explicit particularly supports the onboarding of those from nondominant identities. Since they will be more often othered by the perceptions of culturally dominant identities, this clarity will support their success by uncovering lived values and practices.[14]

Organizations are encouraged to conduct a formalized new employee orientation to ensure an even approach. When doing so, organizations are encouraged to consider being intentional about highlighting how inclusion and diversity align with the organizational strategy or mission and vision. It is more than including photographs and testimonials from colleagues who are part of underrepresented communities. If possible, organizations should focus on not only the external driving forces for inclusion, but also how inclusiveness impacts who they are. To do so, organizations can highlight practices and expectations to support the creation of a positive, healthy, inclusive work environment. Additional components to a thriving orientation program include the following:

- As part of the formal new employee orientation, introduce new hires to professional-social support, such as employee resource groups (also referred to as affinity groups) if they exist.
- Leaders are encouraged to share expectations for communication (platforms, forums, technology, etc.), their approach to leadership, and opportunities for participation in decision-making.
- Reinforce the organization's commitment to continuous improvement and continual learning—the goal being to help individuals feel comfortable asking questions and contributing their input.

As organizations develop orientation programs for newly hired colleagues, here are some key questions to keep top of mind:

- What is absolutely essential for new hires to know before they begin their first day?
- First impressions are set during the interview when applicants are still on the outside looking in. Now that they are colleagues, what impression does the organization want to leave the new colleagues with?
- Are relatively new colleagues (six months to one year tenure) surveyed about their experience during employee orientation?
  - What aspects of new employee orientation did they appreciate?
  - What aspects of new employee orientation did they not appreciate?
  - What was most helpful in terms of acquainting them with the organization?
  - What would they change in order to create a more welcoming experience?
  - Do those surveyed represent a diverse cross section of the organization and of the communities it serves?

Development Stage

There is a commonly replicated office comic theme featuring a CEO speaking with their CFO. The CFO says something like, "What if we invest time and money developing our employees and they leave us?" to which the CEO replies, "What if we don't ...and they stay?" Despite its humorous nature, it illustrates a short-term versus a long-term mindset of investing in your people.

Ensuring an individual is properly oriented to their role creates a firm foundation for their growth and development. When assessing an individual's performance, there is a tendency to measure their proficiency and achievements against their assigned duties and essential functions. If an individual is meeting or exceeding their goals and producing quality work product, they would likely be labeled a high performer. The fallacy of the coveted high performer mark is that it is often based on past and current performance meeting past and current needs. As the needs change over time, so do the factors for evaluating performance. A high performer today may very well be an underperformer down the road.

Forward-thinking organizations will understand how internal and external forces may influence the individual's role and will proactively take steps to meet future needs. Employee development encompasses two essential components: (1) engagement, and (2) involvement. Ensuring individuals are developing and growing is a partnership. Individuals need to be involved in their own development plans, knowing their self-determination is pivotal and therefore providing agency over growth.[15] Conversely, organizations need to engage with their employees to understand and appreciate that they have different life experiences, values, and beliefs that all impact how they learn and grow.

Organization must create opportunities for growth and advancement for all, using an equity mindset that is intentional about viewing employees as individuals. Adopting a culturally intelligent and inclusive approach to learning and development with each as a partner sets a framework for building trust, demonstrating commitment, and making them equal and accountable. Establishing an individual as a responsible party for their own success helps to create trust, provides transparency, and fosters a level of self-determination critical for growth.

Leaders should make a point to articulate their commitment to growth and development throughout the individual's tenure with the organization. Examples of how leaders can create this environment of support include the following:

- Making professional/career development personal and customized for each individual
  - Managers and supervisors should set aside time to connect with their direct reports at least quarterly to discuss long-term goals and professional objectives.
  - Seek projects to advance learning and skill development as outlined in the yearly plan.
- Encouraging colleagues to seek out a mentor outside of their current reporting structure
  - Be intentional about teaching seasoned colleagues how to be effective mentors in the areas of accountability, sponsorship, growth, providing feedback, and advocacy.
  - Set clear expectations and goals from both the mentor and mentee— "By the end of twelve months, we want to have accomplished xyz."
  - Allow the mentee to drive the process in terms of goals, objectives, and supports.
  - Equip the mentor to provide stretch assignments and give feedback in an assertive but constructive manner.
- Establishing leadership development programs aimed at not only high-performing colleagues but also those who have demonstrated high potential for leadership

Retention Stage

Sir Richard Branson, CEO of Virgin Group, is credited with saying, "Train people well enough so they can leave, treat them well enough so they don't want to."[16] In the earlier comic theme, to the CFO who is worried about investing in people because they might leave the organization, Branson's statement signifies the responsibility of the organization to do right by its people. Simply treating employees equally is not enough. It is necessary to ensure employees are treated in an equitable manner—in the way they desire to be treated. In other words, allow the employee to have a say in what constitutes being "treated well."

The purpose of utilizing the employee life cycle model is to, ultimately, create a high-performing, inclusive, and engaged workforce. An organization that recognizes the importance of inclusion at each stage and implements a culturally intelligent approach should expect to retain a diverse workforce as a result. If an organization is intentional about inclusive outreach and creating a culturally intelligent, exceptional candidate experience, then it will already have taken steps to ensure it has the right talent at the onset. Providing effective onboarding, which reinforces its commitment to inclusion, diversity, and equity, will also have an impact as to shaping how individuals perceive their workspaces. Finally, investing in employees and engaging them as partners in their development will support and create an environment where retention is a result rather than an initiative.

In the grand scheme of things, retention is all about ensuring your employees are highly engaged, valued, motivated, challenged, and treated well.[17] Essentially, the goal is to ensure that you can take into account and mitigate the factors that contribute to voluntary turnover. High turnover not only impacts productivity and morale, but also negatively impacts continuity. In terms of resourcing, the Society of Human Resources Management estimates that every time a salaried employee is replaced, it costs six to nine months' salary on average.[18] A 2019 study conducted by the Work Institute reported that approximately 41.4 million employees in the US left their jobs voluntarily in 2018.[19] For employers who place a high value on inclusion and diversity, this statistic raises two questions: (1) Who is leaving? and (2) Why are they choosing to leave?

When examining employee turnover, utilizing data is an essential requirement. Examine employee turnover data by identifying a meaningful time horizon—typically twelve to eighteen months, but this period will differ depending on each organization's unique circumstances.[20] By reviewing data to identify any broad trends relating to demographics, organizations can see if any significant patterns emerge. Organizations should consider the following questions:

- Of those who have left in the past twelve to eighteen months (or other specified time frame), who are they by demographic (e.g., age, race/ethnicity, disability status, veteran status, sex, gender, gender identity, etc.)?
- Which departments did they support?
- Who were their direct supervisors?
- What types of positions did they occupy?
- How long on average were they in their role before leaving?
- Did they provide any additional insight by way of exit interviews?

In studying this data, organizations will want to be mindful of whether there are any disproportionate rates of turnover based on demographics (i.e., Is there a tendency for individuals who are _____ to leave at greater rates?).

While getting to the reasons behind employee turnover is important, it doesn't solve the problem of the talented individuals an organization already lost. The task for employers is understanding how to retain talented professionals in a culturally competent and intelligent manner. There are literally hundreds of articles, resource guides, and white papers that cover best practices for employee retention. Some of these common best practices often include:

- providing competitive compensation and benefits.
- offering health and wellness programs.
- implementing recognition and rewards programs for tenure or achievements.
- allowing flexible work arrangements or remote assignments.
- giving free snacks and beverages as a perk.

While these best practices are certainly good and have some value, it is important to recognize that they will not be universally received by your employees. Some perks appear wonderful on the surface, while lack of structure around their implementation disadvantages retention by leading to confusion and underutilization of perks. For example, in 2017, Namely, Inc., conducted a study of organizations offering unlimited paid time off (PTO). Its findings indicated that employees with unlimited paid time off had utilized (or planned to utilize) on average thirteen days off per year, compared with traditional PTO plan employees, who utilized on average fifteen days off per year.[21] Granted, there are other factors that are implicated, such as communication of this policy and encouragement of leaders to focus on personal time. The factors that lead to employee turnover tend to differ from individual to individual. Rather than taking a generalist approach to retention, leaders should consider customizing their retention efforts at the individual level.

The Stay Interview

Most are no doubt familiar with exit interviews, and many who have changed employers participated in one as the interviewee. For those not familiar, an exit interview is a meeting that takes place when an individual decides to leave the organization. Typically, the departing employee will meet with either a member of the supervisory team or, more often than not, their human resources representative. During this meeting, the interviewer will want to get a sense of why they are choosing to leave and how they would assess and evaluate their time at the organization. This is often done to pinpoint areas in need of improvement, take note of the climate of the organization, and see if there are any patterns emerging or common themes. These meetings tend to be rather honest since the departing employee has little to fear as relates to retaliation or other perceived consequences. While the exit interview provides great insight, it does little to address the fact that the organization has lost an employee and will now feel the impact of their absence in both morale and the bottom line.

Leaders and managers are encouraged to conduct stay interviews. A stay interview is a meeting that takes place between a direct or indirect report and an organizational leader. Unlike an exit interview, this meeting is proactive in that it is done with the intent to understand how someone is feeling in the organization and what they may need in terms of support. The purpose of the stay interview is twofold: (1) reinforce the leader's (and the organization's) commitment to its people; and (2) understand how to best support its top talent, remove barriers, and understand needs.

Stay interviews should be conducted at least annually; depending on schedules, workloads, and organizational culture, it could be more frequently. A successful stay interview is dependent on having a leader who is equipped to create an environment of openness and safety. Employees will not be forthcoming in giving genuine feedback if they fear it may have negative consequences. As a good starting point, leaders may want to plant the seed with their employees by conveying something like "I recognize and value your talents and hard work. Because you are one of my key colleagues, I'd like for us to have an informal conversation to help me understand what you like about your role and how I can best support you, and make sure you can bring your true and authentic self to work." Examples of stay interview questions:

- What gets you excited about coming to work each day?
- What are two to three things that you enjoy about working here?
- What are two to three things that you would like to change about working here?
- How would you prefer that I recognize your accomplishments? Do you prefer a personal e-mail from me or the leadership team? Would you prefer more public recognition?
- How do you acknowledge and recognize others?
- If you could change some aspects of your work, what would that look like?

- Are there any skills or talents you have that you'd like to utilize more in your current role?
- What can I do more of or less of as your manager?
- Are there any areas of the organization you'd like to learn more about?
- Is there anything that may come up that would tempt you to leave?

Grand Valley State University Libraries' Approach and Implementation

In moving forward with their efforts, the libraries opted to use Appreciative Inquiry as one of their strategies.[22] The use of powerful, generative questions formed the foundation to establish core values, highlight what is good, identify possible champions, and foster healthy dialogue. The libraries had a goal of moving from a culture of inclusion to one with an active practice of inclusion, diversity, equity, and accessibility in alignment with the "why" of user focus, social justice, and access for all. This shared understanding was further solidified by articulating that all were responsible for respect and cognitive empathy practices, which were seen as baseline needs for inclusion, by adding them to job descriptions and the annual performance evaluation process.

As the libraries considered their upcoming hiring cycle, the challenge was seen as twofold: (1) bringing empathy and a caring approach to our hiring processes in order to demystify them, and 2) evolving and enhancing our culture so that under-represented minorities and identities would be actively welcomed and included. The libraries wanted to bring the same level of caring that they show to users to their recruitment practices. With regard to users, the libraries work to demystify research, make it as intuitive as possible, and create a lasting connection. The libraries understood inclusion and equity as a journey within the context of a predominantly white organization and a predominantly white profession.[23] Since then, we continue to evolve our hiring approach to add more positive aspects.

All searches are important and critical to the long-term health of an organization, yet leadership searches raise the stakes. The first push to renew efforts toward active inclusion occurred in our hiring process for two associate dean (AD) positions. The approach to developing the AD position descriptions also served as an example of active participatory leadership.

In changing our approach to hiring, we hoped to demystify the hiring process. In ensuring a candidate-centered approach, we adopted practices that would reduce the need for accommodations, while inviting these requests. Lastly, the libraries wanted to center the needs of the candidates as preparations for hiring were made, thereby challenging habitual practices and biases to ensure that each piece of the process would truly inform decisions and support providing feedback to the candidates.

Supporting Colleagues for Active Inclusion and Equity

The libraries administration collaborated with department heads, faculty, and staff to articulate core workplace principles through appreciative inquiry methodology.[24] Workplace principles articulate how we live our values intentionally. In turn, they serve as an explicit statement of how we collectively approach our work. One of the principles created is to "approach each other with respect and empathy." It set the stage for accountability of how individuals accomplish goals as well as the outcomes of those goals. It also centered the needs for interpersonal skills, such as verbal and nonverbal communication, problem-solving, negotiation and compromise, and conflict resolution.

Developing a shared baseline and language around interpersonal effectiveness led to the creation of a workshop that all faculty and staff attend. The university's work-life consultant developed and offered the workshop. In addition, a faculty- and staff-led series of workshops was implemented to increase the ability to effectively give and receive feedback.[25]

The libraries' efforts toward robust, outcomes-focused peer-to-peer communications and generative approaches were seen as a baseline needed toward inclusion. Overall, the libraries hoped to advance a culture of active practice toward inclusion, diversity, equity, and accessibility throughout the libraries.[26] Through this process, the libraries continued to leverage appreciative inquiry and powerful questions.[27] Generative questions are used in our daily practice in order to reframe concerns into questions, to clarify understanding before making conclusions, and to identify opportunities within challenges.[28] As organizations prepare to ask powerful questions, the use of circular questions, which work to elicit patterns and themes, should be explored.[29] Powerful questions, focusing on what could be, avoid blame and shame, thereby disarming righteous reactions of white fragility.[30]

Candidate-Centered Processes

PREPARING FOR THE SEARCH

As the Grand Valley State University Libraries prepared to fill the two associate dean positions (associate dean of curation, preservation, and publishing services and associate dean of curriculum, research, and user services), the dean facilitated several dialogues aimed at gathering input from throughout the libraries that would inform the AD position descriptions.[31] First, the libraries' leadership reviewed the previous and existing portfolios, position descriptions, and the overall structure of the organization. The team looked for areas it knew it wanted to preserve, for emerging or unassigned priorities that would need to be folded into the AD roles, and for the evolution of interconnected nodes within the libraries' organizational structure. The goals of this exploration were to develop two positions that were equitable in workload and leadership opportunity, provide oversight of the major areas of emphasis in the organization, and require that the successful candidates work collaboratively in order to carry forward the work of the libraries. Following this discussion, library administration shared draft position descriptions with library faculty and staff, inviting them to participate in a number of town hall meetings regarding the positions and upcoming search. Faculty and staff were encouraged to comment on the overall structure of the positions, as well as specific elements within the roles. They were invited to submit suggestions, questions, and ideas, which were recorded in the notes for each town hall meeting. Following these dialogues, library administration shared updated drafts and indicated in each where edits had been made based on faculty and staff input. As a result of these facilitated sessions, some changes were made to the reporting lines to the associate deans and, thus, the organizational structure. Additionally, several strategic areas were identified and divided among the associate deans and dean, such as strategic planning.

Following the finalization of the position descriptions, the dean assembled a search committee, which consisted of several members of the libraries' faculty and staff as well as representatives from university information technology and the provost's office, one of whom served as the inclusion advocate. The committee collaboratively developed and implemented a recruitment plan, wrote the job posting, created interview questions for a phone screening and in-person visits, and finalized an agenda for the interview day. The approach of developing the interview questions and agenda prior to reviewing applicant materials was intentional and achieved several goals. First, it helped the committee stay focused on the position qualifications and minimized the chances of introducing bias into interview questions based on applicant materials. Second, while it is more work at the outset of a search, this practice enabled the committee to provide more focus on candidate experience during each stage of the search process. Lastly, it kept the search moving as efficiently as possible, which ultimately is a more empathetic, candidate-focused process.

AD WRITING

In preparing to advertise the positions, a hiring FAQ was developed to provide additional information to applicants about the university and the surrounding area.[32] It also included the compensation package as well as information from human resources about benefits and employee wellness. The intent in pulling this information together was to be as transparent as possible about salary, the organization, and the local area in order to give applicants access to information that could inform their decision on whether or not to apply.

Care was taken to write the job posting to emphasize qualities and skills, such as leadership ability, flexibility, comfort with ambiguity, and confident humility.[33] The job posting was reviewed to identify any areas where gendered language had been used and, as feasible, to edit the ad for gender neutrality. Feelings of belonging that are elicited by a job posting matter in creating job appeal; language that appears to cater to one identity creates a barrier for applicants of other identities.[34]

Job description language can be reframed to avoid implicit bias such as the following:
- Male-biased phrasing
  - Change "who thrive in a competitive atmosphere..." to "who are motivated by goals..."
  - Change "candidates who are assertive..." to "candidates who are go-getters..."
- Female-biased phrasing
  - Change "we are a community of concerned..." to "we are a team focused on..."
  - Change "have a polite and pleasant style..." to "are professional and courteous..."

- o Change "nurture and connect with customers" to "provide great customer service"[35]
- Racism and white-centered phrasing
  - o Include meaningful commitment to inclusion and diversity in your job ad.
  - o Link to more material about inclusion that demonstrate your commitment and actions.
  - o Change "national identity" to "ability to work in [the country of work]."
- Ageist phrasing
  - o Avoid "young," "energetic."
  - o Change "recent college graduate only" to "open to new career."
- Classist and privileged phrasing
  - o Limit the number of qualifications, focusing on must haves. "Studies have shown that many women won't apply for a job they do not 100% qualify for, whereas men will apply for a position they feel they're only 60% qualified for."[36]
  - o Change the requirement "must own a vehicle" to "has a driver's license" (if the job requires significant car travel).
- Ableist phrasing
  - o Change "energetic" to "dedicated."
  - o Review any physical requirements, such as "lift 50 lbs," to either remove it or align with the required core duties.
  - o Challenge the need for "ability to walk, sit, and stand for long periods of time."

The dean and members of the search committee were intentional in crafting a limited number of position requirements, which prioritized soft skills, such as professional acuity, leadership, and interpersonal skills. The job posting provided room for growth in specific portfolio areas, such as facilities, strategic planning, workforce management, and budgeting. The job posting did not require a specific number of years of experience as that can deter otherwise qualified candidates from applying. As a leading practice, we suggest providing candidates with a point person in the organization, typically the search chair or a member of the search committee, to whom they may direct questions along the way.

CANDIDATE EXPERIENCE

Candidates invest their time in the application process, so developing a candidate-focused approach to talent acquisition helps demonstrate that the organization is also investing time in them. A candidate-focused approach in the recruitment and hiring processes requires a significant investment of time and energy on the part of the search committee. In this case, the benefits included successful hires, a more diverse applicant pool, increasingly inclusive hiring practices that have informed future searches, and the growth of professional networks strengthened by positive candidate experiences. There are several ways to demonstrate empathy throughout the application and hiring practices, many of which center on communication. While elements of the hiring process are confidential, a significant amount of information can be shared, particularly regarding the steps in the search process.

TRANSPARENCY AND COMMUNICATION

For applicants in the field of academic librarianship, the process of applying can feel like a one-sided conversation, wherein little communication is received from the hiring organization once application materials have been submitted. While automated update messages to applicants from employment software are helping to improve this situation, a proactive approach on behalf of the search committee can take this further, helping candidates feel connected and informed throughout the stages of the process. Search chairs may be able to customize the generic messages available in their organization's employment software in order to provide candidates with richer contextual information than they might otherwise receive. Another option is sending a follow-up e-mail to provide more information.

In addition to providing prospective applicants with contextual information about the position and organization via the job posting and an FAQ, it is important to engage with applicants at several key stages. First, as the committee reviews applicant materials, using a rubric to mitigate bias and maintain a focus on the qualifications, it will identify those applicants who do not meet the required qualifications. In an applicant-focused search, a leading practice is to notify unqualified applicants as soon as possible that they will not receive an invitation to interview for the position rather than retaining them in the pool for the duration of the search. This respects both the time they have invested in applying and the time they may otherwise spend waiting to hear from the organization. At the application review stage, this may mean a period of several weeks or more where the search committee reviews, discusses, and recommends applicants for interview. For those remaining in the pool, this can feel like a lengthy time with no communication from the organization. To address this, the libraries' practice has evolved to include sending a message to remaining applicants, indicating that the search is in process and that they remain in the pool.

For those applicants whom the search committee invited to participate in a phone interview, the search chairs sent an e-mail communication that included the following:

- The duration of the phone interview, specifying how much time the committee would use for questions and how much time the candidate could expect to ask their questions
- Options for dates and times
- For accessibility purposes:
  - A statement indicating that the committee will send most of the phone interview questions to the candidate, via e-mail, one hour prior to the phone call. This helps prevent candidates from needing to disclose a disability, such as hearing impairment. Further, it offers empathy to the candidates by acknowledging the limitations of technology in phone or Skype interviews.
  - An invitation to request accommodations.
- The names and brief bios of the search committee members
- Information about the time line and process for the search
- The libraries' core workplace principles
- An invitation for the candidate to reach out to the search chairs with any questions they may have

The primary goal of this message is to prepare phone interview candidates with relevant information about the library, the organization, and the process. The message is also written purposefully with an empathetic focus on the candidates as they prepare for their phone interview by demystifying the process as much as possible.

For finalists who were invited to a campus interview, the search committee sent a similar message, which also included the following:

- Detail about travel options and reimbursement of costs, along with a logistics contact person

- Detail about restaurants or meals that will be provided, including
  - links to restaurant menus
  - a request for candidates to share any dietary needs they may have in advance of the visit to ensure that accommodations can be planned
- A detailed interview agenda. Each item on the agenda includes a purpose statement in order to help candidates understand why each component is part of the process and why they will meet with the variety of groups and individuals throughout the day. A sample agenda item:
  - 1:00–1:45
  - Open conversation with library faculty and staff
  - Purpose: ability for candidate to get a sense of colleagues and gauge workplace atmosphere, and for library faculty and staff to interact informally with the candidate
- A presentation prompt, including the duration of the presentation, time for Q&A, available technology, the venue, the general makeup of the audience (i.e., indicating which groups or stakeholders have been invited), evaluation criteria for the presentation, and the purpose of the presentation as part of the interview day

The interview agenda is particularly important to enhance transparency in the process, so it is developed well in advance of sending the invitations for the on-campus interview. In this case, the search committee engaged in dialogue to identify the key stakeholders in the libraries and on campus whom the candidates should meet with during the interview day and then made those choices transparent to the candidates by indicating the purpose for each meeting or activity on the agenda. In order to more fully support inclusion, the committee also left one meeting time open for the discretion of the candidates. They were given several options of university individuals, groups, or centers they could meet with during this time slot, such as a campus tour, meeting with human resources, or meeting with members of campus social justice centers (e.g., the LGBT Center, the Center for Women and Gender Equity, the Office of Multicultural Affairs, etc.). Their selection was known only to an office coordinator managing logistics, ensuring that committee members would not be aware of the selection, thereby reducing the possibility of the candidates' selection introducing bias into the committee deliberations. Reserving this time allowed candidates to explore one aspect of the organization that would be of most interest to them, which served as an expression of empathy by giving them the ability to prioritize their needs during the interview day. Additionally, with regard to candidate needs, several breaks were built into the agenda to give candidates a few moments to reflect, explore the building, replenish beverages, and address other needs they may have.

When meals were included on the interview agenda, the search chairs provided as much information as possible in order to put candidates at ease and to ensure that any dietary needs were addressed. An office coordinator worked directly with the candidates to address dietary needs in advance of the visits. If the meals were at local restaurants, the search chairs provided a link to the restaurant menu and included a statement about attire. For example, one dinner was held the evening prior to the interview day at a fine-dining establishment, so in this case the agenda included the names and titles of all dining companions, as well as a note recommending business attire. For another meal, which was held at the end of the interview day, a more casual restaurant was selected, and the interview agenda included a statement that the dinner companions planned to wear jeans. This level of transparency helps a candidate understand how to prepare and can help remove some of the stressors in the process. It can also give them insight into local and university practices, such as the formality of dress that may be expected at organizational events.

Typically, one of the final meetings of the interview process is a one-on-one dialogue between the candidate and the dean. The dean plans for time to respond to candidate questions, as well as sharing her vision of the libraries and some of the priority initiatives. This meeting also builds empathy into the hiring process by providing a venue for the dean to share as much as possible about the next steps in the process, including time line, campus requirements, and her approach to salary negotiation.

INTERVIEWING PROCESS

The search committee developed phone and in-person interview questions prior to reviewing applicant materials. This helped mitigate bias that may be introduced to the process by virtue of reading applications and becoming aware of the strengths, successes, and growth areas of the applicants. To keep the questions focused on required qualifications, the committee was asked to develop questions and indicate which required or preferred qualification the question addressed. Further, the committee collaboratively developed success criteria for each question. The success criteria represent the concepts that the committee agrees the question is seeking. In other words, the criteria do not answer the question or dictate how a candidate should answer the question; rather, they are a way for the committee to ensure that the group is interpreting the question similarly. They also seek an established and shared understanding of what success looks like. The following is a sample question from the associate dean search:

> Please describe a multi-partner project or initiative that you have participated in or led. What did you learn from your experience? *[success criteria: collaboration, project management, relationship building, vision]*

The committee also wrote follow-up prompts that could be used with the questions if needed to support a candidate or seek greater clarity. Writing them in advance of the interview ensured that the prompts would be consistent across candidates. During the search committee interview with candidates, each candidate was provided with a printed copy of the questions, with space to take notes. Success criteria and prompts were removed from the candidate copy. The candidates were informed that the questions would be collected from them at the end of the meeting in order to protect the confidentiality of the process.

Following each on-campus visit by a finalist, the search chairs sent a feedback survey to anyone who had participated in a portion of the interview day or who had interacted directly with the candidates. The survey framed the feedback in terms of the position requirements, and while it did ask submitters to indicate which meetings they had participated in, it did not require them to identify themselves. Those responses were available to the search committee after the campus visits had concluded.

BUILDING INCLUSION INTO THE PROCESS

By rooting the processes in empathy and respect, we remember that we are not only interviewing the candidates, they are interviewing us too. We also remember that though job searches will always be stressful, we can do a lot to make it smoother and a healthy process. Further, by centering the candidates' ability to succeed, inclusion becomes an easy focus. Removing barriers to success for candidates led to inclusive, high-empathy practices. When employers think about what information, communications, and tools most candidates would need to make informed decisions, making bold choices that help candidates bring their authentic self to the process, they are inherently bringing the concept of universal design to play.

We started by thinking of recruitment planning as a holistic life-cycle process that started from agreeing to fill a job to the end of onboarding.[37] Instead of acting as if candidates should be grateful for the opportunity to apply, we looked at recruitment as an opportunity to find long-term colleagues and allies. We began to use ads as a means of helping candidates early not only to learn what we are looking for, but also to think about what is in it for them. Considerations include the following:

- deciding where to advertise
- articulating goals for the role as well as the organizational needs
- determining whether the search team is equipped for success
- describing what the candidate will gain in the role

Thinking about the possible fear and obstacles to considering a relocation, we began to take the guesswork out of the regional information, out of the pay scale, and out of the benefits umbrella. We sought to answer many of the common questions that cause candidates to self-select out because the risk of not knowing is too great. A lack of clarity about support and pay range is a key reason underrepresented candidates do not apply.

Onboarding Preparedness

Because the first few weeks in a new organization are so critical to success, the libraries critically examined the onboarding process for new hires. In this examination, it became apparent that procedures were largely decentralized, with departments in the libraries implementing differing practices, leading to a fragmented onboarding experience. In response, the libraries' business administrator gathered feedback from recent hires and worked closely with department heads and managers to centralize, update, and add some needed structure to the onboarding practices. One notable change was the creation of a central onboarding document, which indicated that each new employee would connect with library leadership within the first two months of employment. Another improvement was streamlining and centralizing the preparation for the new employee's arrival. This task had been somewhat distributed across the organization, but moved into the purview of the dean's office. Now, an office coordinator prepares for the employee's arrival by ensuring that they are added to directories and have a name tag, a name plate for their workspace, basic office supplies, university-issued login credentials, a parking pass, and a plan for the first few days of employment.

In general, an effort was made to make the libraries' workplace culture and values apparent during the onboarding process while introducing new hires to as many colleagues as possible.[38] Some examples included adding more explicit information about professional development, priority initiatives, organizational structure, vision, and cross-department collaboration. In much the same way that the hiring process became more empathetic and candidate-focused, the onboarding process was intentionally updated to be more employee-focused and consistent.

Moving toward Inclusive Hiring

Though organizational change is never quick and never easy, it is important to make it part of ongoing expectations so that change is the status quo. Inclusion cannot succeed so long as it is an individual's or small group's responsibility. It cannot exist as an intervention or series of interventions. It will grow through systematic change that leverages systems thinking, and it will die by the actions of individuals' everyday actions and words.[39]

The first step toward engaging in an empathy-driven, inclusive hiring process is to question each part of the process from a candidate's point of view. An organization can begin by asking change-focused questions and making space for the difficult conversations that need to occur. Questions to begin the journey include following:

- What are we doing?
  - What makes each of these components important?
  - What purpose does each of these components serve?
  - Which components support decision-making? Which are most critical?
  - How do these components align with the position requirements?
- What approaches are great? Which could be improved?
- What do the words mean?
  - In thinking about requirements, it is key to create shared understanding. This can be done by creating working definitions. Doing so begins to set up new colleagues for success.

- o *Fit* is both an oft-used word and a reviled word. It is coded language to maintain the dominant culture of an organization. For example, "whether you would be willing to invite someone home for dinner" is often relied upon to assess fit. However, it is important to articulate what is required for someone to succeed in the role and the organization, not whether we would invite them to dinner.
- How will we sustain the change (moving beyond the one-shot intervention)?
- How do we define success clearly and objectively?

Developing rules of engagement, which serve as collective agreements for interacting, can be critical a critical tool in this change effort. They can provide clear expectations, support a process focus, and enable shared behaviors.

Conclusion

Petit à petit, l'oiseau fait son nid.
[Little by little, the bird makes its nest]

—French saying

The quote above highlights the need for perseverance and consistency. High-empathy hiring is part of a wider culture change. Hiring is only the first step in connecting with future colleagues who, after going through an inclusive hiring process, will expect an inclusive workplace. While employers showcase the best they have to offer in the recruitment phase, they must ensure that they continue to do so by living their values and authentic practices.

Identifying your organization's readiness for more inclusive practices is a first and crucial step toward creating a healthy work culture for dominant and nondominant identities. A culture where even basic disagreements cannot be resolved peer-to-peer will need to develop the necessary baseline communication skills before it can move into active inclusion. A culture where change and learning are key expectations may review its processes and procedures to gather whether these create barriers for colleagues of nondominant identities. We see inclusion as a state of being that we seek and sustain, which leverages the tactics of liberation, including anti-racism, anti-sexism, and anti-ableism.

In having the belief that everyone is doing their best and yet can do better moving forward, organizations can keep a constructive focus through engagement by the whole. Leveraging micro-appreciative practices can encourage peer-to-peer mentorship, support systems of accountability that focus on strengths and articulate unacceptable behavior, and identify a network of partners for change.[40] The core practices of appreciative inquiry combined with systems thinking can identify root systemic issues that are obstacles to inclusion and therefore explore alternative solutions. As organizations move to change, particularly with a focus on diversity and inclusion, there are great benefits to identifying the core of what is good, which will be preserved. An organization can leverage appreciative inquiry to discuss what is best in its people and what they value most.[41] By preserving the core, the change becomes growth, evolution, and aligned with core values. This appreciative approach can help with white fragility by avoiding blame and shame. Some of the powerful questions to ask include these: Describe a time you felt absolutely at your best working here. Who else was involved? How did you know you were succeeding?[42] Eventually, the dialogue can shift to how inclusion and diversity might support the "why" of the organization.

To advance diversity, equity, and accessibility, organizations must focus on creating an inclusive environment. Inclusive environments are conditions precedent for success. Hiring without healthy retention strategies that support each individual's backgrounds and hopes is simply another lip service program to check off on a strategic plan. Without a commitment to an inclusive culture with associated proactive practices, diversity hiring (for the sole purpose of diversity) can cause harm.

Additionally, organizations must remember that every interaction with a potential candidate is helping you build a network for future recruitment. These interactions also serve as the beginning of the relationships that a hired candidate will form. For Grand Valley State University Libraries, the outcome has been an exceptional candidate experience and an intentional onboarding strategy, which are anchored in an active practice of inclusion for all colleagues. Increasingly the culture of compassion and care associated with the practice of inclusion is leading to candidates and colleagues acknowledging a sense of belonging and safety within the organization.[43]

Appendix 2A

2017 ASSOCIATE DEAN SEARCH POSITION AD
Two Associate Dean Positions, Grand Valley State University, Michigan

Grand Valley State University (GVSU) Libraries is seeking nominations and applications for two Associate Deans (ADs) to provide leadership to a thriving and risk-taking organization. GVSU Libraries embarked on an exciting path of evolution and continued exploration with the arrival of a new Dean. Serving as a nexus for quality education and with a visionary focus on student experience, the libraries play a critical role in advancing a liberal education through intellectual partnership with faculty and students throughout the university.

LEAD—The two ADs along with the Dean and Department Heads will provide vision and leadership in a shared governance model with faculty members, staff and student employees, which includes five locations across two campuses. The ADs provide strategic oversight within the Libraries, working collaboratively across campus, with the local community, and with national and international partners to create and support traditional and cutting edge services designed to meet the current and emergent needs of students, faculty, and staff, with a strong student experience focus in line with liberal education.

As key members of the Grand Valley State University Libraries' senior management team, the ADs ensure organizational effectiveness and efficiency and share in responsibility for decision-making, resource management, and development of policies for operations and services as well as library-wide planning, assessment and programming. While each AD position has individual areas of responsibility, both ADs should adopt a holistic, library-wide view in terms of strategic planning, communication, and fostering an environment of innovation. The ADs are also expected to play a leadership role in promoting teamwork, diversity, and inclusiveness within GVSU University Libraries and the campus. In addition, ADs participate in relevant campus, consortia, or multi-institutional groups.

COLLABORATE—We invite applicants who have innovative and creative approaches to empowering and mentoring faculty and staff, leading collaborative projects, seeing the opportunities offered in problems, and transforming services to meet user needs. Candidates must understand the broad landscape of current trends in academic libraries and higher education as well as have a commitment to student experience, inclusion and accessibility. As faculty members in the Libraries, they maintain an agenda in research, scholarly publications and professional service activities in line with expectations at the Grand Valley State University Libraries.

GROW—After the previous ADs placed externally as Deans and the Dean retired, the Dean collaboratively re-envisioned the AD positions with faculty and staff, creating a connected strategic portfolio model. The ADs will need strengths in multiple areas, the ability and interest to grow in other areas, and the flexibility to work towards library-wide goals. By being growth-focused, the ADs will be able to shift responsibilities as needed to support an effective and agile organization that changes and adapts to needs over time.

EVOLVE—As the Libraries evolve, the portfolios of responsibility are likely to shift and change as areas of focus are re-imagined. GVSU Libraries has been using Appreciative Inquiry and participatory methodology to discover its next evolution. We hope to have the ADs deeply engaged in developing the dream stage of the next evolution and defining their own roles further, as such a comfort with creative ambiguity is an ingredient for success.

By making explicit our values and taking informed risks through an entrepreneurial culture, GVSU Libraries are a critical partner recognized across campus. Collaborations are a critical part of our success at GVSU. Here is a sampling of partnerships involving campus and other key stakeholders:
- Division of Inclusion and Equity: http://www.gvsu.edu/inclusion/
- Division of Student Services: http://www.gvsu.edu/studentservices/
- Faculty Teaching and Learning Center: https://www.gvsu.edu/ftlc/
- Instructional Design for eLearning and the Technology Showcase: http://www.gvsu.edu/elearn
- Instructional Design for eLearning (IDeL): http://www.gvsu.edu/idel/
- Knowledge Market: https://www.gvsu.edu/library/km/
- Open Education Resources: http://scholarworks.gvsu.edu/oer/
- Office of Undergraduate Research: https://www.gvsu.edu/ours/
- Publishing Services: http://scholarworks.gvsu.edu/journals.html
- Steelcase: https://www.steelcase.com/

- Scholar Works: http://scholarworks.gvsu.edu/
- Van Andel Research Institute: https://www.vai.org/

Discover the compensation package by reading the Compensation FAQ (https://gvsu.edu/library/adsearch), visiting the GVSU Wellness website (https://www.gvsu.edu/bewellgv), or the GVSU HR site (https://www.gvsu.edu/hro).

Learn more about the positions by reading the position descriptions for AD Curriculum, Research & User Services (CRUS) at https://gvsu.edu/library/adcurriculum and AD Curation, Publishing & Preservation Services (CPPS) at https://gvsu.edu/library/adcuration

Interested in applying? Go to Curriculum, Research & User Services at http://jobs.gvsu.edu/cw/en-us/job/492722 or Curation, Publishing & Preservation Services at http://jobs.gvsu.edu/cw/en-us/job/492723

Questions? Feel free to contact Annie Bélanger, search committee co-chair and Dean via email annie.belanger@gvsu.edu or telephone 616-331-2621.

Qualifications

REQUIRED

- Master's Degree from a program accredited by the American Library Association (ALA) or from a program in a country with a formal accreditation process as identified by ALA;
- Demonstrated progression of increasingly responsible, relevant, and professional work experience, with a particular expertise and passion for the delivery of user-centered services and/or infrastructure;
- Strong leadership skills, including keen analytical and conceptual abilities and demonstrated ability to lead collaborative organizational change, inspire innovation, and delegate responsibility appropriately;
- Strong interpersonal and public communication skills including ability to serve as an advocate and spokesperson for the Libraries;
- Demonstrated engagement in areas associated with portfolios;
- Strong record of collaboratively working with all levels of library personnel, as well as stakeholders and students;

- Experience with personnel development and management (faculty, staff, student and graduate student assistants, staff development, coaching, mentoring, supervision, hiring, etc.);
- Strong commitment to user experience, with the ability to view issues from Libraries and university wide perspectives;
- Evidence of partnership development and project initiation;
- Evidence of implementation of emerging trends in higher education in the areas of focus;
- Evidence of working creatively, collaboratively, and effectively in a leadership role in promoting teamwork, diversity, equality, and inclusiveness;
- Strong comfort with creative ambiguity;
- Evidence of research, publication, and service consonant with university standards for tenure.

PREFERRED

- Experience in developing and implementing strategic plans, operational plans and large projects;
- Experience with budget management;
- Demonstrated facility with data analysis;
- Demonstrated project management skills;
- Experience in consortia and multi-institutional program development;
- Experience in an academic library or research environment;
- Experience in publisher and vendor negotiations and collaborations.

Appendix 2B

POWERFUL AND GENERATIVE QUESTIONS

"Powerful questions are a reflection of committed listening and understanding the other person's perspective that is confirmed through paraphrasing. This suggests a progression from listening, paraphrasing for understanding, and then asking powerful questions that yield clarity or mediation of thinking."[44] Powerful questions are open-ended questions with no hidden agenda and meant to help the receiver of the question.

Powerful questions
- "generat[e] curiosity and encourag[e] creativity"
- "stimulat[e] reflective conversation"
- "surfac[e] underlying assumptions"
- "explor[e] with genuine curiosity"
- "d[o] not imply intent"
- "us[e] neutral language and tone"[45]

Powerful questions
- are open-ended
- start with "what if," "how might we," and "why"
- include a clear scope
- have a positive intent
- seek to move inquiry forward[46]

Example of generative questions
- "What about this library makes you especially glad you work here?"
- "What do you value most?"
- "What has inspired you to get engaged?"
- "What do you ...hope to contribute?"
- "Thinking back on [the] year, please share a high point when" you felt valued.
- "What are all the possibilities for collaboration between our departments?"
- "What challenges might come our way? ...How might we meet them?"
- "What would someone with different beliefs say about our decisions?"[47]

- How might we move forward together?

Reframing concerns and questions is a way to create powerful questions:
1. "Name it: Name the problem or concern—often a negative statement."
2. "Flip it: Flip it to its opposite—often a positive statement."
3. "Frame it: Frame it in reality—a generative question or set of questions"[48]

Examples:
- "Why did this fail? > We want to succeed. > What could success look like? What did go well? How do we build on what went well?"
- "No one ever tells me anything." > How would you like to be communicated with? I would like to have regular updates. > How can you contribute to open communications?"[49]

Further, closed questions can be evolved to open questions as well as generative ones.
- "Closed: Do you have experience? > Open: What experience do you have? > Generative: How might your experience impact our success?"[50]

Acknowledgment

The authors wish to acknowledge Abigail Smathers, a dean's office student colleague, for her help with the bibliography and footnote citation formatting.

Notes

1.   American Library Association, "Libraries: An American Value," February 3, 1999, http://www.ala.org/advocacy/intfreedom/americanvalue.
2.   Kathy Rosa and Kelsey Henke, *2017 ALA Demographic Study* (Chicago: American Library Association, 2017), https://www.ala.org/tools/sites/ala.org.tools/files/content/Draft%20of%20Member%20Demographics%20Survey%2001-11-2017.pdf.
3.   Jaena Alabi, "Racial Microaggressions in Academic Libraries: Results of a Survey of Minority and Non-minority Librarians, *Journal of Academic Librarianship* 411, no. 1 (2015): 47–53, https://doi.org/10.1016/j.acalib.2014.10.008; Ione T. Damasco and Dracine Hodges, "Tenure and Promotion Experiences of Academic Librarians of Color," *College and Research Libraries* 73, no. 3 (2012): 279–301, https://doi.org/10.5860/crl-244.
4.   Myrna Morales, Em Claire Knowles, and Chris Bourg, "Diversity, Social Justice, and the Future of Libraries," *portal: Libraries and the Academy* 14, no. 3 (2014), 439.
5.   Susan VanDeventer Iverson, "Camouflaging Power and Privilege: A Critical Race Analysis of University Diversity Policies," *Educational Administration Quarterly* 43, no. 5 (December 2007): 606, https://doi.org/10.1177/0013161X07307794.

6.   The Grand Valley State University inclusion advocate (IA) program develops individuals to serve a specialized role on search committees. The IA title requires continuing education on an annual basis, which is typically related to hiring and inclusion topics. The IA is intended to facilitate dialogue around inclusive talent acquisition and ensure that faculty and staff searches are conducted in an equitable manner. As an official member of the search committee, the IA is expected to participate in all committee meetings and in the completion of materials for final referral to the appointing officer or dean. The IA is intended to be an advisor for inclusive talent acquisition, a facilitator of inclusive and equitable deliberation, and an objective voice supplementing the search committee members. Grand Valley State University, "Inclusion Advocates Program," Affirmative Action/Equal Employment Opportunity, last updated March 27, 2020, http://www.gvsu.edu/affirmative/inclusion-advocates-program-33.htm.

7.   Jane E. Dutton, Kristina M. Workman, and Ashley E. Hardin, "Compassion at Work," *Annual Review of Organizational Psychology and Organizational Behavior* 1, no. 1 (2014): 277–304.

8.   Leading practices are dynamic and evolving. They are the emergent practices that are more efficient and effective at delivering an outcome based on the constraints and culture of the organization they are being implemented in. Best practices purport to be the best methods, techniques, or processes that are believed to be more effective than any other method, technique, or process. The difference rests in that there is no assumption that a leading practice is universally the best or that it could be applied to all situations or organizations.

9.   Asha Nagendra, "Paradigm Shift in HR Practices on Employee Life Cycle Due to Influence of Social Media," *Procedia Economics and Finance* 11 (2014): 197–207.

10.   Kristina Martic, "Everything You Need to Know about Full Life Cycle Recruiting," *TalentLyft* (blog), January 12, 2018, https://www.talentlyft.com/en/blog/article/88/what-is-full-life-cycle-recruiting.

11.   Benjamin Schneider, "The People Make the Place," *Personnel Psychology* 40 (1987): 437–53.

12.   Murray R. Barrick and Laura Parks-Leduc, "Selection for Fit," *Annual Review of Organizational Psychology and Organizational Behavior* 6 (January 2019): 171–93, https://doi.org/10.1146/annurev-orgpsych-012218-015028; Jon Billsberry, "Selecting for Fit: A Direct Test of Schneider's Selection Proposition (paper presented at Academy of Management Annual Meeting, New Orleans, LA, August 2004), https://doi.org/10.5465/ambpp.2004.13864354.

13.   Paul Falcone, "Effective Onboarding Should Last for Months," SHRM, April 24, 2018, https://www.shrm.org/resourcesandtools/hr-topics/talent-acquisition/pages/effective-onboarding-should-last-for-months.aspx.

14.   Sarah Mayorga-Gallo and Elizabeth Hordge-Freeman, "Between Marginality and Privilege: Gaining Access and Navigating the Field in Multiethnic Settings," *Qualitative Research* 17, no. 4 (2016), 377–94, https://doi.org/10.1177/1468794116672915; Iverson, "Camouflaging Power and Privilege."

15.   Elaine Z. Jennerich, "The Long-Term View of Library Staff Development: The Positive Effects on a Large Organization," *College and Research Libraries News* 67, no. 10 (2006), 612–14, https://doi.org/10.5860/crln.67.10.7701.

16.   Richard Branson (@richardbranson), Twitter post, March 27, 2014, 12:23 p.m., https://twitter.com/richardbranson/status/449220072176107520.

17.   Joanne G. Marshall et al., "Workforce Issues in Library and Information Science 2 (WILIS 2): Implementing a Model for Career Tracking of LIS Graduates" (poster presented at iConference, University of North Carolina at Chapel Hill, February 8–11, 2009), https://www.ideals.illinois.edu/handle/2142/15328.

18. Christina Merhar, "Real Cost of Losing an Employee | 2019," *PeopleKeep* (blog). February 4, 2016, https://www.peoplekeep.com/blog/bid/312123/employee-retention-the-real-cost-of-losing-an-employee (page content changed).

19. Thomas F. Mahan et al., *2019 Retention Report* (Franklin, TN: Work Institute, 2019), 7, https://info.workinstitute.com/hubfs/2019%20Retention%20Report/Work%20Institute%202019%20Retention%20Report%20final-1.pdf.

20. When determining an appropriate time horizon for baseline purposes, it is important to factor in additional variables that may be outside the norm. For example, the dates of any changes in personnel policies or newly hired leadership may skew the data by impacting turnover. The baseline should represent standard operations and conditions against which historical and current data can be measured.

21. Rachel Bolsu, "How to Implement an Effective Unlimited Vacation Policy," *Namely* (blog), November 1, 2018, https://blog.namely.com/unlimited-vacation-policy.

22. Appreciative Inquiry is a strengths-based, positive approach to leadership and organizational change. It can be used by individuals, teams, organizations, and communities. It helps move toward a shared vision of the future through deep engagement in what is good and what could be. It focuses on leveraging these strengths rather than weaknesses. Appreciative Inquiry is grounded in five core principles: "constructionist, simultaneity, anticipatory, poetic, and positive". It is grounded in the concept that we move in the direction of what we study. Therefore, the questions we ask are fateful in driving energy and focus.
It was first developed in the 1980s by David Cooperrider and Suresh Srivasta. David Cooperrider, "What Is Appreciative Inquiry?" David Cooperrider and Associates, 2012, https://www.davidcooperrider.com/ai-process/. See also 5 Classic Principles of AI, Appreciative Commons, https://appreciativeinquiry.champlain.edu/learn/appreciative-inquiry-introduction/5-classic-principles-ai/

23. Rosa and Henke, *2017 ALA Demographic Study*.

24. Libraries core workplace principles: (1) ask how this benefits our students; (2) sustain an entrepreneurial culture; (3) take informed risks; and (4) approach each other with respect and empathy. Grand Valley State University Libraries Programmatic Review Process Guide. 2020. https://scholarworks.gvsu.edu/cgi/viewcontent.cgi?article=1009&context=library_reports See also David L. Cooperrider, Diana Whitney, and Jacqueline M. Stavros, *Appreciative Inquiry Handbook*, 2nd ed. (Brunswick, OH: Crown Custom Publishing and San Francisco: Berrett-Koehler, 2008).

25. Ashley Rosener et al., "Leading from the Center: Reimagining Feedback Conversations at an Academic Library," *In the Library with the Lead Pipe*, September 18, 2019, http://www.inthelibrarywiththeleadpipe.org/2019/reimagining-feedback/.

26. More information about the libraries' commitment to inclusion, diversity, equity, and accessibility can be found at Grand Valley State University, "IDEA: Inclusion, Diversity, Equity, and Accessibility," University Libraries, last updated August 13, 2021, https://www.gvsu.edu/library/idea-inclusion-diversity-equity-and-accessibility-84.htm.

27. Powerful questions are open-ended and empower the respondent to choose the direction they take. They create possibilities, encourage discovery, and seek infinite imagination. They elicit a thought process. Attributes of powerful questions include these: it is short and precise, it is a single question, it is provocative, it is open-ended, it invites creative ambiguity, it is without assumptions, and it focuses on real issues. Find out more by reading Eric E. Vogt, Juanita Brown, and David Isaacs, *The Art of Powerful Questions* (Mill Valley, CA: Whole Systems Associates, 2003), https://www.sparc.bc.ca/wp-content/uploads/2020/11/the-art-of-powerful-questions.pdf.

28. Generative questions are a type of powerful questions. They are meant to work on the issue at hand, bringing valuable insights even if the issue is not resolved. They are questions that, if answered, could make the most difference to the future of the conversation, situation, or exploration. They ask what if, how might we, and what would it take to.

29. Sarah Lewis, Jonathan Passmore and Stefan Cantore, *Appreciative Inquiry for Change Management* (Philadelphia: Kogan Page Limited, 2008), 72

30. Robin DiAngelo, *White Fragility* (Boston: Beacon Press, 2018), 123.

31. Grand Valley State University is a master's comprehensive public university with a liberal education mission. It has three campuses located in Allendale and Grand Rapids, Michigan. Grand Valley has an enrollment of nearly 24,000 students, with 138 academic programs.

    The libraries have four locations spread across the three campuses: Mary Idema Pew Library Learning and Information Commons; Seidman House—Special Collections and Archives; Steelcase Library, which includes Curriculum Materials Library; and the Frey Learning Resource Center. The locations have different hours, while covering 7 a.m. to 12 a.m. At the time of this process, the libraries had 72 full-time-equivalent employees and close to 120 student colleagues. The employees include unionized paraprofessionals, professional librarians with faculty status, and professional staff.

32. Grand Valley State University Libraries' Hiring FAQ and other hiring material samples as of February 1, 2020, can be found at Grand Valley State University, "Job Opportunities at GVSU Libraries FAQ," Library Reports and Communication, ScholarWorks@GVSU, accessed February 1, 2020, https://scholarworks.gvsu.edu/library_reports/8.

33. Appendix 2A includes the ad used for the associate dean search in 2017, which used these leading practices.

34. Danielle Gaucher, Justin Friesen, and Aaron C. Kay, "Evaluating That Gendered Wording in Job Advertisements Exists and Sustains Gender Inequality," *Journal of Personality and Social Psychology* 101, no. 1 (2011): 109–28.

35. Scott Ayotte, Sarah Beaubien, and Annie Bélanger, "Towards High-Empathy Hiring: Implementing Leading Practices for More Inclusive Recruitment" (presentation, Michigan Academic Library Association Annual Conference, Saginaw Valley State University, Saginaw, MI, May 17, 2019), slide 20, https://scholarworks.gvsu.edu/library_presentations/80/.

36. Ayotte, Beaubien, and Bélanger, "Towards High-Empathy Hiring," slide 22.

37. In essence, full cycle recruiting.

38. Bruce Keisling and Melissa Laning, "We Are Happy to Be Here: The Onboarding Experience in Academic Libraries," *Journal of Library Administration* 56, no. 4 (2016): 391–92, https://doi.org/10.1080/01930826.2015.1105078.

39. Tatiana Bryant, Hillary Bussel, and Rebecca Halpern, "Being Seen: Gender Identity and Performance as a Professional Resource in Library Work," *College and Research Libraries* 80, no. 6 (2019): 804–26, https://doi.org/10.5860/crl.80.6.805.

40. Jim Burklo, "Microaffection: The Antidote to Microagression," Huffington Post, November 24, 2015, last updated November 23, 2016, http://www.huffingtonpost.com/jim-burklo/microaffection_b_8631396.html; Michelle McQuaid, "How to Create Appreciative Micro Moments," podcast audio, *Making Positive Psychology Work* 12: Maureen McKenna, https://www.michellemcquaid.com/podcast/mppw-12-maureen-mckenna/.

41. Cooperrider, Whitney, and Stavros, *Appreciative Inquiry Handbook*.

42. Lewis, Passmore, and Cantore, *Appreciative Inquiry*, 72.

43. Grand Valley State University Libraries provides an opportunity for nonselected candidates to receive feedback; frequently, candidates (selected and nonselected) provide positive

feedback about the hiring process. The libraries collect data on their leaders yearly, with notable notation of a positive and supportive work culture.

44. Kathryn Kee et al., *Results Coaching* (Thousand Oaks, CA: Corwin, 2010), 62.
45. Annie Bélanger and Preethi Rao, "The Art of Questioning: Using Powerful Questions and Appreciative Inquiry Conversations to Understand Values and Needs" (presentation, Michigan Academic Library Association Annual Conference, Presentation, Saginaw Valley State University, Saginaw MI, May 17, 2019), 13, https://scholarworks.gvsu.edu/library_presentations/79.
46. Bélanger and Rao, "Art of Questioning," 15.
47. Bélanger and Rao, "Art of Questioning," 16–18, 20.
48. Bélanger and Rao, "Art of Questioning," 22.
49. Bélanger and Rao, "Art of Questioning," 23–24.
50. Bélanger and Rao, "Art of Questioning," 25.

Bibliography

AI Commons. "5 Classic Principles of AI, Appreciative Commons", retrieved November 11, 2021 https://appreciativeinquiry.champlain.edu/learn/appreciative-inquiry-introduction/5-classic-principles-ai/

Alabi, Jaena. "Racial Microaggressions in Academic Libraries: Results of a Survey of Minority and Non-minority Librarians." *Journal of Academic Librarianship* 41, no. 1 (January 2015): 47–53. https://doi.org/10.1016/j.acalib.2014.10.008.

American Library Association. "Libraries: An American Value." February 3, 1999. http://www.ala.org/advocacy/intfreedom/americanvalue

Ayotte, Scott, Sarah Beaubien, and Annie Bélanger. "Towards High-Empathy Hiring: Implementing Leading Practices for More Inclusive Recruitment." Presentation, Michigan Academic Library Association Annual Conference, Saginaw Valley State University, Saginaw, MI, May 17, 2019. https://scholarworks.gvsu.edu/library_presentations/80/.

Barrick, Murray R., and Laura Parks-Leduc. "Selection for Fit." *Annual Review of Organizational Psychology and Organizational Behavior* 6 (January 2019): 171–93. https://doi.org/10.1146/annurev-orgpsych-012218-015028.

Bélanger, Annie, and Preethi Rao. "The Art of Questioning: Using Powerful Questions and Appreciative Inquiry Conversations to Understand Values and Needs." Presentation, Michigan Academic Library Association Annual Conference, Saginaw Valley State University, Saginaw MI, May 17, 2019. https://scholarworks.gvsu.edu/library_presentations/79.

Billsberry, Jon. "Selecting for Fit: A Direct Test of Schneider's Selection Proposition." Paper presented at Academy of Management Annual Meeting, New Orleans, LA, August 2004. https://doi.org/10.5465/ambpp.2004.13864354.

Bolsu, Rachel. "How to Implement an Effective Unlimited Vacation Policy." *Namely* (blog), November 1, 2018. https://blog.namely.com/unlimited-vacation-policy.

Branson, Richard (@richardbranson). "Train people well enough so they can leave, treat them well enough so they don't want to." Twitter post, March 27, 2014, 12:23 p.m. https://twitter.com/richardbranson/status/449220072176107520.

Bryant, Tatiana, Hillary Bussel, and Rebecca Halpern. "Being Seen: Gender Identity and Performance as a Professional Resource in Library Work." *College and Research Libraries* 80, no. 6 (2019): 804–26. https://doi.org/10.5860/crl.80.6.805.

Burklo, Jim. "Microaffection: The Antidote to Microaggression." Huffington Post, November 24, 2015, last updated November 23, 2016. http://www.huffingtonpost.com/jim-burklo/microaffection_b_8631396.html.

Cooperrider, David. "What Is Appreciative Inquiry?" David Cooperrider and Associates, 2012. https://www.davidcooperrider.com/ai-process/.

Cooperrider, David L., Diana Whitney, and Jacqueline M. Stavros. *Appreciative Inquiry Handbook: For Leaders of Change*, 2nd ed. Brunswick, OH: Crown Custom Publishing and San Francisco: Berrett-Koehler, 2008.

Damasco, Ione T., and Dracine Hodges. "Tenure and Promotion Experiences of Academic Librarians of Color." *College and Research Libraries* 73, no. 3 (2012): 279–301. https://doi.org/10.5860/crl-244.

DiAngelo, Robin. *White Fragility: Why It's So Hard for White People to Talk about Racism.* Boston: Beacon Press, 2018.

Dutton, Jane E., Kristina M. Workman, and Ashley E. Hardin. "Compassion at Work." *Annual Review of Organizational Psychology and Organizational Behavior* 1, no. 1 (2014): 277–304.

Falcone, Paul. " Effective Onboarding Should Last for Months." SHRM, April 24, 2018. https://www.shrm.org/resourcesandtools/hr-topics/talent-acquisition/pages/effective-onboarding-should-last-for-months.aspx.

Gaucher, Danielle, Justin Friesen, and Aaron C. Kay. "Evaluating That Gendered Wording in Job Advertisements Exists and Sustains Gender Inequality." *Journal of Personality and Social Psychology* 101, no. 1 (2011): 109–28.

Grand Valley State University. "IDEA: Inclusion, Diversity, Equity, and Accessibility." University Libraries, last updated August 13, 2021. https://www.gvsu.edu/library/idea-inclusion-diversity-equity-and-accessibility-84.htm.

———. "Inclusion Advocates Program." Affirmative Action/Equal Employment Opportunity, last updated March 27, 2020. https://www.gvsu.edu/affirmative/inclusion-advocates-program-33.htm

———. "Job Opportunities at GVSU Libraries FAQ." Library Reports and Communication, ScholarWorks@GVSU. Accessed February 1, 2020. https://scholarworks.gvsu.edu/library_reports/8.

———. "Programmatic Review Process Guide. University Libraries, last updated August 2020. https://scholarworks.gvsu.edu/cgi/viewcontent.cgi?article=1009&context=library_reports

Iverson, Susan VanDeventer. "Camouflaging Power and Privilege: A Critical Race Analysis of University Diversity Policies." *Educational Administration Quarterly* 43, no. 5 (December 2007): 586–611. https://doi.org/10.1177/0013161X07307794.

Jennerich, Elaine Z. "The Long-Term View of Library Staff Development: The Positive Effects on a Large Organization." *College and Research Libraries News* 67, no. 10 (2006): 612–14. https://doi.org/10.5860/crln.67.10.7701.

Kee, Kathryn, Karen Anderson, Vicky Dearing, Edna Harris, and Frances Shuster. *Result Coaching: The New Essential for School Leaders.* Thousand Oaks, CA: Corwin, 2010.

Keisling, Bruce, and Melissa Laning. "We Are Happy to Be Here: The Onboarding Experience in Academic Libraries." *Journal of Library Administration* 56, no. 4 (2016): 381–94. https://doi.org/10.1080/01930826.2015.1105078.

Lewis, Sarah, Jonathan Passmore, and Stefan Cantore. *Appreciative Inquiry for Change Management: Using AI to Facilitate Organizational Development.* Philadelphia: Kogan Page Limited, 2008.

Lupfer, Elizabeth. "The Social Workplace Employee Lifecycle." Image. The Social Workplace, July 2014, last updated August 2017. http://thesocialworkplace.com/thesocialworkplaceemployeelifecycle2014b-140805182512-phpapp02-2/.

Mahan, Thomas F., Danny Nelms, Christopher R. Bearden, and Brantley Pearce. *2019 Retention Report*. Franklin, TN: Work Institute, 2019. https://info.workinstitute.com/hubfs/2019%20Retention%20Report/Work%20Institute%202019%20Retention%20Report%20final-1.pdf.

Marshall, Joanne G., Jennifer Craft Morgan, Victor W. Marshall, Deborah Barreau, Barbara B. Moran, Paul Solomon, Susan R. Rathbun-Grubb, et al. "Workforce Issues in Library and Information Science 2 (WILIS 2): Implementing a Model for Career Tracking of LIS Graduates." Poster presented at iConference, University of North Carolina at Chapel Hill, February 8–11, 2009. https://www.ideals.illinois.edu/handle/2142/15328.

Martic, Kristina. "Everything You Need to Know about Full Life Cycle Recruiting." *TalentLyft* (blog), January 12, 2018. https://www.talentlyft.com/en/blog/article/88/what-is-full-life-cycle-recruiting.

Mayorga-Gallo, Sarah, and Elizabeth Hordge-Freeman. "Between Marginality and Privilege: Gaining Access and Navigating the Field in Multiethnic Settings." *Qualitative Research* 17, no. 4 (2016): 377–94. https://doi.org/10.1177/1468794116672915.

McQuaid, Michelle. "How to Create Appreciative Micro Moments." Podcast audio. *Making Positive Psychology Work* 12: Maureen McKenna. https://www.michellemcquaid.com/podcast/mppw-12-maureen-mckenna/.

Merhar, Christina. "Real Cost of Losing an Employee | 2019." *PeopleKeep* (blog), February 4, 2016. https://www.peoplekeep.com/blog/bid/312123/employee-retention-the-real-cost-of-losing-an-employee (page content changed).

Morales, Myrna, Em Claire Knowles, and Chris Bourg. "Diversity, Social Justice, and the Future of Libraries." *portal: Libraries and the Academy* 14, no. 3 (2014): 439–51.

Nagendra, Asha. "Paradigm Shift in HR Practices on Employee Life Cycle Due to Influence of Social Media." *Procedia Economics and Finance* 11 (2014): 197–207.

Rosa, Kathy, and Kelsey Henke. *2017 ALA Demographic Study*. Chicago: American Library Association, 2017. https://www.ala.org/tools/sites/ala.org.tools/files/content/Draft%20of%20Member%20Demographics%20Survey%2001-11-2017.pdf.

Rosener, Ashley, Emily Frigo, Susan Ponischil, Annie Bélanger, Jacklyn Rander, and Elisa Salazar. "Leading from the Center: Reimagining Feedback Conversations at an Academic Library." *In the Library with the Lead Pipe*, September 18, 2019. http://www.inthelibrarywiththeleadpipe.org/2019/reimagining-feedback/.

Schneider, Benjamin. "The People Make the Place." *Personnel Psychology* 40 (1987): 437–53.

Vogt, Eric E., Juanita Brown, and David Isaacs. *The Art of Powerful Questions: Catalyzing Insight, Innovation, and Action*. Mill Valley, CA: Whole Systems Associates, 2003. https://www.sparc.bc.ca/wp-content/uploads/2020/11/the-art-of-powerful-questions.pdf.

CHAPTER 3

Gendered Ageism as a Barrier to Tenure-Track Librarianship

Sally Stieglitz

Introduction

Background of Population and Emergent Issue

Librarianship is known to be a largely female profession, with women comprising 79 percent of all librarians and 82.6 percent of graduates of master of library science (MLS) programs.[1] It is also a profession frequently entered as a second career and consequently at a later age.[2] Conservatively, 32.2 percent of female MLS graduates are over age forty within the first five years of their professional careers as librarians.[3] Does the intersection of these identities create a large pool of older female new librarians who will apply for entry-level positions while subject to all the stigmas and biases associated with being an aging woman in the workplace? A lack of available data on the relationship between gender, age, and joining the academic library workforce leaves room for further exploration of this topic and underlies a significant gap in scholarship. In the absence of pertinent data, the topic is illuminated through examination and analysis of literature on mainstream workplace gendered ageism and on the narrower focuses of gendered ageism in libraries and academia.

According to the World Health Organization, ageism is the most socially accepted of prejudices and "may now be even more pervasive than sexism

and racism."[4] Within the United States, legislation has been enacted to protect workers from ageism and establishes age forty as a threshold for those legal protections.[5] As a general workplace issue, "ageism is particularly evident when unemployed and searching for work."[6] Notably, in all workplaces, "particular attention needs to be paid to older female employees and their battle with gendered ageism," which is widely recognized as a significant obstacle to gainful employment.[7]

How might gendered ageism in the workplace impact opportunities for new female librarians hoping to pursue full-time appointments in academic librarianship? This chapter explores the interrelationship between gender bias and ageism that affects female librarians over the age of forty who are recent graduates of library and information science (LIS) master degree programs through an examination of scholarly, popular, and professional literature published between 2000 and 2019.

Across all genres and formats of publications, persistent themes emerge: that older women are judged negatively on age when seeking employment and that the hallmarks of this bias are evident and influential in academic libraries looking to recruit for full-time positions. Older female candidates in libraries are instead considered by some as best suited to part-time or temporary work.[8] These discriminatory attitudes toward older female candidates converge sharply to create a barrier to their full-time employment as academic librarians, positions that would offer them the greatest opportunities for income, professional advancement, job security, workplace benefits, and quite significantly, institutional support for their own scholarship, which is a standard requirement for advancement in the academy.

Research Methods and Scope

To examine current and recent attitudes toward new female librarians in academia, this study undertook a review of scholarly, popular, and professional literature published between the years 2000 and 2019 on the topics of ageism and gendered ageism. The literature examined looked at the broader general workplace and the narrower topics of library and academic workplaces. A limitation on the methodology was the sparse availability of literature specifically addressing gendered ageism in academic librarianship. Where available, demographic data was examined from government agencies and from American Library Association member studies. A notable limitation of American Library Association member studies is that they are not representative of the entire profession, but limited to those who opted to join the organization.

Each type of article reviewed offered different insights into the attitudes and expectations at play in the workforce. As a whole, the literature review suggests strongly that there is a pervasive and persistent barrier to tenure-track employment in academic libraries for new female librarians over the age of forty. (An operational definition of tenure track is included in the following section of the chapter.)

This study was originally presented in 2019 at the American Library Association (ALA) Annual Conference, Association of College Research Libraries (ACRL), Women and Gender Studies Section poster session, in Washington, DC. Since then, additional but limited research has been conducted by the author to explore the related subject of guidelines issued by ACRL with the intent of abating and preventing discriminatory hiring practices.

Research Terms Defined

Although not all academic libraries frame full-time employment as tenure-track, for purposes of this research, the term *tenure-track librarianship* (employment that offers greater salary, benefits, job security, and potential for professional advancement than part-time or adjunct librarian positions) is used here as a convenient term to represent all full-time permanent academic librarian employment, while also recognizing that many academic libraries do not characterize their permanent full-time employment as tenure-track. This allows for a more succinct exploration of gendered ageism in full-time academic librarianship, while recognizing that there are certainly differing systems and terminology for full-time employment at every academic library.

Older candidates, later-in-life librarians, and other similar terms may be used interchangeably to identify women who enter the librarian workforce at an age where gendered ageism begins to impact their potential employment. As will be discussed below, the range of ages at which this becomes impactful varies within the scholarship, but has been identified as beginning as early as age thirty-five.[9] Naturally there is no upper age limit identified, as new female librarians may opt to enter the workforce at any age.

Gaps in the Scholarship

There is not much data or scholarship on the experiences of older women who were unable to access tenure-track positions. They seem largely invisible to institutional and professional fact-gathering efforts on diversity within academic librarianship. With respect to part-time, adjunct, or lecturer librarians, "a review of the literature revealed a dearth of studies specifically focused on the experience of academic librarians outside the tenure track."[10] A recent ALA study of member demographics (2017) was described as "limited with respect to the variety of data collected."[11] The lack of data on the experiences of older female new librarians both creates a gap in the scholarship and suggests a tacit understanding by LIS scholars that their workplace experiences are unworthy of study and remediation. Writings on gendered ageism in other pink collar professions may also be probative for future study (e.g., nursing and teaching[12]) to consider if professional demographic similarities are informative.

To the extent that there has been generational research within LIS, it has not looked deeply at the idea of gendered ageism (as opposed to ageism against all). Rather, it has instead had "a focus on a singular marker of identity (age or generational cohort) while race, sexual orientation, gender expression, ethnicity and other markers are conspicuously absent."[13] This lack of examination of intersecting identities is problematic as it fails to fully examine the nuances of ageist workplace practices. Certainly more work needs to be done to consider the implications of the interplay between all these understudied identities and the impact of their intersections in hiring practices. Future research could consider the implications of race on workplace gendered ageism to discern its impact on hiring.

Outside of LIS, age discrimination in the workplace is also a notably understudied topic. There is, again, a paucity in the scholarship across all professions and disciplines.[14] Once again, the research has not focused on the intersection of multiple identities, but rather has had a single axis approach.[15] "What research has been conducted on age-based prejudice and discrimination demonstrates it to be surprisingly pervasive, potentially infecting numerous societal facets."[16] Nevertheless, much of that research generally neglects consideration of gender as a factor.[17]

The absence of data and scholarship, both within and without LIS, raises the question as to why this area is understudied and, further, what insights might be gained from future scholarship. For purposes of this study on barriers faced by older female new librarians, only the latter issue is addressed; the former is reserved for future scholarship.

FIGURE 3.1

Ages of female librarians five years post ALA-accredited MLS (Data: Dan Albertson, Kaitlyn Spetka, and Kristen Snow, eds., *Library and Information Science Education Statistical Report 2015* [Westford, MA: ALISE (Association for Library and Information Science Education), 2015], https://ali.memberclicks.net/assets/documents/statistical_reports/2015/alise_2015_statistical_report.pdf.)

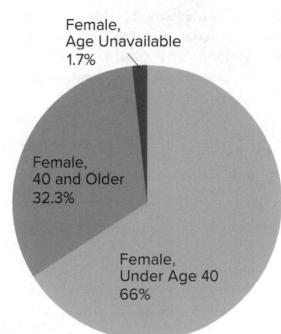

Female, Age Unavailable 1.7%

Female, 40 and Older 32.3%

Female, Under Age 40 66%

Findings and Discussion

Ageism and Employment Law

The United States of America prohibits age discrimination in employment against people over the age of forty, as enacted in The Age Discrimination in Employment Act of 1967 (ADEA), 29 U.S.C. § 621-634. The related Congressional Statement of Findings and Purpose states clearly that "the setting of arbitrary age limits regardless of potential for job performance has become a common practice, and certain otherwise desirable practices may work to the disadvantage of older persons."[18] Unfortunately for older job seekers, age discrimination laws are focused most strongly on ageism's effect on job loss or on workplace promotions, rather than on the role of age discrimination in the hiring process.[19] Ironically, however, age discrimination "occurs more often in the group of job seekers than [to] those in employment."[20]

Certainly, the impact of age discrimination in securing employment is pervasive. "More than 3 of 4 older workers [have] said their age was an obstacle to finding a job."[21] Nevertheless, "after 50 years of a federal law whose purpose is to promote the employment of older workers based on ability, age discrimination remains too common and too accepted. Indeed, 6 out of 10 older workers have seen or experienced age discrimination in the workplace and 90 percent of those say it is common."[22] Tellingly, despite ADEA, ageism is actually on the rise and is considered socially acceptable.[23]

Workplace Age Discrimination Begins Early and Is Not Gender Neutral

Although one may imagine the elderly to be the stereotypical victims of workplace age discrimination, in reality universal workplace ageism often starts much sooner and certainly "negative attitudes begin to rise around age 40."[24] It may come as a surprise to learn that workplace age discrimination may even start as early as age thirty-five, an age generally considered quite youthful, and is especially notable for entry-level jobs.[25]

The literature confirms that "despite the gradual and persistent increase in female employment, women as a group remain at a disadvantage to men as a group in respect to equal treatment at work."[26] Ageism is also not equal in its treatment. "There seems to be little recognition as yet of the gender components of ageism, with public policy discussion on age discrimination legislation persisting to treat the concept as gender neutral."[27] However, it has been clearly established that "the nature of ageism experienced by older women is qualitatively different from men" across all professions.[28]

In point of fact, "women, especially older women but also those at middle age, were subjected to more age discrimination than older men."[29] Notably, "women are often interpreted to be 'old' already rather early, sometimes when they are just over 40,"[30] and the closer women get to retirement age, the more robust the evidence of age discrimination in hiring practices.[31] The qualitative and quantitative divisions of ageism experiences are a strong argument that ageism must be studied through the lens of gender. The two distinct threads of the impact of gender cannot be ignored: first, that ageist hiring bias is an earlier impediment for female job applicants than for males, and second, that women are impacted by ageism in hiring more frequently than men are.

Once acknowledging that it is undeniable and problematic "that women and men experience age, aging, and ageism in different ways in organizations and management,"[32] the existing literature has then sought to unearth the roots of this difference in treatment, adding, ironically, that men will benefit from a beneficial association of age with wisdom and experience whereas for women, age will serve only to increase their invisibility.[33]

The qualitative difference in the bias against women has sometimes been expressed, in the literature, as a double jeopardy (age and gender), and sometimes as a triple jeopardy (age, gender, and appearance). In the literature on higher education, this third, appearance-based stigma has been labelled as "lookism," an experience in which female candidates are judged for employment merit based on their attractiveness.[34] These three biases against older women, age, gender, and lookism, make older female candidates experience ageism in a way that must be acknowledged and addressed in EDI discussions.

A closer examination of the concept of "lookism" has revealed that the impact of an attractive (or unattractive) appearance for a female job candidate is subtle in the search process, resulting in assigning negative or positive attributes to candidates. "Researchers consistently find that favorable personality traits are attributed to attractive people and that attractive people receive more favorable outcomes such as salary increases and job opportunities than do unattractive people."[35] Thus, an attractive and young candidate may have workplace merit ascribed to her based on appearance rather than based on her demonstrable skills, experience, or scholarship in a kind of reverse ageism, skewing the playing field even further for a candidate who is less attractive or young. It is not simply that the older, less attractive candidate is less likely to be hired; it is also that a more attractive, younger candidate is more likely to be hired, to be given better compensation packages, and to receive more opportunities to shine in the workplace. As explained in the literature, "age may be entangled with physical attractiveness when considering discrimination against women, given that attractive people have been found to experience enhanced career success and earnings."[36] Thus, an older woman with significant professional accomplishments may not be appropriately considered for employment, promotion, or compensation as age stigma will detract from her accomplishments. Conversely, professional doors may open for the younger, attractive female candidate, perhaps irrespective of her accomplishments. This double (or triple) standard of aging allows men to be "valued for their accomplishments (which increase with age), whereas women are valued for their appearance (which diminishes with age)."[37] The relationship between youth and attractiveness and access to employment is troubling for its existence and also for the way it is accepted by professional communities, as discussed below.

Professional Advice to Older Candidates

Consequently, and not surprisingly, well intended and misguided advice to older candidates suggests undertaking substantial efforts to appear younger and to conceal clues to one's age. The advice offered to older candidates on combating ageism in hiring is, frankly, to try to pass as a younger candidate. Professional advice to counter ageism in hiring includes using hair dye; losing weight; updating one's hairstyle, wardrobe, and eyeglasses; rejuvenating the appearance of one's skin with cosmetic products and plastic surgery; and whitening one's teeth.[38] For professional documents and for a candidate's online presence, the advice includes not putting photos on professional networking sites, hiding one's children on social media sites, considering whether a first name indicates a certain generation (e.g., be "Liz" rather than "Betty"), removing graduation dates from resumes, editing resumes to eliminate experiences from more than ten years prior, using youth-oriented language and the latest buzzwords, changing one's e-mail addresses to remove any indicators of age, and using Gmail rather than an (outdated) AOL or Hotmail account.[39] These strategies are characterized as "concealments" in the scholarly literature on ageism and are disconcerting when considered through the lens of EDI.[40]

Certainly, within the contexts of academia and librarianship, there is no reluctance in voicing these ageist stereotypes and encouraging older candidates to attempt to "pass" for younger than their actual age. One *American Libraries* column ("Working Knowledge") offering librarians advice to counter ageism suggested, "Do you look your age? Maybe it's time for a not-so-extreme makeover—consider coloring your hair, updating your wardrobe, and getting advice from impartial parties about how you look and sound."[41] The perhaps well-intentioned professional advice masks subtle ageist treatment.[42] In this context, it is not surprising that "older individuals hesitate to put a professional headshot on their social media profiles for fear of being dismissed as 'too old,' having out-of-date skills, or expecting too high a salary."[43] The reality of ageism in hiring compels concealments and fear of discovery among candidates who have been told by their profession that they are undesirable and unwelcome for reasons of identity. This is most true for female candidates who face a harsher judgment based on their age, appearance, and attractiveness.

The Halo Effect

The flip side of the coin of bias against older candidates is the workplace's clear and unabashed preference for the young and attractive candidate. "There's a benefit to youth that can't be expressed. And, that's a flat out discriminatory deal."[44] Sometimes termed a "halo effect," the preference for the physically attractive candidate expresses itself by assigning favorable personality traits to the more attractive candidates.[45] Succinctly, "in a culture where youth and beauty are desirable, older people are at a disadvantage."[46] And while youthful job applicants may benefit from the halo effect, older applicants instead have a "negative halo." "That is, because older people are perceived as generally unattractive, they are also seen as having negative traits and abilities."[47] Also known as appearance stigma, being perceived as less attractive is "both socially and academically costly."[48] For women, a potential employer's judgment on one's appearance is even more impactful. "The notion that women are valued in accordance to the conditions ascribed to their youth (sexual appeal, reproductive capacity) has meant that older women have tended to be …more harshly affected [than younger women],"[49] despite the obvious lack of correlation between youthful fertility and workplace value.

Ageism Addressed in Academic Librarianship

"Age discrimination is a concern for a growing number of library school graduates who have chosen to change careers or enter the workplace later in their life,"[50] and also affects employment opportunities for women over forty in academia in general.[51] One article states baldly that "it's time for colleges to admit that they don't seriously consider older applicants for faculty jobs."[52] Another writes, "For women in academia as in Hollywood, appearance counts."[53] The majority of new female librarians may face this bias if they pursue positions in academic libraries. As "female academic late starters," they will be "perceived as old, rather than being in their mid career."[54]

The literature reveals that aspects of academic librarianship, interestingly, hew quite closely to professions in which gendered ageism has been observed to have the greatest impact. Research suggests ageism is most conspicuous in professions with components of public service, a requirement of technological skills, or both.[55] Since library science has a deep dependence on workers with both technological and customer service skills, it is likely a field in which gendered ageism may have deep impact.

In academic librarianship, both reference services and access services jobs highly prize strong customer service skills. The impact of gendered ageism in customer service jobs is even more significant in "pink collar jobs" where "image, both to the public and in general, may be particularly important for women."[56] Librarianship is so firmly female in public perception and in practice that it has been termed a pink collar ghetto.[57]

The second type of field found to be highly impacted by gendered ageism is a profession with expectations of technological expertise.[58] Likewise, academic librarianship is deeply dependent on emerging technologies and often seeks job candidates with tech skills that are enumerated as required or preferred competencies in position descriptions. These twin expected professional competencies of customer service and technical proficiency make hiring in academic librarianship especially vulnerable to ageist bias.

Ageist Stereotypes Refuted by Scholarship

Ageist stereotypes persist in the workplace even when refuted by scholarship.

> Lingering behind the view that older people do not fit certain company profiles are alleged concerns about future, job-specific performance. The perception of older workers as unwilling or unable to keep up with the demands of a changing workforce is noted across a variety of contexts.[59]

Negative traits assigned to older workers include stubbornness, low adaptability, low energy, lower motivation, less productivity, difficulty being trained or retrained, a greater likelihood of burnout, resistance to change, reduced creativity, an unwillingness to report to younger managers, a reluctance to travel for work, a lack of digital skills, being more costly both in terms of salary and benefits, being more likely to be ill or absent, and generally being less competent than their younger colleagues.[60] Scholarship has also identified negative ageist stereotypes particular to older women, to wit, that they lack stamina, are not tech savvy, want to slow down, and aren't invested in their careers.[61] These perceived deficits are also sometimes considered irremediable. For example, in academic libraries, concern has been expressed that older candidates are not only "increasingly behind the technological curve," but also unable to develop any technical expertise.[62] And although aging is often associated in a general way with increases of desirable personality traits such as conscientiousness, organization, discipline, agreeableness, warmth, generosity,[63] all of which should enhance a candidate in the eyes of a search committee, unsurprisingly, "positive older age stereotype characteristics are viewed less favorably as criteria for job hire."[64]

Although facts are stubborn things, so are stereotypes. "Study findings were surprising in that many human resource professionals seemed to hold stereotypical opinions about age groups based primarily on anecdotal rather than empirical evidence."[65] "Unfounded assumptions about age and ability continue to drive age discrimination in the workplace. Research on ageist stereotypes demonstrates that most people have specific negative beliefs about aging and that most of those beliefs are inaccurate."[66] Ironically, data suggests that "every aspect of job performance gets better as we age,"[67] but the ageist stereotypes about suitability for employment persist despite clear scholarship to the contrary.

For example, the stereotypes of technological skills being a strength particular to younger applicants has been examined and found without merit. "Young people do not inherently possess" digital skills, and "exposure to technology cannot be equated with ability to use it."[68] In academia, "power users among senior professors say that while not all of their peers take the time to master the latest technological offerings, many live as comfortably with digital advances as anyone can."[69] Work performance similarly does not decline as one gets older, but the perception that it does persists nonetheless. "In the workplace, despite considerable research indicating that job performance does not decrease with age, evidence indicates that older job applicants are rated less positively than younger ones, even when they are similarly qualified."[70]

Tenure Track and ROI

The concept of return on investment (ROI) also plays a significant role in ageist hiring decisions. "Implicit in management's goals of profitability and cost containment is the expectation that individuals who are promoted or trained should have a long enough future with the company for the company to recoup its investment."[71] That commitment of time and costs to training a candidate who might retire within a few years may seem unappealing to a search committee. In academia, tenure-track hiring is often considered an investment in a faculty member and may not be considered a worthwhile ROI when the candidates are older.[72] Academic "departments may be concerned that if they hired someone who was 60, that candidate would enjoy relatively few productive years and stay on as deadwood for another 15."[73] "Hirers may, therefore, have strong preference for stereotypically younger candidates if the investment is viewed as long- rather than short-term."[74] Yet when examined more closely, an impending retirement from the workforce is not a strong rationale for disregarding older applicants as, according to the US Bureau of Labor Statistics, across professions, most people are working later in life.[75] In fact, "the labor force participation rate is expected to increase fastest for the oldest segments of the population—most notably, people ages 65 to 74 and 75 and older—through 2024."[76]

Moreover, the argument that hiring young candidates is investment in future returns flies in the face of data establishing that younger candidates are quite often likely to change jobs and to change them with greater frequency than their older counterparts. Millennials (birth year between 1981 and 1996) have been identified as a "job-hopping generation," the most likely generation to switch jobs.[77] "In contrast, a review of moderators of workplace discrimination research revealed evidence for the opposing hypothesis—that older workers are a better long-term investment because they are less likely to quit."[78] In this light, the ROI argument loses validity as an excuse for ageist hiring practices.

A second thread of ROI arguments is that, from a cost overhead perspective, older workers are considered more expensive[79] and "younger workers ...are viewed as cheaper and more worthy of the long-term investment."[80] A résumé filled with experiences may create an impression of higher salary expectations and, although "a robust professional track record should be an accomplishment; instead, many job candidates find it relegates them to 'overqualified' status. They are left to wonder if 'overqualified' translates to 'too expensive,' 'likely to bolt at another opportunity,' or is it simply a polite way of saying 'too old'?"[81] Implicit in this bias is the assumption that older workers expect higher salaries irrespective of the relative level of the position being advertised; however, new librarians of any age would likely be expecting compensation in the same salary range as all other candidates, basing it on their years of experience in the field of librarianship, on marketplace norms, and not on their respective ages.

Beyond institutional expectations of a long-term commitment by younger candidates, the value assigned to young workers is also associated with a boost to a workplace's image. The halo effect of youthful workers is seen as essential to an institution's success. "Age has been, and continues to be, an important cultural dimension of status in our society."[82] The stereotypical values of youth—that is, energy, growth, stamina, and creativity—are positive image and brand stories for the institution. As noted in the literature, "libraries need to attract and maintain as many young people as possible to the profession. Without an influx of youth, librarianship could lose its vitality and a source of new ideas."[83] Specifically, the very survival of the profession is linked to hiring young employees.

Across Professions, Expectations for Older Workers to Step Aside

The literature also reveals an outright expectation that older workers should step aside for younger workers or otherwise be accused of taking jobs away from millennials.[84] This discrimination by gatekeepers is seen as legitimate and fair and within their discretion.[85] Young hires are seen as representative of the future of organizations.[86] Older candidates who do not know their place are viewed as a challenge to this concept, and "the risk for generational tension will be particularly ripe if the younger generations view older ones as increasingly overstepping their boundaries"[87] The literature on academic libraries particularly explains that baby boomers are expected to get out of the way of the Gen Xers and millennials.[88] "Those who stay in their [academic librarian] roles past 65 can limit promotional prospects for others, reduce the number of new hires and increase overall labor costs for their institutions."[89] In sum, "ageist attitudes and discrimination result in lower levels of overall organizational commitment for older workers, and a 'push' out of a particular workplace or full-time employment."[90] This push out, or expectation to step aside, may play a role in hiring decisions for tenure track when candidate pools include older female new librarians.

When one door closes, another one opens; unfortunately, the second door leads to a second class opportunity for employment. The literature acknowledges that while discouraged from pursuing or continuing tenured employment in academia, older workers are often considered good candidates for those non-tenure-track positions, the conventional wisdom being that "candidates in their 50s and 60s can be very competitive for other types of teaching positions on fixed term contracts, such as lectureships."[91] The stereotype that older candidates will be physically and cognitively unable to perform at the appropriate level creates an ingrained preference for younger employees, even when inexperienced, as new hires, compelling the older workers to accept temporary and part-time employment.[92] Older applicants are dismissed preemptively as being uninterested in full-time employment. "Members of the Traditionalist Generation have worked full time for 30 to 40 years and are more than likely not willing to start working full-time again. Consider them for part time work instead."[93] These ageist assumptions and biases frame older applicants as belonging in "low-status roles."[94] In academia, those low-status roles are part-time, lecturer, and adjunct faculty roles. Unlike tenure-track positions, part-time, adjunct, and lecturer employment does not have an implicit expectation of long-term service to an institution, and concomitantly, no obligation of long-term employment from that institution. The non-tenure-track option is an entryway to academic librarianship that, for older candidates, may never provide a stepping stone to the more desirable full-time positions because ironically, as each mature candidate gains greater experience in academic libraries, she also grows older and, accordingly, less appealing as a new full-time hire.

Why Age Bias Is Pervasive and Persistent

It is worthwhile to acknowledge that ageist bias is not necessarily a conscious decision and that negative sentiments toward older applicants can be subtle and unintended in the processes of recruitment and hiring. "Ageism covers both implicit and explicit thoughts, feelings and behaviors that are based on prejudices and myths concerning people of older age."[95] Both pervasive and powerful, generational rhetoric is tied to the life cycle.[96] "Human beings are not neutral in their judgement and behaviour but instead have experience-based associations and preferences (or aversions) without consciously being aware of them."[97] Bias against age, unlike other hiring biases, may spring more from anxiety about one's own inevitable aging than a bias against the other. "When confronted with the realization of their own mortality, people push away reminders of eventual death (i.e., older people) and identify more closely with similar others (i.e., younger or middle aged people)."[98] One negative feeling associated with age is anxiety. "The elderly remind us that youth and beauty will fade; that illness and disability, along with the social isolation they can cause, are likely; and that death is a certainty for everyone."[99] Another is the role, again, of relative attractiveness. Older people "are allegedly unattractive and representative of undesirable traits from which people dissociate themselves."[100] The combination of these sentiments, whether conscious or not, intentional or not, are obstacles to the hiring of older candidates.

How Candidate Searches Incorporate Ageist Bias

Ageist bias results in ageist actions, whether conscious or not, against older workers.[101] Bias against older applicants may be present throughout all stages of the candidate search, including the creation and distribution of the job description. Coded language that reflects a preference for younger applicants, or "dog whistles," in job postings can be targeted to attract younger applicants. These dog whistles include descriptions of the ideal candidate as energetic, recent graduates, digital natives, and emerging leaders.[102] In the evaluation process, discussion of fit, needs, image, and again energy level have also been identified as dog whistles.[103] One study found "problems of appearance and 'team fit' as more formidable barriers to employment" than skills deficits.[104]

Promotion of jobs through social media has also been considered an attempt to reach younger candidates and exclude the older potential applicants.[105] By contrast, older workers, called "digital immigrants," are deliberately excluded through microtargeting practices in job postings.[106]

> After having resumes ignored over and over, some older job applicants begin to search job descriptions for "code" phrases (one question that generated a high volume of discussion on an LIS career options LinkedIn group was whether the descriptor "high energy" was actually a signal that the employer was looking for young applicants.[107]

Advertising for young applicants through microtargeting and dog whistles is not gender neutral either.

> There is an undeniable body of evidence showing that bias against women operates in recruitment and selection processes already for early-career female researchers. Bias can creep in when advertising positions, in the composition and working methods of selection committees and in the language itself of evaluations.[108]

Since appearance bias skews more heavily against older female candidates, they are more likely to be dismissed from consideration for employment, regardless of professional or academic achievement.

Age and Gender as EDI Concerns

Is ageism fundamentally different from other diversity categories, and if so, what place does it have in EDI policies? "It is argued that the dynamic quality of age and ageing make it harder to identify a static disadvantaged group."[109] Gender, by contrast, as a diversity category is well recognized as squarely within EDI concerns. However, it is "difficult to disentangle the discriminatory effects of age and gender."[110]

The "widespread preference for young workers" for tenure-track positions "has been extensively documented."[111]

> While many institutions of higher education have centers on campus that deal with civility, diversity, and inclusion, some feature ageism less prominently than the core diversity topics that they discuss. So job candidates, staff members, faculty and non-traditional students who may experience ageism may also feel alienated on campus.[112]

The literature makes it clear that, "despite its prominence, ageism doesn't hold the place it should in the diversity conversation. Ageism is a reality that complicates life for many Americans. Job seekers are particularly vulnerable."[113] In the absence of vigorous efforts by the academy to remedy ageism, other scholarly voices have emerged in protest. In its "Statement on Age Discrimination (Updated 2017)," for example, the American Historical Association addressed "troubling evidence of age discrimination within the history profession," particularly "discrimination against older applicants in both position announcements and in the hiring process."[114] With respect to late-in-life PhDs, the corollary to this study's late-in-life librarians, the American Historical Association observes that

> such candidates have received the same training as their younger colleagues, and have benefitted from more extensive life experience; yet search committees sometimes tend to be biased against those whose lives do not fit traditional patterns.... The use of such [ageist] criteria at any stage in the search and hiring process is unprofessional and illegal.[115]

ACRL, the division of the American Library Association charged with supporting the work of academic librarians, addresses age discrimination in only a cursory way in their "Diversity Standards: Cultural Competency for Academic Libraries." The document explains that "diversity is an essential component of any civil society" and cautions only that "cultural competence includes knowing and acknowledging how fears, ignorance, and the '-isms' (racism, sexism, ethnocentrism, heterosexism, ageism, able-bodiedism, and classism) have influenced their attitudes, beliefs, and feelings."[116] ACRL also offers four online guides with the associated subject of EDI, but in those guides there is no fuller discussion of ageism. For example, a search for the word *age* in the *ACRL Equity, Diversity, and Inclusion* online guide returned zero results. Within that same guide, *race* returned one result, *gender* one result, *ethnic* three results, and *lgbt*, *lgbtq*, and *lgbtqia* returned a total of four results.[117]

Why is age given short shrift in EDI discussions by ACRL? It may be, in part, because hiring older librarians (looking at age alone) doesn't increase diversity in the profession. There are certainly plenty of female academic librarians over the age of forty in tenured positions. The hiring of new female librarians over age forty also wouldn't offer students of diverse backgrounds any increased opportunity to see themselves reflected in faculty. Clearly, combating ageism is more about equity than diversity.

However, when framed in the context of the disparate impact of gender on ageism for hiring decisions, it is clearer that ageism is indeed an appropriate EDI concern. "When examined through today's understanding of how discrimination operates, age discrimination is more like, than different from, other forms of discrimination."[118] Moreover, it is well established that treating female candidates differently is considered squarely in the wheelhouse of EDI, and, if equity is to be considered of equal importance to diversity and inclusion, institutions of higher education and library professional associations will need to step up their efforts to promote equity in hiring practices. These efforts could include crafting statements and tool kits to counter ageist bias in the recruitment and hiring processes and expressing more than fainthearted objections to the practice of ageism.

Conclusion

From this review of the literature, it is clear that ageism is likely to be pervasive in hiring practices in academic libraries and that age bias is gendered both in that it starts earlier for female candidates and in that it has a greater negative impact on them. The pernicious belief that entry-level tenure-track positions are the rightful domain of younger librarian candidates and the corollary conviction that non-tenure-track work is best suited for older workers create an unfair diversion of older female new librarians away from the employment that would offer them their greatest potential for professional advancement, compensation, job security, benefits, and opportunities for scholarship. These unacknowledged and unchecked biases may create a significant barrier to tenure-track librarianship positions for female new librarians over age forty. This barrier is sustained by tacit and explicit acceptance of the ageist and sexist hiring biases and the openly expressed sentiment that this diversion of older candidates from tenure track is a reasonable policy. Despite extensive scholarship and data to the contrary about the abilities and potential of older candidates, and despite federal law against age discrimination in employment decisions, professional policies are currently weak expressions of compliance rather than concerted EDI efforts to oppose and overcome ageism.

To move forward, essentially to deconstruct this barrier, a barrier that is more substantial for women than for men, academic libraries must first acknowledge the existence of ageist bias against candidates for full-time librarian jobs and then express overtly and clearly that the bias is wrong, illegal, unethical, and unprofessional.

It is key to emphasize that attempts to remedy ageist hiring practices should never work in opposition to the important goal of creating a racially and ethnically diverse workforce. Ideally, hiring committees will take into account both the desire to diversify their staffs and the awareness of ageist biases. Moreover, to the extent that new female librarians over age forty are also librarians of color, they could face triple discrimination: age, race, and gender. Awareness of all these implicit biases is essential to make the hiring process truly equitable, diverse, and inclusive, acknowledging the complexities of our population: gender, race, ethnicity, age, disability, and more.

Steps that could facilitate this include requiring testing for implicit ageist bias for search committee members, dedicated scrutiny of position announcements through the lens of ageism to remove possible dog whistles, rewriting of institutional hiring policies to include explicit anti-ageist initiatives, and offering tool kits of resources on avoiding ageism, as is done for other EDI concerns. If the goal of equity is sincere, then the efforts to achieve equity must be commensurate for all candidates. In the absence of direct and intentional efforts to dismantle the barrier, the obstacles faced by older new female librarians will persist, to the detriment of both those candidates and the academic library profession.

Notes

1. AFL-CIO Department for Professional Employees, "Library Professionals: Facts and Figures," 2019, https://dpeaflcio.org/wp-content/uploads/Library-Workers-Facts-Figures-2019.pdf (page discontinued).
2. Gail Munde, "Considerations for Managing an Increasingly Intergenerational Workforce in Libraries," *Library Trends* 59, no. 1–2 (2010): 94.
3. Dan Albertson, Kaitlin Spetka, and Kristen Snow, eds, *Library and Information Science Education Statistical Report 2015* (Westford, MA: ALISE [Association for Library and Information Science Education], 2015), Table II-8-c-2-ALA, https://ali.memberclicks.net/assets/documents/statistical_reports/2015/alise_2015_statistical_report.pdf.
4. World Health Organization, "Frequently Asked Questions: Ageism," https://www.who.int/ageing/features/faq-ageism/en/.
5. US Equal Employment Opportunity Commission, "Age Discrimination," https://www.eeoc.gov/age-discrimination.
6. Ellie D. Berger and Douglas W. Hodgins, "Policy Brief No. 7—Age Discrimination and Paid Work," *Population Change and Lifecourse Strategic Knowledge Cluster Research/Policy Brief* 1, no. 3 (2012): article 2, p. 1, https://ir.lib.uwo.ca/pclc_rpb/vol1/iss3/2.
7. Berger and Hodgins, "Age Discrimination," 1.
8. Jason Martin, "I Have Shoes Older Than You: Generational Diversity in the Library," *Southeastern Librarian* 54, no. 3 (2006): 9.
9. Joanna Lahey, "Age Discrimination in the Workplace Starts as Early as 35, " PBS NewsHour, January 15, 2016, https://www.pbs.org/newshour/economy/age-discrimination-in-the-workplace-starts-as-early-as-35.
10. Jared A. Rex, Jennifer L. A. Whelan, and Laura L. Wilson, "Tenure Not Required: Recasting Non-tenured Academic Librarianship to Center Stage," in Recasting the Narrative: The Proceedings of the ACRL 2019 Conference, ed. Dawn M. Mueller (Chicago: Association of College and Research Libraries, 2019), 440, https://www.ala.org/acrl/sites/ala.org.acrl/files/content/conferences/confsandpreconfs/2019/TenureNotRequired.pdf.
11. Rex, Whelan, and Wilson, "Tenure Not Required," 450.
12. Carolyn Buppert, "I Believe I'm a Victim of Ageism. What Recourse Do I Have?" Medscape, October 8, 2018, https://www.medscape.com/viewarticle/903024; Rosalyn George, "Older Women Training to Teach," *Gender and Education* 10, no. 4 (1998): 417–30, https://doi.org/10.1080/09540259820844.
13. Carolyn Caffrey Gardner and Elizabeth Galoozis, "False Narratives of Generational Difference in Academic Libraries: Toward an Intersectional Approach," *Library Quarterly* 88, no. 2 (2018): 185, https://doi.org/10.1086/696582.
14. Michael S. North and Susan T. Fiske, "An Inconvenienced Youth? Ageism and Its Potential Intergenerational Roots," *Psychological Bulletin* 138, no. 5 (2012): 982–97, https://doi.org/10.1037/a0027843; National Institutes of Health Public Access author manuscript, PubMed Central, 1, https://www.ncbi.nlm.nih.gov/pmc/articles/PMC3838706/pdf/nihms524581.pdf.
15. Gardner and Galoozis, "False Narratives," 188.

16. North and Fiske, "An Inconvenienced Youth," PubMedCentral, 2.
17. Berger and Hodgins, "Age Discrimination," 3.
18. US Equal Employment Opportunity Commission, "The Age Discrimination Employment Act of 1967," https://www.eeoc.gov/laws/statutes/adea.cfm.
19. Chris Tomlinson, "Age Discrimination Is OK Sometimes," *Houston Chronicle*, April 18, 2017, https://www.houstonchronicle.com/business/columnists/tomlinson/article/Age-discrimination-is-OK-sometimes-11078275.php.
20. Justyna Stypinska and Konrad Turek, "Hard and Soft Age Discrimination: The Dual Nature of Workplace Discrimination, " *European Journal of Ageing* 14, no. 1 (2017): 51, https://doi.org/10.1007/s10433-016-0407-y.
21. US Equal Employment Opportunity Commission, "The State of Age Discrimination and Older Workers in the U.S. 50 Years after the Age Discrimination in Employment Act (ADEA)," 2018, https://www.eeoc.gov/eeoc/history/adea50th/report.cfm (page discontinued).
22. US Equal Employment Opportunity Commission, "State of Age Discrimination."
23. Valerie Bolden-Barrett, "Why Ageism Is the Most Acceptable Form of Workplace Discrimination," HR Dive, December. 15, 2016, https://www.hrdive.com/news/why-ageism-is-the-most-acceptable-form-of-workplace-discrimination/432422/; World Health Organization, "Frequently Asked."
24. Gilbert C. Gee, Eliza K. Pavalko, and J. Scott Long, "Age, Cohort and Perceived Age Discrimination: Using the Life Course to Assess Self-Reported Age Discrimination," Social Forces 86, no. 1 (January 2007): 268, https://doi.org/10.1353/sof.2007.0098.
25. Lahey, "Age Discrimination."
26. Helen Walker et al., "Women's Experiences and Perceptions of Age Discrimination in Employment: Implications for Research and Policy," *Social Policy and Society* 6, no. 1 (2007): 38, https://www.cambridge.org/core/journals/social-policy-and-society/issue/644E8034F6DF8B89DCB6A133553CF50D.
27. Colin Duncan and Wendy Loretto, "Never the Right Age? Gender and Age-Based Discrimination in Employment," *Gender, Work and Organization* 11, no. 1 (2004): 112, https://doi.org/10.1111/j.1468-0432.2004.00222.x.
28. Michael McGann et al., "Gendered Ageism in Australia: Changing Perceptions of Age Discrimination among Older Men and Women," *Economic Papers* 35, no. 4 (2016): 375, https://doi.org/10.1111/1759-3441.12155
29. US Equal Employment Opportunity Commission, "State of Age Discrimination."
30. Marjut Jyrkinen, "Women Managers, Careers and Gendered Ageism," *Scandinavian Journal of Management* 30, no. 2 (2014): 182, https://doi.org/10.1016/j.scaman.2013.07.002.
31. David Neumark, Ian Burn, and Patrick Button, "Is It Harder for Older Workers to Find Jobs? New and Improved Evidence from a Field Experiment," Working Paper No. 21669, National Bureau of Economic Research, November 2017, p. 2, https://www.nber.org/papers/w21669.
32. Marjut Jyrkinen and Linda McKie, "Gender, Age and Ageism: Experiences of Women Managers in Finland and Scotland," *Work, Employment and Society* 26, no. 1 (2012): 62, https://doi.org/10.1177/0950017011426313.
33. Katrina Pritchard and Rebecca Whiting, "Taking Stock: A Visual Analysis of Gendered Ageism," *Gender, Work & Organization* 22, no 5 (2015): 510–28, https://doi.org/10.1111/gwao.12090; Open Research Online, Open University, 26, https://oro.open.ac.uk/42199/1/__userdata_documents8_klp348_Documents_Papers_Versions%20for%20Biron_Taking%20Stock%20Final%20for%20oro.pdf.
34. Jyrkinen and McKie, "Gender, Age and Ageism," 62.

35. Meghan C. McLean, "Gender and Ageism: The Role of Aesthetic Preference in the Aging Double Standard" (MS thesis, Rutgers University, 2015), ii, https://rucore.libraries.rutgers.edu/rutgers-lib/46387/.

36. Jacqueline Granleese and Gemma Sayer, "Gendered Ageism and 'Lookism': A Triple Jeopardy for Female Academics," *Women in Management Review* 21, no. 6 (2006): 502, https://doi.org/10.1108/09649420610683480.

37. McLean, "Gender and Ageism," ii.

38. Ellie D. Berger, "Managing Age Discrimination: An Examination of the Techniques Used When Seeking Employment," *Gerontologist* 49, no. 3 (2009): 326–28, https://academic.oup.com/gerontologist/article/49/3/317/747279; Julie Shifman, "Job Interview Advice Older Women Don't Want to Hear," NextAvenue, December 10, 2012, https://www.nextavenue.org/job-interview-advice-older-women-dont-want-hear/.

39. Bill Murphy Jr., "Not Getting Hired: Maybe People Think You're Too Old," Inc., November 2, 2015, https://www.inc.com/bill-murphy-jr/how-to-make-employers-think-youre-younger.html.

40. Berger, "Managing Age Discrimination," 322.

41. Elisa F. Topper, "Working Knowledge: Fighting Age Discrimination," *American Libraries Magazine* 35, no. 10 (November 2004): 60, https://www.jstor.org/stable/25649363.

42. North and Fiske, "Inconvenienced Youth," PubMedCentral, 3.

43. Kim Dority, "For Librarians Battling Age Discrimination: Ageism in the LIS Profession," *LibGig* (blog), https://www.libgig.com/librarians-battling-age-discrimination/.

44. Nicole Javorsky, "Older Workers Are Organizing to Fight Ageism on the Job," *City Limits*, April 11, 2018, https://citylimits.org/2018/04/11/older-workers-organize-to-resist-stereotypes-and-discrimination/.

45. McLean, "Gender and Ageism," ii.

46. McLean, "Gender and Ageism," ii.

47. North and Fiske, "Inconvenienced Youth," PubMedCentral, 5.

48. McLean, "Gender and Ageism," 1.

49. Walker et al., "Women's Experiences," 39.

50. Elisa F. Topper, "Reverse Age Discrimination," *New Library World* 110, no. 3/4 (2009): 188, https://doi.org/10.1108/03074800910941374.

51. ECDL Foundation, *The Fallacy of the "Digital Native"* (Dublin, Ireland: ECDL Foundation, 2014), https://ec.europa.eu/futurium/en/system/files/ged/the_fallacy_of_the_digitalnative_-_ecdl_foundation.pdf.

52. Robert J. McKee, "The Age(ism) of Diversity," Inside Higher Ed, August 13, 2014, https://www.insidehighered.com/advice/2014/08/13/essay-age-discrimination-faculty-hiring.

53. Evelyn Tsitas, "How Hot Are You? The Harsh Truth about Gendered Ageism in Academia," *100 Days to the Doctorate* (blog), April 28, 2015, https://100daystothedoctorate.wordpress.com/2015/04/28/how-hot-are-you-the-harsh-truth-about-gendered-ageism-in-academia/.

54. Granleese and Sayer, "Gendered Ageism and 'Lookism'," 508.

55. Vincent J. Roscigno et al., "Age Discrimination, Social Closure and Employment," *Social Forces* 86, no. 1 (2007), 324, https://doi.org/10.1353/sof.2007.0109; Raj Mukherjee, "Ageism in the Tech Industry." *Indeed Blog*, October 19, 2017, http://blog.indeed.com/2017/10/19/tech-ageism-report/.

56. Roscigno et al., "Social Closure," 324.

57. Kelly, "Pink-Collar Ghetto," *Ms. Librarian* (blog), February 25, 2013, http://kellyatthelibrary.blogspot.com/2013/02/pink-collar-ghetto.html.

58. Mukherjee, "Tech Industry."

59. Roscigno et al., "Social Closure," 323.

60. Munde, "Considerations for Managing," 95; Lahey, "Age Discrimination"; Tomlinson, "Age Discrimination Is OK"; Jon Shields, "Age Discrimination: Older Applicants vs. 'Young Pretty People,'" Jobscan, March 5, 2018, https://www.jobscan.co/blog/age-discrimination-older-applicants-vs-young-pretty-people/; Berger and Hodgins, "Age Discrimination," 2; Javorsky, "Older Workers Are Organizing"; B. Evan Blaine and Kimberly J. McClure Brenchley, "Understanding Age Stereotypes and Ageism," in *Understanding the Psychology of Diversity*, ed. B. Evan Blaine and Kimberly J. McClure Brenchley (Thousand Oaks, CA: Sage, 2017), 188; Nathaniel Reade, "The Surprising Truth about Older Workers," *AARP The Magazine*, last updated September 2015, https://www.aarp.org/work/job-hunting/info-07-2013/older-workers-more-valuable.html.

61. Bonnie Marcus, "Age Discrimination and Women in the Workplace: How to Avoid Getting Pushed Out," *Forbes*, May 12, 2018, https://www.forbes.com/sites/bonniemarcus/2018/05/12/age-discrimination-and-women-in-the-workplace-heres-how-to-avoid-getting-pushed-out/#3dd6359e2c4a.

62. David W. Lewis and Kindra Orr, "The Age Demographics of Librarians and the Organizational Challenges Facing Academic Libraries," *Library Leadership and Management* 32, no. 3 (2018): 10, https://scholarworks.iupui.edu/handle/1805/16537.

63. Karen Kersting, "Personality Changes for the Better with Age," *Monitor on Psychology* 34, no. 7, (July/August 2003): 14, http://www.apa.org/monitor/julaug03/personality.

64. Dominic Abrams, Hannah J. Swift, and Lisbeth Drury, "Old and Unemployable? How Age-Based Stereotypes Affect Willingness to Hire Job Candidates," *Journal of Social Issues* 72, no. 1 (2016): 105, https://doi.org/10.1111/josi.12158.

65. Munde, "Considerations For Managing," 93.

66. US Equal Employment Opportunity Commission, "State of Age Discrimination."

67. Reade, "Surprising Truth."

68. ECDL Foundation, *Fallacy*, 1, 2.

69. Lawrence Biemiller, "Technology? It's Just Another Knitting Needle," *Chronicle of Higher Education*, September 17, 2017, https://www.chronicle.com/article/These-Tech-Savvy-Professors/241183.

70. North and Fiske, "Inconvenienced Youth," PubMedCentral, 2.

71. Roscigno et al., " Social Closure," 326.

72. Tomlinson, "Age Discrimination Is OK."

73. John Cawley, "Older and on the Market," *Chronicle of Higher Ed Vitae*, July 6, 2015, https://chroniclevitae.com/news/1056-older-and-on-the-market (page discontinued).

74. Abrams, Swift, and Drury, "Old and Unemployable," 107.

75. Mitra Toossi and Elka Torpey, "Older Workers: Labor Force Trends and Career Options," Career Outlook, US Bureau of Labor Statistics, May 2017, https://www.bls.gov/careeroutlook/2017/article/older-workers.htm.

76. Toossi and Torpey, "Labor Force Trends."

77. Michael Dimock, "Defining Generations: Where Millennials End and Generation Z Begins," Pew Research Center, January 17, 2019, https://www.pewresearch.org/fact-tank/2019/01/17/where-millennials-end-and-generation-z-begins/; Amy Adkins, "Millennials: The Job Hopping Generation," *Gallup Business Journal*, May 12, 2016, https://www.gallup.com/workplace/236474/millennials-job-hopping-generation.aspx.

78. Abrams, Swift, and Drury, "Old and Unemployable," 107.

79. Bolden-Barrett, "Why Ageism Is."

80. Roscigno et al., "Social Closure," 315.

81. Ellen Hoenigman Meyer, "Ageism in the Job Hunt," HigherEdJobs, June 27, 2016, https://www.higheredjobs.com/articles/articleDisplay.cfm?ID=969.

82. Roscigno et al., "Social Closure," 313.
83. Martin, "Shoes Older Than You," 8.
84. Tomlinson, "Age Discrimination Is OK"; North and Fiske, "Inconvenienced Youth," PubMedCentral, 10.
85. Roscigno et al., "Social Closure," 318,
86. Pritchard and Whiting, "Taking Stock," Open Research Online, 2.
87. North and Fiske, "Inconvenienced Youth," PubMedCentral, 10.
88. Lewis and Orr, "Age Demographics of Librarians,"12.
89. Lewis and Orr, "Age Demographics of Librarians," 14.
90. Roscigno et al., "Social Closure," 315.
91. Cawley, "Older and on the Market."
92. Blaine and McClure Brenchley, "Understanding Age Stereotypes, 196.
93. Martin, "Shoes Older Than You," 9.
94. Abrams, Swift, and Drury, "Old and Unemployable," 117.
95. Jyrkinen, "Women Managers,"176.
96. Gardner and Galoozis, "False Narratives," 188.
97. League of European Research Universities, *Implicit Bias in Academia: A Challenge to Meritocratic Principle and to Women's Careers—and What to Do about It*, Advice Paper no. 23 (Leuven, Belgium: LERU, January 2018), 3, https://www.leru.org/files/implicit-bias-in-academia-full-paper.pdf.
98. North and Fiske, "Inconvenienced Youth," PubMedCentral, 4–5.
99. Blaine and McClure Brenchley, "Understanding Age Stereotypes," 191.
100. North and Fiske, "Inconvenienced Youth," PubMedCentral, 7.
101. Roscigno et al., "Social Closure," 316–18.
102. Bolden Barrett, "Why Ageism Is"; Shields, "Young Pretty People"; Kenneth Terrell, "Age Discrimination Law Turns 50," AARP, December 14, 2017, https://www.aarp.org/work/working-at-50-plus/info-2017/adea-age-discrimination-fd.html; Pamela DeLoatch, "Outlawed for 50 Years, Age Discrimination Remains Employment's 'Open Secret,'" HR Dive, January 9, 2018, https://www.hrdive.com/news/outlawed-for-50-years-age-discrimination-remains-employments-open-secret/515407/; Annoyed Librarian, "Age Discrimination in Libraries," *Annoyed Librarian* (blog), *Library Journal*, February 8, 2016, http://lj.libraryjournal.com/blogs/annoyedlibrarian/2016/02/08/age-discrimination-in-libraries/ (page discontinued).
103. Roscigno et al., "Social Closure," 323.
104. Jocelyn Handy and Doreen Davy, "Gendered Ageism: Older Women's Experiences of Employment Agency Practices," *Asia Pacific Journal of Human Resources* 45, no. 1 (January 2007): 85, https://doi.org/10.1177/1038411107073606.
105. Deloatch, "Open Secret."
106. US Equal Employment Opportunity Commission, "State of Age Discrimination."
107. Dority, "For Librarians Battling."
108. League of European Research Universities, *Implicit Bias*, 4.
109. Pritchard and Whiting, "Taking Stock," Open Research Online, 4.
110. Pritchard and Whiting, "Taking Stock," Open Research Online, 5.
111. Beryl Lieff Benderly, "Adjuncts and Age Discrimination," *Careers* (blog), *Science*, September 29, 2014, https://www.science.org/content/article/adjuncts-and-age-discrimination.
112. Meyer, "Ageism in the Job Hunt."
113. Meyer, "Ageism in the Job Hunt."

114. American Historical Association, "Statement on Age Discrimination (Updated 2017),"
     January 5, 2017, https://www.historians.org/jobs-and-professional-development/
     statements-standards-and-guidelines-of-the-discipline/statement-on-age-discrimination.
115. American Historical Association, "Statement."
116. Association of College and Research Libraries, "Diversity Standards: Cultural Compe-
     tency for Academic Libraries (2012)," https://www.ala.org/acrl/standards/diversity. As of
     2021, ACRL with ALA's Office for Diversity, Literacy and Outreach Services (ODLOS);
     the Public Library Association (PLA); and the Association of Research Libraries (ARL) is
     developing a framework for cultural proficiencies in racial equity. See the ACRL Equity,
     Diversity and Inclusion online guide, Cultural Competencies tab, https://acrl.libguides.
     com/EDI/culturalcompetencies.
117. Association of College and Research Libraries, "Diversity Standards."
118. US Equal Employment Opportunity Commission, "State of Age Discrimination."

Bibliography and Additional Resources

Abrams, Dominic, Hannah J. Swift, and Lisbeth Drury. "Old and Unemployable? How
    Age-Based Stereotypes Affect Willingness to Hire Job Candidates." *Journal of Social Issues*
    72, no. 1 (2016): 105–21. https://doi.org/10.1111/josi.12158.
Adkins, Amy. "Millennials: The Job Hopping Generation." *Gallup Business Journal*, May 12,
    2016. https://www.gallup.com/workplace/236474/millennials-job-hopping-generation.aspx.
AFL-CIO Department for Professional Employees. "Library Professionals: Facts and Figures."
    2019. https://dpeaflcio.org/wp-content/uploads/Library-Workers-Facts-Figures-2019.pdf
    (page discontinued).
Albertson, Dan, Kaitlyn Spetka, and Kristen Snow, eds. *Library and Information Science Educa-
    tion Statistical Report 2015*. Westford, MA: ALISE (Association for Library and Information
    Science Education). 2015. https://ali.memberclicks.net/assets/documents/statistical_
    reports/2015/alise_2015_statistical_report.pdf.
American Historical Association. "Statement on Age Discrimination (Updated 2017)."
    January 5, 2017. https://www.historians.org/jobs-and-professional-development/
    statements-standards-and-guidelines-of-the-discipline/statement-on-age-discrimination.
American Library Association. "About NMRT." https://www.ala.org/rt/nmrt/about-nmrt.
———. "Diversity Counts 2009–2010 Update." https://www.ala.org/aboutala/offices/diversity/
    diversitycounts/2009-2010update.
———. "Equity, Diversity, and Inclusion." https://www.ala.org/advocacy/diversity.
Annoyed Librarian. "Age Discrimination in Libraries." *Annoyed Librarian* (blog), *Library
    Journal*, February 8, 2016, http://lj.libraryjournal.com/blogs/annoyedlibrarian/2016/02/08/
    age-discrimination-in-libraries/ (page discontinued).
Association of College and Research Libraries. "Diversity Standards: Cultural Competency for
    Academic Libraries (2012)." https://www.ala.org/acrl/standards/diversity.
Association of American Colleges and Universities. "Diversity, Equity, & Inclusive Excellence."
    https://www.aacu.org/resources/diversity-equity-and-inclusive-excellence.
Association of College and Research Libraries. "Equity, Diversity, and Inclusion." http://www.
    ala.org/acrl/aboutacrl/directoryofleadership/committees/racialethnic.

Benderly, Beryl Lieff. "Adjuncts and Age Discrimination." *Careers* (blog), *Science*, September 29, 2014. https://www.science.org/content/article/adjuncts-and-age-discrimination.

Berger, Ellie D. "Managing Age Discrimination: An Examination of the Techniques Used When Seeking Employment." *Gerontologist* 49, no. 3 (2009): 317–32. https://academic.oup.com/gerontologist/article/49/3/317/747279.

Berger, Ellie D., and Douglas W. Hodgins. "Policy Brief No. 7—Age Discrimination and Paid Work." *Population Change and Lifecourse Strategic Knowledge Cluster Research/Policy Brief* 1, no. 3 (2012): article 2. https://ir.lib.uwo.ca/pclc_rpb/vol1/iss3/2.

Biemiller, Lawrence. "Technology? It's Just Another Knitting Needle." *Chronicle of Higher Education*, September 17, 2017. https://www.chronicle.com/article/These-Tech-Savvy-Professors/241183.

Blaine, B. Evan, and Kimberly J. McClure Brenchley. "Understanding Age Stereotypes and Ageism." In *Understanding the Psychology of Diversity*. Edited by B. Evan Blaine and Kimberly J. McClure Brenchley, 185–202. Thousand Oaks, CA: Sage 2017.

Bodner, Ehud, Yoav S. Bergman, and Sara Cohen-Fridel. "Different Dimensions of Ageist Attitudes among Men and Women: A Multigenerational Perspective." *International Psychogeriatrics* 24, no. 6 (July 2012): 895–901. https://doi.org/10.1017/s1041610211002936.

Bolden-Barrett, Valerie. "Why Ageism Is the Most Acceptable Form of Workplace Discrimination." HR Dive, December 15, 2016. https://www.hrdive.com/news/why-ageism-is-the-most-acceptable-form-of-workplace-discrimination/432422/.

Buppert, Carolyn. "I Believe I'm a Victim of Ageism. What Recourse Do I Have?" Medscape, October 8, 2018. https://www.medscape.com/viewarticle/903024.

Cawley, John. "Older and on the Market." *Chronicle of Higher Ed Vitae*, July 6, 2015. https://chroniclevitae.com/news/1056-older-and-on-the-market (page discontinued).

Chu, Melanie. "Ageism in Academic Librarianship." *Electronic Journal of Academic and Special Librarianship* 10, no. 2 (Summer 2009). https://southernlibrarianship.icaap.org/content/v10n02/chu_m01.html.

DeLoatch, Pamela. "Outlawed for 50 Years, Age Discrimination Remains Employment's 'Open Secret.'" HR Dive, January 9, 2018. https://www.hrdive.com/news/outlawed-for-50-years-age-discrimination-remains-employments-open-secret/515407/.

Dimock, Michael. "Defining Generations: Where Millennials End and Generation Z Begins." Pew Research Center. January 17, 2019. https://www.pewresearch.org/fact-tank/2019/01/17/where-millennials-end-and-generation-z-begins/.

Dority, Kim. "For Librarians Battling Age Discrimination: Ageism in the LIS Profession." *LibGig* (blog). https://www.libgig.com/librarians-battling-age-discrimination/.

Duncan, Colin, and Wendy Loretto. "Never the Right Age? Gender and Age-Based Discrimination in Employment." *Gender, Work and Organization* 11, no. 1 (2004): 95–115. https://doi.org/10.1111/j.1468-0432.2004.00222.x.

ECDL Foundation. *The Fallacy of the "Digital Native": Why Young People Need to Develop Their Digital Skills*. Dublin, Ireland: ECDL Foundation, 2014. https://ec.europa.eu/futurium/en/system/files/ged/the_fallacy_of_the_digitalnative_-_ecdl_foundation.pdf.

Farber, Henry S., Dan Silverman, and Till M. Von Wachter. "Factors Determining Callbacks to Job Applications by the Unemployed: An Audit Study." *RSF: The Russell Sage Foundation Journal of the Social Sciences* 3, no. 3 (2017): 168–201. https://doi.org/10.7758/rsf.2017.3.3.08.

Fox Rothschild, Attorneys-at-Law. "We're on the Hunt for Young, Fit and Competent Employees." Employment Discrimination Report, November. 6, 2014. https://employmentdiscrimination.foxrothschild.com/2014/11/articles/general-employment-discrimination/age-discrimination-another-category/were-on-the-hunt-for-young-fit-and-competent/.

Gardner, Carolyn Caffrey, and Elizabeth Galoozis. "False Narratives of Generational Difference in Academic Libraries: Toward an Intersectional Approach." *Library Quarterly* 88, no. 2 (2018): 177–92. https://doi.org/10.1086/696582.

Gee, Gilbert C., Eliza K. Pavalko, and J. Scott Long. "Age, Cohort and Perceived Age Discrimination: Using the Life Course to Assess Self-Reported Age Discrimination." *Social Forces* 86, no. 1 (January 2007): 265–90. https://doi.org/10.1353/sof.2007.0098.

George, Rosalyn. "Older Women Training to Teach." *Gender and Education* 10, no. 4 (1998): 417–30. https://doi.org/10.1080/09540259820844.

Granleese, Jacqueline, and Gemma Sayer. "Gendered Ageism and 'Lookism': A Triple Jeopardy for Female Academics." *Women in Management Review* 21, no. 6 (2006): 500–517. https://doi.org/10.1108/09649420610683480.

Handy, Jocelyn, and Doreen Davy. "Gendered Ageism: Older Women's Experiences of Employment Agency Practices." *Asia Pacific Journal of Human Resources* 45, no. 1 (January 2007): 85–99. https://doi.org/10.1177/1038411107073606.

Javorsky, Nicole. "Older Workers Are Organizing to Fight Ageism on the Job." *City Limits*, April 11, 2018. https://citylimits.org/2018/04/11/older-workers-organize-to-resist-stereotypes-and-discrimination/.

Jyrkinen, Marjut. "Women Managers, Careers and Gendered Ageism." *Scandinavian Journal of Management* 30, no. 2 (2014): 175–85. https://doi.org/10.1016/j.scaman.2013.07.002.

Jyrkinen, Marjut, and Linda Mckie. "Gender, Age and Ageism: Experiences of Women Managers in Finland and Scotland." *Work, Employment and Society* 26, no. 1 (2012): 61–77. https://doi.org/10.1177/0950017011426313.

Kelly. "Pink-Collar Ghetto." *Ms. Librarian* (blog), February 25, 2013. http://kellyatthelibrary.blogspot.com/2013/02/pink-collar-ghetto.html.

Kersting, Karen. "Personality Changes for the Better with Age." *Monitor on Psychology* 34, no. 7 (July/August 2003): 14. http://www.apa.org/monitor/julaug03/personality.

Lahey, Joanna. "Age Discrimination in the Workplace Starts as Early as 35." PBS NewsHour, January 15, 2016. https://www.pbs.org/newshour/economy/age-discrimination-in-the-workplace-starts-as-early-as-35.

League of European Research Universities. *Implicit Bias in Academia: A Challenge to Meritocratic Principle and to Women's Careers—and What to Do about It.* Advice Paper no. 23. Leuven, Belgium: LERU, January 2018. https://www.leru.org/files/implicit-bias-in-academia-full-paper.pdf.

Lewis, David W. and Kindra Orr. "The Age Demographics of Librarians and the Organizational Challenges Facing Academic Libraries." *Library Leadership and Management* 32, no. 3 (2018): 1–24. https://scholarworks.iupui.edu/handle/1805/16537.

Marcus. Bonnie. "Age Discrimination and Women in the Workplace: How to Avoid Getting Pushed Out." *Forbes*, May 12, 2018. https://www.forbes.com/sites/bonniemarcus/2018/05/12/age-discrimination-and-women-in-the-workplace-heres-how-to-avoid-getting-pushed-out/#3dd6359e2c4a.

Martin, Jason. "I Have Shoes Older Than You: Generational Diversity in the Library." *Southeastern Librarian* 54, no. 3 (2006): 4–11.

McGann, Michael, Rachel Ong, Dina Bowman, Alan Duncan, Helen Kimberley, and Simon Biggs. "Gendered Ageism in Australia: Changing Perceptions of Age Discrimination among Older Men and Women." *Economic Papers* 35, no. 4 (2016): 375–88. https://doi.org/10.1111/1759-3441.12155.

McKee, Robert J. "The Age(ism) of Diversity." Inside Higher Ed, August 13, 2014. https://www.insidehighered.com/advice/2014/08/13/essay-age-discrimination-faculty-hiring.

McLean, Meghan C. "Gender and Ageism: The Role of Aesthetic Preference in the Aging Double Standard." MS thesis, Rutgers University, 2015. https://rucore.libraries.rutgers.edu/rutgers-lib/46387/.

Meyer, Ellen Hoenigman. "Ageism in the Job Hunt." HigherEdJobs, June 27, 2016. https://www.higheredjobs.com/articles/articleDisplay.cfm?ID=969.

Mukherjee, Raj. "Ageism in the Tech Industry." *Indeed Blog*, October 19, 2017. http://blog.indeed.com/2017/10/19/tech-ageism-report/.

Munde, Gail. "Considerations for Managing an Increasingly Intergenerational Workforce in Libraries." *Library Trends* 59, no. 1–2 (2010): 88–108.

Murphy Bill, Jr. "Not Getting Hired: Maybe People Think You're Too Old." Inc., November 2, 2015. https://www.inc.com/bill-murphy-jr/how-to-make-employers-think-youre-younger.html.

Neumark, David, Ian Burn, and Patrick Button. "Age Discrimination and Hiring of Older Workers. FRBSF Economic Letter. Federal Reserve Bank of San Francisco, February 27, 2017. https://www.frbsf.org/economic-research/publications/economic-letter/2017/february/age-discrimination-and-hiring-older-workers/.

———. "Is It Harder for Older Workers to Find Jobs? New and Improved Evidence from a Field Experiment." Working Paper No. 21669. National Bureau of Economic Research, November 2017. https://www.nber.org/papers/w21669.

North, Michael S., and Susan T. Fiske. "An Inconvenienced Youth? Ageism and Its Potential Intergenerational Roots." *Psychological Bulletin* 138, no. 5 (2012): 982–97. https://doi.org/10.1037/a0027843; National Institutes of Health Public Access author manuscript, PubMedCentral, https://www.ncbi.nlm.nih.gov/pmc/articles/PMC3838706/pdf/nihms524581.pdf.

Pritchard, Katrina, and Rebecca Whiting. "Taking Stock: A Visual Analysis of Gendered Ageism." *Gender, Work and Organization* 22, no. 5 (2015): 510–28. https://doi.org/10.1111/gwao.12090. Open Research Online, Open University, https://oro.open.ac.uk/42199/1/__userdata_documents8_klp348_Documents_Papers_Versions%20for%20Biron_Taking%20Stock%20Final%20for%20oro.pdf.

Reade, Nathaniel. "The Surprising Truth about Older Workers." *AARP The Magazine*. Last updated September 2015. https://www.aarp.org/work/job-hunting/info-07-2013/older-workers-more-valuable.html.

Rex, Jared A., Jennifer L. A. Whelan, and Laura L. Wilson. "Tenure Not Required: Recasting Non-tenured Academic Librarianship to Center Stage," in *Recasting the Narrative: The Proceedings of the ACRL 2019 Conference*. Edited by Dawn M. Mueller, 439–58. Chicago: Association of College and Research Libraries, 2019. https://www.ala.org/acrl/sites/ala.org.acrl/files/content/conferences/confsandpreconfs/2019/TenureNotRequired.pdf.

Roscigno, Vincent J., Sherry Mong, Reginald Byron, and Griff Tester. "Age Discrimination, Social Closure and Employment." *Social Forces* 86, no. 1 (2007): 313–34. https://doi.org/10.1353/sof.2007.0109.

Shields, Jon. "Age Discrimination: Older Applicants vs. 'Young Pretty People.'" Jobscan, March 5, 2018. https://www.jobscan.co/blog/age-discrimination-older-applicants-vs-young-pretty-people/.

Shifman, Julie. "Job Interview Advice Older Women Don't Want to Hear." NextAvenue, December 10, 2012. https://www.nextavenue.org/job-interview-advice-older-women-dont-want-hear/.

Stypinska, Justyna, and Konrad Turek. "Hard and Soft Age Discrimination: The Dual Nature of Workplace Discrimination." *European Journal of Ageing* 14, no. 1 (2017): 49–61. https://doi.org/10.1007/s10433-016-0407-y.

Terrell, Kenneth. "Age Discrimination Law Turns 50." AARP, December 14, 2017. https://www.aarp.org/work/working-at-50-plus/info-2017/adea-age-discrimination-fd.html.

Tomlinson, Chris. "Age Discrimination Is OK Sometimes." *Houston Chronicle*, April 18, 2017. https://www.houstonchronicle.com/business/columnists/tomlinson/article/Age-discrimination-is-OK-sometimes-11078275.php.

Topper, Elisa F. "Reverse Age Discrimination." *New Library World* 110, no. 3/4 (2009): 188–90. https://doi.org/10.1108/03074800910941374.

———. "Working Knowledge: Fighting Age Discrimination." *American Libraries Magazine* 35, no. 10 (November 2004). https://www.jstor.org/stable/25649363.

Toossi, Mitra, and Elka Torpey. "Older Workers: Labor Force Trends and Career Options." Career Outlook, US Bureau of Labor Statistics, May 2017. https://www.bls.gov/careeroutlook/2017/article/older-workers.htm.

Tsitas, Evelyn. "How Hot Are You? The Harsh Truth about Gendered Ageism in Academia." *100 Days to the Doctorate* (blog), April 28, 2015. https://100daystothedoctorate.wordpress.com/2015/04/28/how-hot-are-you-the-harsh-truth-about-gendered-ageism-in-academia/.

US Equal Employment Opportunity Commission. "Age Discrimination." https://www.eeoc.gov/age-discrimination.

———. "The Age Discrimination Employment Act of 1967." https://www.eeoc.gov/laws/statutes/adea.cfm.

———. "The State of Age Discrimination and Older Workers in the U.S. 50 Years after the Age Discrimination in Employment Act (ADEA)." 2018. https://www.eeoc.gov/eeoc/history/adea50th/report.cfm (page discontinued).

US Department of Labor, Women's Bureau. "Older Women and Work: A Fact Sheet." 2014. https://www.dol.gov/wb/resources/older_women_and_work.pdf (page discontinued).

Vinopal, Jennifer. "Are We Talking Enough about Gender Bias and Discrimination in the Library Profession?" Jennifer Vinopal website, December 5, 2013. http://vinopal.org/2013/12/05/are-we-talking-enough-about-gender-bias-and-discrimination-in-the-library-profession/.

Walker, Helen, Diane Grant, Mark Meadows, and Ian Cook. "Women's Experiences and Perceptions of Age Discrimination in Employment: Implications for Research and Policy." *Social Policy and Society* 6, no. 1 (2007): 37–48. https://www.cambridge.org/core/journals/social-policy-and-society/issue/644E8034F6DF8B89DCB6A133553CF50D.

World Health Organization. "Ageing and Life Course." https://www.who.int/ageing/en/.

———. "Frequently Asked Questions: Ageism." https://www.who.int/ageing/features/faq-ageism/en/.

CHAPTER 4

Desperately Seeking Librarians with a Disability

Kenneth D. Litwak

Introduction

In the spring of 2019, the Diversity in Academic Libraries interest group of CARL, the California Academic and Research Libraries, held a workshop that focused on diversity, inclusion, and equity for persons of color. That is an important issue. However, there have not been, to my knowledge, workshops or conference sessions on diversity and inclusion of people with an apparent disability in academic libraries. There are no organizations or programs for academic librarians with a disability.[1] Researchers will search in vain for scholarly articles on librarians with disabilities, as there is very little.[2] Library literature has numerous articles on racial diversity, inclusion, and equity but scant attention to diversity and inclusion of librarians with disabilities, though research on librarians with disabilities is slowly increasing. Joanne Oud emphasizes the disparity regarding the attention paid to equity and inclusion on racial and ethnic minorities. She states,

> There appears to be increasing awareness of and attention paid to equity concerns within the profession. Little of this diversity and equity discussion within librarianship has

focused on disability, even though librarians with disabilities form a substantial minority within the profession.[3]

According to the World Health Organization, approximately 15 percent of people in the world have a disability.[4] This suggests that "people with disabilities are underrepresented in librarianship and library work."[5] According to the National Center for Education Statistics, 19 percent of undergraduates in the United States report having a disability.[6] While I am especially interested in those with an apparent disability, I have not found statistics on visible or apparent versus "invisible" disabilities. Research has shown that many academic librarians "pass,"—that is, do not appear to have a disability, even though their daily lives may be affected significantly by their disability.[7] Therefore, these librarians are not part of the survey results. Students with disabilities will look in vain generally if they want to find a librarian who likewise has a disability. An ALA survey in January 2017 shows that out of 37,666 ALA respondents, only 2.91 percent disclosed having a disability.[8]

The focus of this study is the presence or lack of full-time academic librarians who have an apparent disability, particularly those who had an apparent disability when they were interviewed for their positions. A visible or apparent disability has visible or recognizable features or characteristics.[9]

In the literature on disabilities, some use the language "a disabled person." Others use the language "a person with a disability." I will use the latter because it emphasizes that people are more than their disability. A disability is a trait, but it does not define individuals, even as a particular racial or ethnic background does not define a person.

Survey Methodology

In mid-2019, I conducted a survey, Diversity and Disability in Academic Librarianship, to gather information about how many academic librarians have a disability and how many of those had the apparent disability at the time that they were interviewed. Having been told by a search committee chair that I was not offered the position because of concerns about my eyesight, this issue is of personal importance. I have a visual impairment and wonder how it might be affecting the outcomes of interviews I have had.

As part of the survey, I sought to learn what sorts of schools—for example, private colleges or large research universities—have librarians who have an apparent disability. The survey also asked respondents why they think so few librarians with disabilities are hired and how an applicant for a librarian position who has a disability can improve the chances of getting hired as a full-time librarian. The survey focuses on apparent physical and sensory disabilities. While other sorts of disabilities exist and present challenges, "invisible" disabilities are not likely to affect an interview. Interviewers for an academic librarian position are not as likely to notice conditions such as a learning disability.

This survey was done with SurveyMonkey, and I invited participants on several librarian mailing lists, such as Uniaccess, an ACRL interest group focused on access issues. The survey was anonymous, and the results do not take into account possible duplication by multiple individuals at a given institution. Thus, they may not be an accurate representation of any specific institution. Nevertheless, the results suggest that relatively few academic libraries have a librarian who has an apparent disability. The survey results are analyzed, and implications and future research directions are suggested.

There were a total of sixty respondents; the number of respondents was too small to be able to determine definitive patterns. The quantitative results are, however, consistent with the results of other studies. The survey had seven questions. For questions that seek textual responses, such as question six, the text below represents quotations except for very minor spelling or grammatical corrections. The textual responses are the most significant data from the survey. I have presented all the survey data in the appendix. The survey results will be presented briefly and then analyzed in more detail. In spite of the sample size and duplicates, the numbers suggest that, while it is possible for someone with a disability to be hired to be an academic librarian, the odds are definitely against such a possibility.

Survey Results

Question One

"Are there any full-time librarians at your institution who have an apparent physical or sensory disability?"

Twenty-one respondents (35.0%) said yes, while there were twenty-nine negative responses (48.33%). Ten respondents (16.66%) did not know. A physical disability would include conditions such as difficulty walking because of a leg injury or deformity. Sensory disabilities would be primarily related to eyesight and hearing.

Having 35 percent of respondents say that their institution has at least one full-time librarian with an apparent physical or sensory disability at first sight looks promising. As will become apparent below, however, this does not tell the whole story.

Question Two

"If you answered 'Yes' to question one, how many persons with disabilities are full-time librarians at your library/institution?"

The most common response to this question was one, while the numbers ranged from one to five. The total number of these librarians is thirty-one. A much larger sample, perhaps with some mechanism to avoid duplication, would be of significant help in forming a more accurate picture.

Question Three

"How many full-time librarians are there in your library/institution?"

There were fifty-eight respondents, with responses that ranged from one to 150. The number of full-time librarians represented by the answers to question two is very small compared to the total number of librarians represented by question three, which is 825. The percentage of librarians with disabilities, according to this data, is 3.75 percent. This is consistent with other studies, even though the data set is relatively small and may contain duplicates.

Question Four

"Are you aware of any current or previous full-time librarians at your institution who had an apparent physical or sensory disability at the time of their interview(s) for the position?"

Out of sixty responses, eleven respondents said yes. The overall percentage of full-time librarians with a disability is only 3.75 of the 825 librarians reported. Oud reported estimates of 3.7 percent for the United States and 5.9 percent for Canada.[10] A survey of Canadian librarians found that of all those who said they had a disability, only 14 percent said it was visible.[11] Therefore, the comparison is only a general result, not a precise result. However, this low percentage corresponds with what others have reported.[12]

All sixty respondents answered this question; 22.4 percent of respondents stated that the full-time librarian had an apparent disability at the time of the interview. In this survey, of the (possibly) thirty-one librarians who were known to have a visible disability, eleven had it at the time of the interview, or 35.4 percent. This suggests that about one of every three full-time librarian with an apparent disability had it at the time of their job interviews at these institutions. The small sample size makes it difficult to generalize about the librarian profession.

Question Five

"Compared to the percentage of students with disabilities at many institutions, there are relatively few full-time academic librarians across institutions who have an apparent physical or sensory disability. Why do you think this is the case?"

This question seeks insights on why the percentage of students with a disability is so high compared to the percentage of academic librarians with a disability. Of the 19 percent of students who reported that they had a disability, we do not know how many of those had apparent disabilities.

Forty-nine people answered this, with eleven respondents skipping it. See the appendix for the responses.

Question Six

"Can you suggest any steps an applicant with an apparent physical or sensory disability might take in cover letters, interviews, etc. to improve her or his chances for being hired?"

This question seeks ideas for how someone with an apparent disability might get through the issues involved in a job search with an apparent disability. Forty-five respondents answered this question. See the appendix for all the answers.

Question Seven

This question asked respondents what type of academic institution they are affiliated with. All sixty respondents answered this question. Responses came primarily from state colleges or universities and private liberal arts colleges or universities.

In order to assure anonymity, the survey does not connect responses to other questions with the respondent type of institution. Presumably, the number of librarians in general would be related to the type and size of an institution.

Analysis of Responses

This analysis pertains primarily to the textual responses, which are not affected by sample size. The answers to question five reflect a diversity of opinions, such as, "Don't know," "Prejudice," and the physical demands of an academic librarian are beyond what someone with a disability could do. The answers to question five point to the following, with some of the responses that suggest each point.

- prejudice: 2, 3, 15, 37, 43, 49
- lack of interest in hiring those with apparent disabilities: 12, 15, 20, 28
- doubt about the assertion of the question, as suggested by 4, 47, and perhaps 33
- belief that those with disabilities do not apply for academic librarian positions: 1, 23, 24, 29, 36
- belief that those with disabilities could not perform the required duties: 3, 7, 10, 14, 21

Many respondents said that a disability means one cannot perform the job duties. As noted by other authors who are pushing for more ethnic and racial diversity, the library field should take a hard look at the requirements it is listing, such as the ability to drive, sit for long periods of time, or lift a specific amount of weight. Does anyone in the library really need to lift fifty pounds? Or even ten pounds? Library administrators should think hard about whether these skills are really necessary for the job being posted.

Ableism or bias against those with disabilities was a frequent theme in the responses. Lois A. Weiss asserts,

> Despite increased disability awareness and the advancement of disability rights laws, the stigma of disabilities continues to be a problem in our country. Ableism is the outcome of negative attitudes towards disabilities perpetuating the belief that being able-bodied is preferable over being disabled.[13]

This could be stated even more strongly. There are many societal systems that seek to control identities, "constantly emphasizing the fictive necessity of achieving normalcy in all aspects of life."[14] Disability is often seen as lack, failure, or loss.[15] Several survey respondents asserted that this bias or prejudice is the main reason that there are not more academic librarians with disabilities. Research has shown bias is a definite factor, if not the most important factor.[16] Respondents to question five identified other factors, such as the fact that some institutions are paying lip service to diversity but not genuinely seeking diversity, doubt that there is "an intentional planning to recruit for diversity," and library buildings that are not ADA-compliant. Some respondents doubt the assertion of question five, which suggests these respondents are not familiar with the studies on this issue. Curiously, as disability studies on employment show, employers will speak positively about the idea of hiring someone with a disability, but the reality is that they do not hire those with disabilities.[17] In theory, the Americans with Disabilities Act (ADA) should help prevent discrimination. However, it is mostly used by people with disabilities who are already employed. Those seeking employment cannot use this law because they cannot demonstrate that they were discriminated against because of their disability.[18]

Among the responses to question six, the answer "Mention being disabled. Hirers are looking for diversity," seems to go against the grain of available data, both in the responses in this survey and other studies. There is significant encouragement to hire racially and ethnically diverse librarians. Evidence is lacking that academic libraries are encouraged to hire librarians with disabilities. On the contrary, as responses to questions five and six indicate, the best strategy seems to be to not mention it and try to "pass."

Ableism seems to trump all facts. Emphasizing the value of a diverse workforce might succeed, but the applicant would need to show how her or his disability contributes to that value. Some respondents stressed the need for the applicant to do a good interview by being prepared, "taking a strengths-based approach," and demonstrating in a presentation that disability does not hinder performance. This is the sort of advice all applicants with or without disabilities need to follow. If the disability is apparent, the applicant would do well to address how he or she can perform the job well, regardless of the disability. It would be interesting to know if answers like "no" or "not in particular" mean that the respondent cannot think of anything or if the respondent thinks that there is no way to overcome the apparent disability of the candidate.

As noted in a recent *Chronicle of Higher Education* advice piece, there are stated criteria for positions and hidden criteria for positions.[19] Assumptions about the significance of a disability would fit into this latter category. As several survey participants stated, it is important for an applicant with a disability to show a search committee that, with or without accommodations, the candidate can perform the responsibilities of the position effectively. If accommodations are needed for an interview, an applicant may need to contact the human resources department of the institution after an invitation to an interview has been given in order to have accommodations in place for the interview. An interview for someone with a disability may well be harder than it is for others, but the core of the interview should be about how an applicant fulfills the job expectations.

It is important that a disability be presented in the context of a job and its requirements. If an applicant can perform a job fully with a reasonable accommodation, the applicant should say so. If the interviewers do not bring up the subject of an apparent disability, the survey responses suggest that the applicant should bring it up in order to answer any questions the search committee members might have but think are illegal to ask. It is even better to state that one has a disability and can perform the job well with a reasonable accommodation and state what that accommodation is.[20] If an applicant knows that the library is seeking a librarian with a disability, visible or invisible, it may be beneficial to disclose up front. One study showed that a person with an invisible disability is sixteen times more likely to be hired than one with a visible disability.[21]

Participants offered suggestions for how someone with an apparent disability could get hired for a full-time position. The applicant should make sure that application materials are the best possible. The materials need to make a clear case that the applicant qualifies fully for the position with or without reasonable accommodations. Respondents disagreed over whether to disclose a disability in a cover letter or wait until an interview. One respondent said to "Note in cover letter the strengths that the disability gives the candidate." There are other advocates of disclosing in a cover letter.[22] Another stated, however, that "They shouldn't need to address this in a cover letter. We should be hiring regardless of disability status."[23] Once an institution invites an applicant for an interview, it is up to the candidate whether or not to disclose a disability.

Under the Americans with Disabilities Act, potential employers cannot ask for information about a disability, but they can ask how an apparent disability will affect how well the candidate can perform the job duties. If an applicant cannot hide the disability, then somewhere in the interview, the job seeker should bring up the disability in order to show that she has excellent qualifications and possibly mention accommodations needed to succeed in the position. Depending upon the institution and context, it may be advantageous to stress that the disability will make the library personnel more diverse and better able to serve patrons with disabilities or members of other marginalized groups.

Some respondents spoke of presenting disabilities as an asset. They suggested looking for opportunities in an interview to present a disability as an asset. The disability should not be used as an excuse for why an applicant cannot meet the job requirements. It may, however, improve a candidate's chances by stressing how the efforts to succeed despite the disability show that the person would do well in the position. Also, for schools that are serious about diversity, inclusivity, and equity, hiring someone with a disability will definitely diversify the library staff. In addition, the presence of a librarian with a disability may suggest to students that it is acceptable to be different themselves. It may also provide a librarian for a student with a disability to consult with who has a better understanding of what it means to live with a disability. This does not mean that having a disability guarantees that the librarian can be more empathetic or helpful to a student with a disability. It may, however, avoid negative situations. Librarians with disabilities may have more insight into ways to make libraries more accessible.

Research has shown that the better the attitudes of academic librarians toward persons with disabilities, the more services are developed to aid those persons.[24] With a growing number of students with disabilities entering higher education, the need for such services will increase. Positive attitudes of academic librarians develop through contact with persons who have disabilities. This contact could be with family, friends, coworkers, or others.

Future Research

Going forward, I want to interview academic librarians with apparent disabilities to learn about their experience, including the job application process. Also, I would like to get a larger sample size. While the survey points to some realities of searching for academic librarian jobs, the sample size is too small to make definite conclusions. I also want to gather data about the precise connections between type of institution and presence of librarians who have a disability at the time of hiring. This is important because it could guide an applicant in deciding which positions to apply for. The issue of what percentage of graduates of library schools have an apparent disability would be helpful to know, and I hope to find ways to obtain that sort of data. It would also be useful to find a way to determine why people with disabilities self-select by deciding to not try to become an academic librarian, though again, this could be very difficult to research. The survey results suggest that, while some full-time academic librarians have a disability, they are a very small minority, at least in the USA. A portion of these librarians may have had an apparent disability at the time of their interviews. The survey participants indicated that there are multiple reasons why the number of full-time academic librarians with an apparent disability is so small. Some people might have recognized that their disability or disabilities would keep them from performing the duties of a librarian. Others might have entered library school but did not graduate. The survey as well as the research I looked at for this essay show that many people with an apparent disability are not hired. Is this related to bias or prejudice against them because of their disability? Or are there other factors outside of an applicant's control? It would be difficult to determine how many otherwise qualified librarians with a disability were not hired due to ableism.

In higher education, disability is seen as a deficit, and as Moeller observes, "the deficit model of disability …frames disability as a medically certifiable 'problem' to be 'solved' in some manner.…" Higher education views disability as an exception that does not fit in the academic environment.[25] Therefore, even the definition of professionalism for academic librarians can exclude those with disabilities because their disability makes them an exception.[26] This is no different from other forms of bias, such as racial discrimination. Academic libraries and their institutions need to take steps to end this discrimination, not claim they do not discriminate, even though they clearly seem to reject those with disabilities because they have disabilities. If 19 percent of undergraduates have a disability but fewer than 4 percent of academic librarians have a disability, the library profession, at least in the United States, falls far short of being as inclusive as student populations. Given this stark difference, it is fair to say that academic libraries have a long way to go in making employment for this marginalized group equitable or inclusive. This implies that a prospective academic librarian with a disability faces a difficult task in getting hired by an academic library. The survey suggests several significant issues for getting hired as a full-time academic librarian with a disability.

There should be an increased focus in library literature on the status and plight of those with disabilities who seek academic librarian positions. There is a huge need for organizations that can support academic librarians and those seeking to become librarians who have disabilities. We want a truly diversified, inclusive, and equitable profession, and that must include librarians with disabilities.

Appendix

COMPLETE SURVEY RESULTS

Question One

Are there any full-time librarians at your institution who have an apparent physical or sensory disability?

Responses	Number of Responses	Percentages
Yes	21	35
No	29	48.33
Do Not Know	10	16.66

Question Two

If you answered "Yes" to question one, how many persons with disabilities are full-time librarians at your library/institution?

Number of F/T Librarians with a Disability	Number of Respondents
0	8
1	15
2	2
3	1
4	1
5	1 (Respondent said this was approximate.)
Total Number of Librarians with a Disability	31

Question Three

How many full-time librarians are there in your library/institution?

Number of Librarians	Number of Respondents
1	4
2	3
3	6
4	4
5	6
6	2
7	2
8	3
9	5
10	3
11	2
12	2
14	1
15	2
17	1
19	1
24	2
25	3
30	1
40	1
43	1
44	1
70	1
150	1
Total Librarians given by Respondents	825

Question Four

Are you aware of any current or previous Are you aware of any current or previous full-time librarians at your institution who had an apparent physical or sensory disability at the time of their interview(s) for the position?

| Yes | 11 |
| No | 49 |

Question Five

Compared to the percentage of students with disabilities at many institutions, there are relatively few full-time academic librarians across institutions who have an apparent physical or sensory disability. Why do you think this is the case?

1. Perhaps the perceived physical demands of shelving and moving print materials?
2. I think librarians hide their disabilities, so I wouldn't necessarily agree with this take.
3. Prejudice and assumptions (some correct) about how the physical work involved (carrying, bending, stooping, climbing) would require significant reshaping of the physical space to accommodate some disabilities. However, accommodations would be small for some positions (e.g., instructional).
4. I do not know if this is the case.
5. People hide them as much as possible to avoid stigma.
6. I can't speculate. In the past we employed a library technician with an "apparent physical or sensory disability" which, after some technical accommodations, did not hinder them at work.
7. Many workplaces, libraries included, are not accommodating to persons with disabilities up front. To get an accommodation is often something an employee has to fight for. This is particularly true at my campus—an urban campus—where we don't offer flexible scheduling unless it's specifically requested and then approved by our ADA compliance officer.
8. All students are accepted; all applicants are not.

9. Graduate study might eliminate some folks, particularly with visual impairment (not much available digitally years ago). Also, folks in beginning positions may have need to be more physically capable (i.e., carrying or moving stacks of books; libraries may not be completely accessible; etc.).

10. Entry-level librarian positions often deal with circulation or page-like activities, which often include physical activities. People with physical or sensory disabilities may also use and find information in ways that are different from established practices that librarians use.

11. Librarians have probably not disclosed non-apparent disabilities for a variety of reasons.

12. Lip service is paid to inclusiveness, but not practiced in hiring or promotion.

13. don't know. It's a good question.

14. Some disabilities disqualify one from most of the things academic librarians do (plenty of movement around building, plenty of communication with all sorts of people). Many libraries are older buildings with little in the way of physical accommodations for disability.

15. Disability equals imperfection and leaders must look perfect.

16. Because workload is so heavy among academic libraries, administration is more concerned with their bottom lines than providing equity and accommodations.

17. I would think it's a case of numbers. The ratio of students to librarians is much larger.

18. I think there are more people with disabilities that are not apparent. Otherwise, librarianship can be difficult for people with apparent disabilities—for example, someone in a wheelchair may have a difficult time reaching shelves and navigating the library.

19. There could be many reasons, and "apparent" could be defined variously. We have librarians with obvious visual and hearing challenges—is that within your scope for "apparent"? Some explain their disability, some do not. I don't believe there are many actual librarians in wheelchairs, etc.—certainly none in my library school years (my own or those surrounding or recently).

20. I don't think there is an intentional planning to recruit for diversity.

21. The profession generally requires the ability to see and work with the materials?

22. I am baffled by this, and am not sure why.

23. People with disabilities are not encouraged to pursue librarianship, few scholarships, and often physical requirements ("able to lift 50 lbs.") are included in library positions when they shouldn't be—I have NEVER had to lift more than 5 books in my position as an academic librarian and I'm sure even then, I would have been able to get around doing it if I had to.

24. I am not sure, maybe people with apparent disabilities are not choosing to be librarians. Perhaps the field needs to be intentional about encouraging and welcoming people with disabilities.

25. Unwilling to say without doing research. I worked with a profoundly hearing-impaired librarian at one position, and the situation was met successfully with accommodations. Some disabilities would present some very challenging problems to overcome, and I understand from our institutional personnel training sessions that corporations can use the reasoning of "undue hardship" and "reasonable accommodation" as an opt-out.

26. I think many more students are being diagnosed with disabilities now. Many who are currently employed may have a disability (Autism Spectrum, ADHD, etc.) but not be officially diagnosed. Others with a diagnosis may have been discouraged from pursuing higher education.

27. Many institutions are not entirely ADA-compliant and many job postings have physical requirements (which many times seem unnecessary).

28. HR is reluctant to hire people with disabilities in any industry.

29. They may lack confidence to apply for those positions and we do not seek them out.

30. I think a lot of library buildings are not ADA compliant due to lack of funding and/or the age of the building.

31. Perhaps people with these types of disabilities do not seek out the opportunity to become a librarian and feel other types of work are better suited to them for various reasons. I work for a public institution, so any discrimination based on apparent disability would be highly illegal.

32.   Most librarian jobs I've seen posted list a requirement of being able to lift 20 or 25 lbs. I also know that many offices in higher ed have the awful fluorescent lights, and that isn't great for visual sensitivities.

33.   I'm concerned about your use of "apparent"—we have librarians with some serious health issues for whom we have made accommodations but I don't think the issues are obvious.

34.   a graduate degree can be a barrier to people with disabilities and the perception that people with disabilities can't do as good a job as those who don't have any disabilities

35.   I don't know that this is true

36.   I have been involved with many librarian searches and have never interviewed anyone with a physical or sensory disability. Perhaps they don't think this is a field that can accommodate their disabilities.

37.   unconscious prejudice, i.e., thinking it would be too difficult for a person with physical/sensory disabilities to do what is required in most libraries.

38.   Not sure. Maybe there aren't many people with disabilities that go to library school. For certain positions, mobility and good eye sight are required but I definitely think there are positions that would welcome all people.

39.   Perhaps libraries aren't thought to be friendly toward employees or patrons with these disabilities?

40.   I'm not sure because I would think librarianship would lend itself more readily to necessary accommodations than many other careers. What percentage of adults with apparent physical or sensory disability are employed full time? How does the relative percentage compare for librarianship? Is there better representation among library staff or part-time librarians than full-time librarians?

41.   As a part of many interview committees, I do not recollect anyone with an apparent physical or sensory disability.

42.   My guess is that they retired, reassigned or are not hired based on what physical/sensory issues would impact provision of service or ability to do the job as described.

43.   Prejudice

44.   I would be speculating.

45. Perhaps librarianship is not considered a good career path by individuals with physical or sensory disabilities.
46. Unsure
47. Where is the research that this is true?
48. Don't know
49. Ableism: assumption that any disability makes an applicant incapable of performing job duties.

Question Six

Can you suggest any steps an applicant with an apparent physical or sensory disability might take in cover letters, interviews, etc. to improve her or his chances for being hired?

Here are the responses:

1. Perhaps indicate prior successes in accomplishing similar tasks to those specified in the job description with reasonable accommodation
2. Mention being disabled. Hirers are looking for diversity.
3. No
4. Emphasize how many accommodations would help many library users (the universal design principle).
5. Can't think of any
6. Note in cover letter the strengths that the disability gives the candidate.
7. Speak to the importance of supporting a diverse workforce and their commitment to contributing to a welcoming environment.
8. Most academic library job interviews require a presentation. The candidate should show their strengths in that area.
9. Give examples of what he/she can do or has done in the past related to the position he/she is applying for.
10. I don't think this is the issue.
11. Promote their skills that support the specific job requirements.
12. Be the best qualified candidate.
13. If the applicant is willing, explain how the apparent disability is handled as to alleviate any concerns about suitability for the position.
14. Perhaps clues in how the disabilities are accommodated.
15. No

16. I think taking a strengths-based approach is best for all candidates, regardless of physical or sensory ability.

17. No

18. I'm not sure if this would help but I would be interested in how their disability has made them more effective at their job or how they work around the issue. I'm not certain how that can be addressed in cover letters but it could be worked into interview answers.

19. Perhaps volunteering information about how she would perform the job with reasonable accommodation (this question I believe is legal in an interview situation).

20. Just the suggestions I would give to anyone—tailor the letter/resume to the position, research the institution and come with questions and send a thank you note afterwards.

21. Not in particular

22. If they choose to disclose, then they may offer examples of adaptations/accommodations they or previous employers have made as well as emphasizing the positive impact of having a diversely abled faculty can have on a similarly diverse student body. I think the interview would be a better forum for a candidate to share this information. Addressing how the disability may impact work (if at all) would be helpful. We perceive that disabilities may impact work but this may not be the case. If it is the case, employers would have to weigh whether this impact is significant or no more an impediment than a worker with no apparent disabilities but who does not work well in a team.

23. No

24. I have sensory issues and purposefully do not mention it as I don't feel protected

25. I couldn't raise it in interviews, etc. but you could. Possibly address what helps you succeed at the work, be it technical/ergonomic/space or other accommodations.

26. I don't know. As a person with a non-obvious disability, I have spent years not disclosing my needs due to fear of retribution/rejection. I would like to say that it would be a good idea for a person with an apparent disability to be upfront about it, and ADA accommodations, but I'm not sure that would necessarily help improve chances of being hired.

27. Explain the disability and how they are able to overcome it/mitigate its effect on the workplace. All we are concerned with is that the disability won't impede their ability to do the job as well as their non-disabled colleagues.

28. Highlight ways in which they have demonstrated their competency with a minimum of necessary interventions.

29. Highlight how their disability can help enhance students' experiences in inclusiveness, diversity, understanding, and connecting with those who may also have differing abilities.

30. If they choose to disclose, then they may offer examples of adaptations/accommodations they or previous employers have made as well as emphasizing the positive impact of having a diversely abled faculty can have on a similarly diverse student body.

31. Explain how it will be possible to perform the various required duties despite the disability.

32. Don't hide the disability nor make excuses for having one.

33. I think candidates should call out any potential discrimination by indicating that given the rise of students with disabilities, they would be better able to serve and represent that growing population.

34. I guess I would appreciate it being addressed in a cover letter, so my institution could be better prepared to offer her accommodations.

35. Don't mention that you have a disability. I believe it's illegal for an employer to discriminate against people with disabilities, but it happens, especially at the resume review stage.

36. They shouldn't need to address this in a cover letter. We should be hiring regardless of disability status.

37. Promote their experience in advocating for inclusiveness.

38. Show how they can compensate?

39. Expressing how the applicant has initiated creative solutions to the challenges of their disability would be one effective step.

40. IGNORE PHYSICAL REQUIREMENTS ON JOB ANNOUNCEMENTS. Don't ever answer a question about your disability that makes you feel uncomfortable. Be as matter-of-fact as possible ("That won't be an issue.") and ask your interviewers about the work they do to accomidate [sic] the disabilities of students and staff.

41. Just need to sell their abilities that they can do the job. Physical disabilities should not affect the outcome.

42. None. Once there is a face to face interview—it's usually over.

43. It is my understanding that individuals on the autism spectrum may have more difficulty answering interview questions when there are multiple interviewers. Nearly every interview I have participated in (as an interviewee or interviewer) has involved at least 3, more often 4–5 interviewers. Perhaps individuals with this difficulty could be accommodated through video conferencing; one representative from the hiring committee could conduct the interview while other members observe via video.

44. We attempted to interview someone with a hearing disability this past year but he never responded to our attempts to reach him. This is the only time that I can remember someone with a disability even applying for one of our jobs. So the issue to me is whether or not the applicants even exist or how someone might present themselves in an interview situation. I am not sure there are many individuals out there to recruit.

45. I don't know if I would mention in the cover letter, but perhaps mention during a pre-interview or during the planning for actual interview what needs the applicant has.

Question Seven

Is your institution a
- State College or University
- Private major research…
- Private liberal arts…
- Other (please specify).

Type of Institution	Number of Respondents	Percentage of Respondents
State College or University	23	38.333
Private major research university	0	0.0
Private liberal arts college or university	22	36.666
Other	15	25.0

Notes

1. Joanne Oud "Systemic Workplace Barriers for Academic Librarians with Disabilities,"
    College and Research Libraries 80, no. 2 (March 2019): 169, https://crl.acrl.org/index.php/
    crl/article/view/16948.
2. Oud, "Systemic Workplace Barriers," 169.
3. Joanne Oud, "Academic Librarians with Disabilities: Job Perceptions and Factors Influ-
    encing Positive Workplace Experiences," *Partnership: The Canadian Journal of Library and
    Information Practice and Research* 13, no. 1 (2018): 2, https://doi.org/10.21083/partnership.
    v13i1.4090.
4. World Health Organization and World Bank, *World Report on Disability: Summary*
    (Geneva, Switzerland: World Health Organization, 2011), 8, http://whqlibdoc.who.int/
    hq/2011/WHO_NMH_VIP_11.01_eng.pdf.
5. Amelia Koford, "People with Disabilities" in *Encyclopedia of Library and Information
    Services*, 4th ed., ed. John D. McDonald and Michael Levine-Clark (Boca Raton, FL: CRC
    Press, 2018), 3579.
6. National Center for Education Statistics, *Digest of Education Statistics, 2017*, NCES 2018-
    070 (Washington, DC: US Department of Education, 2019), chapter 3, https://nces.ed.gov/
    fastfacts/display.asp?id=60 (information from 2017 removed from page). Over half of
    undergraduates reporting disabilities report learning and psychological disabilities such
    as attention deficit disorder, depression, etc. that may not be "visible" (National Center
    for Education Statistics, *Characteristics and Outcomes of Undergraduates with Disabilities*,
    NCES 2018-432 [Washington, DC: US Department of Education, December 2017], 33,
    table 6, https://nces.ed.gov/pubs2018/2018432.pdf). Nevertheless, a library that has made
    disabled librarians feel welcome may more easily make disabled students feel welcome,
    no matter the type of disability, and the lack of opportunities for disabled librarians is an
    equity issue.
7. Robin Brown, and Scott Sheidlower, "Claiming Our Space: A Quantitative and Qualitative
    Picture of Disabled Librarians," *Library Trends* 67, no. 3 (Winter 2019): 471–86, https://doi.
    org/10.1353/lib.2019.0007.
8. Kathy Rosa and Kelsey Henke, *2017 ALA Demographic Study* (Chicago: American Library
    Association, 2017), https://www.ala.org/tools/sites/ala.org.tools/files/content/Draft%20
    of%20Member%20Demographics%20Survey%2001-11-2017.pdf.
9. Karisa Teindl et al., "Does Visibility of Disability Influence Employment Opportunities and
    Outcomes? A Thematic Analysis of Multi-stakeholder Perspectives," *Journal of Vocational
    Rehabilitation* 49, no. 3 (2018): 368, https://doi.org/10.3233/JVR-180980.
10. Oud, "Systematic Workplace Barriers," 169.
11. Oud, "Academic Librarians with Disabilities," 8.
12. Christine M. Moeller, "Disability, Identity, and Professionalism: Precarity in Librarianship,"
    Library Trends 67, no. 3 (Winter 2019): 462, https://doi.org/10.1353/lib.2019.0006.
13. Lois A. Weiss, "Understanding Faculty Members Living with Disabilities in Higher
    Education" (EdD diss., Ball State University, 2016), iv, https://cardinalscholar.bsu.edu/
    handle/123456789/200563. Weiss cites (Siebers, 2008) as a source for these ideas, but I
    have been unable to find these precise statements in Tobin Siebers, *Disability Theory* (Ann
    Arbor: University of Michigan Press, 2008).
14. Shahd Alshammari, "A Hybridized Academic Identity: Negotiating a Disability within
    Academia's Discourse of Ableism," in Negotiating Disability: Disclosure and Higher
    Education, ed. Stephanie L. Kerschbaum, Laura T. Eisenman, and James M. Jones (Ann

Arbor: University of Michigan Press, 2017), 27, https://www.jstor.org/stable/10.3998/mpub.9426902.6.

15. Alshammari, "Hybridized Academic Identity," 27.
16. Oud, "Systemic Workplace Barriers," 173.
17. Oud, "Systemic Workplace Barriers," 190.
18. Doris Zames Fleischer and Frieda Zames, *The Disability Rights Movement* (Philadelphia: Temple University Press, 2011), 110–11, https://www.jstor.org/stable/j.ctt14bt7kv.
19. Brian Leiter, "Academic Ethics: 'Hidden' Hiring Criteria," *Chronicle of Higher Education*, January 30, 2018, https://www.chronicle.com/article/Academic-Ethics-Hidden-/242381?cid=wcontentgrid.
20. Richard Pimentel, "The Art of Disclosing Your Disability," Milt Wright & Associates (website), accessed January 14, 2020, http://www.miltwright.com/articles/ArtOfDisclosingYourDisability.pdf.
21. Teindl et al., "Visibility of Disability," 368.
22. Pimentel, "Disclosing Your Disability"; Career Center, University of California, Berkeley, "Disclosing a Disability," accessed January 14, 2019, https://career.berkeley.edu/Tools/DisclosingADisability.
23. In my own personal interaction with other job seekers in forums about getting library positions and talking with others in person on this topic, the opinion has been unanimous that cover letters that disclose disabilities never result in interviews. This does not prove that such disclosure will get an applicant for a position rejected. However, as there are far too many unknowns in the application process to draw any firm conclusions. I have not seen any studies on this particular issue, and it would be difficult to develop statistical data.
24. Henry C. Dequin, Irene Schilling, and Samuel Huang, "Attitudes of Academic Librarians toward Disabled Persons," *Journal of Academic Librarianship* 14, no. 1 (March 1988): 30. While this research is dated, its point that attitudes are influenced far more by contact with persons with a disability than information about disability likely still holds true.
25. Moeller, "Disability," 458.
26. Moeller, "Disability," 458.

Bibliography

Alshammari, Shahd. "A Hybridized Academic Identity: Negotiating a Disability within Academia's Discourse of Ableism." In *Negotiating Disability: Disclosure and Higher Education*. Edited by Stephanie L. Kerschbaum, Laura T. Eisenman, and James M. Jones, 25–38. Ann Arbor: University of Michigan Press, 2017. https://www.jstor.org/stable/10.3998/mpub.9426902.

Brown, Robin, and Scott Sheidlower. "Claiming Our Space: A Quantitative and Qualitative of Disabled Librarians." *Library Trends* 67, no. 3 (Winter 2019): 471–86. https://doi.org/10.1353/lib.2019.0007.

Career Center, University of California, Berkeley. "Disclosing a Disability." Accessed January 14, 2019. https://career.berkeley.edu/Tools/DisclosingADisability.

Dequin, Henry C., Irene Schilling, and Samuel Huang. "Attitudes of Academic Librarians toward Disabled Persons." *Journal of Academic Librarianship* 14, no. 1 (March 1988): 28–31.

Fleischer, Doris Zames, and Frieda Zames. *The Disability Rights Movement: From Charity to Confrontation*. Philadelphia: Temple University Press, 2011. https://www.jstor.org/stable/j.ctt14bt7kv.

Koford, Amelia. "People with Disabilities." In *Encyclopedia of Library and Information Services*, 4th ed. Edited by John D. McDonald and Michael Levine-Clark, 3573–83. Boca Raton, FL: CRC Press, 2018.

Leiter, Brian. "Academic Ethics: 'Hidden' Hiring Criteria." *Chronicle of Higher Education*, January 30, 2018. https://www.chronicle.com/article/ Academic-Ethics-Hidden-/242381?cid=wcontentgrid.

Moeller, Christine M. "Disability, Identity, and Professionalism: Precarity in Librarianship." *Library Trends* 67, no. 3 (Winter 2019): 455–70. https://doi.org/10.1353/lib.2019.0006.

National Center for Education Statistics. *Characteristics and Outcomes of Undergraduates with Disabilities*, NCES 2018-432. Washington, DC: US Department of Education, December 2017. https://nces.ed.gov/pubs2018/2018432.pdf.

———. *Digest of Education Statistics, 2017*, NCES 2018-070. Washington, DC: US Department of Education, 2019. https://nces.ed.gov/fastfacts/display.asp?id=60 (information from 2017 removed from page).

Oud, Joanne. "Academic Librarians with Disabilities: Job Perceptions and Factors Influencing Positive Workplace Experiences," *Partnership: Canadian Journal of Library and Information Practice and Research* 13, no. 1 (2018). https://doi.org/10.21083/partnership.v13i1.4090.

———. "Systemic Workplace Barriers for Academic Librarians with Disabilities." *College and Research Libraries* 80, no 2 (March 2019): 169–94. https://crl.acrl.org/index.php/crl/article/ view/16948.

Pimentel, Richard. "The Art of Disclosing Your Disability." Milt Wright & Associates (website). Accessed January 14, 2020. http://www.miltwright.com/articles/ArtOfDisclosingYourDis-ability.pdf.

Rosa, Kathy, and Kelsey Henke. *2017 ALA Demographic Study*. Chicago: American Library Association, 2017. https://www.ala.org/tools/sites/ala.org.tools/files/content/Draft%20of%20 Member%20Demographics%20Survey%2001-11-2017.pdf.

Siebers, Tobin. *Disability Theory*. Ann Arbor: University of Michigan Press, 2008.

Teindl, Karisa, Sandra Thompson-Hodgetts, Marghalara Rashid, and David B. Nicholas. "Does Visibility of Disability Influence Employment Opportunities and Outcomes? A Thematic Analysis of Multi-stakeholder Perspectives." *Journal of Vocational Rehabilitation* 49, no. 3 (2018): 367–77. https://doi.org/10.3233/JVR-180980.

Weiss, Lois A. "Understanding Faculty Members Living with Disabilities in Higher Education." EdD diss., Ball State University, 2016. https://cardinalscholar.bsu.edu/ handle/123456789/200563.

World Health Organization and World Bank. *World Report on Disability: Summary*. Geneva, Switzerland: World Health Organization, 2011. http://whqlibdoc.who.int/hq/2011/WHO_NMH_VIP_11.01_eng.pdf.

CHAPTER 5

Mentoring and Diversity

Barbara Lewis, Matt Torrence, Tomaro Taylor, and Meghan Cook

Introduction

Establishing a diverse, equitable, and inclusive (DEI) workforce begins with the culture of the organization. Hiring policies and practices that support and facilitate diversity, inclusion, and equity are critical features of building a workforce that is representative of society. Most of us don't have that much influence on the hiring practices of our library, but we can all be leaders, and all are responsible for creating and maintaining a welcoming and inclusive environment for a diverse array of newcomers. One area in which we can be influential is the mentoring of new employees. Effective mentoring can have a tremendous impact on whether a new employee feels welcomed and included and stays with the organization in the long term.[1]

The University of South Florida (USF) Libraries are embarking on an ambitious and strategic hiring plan. In the next five years, it is anticipated that approximately fifty new employees will join the libraries to enhance, support, and sustain both new and upcoming initiatives. It can be a challenge for newcomers to be integrated into an existing organizational culture and for an established culture to evolve and incorporate the strengths of new employees. Therefore, a Mentoring Program Exploration Group (MPEG) was established to consider how faculty and staff at the Tampa Campus Library, with likely new partners from other campus locations, can establish and maintain a culture of formal

121

and diverse mentorship among all library employees. A committee of library faculty and professional staff from Library Student Success, Research Platform Teams, and Special Collections determined that such an endeavor is possible with the right groundwork, strong commitments of participation from potential mentors and mentees, and continuous assessment. This chapter will present the recommendations of the MPEG while focusing on the lessons learned from the participants in the Dr. Henrietta M. Smith Residency Program, which promotes and encourages diversity in the USF Libraries, whose experiences have contrasted with those of other new hires.

Literature Review

The preponderance of research on mentoring focuses on the recruitment and hiring practices of libraries, but there is limited mention of diversity, equity, or inclusion. This literature review includes a blend of current articles about general mentoring in libraries and highlights from those works that do address the issues of diversity. The focus for this review will be given to recent examples at academic libraries, but other examples are included for consideration and examination.

A number of excellent and comprehensive reviews of mentoring programs provide the foundation for this journey into mentoring in academic libraries. For example, the article "A Scoping Review of Mentoring Programs for Academic Librarians" offers a high-quality analysis of the various types of mentoring programs that exist in this environment. Particularly interesting in this work is the section on "incentives" and making them "tangible" for all involved parties.[2] This type of measurable benefit, financial or other, is a key element that is not to be overlooked, along with the benefits to, in most cases, junior or new professionals. Another excellent article for succinct, but comprehensive coverage of this subject is the work "Leadership and Leadership Development in Academic Libraries: A Review." Well outlined in this article are fundamental elements of leadership capabilities, including types and levels of leadership expectations and competencies, while also highlighting vague, or undefined, elements of leadership as they relate to mentoring and mentoring programs.[3]

The topic of mentoring also garners monographic attention. The chapter "Mentoring in Academic Libraries" shines for its attention to the concepts of formal and informal mentoring, as well as providing an excellent review of best practices from the literature.[4] While this work is slightly dated, it offers another good and foundational study of the subject. Other interesting analyses include Hussey and Campbell-Meier's work in summarizing the mentoring culture in the world of library and information science.[5] With a focus on topics such as trust and the importance of value, this article delves more deeply into the history and sociology of academic library work. A final suggestion for an overview study, but with a unique focus, is a white paper with a helpful section on coaching. This work simplifies and explains the concept of coaching and how it relates to, differs from, and overlaps with mentoring.[6]

Broad coverage is wonderful, but helpful information may also be garnered from case studies and intensive examination of some of the specific elements of mentoring. There are several excellent articles that well represent important topics specific to management of personnel and the management of mentoring programs. One such case study, for example, covers the formation of committees or groups, as well as the importance of inclusivity, matching of mentors and mentees, and selecting the proper systems for official and unofficial mentoring for various types of academic libraries.[7] Another excellent work offers critical insight into the intricacies of official and unofficial mentoring, in addition to excellent ideas on how to choose the proper system for varying types of academic library settings.[8] Success with mentoring requires effort and common understanding from both partners, as well as from all levels of library employees.

Diversity-specific publications and research in academic libraries are more difficult to locate, but quality content is available. Boyd, Blue, and Im authored an excellent study and evaluation of diversity in residency programs, with some additional content on mentoring and retention in this realm.[9] This work covers a history of diversity initiatives, relevant training, and the impact of various social programs and efforts in recent times. This was, perhaps, the most commonly cited work in this specific arena, and it is filled with helpful information on a variety of formal and informal mentoring topics, such as the influence of diversity on the selection process, acculturation to other academic units on campus, and the types of activities included in residency programs. In addition, mentoring and diversity is covered by an article titled "Purposeful Mentoring in Academic Libraries." While the attention to diversity is brief, this work attentively covers the benefits of mentoring, including legacy and succession planning, reverse mentoring, and salutary benefits. The text additionally makes specific reference to these benefits as they relate to minorities in the profession.[10]

While there are relatively few journal articles on diversity in library mentoring, there are useful academic library websites that address this topic. Iowa State provides one good example, which explains the diversity initiatives of its residency program, including procedures, benefits, and a time line.[11] The same may be said for ACRL, which offers a brief, but useful description of its mentoring program for underrepresented groups.[12] These programs, along with the USF Tampa Library's Dr. Henrietta M. Smith Residency Program, make it clear that information is available with a focus on diversity in library training and mentorship.

Turning back to general mentoring issues, this review will close with the subjects of succession planning, actual experiences of mentees, and assessment. With a focus on management and leadership, "Succession Planning through Mentoring in the Library" addresses how mentorship can be effectively used for human resources and future strategic planning.[13] This work is relatively current and combines elements of both business and library literature and highlights the importance of diversity in academic libraries in both recruitment and leadership.[14] And with the good, there must be some bad, and this is represented well by a nonlibrary article, "Are Bad Experiences Stronger Than Good Ones in Mentoring Relationships? Evidence from the Protégé and Mentor Perspective." While not focused on LIS topics, the article makes a strong case that a negative experience can be just as important or beneficial as a positive one.[15] Learning from mistakes may be cliché, but it's as prevalent in the library world as any other area of work or study.

There are numerous efforts on the assessment of library mentoring programs. A very recent work, "Mixed-Methods Assessment of a Mentoring Program," is focused on libraries and outlines the benefits, as well as policies and practices, related to the use of focus groups and feedback.[16] This work is properly heavy on statistical results and useful conclusions and discussion. And while not entirely focused on mentoring, "Funding, Time, and Mentoring: A Study of Research and Publication Support Practices of ARL Member Libraries" considers how peer and administrative support and mentorship can impact librarians at all levels in terms of publications and other measurable elements of academic production. Of particular interest is the chart that demonstrates the markedly higher prevalence of mentoring programs in academic libraries where faculty are required to publish for promotion (90 percent) when compared to those that are not (50 percent).[17]

USF Library History and the MPEG Project

The USF Libraries have a long, albeit inconsistent, history of supporting both formal and informal mentorship of library employees who are directly engaged in professional library activities. Graduate students enrolled in the university's library and information science master's program and new faculty librarians have often been the most likely candidates for engaging in an on-site mentoring relationship with an experienced librarian. Library and information science master's students in the Tampa Library's Graduate Assistant program, which ran from 1976 until 2013, typically received informal mentorship via group meetings led by program coordinators, professional development workshops with librarians, and on-the-job training, and they worked closely with incumbent librarians on projects. Visiting Instructor Librarians hired under the Dr. Henrietta M. Smith Residency Program,[18] as well as a few more recent hires, were assigned formal mentors to facilitate onboarding and help librarians adjust to the profession and professional work environment. The dissolution of the Graduate Assistants program; reduced funding to support the Residency; and slowed hiring due to reorganization, restructuring, and campus freezes have rendered even the spottiest of efforts fairly nonexistent.

In 2018, the dean of the USF Libraries announced an ambitious and strategic plan to hire roughly fifty employees over a five-year period. New employees would comprise not only professional librarians but other professional and nonprofessional positions as well. The announcement was met by one of our chapter authors with the question "Will new employees receive mentoring?" For the short term, a mentoring program could facilitate integration of new employees into the USF Tampa Library's workplace culture. For the long term, with the promise of so many new hires—who may or may not have library or information science backgrounds—it would be advisable for the library to formalize mentor relationships on an institutional level. Library administration's hiring plan provided the perfect opportunity to implement formal mentorship activities as part of every new employee's job.

The Mentoring Program Exploration Group (MPEG) formed after the hiring plan was announced. The group, made up of volunteers from the library's Research and Instruction unit—which consisted of Library Liaison Services, the

Research Platform Teams, and Special Collections—worked together to determine how current faculty and staff at the USF Tampa Library could establish and maintain a culture of mentorship among all library employees. Outwardly, the group may have appeared somewhat limited in focus and scope, as we were all part of the library's public service units. However, our diverse backgrounds and experience lent to our push to recommend a plan that would build a foundation for a sustainable and effective program.

- Member 1: A PhD candidate with a professional, nonfaculty appointment whose educational and work history are outside of library and information science. The employee had worked at the USF Tampa Library for less than one year and had not received formal mentoring.
- Member 2: A second-career librarian whose work has included significant outreach, leadership, and supervisory responsibilities in fifteen years of service.
- Member 3: A former graduate assistant and the first Dr. Henrietta M. Smith Resident Librarian who received both formal and informal mentorship from senior librarians during the early career stage.
- Member 4: A career librarian who served as formal mentor of the second Dr. Henrietta M. Smith Resident Librarian.

The Dr. Henrietta M. Smith residents brought new and diverse life experience to the library workforce and significant professional opportunities to the residents. However, one consequence is that the residents were expected to be the voice of their minority group and to lead other diversity initiatives in the libraries. This can be challenging and cause stress. More importantly, it put added emphasis on their minority status, which can further separate them as other. It can also contribute to the misguided conception that members of minority groups are monolithic rather than diverse in their experiences, opinions, and needs. Because of our different experiences as mentees, mentors, or both, we brought a range of opinions about how a mentoring program should take shape at the USF Tampa Library. After brainstorming initial ideas, we turned to the literature to determine whether our ideas had proven effective at other institutions, if they had been tried at all, and to discover ideas we had not considered. Our initial goal wasn't to establish the mentoring program per se, but to investigate and recommend policies and practices to formalize mentorship at all levels of the institution. Of utmost importance from our shared perspectives is the idea of involving all levels of employees in formal mentor opportunities, especially since our aggressive hiring plan included many professional nonfaculty positions. Not only does this increase the possible assessment capacity of mentor/mentee relationships within the library, but it also affords opportunities for students, staff, administrative personnel, and promotion-track faculty to grow professionally in the ways most suited for furthering their careers—not just library students and library faculty, as attempted in the past, but all personnel employed by the library. As our literature review suggests, this approach was not common in academic institutions.

The MPEG Recommendations

Keywords

Mentoring can mean many things to many people and those differences can lead to confusion and misunderstanding. Therefore, through our exploration process, we agreed on the definitions of the terms listed here.

- *Mentoring Program:* A formal structure designed to build workplace and professional expertise through the pairing of established and new professionals at the USF Libraries. In addition, the Mentoring Program should also facilitate the inclusion of new employees in formal and informal activities of the Libraries.
- *Mentor:* A dependable and collegial contact who can be relied on for both general and professional guidance. A mentor cannot be a mentee's immediate supervisor but can be a supervisor in a unit or department external to the mentee's primary areas of responsibility.
- *Mentee:* A new USF Libraries employee who would benefit from dependable, collegial, and professional guidance beyond the relationships that typically develop from working with colleagues and that also extends beyond the university's and libraries' initial onboarding processes. A mentee can also be an incumbent employee who has moved into or wants to move into a new position and needs guidance.
- *Coach:* A USF Libraries employee who serves in the informal capacity of providing advice to newer employees. Coaches do not actively provide career development guidance, but rather serve to help colleagues navigate their professional enculturation and personal inclusion within the libraries.

- *Mentoring Ambassador:* A USF Libraries employee who serves as and impartial party with whom mentors and mentees can speak confidentially about their mentoring relationships. This may include, among other things, commitment issues, personality issues, or lack of mentor experience in an area the mentee wishes to develop. Ambassadors could recommend ways to improve the relationship, the addition of a new mentor for a specific purpose, or the dissolution of the mentoring relationship.
- *Library employees:* Faculty, staff, administrative and professional, postdoctoral, and graduate-level workers at the USF Libraries. For the purposes of this document, undergraduate student workers are excluded from the "library employees" category. However, mentoring practices may be applied to student workers.

Mentoring Committee

The first and most important recommendation of the MPEG was that a Mentoring Committee be formally established and charged by Library Administration. Initially, the MPEG group was conceived by the USF Tampa Library Faculty Group. However, the MPEG agreed that any employee may have ideas and skills to contribute to the Mentoring Program and that all employees should be able to participate in the Mentoring Program. The MPEG therefore recommended that membership on the Mentoring Committee should be open to all faculty, administrative/professional, and staff employees and should include diverse representation. In addition, the Mentoring Committee should work with the library's new Diversity Committee to ensure that both programs are complementary in their goals and activities and that mentors and mentees are provided the necessary development, training, and networking opportunities related to diversity, equity, and inclusion. The Mentoring Committee will:

- Identify and compile a database of current USF Libraries employees willing to participate in the libraries' Mentoring Program, as either mentors or mentees. In a previous project, the library developed a skills inventory database for each employee, which may be included in the Mentoring Program database to help identify areas of mentor expertise. As new employees join the organization, their information will be added to the database to help pair them with an appropriate mentor.

- Develop guidelines for Mentoring Ambassadors who will help mentees and mentors navigate the process, be a sounding board for issues, and be an ally and provide a safe zone when needed.
- Define the types of mentorship opportunities that will be available (project, promotion, professional development, social, etc.). It should be noted that different mentorship opportunities may result in a mentee having more than one mentor for specific purposes. For example, one mentor could work with the mentee on scholarship and creative activities, such as a presentation or publication. Another mentor could work with the mentee to identify service opportunities within the University of South Florida or within professional organizations.
- Develop mentoring program guidelines and best practices, which are based on experience gained during implementation of the program, investigation into mentoring programs at other institutions, and continuous review of the literature.
- Develop or identify training opportunities for mentors and ambassadors, acknowledging that mentorship is not an intuitive skill, such as:
  - in-person training workshops or programs that are internally developed (e.g., Mentor the Mentor and Implicit Bias) or available through professional organizations
  - web-based training workshops, such as those available through ALA webinars
  - online training modules that are internally developed or available through virtual learning tools, such as LinkedIn Learning
  - readings, such as those on the reading list below and on the Diversity, Equity, and Inclusion subject guide, which identifies diverse classes and provides resources for continued learning and understanding about each[19]
- Identify formal diversity initiatives at the university in which mentors and mentees can participate, including committees (e.g., Faculty Senate Council on Racial Justice, USF Libraries Diversity Committee), webinars and panel discussions (e.g., I'm Speaking Series: Conversations That Move, Enlightenment Series), and reading and discussion groups (e.g., Dismantling Racism Study Circles, Antiracist Reading Group).
- Develop a list of diverse social, cultural, and professional organizations at USF and in the community and encourage mentors and ambassadors

to become familiar with these opportunities in which new employees may participate.

New Employee Orientation

PHASE 1

In order to acclimate to and be welcomed into the diverse culture of the University of South Florida, all new employees are required to participate in orientation at the university level. This includes the typical introduction to available benefits; the history, mission, and strategic plan of the university; a campus tour; and the metrics and performance standings of the university. However, orientation at the USF Libraries level has historically been the responsibility of the department in which the employee's primary duties will be performed. This can result in a lack of knowledge about the overall functioning of the USF Libraries and the purpose, contributions, goals, and personnel of other departments. With this in mind, MPEG recommended the following:

- A four-to-six-week onboarding process, initiated by library Human Resources, that includes an employee handbook or manual with information about all USF Libraries departments—personnel, contact information, overview/summary of department function, and so on. The manual should include substantial information about the new employee's primary department and other departments the employee may work with. The Mentoring Committee will work with the libraries' Human Resources unit to finalize a new employee orientation process and handbook.
- Introduce all new employees to the mentoring program during the onboarding process, even though new hires will not be paired with mentors at that time. Based on a new employee's experience and areas of expertise, they may gravitate toward specific individuals, they may elect to have the Mentoring Committee recommend a mentor, or they may choose not to have a mentor at all. It is, however, recommended that all new library faculty (one to five years of experience) receive an assigned mentor and actively participate in the mentoring program because of the research and professional service requirements of faculty positions.

- Formally discuss the mentoring program with all new employees. It should also be stressed that, in addition to the professional aspects and advantages of mentoring, participation in the Mentoring Program also provides an opportunity to learn about the USF Libraries' culture and to become a participating member of the library community. In addition, information about the Mentoring Program should be included in the employee handbook.
- Determine which new employees will participate in the mentoring program, whether as a result of requirement or self-selection, and facilitate the selection of appropriate mentors from a professional and cultural perspective. This will largely be based on the information collected in the Mentoring Program database.

Phase 2

Once an employee completes the orientation and onboarding processes, they are generally expected to independently assume control of their job assignment. For newer professionals, this can be a difficult transition period filled with uncertainty and unclear expectations, which a mentor can help alleviate. MPEG recommended that the Mentoring Committee do the following:

- Help mentees identify mentors approximately three to five weeks after employees begin working at the USF Libraries. This will allow the parties to become acquainted with each other without interfering with formal USF new employee, library, and departmental orientations, which usually occur in the first few weeks of employment.
- Help determine the minimum and maximum lengths of time (one, two, three semesters) mentors and mentees will be paired together. Relationship duration will be based on the new employee's academic library experience and mentor relationship goals. MPEG recommends a minimum of two semesters for most mentor-mentee relationships.
- Help mentors and mentees develop relationship goals that outline measurable expectations. These should be documented and agreed upon by both parties and may be used as part of the Mentoring Program assessment.
- Encourage mentors and mentees to schedule weekly, biweekly, or monthly meeting times, depending on their expectations and schedules.

If both parties agree, the meetings may take place in an informal setting, such as over lunch.

Phase 3

As employees settle into their new positions, and as their mentoring relationships develop, mentors and mentees will need to reevaluate their initial expectations. MPEG recommended the following, which will provide some of the information needed for assessment and continuous improvement of the mentoring program:

- Monthly mentoring program meetings, led by a member of the Mentoring Committee, to allow mentors and mentees to discuss what is working or not working at the programmatic level. Ideally, these meetings will include all current mentors and mentees. Additional meetings of mentees only or mentors only may also be called if deemed necessary.
- Monthly check-ins with the mentor and mentee to discuss their experiences and understand how and whether their relationship changes over time.
- Selection and training of Mentoring Program Ambassadors, who will be available to mentees and mentors to discuss any issues they would rather not discuss in open meetings.

Phase 4

Every program should practice assessment to improve its operation and outcomes. For this program, it is also necessary to assess the growing culture of mentorship in the USF Libraries. MPEG recommended the following:

- The Mentoring Committee will create and implement an assessment plan based on monthly meeting records, check-in meeting records, and qualitative interviews to evaluate the effectiveness and sustainability of the mentoring program and to assess the growing culture of mentorship in the USF Libraries. While general surveys of the participants' experiences may facilitate understanding of the program's effectiveness, longer-range studies may be more appropriate for determining the program's value and establishing data collection baselines. This could include participation in the exit interview process for mentees who choose to leave the organization. In addition, the committee should periodically evaluate the assessment plan to ensure that it evolves with the mentoring program.

- The Mentoring Committee will establish data collection baselines and implement a calendar for consistent data collection. Significant research is needed into existing assessment programs at other institutions, business as well as academic.
- The Mentoring Committee will investigate and consider development of a reverse mentoring aspect of the program, such as new employees with technical skills helping incumbent employees to develop those skills, as a way to further establish mentorship as a community of practice and emphasize that we can all learn from each other.

POST-IMPLEMENTATION PHASE

Since the MPEG recommended that a mentee-mentor relationship should not be less than two semesters, the official post-implementation phase will begin two semesters after the first mentor-mentee relationship is initiated. The final recommendations from the MPEG are for the Mentoring Committee to do the following:

- Document what is learned during the Mentoring Program implementation in the form of best practices for creating and sustaining a culture of mentorship at the USF Libraries.
- Compile, analyze, and summarize the gathered assessment data and make recommendations for continuous improvement of the Mentoring Program.
- Provide an annual report to management on the activities, achievements, and assessment of the Mentoring Program.

The Present and Future of Mentoring at the USF Libraries

Present efforts, guided by the MPEG report, include the initiation of a Mentoring Committee for the USF Libraries consisting of faculty, administrative/professional, and staff employees. The formal charge given to the committee by the administration is to develop, implement, and assess a Mentoring Program for new and current employees of the libraries. Following the MPEG recommendations, the new Mentoring Committee will:

- work with the libraries' Human Resources department to develop and finalize an employee handbook for proper and consistent onboarding

- define the types of mentorship opportunities that will be available (e.g., project, promotion, professional development, social, etc.) and match the appropriate people to each other
- develop mentoring program guidelines, in-person training workshops, and online training modules
- collaborate with the libraries' Diversity Committee and search committees to ensure the goals and activities of all groups are aligned and complementary
- create an assessment plan for evaluating the effectiveness and sustainability of the mentoring program, as well as how to improve it
- establish best practices for sustaining a culture of mentorship at the USF Libraries

The new Mentoring Committee is in its infancy. Therefore much still needs to be done to satisfy the charge. In addition, budget issues related to the coronavirus pandemic have caused a temporary hiring freeze at the university. Therefore, mentoring activities are currently focused on existing employees and will be for the foreseeable future. We have introduced employees to the mentoring program, developed a website (https://guides.lib.usf.edu/mentoring), and begun recruiting mentors and mentees.

There are many factors that impact mentoring, and this committee will evaluate short-term tactical goals versus long-term strategic goals. Down the road, the hope is that an environmental and cultural shift will occur that allows for new and current employees to feel included and supported in their role in the library. We are in a period of potential positive change with the addition of diverse employees with varied skill sets into the professional, cultural, and social channels of the libraries and the formation of institutional diversity initiatives at the university. Therefore, the success of the Mentoring Program, the Mentoring Committee, and the USF Libraries hiring program will be measured by the successful inclusion of new employees into the USF Libraries culture, the retention of all employees, the professional pathways created that lead to success for all parties involved, including the library, and the evolution of the existing organizational culture to welcome and include a diverse community of newcomers and incumbent employees and incorporate their strengths.

MPEG Reading List

Although all of the members of the MPEG had previous mentee or mentor experience, our knowledge of activities outside the USF Libraries was limited. The following resources are a few of those identified and read by the MPEG to help us learn about mentoring practices within the academic library community:

Bruxvoort, Diane. "Mentoring in Academic Libraries." In *Workplace Culture in Academic Libraries: The Early 21st Century*. Edited by Kelly Blessinger and Paul Hrycaj, 251–62. Oxford: Chandos, 2013.

Colosimo, April, Robin Elizabeth Desmeules, and Dawn McKinnon. "Whole-Person Mentoring for Every Stage of Careers in Librarianship." *Library Leadership and Management* 32, no. 1 (2017): 1–13.

Cogell, Raquel V., and Cindy A. Gruwell, eds. *Diversity in Libraries: Academic Residency Programs*. Westport, CT: Greenwood Press, 2001.

Fyn, Amy F. "Peer Group Mentoring Relationships and the Role of Narrative." *Journal of Academic Librarianship* 39, no. 4 (2013): 330–34.

Garrison, Julie. "Academic Library Residency Programs and Diversity." *portal: Libraries and the Academy* 20, no. 3 (2020): 405–09. https://doi.org/10.1353/pla.2020.0020.

Henrich, Kristin J., and Ramirose Attebury. "Communities of Practice at an Academic Library: A New Approach to Mentoring at the University of Idaho." *Journal of Academic Librarianship* 36, no. 2 (2010): 158–95.

Hodges, Sue. *Leading Libraries: Briefing Paper on Coaching and Mentoring*. London: SCONUL, 2017.

Lorenzetti, Diane L., and Susan E. Powelson. "A Scoping Review of Mentoring Programs for Academic Librarians." *Journal of Academic Librarianship* 41, no. 2 (2015): 186–96. https://doi.org/10.1016/j.acalib.2014.12.001.

Mavrinac, Mary Ann, and Kim Stymest. *Pay It Forward: Mentoring New Information Professionals*. Chicago: Association of College and Research Libraries, 2012.

Smigielski, Elizabeth M., Melissa A. Laning, and Caroline M. Daniels. "Funding, Time, and Mentoring: A Study of Research and Publication Support Practices of ARL Member Libraries." *Journal of Library Administration* 54, no. 4 (2014): 261–76. https://doi.org/10.1080/01930826.2014.924309.

Notes

1. Jennifer A. Bartlett, "Paying It Forward, Giving It Back: The Dynamics of Mentoring," *Library Leadership and Management* 27, no. 4 (2013): 1–6, http://works.bepress.com/ jenbartlett/11/; J. Denard Thomas, Laura Gail Lunsford, and Helena A. Rodrigues, "Early Career Academic Staff Support: Evaluating Mentoring Networks," *Journal of Higher Education Policy and Management* 37, no. 3 (2015): 320–29, https://doi.org/10.1080/13600 80X.2015.1034426.
2. Diane L. Lorenzetti and Susan E. Powelson, "A Scoping Review of Mentoring Programs for Academic Librarians," *Journal of Academic Librarianship* 41, no. 2 (2015): 186–96, https:// doi.org/10.1016/j.acalib.2014.12.001.
3. Gabrielle Ka Wai Wong, "Leadership and Leadership Development in Academic Librar-ies: A Review," *Library Management* 38, no. 2/3 (2017): 153–66, https://doi.org/10.1108/ LM-09-2016-0075.
4. Diane Bruxvoort, "Mentoring in Academic Libraries," in *Workplace Culture in Academic Libraries: The Early 21st Century*, ed. Kelly Blessinger and Paul Hrycaj (Oxford: Chandos, 2013), 251–62.
5. Lisa K. Hussey and Jennifer Campbell-Meier, "Is There a Mentoring Culture within the LIS Profession?" *Journal of Library Administration* 57, no. 5 (2017): 500–516, https://doi.org/10 .1080/01930826.2017.1326723.
6. Sue Hodges, *Leading Libraries* (London: SCONUL, October 2017), https://www.sconul. ac.uk/publication/briefing-paper-on-coaching-and-mentoring.
7. April Lynn Colosimo, Robin Elizabeth Desmeules, and Dawn McKinnon, "Whole Person Mentoring for All Stages of the Library Career," *Library Leadership and Management* 32, no. 1 (2017): 1–13, https://journals.tdl.org/llm/index.php/llm/article/view/7234/6437.
8. Bartlett, "Paying It Forward."
9. Angela Boyd, Yolanda Blue, and Suzanne Im, "Evaluation of Academic Library Residency Programs in the United States for Librarians of Color," *College and Research Libraries* 78, no. 4 (2017): 472–511, https://doi.org/10.5860/crl.78.4.472.
10. Kevin M. Ross, "Purposeful Mentoring in Academic Libraries," *Journal of Library Adminis-tration* 53, no. 7–8 (2013): 412–28, https://doi.org/10.1080/01930826.2013.882195.
11. Iowa State University Library, "Residency Program," accessed January 3, 2020, https:// www.lib.iastate.edu/about-library/library-diversity/residency.
12. Association of College and Research Libraries, "The ACRL Dr. E. J. Josey Spectrum Scholar Mentor Program," September 1, 2006, https://www.ala.org/acrl/membership/mentoring/ joseymentoring/mentorprogram.
13. Julie Ann Leuzinger and Jennifer Rowe, "Succession Planning through Mentoring in the Library," *Library Leadership and Management*, 31, no. 4 (2017): 1–22, https://journals.tdl. org/llm/index.php/llm/article/view/7212.
14. Ross, "Purposeful Mentoring."
15. Lillian T. Eby, Marcus M. Butts, Jaime Durley, and Belle Rose Ragins, "Are Bad Experiences Stronger Than Good Ones in Mentoring Relationships? Evidence from the Protégé and Mentor Perspective," *Journal of Vocational Behavior* 77, no. 1 (2010): 81–92, https://doi. org/10.1016/j.jvb.2010.02.010.
16. Karen Harker et al., "Mixed-Methods Assessment of a Mentoring Program," *Journal of Library Administration* 59, no. 8 (2019): 873–902, https://doi.org/10.1080/01930826.2019.1 661745.
17. Elizabeth M. Smigielski, Melissa A. Laning, and Caroline M. Daniels, "Funding, Time, and Mentoring: A Study of Research and Publication Support Practices of ARL Member

Libraries," *Journal of Library Administration* 54, no. 4 (2014): 261–76, https://doi.org/10.10
80/01930826.2014.924309.

18. Tomaro I. Taylor, "Changing the Faces of Librarianship: The Dr. Henrietta M. Smith Residency at USF," *Florida Libraries* 48, no. 2 (2005): 12–14.
19. University of South Florida Libraries, "Diversity, Equity, and Inclusion," LibGuide, last updated August 24, 2021, https://guides.lib.usf.edu/diversity.

Bibliography

Association of College and Research Libraries. "The ACRL Dr. E. J. Josey Spectrum Scholar Mentor Program." September 1, 2006. https://www.ala.org/acrl/membership/mentoring/joseymentoring/mentorprogram.

Bartlett, Jennifer A. "Paying It Forward, Giving It Back: The Dynamics of Mentoring." *Library Leadership and Management* 27, no. 4 (2013): 1–6. http://works.bepress.com/jenbartlett/11/.

Boyd, Angela, Yolanda Blue, and Suzanne Im. "Evaluation of Academic Library Residency Programs in the United States for Librarians of Color." *College and Research Libraries* 78, no. 4 (2017): 472–511. https://doi.org/10.5860/crl.78.4.472.

Bruxvoort, Diane. "Mentoring in Academic Libraries." In *Workplace Culture in Academic Libraries: The Early 21st Century*. Edited by Kelly Blessinger and Paul Hrycaj, 251–62. Oxford: Chandos, 2013.

Colosimo, April Lynn, Robin Elizabeth Desmeules, and Dawn McKinnon. "Whole Person Mentoring for All Stages of the Library Career." *Library Leadership and Management* 32, no. 1 (2017): 1–13. https://journals.tdl.org/llm/index.php/llm/article/view/7234/6437.

Eby, Lillian T., Marcus M. Butts, Jaime Durley, and Belle Rose Ragins. "Are Bad Experiences Stronger Than Good Ones in Mentoring Relationships? Evidence from the Protégé and Mentor Perspective." *Journal of Vocational Behavior* 77, no. 1 (2010): 81–92. https://doi.org/10.1016/j.jvb.2010.02.010.

Harker, Karen, Erin O'Toole, Setareh Keshmiripour, Marcia McIntosh, and Catherine Sassen. "Mixed-Methods Assessment of a Mentoring Program." *Journal of Library Administration* 59, no. 8 (2019): 873–902. https://doi.org/10.1080/01930826.2019.1661745.

Hodges, Sue. *Leading Libraries: Briefing Paper on Coaching and Mentoring.* London: SCONUL, October 2017. https://www.sconul.ac.uk/publication/briefing-paper-on-coaching-and-mentoring.

Hussey, Lisa K., and Jennifer Campbell-Meier. "Is There a Mentoring Culture within the LIS Profession?" *Journal of Library Administration* 57, no. 5 (2017): 500–516. https://doi.org/10.1080/01930826.2017.1326723.

Iowa State University Library. "Residency Program." Accessed January 3, 2020. https://www.lib.iastate.edu/about-library/library-diversity/residency.

Leuzinger, Julie Ann, and Jennifer Rowe. "Succession Planning through Mentoring in the Library." *Library Leadership and Management* 31, no. 4 (2017): 1–22. https://journals.tdl.org/llm/index.php/llm/article/view/7212.

Lorenzetti, Diane L., and Susan E. Powelson. "A Scoping Review of Mentoring Programs for Academic Librarians." *Journal of Academic Librarianship* 41, no. 2 (2015): 186–96. https://doi.org/10.1016/j.acalib.2014.12.001.

Ross, Kevin M. "Purposeful Mentoring in Academic Libraries." *Journal of Library Administration* 53, no. 7–8 (2013): 412–28. https://doi.org/10.1080/01930826.2013.882195.

Smigielski, Elizabeth M., Melissa A. Laning, and Caroline M. Daniels. "Funding, Time, and Mentoring: A Study of Research and Publication Support Practices of ARL Member

Libraries." *Journal of Library Administration* 54, no. 4 (2014): 261–76. https://doi.org/10.1080/01930826.2014.924309.

Taylor, Tomaro I. "Changing the Faces of Librarianship: The Dr. Henrietta M. Smith Residency at USF." *Florida Libraries* 48, no. 2 (2005): 12–14.

Thomas, J. Denard, Laura Gail Lunsford, and Helena A. Rodrigues. "Early Career Academic Staff Support: Evaluating Mentoring Networks." *Journal of Higher Education Policy and Management* 37, no. 3 (2015): 320–29. https://doi.org/10.1080/1360080X.2015.1034426.

University of South Florida Libraries. "Diversity, Equity, and Inclusion." LibGuide. Last updated August 24, 2021. https://guides.lib.usf.edu/diversity.

Wong, Gabrielle Ka Wai. "Leadership and Leadership Development in Academic Libraries: A Review." *Library Management* 38, no. 2/3 (2017): 153–66. https://doi.org/10.1108/LM-09-2016-0075.

CHAPTER 6

Bare Witness

Library Leaders of Color Tell Their Stories of Advancing into Senior Leadership Positions

Kimberley Bugg

Events such as the 1964 E. J. Josey's speech before ALA and the 2018 ALA Presidents' Program serve as mileposts on a laggard path toward creating a diverse and inclusive workforce in libraries. While libraries and library associations understand the value of a diverse workforce, attempts to increase racial and ethnic diversity among librarians, although well-documented, are primarily focused on recruitment efforts.[1] However, creating a diverse workforce requires attention to recruitment, retention, and advancement equally.[2] While related, each focuses on different aspects of the workforce and requires separate examination. This chapter focuses on advancement because it is not enough to recruit or retain people of color in libraries; it is also essential to promote them to create diversity throughout the pipeline. Although there is a growing body of research concerning the barriers that librarians of color face with retention and advancement, little is known about those who manage to persist and advance to senior-level positions, due partially to insufficient data and scholarship on workforce diversity at the position level. To address that gap, this examination utilizes a narrative inquiry approach called critical incident to gain an understanding of the lived experiences of twelve senior-level library leaders of color,[3]

hereinafter referred to as library deans,[4] to identify strategies useful in supporting the advancement of more librarians of color into senior leadership positions.

Narrative inquiry is a qualitative methodology that utilizes storytelling to examine phenomena. It is useful for examining and contextualizing lived experiences (i.e. life-stories). This approach, which can take the form of a biography or story, is useful for many reasons, including allowing an individual (the narrator) to express intention and assign merit from their unique perspective. Often the story that an individual chooses provides information about their identity and beliefs, and offers a way for them to make sense of past events.[5] For this study, narrative inquiry is coupled with critical incidents to narrow the focus of the story on events that the narrator considered significant to their advancement. The critical incident structure has been used in leadership studies to allow the narrator to identify circumstances or experiences that explain their leadership trajectory. Simultaneously, the outcome (e.g., an achievement, a current role, or a present self) gives context to the story.[6] Because such a narrative device is reflective, it allows the library deans to create connections between events they consider relevant to their current position and professional growth.[7] However, a life story is not just about the critical incidents in a leader's life; instead, such a story is also a reflection of that individual's interpretations of an experience. While the story reflects a particular context, the narrator decides which aspects of the story to highlight.[8] As a result, how the story is told is often just as important as the story because it shows the leader's perception of themselves. Because narrative inquiry is a qualitative way to understand, quantitative validation devices are not appropriate. However, it is still possible to confirm truthfulness and accuracy.[9] For this study, library deans were asked to submit their curriculum vitae prior to telling their stories. These documents were used during the distilling process (i.e., listening to the recorded stories repeatedly to find meaning) to establish timelines, confirm historical references in stories, further identify trends, and assess commonalities among these library deans. This allows others to make sense of their career progression, particularly their time as middle managers, to garner strategies for and understand the challenges inherent in the advancement of librarians of color to senior-level library leadership positions.

From this process, ten themes emerged:

- education,
- professional experience (i.e., work history),
- career trajectory (i.e., how one advances),

- professional development,
- participation in formal library leadership programs,
- mentorship,
- motivation,
- position attainment,
- social capital,
- and resiliency.

Education

While the deans represent diverse educational experiences, some educational commonalities exist, and it may be useful to relate their educational background to their current position and path to senior leadership. Of course, all the deans possess an MLS from an ALA-accredited university. Interestingly, the longer the dean has been a librarian, the fewer degrees they had. None of the deans with more than ten years in the position had a secondary master's degree in a different discipline. Those who did hold a secondary master's degree did so in various fields, including business administration, music, history, literature, environmental science, and education. Four deans completed doctorate degrees (or the equivalent): two in library science, one an EdD, and one a Juris Doctor.

Additionally, there might be a relationship between where they went to school and where they worked. For example, the two deans that attended Ivy League universities for either undergraduate or graduate studies also worked at Ivy League universities. The three deans who earned degrees from Historically Black Colleges and Universities (HBCUs) were the only deans to work at HBCUs, and the three deans who obtained undergraduate degrees from universities outside of the US were the only deans to later work as librarian-managers in universities outside of the country.

Professional Experience (Work History)

The deans worked in various types of libraries, both domestically and internationally. They all spent some time as middle managers.

- Seven deans worked for the Association of Research Libraries (ARL) member libraries in their careers. All but one served as a middle manager in an ARL library during their career.
- Seven deans began their academic librarian careers at an ARL library.
- Seven deans worked as a middle manager in an ARL library.
- Three deans currently serve as library deans for ARL libraries. (None of the deans moved from serving as a dean of an ARL to serving as dean of a non-ARL library.)
- One dean worked in an ARL library for their entire library career. The other deans with ARL experience fluctuated between different libraries, including community colleges, statewide university library systems, specialized libraries, and public libraries.
- Two deans have experience working for a public library.
- None of the deans indicated any work experience at for-profit libraries during their careers as librarians.

Career Trajectory

All but one of the librarians in this study spent time in both the first and third phases of middle management (the one exception had spent time as a library dean in a specialized library without an MLS before becoming a credentialed librarian). Three deans spent time in the second phase of middle management at the academic libraries that offer this phase. Each dean stayed in the first phase of middle manager for at least seven years, but not more than ten years. However, some moved out of the third phase faster—from a minimum of sixty days to a maximum of ten years. There also appears to be more lateral position movement in the third phase of middle management. In that phase, one librarian held three different positions before moving into a deanship. It was also common at this level for deans to move from a more specialized associate dean (AD) position (e.g., associate dean of public services) to an associate dean position or its equivalent where they oversaw operations for the entire library or library system. Several deans held interim deanships before moving into a permanent position (25 percent). One dean had an interim deanship twice at two different libraries. Another worked (in this order) as an AD, an interim dean, a department AD, an AD responsible for the entire library, and finally as a dean. Seventy-five percent of the participants are currently in their first deanship.

Professional Development

In telling their life stories, all of the library deans expressed an understanding of the value of participation in short professional development workshops. They all felt these experiences, including "courses offered by their institution's human resources department or other on-campus leadership training" and "ARL Leadership Development classes," allowed them to prepare for leadership positions and hone their leadership skills. By taking "advantage of every bit of leadership training offered," as one participant remarked, they were exposed to the business of leadership, learned the vocabulary, and gained greater understanding about the influence of organizational culture.

Participation in Formal Library Leadership Programs

The deans repeatedly mentioned that they found professional development that focused on library leadership invaluable for their ability to advance into a senior leadership position. Formal library leadership development includes those programs that focus on building and increasing particular leadership competencies for librarians. These programs take the form of short-term residencies (three weeks or less) where participants devote time to strengthening their leadership, cultivating new relationships with peers, and connecting with individuals with more experience. Also, it appears that the value of participating in library leadership development for career advancement increased over time since participants with shorter tenure in the profession were more likely to participate in a leadership institute designed for library leaders. The most commonly attended leadership development training programs by those interviewed were Leadership Institute for Academic Librarians hosted by Harvard Graduate School of Education; Frye Leadership Institute (now called the Leading Change Institute); the University of California, Los Angeles, Senior Fellows Program; and the ARL Leadership and Career Development Program. Other formal library leadership development institutes that they participated in include the University of Minnesota Early Career Institute and the Snowbird Leadership Institute. They described their participation in the library-focused leadership training as good exposure for other leadership opportunities. Several library deans indicated that at least one of these library-focused leadership opportunities serves as a potential candidate list for libraries looking to fill leadership vacancies within their organizations, reinforcing the power of attending as an advancement strategy.

Mentorship

For the majority of the current deans, mentorship was primarily informal. Only four of the deans perceived that they had official mentors during their careers, all of whom mentioned that these formal mentors were assigned as a part of their participation in one or more formal leadership institutes. However, many said informal personal and professional mentors supported and contributed to their interest in advancement. These people served as "advisors" and "facilitators" rather than "mentors." As one dean described

> a mentor is something unique. Someone who sees something in you that no one else has seen supports you because they feel you have something to say that no one else has been able to say and [they] believe in you. A facilitator is someone, to me, that shares an enormous amount of information with you; that information becomes pivotal in how you actually move or navigate the waters that you are into your advantage.... So it is not mentorship, it is hearing, learning, and understanding.

Many deans describe bosses (i.e., library deans, university presidents, and provosts) who supported and encouraged their leadership, leadership training, and leadership advancement during their time as a middle manager. In one story, a dean recalls the university president offered support for their promotion. Others told stories of "really supportive bosses who encouraged them to ask questions." It is important to note that most of these mentors, advisors, and facilitators were not people of color.

Motivation

The deans seemed inherently motivated by their desire to succeed. Three of the deans said they entered the profession already knowing that they wanted to be a library dean. One dean shared, "it was a matter of how and when I would be a dean since I knew that no one would probably give me a deanship right away." In contrast, another shared,

> I came into the profession with the ambition of a deanship, and I just decided that I would get involved in every aspect of the library operation and I quickly became an associate dean which really shaped my leadership because I was involved with every operation.

Others were less organized about advancing to a senior leadership position. As one participant shared,

> I just seized opportunities as they became available to me and was not really focused on necessarily moving up but just doing the things that I wanted to do, it was more about those positions that offered opportunities or provided me with the ability to gain different types of skill sets and to work with people in very different ways and at different levels.

While they did not describe their family members' role as primary to their decisions, their families' inclusion in their stories indicated the importance of family in their value systems and decision-making process. For example, one dean said, "after they [the university] called me, I spoke to my husband, and he said, 'You should go. It could be fun to spend the day talking with them.'" Another dean said, "When the university called, it was good timing. My wife was ready for a change, and my daughter had left for college." For others, the desire to be closer to family was also a motivating factor: "A lot of my decision to take this library dean position was location-driven. I wanted to be close to my family." Similarly, another dean said, "My mother is older and in perfect health, but I just wanted to be closer to her to kind of settle and enjoy this phase."

Position Attainment

Advancement begins with the hiring process, so studying the hiring process of library deans of color could be perceived as critical incidents related to advancement. Yet the stories that participants told about applying, interviewing, and onboarding did not provide compelling information. However, what stood out in these stories was what happened before participants applied for positions.

All but one dean reported that someone (either a headhunter or someone from the library with the vacancy) asked, recommended, or convinced them to apply for the open position. Three deans shared stories about repeatedly declining invitations to apply for new jobs. One dean shared that he asked another dean to recommend him for a library dean position. For other participants, the recommendations were more spontaneous. In one story, the participant assumed the interim library dean position before applying for and receiving the deanship. Collectively, these stories point to the notion that libraries are proactive about hiring at the senior level. They seek out candidates to put into their candidate pool. Further, they suggest that securing a senior-level position might require more than just qualifications but a combination of factors, including social capital.

Social Capital

Social capital is an intangible benefit that someone gains mostly due to their position or status. This gain is primarily based on relationships that create power and advantage for the holder compared to others. This advantage, which is not about the person's network but rather how it creates a leg up, can be leveraged for the owner's benefit.[10] Presumably, people enter the library profession with some social capital based on many things, including familial relationships, class, race, gender, and background. They likely also gain additional social capital based on commonalities with others, such as shared experiences and other commonalities. The network is critical for at least one key reason: somebody recommended each dean in this study for their current position. This is not to suggest that qualification was not a factor, because they each possessed the qualifications consistent with senior library leadership before assuming the role. However, they also knew someone of influence who could recommend them for a position and positively influenced the process in their favor. Each dean shared at least one critical incident in which they used social capital to move something forward or how the lack of social capital stopped them from moving forward. Early in their careers, many of the deans conveyed an understanding of the value of being part of a network of individuals they knew would advocate on their behalf. They also understood what capital they possessed (i.e., status, relationship, etc.) that could be leveraged in their network for their advancement as demonstrated by the two deans who called someone and asked them to recommend them for a position.

For example, one dean said that he would not have succeeded in one of his positions without several forms of social capital. He discussed using his connection to others in the broader organization to help kick off a capital campaign that he was having "trouble getting buy-in for." He explained that the library dean is not only operating at the senior level in the library but as a middle manager (i.e., department head) at the university level, so to know "who the players are at the university level is helpful." He shared, "I called an undergraduate classmate and asked for help getting buy-in." In addition to personal networks, there appear to be a few key relationships essential to academic librarian advancement.

Deans repeatedly mentioned working with Maureen Sullivan and Camila Alire throughout their careers, meeting them early, and staying connected with them in a meaningful way. While the mentions of Maureen and Camila were casual, and no dean spoke directly about their role, one can infer that as former ALA presidents, they both have a tremendous amount of social capital to leverage to support others. They have extensive networks, proven track records of success, and influence, and they are willing to use their capital to assist others.

Resiliency

All the library deans experienced challenges related to race and ethnicity. While the deans' stories about their experiences with discrimination, microaggressions, and racism were quite gripping, their ability to overcome extreme adversity was more compelling. Deans related incidents that ran the gamut from direct acts (e.g., being called a derogatory term) to subtler instances of racism (e.g., being wholly ignored during meetings). Yet two common themes emerged across participants and throughout the life stories that they shared: (1) perceived lack of competency and qualification due to their race or ethnicity and (2) lack of diversity of representation among other senior leaders. Repeatedly, participants shared that not seeing other people of color in leadership positions negatively impacted their confidence concerning their ability to secure a senior leadership position despite being adequately qualified. For instance, the deans described bias for and against them while they were candidates for positions. Deans discussed being encouraged to apply for jobs to add ethnic diversity to the candidate pool or hearing they received an appointment solely because of their race or ethnicity. Many deans told stories of having their qualifications questioned. While a middle manager, one dean was told directly by a subordinate that they were hired solely because they were a person of color. A nonminority direct report said to a different dean that she knew the library hired her only because she is a person of color because she was "woefully under-qualified." In a similar story, another dean recalled overhearing two people they supervised conversing about whether the organization selected the dean because of their race or their qualifications. Yet another dean recalled walking past a break room where her entire staff was having lunch and someone telling her that she did not receive an invite because there was no "diversity quota" required at lunch. Others recalled subtler experiences with racism, including being asked to show ID while sitting in their office and being asked to serve on more committees than other colleagues.

As a part of their stories of encountering diversity-related challenges through subtle or overt racist acts, the deans also spoke about how they deal with these circumstances. They describe coping mechanisms that allow them to thwart feelings of despair and hopelessness while refusing to internalize negative comments. One dean shared that she knows being a minority in an all-white setting places her in the peculiar position of having to represent both herself and every other person in her race. For her, "It is not only how you react but how you act. Recognizing who you are and how you are and living those values is how you survive." Others see themselves as a champion of their race in all-white settings and use those small interactions to speak for themselves and their entire race as an opportunity for activism; as one dean said, "If I have an issue with something that someone said or did on our campus, I am going to speak about it. I do a lot of that." Beyond their central place in their own challenging racism stories, they also see themselves as a part of a community of individuals with shared experiences existing as anomalies in higher education and not just as ethnic and racial minorities. One dean shared,

> My colleagues that are minorities, women, or both, we get together, and we talk about it. We laugh about it, we scream about it, but we also strategize about it. I find the support that we have for each other very helpful.

Interestingly, they intentionally seek out and create these communities at the various places where they work to ensure that they are supported and give others support. As one dean said, "too much systematic and direct racism without someone to help you process it, it will take you down."

Discussion

The findings in this study do not illuminate a single path to senior leadership, and it is not possible to generalize from such a small sample size. Still, the stories told by these twelve deans do highlight a series of personal habits and behaviors that seemingly prepared these librarians of color for leadership. Though not all deans were planning a career in leadership, they described early-career incidents in which they demonstrated leadership attributes including initiative, problem-solving, and decision-making.[11] They shared stories about volunteering to lead new projects in the library or on the college campus where they worked, implementing new workflows, or successfully securing grants that expanded the library's role on campus or brought attention to their library. They accomplished these things while pursuing additional degrees and participating in leadership-specific professional development. These actions could explain why others saw leadership potential in them, nurtured that potential, and selected them for leadership positions. Furthermore, by engaging in these activities, they likely countered job stagnation and increased job satisfaction—two issues that plague retention and advancement for librarians of color.[12] Even though more than half of the deans discussed some desire to pursue library leadership at the beginning of their career, only a couple of deans initially viewed their first middle manager position as a step toward senior leadership. Instead, they found themselves needing a job for reasons that include relocation, a change in status (e.g., gaining a degree), and gaining more skill in a particular area, then applying to open positions that matched their current qualifications. For many deans, middle manager leadership provided the opportunity to function as both a practitioner and a leader, a combination that they were overwhelmingly reluctant to give up when moving from first or second phase middle management to third phase and even senior library leadership. In several instances, library deans found ways to stay connected to the interest that drove them to a career in librarianship (i.e., archives, medical librarianship, and law) through association-level committee work, civic engagement, and social activities.

Even though the deans recalled some distressing incidents about being treated unfairly and unfairly judged based on their race, they presented these stories casually and without anger. Instead, they shared these stories as if they expected and prepared to encounter and handle such situations. They also described coping skills that involved discussing, confronting, and looking for support for the issue. Additionally, they supported others with similar problems and championed racial equity in their workplace and other settings. They also conveyed some competencies in this area that stemmed not from career training and development, but perhaps from their personal histories. Particularly for the African Americans deans that described these situations, they specifically related them to childhood, college experiences, and other experiences outside of the workplace where similar discrimination had occurred.

Further, they seemed to understand the mental burden that having to "work twice as hard" and be "twice as good" as their white counterparts for near-equal consideration has on people of color and the pressure that it applies to their success; yet they leverage it as a catalyst for maintaining excellence even in the face of adversity. Beyond the internalized expectation of being twice as good, there is also a strong sense of self-efficacy commonly conveyed in their stories of self-confidence, self-motivation, and self-resiliency. Participants attributed these behaviors to many different sources, including upbringing, personality, and repeatedly overcoming challenges that served as a springboard into senior library leadership.

The shared stories and moments of self-reflection revealed that the deans interviewed for this study possess a keen insight into their environments that they used to make career decisions. Once they started thinking of leadership as a career path or knew when they could no longer be effective in a particular role, they were emotionally intelligent enough to quickly assess what capital they needed to advance to a new position. The deans spoke of seeking more challenging work in their stories even if that meant making job changes, creating strategic work allies, and creating coping mechanisms for racism. Perhaps the most profound skill widely shared among the deans was their ability to cope and thrive in highly racialized situations.

Of all the methods that supported advancement, formal mentorships were the least utilized by these deans. Stories of strong mentor relationships were mostly missing from the critical incidents the deans shared. A few talked about relationships that grew out of participation in leadership training or individuals who guided them in a mentor way. However, only one participant mentioned a formal and sustained mentorship that was initiated at work by the library dean who suggested he attend a leadership institute and served as his mentor in that program. While these leaders were successful at advancing to senior library leadership positions mostly without formal mentors, this contradicts the large body of literature that suggests that formal mentorship is critical to advancement and is worthy of further study.[13]

Next Steps

This chapter does not fully address why so few librarians of color advance to senior library leadership positions. However, it does point to some of the obstacles that require further exploration that might keep more librarians of color from advancing, such as lack of formalized mentors, racialized discrimination, and lacking social capital. Additional topics emerged in these rich and varied conversations worthy of study in future research on various topics including

- work-life balance issues for library leaders,
- the impact of personal relationship development as a coping mechanism, gender, relocation,
- role of family in leadership pursuits, and
- resonant leadership for library leaders of color.

Also, this study investigated the behaviors of only a select few library deans of color in senior leadership positions. However, it might help to identify and study individuals who desired but were not successful at attaining senior library leadership positions to understand the role that social capital, networking, and mentoring or the lack thereof might have played.

For librarians of color interested in advancement, this study can serve as a set of best practices. Not only did the study point to specific and common behaviors and attributes of leadership for librarians interested in advancing to senior leadership to emulate. The leaders participating in the study also made recommendations or offered "guiding principles" that they enacted that provide helpful strategies for senior-leadership job attainment:

- Get to know your boss's boss.
- It is not enough to be able to say that you have experience. You have to be able to share a vision of a direction or give people some encouraging sorts of ideas about how the future of the libraries is going to work.
- Think about the job as part of the broader campus culture. You have to see the library at the different levels of the organization.
- Don't think of your time at a library in time increments; think about it in accomplishments, "What did I accomplish? Can I accomplish more?" If the answer is no, then it's time to move on.

- When you start thinking that you can do your boss's job better than they can, then it might be time to look at advancing.[14]
- Make opportunities for yourself.
- Take the assignments that people are less interested in and use them to engage people at higher levels and outside the library.
- Don't put your career first, before friends and family.
- Don't be afraid to fail because failing is a part of success.
- Great lessons are learned by failing.
- Talk about your weaknesses because nobody is perfect. See them as professional development opportunities to work on and ask others to help you work on them.
- Even if you want to be a dean one day, follow your passions; they guide you.
- It helps to interview when you already have a job because you can just be yourself and if it works out, great. If not, at least you already have a job, so it is not that big a deal.
- Figure out what kind of person you are, how you feel about leadership and management, what are your values, what kind of organization do you want to create.
- Always take the time to talk to someone about their career path or librarianship because someone did this for me.
- It is part of our purpose to give back, help each other, and make it easier for others, even when it's uncomfortable.
- Preparation is vital for everyone but especially for people of color.
- Preparation, education, and credentials are essential. Think of the PhD as one way to gain credentials.
- Get a variety of experiences before becoming a dean.
- The library world is small, so being social is as important as being professional.

It makes sense that the library deans primarily describe their personal efforts and attributes that led them to a senior-level library leadership position because this qualitative approach asks them to assume the first-person perspective of an autobiography. However, it is presumptuous to assume that these deans' success is attributed only to their efforts since effort does not always equal success. It was imperative that their commitment and drive met opportunities provided by gatekeepers, who are mostly not other librarians of color. For gatekeepers, library leaders, and others interested in promoting and advancing library leaders of color, the following recommendations were garnered from the library deans:

- Formally mentor librarians of color.
- Leaders can also become more thoughtful about the candidate pool.
- Cultivate staff who currently work for or with you to fill open positions.
- Nurture and create potential when possible.
- Examine your network and move beyond working with those they have always worked with or are familiar with.

Ultimately, it is possible for libraries to increase and sustain a diverse workforce by giving greater attention to promoting and advancing librarians of color. Hopefully, the insights provided here will quicken the pace and swell the ranks.

Notes

1. Janice Y. Kung, K-Lee Fraser, and Dee Winn. "Diversity Initiatives to Recruit and Retain Academic Librarians: A Systematic Review." *College and Research Libraries* 81, no. 1 (2020): 96–108, https://doi.org/10.5860/crl.81.1.96.
2. Teresa Y. Neely and Lorna Peterson, "Achieving Racial and Ethnic Diversity among Academic and Research Librarians: The Recruitment, Retention, and Advancement of Librarians of Color—A White Paper," *College and Research Libraries News* 68, no. 9 (2007): 562–65.
3. Leonard Webster and Patricia Mertova define critical incidents as events that had a profound effect on an individual at a particular time and caused a change. Leonard Webster and Patricia Mertova, *Using Narrative Inquiry as a Research Method*. London: Routledge, 2007: 59.
4. *Library dean* is used as a catchall phrase to represent the senior-ranking member of library staff. The word stands for titles such as *library director, university librarian, associate provost of libraries*, etc.
5. David B. Pillemer, "Momentous Events and the Life Story," *Review of General Psychology* 5, no. 2 (2001): 123–34; Boas Shamir and Galit Eilam, "'What's Your Story?' A Life-Stories Approach to Authentic Leadership Development," *Leadership Quarterly* 16, no. 3 (2005): 395–417.
6. Boas Shamir, Hava Dayan-Horesh, and Dalya Adler, "Leading by Biography: Towards a Life-Story Approach to the Study of Leadership," *Leadership* 1, no. 1 (2005): 13–29.
7. Gina Scott Ligon, Samuel T. Hunter, and Michael D. Mumford, "Development of Outstanding Leadership: A Life Narrative Approach," *Leadership Quarterly* 19, no. 3 (2008): 312–34.
8. Pillemer, "Momentous Events."
9. Webster and Mertova, *Using Narrative Inquiry*.
10. Scott E. Seibert, Maria L. Kraimer, and Robert C. Liden, "A Social Capital Theory of Career Success," *Academy of Management Journal* 44, no. 2 (2001): 219–37.
11. Peter Hernon, Ronald R. Powell, and Arthur P. Young, "University Library Directors in the Association of Research Libraries: The Next Generation, Part One," *College and Research Libraries* 62, no. 2 (2001): 116–46.

12. Ashley E. Bonnette, "Mentoring Minority Librarians up the Career Ladder," *Library Leadership and Management* 18, no. 3 (2004): 134–39.
13. See a sample of the mentoring literature within and outside LIS: Camila A. Alire, "The New Beginnings Program: A Retention Program for Junior Faculty of Color," *Journal of Library Administration* 33, no. 1–2 (2001): 21–30; Teresa Y. Neely and Kuang-Hwei Lee-Smeltzer, *Diversity Now* (New York: Haworth Information Press, 2002); Christopher Avery, Susan Athey, and Peter Zemsky, "Mentoring and Diversity," *American Economic Review* 90 no. 4 (2000): 765–86.
14. Half of the deans in this study made this recommendation.

Bibliography

Alire, Camila A. "The New Beginnings Program: A Retention Program for Junior Faculty of Color." *Journal of Library Administration* 33, no. 1–2 (2001): 21–30.

Avery, Christopher, Susan Athey, and Peter Zemsky. "Mentoring and Diversity." *American Economic Review* 90, no. 4 (2000): 765–86.

Bonnette, Ashley E. "Mentoring Minority Librarians up the Career Ladder." *Library Leadership and Management* 18, no. 3 (2004): 134–39.

Hernon, Peter, Ronald R. Powell, and Arthur P. Young. "University Library Directors in the Association of Research Libraries: The Next Generation, Part One." *College and Research Libraries* 62, no. 2 (2001): 116–46.

Kung, Janice Y., K-Lee Fraser, and Dee Winn. "Diversity Initiatives to Recruit and Retain Academic Librarians: A Systematic Review." *College and Research Libraries* 81, no. 1 (2020): 96–108. https://doi.org/10.5860/crl.81.1.96.

Ligon, Gina Scott, Samuel T. Hunter, and Michael D. Mumford. "Development of Outstanding Leadership: A Life Narrative Approach." *Leadership Quarterly* 19, no. 3 (2008): 312–34.

McAdams, Dan P. "The Psychology of Life Stories." *Review of General Psychology* 5, no. 2 (2001): 100–122.

Neely, Teresa Y., and Kuang-Hwei Lee-Smeltzer. *Diversity Now: People, Collections, and Services in Academic Libraries: Selected Papers from the Big 12 Plus Libraries Consortium Diversity Conference.* New York: Haworth Information Press, 2002.

Neely, Teresa Y., and Lorna Peterson. "Achieving Racial and Ethnic Diversity among Academic and Research Librarians: The Recruitment, Retention, and Advancement of Librarians of Color—A White Paper." *College & Research Libraries News* 68, no. 9 (2007): 562–65.

Pillemer, David B. "Momentous Events and the Life Story." *Review of General Psychology* 5, no. 2 (2001): 123–34.

Seibert, Scott E., Maria L. Kraimer, and Robert C. Liden. "A Social Capital Theory of Career Success." *Academy of Management Journal* 44, no. 2 (2001): 219–37.

Shamir, Boas, Hava Dayan-Horesh, and Dalya Adler. "Leading by Biography: Towards a Life-Story Approach to the Study of Leadership." *Leadership* 1, no. 1 (2005): 13–29.

Shamir, Boas, and Galit Eilam. "'What's Your Story?' A Life-Stories Approach to Authentic Leadership Development." *Leadership Quarterly* 16, no. 3 (2005): 395–417.

Webster, Leonard, and Patricia Mertova. *Using Narrative Inquiry as a Research Method: An Introduction to Using Critical Event Narrative Analysis in Research on Learning and Teaching.* London: Routledge, 2007.

SECTION II
Professional Development

CHAPTER 7

Your Workforce Is More Than You Think

Looking at Diversity and Inclusion with Student Workers

Melanie Bopp

Many human resources departments conduct training sessions for both full- and part-time staff, but this still overlooks a significant group of individuals working in the average academic library: student employees. At Northeastern University Library, student workers in Information Delivery and Access Services (IDEAS) outnumbered full-time staff five to one. How an institution defines *employees* will affect how student workers are considered in terms of diversity outreach, and training. Generally speaking, however, student workers are considered more student than worker. Unfortunately, student workers are frequently omitted from training opportunities that could benefit them both now and in future positions post-degree.

Defining Employees

When an institution considers employees, it is generally considering only full-time, usually benefits-eligible employees. Many institutions will include further designations of employees: temporary, part-time, and contractors, to name a few. Student employees are rarely considered employees—they are students first, after all.

What defines employees at any institution? They are compensated for work contributed, usually specializing in a particular department or function. The institution, at whatever level, controls how the work is accomplished. In the 2002 article "What Is an Employee? The Answer Depends on the Federal Law," the author quotes *Black's Law Dictionary*, stating it

> defines "employee" as "a person in the service of another under any contract of hire, express or implied, oral or written, where the employer has the power or right to control and direct the employee in the material details of how the work is to be performed.[1]

By this definition, by any definition, student workers are institutional employees.

Even in a student-focused organization or department, work cannot and should not be fully separated from a student worker's status as a student. Students bring an interesting and different perspective to their position tasks. Anecdotal evidence at Northeastern University has led to pursuing peer relationships to help reduce library anxiety, something that has been seen at libraries across the country. As Bodemer says, "Academic libraries would be remiss in not seeking to harness peer learning dynamics to enhance student learning and success."[2] Most of the literature found, however, focuses on peer-to-peer reference and programs that help with the library anxiety of the user. At the time of starting the training program discussed in this chapter, similar literature on the effects of other types of peer training was a lot harder to obtain. To get answers to questions that students don't want to pose for fear of appearing unprepared in front of faculty or staff (for undergraduates, in front of "real adults"), pressure is reduced when they can instead ask a peer. This aspect—combined with shared pressures of university life—can help form a relationship between students that simply cannot be matched by those between students and staff.

In the end, the focus must be on balancing both the student and the employee dynamics while providing student workers the resources they need to succeed in both arenas.

Hiring a Diverse Student Group

Hiring student workers is a never-ending process. Naturally, students always come and go on the academic calendar and leave upon graduation. As a result, it is all too easy to hire warm bodies to help cover service points and get basic tasks completed. Why invest time on a student workforce that is inevitably going to change in a few months?

In a 2018 study of the literature, most of the literature reviewed did not discuss recruitment of diverse populations or Federal Work-Study (FWS) funding models. Incorporating FWS funding models is essential in capturing a diverse range of socioeconomic backgrounds. Twenty-three studies (10.65 percent) noted recruiting diverse student populations, while six studies (2.78 percent) explicitly mentioned not recruiting diverse students. One hundred eighty-seven studies (86.57 percent) did not discuss the topic at all. Thirty-eight studies (17.59 percent) mentioned utilizing FWS positions, and more than half of the studies reviewed (58.33 percent) did not consider whether student employee positions are funded by FWS programs.[3] Further, the review noted that "very few studies noted the importance of recruiting and employing students (and staff) from different backgrounds in order to reflect the diverse campus."[4]

At Northeastern University, staff wanted to make a concerted effort to have both a skilled student workforce and a representative one. Northeastern is ranked at number thirty-two nationwide for diversity in general, and above average in diversity among the student population: More than 50 percent of the entire student body is non-White.[5] Looking specifically at the undergraduate population of approximately 18,000, this number is just under 50 percent. Eighteen percent of the student population is international, some of which is non-white.[6] This is not to say staff purposefully chose to hire students of certain backgrounds, cultures, sexualities, and so on. Instead, by creating a standardized hiring process making use of a rubric for specific qualifications for individual positions, but still allowing flexibility based on library needs, staff both had a straightforward evaluation method and removed the temptation everyone has to surround themselves with the familiar.

Staff Training and Standardization

Prior to the changes in the library's hiring and training program, some hiring decisions had been made based on student schedules, and onboarding for student workers was done mainly via an e-mail with documentation attached for them to read and a checklist for staff to go through to cover the basics. This was then followed by tossing the student into the proverbial deep end: the job itself. While some check-ins were scheduled by individual supervisors, they were not routinely deployed across the board. There was little in place for student leads to learn how to manage their fellow student workers. Some staff supervisors relied on student referrals for new hires to avoid placing an open position on the university's student employment website. While IDEAS did not create a full program for student supervisors, IDEAS staff were encouraged to attend university training for managers, explore other human resources programs related to their positions, and participate in diversity and inclusion training as created by one of the department librarians partnering with Northeastern's Office of Diversity and Inclusion.

Diversity training was optional at the staff level at Northeastern University. However, IDEAS wanted to ensure full-time staff were prepared and knowledgeable regarding diversity and inclusion throughout the hiring and training processes for student workers. Those supervising students created templates for various parts of the process, including job descriptions, interview rubric, and the process of reviewing applications. To eliminate as much potential bias as possible, reviewing applications involved hiding the spreadsheet columns for names and using student ID numbers as identifiers. Once the initial applications were reviewed, résumés would come into play, so familiarity or lack thereof for recognizable names would not apply within initial consideration. The simple act of removing an applicant name removed the chance of applying racial or gendered characteristics during the beginning of the applicant review process.

As part of the university's diversity and inclusion initiatives, staff were encouraged to take advantage of training offered by university human resources, especially on topics like handling potentially emotionally charged situations, using managerial skills, and furthering their professional development. IDEAS as a department invested in various webinars when possible. The topics including dealing with angry patrons, team building, communication, and student worker programs. Staff used ideas learned from all these experiences to build a manageable and implementable student worker hiring and training program.

Standardizing the Hiring Process

Standardizing the hiring process is a multistep project, from the application to the interview, and through the onboarding and training process. This process has been discussed for decades; a 2000 article stated:

> The lack of standardized hiring practices ...created the need to conduct interviews whenever a specific vacancy occurred. Supervisors, without clear criteria of what they were looking for in the selection interview, subjected candidates to protracted interviews only to reject them as not acceptable. Without statewide agreement on screening criteria, the same applicants were interviewed in several different regions. And without valid criteria for rejection, the register was filled with "deadwood," candidates who had been interviewed several times and rejected.[7]

Of interest was representing the student body, which is already diverse. Staff embraced the idea that "inclusion is how you use that diversity, how you include diverse people, how you make them feel valuable."[8]

The hiring process for a new position, or for filling a pre-existing one, begins with the job description and application. Whether job descriptions are posted on the library's website or a campus student employment website, they should be regularly examined to make certain that the description accurately represents the position. IDEAS staff carefully read through pre-existing job descriptions for specific things to address:

- Long sentences and paragraphs of text needed to be updated to make information easier to comprehend for students who speak English as a second language and those with learning disabilities.
- Any pronouns needed to be changed to a neutral "they/them" for inclusivity.
- Any qualifications, whether required or preferred, should be clearly defined.
- Any qualifications should be reconsidered for necessity. For example, does a student stacks worker need extensive customer service experience?

Staff undertook the same examination of applications students were required to complete through Northeastern University's student employment office. Did the information gathered match what student supervisors needed to make an informed hiring decision? Was this information necessary? Some information, such as a résumé or how many years of their degree the student had completed, was required by the student employment office and therefore was not optional for staff to remove. Some questions, however, had been used across the board for all positions, whether or not they were customer-facing. Did staff need the full customer service history for an interlibrary loan student worker? Did circulation assistants need to expand on their project management skills? Staff wanted to ensure certain characteristics that are more desired for customer-facing positions were not also being asked of students who would rarely, if ever, work directly with users.

The interview process was given similar scrutiny, with introduction of a standardized question list and schedule, more reminiscent of standard librarian interviews.[9] Previously, questions focused mainly on scheduling needs, touching only on the basics of the position description and the student's job history and relevant experiences.

Depending on the position, an interview may take less than thirty minutes, but scheduling thirty minutes for each interview gives applicants more time for questions and clarification of the position and gives staff time to follow up on any previous responses and review the applicant's rubric. Maintaining a stricter schedule can help staff resist the urge to chat with students and is particularly useful for those new to the student hiring process.

While standardization generally entails creating a level playing field, staff must balance equity with equality. Creating a situation where everyone is judged on the same basis may be equal, but is it actually fair? Every applicant for a position is asked the same questions, and if they do not provide something requested, they will be removed from consideration. However, the process structure does permit some flexibility. Staff have e-mailed a student about a question they didn't answer or to ask them to submit a résumé not included in the initial application. This has been particularly useful with international students, who do not always understand the question as posted. One applicant, when asked whether they had library experience, replied they used the library regularly. Staff were able to contact this student directly with a carefully phrased communication to avoid embarrassing the student.

During the interview, similar strategies can be applied. Situational questions allow staff to determine not necessarily how a student may interpret policy, but their initial reaction to a situation. Is their first instinct to call a supervisor? Will they attempt to address it themselves? For example, if an alarm goes off, one might recommend alerting the appropriate authorities, while another might investigate the situation and decide whether to evacuate. IDEAS staff prefers the latter response, which shows initiative and independent problem-solving.

One unique aspect to interviews for service desk positions in IDEAS was our interview location, the workroom directly behind the main service point. Northeastern University Library is particularly busy—with around 2.2 million entries per year—and the help and information desk is busy around the clock. Using this space for interviews not only represents more accurately the environment in which students will be working, but it also allows staff to observe how candidates react to potential interruptions in a real-life work environment. The ability to handle interruptions while serving the public mattered for some positions more than others and could be incorporated into the rubric as needed.

For IDEAS positions at Northeastern, many student applicants for non-work-study positions were international students, specifically from India. As a result, most position advertising was accomplished by word of mouth to mostly Indian students. When looking to hire, staff frequently ask for recommendations from current students who are acquainted with the needs of the position. However, this resulted in a fairly homogeneous student group, even if that group was comprised of minority students. Wishing to create a student team that more closely reflected the student body, staff worked with the library's Marketing and Communications department to create electronic slides for digital displays and a half-page handout that students seeking employment could take with them, complete with a QR code linked to the student employment website. Also included were basic instructions on how to create a job alert through the student employment website to be notified when the library posted an available position.

While all this sounds fairly standard and straightforward, when it was combined with training and addition of a rubric, staff were able to increase their reach to potential student workers and conduct the interview and hiring process more equitably. Circulation assistants had been historically white American students; after implementing the new procedures, the department added three international students (one each from China, India, and South Africa), and even part-time positions saw an increase in students from countries outside of India, including China, Korea, France, and Paraguay. In addition to the international students, IDEAS increased hiring within American ethnic minorities, including most recently two Black students, four Asian American students, and two other American students of color.

Importance of a Rubric

The decision to use an official rubric adjusted for each individual student position arose from the need to streamline the process for staff. Once we started implementing rubrics, staff realized the quantitative format worked to the students' benefit.

The benefit of a rubric is most noticeable when there is a high volume of applicants for a position, but it is valuable at every level of staffing. The rubric quantifies what staff seek in a student worker; for IDEAS, this was mainly communication and customer service skills. The rubric shown in figure 7.1 was adapted for a leads position involved in training new student workers and acting as a bridge between staff and students.

There were initial concerns that emphasis on communication and spoken English would disadvantage international students. As the rubric developed, however, staff discovered there was no perceptible difference in scoring between international and domestic students on communication issues. While a number of international students would occasionally struggle over vocabulary or library-specific terminology, they consistently provided qualities staff were looking for in customer service, such as engagement in conversation and ability to share pertinent information. There was a similar conversation about eye contact in the rubric being potentially discriminatory toward students on the autism spectrum. Supervisors hiring for more back-of-house positions adapted these categories to ones more suitable for these tasks, such as attention to detail.

This quantitative over qualitative approach has helped staff remove any gut feeling reactions to interviews, reactions that have been shown to result in hiring within one's own group, whether racially, by gender identity, or by ethnicity.[10] When students fit between multiple scores—for example, they have some teaching experience, but not much in customer service—staff had the leeway to fractionalize the score to a 2.5. The end result was a distinct framework staff could use for decision-making, still allowing for some flexibility within that structure. This same framework could also be used when students confronted staff when they were not hired for the position. When staff needed to respond, they were armed with specific reasons they could reference to justify their decision. They could also provide positive feedback or perhaps direct the student to more suitable positions. This same rubric was later adopted when recruiting office support staff positions, assisting in evaluating a large number of applicants with quantifiable criteria.

FIGURE 7.1

Hiring Rubric – Access Leads

Score Levels	Application and Resume	Experience
4	• Includes resume with applicable and supporting positions. • No spelling, grammatical, or punctuation errors. • High-level use of vocabulary and word choice.	• Has significant proctor/security service experience. • Has successful strategies for and/or experience with handling problems, dissatisfied users, and/or emergencies. • Has significant teaching experience.
3	• Includes resume with supporting positions. • Few (1 to 3) spelling, grammatical, or punctuation errors. • Good use of vocabulary and word choice.	• Has significant customer service experience. • Has some strategies for and/or experience with handling problems, dissatisfied users, and/or emergencies. • Has some teaching experience.
2	• Includes resume. • Minimal (3 to 5) spelling, grammatical, or punctuation errors. • Low-level use of vocabulary and word choice.	• Has customer service experience. • Has little strategies for and/or experience with handling problems, dissatisfied users, and/or emergencies. • Demonstrates hesitancy in training others.
1	• Does not include resume. • More than 5 spelling, grammatical, or punctuation errors. • Poor use of vocabulary and word choice.	• Has no customer service experience. • Has no strategies for and/or experience with handling problems, dissatisfied users, and/or emergencies. • Does not feel comfortable in teaching others.

FIGURE 7.1

Hiring Rubric – Access Leads

Score Levels	Other Considerations	Interview
4	• Provides significant useful information. • Has excellent spoken English communication skills. • Follows directions. • Demonstrates ability to teach others.	• Arrives on time (and not too early), and is ready to start on schedule. • Gives well-constructed, confident responses that are genuine. • Sits up straight, excellent posture; looks relaxed and confident; establishes eye contact with interviewers.
3	• Provides useful information. • Has good spoken English communication skills. • Suggests ability to teach others.	• Arrives on time, and is ready to start on schedule. • Gives well-constructed responses, does not sound rehearsed, student somewhat hesitant or unsure. • Sits up straight, good posture; establishes eye contact with interviewers during the interview 80–90%of the time.
2	• Provides basic information. • Has basic spoken English communication skills. • Follows basic directions.	• Arrives late or early, but communicates problem and addresses it upon arrival. • Gives well-constructed responses, but sounds rehearsed or unsure. • Sits up straight; average posture; establishes eye contact with interviewers during the interview 70–80% of the time.
1	• Provides inconsistent information. • Lacks clear spoken English communication skills. • Does not follow basic directions.	• Arrives significantly late or early. May also expect interviewer to change schedule to match arrival. • Answers with "yes" or "no" and fails to elaborate or explain; talks negatively about past employers. • Does not look at persons involved in the interview process; keeps head down; minimal eye contact; does not have good posture; slouching.

Training a Diverse Student Group

Student worker training at Northeastern Library consists of task-specific training and employee-specific training. Task-specific training encompasses how to perform a specific task—shelve a book, answer a basic reference question, help a library user. Employee-specific training covers how schedules work or any behavioral expectations. Most student supervisors have traditionally focused on task training, with employee training mostly being handled through a checklist. This plan was lacking in several areas that produce a well-rounded employee, those areas that would make a student worker an attractive employee in their future but would also provide immediate benefits to the library.

IDEAS student supervisors wanted to expand on the checklist they had been using, so they designed a series of student basics quizzes. Initially, these quizzes were all in Qualtrics, with students given a set time period in which to complete them. While these quizzes were helpful, the complexity of Qualtrics was far beyond what staff needed for student training. The quizzes were later transferred to LibWizard from Springshare, which was both easier and more intuitive for staff, but still had the necessary features available, such as conditional logic. Staff then created a student training manual in LibGuides, linking or embedding all student training quizzes to it for ease of access.

This simpler platform also helped staff create additional training, including situational awareness, train the trainer, and diversity and inclusion. Staff worked with the Office of Institutional Diversity, Equity and Inclusion, pulled materials from human resources training, and scoured a variety of other resources to make something that was Northeastern-specific. While some of these training modules are still in development, staff felt it was responsible to provide professional development and training at this level, as the work experience students receive directly impacts their future career path.

The overall strategy was to create a training program that was inclusive, in terms of both topics covered and also the wide variety of students being hired. Staff were committed to eliminating as much library jargon as possible, so we added a link to a multilingual glossary,[11] which student staff can access to communicate with students unfamiliar with library terminology and which can also be adapted as a training module at some point in the future.

Training time has been moved to a fully on-the-clock model to eliminate the time students had previously spent outside work reading through documentation.

This time had taken an economic toll that not all students could absorb. Students at the help and information desk were given time off the desk to give them additional time to learn without an audience, which was particularly helpful for students with mental disabilities. Staff also resumed annual student worker orientations, which are "one of the best ways to get students to start with consistent knowledge while also minimizing the time spent."[12] These orientation sessions were mandatory, with those few students unable to attend required to complete an electronic version. They generally combined the information needed with activities and pizza. In fall 2019, this orientation included escape rooms designed by a library staff member, where students from different positions within IDEAS were paired together. These events over the past four years have proven to be both an effective training tool and something the students look forward to each year.[13]

One additional step was to create an intermediary position, called student lead. These leads assisted in training students, acting as peer trainers as well as serving as intermediary between student workers and staff. Leads were indispensable when staff were revising the department's training materials. They were asked to review drafts and met with their supervisor to provide input. Leads tested new online training quizzes, provided feedback on phrasing and question organization, and provided support to students completing the quizzes.

Staff ultimately resolved that the best way to train diverse student staff was to provide a wide range of materials to suit a variety of learning styles and resources readily available at point of need. By being clear on expectations, creating a peer training program, and making certain that information students needed to perform their jobs was easily obtainable, they made the training process easier for both students and staff. Because we followed a peer training module, staff could be released to address higher-level tasks, student leads gained valuable skills, and new student workers experienced more comfortable and productive training sessions.

Diversity Training

When a new employee starts at Northeastern University, before receiving training on specific job functions, there is a series of mandatory training sessions that covers a variety of higher-level issues, such as ethics, workplace violence, and diversity and inclusion. IDEAS staff wanted to promote the understanding to both student workers and library administration that student worker positions are real jobs that can teach more than just task-based behavior. Diversity was the first component of this section of the department's training program.

Northeastern University's Office of Diversity, Equity, and Inclusion OIDI was an excellent resource to initiate training for library student workers.[14] This office is home to the university's diversity program, partners with outside groups as appropriate, and underwrites funding for diversity and inclusion initiatives at the university, including those spearheaded by students. IDEAS staff met with the associate director of OIDI to discuss any pre-existing training options that might be applicable, but both parties soon realized there was not yet anything geared toward student employees in a customer service setting.

As library staff were already using LibWizard for student training quizzes, they decided the tutorial function in the same system would be an ideal software for student worker diversity training. LibWizard tutorials combine a presentation-style slide system with a space for notes, and any questions or responses the creator wants to add to make it more interactive. Staff used a combination of images (including animated GIFs), text, embedded websites, and embedded videos (complete with transcript) to make the tutorials more interactive (see figure 7.2). The training covered implicit bias (including a link to Harvard University's Project Implicit[15]), some information on diversity and discrimination in the workplace, and space for trainees to reflect on their own experiences. Staff also included an optional space for student feedback—for example, some students provided feedback about the quiz itself, and others asked for more information on certain topics.

FIGURE 7.2
Image from LibWizard tutorial student worker diversity training

While student workers are not required to take the diversity training module, several have opted to take it regardless.[16] One student worker, seeking additional responsibilities, asked to participate in developing the module, taking the quiz during its construction and writing out transcripts for the video. Overall, response to the diversity training module has been positive, based on student feedback via both an open comments area in the quiz itself and informal conversations with supervisors. While only a portion of students have taken it, they not only found it helpful, but also were interested in applying some of the training on a regular basis. One student recommended that staff query students about their experiences with possible biases as a reflection so the situation remains fresh and functions as a more useful learning tool (see figure 7.3).

Question:
If you have any questions or feedback, please use this space to share it. If you would like a response, please include your name, as this training module is completely anonymous.

Response:
It was a really great quiz. A lot of things included was interesting like Microaggression, bias, and diversity. Video resource on the Diversity and bias was really a great example. Suggestion: Regarding the question on do you feel biased or did you make any assumption about anyone? These forms could provide a great value if it asks every employee on monthly basis. Doing that might eliminate the case where the employee has faced such situation but have now forgotten about that. Overall it was great experience giving this quiz

---

FIGURE 7.3
Student suggestion in response to diversity training tutorial

This training was shared with OIDI, which passed it along to the campus's athletics department, which was interested in creating something similar for student employees working at one of the gyms. Library staff met with the student supervisor there, discussing outcomes of the library training, how it was created, and what could have been done differently. Athletics student workers are starting to receive some diversity and bias training, based both on what the library did and on other trainings available from OIDI.

In an effort to further improve training and awareness for student workers, several library staff have met with Northeastern's Disability Resource Center (DRC) to discuss particular challenges of students with disabilities and clarify DRC's role in the process. Staff have seldom encountered disability issues in diversity training options at Northeastern, which frequently focused on race and gender, and wanted to ensure that student workers were familiar with the potential differences in services needed for students with disabilities, such as providing a printout or pulling materials for users. Moreover, it was helpful to educate student workers about legal issues related to access, such as service animals versus emotional support animals.

Further, staff must also take invisible disabilities into consideration in building training, such as potential chronic illnesses or mental illnesses that may require adjustments to standard library services. Students are frequently not included in these conversations and so must refer these issues to staff. Some training must be provided about how to address library users with different needs, but it ultimately comes down to paying attention to the person being helped, listening to what they are actually asking for, being patient, and building an understanding of services and possibilities.

The key takeaway for staff, however, was that diversity training is never truly completed. The training was created, but new topics and components have been added, including service animals, video transcripts, additional reflection questions, and an ever-evolving list of additional resources, including books, videos, and even blog posts for further reading.

Outcomes of Student Diversity and Inclusion

The end result of diversity training and active diversity recruitment has been three-fold at Northeastern: higher student worker retention (see appendix 7B), a more dedicated student worker group, and a position for students that more accurately reflects what they will experience in the professional workplace. Northeastern University prides itself on preparing students for the work world: hiring instructors actively engaged in their fields, investing in a comprehensive and intensive cooperative education program, and offering advanced training. Employees are expected to understand ethical concerns encountered within their position, as well as understanding the fundamentals of diversity and inclusion and providing the best service possible. Initiating this education in a student worker position provides advantages in later work life.

Moreover, reframing student worker employment as professional experience reinforces the individual's commitment to the position. When staff regard a student worker position as a job, students are more likely to respond in kind. IDEAS has experienced a decrease in last-minute schedule changes for some of its student positions as more training and flexibility have been incorporated. More students ask to increase their involvement or undertake more challenging projects. There has also been an increase in students asking for references from their library positions and asking how best to frame their library experience for résumés and job interviews.

Increased dedication to their positions and the library has augmented retention for IDEAS. Over the past three years, one unit went from needing to hire additional backups each semester to hiring once a year at the beginning of the fall semester and then occasionally an additional worker in the spring. When looking at the data, the shortest employment period for student workers in this position increased from less than one full month in 2014 to twelve months in 2018. Unfortunately, the pandemic in early 2020 severely impacted the 2019 hire numbers—of the four backup supervisor student workers hired in 2019, three were hired in December and one was hired in November. As the library shut down in early March 2020, those employment terms were heavily influenced by outside forces.

IDEAS believes that because it hires and trains for diversity, student workers from all backgrounds feel welcomed and valued and that their experiences are validated. Similarly, the University of Las Vegas Libraries created a peer research coach program, intentionally focusing on diversity in hiring:

> Diversity is intentionally fostered by recruiting diverse student employees through the Mason Undergraduate Peer Research Coach Program.... The hope is that by offering extensive training programs, by celebrating the peer coaches' individual and unique identities, and by engaging in other co-curricular activities, such as semesterly book discussions that amplify voices from people of color, that program participants feel their lived experiences and identities are important and valued.[17]

These changes to the student worker experience at Northeastern have helped student workers feel they are contributing to the library and their university on a higher level, rather than simply checking out a book or scanning an ID. Students have begun soliciting feedback from their supervisors on how best to market their library-based skills. They regard their library positions as true employment experiences. Although this was not a consideration for the changes to the student worker program, the increased diversity of student workers and improved training could potentially result in more diverse students interested in library school and entering the profession with relevant and extensive experiences.

Appendix 7A

SAMPLE STUDENT WORKER INTERVIEW SCHEDULE

- Five minutes for introduction and the standard "tell me about yourself" question. Some students without interview or job experience may need some prompting: "What's your major?" "Where are you from?" etc.
- Five minutes for position explanation, including expected day-to-day tasks and general schedule expectations. Leave some time for student questions and confirm understanding of explanation. Ensure the explanation and all descriptions are free of library jargon or are not overly complicated.
- Ten minutes for position-specific questions including
- Please tell me about your customer service experience.
- Do you have any library experience?
- If applicable, five minutes for situational questions, acknowledging that the applicant is not familiar with specific policies and procedures such as
  - A patron is causing a disturbance. What would you do?
  - There is a problem with the project you are assigned. What do you do?
- Five minutes for applicant questions and wrap-up.

Appendix 7B

SUMMARY OF APPROXIMATE TIME SPENT WORKING FOR THE LIBRARY BY BACKUP SUPERVISOR STUDENT WORKERS, BEGINNING 2014

Year	2014	2015	2016	2017	2018	2019
Number of New Hires	13	7	8	8	7	4
Average number of months employed	7.7	14	14.6	17.3	17.1	4
Longest employment term by months	27	32	43	39	22	
Shortest employment term by months	0	2	6	2	12	

Note: 2019 hires and employment averages were affected by closures for COVID-19. Shortest and longest employment terms are not included as a result.

Notes

1. Charles J. Muhl, "What Is an Employee? The Answer Depends on the Federal Law." *Monthly Labor Review* 125, no. 1 (January 2002): 3, https://www.bls.gov/opub/mlr/2002/01/art1full.pdf.
2. Brett B. Bodemer, "They CAN and They SHOULD: Undergraduates Providing Peer Reference and Instruction," *College and Research Libraries* 75, no. 2 (March 2014): 162, https://doi.org/10.5860/crl12-411.
3. Rosan Mitola, Erin Rinto, and Emily Pattni, "Student Employment as a High-Impact Practice in Academic Libraries: A Systematic Review," *Journal of Academic Librarianship* 44, no. 3 (May 2018): 352–73. https://doi.org/10.1016/j.acalib.2018.03.005.
4. Mitola, Rinto, and Pattni, "Student Employment."
5. Northeastern University, "Northeastern Demographics and Diversity Report," College Factual, accessed August 11, 2020, https://www.collegefactual.com/colleges/northeastern-university/student-life/diversity/.
6. Northeastern University, "Diversity at Northeastern," Undergraduate Admissions, https://www.northeastern.edu/admissions/student-life/diversity-at-northeastern/.
7. Freda Bernotavicz and Amy Locke, "Hiring Child Welfare Caseworkers: Using a Competency-Based Approach," *Public Personnel Management* 29, no. 1 (Spring 2000): 33, https://doi.org/10.1177/009102600002900103.

8.   Doug Ross. "The Evolving Workplace: The Evolving Workplace: Having a Diverse
      Workforce Also Means Greater Emphasis on Sensitivity Training and Hiring Practices,"
      Northwest Indiana Business Magazine, December 2019/January 2020, 41, https://nwindi-
      anabusiness.com/article/the-evolving-workplace/.
9.   See appendix 7A for standardized interview outline.
10.   Chun-Hsi Vivian Chen, Hsu-Mei Lee, Ying-Jung Yvonne Yeh, "The Antecedent and
      Consequence of Person–Organization Fit: Ingratiation, similarity, hiring recommendations
      and job offer," *International Journal of Selection and Assessment* 16, no. 3 (2008): 210-219.
      https://doi.org/10.1111/j.1468-2389.2008.00427.x. Also see Lauren A. Rivera, "Hiring as
      Cultural Matching: The Case of Elite Professional Service Firms," *American Sociological
      Review* 77, no 6 (2012): 999-1022. https://doi.org/10.1177%2F0003122412463213.
11.   Association of College and Research Libraries, Instruction Section, "Multilingual
      Glossary for Today's Library Users," accessed January 17, 2020, https://acrl.ala.org/IS/
      instruction-tools-resources-2/pedagogy/multilingual-glossary-for-todays-library-users/.
12.   Julia McKenna, "So Many Students, So Little Time: Practical Student Worker Training in
      an Academic Library," *Journal of Access Services* 17, no. 2 (2020): 74, https://doi.org/10.108
      0/15367967.2020.1718505.
13.   As one such student said in an e-mail request for a reference, "I miss orientation! Some of
      my favorite college memories are from working at the library, and I met [my boyfriend]
      there!"
14.   Northeastern University, "Our Vision of Diversity," Institutional Diversity, Equity and
      Inclusion, https://provost.northeastern.edu/odei/.
15.   Project Implicit home page, https://implicit.harvard.edu/implicit/.
16.   Other optional training modules include situational awareness training, a harassment
      presentation, and a customer service module complete with staff acting, which was a favor-
      ite of many student workers.
17.   Erin Rinto, Rosan Mitola, and Kate Otto, "Reframing Library Student Employment as a
      High-Impact Practice: Implications from Case Studies," *College and Undergraduate Librar-
      ies* 26, no. 4 (2019): 264, https://doi.org/10.1080/10691316.2019.1692747.

Bibliography

Association of College and Research Libraries, Instruction Section. "Multilingual Glos-
      sary for Today's Library Users." Accessed January 17, 2020. https://acrl.ala.org/IS/
      instruction-tools-resources-2/pedagogy/multilingual-glossary-for-todays-library-users/.
Bernotavicz, Freda, and Amy Locke. "Hiring Child Welfare Caseworkers: Using a Competen-
      cy-Based Approach." *Public Personnel Management* 29, no. 1 (Spring 2000): 33–42. https://
      doi.org/10.1177/009102600002900103.
Bodemer, Brett B. "They CAN and They SHOULD: Undergraduates Providing Peer Reference
      and Instruction." *College and Research Libraries* 75, no. 2 (March 2014): 162–78. https://doi.
      org/10.5860/crl12-411.
Chen, Chun-His Vivian, Hsu-Mei Lee, and Ying-Jung Yvonne Yeh. "The Antecedent and
      Consequence of Person–Organization Fit: Ingratiation, similarity, hiring recommendations
      and job offer." *International Journal of Selection and Assessment* 16, no. 3 (2008): 210-219.
      https://doi.org/10.1111/j.1468-2389.2008.00427.x.
McKenna, Julia. "So Many Students, So Little Time: Practical Student Worker Training in an
      Academic Library." *Journal of Access Services* 17, no. 2 (2020): 74–82. https://doi.org/10.1080
      /15367967.2020.1718505.

Mitola, Rosan, Erin Rinto, and Emily Pattni. "Student Employment as a High-Impact Practice in Academic Libraries: A Systematic Review." *Journal of Academic Librarianship* 44, no. 3 (May 2018): 352–73. https://doi.org/10.1016/j.acalib.2018.03.005.

Muhl, Charles J. "What Is an Employee? The Answer Depends on the Federal Law." *Monthly Labor Review* 125, no. 1 (January 2002): 3–11. https://www.bls.gov/opub/mlr/2002/01/art1full.pdf

Northeastern University. "Diversity at Northeastern." Undergraduate Admissions. https://www.northeastern.edu/admissions/student-life/diversity-at-northeastern/.

———. "Northeastern Demographics and Diversity Report." College Factual. Accessed August 11, 2020. https://www.collegefactual.com/colleges/northeastern-university/student-life/diversity/.

———. "Our Vision of Diversity." Institutional Diversity and Inclusion. https://provost.northeastern.edu/oidi/.

Project Implicit home page. https://implicit.harvard.edu/implicit/. Rinto, Erin, Rosan Mitola, and Kate Otto. "Reframing Library Student Employment as a High-Impact Practice: Implications from Case Studies." *College and Undergraduate Libraries* 26, no. 4 (2019): 260–77. https://doi.org/10.1080/10691316.2019.1692747.

Rivera, Lauren A. "Hiring as Cultural Matching: The Case of Elite Professional Service Firms." *American Sociological Review* 77, no 6 (2012): 999-1022. https://doi.org/10.1177%2F0003122412463213.

Ross, Doug. "The Evolving Workplace: Having a Diverse Workforce Also Means Greater Emphasis on Sensitivity Training and Hiring Practices." *Northwest Indiana Business Magazine.* December 2019/January 2020. 38–41. https://nwindianabusiness.com/article/the-evolving-workplace/.

CHAPTER 8

Introducing Cultural Competency in Libraries

A Case Study in Grassroots Professional Development

Katherine Kapsidelis and Elizabeth Galoozis

Introduction

The case study described in this chapter examines a series of internal trainings on diversity, equity, and inclusion (DEI) topics that took place at the University of Southern California Libraries in 2017 and 2018. The professional development trainings were organized by an ad hoc group who planned the initiative in order to develop a shared understanding of DEI issues among library employees.

In addition to providing a detailed description of the content covered in each of these workshops, this chapter will describe and analyze the planning process, along with successes and challenges, of this training series. The authors—who were part of the planning committee—will reflect on their inspirations and goals for the workshops and the ways they sought to assess the effectiveness of the program and to keep the momentum going after its conclusion. Our goal is

to provide a model of implementing DEI-related initiatives through grassroots planning.

Context and Inspiration

The University of Southern California (USC) is a large research university located in Los Angeles, California. USC Libraries comprises several libraries and over 200 faculty and staff members. Most libraries are on the University Park Campus; the exception is the Norris Medical Library, which is located about seven miles away from the main campus on the USC Health Sciences Campus.

In 2016, the USC provost's office instituted a new Diversity Council and required all schools and academic units, including the library, to develop a five-year diversity and inclusion plan.[1] While the library was responsible for naming diversity and inclusion liaisons from its faculty, the plan itself was drafted using input from all employees. No official committee or task force was assembled within the library to implement the diversity and inclusion plan; everyone was tasked with determining their own contributions and initiatives. Around the same time, the library released a new strategic plan, which in its vision statement calls for "a culture of commitment to our community and our colleagues and to developing diverse collections, services, spaces, and programs that embody that dedication."[2] So while DEI-related work was certainly happening in the library and across the university before 2016, these high-level initiatives spurred many of us to consider how we could contribute.

In the spring of 2017, the annual call for Dean's Challenge Grants came out. Dean's Challenge Grants are a program in the USC Libraries through which the dean of the library funds one-time programs or projects, defined broadly as innovative. Many of us were seeking opportunities to put theory into action and were eager to connect both the diversity and inclusion plan and the strategic plan to our proposals. One author (Elizabeth) invited a group of library employees (including the other author, Katherine) to participate in the grant initiative.[3] We decided to propose a program that would, as a first step, seek to develop a shared understanding of concepts and issues related to diversity, equity, and inclusion among USC Libraries employees. To focus our work and connect it to academic libraries, we explicitly concentrated on the first standard of the "Diversity Standards" of the Association of College and Research Libraries (ACRL), which enjoins library workers to "develop an understanding of their own personal and cultural values and beliefs as a first step in appreciating the importance of multicultural identities" in their institutions.[4]

As detailed below, we proposed, and received funding for, a set of trainings and resources for the 2017–2018 academic year. The funding provided by the internal grant was used to provide honoraria for speakers and workshop refreshments; the awarding of the grant also helped signal the support of the library's administration for the workshop series.

The Workshops

Our goal was a substantial one: to begin developing a shared understanding of diversity, equity, and inclusion issues among library employees. The bulk of our program consisted of a series of workshops that sought to train colleagues in baseline diversity-related cultural competence. ACRL, using a definition from the National Association of Social Workers, describes "cultural competence" as

> [a] congruent set of behaviors, attitudes, and policies that enable a person or group to work effectively in cross-cultural situations; the process by which individuals and systems respond respectfully and effectively to people of all cultures, languages, classes, races, ethnic backgrounds, religions, and other diversity factors in a manner that recognizes, affirms, and values the worth of individuals, families, and communities and protects and preserves the dignity of each.[5]

Writing in the *Library Quarterly,* Patricia Montiel-Overall defines cultural competence as a "highly developed ability to understand and respect cultural differences and to address issues of disparity among diverse populations competently."[6]

We believed that a starting place for developing cultural competence was to foster a shared understanding of DEI ideas and issues and to encourage individual reflection on these concepts and how they connected with our work in the library. Beginning with individual understanding and action is also an approach advocated by proponents of "cultural humility." Within a library context, Hurley, Kostelecky, and Townsend define cultural humility as

> the ability to maintain an interpersonal stance that is other oriented in relation to aspects of cultural identity that are

most important to the other person, the ability to recognize
the context in which interactions occur, and a commitment
to redress power imbalances and other structural issues to
benefit all parties.[7]

Twanna Hodge argues that to practice cultural humility, we must begin by interrogating our own explicit and implicit cultural biases as a first step toward understanding and mitigating how these inevitable biases impact our work in libraries.[8] A practice of cultural humility does not ask practitioners to learn the relevant cultural knowledge needed to understand or even identify the multiple identities that all patrons bring to the library; rather, it encourages individuals to be thoughtful and reflective in their interactions with others, keeping the impact of culture and bias in mind.[9] We aimed to work toward this kind of thoughtfulness and reflection through our workshops.

We also felt that it was important to disrupt the ideas of objectivity and neutrality. These concepts have been especially pernicious in libraries, which often center majority cultures as "objective" or "neutral." For example, regarding race, Robin DiAngelo writes the "belief in objectivity, coupled with positioning white people as outside of culture (and thus the norm for humanity), allows whites to view themselves as universal humans who can represent all of human experience."[10] We wanted participants to understand that microaggressions, bias, and racism are not problems that "others" have, but are rather issues that everyone—and especially white people, or those whose identities are considered "outside of culture" in libraries—has a responsibility to understand, confront, and redress.[11]

It was a challenge, however, to transform these ambitions into workshops that would be manageable in terms both of content for participants and of logistics for our planning team. The committee included members from both campuses who worked at different levels of the library hierarchy—including a contract librarian, heads of libraries, and a member of library administration—and who had varying job responsibilities. During initial planning sessions for the workshop series, we defined an explicit learning goal for each workshop (as detailed below). In order to accommodate different ways of learning, we also varied the method by which information was conveyed: via presentations, as part of interactive sessions, and through experiential and skills-based sessions. Another challenge was the distance that separates libraries located on USC's two campuses. For our second training, we were able to offer our workshop twice, once on each campus—but scheduling and other logistical difficulties prevented us from offering second sessions for the other trainings.

Each workshop was facilitated by an expert outside the library. We leveraged our connections on campus and in the community to bring in experts who could speak authoritatively on DEI issues, but were also mindful of the importance of explicitly connecting the workshops to libraries and to the specific issues of our workplace. Our intention was for each workshop to build upon the previous ones, but also to be understandable for those unable to attend every one. The workshops were open to all library employees.

The first workshop's goal was to create a shared vocabulary by establishing definitions for diversity concepts and to discuss racial climate research in higher education. Shaun Harper had recently joined USC as the executive director of the new Race and Equity Center and kicked off the workshop series by addressing these topics. In meetings leading up to the first workshop, Dr. Harper asked us about what we saw as particular DEI-related challenges in the library, in order to focus on specific concepts. Some of the challenges we discussed were creating inclusive physical and digital spaces; mitigating bias when interacting with patrons (particularly around nationality); and making assumptions (by both patrons and fellow library employees) about library employees (for instance, assuming that women are less authoritative).

In his presentation, Dr. Harper laid a foundation by summarizing his extensive research on racial climates in higher education and introduced us to concepts like "onlyness" ("the psychoemotional burden of having to strategically navigate a racially politicized space occupied by few peers, role models, and guardians from one's same racial or ethnic group"[12]) and "stereotype threat" ("being at risk of confirming, as self-characteristic, a negative stereotype about one's group"[13]). He also shared findings specific to USC and discussed that although faculty and staff aspire to equity, very few are trained in it—and that race was perceived as a taboo topic of discussion on campus. He then invited us to reflect on diversity and equity within the library, collecting anonymous notecards from participants responding to the prompt "Write one diversity-related question you have long had, but haven't felt comfortable openly discussing it with colleagues in the USC Libraries." This led to a rich discussion on difficult issues that were particular to our library and also highlighted some uncomfortable truths—such as how much more racially diverse our staff is than our faculty (both at USC Libraries and USC more generally).

The goal of the second workshop was to define microaggressions and discuss them in the context of USC Libraries. We invited Cynthia Mari Orozco, librarian for equitable services at East Los Angeles College and founder of the *Microaggressions in Librarianship* blog,[14] to lead us in addressing this goal. In our preliminary discussions, we discussed what we aspired to get out of the workshop: to define microaggressions and what falls under that definition; to focus on individual strategies rather than one-off solutions; and to begin to create a culture of support for combating microaggressions and their effects. We had noted from Dr. Harper's workshop that participants responded well to anonymous interactivity and worked with Ms. Orozco to incorporate this technique. Ahead of time, she solicited examples of microaggressions from libraries employees through an online survey, using a definition from Derald Wing Sue and colleagues: "Racial microaggressions are brief and commonplace daily verbal, behavioral, or environmental indignities, whether intentional or unintentional, that communicate hostile, derogatory, or negative racial slights and insults toward people of color."[15] Participants were asked in the same survey if they had ever witnessed specific types of microaggressions in their work at the USC Libraries, from patrons or from library faculty and staff. We provided seven types of microaggressions as examples:

- members of dominant groups being called on, listened to, or praised more than members of nondominant groups in meetings or other situations
- dismissal of requests for equitable treatment (e.g., using preferred pronouns or accommodating disabilities)
- denial of privacy (e.g., commenting on or asking about disability or medical status)
- use of language that is racist, sexist, ableist, homophobic, and so on
- ascribing stereotypical characteristics to a certain group
- environmental microaggressions in the climate of the library
- assigning work based on race, gender, language, age, or other characteristics rather than on ability

Each category was checked off by at least four library employees who responded to the survey.

Ms. Orozco led two workshops, one at the University Park Campus and another at the Norris Medical Library on the Health Sciences Campus. The pre-workshop survey not only allowed participants to contribute examples anonymously, but also gave them time to think through the provided definitions and examples of microaggressions. During the workshops, Ms. Orozco guided the discussion and the analysis of some of the scenarios that had been submitted. She also led the group in creating a set of strategies for addressing the microaggressions illustrated by the examples.

The goal of the third workshop was to become aware of how algorithms (among other factors) can unconsciously bias our work at both an organizational and an individual level and to learn how to actively work to interrupt bias. Two faculty members at USC presented different portions of the workshop. First, Safiya Umoja Noble (then of the Annenberg School for Communication) presented on her research on bias in search engines, libraries, and other information settings in order to ground our discussion. Specifically, Dr. Noble defined unconscious bias, differentiated it from microaggressions, and discussed bias in libraries and information systems in general, including in library workplaces and workforces.

In the second half of the workshop, Anita Dashiell-Sparks, associate dean of equity, diversity and inclusion at the School of Dramatic Arts, led participants in a training on interrupting bias in different library-based scenarios. Ms. Dashiell-Sparks began by leading us through an exercise using an "identity wheel" to identify external and internal parts of our individual identities and then related them to privilege and impression through one-on-one discussion in pairs. She also introduced us to the resource "To Equalize Power among Us: Tools for Change," which adapts questions and actions from *Breaking Old Patterns, Weaving New Ties: Alliance Building* by Margo Adair and Sharon Howell.[16] These questions and actions prompted us to consider ways of identifying and interrupting bias; for example, "Do I take responsibility for, think for, or speak for others?" and "Appreciate efforts that point out my mistakes or lack of awareness."

A final component of the grant project was a brainstorming meeting, which was open to all library employees. This meeting served as an opportunity to discuss what we had learned during the training series and to apply it directly to our workplace by developing tangible next steps related to DEI issues. Participants were invited to identify problems and to share ideas on concrete ways that we could work to expand the diversity and inclusiveness of the library, its services and collections, and the environment for its employees. Those unable to attend the meeting were invited to provide feedback virtually. These ideas grew into the agenda of the Diversity, Equity, and Inclusion Working Group, discussed in further detail later in the chapter.

To assess the quality and the impact of the program, we sent participants a survey after each training that provided an opportunity for feedback and reflection. Of the sixty-three responses that we received over the course of the workshop series, we received no ratings (on a five-point scale from Poor to Excellent) lower than average—and fifty-nine participants rated the trainings as either excellent or good. The survey also invited respondents to reflect on something that they might "do differently in your approach to working with patrons, instruction, and/or collections as a result of this training." In their responses, those who had attended the trainings discussed a variety of ideas for incorporating new knowledge about DEI topics into their work with colleagues, the public, and students. One wrote about setting up rules of engagement to foster more respectful and open discourse before meetings and classes; several discussed approaching others with more mindfulness and awareness of the way their actions can contribute to the creation of a more inclusive environment. Others reflected on the ways that institutions can reinforce bias and on how this might influence individual action. Although it is difficult to measure real-world behavioral impact, these responses show that those who attended the workshops made connections between the trainings and their work in the library.

Continuing Momentum and Lessons Learned

At the conclusion of the grant year, the group found ourselves with a long list of ideas to further implement the library's diversity and inclusion plan and wanted to put into action the knowledge we had gained during the workshops. In the absence of a formal body to enact these recommendations, the grant group decided to stay together to coordinate and prioritize efforts. Over time, we began actively working to recruit new members to what we decided to call the Diversity, Equity, and Inclusion Working Group (DEIWG). At our first post-grant meeting, we categorized the ideas of our colleagues into five broad themes: language, recruitment, physical space, patron/student and faculty engagement, and training and education.

One of our first projects was to create a *Diversity and Inclusion Resource Guide* that documented and reinforced concepts covered in the workshop. In addition to summarizing key ideas, definitions, and other takeaways from the trainings, the guide provided contextual information about the USC community. The authors were inspired by a presentation about diversity training at Loyola Marymount University; the presenters had led a campus-wide diversity training day, accompanied by a resource guide on which we modeled our own guide. The presenters highlighted the value of their resource guide in extending participants' learning and emphasized the importance within their guide of acknowledging minority and dominant populations as an initial step toward understanding.[17] The guide therefore included statistical information about the demographic makeup of library employees as well as USC's students, faculty, and staff. The committee worked with the library's in-house graphic designers to create a polished brochure that was professionally printed. The resource guide was distributed across USC Libraries, reaching those who may not have been able to attend the workshops; an electronic version is also internally available. It is also now given to new library employees as part of their onboarding.

The DEIWG found that our work organizing the trainings had provided us with the experience and authority to tackle other projects within the library. Spurred by conversations during the workshops, for example, we were able to immediately institute the inclusion of a diversity statement as part of the library's faculty hiring process. We organized workshops and meetings that addressed issues raised in the trainings and invited Dr. Noble to return to the libraries to speak at a DEI-themed Wikipedia edit-a-thon that took place as part of a campus-wide DEI week. Our committee also worked with a variety of partners within the library, particularly our faculty and staff governance organizations, to build recognition programs across departments in order to celebrate a wide variety of accomplishments and strengths. At the time of writing this chapter, other new projects include diversity reviews of our collections and increased efforts to make our resources and services more accessible to all patrons.

Discussions from our brainstorming session also helped us identify needs that could be addressed when outside opportunities arose. For example, participants from the brainstorming session identified the language on our websites and research guides as an area where the library could improve. So when we saw that ACRL was offering a webcast on how to use plain language to make web-based resources more accessible, we knew there would be an audience for an organized viewing. This kind of momentum, as well as the increased awareness that the workshops created for action on DEI projects within the library, was a key success of the training series.

Important successes from the planning process included determining clear and thoughtful learning outcomes and varying the ways that information was presented to accommodate different learning preferences. Establishing these ideas as part of our proposal outline in the early stages of our planning process helped to guide the later work of the committee, making it easier for the group to work efficiently and collectively. Additionally, the creation of the *Diversity and Inclusion Research Guide* at the end of the training series institutionalized the concepts covered in the trainings while also making them accessible for those who were not able to attend. The guide also provided contextual institutional information to frame all of our work.

Based on our experience with this project, there are a few key aspects that we would change if we planned another workshop series. First, we would seek to more precisely measure the impact of the training series by developing larger-scale assessments—such as, for example, by conducting library-wide climate surveys before and after the trainings. The individual workshop surveys provided valuable feedback, but their scope was limited—and we have found it difficult to quantify broader change.

Second, we would form a more inclusive organizing committee. Our group came together based around a shared interest in DEI issues and was not formed to be intentionally representative of library employees. Our planning committee did include librarians from both campuses, which helped us to be thoughtful and proactive about attempting to make the trainings as accessible as possible for employees who do not work on the main campus. However, missing from the group were members of library staff without faculty status, in addition to representatives of some departments, such as Technical Services and Information Technology. Staff attendance at the workshops was low relative to that of faculty, and the inclusion of staff on the committee may have helped us to anticipate and address this issue. Similarly, while some student workers were invited to the workshops, none ultimately attended. A more representative committee may have been able to identify improvements to the workshops that would have increased their relevance or accessibility.

Finally, we could have done more during the workshop series to directly address and challenge white privilege—either during the trainings we had or by planning an additional session that focused specifically on the issue. The pervasiveness and persistence of white privilege—and its pernicious effects in higher education, libraries, and the country—demand greater attention and action.

Our trainings have raised many issues that the new DEI working group is seeking to address through ongoing initiatives. This has highlighted the importance of dedicating ongoing resources to DEI trainings and initiatives—and points to a limitation of grassroots efforts such as the one described in this chapter. Although our project allowed us to experiment and plan a training series with a minimum of bureaucratic impediments, it has become clear to us that formal recognition and support is crucial to enabling larger and more systemic changes within an institution the size of USC Libraries. Ultimately, grassroots efforts must work in conjunction with institutional initiatives to make progress toward the goals outlined in this chapter.

Conclusion

To practice cultural humility is to engage in an ongoing effort—and beginning efforts like these workshops are helpful, since seeking to address diversity, equity, and inclusion issues can be overwhelming. Institutionalized discrimination and systemic oppression demand responses on an equivalent scale, and approaching DEI work in a piecemeal or a time-limited fashion can cause more harm than good. However, we found value in this training series as a foundational step, and hope that it can serve as a model for other libraries. We believe that even libraries with robust DEI programs could benefit from a similar workshop model as it is important to periodically reinforce the understanding of DEI concepts that can sometimes feel hollow when they are used as superficial buzzwords. Revisiting key terms is also an opportunity to cultivate a deeper and more nuanced understanding, and we found that the act of creating a consensus through discussion can also provide a springboard that allows for swift implementation of new initiatives.

Notes

1. University of Southern California, "Diversity at USC," accessed January 8, 2020, https://diversity.usc.edu/ (page content changed).
2. "USC Libraries Strategic Plan," last updated November 2017, https://libraries.usc.edu/sites/default/files/usc_libraries_strategic_plan_update_nov_2017.pdf.

3. The group consisted of Elizabeth Galoozis (head of information literacy); Cynthia Henderson (formerly associate dean of the Health Sciences Libraries and one of the libraries' diversity and inclusion liaisons); Karen Howell (head of Leavey Library and the other diversity and inclusion liaison); Katherine Kapsidelis (formerly reference and instruction librarian for special collections); Karin Saric (information services librarian for health sciences); and Marje Schuetze-Coburn (associate dean for faculty affairs).
4. Association of College and Research Libraries, "Diversity Standards: Cultural Competency for Academic Libraries," 2012, https://www.ala.org/acrl/standards/diversity.
5. Association of College and Research Libraries, "Diversity Standards."
6. Patricia Montiel Overall, "Cultural Competence: A Conceptual Framework for Library and Information Science Professionals," *Library Quarterly* 79, no. 2 (April 2009): 176, https://doi.org/10.1086/597080.
7. David Hurley, Sarah Kostelecky, and Lori Townsend, "Cultural Humility in Libraries," *Reference Services Review* 47, no. 4 (August 2019): 549, ProQuest.
8. Twanna Hodge, "Integrating Cultural Humility into Public Services Librarianship," *International Information and Library Review* 51, no. 3 (July 3, 2019): 268–74. https://doi.org/10.1080/10572317.2019.1629070.
9. Hurley, Kostelecky, and Townsend, "Cultural Humility," 550–51; Adilene Rodgers, "Cultural Humility in Librarianship: What Is It?" *Teen Librarian Toolbox* (blog), *School Library Journal*, November 12, 2018, https://www.teenlibrariantoolbox.com/2018/11/cultural-humility-in-librarianship-what-is-it/.
10. Robin DiAngelo, "White Fragility," *International Journal of Critical Pedagogy* 3, no. 3 (2011): 59.
11. DiAngelo, "White Fragility," 55.
12. Shaun R. Harper et al., "Race and Racism in the Experiences of Black Male Resident Assistants at Predominantly White Universities," *Journal of College Student Development* 52, no. 2 (March 2011): 190.
13. Claude M. Steele and Joshua Aronson, "Stereotype Threat and the Intellectual Test Performance of African Americans," *Journal of Personality and Social Psychology* 69, no. 5 (1995): 797.
14. *Microaggressions in Librarianship* blog, accessed January 8, 2020, https://lismicroaggressions.tumblr.com/.
15. Derald Wing Sue et al., "Racial Microaggressions in Everyday Life: Implications for Clinical Practice," *American Psychologist* 62, no. 4 (2007): 271.
16. Margo Adair and Sharon Howell, *Breaking Old Patterns, Weaving New Ties* (San Francisco: Tools for Change, 1994).
17. Elisa Slater-Acosta et al., "A Change Is Gonna Come: Renewing Information Workers' Commitment to Social Justice" (presentation, California Academic and Research Libraries Conference, Redwood City, CA, April 13–15, 2018) http://conf2018.carl-acrl.org/wp-content/uploads/2018/08/carl2018proceeding_acosta_engage_changeisgonna.docx.

Bibliography

Adair, Margo, and Sharon Howell. *Breaking Old Patterns, Weaving New Ties: Alliance Building.* San Francisco: Tools for Change, 1994.
Association of College and Research Libraries. "Diversity Standards: Cultural Competency for Academic Libraries." 2012. https://www.ala.org/acrl/standards/diversity.

DiAngelo, Robin. "White Fragility." *International Journal of Critical Pedagogy* 3, no. 3 (2011): 54–70.

Harper, Shaun R., Ryan J. Davis, David E. Jones, Brian L. McGowan, Ted N. Ingram, and C. S. Platt. "Race and Racism in the Experiences of Black Male Resident Assistants at Predominantly White Universities." *Journal of College Student Development* 52, no. 2 (March 2011): 180–200.

Hodge, Twanna. "Integrating Cultural Humility into Public Services Librarianship." *International Information and Library Review* 51, no. 3 (2019): 268–74. https://doi.org/10.1080/1057 2317.2019.1629070.

Hurley, David, Sarah Kostelecky, and Lori Townsend. "Cultural Humility in Libraries." *Reference Services Review* 47, no. 4 (August 2019): 544–55. ProQuest.

Microaggressions in Librarianship website. Accessed January 8, 2020. https://lismicroaggressions.tumblr.com/.

Montiel-Overall, Patricia. "Cultural Competence: A Conceptual Framework for Library and Information Science Professionals." *Library Quarterly* 79, no. 2 (April 2009): 175–204. https://doi.org/10.1086/597080.

Rodgers, Adilene. "Cultural Humility in Librarianship: What Is It?" *Teen Librarian Toolbox* (blog), *School Library Journal*, November 12, 2018. https://www.teenlibrariantoolbox.com/2018/11/cultural-humility-in-librarianship-what-is-it/.

Slater-Acosta, Elisa, Aisha Conner-Gaten, Javier Garibay, Rhonda Rosen, and Desirae Zingarelli-Sweet. "A Change Is Gonna Come: Renewing Information Workers' Commitment to Social Justice." Presentation, California Academic and Research Libraries Conference, Redwood City, CA, April 13–15, 2018. http://conf2018.carl-acrl.org/wp-content/uploads/2018/08/carl2018proceeding_acosta_engage_changeisgonna.docx.

Steele, Claude M., and Joshua Aronson. "Stereotype Threat and the Intellectual Test Performance of African Americans." *Journal of Personality and Social Psychology* 69, no. 5 (1995): 797–811.

Sue, Derald Wing, Christina M. Capodilupo, Gina C. Torino, Jennifer M. Bucceri, Aisha Holder, Kevin L. Nadal, and Marta Esquilin. "Racial Microaggressions in Everyday Life: Implications for Clinical Practice." *American Psychologist* 62, no. 4 (2007): 271–86.

University of Southern California. "Diversity at USC." Accessed January 8, 2020. https://diversity.usc.edu/ (page content changed).

USC Libraries. "USC Libraries Strategic Plan." Last updated November 2017. https://libraries.usc.edu/sites/default/files/usc_libraries_strategic_plan_update_nov_2017.pdf.

CHAPTER 9

Embracing a Culture of Humility, Diversity, and Inclusion

A Case Study of an Academic Library's Radical Compassion Programming

Latanya N. Jenkins and Elizabeth L. Sweet

> "Me pinto a mí misma porque soy a quien mejor conozco."
> —*Frida Kahlo*

Since all graduates of LIS programs will potentially serve communities of color, curricula should prepare all students for this eventuality. Innovative curriculum design is the area of greatest potential and can be reflected in targeted course plans or through service learning opportunities, providing students with the option to specialize in services for cultural communities. It is only through a curriculum with an embedded diversity worldview that LIS can take steps away from... [the] charge that institutional racism exists within our LIS programs.[1]

Academic librarians' educational endeavors and training include supporting the work and research of all library users. Information professionals develop skills and knowledge that help researchers and scholars facilitate not only how to locate information, but also how to critically analyze and assess the legitimacy of that information. However, research demonstrates that positionality and identity complicate attempts to be neutral in terms of both interpretations of material and professional practice.[2] Rarely are librarians afforded opportunities to assess their own identity or to think critically about how it may influence or have an impact on their interactions with library users. As the Black Lives Matter movement and the recent murders of George Floyd and Breonna Taylor have crystallized for many in the United States, racism has been a deepseated part of how we see and interpret the world. Higgins and Stark argue that implicit bias linked to the overwhelmingness of white librarians in the libraries prioritizes dominant voices in society, decreases the chance of accessing information about less dominant voices, and negatively impacts the experiences of library users.[3] It is important to understand and acknowledge implicit bias as linked to individual histories, especially racial histories, because they shape unique experiences, relationships, structures, and approaches to everyday life and professional practice.

In developing Temple University's Paley Library workshop series on Radical Compassion, the goal was to help library staff be more open and understanding toward library users and peers from diverse backgrounds and to become more aware of the power of words and body language during interactions with library users and colleagues.

Professionals, broadly, have been encouraged to embrace *cultural competence* as a way to broaden their engagement with communities that are not their own.[4] A cultural competence approach views cultural differences as a kind of knowledge that can be learned. It is guided by an assumption that professionals have the capability to "learn a culture." This assumption would include an ability wholly to learn language, history, social norms, cultural rituals, and values, among other aspects of a culture. "Its proponents hold that once practitioners (and the institutions they work in) become culturally competent, they will be able to take direct action and engage with people from different cultures in a way that is efficient, respectful, and effective."[5] "The word *competence* implies that culture… is finite and static";[6] it does not acknowledge the dynamism and complexities encompassed by diverse cultures.

Professionals could practice a more collective and collaborative approach to knowledge creation and interpretation instead by embracing *cultural humility* as a framework to guide ongoing self-reflection. Cultural humility begins with professionals committing to open-ended introspection—an opportunity to learn from others in a humble manner with radical compassion. For our purposes, *radical compassion* is the deliberate act of love, empathy, care, and kindness; as opposed to only compassion, which is a feeling of sympathy or concern for the suffering of others. Radical compassion is a counterintuitive, but powerful response to fear, hatred, and supremacy of any kind and is rooted in action, not just feelings of empathy. Coupling cultural humility and radical compassion provides a path to embrace diversity, push for inclusion, and advocate for equity. Librarians are in an excellent position to strengthen communities by using cultural humility to create an environment of radical compassion. Individual institutions have the option of developing programs for professional development and personal growth that encourage reframing librarians' work with library users to challenge dominant social and political relationships, specifically professional/nonprofessional binaries that divide rather than unite. Institutions should support and encourage efforts to create and build spaces where kind, caring, and empathetic voices can flourish, learn, and grow. Library administrators should value librarians who embrace cultural humility as assets to the communities they serve.

Temple University is considered to be a very diverse educational institution. James Hilty describes Temple's deliberate efforts "throughout its history [to] purposely cultivate an aura of diversity... and became more diverse, in terms of both gender and racial ethnicity."[7] More recently, however, diversity among faculty and students by race has been decreasing.[8] Multiple efforts to develop opportunities for growth and create environments of support for diversity are ongoing. For example, Temple University's faculty senate Committee on the Status of Faculty of Color (FOC) facilitates programs and activities that aim to support diversity work across the campus. Both Jenkins and Sweet were members of that committee in 2016, when the Academic Center for Research in Diversity (ACCORD) at Temple and the FOC organized a diversity workshop attended by participants from across campus on "Defining and Defying Microaggressions" (figure 9.1) The session employed body-map storytelling to encourage self-reflection and visceral memory regarding incidences of racism or discrimination that participants had experienced or witnessed.

In developing the series on Radical Compassion, the goal was to help library staff be more open and understanding toward library users and peers from diverse backgrounds and to become more aware of the power of words and body language during interactions with library users and colleagues. We believe that cultural humility could not only prevent demeaning or problematic interactions, but also provide a path for responding appropriately once a transgression occurs. Additionally, cultural humility creates an inclusive work environment whereby librarians and information professionals can promote and embrace thinking and communicating effectively from a place of equality rather than a place of superiority. Once information professionals learn and embrace cultural humility, library services will improve and radical compassion will emerge.

FIGURE 9.1
ACCORD "Defining and Defying Microaggressions" workshop, 2016.

In the fall of 2018, the Continuing Education Committee at Temple's Samuel L. Paley Library organized a workshop called "Radical Compassion: Gender and Cultural Humility in the Workplace" as part of the Radical Compassion series to challenge the embedded neutral assumption linked to librarians' work. Before the start of the workshop, participants read an article on cultural humility, which gave everyone a chance to ask questions or make comments about the concept. Providing this background reading also allowed participants to start from the same place of knowledge before embarking on the self-reflective journey and to view the workshop as an ongoing self-development activity. Using the framework of cultural humility as defined above, we asked twenty-five library staff members, librarians, and administrators to engage in self-reflection by asking them to "locate themselves," and used body-map storytelling to document visually their identities and the power dynamics these identities carry. As we locate ourselves, cultural humility enables us to practice radical compassion, which is an antidote to the current national climate of white supremacy and hatred. In this chapter, we also suggest how the Radical Compassion series could fit with other types of learning opportunities and experiences for professional development. Below we include questions that information professionals can use to guide and inspire self-reflection and work toward radical compassion—thereby creating a better work environment for everyone and a better space for library users.

The concept of cultural humility, developed by Melanie Tervalon and Jann Murray-Garcia, insists that professionals have an obligation to pursue practices that illuminate the prevailing power position of experts in the field.[9] Cultural humility contests the belief that one can actually become competent in another culture (which is the theory of cultural competence). Instead, cultural humility pursues a practice and ongoing recognition and evaluation of power imbalances. It marks an intentional effort to rebalance power inequities. The goal is to develop "non-paternalistic" collaboration with library users.[10] In the current political climate, cultural humility becomes even more urgent as librarians guide researchers during information exchange and knowledge creation.

Cultural humility encourages practitioners to "relinquish" their position as expert.[11] Institutional accountability through cultural humility is also an important component of system change.[12] While cultural humility was developed with medical practitioners and social workers in mind, it can shift the dynamics of librarians' interactions with the public in such a way as to support and embrace diversity rather than try to manage it with a demonstrated competence or knowledge about the other. Cultural humility is a way to practice "transmodernism," a term used by Latin American scholars to counterbalance European philosophical reliance on modernism that sees European thinking and ideas about technology and art as superior to other approaches to knowledge and experience, which are labeled as backward.[13] It could enable librarians, via self-reflection, to uncover the overreliance on and unjustifiable valorization of US white settler knowledge, perspective, and beliefs that dominate library resources and library school education. Cultural humility also provides a process for librarians to assess how their positions of power and privilege have influenced their professional practice. Within this framework, professionals acknowledge they are not able to be competent in another culture, but rather have the obligation to examine their own culture and position as a professional, to disclose their biases, limited vision, and privileges, to understand "the ways their culture influences their personal attitudes, values and beliefs."[14] Self-reflection sets the groundwork for cultural humility and could strengthen the possibilities of the "radicality" of opening up opportunities for equal partnerships and decentering the power of the expert.

Since cultural competence is linked to colonial thinking and Western dominance placing practitioners in the position of knower and others in the position of known, cultural humility is a more inclusive approach. If librarians embrace cultural humility, we can expect a weakening in the philosophical grip of US white settler colonial beliefs and values. If library school curricula incorporate activities such as "locating oneself" to train librarians on how to engage in ongoing self-reflection and self-critique,[15] not only of their work, but also of who they are—their social, cultural, and racial identities—there is a chance to move toward radical compassion as a driving factor for libraries and their work environment.

While radical compassion has its philosophical roots in theological analysis, particularly related to Christianity, we are using it here in a secular manner to depict a move away from objectivity and individuality to a more collaborative, loving self-reflection that leads to radical compassion. Radical compassion is, for us, the ability to deeply see and embrace the humanity in others and link that embrace to service. We want the actual process of service provision to be driven by compassion, not a narrow notion of expertise or professionalism; those are secondary aspects of the role and the easy part of being a librarian. It is much harder and requires significant effort to engage in radical compassion as we describe it here.

Methods of Self-Reflection

Below we document the process followed in the workshop "Gender and Cultural Humility in the Workplace" to first "locate" oneself and then link that exploration to historical and contemporary experiences and relationships. We point to the intentionality of the program as well as its clear goals, demonstrable outcomes, and transferable strategies.

In the process of locating oneself, we sometimes need to grieve some aspects of our identities and histories, which is not about guilt or blame; it is an acknowledgment of how our histories and how our people (the groups of people with whom we most identify) might have negatively affected others or been impacted negatively by others. By locating ourselves and understanding what that location means—that is, our positionality[16]—we are better equipped to practice cultural humility. We have a better sense of who we are at this moment and are able to engage in an ongoing analysis as we change and understand more about ourselves and our relation to others, in different places, times, and circumstances. In this practice, we reject Descartes's declaration "I think, therefore I am" as one of the foundational philosophical underpinnings of Western thought. We acknowledge our existence and experiences are a result of history, time, space, and relationships. By locating oneself, we are actively engaging in a decolonial practice that would serve librarians as a check on privilege or lack thereof, de-emphasize expert position, and ground practice in cultural humility.

For the workshop, we decided to use body-map storytelling as an activity to help in the process of locating oneself. The guiding questions for this activity allow participants to reflect on their own power. The body is a subject that can be political and cultural, and its power changes in time and space in accordance with a diversity spectrum, which is why body-map storytelling is an appropriate way to facilitate self-reflection.

Body-map storytelling, or mapping stories on paper images of bodies, not only helps in self-reflection of the many aspects of intersectionality, but also allows participants to better understand how to address and navigate stressors in the workplace that accompany working through those challenges and how to recognize when to seek support. This is an active learning process rather than a lecture, in which participants have to be engaged and intentional about their contribution. This process enables multiple opportunities to engage with the complexity of concepts like diversity and inclusion.

Body-map storytelling is a holistic and nonlinear data creation technique that can document intersecting temporal and spatial events, processes, and experiences that include feelings, emotions, and perceptions, while also visually engaging bodies and spaces around these bodies.[17] Historical and contemporary stories can be transmitted through symbols, shapes, colors, and images.[18] Since the 1980s, body mapping has been used by medical doctors[19] and with HIV-positive people to raise awareness and self-esteem,[20] to document migration experiences and health concerns of undocumented workers,[21] and to explore women's experiences with violence.[22] Each person responds to questions by painting, drawing,

TABLE 9.1

Workshop questions

Questions: Locating Oneself using Body Map Storytelling
1. Draw the history of your people on your body.
2. How is that history in/on your body?
3. Draw the impact of your people on others around your body and/or the impact of other people on your (people) body.
4. Draw how your identities intersect with intersectional racism
5. Draw how your stories connect to the stories of others.
6. What is your location and how does it affect your interactions with patrons?

and/or pasting objects into their life-sized or smaller body silhouette. Participants were invited to reflect on their answers to the questions in table 9.1 on their body maps. We then asked the mappers to describe the meaning of their finished maps. After everyone completed their body maps, we asked participants to think about their location and identify how it affects their interactions with library users. See figures 9.2 and 9.3 for examples of body maps from the workshop.

Analysis and Use of Body Maps

Throughout the workshop, the series of questions in table 9.1 allowed participants to map their roots and history, their relationships to other groups, and the intersection of their identities, and to advance their understanding of self. It was difficult for some participants to work through this activity. It is challenging to take off the neutral hat that is embedded in Western thinking and training and dig into the historical and contemporary location of oneself. Self-reflection is contrary to the idea that professionalism means avoiding the intrusion/dominance of identity and experiences as guiding everyday practice.

Figures 9.2 and 9.3 are example maps from the workshop utilizing the aforementioned questions. In figure 9.2, the mapper acknowledged her African and Caribbean heritage and its colonial influences, identified by the crown and the castle in the background, and the privileges that the mapper has in terms of education and nationalities, represented by the pencil and flags, respectively. The changing globe and the jewels show the benefits that others have gleaned from the resources of others and identify history over time. History is drawn as a teardrop and a chained hand, which represents the losses of freedom seekers—life, family, educational attainment, and so on. The purse shows the stolen resources, and the cook's serving spoon represents the role her family has had over the course of time in feeding multitudes. The jewel with the black sash represents the struggle for justice that all people will face if they choose not to fight collectively for one another. In terms of service, the unicorn shows that the mapper has a unique talent for finding other people's talents and helping them increase their own attributes and attainment, whether it's activities she enjoys, like travel, writing, or chatting about other people's lives. This map documents the intersection of identities of space, time, and relationships. The mapper is reflecting on the European colonial reach from Africa to the Caribbean and the economic extractions as part of that process. These events are linked to contemporary struggles for social justice. The yellow ribbons link the body of the mapper with times, places, events, and individual characteristics. This mapper's self-reflection is emblematic of historical inequality, but also of hope, resistance, and

FIGURE 9.2
Sample body map from workshop

FIGURE 9.3
Sample body map from workshop

opportunities. Sharing her map and explaining its attributes to her colleagues opened up dialogue about historical and concurrent issues of injustice and the ways interactions with library users can replicate these injustices even without conscious decision-making. The discussion highlighted the need to be intentional in attempts to redress injustice and inequality in service provision.

In figure 9.3, the mapmaker directly documents multiple identities as Asian and American and shows her solidarity in the words "Asians 4 Black Lives." She has many people in her thoughts as they are emanating from her head. She has education through books, but there is also an empty bowl with a question mark. This body map shows a black diamond that could represent wealth turned into a pacifier, which is on the floor away from her body. She is wrapped in a US flag including a heart and a full bowl; there is a cross below with green and brown colors connecting her to ancestral lands and a padlock on her mouth. Her identity is complicated, and she is questioning and speaking, but also silenced. This body map was created in 2018. We hope that the padlock has been broken and the bowl has been filled with solidarity.

For both coauthors, a way forward is to institute a culture of humility and radical compassion from library school curriculum to everyday practice in libraries. We hope that via changes to curriculum, continuing education opportunities, and a commitment by leaders in libraries, self-reflection becomes the norm for librarians in their engagement with library users and each other. These opportunities will use radical compassion as a way to embrace cultural diversity through "dynamic engagement between cultures, their values, beliefs, and ways of knowing."[23]

While we did not conduct a formal assessment of the workshop, we received immensely positive feedback from participants. The participants universally said that it really made them think about who they are and how they interact with others in the library. After the workshop, other librarians and staff, who had heard good things, asked if we would do it again so they could participate. The sole librarian, who participated virtually, said that she would have benefited more by in-person attendance, as she was not able to see the other participants' works, nor share her creation. The opportunity to engage in self-reflection really seemed to shift thinking, but it was not effortless. We, as facilitators, had to take care to support what was for some a difficult and uncomfortable process. By the end, however, everyone wanted to keep their body map, and some participants put their respective maps on their office walls. We interpret this as a sign that the workshop was important and participants wanted a reminder of their work in locating themselves.

If LIS programs prioritize educational opportunities to overcome institutional barriers to diversity, inclusivity, and equity, that work should be reinforced by librarians and information professionals. Creating workshops that provide opportunities for self-reflection and growth can help institutions combat the structural impediments experienced by staff and library users with a variety of backgrounds and life experiences. It is vital that colleges and universities, as a part of educational advancement, support opportunities for better understanding among peers and provide spaces conducive to openness and growth. While growth and self-reflection take time and energy, librarians and information professionals should welcome the opportunity for it. Especially in the context of Black Lives Matter, professional development that would put into practice the professed commitment to diversity, inclusion, and equity definitely should garner support. In our current political climate, with the quadruple crises of the pandemic, climate change, economic depression, and racist police brutality/deep structural racism, the use of radical compassion will allow librarians and patrons to be empowered through trust and transparency. It is vital that colleges and universities, as a part of educational advancement, support opportunities for better understanding among peers and provide spaces conducive to openness and growth. Librarians and information professionals should have chances for deep reflection on their own privilege and "incorporate cultural humility as an objective in community-engaged learning, such as internships, community-based research, and service learning courses."[24]

Notes

1.   Lorienne Roy, "Diversity: Then Is Now. Commentary on Carter, J. R. (1978) Multicultural Graduate Library Education (*Journal for Education for Librarianship*, 18[4], 295–314)," *Journal of Education for Library and Information Science* 56, no. 1 (Winter 2015): 1–2.
2.   Elizabeth L. Sweet, "Cultural Humility: An Open Door for Planners to Locate Themselves and Decolonize Planning Theory, Education, and Practice," *Ejournal of Public Affairs*, August 23, 2018, http://www.ejournalofpublicaffairs.org/cultural-humility/.
3.   Molly Higgins and Rachel Keiko Stark, "Mitigating Implicit Bias in Reference Service and Literature Searching," in *Diversity, Equity, and Inclusion in Action: Planning, Leadership, and Programming*, ed. Christine Bombaro (Chicago: ALA Editions, 2020), 61.
4.   Sweet, "Cultural Humility."
5.   Sweet, "Cultural Humility," 6.
6.   Sweet, "Cultural Humility," 6.
7.   James W. Hilty, *Temple University: 125 Years of Service to Philadelphia, the Nation, and the World* (Philadelphia: Temple University Press, 2010), 272.

8. Elizabeth L. Sweet, Karen Marie Turner, and Kimmika Williams-Witherspoon, "Three Senior Scholars of Color Discuss Their Research and Diversity at Temple," *Faculty Herald* 44, no. 5 (2014): 1, 4–5, http://www.temple.edu/herald/44_5/ThreeSeniorScholarsDiscuss. htm (page discontinued).

9. Melanie Tervalon and Jann Murray-Garcia, "Cultural Humility versus Cultural Competence: A Critical Distinction in Defining Physician Training Outcomes in Multicultural Education," *Journal of Health Care for the Poor and Underserved* 9, no. 2 (May 1998): 117–25, https://doi.org/10.1353/hpu.2010.0233.

10. Tervalon and Murray-Garcia, "Cultural Humility versus Cultural Competence," 117.

11. Laurie Ross, "*Notes from the Field*: Learning Cultural Humility through Critical Incidents and Central Challenges in Community-Based Participatory Research," *Journal of Community Practice* 18, no. 2–3 (2010): 318, https://doi.org/10.1080/10705422.2010.490161.

12. Tervalon and Murray-Garcia, "Cultural Humility versus Cultural Competence," 122.

13. Enrique D. Dussel, "Transmodernity and Interculturality: An Interpretation from the Perspective of Philosophy of Liberation," *Transmodernity* 1, no. 3 (2012): 28–59.

14. Joshua N. Hook et al., "Cultural Humility: Measuring Openness to Culturally Diverse Clients," *Journal of Counseling Psychology* 60, no. 3 (2013): 353, https://doi.org/10.1037/ a0032595.

15. Self-reflection and self-critique would also lessen instances of "vocational awe," which refers to the set of ideas, values, and assumptions librarians have about themselves and the profession that result in beliefs that libraries as institutions are inherently good and sacred, and therefore beyond critique. See Fobazi Ettarh, "Vocational Awe and Librarianship: The Lies We Tell Ourselves," *In the Library with the Lead Pipe*, January 10, 2018, http://www. inthelibrarywiththeleadpipe.org/2018/vocational-awe/.

16. Feminist geographers among others have argued that knowledge is a product of the biases, privileges, and power of its creator and that these positions constitute their positionality and make all knowledge partial knowledge. For a review of positionality, see Gilian Rose, "Situating Knowledges: Positionality, Reflexivities and Other Tactics," *Progress in Human Geography* 21, no. 3 (1997): 305–20, https://doi.org/10.1191/030913297673302122.

17. Denise Gastaldo et al., *Body-Map Storytelling as Research* (Toronto: Centre for Support and Social Integration Brazil-Canada and Centre for Spanish-Speaking Peoples, 2012), 10, http://www.migrationhealth.ca/undocumented-workers-ontario/body-mapping.

18. Gastaldo et al., *Body-Map Storytelling*, 5.

19. Andrea Cornwall, "Body Mapping in Health RRA/PRA," *RRA Notes*, no. 16 (1992): 69–76, PLA Notes CD-ROM 1988–2001, IIED London, https://pubs.iied.org/sites/default/files/ pdfs/migrate/G01449.pdf.

20. Art2Be in partnership with Kenyan-German Development Cooperation in Healthcare, Art2Be: Art Therapy for Positive Living and Social Change website, February 23, 2012, https://web.archive.org/web/20120223114018/http://www.art2bebodymaps.com/index. php?option=com_content&task=view&id=42&Itemid=86.

21. Gastaldo et al., *Body-Map Storytelling*.

22. Elizabeth L. Sweet and Sara Ortiz Escalante, "*Engaging Territorio Cuerpo-Tierra* through Body and Community Mapping: A Methodology for Making Communities Safer," *Gender, Place and Culture* 24, no. 4 (2017): 594–606, https://doi.org/10.1080/09663 69X.2016.1219325.

23. William C. Welburn, "Do We Really Need Cultural Diversity in the Library and Information Science Curriculum?" *Journal of Education for Library and Information Science* 35, no. 4 (1994): 328, https://doi.org/10.2307/40323026.

24. Ross, "*Notes from the Field*," 332.

Bibliography

Art2Be in partnership with Kenyan-German Development Cooperation in Healthcare. Art2Be: Art Therapy for Positive Living and Social Change website. February 23, 2012. https://web.archive.org/web/20120223114018/http://www.art2bebodymaps.com/index. php?option=com_content&task=view&id=42&Itemid=86.

Cornwall, Andrea. "Body Mapping in Health RRA/PRA." *RRA Notes*, no. 16 (1992): 69–76. PLA Notes CD-ROM 1988–2001. IIED London. https://pubs.iied.org/sites/default/files/pdfs/migrate/G01449.pdf.

Dussel, Enrique D. "Transmodernity and Interculturality: An Interpretation from the Perspective of Philosophy of Liberation." *Transmodernity* 1, no. 3 (2012): 28–59.

Ettarh, Fobazi. "Vocational Awe and Librarianship: The Lies We Tell Ourselves." *In the Library with the Lead Pipe*, January 10, 2018. http://www.inthelibrarywiththeleadpipe.org/2018/vocational-awe/.

Gastaldo, Denise, Lilian Magalhães, Christine Carrasco, and Charity Davy. *Body-Map Storytelling as Research: Methodological Considerations for Telling the Stories of Undocumented Workers through Body Mapping*. Toronto: Centre for Support and Social Integration Brazil-Canada and Centre for Spanish-Speaking Peoples, 2012. http://www.migrationhealth.ca/undocumented-workers-ontario/body-mapping.

Higgins, Molly, and Rachel Keiko Stark. "Mitigating Implicit Bias in Reference Service and Literature Searching," In *Diversity, Equity, and Inclusion in Action: Planning, Leadership, and Programming*. Edited by Christine Bombaro, 59–72. Chicago: ALA Editions, 2020.

Hilty, James W. *Temple University: 125 Years of Service to Philadelphia, the Nation, and the World*. Philadelphia: Temple University Press, 2010.

Hook, Joshua N., Don E. Davis, Jesse Owen, Everett Worthington, and Shawn Utsey. "Cultural Humility: Measuring Openness to Culturally Diverse Clients." *Journal of Counseling Psychology* 60, no. 3 (2013): 353–66. https://doi.org/10.1037/a0032595.

Jenkins, Latanya N. *Body Map*. Created in "Gender and Cultural Humility in the Workplace" workshop. Temple University Libraries, 2018.

Montaniel, Katerina. *Body Map*. Created in "Gender and Cultural Humility in the Workplace" workshop. Temple University Libraries, 2018.

Rose, Gilian. "Situating Knowledges: Positionality, Reflexivities and Other Tactics." *Progress in Human Geography* 21, no. 3 (1997): 305–20. https://doi.org/10.1191/030913297673302122.

Ross, Laurie. "*Notes from the Field*: Learning Cultural Humility through Critical Incidents and Central Challenges in Community-Based Participatory Research." *Journal of Community Practice* 18, no. 2–3 (2010): 315–35. https://doi.org/10.1080/10705422.2010.490161.

Roy, Lorienne. "Diversity: Then Is Now. Commentary on Carter, J. R. (1978) Multicultural Graduate Library Education (*Journal for Education for Librarianship*, 18[4], 295–314)." *Journal of Education for Library and Information Science* 56, no. 1 (Winter 2015): 1–2.

Sweet, Elizabeth L. "Cultural Humility: An Open Door for Planners to Locate Themselves and Decolonize Planning Theory, Education, and Practice." *Ejournal of Public Affairs*, August 23, 2018. http://www.ejournalofpublicaffairs.org/cultural-humility/.

Sweet, Elizabeth L., and Sara Ortiz Escalante. "*Engaging Territorio Cuerpo-Tierra* through Body and Community Mapping: A Methodology for Making Communities Safer." *Gender, Place and Culture* 24, no. 4 (2017): 594–606. https://doi.org/10.1080/0966369X.2016.1219325.

Sweet, Elizabeth L., Karen Marie Turner, and Kimmika Williams-Witherspoon. "Three Senior Scholars of Color Discuss Their Research and Diversity at Temple." *Faculty Herald* 44, no. 5 (2014): 1, 4–5. http://www.temple.edu/herald/44_5/ThreeSeniorScholarsDiscuss.htm (page discontinued).

Tervalon, Melanie, and Jann Murray-Garcia. "Cultural Humility versus Cultural Competence: A Critical Distinction in Defining Physician Training Outcomes in Multicultural Education." *Journal of Health Care for the Poor and Underserved* 9, no. 2 (May 1998): 117–25. https://doi.org/10.1353/hpu.2010.0233.

Welburn, William C. "Do We Really Need Cultural Diversity in the Library and Information Science Curriculum?" *Journal of Education for Library and Information Science* 35, no. 4 (1994): 328–30. https://doi.org/10.2307/40323026.

CHAPTER 10

Cultural Intelligence in Academic Libraries

Michele A. L. Villagran

According to Wang and Su, cultural intelligence is identified as one of the most important leadership attributes for developing library leaders.[1] Cultural intelligence (CQ) was officially defined in 2003 by Earley and Ang as "an individual's capability to function effectively in situations characterized by cultural diversity."[2] It is how one can successfully adapt to new cultural settings, including national, ethnic, organizational, generational, and so on.[3]

This chapter will offer a glimpse into how cultural intelligence can be and is being applied within academic libraries by library staff. Cultural intelligence is a model that colleges and universities are leveraging to achieve diversity, equity, community, and inclusive excellence in the areas of staff development, recruitment and hiring, and instruction. Organizations continue to demonstrate their commitment to creating an inclusive and culturally intelligent campus community. As we consider the phenomenon of cultural intelligence, it is important to begin with some background on cultural competence and cultural intelligence.

Background

The emergence of cultural competence literature traces back to the 1990s, originating from the health, social work, and psychology professions. According to Leung and colleagues, *cultural competence* is an overarching term for many concepts related to intercultural effectiveness. They examined thirty cultural competence models with over 300 concepts that covered many cultural competence characteristics, including attitudes, personality traits, and world-wide views.[4] The models differed in focus, scope, and domains. The term 'cultural competence' entered into the library and information science profession in 1999.[5] Montiel-Overall, Villaescusa Nunez, and Reyes-Escudero further discuss a framework, in 2016, foundational to understanding cultural competence for libraries based on a social work theory, defining it as

> The capacity to recognize the significance of culture in one's own life and in the lives of others; to acquire and respectfully use knowledge of diverse ethnic and cultural groups' beliefs, values, attitudes, practices, communication patterns, and assets to strengthen LIS programs and services through increased community participation; to bridge gaps in services to communities by connecting them with outside resources; to recognize socioeconomic and political factors that adversely affect diverse populations; and to effectively implement institutional policies that benefit diverse populations and communities.[6]

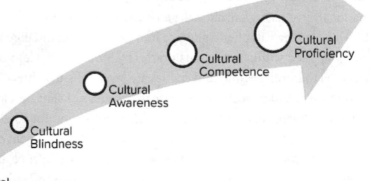

FIGURE 10.1
Cultural competence continuum
(Adapted from Terry L. Cross, Barbara J. Bazron, Karl W. Dennis, and Mareasa R. Isaacs, *Towards a Culturally Competent System of Case* [Washington, DC: CASSP Technical Assistance Center, Georgetown University Child Development Center, 1989], https://files.eric.ed.gov/fulltext/ED330171.pdf.)

This definition alone illustrates just how complex cultural competence is. As Cross and colleagues explained in the social work field, cultural competence is seen as a continuum where one is continually improving upon one's own competence (see figure 10.1).[7] It is similar to a journey where we each are continually improving.

Montiel-Overall expressed it as "the ability of professionals to understand the needs of diverse populations."[8] Cooke further adapted the model of Cross and colleagues to include cultural humility. Cultural humility focuses on "examining and identifying underlying issues that produce instances of inequality in the diverse communities we serve."[9] Cultural intelligence is the capability to work effectively across cultures and relates to cultural competence. CQ is a form of intelligence that can be measured and developed.

Harris as quoted in Hudson-Ward suggests that values-based diversity has a place in libraries, as these are characteristics that we each bring into the workplace that impact our thoughts and actions there.[10] Values-based diversity is defined as a management philosophy in which the values that individuals bring into the workplace (such as differences in communication styles, work ethics, and motivational factors) are elevated as diversity issues.[11] Values-based diversity is similar to cultural intelligence in that we all have our own cultural values that are a part of us, and we carry them with us and exhibit them in the workplace. Therefore, we may need to adapt or modify our own communication when we interact with a student.

Cultural competence over the years has been applied to library recruitment, retention, staff training, collections, service, and programming.[12] Duffus and colleagues identified "two staff development objectives to strengthen these values [DEI] within the library: 1) cultivate an inclusive environment by opening dialog among employees, and 2) develop skills and cross-cultural competencies that can be incorporated into daily workflows."[13] Mestre examined academic librarians' experiences with diversity training ten years ago and found that they lacked cultural competence training and therefore were not prepared in the workplace.[14] Wang and Su acknowledge that libraries recognize that diversity within library staff can add value to an organization if managed effectively.[15]

Highlighting the importance of diversity values and standards, the Association of College and Research Libraries (ACRL) adopted diversity standards for academic libraries in 2012. The diversity standards, also known as "Diversity Standards: Cultural Competency for Academic Libraries," are meant to "emphasize the need and obligation to serve and advocate for racial and ethnically diverse constituencies."[16] These are guidelines to ensure that academic librarians are knowledgeable about cultural aspects of diverse populations and that they can illustrate cultural competence with a variety of stakeholders.

Cultural Intelligence

The term *cultural intelligence* has been used synonymously with terms such as *global mindset*, *global competency*, *cultural competence*, and *intercultural competence* within the literature and in discussions. Each of these, however, has its own unique definition. Earley and Ang first introduced the concept of cultural intelligence in 2003, drawing upon Sternberg and Detterman's multidimensional perspective of intelligence. They defined CQ as "a person's capability to adapt effectively to new cultural contexts."[17] The goal of CQ research is to understand why some individuals prosper in culturally diverse situations and others do not. Cultural intelligence differs from other intelligences (such as emotional intelligence) because it focuses on situations and interactions characterized by cultural diversity. Cultural intelligence "assesses multiple aspects of intercultural competence based on theoretically grounded, comprehensive, and coherent framework,"[18] as presented below. Ang and Van Dyne developed a cultural intelligence model or framework that contains four distinct dimensions or elements: metacognitive (drive), cognitive (knowledge), motivational (strategy), and behavioral (action)[19] (see figure 10.2). Based on this research, individuals with high cultural intelligence are utilizing all dimensions. The goal for an individual is to score high on all four dimensions in order to have a high overall cultural intelligence. Even if you are weak in one dimension, you can improve. Examination of each of the four elements is significant to understanding the framework and one's own cultural intelligence level.

FIGURE 10.2

Cultural intelligence model, which includes four distinct dimensions, beginning with drive.

(Adapted from Soon Ang and Linn Van Dyne, "Conceptualization of Cultural Intelligence: Definition, Distinctiveness, and Nomological Network," chapter 1 in Handbook of Cultural Intelligence: Theory, Measurement, and Applications, ed. Soon Ang and Linn Van Dyne [Armonk, NY: M. E. Sharpe, 2008], 3–15.)

Motivational or Drive CQ

Motivational CQ relates to how motivated we are—our intrinsic motivation, our extrinsic motivation and confidence—to work in a cross-cultural situation. This is the first aspect of CQ because it starts with us and is foundational to having diverse interactions. If one is not motivated to engage with others, there is a lack of cultural intelligence. How confident are we in our interactions with diverse patrons in an academic library? Livermore offers as examples that motivational CQ is often increased in organizations when we face our biases and maintain control.[20] The author has found, based on survey of participants over the years,[21] that this first element is often the most overlooked because librarians already assume they have passion and motivation or they wouldn't be in this type of profession.

Cognitive or Knowledge CQ

Cognitive CQ focuses on understanding different cultural practices, values, and norms. This element is important because we need to understand that cultures have differences and that these differences have an impact on decisions we make each day. Within cognitive CQ in the model, there are three key subdimensions that are important to reflect on: business, interpersonal, and sociolinguistic. Each of these may be different for each culture. There are ten cultural dimensions that can also be examined per specific cultural region to understand one's personal value orientations:

- individualism versus collectivism
- low versus high power distance
- low versus high uncertainty avoidance
- cooperative versus competitive
- short term versus long term
- direct versus indirect
- being versus doing
- universalism versus particularism
- non-expressive versus expressive
- linear versus nonlinear[22]

Each of these value orientations offers insight into one's own personal preferences for interacting with other cultures. Note that there is variability in cultural values within national cultures and even within specific groups (e.g., gender, ethnicity), so even if one identifies with a specific cluster, someone who identifies with the same cluster may have different cultural values. There are several assessment tools that can be used to understand these preferences and help train individuals on the differences between values and how to leverage where individuals may be on a continuum. The values vary by individual and are neither good nor bad.

Organizational leaders such as library deans should understand the cultural values of their teams and those of the campus community to ensure that practices are suitable and will be effective. Additionally, the cultural values of external communities served by the university should be examined. Often conflicts occur due to an underlying cultural value. University personnel can conduct a needs assessment of these communities and then utilize the cultural values to learn more about the value orientation preferences of community members. This includes both internal employees and external stakeholders such as students and parents.

Metacognitive or Strategy CQ

Metacognitive CQ relates to one's awareness during interactions with those from different cultures. Our cultural backgrounds and values influence our identities. These help us understand why we behave the way we do. Metacognitive CQ is the third element of the cultural intelligence model and one of the most important because it encourages critical thinking and inspires individuals to assess their own ways of thinking. Asking self-reflective questions can help you to take inventory of where you are with your current thinking, explore what is or is not working, and help you determine what you need to do next.

Librarians can take a cultural inventory assessment, such as the Diversity Wheel,[23] to identify components of their own identities and reflect on how those identities may be more visible in different situations and how those identities may intersect and impact the ways one is viewed or treated by others. Additionally, metacognitive CQ promotes awareness and planning when one encounters a cultural situation. How often have we planned or observed a cultural situation or even debriefed after one? Based on assessments and interviews with librarians working in the United States over the years, the author found that this dimension is often weaker due to the view of time in our country. In general, those working in the Americas do not have time to plan and debrief because we live and operate in such a fast-paced environment. We need to observe a situation and determine how to engage, which requires slowing down and taking time to plan, debrief, and reflect.

Behavioral or Action CQ

Behavioral CQ is how one adapts when relating or working interculturally. It refers to how and if you adapt your verbal and nonverbal actions when interacting in diverse cultural situations. Many organizations offer different types of diversity training to address or help minimize cultural diversity challenges within the workplace. However, the majority of these trainings assume that awareness, understanding, and cultural sensitivity will lead to changes in one's behavior.[24] Changes in any behavior require high cultural intelligence. Some individuals are able to recognize behaviors that influence culture and learn to modify their verbal and nonverbal communication when involved in a cultural situation. One can improve one's behavioral CQ by strengthening one's cognitive knowledge; however, knowledge alone is not the answer.

Cultural Intelligence Training in Academia

Universities have long been institutions that draw students from various backgrounds, which offers the opportunity to foster cultural intelligence. Faculty, administrators, and librarians play a significant role in promoting and ingraining cultural intelligence into their practices as they have regular interactions with students from a variety of cultural backgrounds.

In 2003, the first academic training program on cultural intelligence was launched at Nanyang Technological University.[25] London Business School followed with a similar program focusing on creating diverse teams. With millions of people in higher education around the world, there is a huge opportunity for boosting cultural intelligence. For example, in Dubai, many universities have enhanced their culturally intelligent practices by celebrating and respecting different cultures through an annual festival. Tiffin University launched a cultural intelligence initiative that included training with experiential exercises, case studies, and assessments of levels of cultural intelligence to align its efforts to ensure all students graduate with global competence.[26] Georgia Southern University Libraries, California State University, San Marcos, Library, and California State University, Sacramento, Library recently underwent bias, cultural intelligence, and awareness training, respectively, to support their missions of appreciating diversity and supporting inclusive excellence. Beyond training, cultural intelligence application has also appeared within teaching, curricula, and working with students.

Curriculum in Higher Education

The benefits of embedding cultural intelligence practices in curriculum include advancing inclusivity, reducing stereotyping, and making higher education more attractive to students of color. Nelson Laird examined how diversity is addressed in college courses, including those of Indiana University (IU). In a survey of student engagement at IU, Laird found that fewer than 50 percent of faculty adopted inclusive practices toward course objectives and content in their courses.[27] According to Chun and Evans, department chairs and directors can impact faculty members' inclusion of diversity within the curriculum.[28] A suggestion is for faculty to review colleagues' syllabi and offer feedback on the diversity of their course content. One way for faculty to practice cultural intelligence in their pedagogy is to encourage interaction among members of different cultures.

Faculty and Instruction in Library and Information Studies

How well do library and information studies (LIS) faculty currently introduce cultural competence and cultural intelligence practices into their instruction? Over the years, many scholars have examined how cultural competence has been incorporated, or not, in library and information science education.[29] Tumuhairwe found that huge strides haven't been taken within curriculum development, even though there is evidence of the importance of diversity and cultural aspects to the profession.[30] However, there has been much criticism of the concept of cultural competence within the United States, particularly on whether privilege and racism are addressed.[31] These terms are often lumped under broader umbrella terms such as *multiculturalism* or *diversity*. Pawley encourages LIS educators to "recognize the roots of our racialized thinking" and how these "are still discernible in LIS curriculum."[32]

Curriculum reviews, instructional reviews from peers, professional development training focused on cultural intelligence, and incorporation of cultural intelligence in performance reviews are all possible tactics for embedding cultural intelligence into faculty practices. Embedding cultural intelligence into individual teaching practices is a more inclusive practice allowing instructors to reach students from every cultural background. Foster examined instructional librarians and their incorporation of cultural competence. She found that instructional librarians will be better prepared to connect with and teach students from a variety of backgrounds if cultural competence is considered at each stage of the teaching process.[33] This aligns with pedagogical practices around culturally relevant teaching as defined by Ladson-Billings in 1994 as " that which empowers students intellectually, socially, emotionally, and politically by using cultural referents to impart knowledge, skills and attitudes."[34]

LIS Students

Globalization and multicultural characteristics of society have placed a spotlight on whether educators are able to develop LIS students who are multiculturally educated and globally engaged within their professions. As noted above, Mestre found that academic librarians' diversity training lacked preparation for cultural competence and that all LIS graduates should have a foundational understanding.[35] Kumasi and Franklin Hill examined how well students felt their courses prepared them to become culturally competent practitioners. They found minimal knowledge gains in cultural competence among LIS students at Wayne State University and Syracuse University.[36] Villagran and Hawamdeh further found that progress has been made among United States LIS education accredited programs in increasing multicultural courses that include cultural competence, as evident from courses offered and learning outcomes of courses, but additional recommendations should be taken into consideration.[37] Experiential learning may offer students the chance to reflect on differences and develop skills and values from direct experiences outside a traditional academic setting.

Cultural Intelligence in Academic Libraries

While academic librarians cannot take credit for a student's success, academic libraries can make a great impact. Soria, Fransen, and Nackerud found that students who use the library regularly and get help from librarians are more likely to graduate, and they have higher GPAs than nonusers of the library.[38]

When working with students, academic librarians should consider language, family aspects, communications, self-efficacy, and possible economic factors that impact students. Being empathetic and willing to engage beyond a transactional task will open up the conversation. A librarian must feel motivated to inspire students in a new environment as this may be the first time a student has visited a library.

Cherinet found that cultural intelligence was a frequently mentioned skill in job ads for LIS positions. This is a skill that can "help us to be culturally sensitive to diversified library users and the workforce."[39] According to the "Master of Library and Information Science Skills at Work" annual report from San José State University School of Information, communication and interpersonal skills was the number one skill most in demand by employers in 2018, with employers also desiring experience working with and serving diverse communities in 2019.[40] Utilizing the framework of cultural intelligence, academic librarians can adapt their verbal and nonverbal actions when interacting with those from different backgrounds.

Current Cultural Intelligence Research

The author's current research includes seeking to understand the overall level of cultural intelligence of librarians participating in the study and their viewpoints on the value and importance of cultural intelligence within their universities or colleges in light of diversity initiatives. How is cultural intelligence currently being applied and embedded in diversity practices? What has worked? What best practices can be offered? Where else can we improve? The author has used the cultural intelligence scale to examine this phenomenon specifically within academic law libraries (with the support of a research grant received from American Association of Law Libraries Academic Special Interest Section), special libraries (including academic),[41] and academic libraries within the state of Pennsylvania. For each study, the participants were recruited through their respective association.

The special libraries mixed-methods study included 148 initial respondents who were members of the Special Libraries Association from across the world. The study included the cultural intelligence assessment, demographic questions, and open-ended items. Seventy-three percent were female, 35 percent reported a minority status, and 26 percent were currently working in academic libraries in various roles. The academic law libraries mixed-methods research study included 171 participants from academic law libraries throughout the United States. The study was available to all members of the American Association of Law Libraries Academic Special Interest Section. Almost 50 percent of participants had more than fifteen years of experience working in an academic law library, and job titles varied from reference to public service to instruction to electronic services to director. Twenty-eight percent were from the Midwest, 21 percent from the Northeast, 19 percent from the South, and 26 percent from the West. The Pennsylvania research focused on the College and Research division, but the study was available to all Pennsylvania librarians who were Pennsylvania Library Association members.[42] Qualitative and quantitative data was collected via a survey with 166 responses; 32.5 percent of responses were from those currently working in academic libraries in Pennsylvania. The discussion below offers insights from survey responses and focus group interviews of participants; however, it does not report the full findings, as the full data is currently available in journal publications.

Livermore reveals that individuals who accomplish their objectives regardless of the cultural context (national, generational, ethnic, etc.) have strengths in four key dimensions (CQ Drive, CQ Knowledge, CQ Strategy, and CQ Action).[43] These four dimensions are those of culture intelligence as defined by Ang and Van Dyne. The Cultural Intelligence Scale (CQS) was utilized for these studies. This assessment tool provides a valid and reliable measure of a person's ability to function effectively in culturally diverse situations.[44] The CQS measures the four key dimensions as discussed above. The tool was converted into an electronic survey with additional demographic and open-ended questions. To more deeply understand this phenomenon within the academic library sphere, open-ended questions and focus groups with academic law librarians and academic librarians in special libraries took place after the survey. The open-ended questions were coded and analyzed within NVivo, a qualitative data analysis tool. Follow-up interviews took place with participants from the special libraries and academic law libraries studies. The following five questions will be explored within this chapter:

1. What has been your experience with the term *cultural intelligence*?
2. What do you believe is the value of cultural intelligence to academic libraries/to your library?
3. How important is cultural intelligence in your current role?
4. What has gone well due to CQ within your organization?
5. What is one change or recommendation you would suggest ensuring cultural intelligence is embedded within your library?

Each of these questions offers insight into the foundational understanding of cultural intelligence by academic librarians, the value participants believed it brought to their library or to academic libraries, and how important they felt it is in their current position.

Experience with Term *Cultural Intelligence*

The majority of participants identified as having either limited experience or no experience at all with the term *cultural intelligence* in their library. Some have heard about, read about, or had experience with the term, but in a specific situation (e.g., attended a training, read an article, attended a webinar, etc.). There is significant value in knowing what participants thought of cultural intelligence as a benchmark in this study. Figure 10.3 offers a visual representation of key terms participants expressed when considering these questions.

FIGURE 10.3

Word cloud of study participants' experience with the term *cultural intelligence*

One academic law librarian commented, "I understand it is a skill or competency that is important for interacting with people from unknown or different cultural backgrounds." Another agreed that their library has different people from various nationalities. Interestingly, another participant viewed cultural intelligence as a negative because the participant "only found it used in describing deficits in behavior… never describing strengths." Participants did comment that the phrase can be associated with "cultural sensitivity," "awareness," "code switching," "synonymous to diversity," "cultural competence," "inclusivity," and "emotional intelligence." One described cultural intelligence as "being like emotional intelligence but more limited to being mindful of whether others might perceive comments and actions as being racist, ageist, or insensitive to LGBTQ issues." Another respondent thought cultural intelligence was part of emotional intelligence and a soft skill that they utilize in their workplace.[45]

Value of Cultural Intelligence

Participants believed that cultural intelligence is valuable in a variety of ways, given the diverse cultural backgrounds of the students they support. When asked about the ways in which cultural intelligence could be valuable, respondents most frequently mentioned that CQ could be valuable when working with students and patrons (see figure 10.4). For example, one respondent expressed, "We cannot properly teach our students if we do not recognize the differences in culture and how these differences impact learning." This confirms what we discussed earlier about faculty teaching practices and their own cultural intelligence within the classroom.

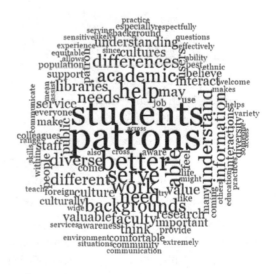

FIGURE 10.4

Word cloud of study participants' understanding of the value of cultural intelligence

Service was also another area where respondents thought cultural intelligence could bring value to the library. "It is extremely important to gain an understanding of cultural intelligence because the patron population will come from all walks of life and cultures," stated one participant. Another expressed that the workforce is becoming more diverse and that cultural intelligence could assist them with working with various generations. It is extremely valuable as "it helps you do a better job... our job is to support ALL of our faculty and students, not merely the ones who look/think like us." This refers to affinity bias, an unconscious bias we have that makes us gravitate to those who resemble ourselves. "Cultural intelligence practices help us root out bias in performing our job... it is another aspect of providing equitable treatment to all," explained another participant. In conjunction with service and bias is the notion of making users feel welcome. One participant found that "making users feel welcome makes it more likely that they will be comfortable coming to librarians with questions they have, and that gives us more opportunities to help them be as successful as possible." Other key themes that emerged with this question included enhanced communication, improved interactions, empathy and respect of others, and awareness.

Importance of Cultural Intelligence

Academic librarian participants personally felt that cultural intelligence is important in their current role; however, there has been some resistance organizationally and with management in some organizations. "The lack of cultural intelligence of my managers made it impossible for them to use my ideas," said one respondent. Another argued that it is important, but "my workplace doesn't put enough emphasis on it for the whole office."

Many believed it was important related to their teaching efforts and making patrons and students feel welcome. "Having an understanding of how to create comfort across different cultures is vital in that mission," stated one librarian. Public-facing librarians found it was of critical importance to their role because "they must be prepared for all types of interactions." One librarian said, "it is a fundamental skill that helps both navigate cross-cultural cultural interactions and prime the brain for dealing with whatever comes your way in the library regardless of its origin in cultural difference." Figure 10.5 is a word cloud of terms that appeared most within this question.

FIGURE 10.5
Word cloud of study participants' understanding of the importance of cultural intelligence

Given this research is still in progress, additional themes may appear that contribute to the value and importance of application of cultural intelligence in academic libraries.

Positive Examples of Cultural Intelligence

Communication, culture, and *people* were each associated with positive examples of what has gone well due to cultural intelligence within their organization when this question was asked in follow-up interviews of academic librarians in the special libraries study. An academic librarian participant commented that "coworkers were curious to get to know you if they didn't know you and were open to learning more about you." Another expressed similar notions in that "open communication has helped them to get to know one another. Working closely together over policy decisions and being inclusive of all voices in the process has brought them closer together." Another participant reinforced what that participant stated: "Communication has been seen as key to develop trust among coworkers. Offering others the opportunity to express their own viewpoints has helped them develop a closer working relationship."

In another example, a participant expressed how their national culture has forced them to learn about and understand cultural differences about their counterparts' own culture. The participant viewed this as a positive example because it gave them "the opportunity to become more willing to learn about others' cultural backgrounds and to try and understand people better." It has been through cultural training and role modeling within the library that the participant felt positive behaviors are being sustained.

Participants did express that in order for cultural intelligence to be embedded within their library that their leadership must be on board. "There needs to be a collaborative and inclusive approach that is adopted across the board." At least five participants who were interviewed suggested that "human resources and hiring managers be more involved in cultural intelligence so they can raise awareness and train others. This would help to foster more open dialogue with coworkers." The following were additional ideas offered to develop and begin implementing cultural intelligence in libraries.

Developing and Implementing Cultural Intelligence

One of the best ways to develop a culturally intelligent organization is to help the librarians improve their own cultural intelligence through experiences, trainings, and personal development. It is one thing to teach librarians about being aware and sensitive about differences, but it is entirely different when a leader needs to integrate people from different cultures into the same institution or even department. Leadership can conduct an organizational culture audit by asking questions such as these about culturally intelligent practices:

- Do policies and procedures reflect a culturally intelligent approach?
- What cultures are represented and underrepresented within the organization?
- How have departments and teams engaged with diverse representation?

- Does the leadership support and promote culturally intelligent behaviors?
- Is cultural intelligence considered when recruiting, hiring, and retaining librarians?[46]

Pairing a cultural intelligence assessment with training afterward focused on strategies to enhance each of the four dimensions of CQ can help individuals come up with a personalized development plan to improve their cultural intelligence. The plan should include actions to take over the next thirty, sixty, and ninety days with check-in accountability meetings with a partner. A library can hold ongoing dialogue conversations about topics related to cultural intelligence, events can be planned with cultural intelligence in mind, and any initiatives should consider how CQ should show up in the workplace.

Taking action to diversify hiring practices is also a step toward developing a culturally intelligent workforce versus hiring based only on fit. This may include altering procedures, job descriptions, and processes to eliminate criteria that can promote bias; working toward a diverse set of interviewers; and reflecting on how your organization is defining specific terms such as *diversity* and *inclusion*. Improving communication skills within hiring practices and understanding how others may view or perceive this communication in distinctive ways can enhance your cultural intelligence.

Conclusion

Developing and implementing cultural intelligence takes effort on the part of individuals and organizations. Through experiences, reflections, observation, and practice, we can increase our cultural intelligence. Helping librarians improve their cultural intelligence through training, personal development, and practical application is the best way to develop culturally intelligent libraries. Considering our biases and assumptions is foundational to developing our own cultural intelligence and a first step to understanding others. Administrators and human resources departments within these organizations can incorporate cultural intelligence training into onboarding and professional development. This chapter presents an opportunity for academic libraries to develop culturally intelligent organizations and to take action to better serve their stakeholders.

Notes

1. Xuemao Wang and Chang Su, "Developing Future Library Leaders in the Context of Globalization with an Analysis on Cultural Intelligence (CQ)," in *Library Management and Marketing in a Multicultural World: Proceedings of the 2006 IFLA Management and Marketing Section's Conference*, ed. James L. Mullins (Munich, Germany: K. G. Saur, 2007): 303–22.
2. Soon Ang and Linn Van Dyne, "Preface and Acknowledgments," in *Handbook of Cultural Intelligence: Theory, Measurement and Applications*, ed. Soon Ang and Linn Van Dyne (Armonk, NY: M. E. Sharpe, 2008), xv.
3. Ang and Van Dyne, "Preface and Acknowledgments."
4. Kwok Leung, Soon Ang, and Mei Ling Tan, "Intercultural Competence," *Annual Review of Organizational Psychology and Organizational Behavior* 1 (2014): 489–519. https://doi.org/10.1146/annurev-orgpsych-031413-091229.
5. John Berry, "Culturally Competent Service," *Library Journal* 124, no. 14 (1999): 112.
6. Patricia Montiel Overall, Annabelle Villaescusa Nunez, and Veronica Reyes-Escudero, *Latinos in Libraries, Museums, and Archives* (Lanham, MD: Rowman & Littlefield, 2016), 23.
7. Terry L. Cross et al., *Towards a Culturally Competent System of Care: A Monograph on Effective Services for Minority Children Who Are Severely Emotionally Disturbed* (Washington, DC: CASSP Technical Assistance Center, Georgetown University Child Development Center, 1989), https://files.eric.ed.gov/fulltext/ED330171.pdf.
8. Patricia Montiel Overall, "Cultural Competence: A Conceptual Framework for Library and Information Science Professionals," *Library Quarterly* 79, no. 2 (2009): 176, https://doi.org/10.1086/597080.
9. Nicole A. Cooke. *Information Services to Diverse Populations* (Santa Barbara, CA: Libraries Unlimited, 2017), 18.
10. Alexia Hudson-Ward, "Eyeing the New Diversity," *American Libraries*, August 18, 2014, https://americanlibrariesmagazine.org/2014/08/18/eyeing-the-new-diversity/.
11. Hudson-Ward, "Eyeing the New Diversity."
12. Overall, "Cultural Competence"; Elizabeth Ramsey, "Cross-cultural Competence for Librarians." *PNLA Quarterly* 78, no. 1 (Fall 2013): 8–10, https://core.ac.uk/download/pdf/61745502.pdf; Mitch Fontenot, "Diversity: A Task Force: Survey of the Literature and Some Possible Trends for Academic Libraries," *Louisiana Libraries* 73, no. 1 (Summer 2010): 8–11; Jenny Lynne Semenza, Regina Koury, and Sandra Shropshire, "Diversity at Work in Academic Libraries 2010–2015: An Annotated Bibliography." *Collection Building* 36, no. 3. (2017): 89–95, https://doi.org/10.1108/CB-12-2016-0038; Association of Research Libraries, "Iowa State University Library Staff Build Cultural Competence to Improve Equity, Inclusion," accessed January 17, 2020, https://www.arl.org/iowa-state-university-library-staff-build-cultural-competence-to-improve-equity-inclusion/.
13. Orolando Augustus Duffus et al., "Diversity from the Inside Out: Eight Years of the UNCG Libraries Diversity Committee," *North Carolina Libraries* 74, no. 1 (2016): 25, http://www.ncl.ecu.edu/index.php/NCL/article/viewFile/728/785.
14. Lori S. Mestre, "Librarians Working with Diverse Populations: What Impact Does Cultural Competency Training Have on Their Efforts?" *Journal of Academic Librarianship* 36, no. 6 (2010): 479–88, https://doi.org/10.1016/j.acalib.2010.08.003.
15. Wang and Su, "Developing Future Library Leaders."
16. Association of College and Research Libraries, "Diversity Standards: Cultural Competency for Academic Libraries," May 4, 2012, http://www.ala.org/acrl/standards/diversity.

17. P. Christopher Earley and Soon Ang, *Cultural Intelligence* (Stanford, CA: Stanford University Press, 2003), 59.

18. Soon Ang, Linn Van Dyne, and Mei Ling Tan, "Cultural Intelligence," in *The Cambridge Handbook of Intelligence*, ed. Robert J. Sternberg and Scott Barry Kaufman, Cambridge Handbooks in Psychology (Cambridge: Cambridge University Press, 2011), 583, https://doi.org/10.1017/CBO9780511977244.030.

19. Soon Ang and Linn Van Dyne, "Conceptualization of Cultural Intelligence: Definition, Distinctiveness, and Nomological Network," in *Handbook on Cultural Intelligence: Theory, Measurement, and Applications*, ed. Soon Ang and Linn Van Dyne (Armonk, NY: M. E. Sharpe, 2008), 3–15.

20. David Livermore, *Leading with Cultural Intelligence* (New York: Amacom, 2010).

21. There is a validated cultural intelligence assessment tool that measures one's cultural intelligence level based on this framework. Linn Van Dyne, Soon Ang, and Christine Koh, "Development and Validation of the CQS," in *Handbook of Cultural Intelligence: Theory, Measurement, and Applications*, ed. Soon Ang and Linn Van Dyne (New York: M. E. Sharpe, 2008), 16–38.

22. Cultural Intelligence Center, "Cultural Values Profile," accessed December 18, 2019, https://culturalq.com/products-services/assessments/cultural-values-profile/cv-profile/; Cultural Intelligence Center, "Research Basis of Cultural Values," https://culturalq.com/wp-content/uploads/2019/03/Research-Basis-of-CV_v.1.19.pdf.

23. "In 1990, Marilyn Loden and Judy Rosener developed a framework for thinking about the different dimensions of diversity within individuals and institutions. Depicted as concentric circles, this 'Diversity Wheel' can be used in many different ways to encourage thinking about values, beliefs, and dimensions of identity for people and organizations." Cultural Competence Learning Institute, "Diversity Wheel," 2020, https://community.astc.org/ccli/resources-for-action/group-activities/diversity-wheel.

24. P. Christopher Earley, Soon Ang, and Joo-Seng Tan, *CQ* (Stanford, CA: Stanford University Press, 2006), 105.

25. Earley, Ang, and Tan, *CQ*, 209–210.

26. Sandra Upton, "Tiffin University Expands CQ Campus-wide," *Cultural Intelligence Center* blog, January 14, 2020, https://culturalq.com/blog/tiffin-university-expands-cq-campus-wide/.

27. Thomas F. Nelson Laird, "Measuring the Diversity Inclusivity of College Courses," *Research in Higher Education* 52, no. 6 (2011)): 572–88, https://doi.org/10.1007/s11162-010-9210-3.

28. Edna Chun and Alvin Evans, *The Department Chair as Transformative Diversity Leader* (Sterling, VA: Stylus, 2014), 223.

29. Fiona Blackburn, "'Cultural Competence Is for Everyone': Cultural Competence in the United States Library and Information Sector. Is It Relevant to Australian Libraries?" *Australian Academic and Research Libraries* 46, no. 3 (2015): 176–93. https://doi.org/10.1080/00048623.2015.1063800.

30. Goretti Kabatangare Tumuhairwe, "Analysis of Library and Information Science/Studies (LIS) Education Today: The Inclusion of Indigenous Knowledge and Multicultural Issues in LIS Curriculum" (paper presented at IFLA WLIC 2013: Future Libraries: Infinite Possibilities, Singapore, August 15–23, 2013), http://library.ifla.org/276/1/125-tumhuwaire-en.pdf.

31. Christine Pawley, "Unequal Legacies: Race and Multiculturalism in the LIS Curriculum," *Library Quarterly* 76, no. 2 (April 2006): 149–68, https://doi.org/10.1086/506955.

32. Pawley, "Unequal Legacies," 153.

33. Elizabeth Foster, "Cultural Competence in Library Instruction: A Reflective Practice Approach," *portal: Libraries and the Academy* 18, no. 3 (2018): 575, https://doi.org/10.1353/pla.2018.0034.

34. Gloria Ladson-Billings, *The Dreamkeepers*, Jossey-Bass Education Series (San Francisco: Jossey-Bass 1994), 17–18.

35. Mestre, "Librarians Working with Diverse Populations."

36. Kafi Kumasi and Renee Franklin Hill, "Are We There Yet? Results of a Gap Analysis to Measure LIS Students' Prior Knowledge and Actual Learning of Cultural Competence Concepts," *Journal of Education for Library and Information Science* 52, no. 4 (2011): 251–64. https://www.jstor.org/stable/41308902.

37. Michele A. L. Villagran and Suliman Hawamdeh, "Cultural Competence in LIS Education: Case Study of United States Ranked Schools," *Multicultural Education Review* 12, no. 2 (2020): 136–55, https://doi.org/10.1080/2005615X.2020.1756091.

38. Krista M. Soria, Jan Fransen, and Shane Nackerud, "Library Use and Undergraduate Student Outcomes: New Evidence for Students' Retention and Academic Success," *portal: Libraries and the Academy* 13, no. 2 (2013): 147–64, https://doi.org/10.1353/pla.2013.0010.

39. Yared Mammo Cherinet, "Blended Skills and Future Roles of Librarians," *Library Management* 39, no. 1/2 (2018): 100, https://doi.org/10.1108/LM-02-2017-0015.

40. San José State University School of Information, "Master of Library and Information Science Skills at Work: A Snapshot of Job Postings Spring 2019," accessed December 2, 2019, https://ischool.sjsu.edu/sites/default/files/content_pdf/career_trends.pdf (2019 information deleted from page).

41. Michele A. L. Villagran, "A Study of the Cultural Intelligence of Special Libraries: Phase 1," *Qualitative and Quantitative Methods in Libraries* 9, no. 2 (June 2020): 285–300, http://www.qqml-journal.net/index.php/qqml/article/view/522; Michele A. L. Villagran, "Impact of Cultural Intelligence within Special Libraries: Focus Group Findings and Results," *Qualitative and Quantitative Methods in Libraries* 9, no. 2 (June 2020), 207–17, http://www.qqml.net/index.php/qqml/article/view/631.

42. Michele A. L. Villagran, "Phenomena of Cultural Intelligence in Pennsylvania Libraries: A Research Study," *Pennsylvania Libraries: Research and Practice* 8, no. 1 (2020): 7–36, https://doi.org/10.5195/palrap.2020.221.

43. Livermore, *Leading with Cultural Intelligence.*

44. Cultural Intelligence Center, "Academic Construct Validity," https://culturalq.com/wp-content/uploads/2019/10/Academic-Constuct-Validity_v.3.19.pdf; David Matsumoto and Hyisung C. Hwang, "Assessing Cross-cultural Competence: A Review of Available Tests," *Journal of Cross-cultural Psychology* 44, no. 6 (August 2013): 849–73, https://doi.org/10.1177/0022022113492891.

45. Note: There has been research to confirm that there are differences between cultural intelligence and emotional intelligence. Kerri A. Crowne, "The Relationships among Social Intelligence, Emotional Intelligence and Cultural Intelligence," *Organization Management Journal* 6, no. 3 (2009): 148–63, https://doi.org/10.1057/omj.2009.20; Thomas Rockstuhl et al., "Beyond General Intelligence (IQ) and Emotional Intelligence (EQ): The Role of Cultural Intelligence (CQ) on Cross-border Leadership Effectiveness in a Globalized World," *Journal of Social Issues* 67, no. 4 (December 2011): 825–840, https://doi.org/10.1111/j.1540-4560.2011.01730.x.

46. SHRM Foundation, *Cultural Intelligence* (Alexandria, VA: SHRM, 2015), 16, https://www.shrm.org/hr-today/trends-and-forecasting/special-reports-and-expert-views/Documents/Cultural-Intelligence.pdf.

Bibliography

Ang, Soon, and Linn Van Dyne, eds. *Handbook of Cultural Intelligence: Theory, Measurement and Applications.* New York: Routledge, 2008.

Ang, Soon, Linn Van Dyne, and Mei Ling Tan. "Cultural Intelligence." In *The Cambridge Handbook of Intelligence.* Edited by Robert J. Sternberg and Scott Barry Kaufman, 582–602. Cambridge Handbooks in Psychology. Cambridge: Cambridge University Press, 2011. https://doi.org/10.1017/CBO9780511977244.030.

Association of College and Research Libraries. "Diversity Standards: Cultural Competency for Academic Libraries." May 4, 2012. http://www.ala.org/acrl/standards/diversity.

Association of Research Libraries. "Iowa State University Library Staff Build Cultural Competence to Improve Equity, Inclusion." Accessed January 17, 2020. https://www.arl.org/iowa-state-university-library-staff-build-cultural-competence-to-improve-equity-inclusion/.

Berry, John. "Culturally Competent Service." *Library Journal* 124, no. 14 (1999): 112.

Blackburn, Fiona. "'Cultural Competence Is for Everyone': Cultural Competence in the United States Library and Information Sector. Is It Relevant to Australian Libraries?" *Australian Academic and Research Libraries* 46, no. 3 (2015): 176–93. https://doi.org/10.1080/00048623.2015.1063800.

Cherinet, Yared Mammo. "Blended Skills and Future Roles of Librarians." *Library Management* 39, no. 1/2 (2018): 93–105. https://doi.org/10.1108/LM-02-2017-0015.

Chun, Edna, and Alvin Evans. *The Department Chair as Transformative Diversity Leader: Building Inclusive Learning Environments in Higher Education.* Sterling, VA: Stylus, 2014.

Cooke, Nicole A. *Information Services to Diverse Populations: Developing Culturally Competent Library Professionals.* Santa Barbara, CA: Libraries Unlimited, 2017.

Cross, Terry L., Barbara J. Bazron, Karl W. Dennis, and Mareasa R. Isaacs. *Towards a Culturally Competent System of Care: A Monograph on Effective Services for Minority Children Who Are Severely Emotionally Disturbed.* Washington, DC: CASSP Technical Assistance Center, Georgetown University Child Development Center, 1989. https://files.eric.ed.gov/fulltext/ED330171.pdf.

Crowne, Kerri A. "The Relationships among Social Intelligence, Emotional Intelligence and Cultural Intelligence." *Organization Management Journal* 6, no. 3 (2009): 148–63. https://doi.org/10.1057/omj.2009.20.

Cultural Competence Learning Institute. "Diversity Wheel." 2020. https://community.astc.org/ccli/resources-for-action/group-activities/diversity-wheel.

Cultural Intelligence Center. "Academic Construct Validity." https://culturalq.com/wp-content/uploads/2019/10/Academic-Constuct-Validity_v.3.19.pdf.

———. "Cultural Values Profile." Accessed December 18, 2019. https://culturalq.com/products-services/assessments/cultural-values-profile/cv-profile/.

———. "Research Basis of Cultural Values." https://culturalq.com/wp-content/uploads/2019/03/Research-Basis-of-CV_v.1.19.pdf.

Duffus, Orolando Augustus, Tiffany Henry, Jada Jones, and Stacey Krim. "Diversity from the Inside Out: Eight Years of the UNCG Libraries Diversity Committee." *North Carolina Libraries* 74, no. 1 (2016): 25–29. http://www.ncl.ecu.edu/index.php/NCL/article/viewFile/728/785.

Earley, P. Christopher, and Soon Ang. *Cultural Intelligence: Individual Interactions Across Cultures.* Stanford, CA: Stanford University Press, 2003.

Earley, P. Christopher, Soon Ang and Joo-Seng Tan. *CQ: Developing Cultural Intelligence at Work.* Stanford, CA: Stanford University Press, 2006.

———. "Developing and Implementing a Diversity Plan at Your Academic Library." *Library Leadership and Management* 30, no. 2 (2016): 1–11. https://pdfs.semanticscholar.org/13ba/f3bf97e364f4552d88a256a9c03c72cd3d96.pdf.

Fontenot, Mitch. "Diversity: A Task Force: Survey of the Literature and Some Possible Trends for Academic Libraries." *Louisiana Libraries* 73, no. 1 (Summer 2010): 8–11.

Foster, Elizabeth. "Cultural Competence in Library Instruction: A Reflective Practice Approach." *portal: Libraries and the Academy* 18, no. 3 (2018): 575–93. https://doi.org/10.1353/pla.2018.0034.

Hudson-Ward, Alexia. "Eyeing the New Diversity." *American Libraries*, August 18, 2014. https://americanlibrariesmagazine.org/2014/08/18/eyeing-the-new-diversity/.

Kumasi, Kafi, and Renee Franklin Hill. "Are We There Yet? Results of a Gap Analysis to Measure LIS Students' Prior Knowledge and Actual Learning of Cultural Competence Concepts." *Journal of Education for Library and Information Science* 52, no. 4 (2011): 251–64. https://www.jstor.org/stable/41308902.

Ladson-Billings, Gloria. *The Dreamkeepers: Successful Teachers of African American Children.* Jossey-Bass Education Series. San Francisco: Jossey-Bass, 1994.

Leung, Kwok, Soon Ang, and Mei Ling Tan. "Intercultural Competence." *Annual Review of Organizational Psychology and Organizational Behavior* 1 (2014): 489–519. https://doi.org/10.1146/annurev-orgpsych-031413-091229.

Livermore, David. *Leading with Cultural Intelligence.* New York: Amacom, 2010.

Matsumoto, David, and Hyisung C. Hwang. "Assessing Cross-cultural Competence: A Review of Available Tests." *Journal of Cross-cultural Psychology* 44, no. 6 (August 2013): 849–73. https://doi.org/10.1177/0022022113492891.

Mestre, Lori S. "Librarians Working with Diverse Populations: What Impact Does Cultural Competency Training Have on Their Efforts?" *Journal of Academic Librarianship* 36, no. 6 (2010): 479–88. https://doi.org/10.1016/j.acalib.2010.08.003.

Montiel-Overall, Patricia. "Cultural Competence: A Conceptual Framework for Library and Information Science Professionals." *Library Quarterly* 79, no. 2 (2009): 175–204. https://doi.org/10.1086/597080.

Montiel-Overall, Patricia, Annabelle Villaescusa Nunez, and Veronica Reyes-Escudero. *Latinos in Libraries, Museums, and Archives: Cultural Competence in Action! An Asset-Based Approach.* Lanham, MD: Rowman & Littlefield, 2016.

Nelson Laird, Thomas F. "Measuring the Diversity Inclusivity of College Courses." *Research in Higher Education* 52, no. 6 (2011): 572–88. https://doi.org/10.1007/s11162-010-9210-3.

Pawley, Christine. "Unequal Legacies: Race and Multiculturalism in the LIS Curriculum." *Library Quarterly* 76, no. 2 (April 2006): 149–68. https://doi.org/10.1086/506955.

Ramsey, Elizabeth. "Cross-cultural Competence for Librarians." *PNLA Quarterly* 78, no. 1 (Fall 2013): 8–10. https://core.ac.uk/download/pdf/61745502.pdf.

Rockstuhl, Thomas, Stefan Seiler, Soon Ang, Linn Van Dyne, and Hubert Annen. "Beyond General Intelligence (IQ) and Emotional Intelligence (EQ): The Role of Cultural Intelligence (CQ) on Cross-border Leadership Effectiveness in a Globalized World." *Journal of Social Issues* 67, no. 4 (December 2011): 825–840. https://doi.org/10.1111/j.1540-4560.2011.01730.x.

San José State University School of Information. "Master of Library and Information Science Skills at Work: A Snapshot of Job Postings Spring 2019." Accessed December 2, 2019. https://ischool.sjsu.edu/sites/default/files/content_pdf/career_trends.pdf (2019 information deleted from page).

Semenza, Jenny Lynne, Regina Koury, and Sandra Shropshire. "Diversity at Work in Academic Libraries 2010–2015: An Annotated Bibliography." *Collection Building* 36, no. 3. (2017): 89–95. https://doi.org/10.1108/CB-12-2016-0038.

SHRM Foundation. *Cultural Intelligence: The Essential Intelligence for the 21st Century.* Alexandria, VA: SHRM, 2015. https://www.shrm.org/hr-today/trends-and-forecasting/special-reports-and-expert-views/Documents/Cultural-Intelligence.pdf.

Soria, Krista M., Jan Fransen, and Shane Nackerud. "Library Use and Undergraduate Student Outcomes: New Evidence for Students' Retention and Academic Success." *portal: Libraries and the Academy* 13, no. 2 (2013): 147–64. https://doi.org/10.1353/pla.2013.0010.

Tumuhairwe, Goretti Kabatangare. "Analysis of Library and Information Science/Studies (LIS) Education Today: The Inclusion of Indigenous Knowledge and Multicultural Issues in LIS Curriculum." Paper presented at IFLA WLIC 2013: Future Libraries: Infinite Possibilities, Singapore, August 15–23, 2013. http://library.ifla.org/276/1/125-tumhuwaire-en.pdf.

Upton, Sandra. "Tiffin University Expands CQ Campus-wide." *Cultural Intelligence Center* blog, January 14, 2020. https://culturalq.com/blog/tiffin-university-expands-cq-campus-wide/.

Van Dyne, Linn, Soon Ang, and Christine Koh. "Development and Validation of the CQS." In *Handbook of Cultural Intelligence: Theory, Measurement, and Applications.* Edited by Soon Ang and Linn Van Dyne, 16–38. New York: Sharpe, 2008.

Villagran, Michele A. L. "Impact of Cultural Intelligence within Special Libraries: Focus Group Findings and Results." *Qualitative and Quantitative Methods in Libraries* 9, no. 2 (June 2020), 207–17. http://www.qqml.net/index.php/qqml/article/view/631.

———. "Phenomena of Cultural Intelligence in Pennsylvania Libraries: A Research Study." *Pennsylvania Libraries: Research and Practice* 8, no. 1 (2020): 7–36. https://doi.org/10.5195/palrap.2020.221.

———. "A Study of the Cultural Intelligence of Special Libraries: Phase 1." *Qualitative and Quantitative Methods in Libraries* 9, no. 2 (June 2020): 285–300. http://www.qqml-journal.net/index.php/qqml/article/view/522.

Villagran, Michele A. L., and Suliman Hawamdeh. "Cultural Competence in LIS Education: Case Study of United States Ranked Schools." *Multicultural Education Review* 12, no. 2 (2020): 136–55. https://doi.org/10.1080/2005615X.2020.1756091.

Wang, Xuemao, and Chang Su. "Developing Future Library Leaders in the Context of Globalization with an Analysis on Cultural Intelligence (CQ)." In *Library Management and Marketing in a Multicultural World: Proceedings of the 2006 IFLA Management and Marketing Section's Conference.* Edited by James L. Mullins, 303–22. Munich, Germany: K. G. Saur, 2007.

SECTION III

Leveraging Collegial Networks

CHAPTER 11

Braving Our Blind Spots

Using a Virtual Book Discussion Group to Continue Conversations on Implicit Bias in Libraries

Shannon Jones, Kelsa Bartley, Melissa DeSantis, Ryan Harris, Don Jason, and Dede Rios

Introduction

Increasing the racial and ethnic diversity of the workforce in libraries throughout the United States has been a strategic priority for years, yet statistically the homogeneous nature of library staffs remains the same. Statistics from the American Library Association's *2017 ALA Demographic Study* indicates that librarianship is a largely white female profession.[1] This homogeneity is likely a contributing factor to the implicit bias that individuals from marginalized groups feel in librarianship. An implicit bias occurs when we have attitudes toward people, or associate stereotypes with them, without our conscious knowledge.[2] Growing research indicates that implicit biases impact the actions we take and decisions we make in our personal and professional lives. Every day, each of us makes decisions in our professional lives that impact who gets hired, supported, promoted, and admitted, and which programs get funded. Implicit bias impacts

the decisions we make in our personal lives too, from the neighborhoods in which we choose to live and the schools we attend to the friends with whom we associate. Implicit bias is pervasive in all we do. Its effects are long-lasting and detrimental to the recipient. The key to mitigating implicit bias is awareness and action. Uncovering implicit biases is the first step toward appreciating and leveraging the unique differences that each of us brings to every setting or situation.

In this chapter, the group organizers discuss the use of a virtual book club to provide a forum for dialogue on implicit bias. The authors share insights gained from planning and facilitating a virtual discussion group for over fifty medical librarians using Mahzarin Banaji and Anthony G. Greenwald's book, *Blindspot: The Hidden Biases of Good People* as a platform for safe and thought-provoking dialogue.[3] The discussion groups provided participants the opportunity to share their unique perspectives in a small-group setting. This intimate environment, though virtual, provided increased participant awareness of ingrained narratives learned throughout their lifetimes and afforded opportunities for each to learn more effective ways to communicate across their differences. This team of facilitators worked together to create a bank of questions for each chapter, PowerPoints to share with each group, a shared document for post-session notes, and a communication plan to keep everyone on track. This helped build community and prepare the facilitators, especially for those who lacked experience or confidence in leading online discussion groups. Authors will share insights addressing the benefits and challenges of organizing a virtual book discussion group.

Implicit Bias and Microaggressions Defined

Oxford Learner's Dictionaries define *bias* as a prejudice in favor of or against one thing, person, or group compared with another, usually in a way considered to be unfair.[4] While bias might be a concept that is familiar to many librarians, the purpose of the book club was to allow librarians to gain a deeper understanding of the concept of *implicit bias*. The Kirwan Institute for the Study of Race and Ethnicity defines *implicit bias* as "the attitudes or stereotypes that affect our understanding, actions, and decisions in an unconscious manner. They are "activated involuntarily, without awareness or intentional control. Can be either positive or negative. Everyone is susceptible."[5] Implicit bias is something ingrained in us. It is something we cannot control in most instances. It can unknowingly impact how we interact with our peers and also how we provide services to our patrons. Book club participants agreed that gaining greater insight about our own implicit biases, and their impact on our interactions with others, was important for librarians to know. While the uncontrollable nature of implicit bias can make it a difficult and painful conversation for many, the idea to have frank discussions around the topic is important. Gaining a better understanding of the concept has the potential to allow for reflection and growth, and can impact how librarians engage with colleagues, our patrons, and the world at large.

This understanding of how implicit bias can impact daily interactions is an important one, as many people experience microaggressions on a day-to-day basis. Sue and colleagues define them this way:

> Racial microaggressions are brief and commonplace daily verbal, behavioral, or environmental indignities, whether intentional or unintentional, that communicate hostile, derogatory, or negative racial slights and insults toward people of color. Perpetrators of microaggressions are often unaware that they engage in such communications when they interact with racial/ethnic minorities.[6]

This definition makes it clear that many instances of hostile words, interactions, and behavior can be unintentional at times. Like implicit bias, microaggressions are often insidious in nature and not done in an overt or knowing matter. The fact that so many create this hostile and unfriendly environment without being aware makes it even more dangerous. It is also imperative to note that microaggressions are not limited only to people of color. Microaggressions can also be directed at people due to their gender, sexual orientation, religion, social class, or other personal characteristics, including immigration status.[7] Librarians can face microaggressions in the workplace. A 2014 study by Jaena Alabi discussed the microaggressions experienced by both minority and nonminority academic librarians in the workplace. Some of the experiences included assumption that another librarian would have a lower education because of their race, being ignored at work because of their race, being told that all racial groups have the same obstacles, and acting surprised at another librarian's professional successes because of their race.[8] An awareness that many librarians are experiencing these microaggressions on a day-to-day basis is vital. In doing so, there is the hope that actions can be taken to create a more welcoming environment for all. While this is not an easy task, it is crucial to have an understanding of the concepts of implicit bias and microaggressions to be more prepared to respond to these challenges.

The Book: Blindspot: The Hidden Biases of Good People

One method to support increased awareness about implicit bias was to engage colleagues in reading and discussing Mahzarin Banaji and Anthony G. Greenwald's *Blindspot: Hidden Biases of Good People*. Published in 2013, *Blindspot* has been described as an accessible and authoritative guide to understanding how our brains' cognitive processes create implicit or hidden biases, how we can become aware of them, and how we can begin to mitigate these biases.[9] The book explains how our brains produce visual, memory, and social "mindbugs" while attempting to process and interpret the myriad stimuli, data, and information we are constantly bombarded with. Banaji and Greenwald define mindbugs as "ingrained habits of thought that lead to errors in how we perceive, remember, reason, and make decisions."[10] These cognitive mindbugs create blind spots or gaps in the way we see and remember things and in our social interactions with each other. Blind spots prevent us from seeing the inherent biases that contribute to the creation of stereotypes, explicit prejudices, and widespread systemic discrimination.

Banaji and Greenwald's research led to the development of the Implicit Association Test (IAT) to assist in revealing and assessing levels of hidden bias. The IAT measures attitudes and beliefs that people may be unwilling or unable to report using other methods.[11] The IAT may be especially interesting if it reveals an unknown implicit attitude, perception, or stereotype to the test taker. The IAT was designed to address the psychological concept of dissociation that often occurs between our rational minds and automatic minds. Dissociation is defined as "the occurrence, in one and the same mind, of mutually inconsistent ideas that remain isolated from one another. "[12] We may be thinking one way in our rational minds, but acting based on biases in our automatic minds, to which we can be completely blind. The premise is that we need to become aware of the cognitive dissonance that continually occurs in our everyday lives so that we can be prepared to mitigate the effects of the biases they cause.

The Race IAT was one of the first IATs developed and features prominently in the book *Blindspot*. The authors spend considerable time discussing how biases and stereotypes continue to contribute to systemic racial discrimination in America. However, the book also mentions other significant IATs, such as the Gender-Career IAT, and how gender stereotypes continue to color our perceptions of women in the workplace. There are now fourteen IATs on the Project Implicit website hosted by Harvard University, including IATs on sexuality, religion, weight, age, disability, ethnicity, and skin tone.[13] To date, millions of people have taken IATs, with all the data collected publicly available for further research.

"Outsmarting the Machine," the book's last chapter, offers ideas and examples for outsmarting the cognitive mindbugs that create hidden biases. The authors conclude that eradicating them may be impossible now but are optimistic that becoming aware of them is the first step to reducing the effects of bias on our society and systems.

Book Discussion Groups as a Learning Tool

Blindspot provided the perfect content for discussing implicit bias, which allowed the organizers to focus their energies on developing a virtual learning environment where participants could learn, discuss, and process the implications of biases on their work as information professionals and in their personal lives. Book discussion groups have also become popular on college campuses and within a variety of communities. Universities such as Virginia Commonwealth University, the University of Denver, the University of Miami, and many others sponsor Common Reading programs, where incoming students discuss a common book, often as part of the first-year experience.[14] Penguin Random House maintains a curated list of titles from across all its publishing divisions of books being used in common and community reads programs on its Common Reads website.[15] The website also features an annual list of books used at colleges and universities around the country.[16] Penguin also sponsors its First-Year Experience Conference annually.[17]

Public libraries throughout the US host One City, One Book programs such as Santa Monica Reads; One Book, One San Diego; One Book, Two Villages; One Book, One Philadelphia; Lake Oswego Reads; and Sonoma County Reads to encourage patrons to read and discuss the same book. Many of these public libraries have received grant funding from the National Endowment for the Arts (NEA) Big Read program. The NEA Big Read's goal is to showcase a diverse range of contemporary titles that reflect many different voices and perspectives with the aims of inspiring conversation and discovery.[18] Since its start in 2006, the NEA Big Read has supported approximately seventy-five dynamic community reading programs annually. Each community program that receives an NEA Big Read grant is also provided with resources, outreach materials, and training.[19] The National Network of Libraries of Medicine's Reading Club provides a selection of ready-to-use book titles along with free and downloadable materials designed to help libraries support health information needs in their communities.[20]

Historically, most book discussion groups are held in face-to-face settings, though the online environment is becoming more popular. The book discussion group highlighted in this chapter uses a hybrid model featuring four online and one in-person sessions. The in-person session was held at a professional library conference. The hybrid model has proven to be an exciting engagement format as it offered participants the opportunity to interact and build relationships with new colleagues and those from diverse backgrounds.

Discussion Group Organization and Logistics

The Medical Library Association's (MLA) Discussion Group Program provides participants the opportunity to explore a topic of interest with other professionals and earn continuing education (CE) contact hours for professional development.[21] Groups, consisting of three to ten people, may meet in person or hold discussions online.[22] The programs' goals are to promote professional interchange and provide opportunities for professional growth and development. Participants could claim up to seven hours CE credit depending on their attendance level and the completion of the evaluation form. The program required that groups spend eight hours of time in discussion within twelve months of the starting date. Based on these criteria and the book length, the discussion was divided into four 90-minute monthly sessions and one in-person session to be held at the MLA 2019 Annual Meeting (see table 11.1). *Blindspot* consists of eight chapters, so the group discussed two chapters during each of the four online sessions. The onsite session focused on a discussion of the book's appendixes and other topics the participants proposed. This session was replicated virtually for attendees who were unable to attend the May 2019 conference.

TABLE 11.1
Session Breakdown

Session I January 2019	Chapter 1: Mindbugs Chapter 2: Shades of Truth
Session II February	Chapter 3: Into the Blindspot Chapter 4: Not That There's Anything Wrong with That
Session III March	Chapter 5: Homo Categoricus Chapter 6: The Hidden Costs of Stereotypes
Session IV April	Chapter 7: Us and Them Chapter 8: Outsmarting the Machine
Session V On-site at MLA'19 Annual Conference	Appendix 1: Are Americans Racist? Appendix 2: Race, Disadvantage, and Discrimination Overall discussion feedback Steps for claiming MLA continuing education credit Next Steps

The book discussion group was made possible by a funding award the project leader applied for and received from the National Network of Libraries of Medicine/Southeastern Atlantic Region (NNLM/SEA) on behalf of the African American Medical Librarians Alliance (AAMLA) special interest group (SIG).[23] The initial purpose was to sponsor a ninety-minute session at the 2018 Annual Meeting of the Medical Library Association titled "Transforming Libraries through Implicit Bias Training." Two outcomes emerged from this session: the creation of a four-hour CE course ("Implicit Bias for Information Professionals") and the MLA Reads Virtual Book Club. The latter is discussed in this chapter. Award funding was used in 2018 to pay the featured speaker's travel costs to attend the annual meeting and to purchase twenty-five books to distribute to attendees with the hope that recipients would want to join the virtual discussion. The session featured engaging speakers, hands-on activities, and thought-provoking dialogue. During the informal feedback phase, the session facilitators asked the attendees about potential behavioral changes they might make based on this new knowledge. It was at this time that several attendees expressed a desire to keep the conversation going. Ninety minutes was just not enough time to fully process the implications of implicit bias. The attendees wanted to learn more. They did not want this to be another high-energy conference session that came and went with no real outcomes. At the session's conclusion, at least thirty people indicated an interest in participating in the virtual discussion, and several expressed a willingness to serve as discussion group leaders.

A formal participation invitation was sent to identify prospective participants and additional facilitators immediately following the conference. The organizers used a variety of mechanisms to identify participants, including sending messages to e-mail discussion groups, word of mouth, and marketing at regional conferences and annual meetings. Of those strategies, word of mouth proved to be an effective recruitment strategy as individuals who attended the onsite session encouraged colleagues at their respective institutions to participate. Library professionals from all library types were welcome, though the participants were largely academic and hospital library personnel. Ultimately, ten facilitators were recruited to lead nine groups, and seventy-five librarians signed up to participate. At least one group had co-facilitators. All participant e-mails were added to a Google Group to facilitate easy communication with the participants. The remaining grant funds were used to purchase another fifty books to distribute to the participants. The book was shipped to participants at no cost while a few others opted to acquire their own copy.

Once the books were distributed, the facilitators met virtually to plan the discussion so that it met the MLA Book Club Program requirements. Each facilitator was not only responsible for reading the book but was also assigned to prepare a summary and develop discussion questions for a specific chapter. Facilitators also located supplemental materials to accompany their chapters. These materials included websites, documentaries, and articles that allowed for further exploration of the themes featured in their chapter. All of this work was stored in a Google Drive folder.

The authors used the Google Groups and Drive services extensively throughout the project. The facilitators developed a communication and engagement plan in tandem with the enrollment phase. The plan included the creation of a Google Group to facilitate information exchange with attendees. Support provided included the creation of standard discussion questions, presentation slides, attendance sheets, and other documentation using Google's collaboration and productivity tools.

The organizer's goal was to provide participants options to meet virtually across a variety of days and times and in multiple time zones. All facilitators were asked to identify a consistent date and time to host their discussion group: for example, the first Thursday of the month at 10 a.m. or the second Tuesday of the month at 1 p.m. Facilitators were also asked to indicate which videoconferencing tool (Google Hangouts, Zoom, Webex, etc.) they would use based on personal preference or the tool that was available at their institution. Using this information, the organizers created a group registration form using the Signup Zone scheduling tool.[24] This allowed participants to join the group that worked best for their schedules. Group membership was capped at ten participants per group in addition to the facilitators. During the enrollment phase, participants received a "Meet the Facilitators" handout that included the headshots and bios to use as they were choosing a group.

Once enrollment was complete, a virtual welcome session was held to orient participants to the book club, to set expectations for engaging in respectful discussions, to introduce the facilitators, and to respond to any questions or concerns the participants had.

Facilitator Training

No formal training was offered to facilitators for the first installment of the book club. During the *Blindspot* discussion, facilitators had a series of virtual check-in meetings with organizers and other facilitators. During these meetings, facilitators received informal coaching and were able to ask questions and share concerns. In the evaluation, the facilitators who led the *Blindspot* discussion stated that they would have benefited from training. This suggestion was seen multiple times in the evaluation and heard through anecdotal feedback provided to organizers. Therefore, the organizers of the book club decided to implement training for the next installment of MLA Reads. When the training was implemented, it primarily focused on the mechanics, technology, and interpersonal skills needed to lead virtual book discussions. In hindsight, the training should have focused on guiding difficult conversations and embracing discussion topics that may go beyond facilitators' comfort zones.

There were several planning meetings in the summer and fall of 2018, leading up to the *Blindspot* discussion that launched in January 2019. During these meetings, the organizers and facilitators prepared chapter summaries, wrote chapter discussion questions, and developed icebreaker activities. These efforts provide consistency in the book discussion curriculum. One goal of the meetings was to help the facilitators become comfortable leading a virtual discussion, since many of them had no prior experience doing so. These meetings also provided the facilitators opportunities to bond with one another and share experiences. It also served as a forum for setting expectations and addressing concerns. Some of the initial concerns included using strategies for sparking and guiding dialogue, addressing scheduling conflicts for facilitators and participants, and managing technical issues.

After the *Blindspot* discussion concluded, book club organizers began developing the training for the next installment of MLA Reads. To do this, they identified best practices for leading book clubs and discussion groups in the literature. The organizers adopted some of these practices and modified strategies for a virtual environment. The organizers pulled additional best practices from their experience leading the *Blindspot* discussion. These best practices were used to create the facilitators' training session. The practices identified were divided into two components: what to do before each session and what to do during the session. Additional best practices include tips for guiding the discussion, the importance of body language, and avoiding technology glitches.

The facilitators were not given any formal training in diversity, equity, and inclusion (DEI). Facilitators were not expected to be DEI experts. However, we did expect them to have an eagerness to learn, a growth mindset, and a willingness to share their own experiences. At the inception of the book club, there was no way to anticipate how large it would get or how many facilitators would be needed to guide the participants. Nevertheless, this was a blind spot on the part of the planning committee. All facilitators should have participated in a standard DEI training exercise. This would have given all facilitators a baseline of training. This might have made them more comfortable leading their discussion groups.

Even with no formal DEI training, many facilitators pursued their own training. They read articles, viewed webinars, and listened to podcasts. Several facilitators received implicit bias training prior to signing up to lead discussion groups. They participated in a training session led by Kimberly Reynolds, MD, at the Medical Library Association Annual Meeting in 2018. This training session is where the initial twenty-five copies of *Blindspot* were distributed and where the first wave of facilitators were recruited.

What to Do before the First Virtual Discussion Session

Facilitators were encouraged to complete several tasks prior to leading their virtual session.[25] They were instructed to do the following:

- Finish the book early to allow sufficient time to review the content and prepare for the sessions.
- Be active readers. Facilitators should note specific passages that may spark discussion. Methods include using Post-it Notes, dog-earring pages, as well as underlining and highlighting text. This would allow facilitators to quickly reference specific passages during their group discussions.
- Familiarize themselves with the discussion questions. This allows facilitators to feel more comfortable, relaxed, and confident when reading the questions or guiding conversation back to the questions.
- Engage in consistent and timely communication with group members. Facilitators were encouraged to send e-mail reminders to the group prior to the session. Two to three reminders should be e-mailed at various times leading up to the session. The reminders should include discussion questions, chapter summaries, Zoom or Webex link, and a call-in phone number in the event the videoconferencing technology fails.

What to Do during the First Virtual Discussion Session

During the first session, facilitators were encouraged to determine what motivated members of their group to participate in the book club. Motivation can drive participation. Lack of confidence to speak in a group should not be mistaken for lack of motivation. In addition, knowing the personal motivation for each group member helps a facilitator meet participants' expectations and make the discussions more personalized.[26] Motivation varied from participant to participant. For example, some librarians participated to network with colleagues, while others were looking for a social outlet. Some may enjoy the subject matter and prefer an in-depth conversation, while others may prefer a more lighthearted approach to discussion. Facilitators needed to know this prior to engaging in discussion with their group members. This helped facilitators respond appropriately to group members and ensure everyone felt their voices had significance.[27] Overall, this kept group morale high and kept group members motivated to continue participating in the book club.

To uncover these motivations, facilitators were encouraged to conduct an icebreaker with their groups.[28] This could be as simple as having everyone on the call do a standard introduction. For example, they may state their name and their institutional affiliation, and disclose an interesting fact about themselves. Some facilitators took it a step further and created "virtual seating charts" with group members' headshots and bios. This allowed people to familiarize themselves with group members and put a face to a name.[29] Overall, this process of virtual introductions helped facilitators learn more about their group members. It made group members and facilitators more comfortable with each other. This comfort translated into a better ability to discuss the concepts and themes featured in the book.

The old adage that says first impressions are the most lasting holds true for virtual discussions too. The first session laid the foundation for the participants' entire MLA Reads experience. Therefore, facilitators were encouraged to promote equity. It was critical that facilitators encourage an environment where participants could express their opinions in constructive ways that kept the discussion open to all. Empowering participants to speak their truth was equally important. Facilitators were expected to cultivate virtual environments where people felt that their voice mattered and was heard while balancing participation and engagement so that one person's voice was not excessive. Facilitators were encouraged to keep their own thoughts and opinions in check as well, since their role was to ensure that the discussion progressed.[30]

What to Do during All Virtual Discussion Meetings

The discussion group sessions were very similar to other online discussions. In fact, facilitators were encouraged to pull from previous experiences leading or participating in virtual discussion groups. The subject matter made the discussion groups unique. Given the sensitive nature of DEI topics, maintaining the psychological safety of participants was paramount. Outside of the welcome session, discussion group sessions were not recorded. A commitment was made to upholding "Vegas rules," where conversations that happened in the group stayed in the group. This was important for making the participants feel comfortable sharing personal experiences with the group without fear of them being recorded and disclosed outside of the group. Facilitators were encouraged to do introductions for every meeting, as the possibility of new people joining the session was real. Once names were collected, facilitators were encouraged to use them during the call to create a more personal atmosphere. Facilitators were told to allow the discussion to build naturally. They were encouraged to preserve the momentum of the conversation even if they had to ask discussion questions out of order. They were empowered to go where the conversation led them with the caveat that the conversation should highlight concepts featured in the book.[31]

Facilitator contributions to the discussion should be thoughtful, inviting, and mindful. Accomplishing this requires that facilitators ask the questions and then let others respond prior to expressing their own opinions. In addition, facilitators should keep track of who is participating in the discussion and who is not so that they can invite quieter participants into the conversation.[32] Since the questions were shared by e-mail before the discussion meeting time, facilitators could contact a quiet member prior to the discussion day and ask if they could call on them for a specific question during the virtual discussion. This is done by directing questions to quieter members; for example, "Jayne, what are your thoughts on this chapter of the book?" This gives people who are introverts an opportunity to speak up or share their opinions. Facilitators also offered the option for participants to respond in the chat box and then read the comments aloud to the group, as that may be their preferred method of communication. Some may be too shy to speak out verbally while others may be participating in an open office environment with cubicles or in a public space that requires silence. These strategies worked. They created an open and free dialogue. Participants disclosed their blind spots and implicit biases.

Tips for Guiding the Discussion

There is a fine line between dominating the conversation and guiding the conversation in a virtual book discussion. Facilitators were encouraged to guide the conversation using the following strategies:

- Use a structured approach. For example, they might read a question and say, "Who wants to go first?" Then invite participants to respond in a round-robin fashion to the first question. Then let the dialogue flow naturally.

- Remember the specific role the facilitator plays in the group and stay alert. Since the discussion focused on diversity, equity, and inclusion topics, the conversation had the potential to become emotionally charged and heavy. Facilitators were encouraged to be ready to arbitrate disputes and de-escalate situations. Ultimately, there were very few reported instances of conflict. This may be attributed to facilitators following the best practices and guidelines presented in the training. It may also be attributed to the professional nature of the book club. Participants were discussing this book with colleagues and not personal friends. People will naturally be more circumspect when sharing thoughts and information with professional colleagues.[33]

To make the most of the ninety-minute session, facilitators had to be mindful to rein in tangential conversations and refocus attention to the book. While a little small talk is helpful for building common ground and setting the learning atmosphere, too much small talk could potentially derail a session.[34] Facilitators learned very quickly that the true value of the session was in the dialogue, the connections that were built, and the breakthroughs that some participants were experiencing in their own thinking. During the sessions, the facilitators would make time for participants to discuss the activities and exercises included in the book. One of the first activities in *Blindspot* requires readers to look at two coffee tables that are photographed from different angles. In the photograph, one table appears to be larger than the other table. In reality, the tables are the same size. This exercise and the other activities that followed in the book created an avenue for facilitators to start conversations centered on point of view, perspective, and implicit bias. After completing these exercises and talking about them with their group members, many participants had aha moments. Their blind spots suddenly became apparent to them.

Finally, closing out the session was just as important as the opening. It was critical that facilitators respected participants' schedules by starting and stopping on time. Facilitators used a variety of strategies to bring the conversation to a close. Some shared a favorite quote from the chapter. Others led an informal round-robin, where everyone gave a final thought about the assigned reading. All sessions concluded with a reminder about the date for the next session. If helpful websites, book titles, or other pertinent information was shared in the chat, it was captured and sent to group members via e-mail.

The Importance of Body Language

Some may think that body language would not come into play during a virtual discussion, but that could not be further from the truth. When facilitating a virtual discussion where there is audio and video, facilitators should be sure to keep their eyes on the camera. This allows the facilitator to make eye contact with the participants who are watching on their respective screens and devices. Facilitators should display an open body posture. They should avoid crossing arms and leaning back in the chair. Facilitators should lean into the camera and look engaged with the conversation. Facilitators should avoid fidgeting. Speaking with hand gestures adds emphasis and is acceptable. However, facilitators should avoid twiddling thumbs or tapping pens on the desk. Finally, facilitators should give affirmative gestures such as head nods and smiles.

Best Practices for Avoiding Technology Glitches

Technical difficulties are inevitable when facilitating a book club online. Some facilitators experienced technical difficulties with the virtual conferencing platforms used to facilitate their sessions. For example, the electricity went out at a facilitator's institution during one of her discussion sessions. However, she had previously installed the Zoom app on her phone and was able to pick up the virtual discussion relatively quickly. Another facilitator's institution shut down and rebooted all university computers moments before his group's discussion was slated to begin. Fortunately, he brought his personal laptop to work that day and was able to start his virtual discussion from his backup device.

To minimize these difficulties, facilitators were encouraged to sign into the video conferencing platform ahead of time to ensure it was working that day. Facilitators were told to ensure their group members were familiar with the web conferencing platform prior to the start of the first session. Some facilitators chose to hold a technology practice or training session with their group. This allowed group members to practice using the features such as the chat box and screen sharing prior to their actual session.

Challenges and Pitfalls

Challenges and pitfalls bring opportunities for growth and learning. Despite the amount of preparation that went into planning the discussion, there were pitfalls.

As mentioned in the previous section, some groups experienced technical problems. Some groups had conversations that were too fast- or slow-paced, while some groups experienced a lack of participation. Sadly, some of the preplanned questions fell flat during the discussions. Silence or dead air could be very intimidating to a new facilitator. However, the facilitators were discouraged from panicking but were encouraged to think on their feet. They were told to take the heat off themselves and ask the participants targeted questions to get the conversation moving. For example, a facilitator might ask each member open-ended questions such as, "What did you find the most surprising or interesting about the chapter?" or "What did you learn from this chapter?" Another strategy is for the facilitator to ask each person to choose an excerpt from the month's chapters and read it aloud. Each member can then share their thoughts and highlight the merits and drawbacks of the passage.[35]

New facilitators often found it helpful to shadow an experienced facilitator. Facilitators were invited to attend a session facilitated by a more experienced group leader to inform how they might lead their own session. Participants were made aware of the second facilitator's presence at the beginning of the discussion. Sometimes new facilitators felt overwhelmed with multitasking. Keeping the dialogue flowing while sharing screens, adjusting video and audio, troubleshooting technical problems, and monitoring the chat box was too much. Some facilitators opted to have another facilitator join their call or asked a group member to assist with monitoring the chat box. This allowed for comments in the chat box to be seen and addressed in real time.

Facilitator training was a contributing factor to the success of the virtual book club. The first installment of the book club did not have formal training. It relied on informal meetings and periodic check-ins with facilitators where encouragement and coaching was provided. After the *Blindspot* book discussion concluded, organizers received feedback from facilitators and participants that suggested training for facilitators. It was thought that this training would enhance the book club experience for all participants. Therefore, the training was added. The training focused on the mechanics of leading a virtual book club and did not focus on cultural competency or diversity, equity, and inclusion (DEI) issues. It also did not focus on guiding difficult conversations. This was an oversight on the part of the organizers. Nevertheless, this blind spot provided an opportunity for growth and development. MLA Reads organizers will include cultural competency and DEI topics in future facilitator training sessions.

Evaluation

Two separate evaluations were administered to capture feedback from the participants and facilitators. One evaluation was drafted by the facilitators and sent to all participants, while the other was MLA's standard evaluation for professional development. Participants who sought to claim MLA CE credit were required to complete the later. The organizers hoped members would complete both since they asked different questions.

The facilitators created an evaluation that was sent to all participants. Twenty-two participants completed the evaluation, and the feedback was overwhelmingly positive. Ninety-one percent rated their satisfaction with the book club as very to extremely satisfied, and the same percentage said they would participate in a future book club. The remaining respondents said they might participate in a future book club. The open-ended questions returned numerous positive comments such as these:

- What a wonderful way to get a diverse set of professionals to interact and build community.
- The experience was rewarding, helpful, and a good use of my time.
- This makes me want to get more involved.

Respondents were asked about their interest in selected titles for a future book club, and all respondents selected at least one book they were interested in reading.

The evaluation from MLA consisted of a standard set of questions that could not be altered. This evaluation was seen only by participants who wanted to receive a MLA CE certificate. Forty-one respondents completed the evaluation. The results were overwhelmingly positive, with 78 percent indicating the course exceeded their expectations and the remaining 22 percent indicating that the course met most or all of their expectations. The most powerful part of the evaluation was the responses to the open-ended question asking how participants intend to use what they have learned. Some of the responses included these:

- I have already become more conscious of my actions and the words I use.
- I am catching myself when my own biases rear their ugly heads. This is in both work and personal life.
- I will feel more confident when I have to speak up about issues related to unconscious bias now.

Ninety percent of respondents indicated they strongly agreed that the book club format was engaging. Many respondents indicated their interest in continuing to learn about this topic and their interest in participating in another book club.

Both evaluations asked participants to share suggestions to improve the book club. Some feedback was received during the book clubs and incorporated right away. An example was the request to share the discussion questions with all participants prior to the sessions so that participants had the option to spend time thinking about their responses. There were suggestions to post a schedule of all the sessions so that participants could more easily locate a makeup session if they missed their own session. There were suggestions to provide additional training to facilitators, primarily to help facilitators ensure everyone received a chance to speak. And finally, there were suggestions to have more time to discuss the material.

Lessons Learned

Based on participant evaluations and discussions among the facilitators, it was concluded that book discussions are a rewarding way to cover a topic. As this book chapter was being written, a second book discussion on Dolly Chugh's *The Person You Mean to Be: How Good People Fight Bias* was underway, with nearly 200 participants. There were a few takeaways learned from this experience and changes that have been implemented for the second book discussion.

Although the Welcome Session was recorded, the individual discussion sessions were not. Recording the Welcome Session was a good decision and worked well. It allowed people who could not attend the Welcome Session to review the information while giving participants the ability to speak freely during the individual book club sessions.

On a technical note related to Google Groups, it was learned that it is better for organizers to send the participants a link to the Google Group and require them to request access rather than having the organizers directly add them to the group. For the *Blindspot* book club, the organizers directly added all participants to the Google Group, but this caused confusion for participants as they might have wanted to use a different e-mail address or they didn't recognize the registration was related to the book club and they deleted the message or did not accept the invitation.

Facilitator training should be offered to all facilitators. Serving as a discussion group facilitator was a new experience for some of the leaders. Creating a baseline training for all of the facilitators would likely help the facilitators feel more confident leading their groups. Additionally, providing training related to discussing sensitive topics would likely also increase the facilitator's confidence.

Schedule at least one standing makeup session a month. Even with the best laid plans, unexpected events come up. Every month, a few participants were unable to make their monthly group meeting. Scheduling a monthly makeup session that anyone could attend relieved stress for those participants. The makeup session should occur at the end of the month and after the last regular session.

Create a site to post all of the information related to the book club that participants will need to know. During the book discussion, organizers sent e-mail messages to all participants, but that might not have been the most effective way to share information. A password-protected LibGuide was created for the discussion of *The Person You Mean to Be* so that participants have one place they can go to retrieve information. An added bonus is that most of these sites will allow organizers to capture statistics on how many times the site was accessed and what parts were accessed most often. This information could be useful in terms of assessment. Some of the items on the LibGuide for book discussion two include a list of all the discussion questions, a calendar showing when all the sessions are meeting during each month, and additional resources related to the book. Adding the LibGuide proved especially helpful. Organizers received feedback during the registration phase for the second iteration of the book club that information professionals who worked in hospitals did not have access to certain online platforms. Therefore, these members would not be able to access content at work if the Google platform was going to be the primary communication medium.

Expect that there will be some attrition of participants. Several of the people that signed up to participate dropped out throughout the process. Sometimes participants let the facilitators know why they were dropping out, but other times they simply stopped attending sessions or responding to e-mail. This caused angst for some of the facilitators, but it should be expected. Life happens, so don't take people's need to discontinue participation personally. People have changes that occur in their personal and professional lives, and sometimes they can't meet all of their commitments. It is nice to reach out at least once to individuals who have not responded to e-mail inquiries to let them know their participation has been missed and that they are welcome to rejoin when their schedule allows. It was also helpful to remind participants who withdrew from participating in the discussion that they could still claim MLA credit for the time they had participated. Before the book club begins, in order to help facilitators be prepared to handle these situations, make sure all the facilitators know that participants might drop out.

Holding book club sessions virtually allowed us to interact and build community with a diverse group of informational professionals. The sessions were free to attend, and no funding was needed for travel. This allowed participants who do not receive travel funding and participants with family or mobility issues to participate. Offering sessions in various time zones also gave participants the potential option to participate outside of regular work hours.

Outcomes and Next Steps

The initial book club has inspired continued action, including a second cycle for the book club and individual participants using the template established by the first book club to do their own book club discussions on campus. The overall response to the discussion of *Blindspot* has been positive. Feedback from participants at the onsite session and on the evaluation form indicated a desire to see the book discussion group continue, resulting in planning for cycle two of the book club. The feedback form included a question requesting participant feedback on the book selection for the next discussion. Participants' feedback showed an interest in reading Dolly Chugh's, *The Person You Mean to Be: How Good People Fight Bias*. This book was seen as a natural extension to continue the conversation on implicit bias and how individuals can respond to it. The meetings were planned to occur over a four-month period to coincide with the four major sections of the book, with an in-person discussion to take place at the 2020 MLA Annual Meeting. The second book discussion featured thirty-two facilitators, nineteen groups, 168 regular participants, and two prescheduled makeup sessions. Similar to the first book discussion, organizers received funding from the National Network of Libraries of Medicine, Midcontinental Region, to provide the participants with complimentary copies of the book.[36]

One of the inaugural facilitators shared the work that had been done with his library's Diversity, Equity, and Inclusion (DEI) Committee at the University of North Carolina, Charlotte. The committee liked the idea of facilitating a discussion on issues related to DEI, and the chair of the committee talked to the dean of the library about a possible book club discussion for faculty and staff at the library. When the idea was presented, the dean suggested it expand beyond the library itself and open up to the entire campus community. The first book club discussion took place in January 2020. Because the facilitator had recently read and led discussions on the book *The Person You Mean to Be* by Dr. Chugh, they decided to select that as the first book to discuss. This discussion was not virtual and took place in one 2-hour-long meeting. The book club and discussion were promoted to all faculty, staff, and students. The UNC Charlotte Diversity, Equity, and Inclusion Committee has now created a task group to facilitate these book club discussions on an ongoing basis. The foundation that the virtual book club established made it much easier to facilitate these in-person discussions.

At the University of Virginia, one of the book club facilitators decided to hold in-person book club discussions for faculty and staff. The facilitator used the material created in the LibGuide and discussion questions as the basis of discussion, just the same as the many virtual meeting groups. This was done to make participation easier as the schedule was set to meet the specific schedule needs of those on the campus. The facilitator also thought that because the book discusses sensitive topics, some members might be more willing to share their thoughts and opinions. The in-person sessions have also allowed for some flexibility, allowing for one chapter to be discussed at each meeting for an hour at a time. While using the same book and discussion materials, this in-person session has allowed for creativity in meeting the needs of the members of a specific institution in terms of how often to meet.

A long-term goal for those who have been organizers and facilitators for the book club is to work with the Medical Library Association's annual meeting planners to select a book that the annual meeting attendees could read before coming to the meeting and invite the author to speak at a plenary session. This would be a way to engage a larger group of libraries and to facilitate a larger discussion. The group plans to actively seek out relevant partnerships to continue the vital and important discussions that the book club has helped to facilitate.

Notes

1. Kathy Rosa and Kelsey Henke, *2017 ALA Demographic Study* (Chicago: American Library Association, 2017), https://www.ala.org/tools/sites/ala.org.tools/files/content/Draft%20 of%20Member%20Demographics%20Survey%2001-11-2017.pdf.
2. Perception Institute, "Implicit Bias," accessed January 17, 2020, https://perception.org/ research/implicit-bias/.
3. Mahzarin R. Banaji and Anthony G. Greenwald, *Blindspot* (New York: Delacorte Press, 2013).
4. Oxford Learner's Dictionaries, "Bias," accessed January 10, 2020, https://www.oxfordlearn-ersdictionaries.com/definition/english/bias_1.
5. Cheryl Staats et al., *State of the Science: Implicit Bias Review*, 5th ed. (Columbus: Kirwan Institute for the Study of Race and Ethnicity, Ohio State University, 2017), 10, http://kirwa-ninstitute.osu.edu/implicit-bias-training/resources/2017-implicit-bias-review.pdf.
6. Derald Wing Sue et al., "Racial Microaggressions in Everyday Life: Implications for Clinical Practice," *American Psychologist* 62, no. 4 (May–June 2007): 271, https://doi. org/10.1037/0003-066X.62.4.271.
7. DeEtta Jones, "Understanding Microaggressions: What They Are and How They Affect the Workplace," DeEtta Jones website, June 5, 2018, https://deettajones.com/understand-ing-microaggressions-affect-workplace/ (page discontinued).
8. Jaena Alabi, "Racial Microaggressions in Academic Libraries: Results of a Survey of Minority and Non-minority Librarians," *Journal of Academic Librarianship* 41, no. 1 (January 2015): 47–53, https://doi.org/10.1016/j.acalib.2014.10.008.
9. Matthew Hutson, "'Blindspot: Hidden Biases of Good People' by Mahzarin R. Banaji and Anthony G. Greenwald," *Washington Post*, February 8, 2013, https://www.washingtonpost. com/opinions/blindspot-hidden-biases-of-good-people-by-mahzarin-r-banaji-and-antho-ny-g-greenwald/2013/02/08/4c42d6b8-6a1b-11e2-ada3-d86a4806d5ee_story.html.
10. Banaji and Greenwald, *Blindspot*, 4.
11. Project Implicit. "Overview," Implicit Association Test (IAT), Harvard University, accessed January 9, 2020, https://implicit.harvard.edu/implicit/education.html.
12. Banaji and Greenwald, *Blindspot*, 4.
13. Project Implicit website, https://implicit.harvard.edu/implicit/.
14. Virginia Commonwealth University, "Common Book," accessed January 20, 2020, https:// commonbook.vcu.edu/; University of Denver, "One Book, One DU," accessed January 20, 2020, https://www.du.edu/onebook/index.html (page discontinued); University of Miami, "One Book, One U," accessed on January 20, 2020, https://culture.miami.edu/programs/ one-book/index.html.
15. Penguin Random House, "Common Reads," accessed January 20, 2020, http://common-reads.com/2015/11/01/welcome-new-penguin-random-house-common-reads-website/.
16. Luis Diaz, "What Students Will Be Reading: Campus Common Reading Roundup, 2019–20." Common Reads, Penguin Random House, October 3, 2019, http://common-reads.com/2019/10/03/first-year-reading-2019-campus-roundup/.
17. Penguin Random House, "First-Year Experience Conference," accessed January 20, 2020, http://commonreads.com/2019/11/11/fye2020-registration/.
18. National Endowment for the Arts, "NEA Big Read," October 15, 2019, https://www.arts. gov/national-initiatives/nea-big-read.
19. National Endowment for the Arts, "NEA Big Read."
20. National Library of Medicine, "NNLM Reading Club," National Institutes of Health, accessed January 20, 2020, https://nnlm.gov/all-of-us/nnlm-reading-club/.

21. Medical Library Association, "Discussion Group Program," accessed January 17, 2020, https://www.mlanet.org/page/discussion-group-program.
22. Medical Library Association, "Discussion Group Program."
23. National Library of Medicine, "National Network of Libraries of Medicine, Southeastern/ Atlantic Region," accessed January 17, 2020, https://nnlm.gov/sea (page discontinued).
24. Signup Zone website, accessed January 17, 2020, https://signup.zone/.
25. Erin Collazo Miller, "How to Lead a Successful Book Club Discussion," ThoughtCo, last updated March 7, 2018, https://www.thoughtco.com/lead-a-book-club-discussion-362067.
26. David L. Baker, "Designing and Orchestrating Online Discussions," *MERLOT Journal of Online Learning and Teaching* 7, no. 3 (September 2011), 401–11, ProQuest; John H. Curry and Jonene Cook, "Facilitating Online Discussions at a Manic Pace: A New Strategy for an Old Problem," *Quarterly Review of Distance Education* 15, no. 3 (2014): 1–11, ProQuest.
27. Sophie Haroutunian-Gordon, *Learning to Teach through Discussion* (New Haven, CT: Yale University Press, 2009), https://www.jstor.org/stable/j.ctt1npg01.
28. LitLovers, "How to Discuss a Book," accessed June 27, 2020, https://www.litlovers.com/run-a-book-club/lead-a-book-club-discussion.
29. Edwige Simon, "Ten Tips for Effective Online Discussions," *Transforming Higher Ed* (blog), *Educause Review*, November 21, 2018, https://er.educause.edu/blogs/2018/11/10-tips-for-effective-online-discussions.
30. LitLovers, "How to Discuss a Book."
31. Miller, "How to Lead a Successful Book Club Discussion"; Book Browse, "Leading a Successful Discussion," accessed June 27, 2020, https://www.bookbrowse.com/book-clubs/advice/index.cfm/fuseaction/moderating_meetings; *FreshBooks Blog*, "Six Tips for Running a Book Club at Your Workplace," last updated March 2019, https://www.fresh-books.com/blog/6-tips-for-running-a-book-club-at-your-workplace.
32. Miller, "How to Lead a Successful Book Club Discussion."
33. Book Browse, "Leading a Successful Discussion"; *FreshBooks Blog*, "Six Tips."
34. Miller, "How to Lead a Successful Book Club Discussion."
35. *FreshBooks Blog*, "Six Tips."
36. National Library of Medicine, "National Network of Libraries of Medicine, MidContinental Region," National Institutes of Health, accessed January 17, 2020. https://nnlm.gov/mcr (page discontinued).

Bibliography

Alabi, Jaena. "Racial Microaggressions in Academic Libraries: Results of a Survey of Minority and Non-minority Librarians." *Journal of Academic Librarianship* 41, no. 1 (January 2015): 47–53. https://doi.org/10.1016/j.acalib.2014.10.008.
American Library Association. "Diversity Counts." Accessed January 17, 2020. https://www.ala.org/aboutala/offices/diversity/diversitycounts/divcounts.
Baker, David L. "Designing and Orchestrating Online Discussions." *MERLOT Journal of Online Learning and Teaching* 7, no. 3 (September 2011): 401–11. ProQuest.
Banaji, Mahzarin R., and Anthony G. Greenwald. *Blindspot: Hidden Biases of Good People.* New York: Delacorte Press, 2013.
Book Browse. "Leading a Successful Discussion." Accessed June 27, 2020. https://www.book-browse.com/bookclubs/advice/index.cfm/fuseaction/moderating_meetings%20.

Curry, John H., and Jonene Cook. "Facilitating Online Discussions at a Manic Pace: A New Strategy for an Old Problem." *Quarterly Review of Distance Education* 15, no. 3 (2014): 1–11, ProQuest.

Diaz, Luis. "What Students Will Be Reading: Campus Common Reading Roundup, 2019–20." Common Reads, Penguin Random House, October 3, 2019. http://commonreads.com/2019/10/03/first-year-reading-2019-campus-roundup/.

FreshBooks Blog. "Six Tips for Running a Book Club at Your Workplace." Last updated March 2019. https://www.freshbooks.com/blog/6-tips-for-running-a-book-club-at-your-workplace.

Haroutunian-Gordon, Sophie. *Learning to Teach through Discussion: The Art of Turning the Soul.* New Haven, CT: Yale University Press, 2009. https://www.jstor.org/stable/j.ctt1npg01.

Hutson, Matthew. "'Blindspot: Hidden Biases of Good People' by Mahzarin R. Banaji and Anthony G. Greenwald." *Washington Post*, February 8, 2013. https://www.washingtonpost.com/opinions/blindspot-hidden-biases-of-good-people-by-mahzarin-r-banaji-and-anthony-g-greenwald/2013/02/08/4c42d6b8-6a1b-11e2-ada3-d86a4806d5ee_story.html.

Jones, DeEtta. "Understanding Microaggressions: What They Are and How They Affect the Workplace." DeEtta Jones website, June 5, 2018. https://deettajones.com/understanding-microaggressions-affect-workplace/ (page discontinued).

LitLovers. "How to Discuss a Book." Accessed June 27, 2020. https://www.litlovers.com/run-a-book-club/lead-a-book-club-discussion.

Medical Library Association. "Discussion Group Program." Accessed January 17, 2020. https://www.mlanet.org/page/discussion-group-program.

Miller, Erin Collazo. "How to Lead a Successful Book Club Discussion." ThoughtCo. Last updated March 7, 2018. https://www.thoughtco.com/lead-a-book-club-discussion-362067.

National Endowment for the Arts. "NEA Big Read." October 15, 2019. https://www.arts.gov/national-initiatives/nea-big-read.

National Library of Medicine. "National Network of Libraries of Medicine, MidContinental Region." National Institutes of Health. Accessed January 17, 2020. https://nnlm.gov/mcr (page discontinued).

———. "National Network of Libraries of Medicine, Southeastern/Atlantic Region." Accessed January 17, 2020. https://nnlm.gov/sea (page discontinued).

———. "NNLM Reading Club." National Institutes of Health. Accessed January 20, 2020. https://nnlm.gov/all-of-us/nnlm-reading-club/.

Oxford Learner's Dictionaries. "Bias." Accessed January 10, 2020. https://www.oxfordlearnersdictionaries.com/definition/english/bias_1.

Penguin Random House. "Common Reads." Accessed January 20, 2020. http://commonreads.com/2015/11/01/welcome-new-penguin-random-house-common-reads-website/.

———. "First-Year Experience Conference." Accessed January 20, 2020. http://commonreads.com/2019/11/11/fye2020-registration/.

Perception Institute. "Implicit Bias." Accessed January 17, 2020. https://perception.org/research/implicit-bias/.

Project Implicit website. https://implicit.harvard.edu/implicit/.

Project Implicit. "Overview." Implicit Association Test (IAT), Harvard University. Accessed January 9, 2020. https://implicit.harvard.edu/implicit/education.html.

Rosa, Kathy, and Kelsey Henke. *2017 ALA Demographic Study.* Chicago: American Library Association, 2017. https://www.ala.org/tools/sites/ala.org.tools/files/content/Draft%20of%20Member%20Demographics%20Survey%2001-11-2017.pdf.

Signup Zone website. Accessed January 17, 2020. https://signup.zone/.

Simon, Edwige. "Ten Tips for Effective Online Discussions." *Transforming Higher Ed* (blog), *Educause Review*, November 21, 2018. https://er.educause.edu/blogs/2018/11/10-tips-for-effective-online-discussions.

Staats, Cheryl, Kelly Capatosto, Lena Tenney, and Sara Mamo. *State of the Science: Implicit Bias Review*, 5th ed. Columbus: Kirwan Institute for the Study of Race and Ethnicity, Ohio State University, 2017. http://kirwaninstitute.osu.edu/implicit-bias-training/resources/2017-implicit-bias-review.pdf.

Sue, Derald Wing, Christina M. Capodilupo, Gina C. Torino, Jennifer M. Bucceri, Aisha M. B. Holder, Kevin L. Nadal, and Marta Esquilin. "Racial Microaggressions in Everyday Life: Implications for Clinical Practice." *American Psychologist* 62, no. 4 (May–June 2007): 271–86. https://doi.org/10.1037/0003-066X.62.4.271.

University of Denver. "One Book, One DU." Accessed January 20, 2020. https://www.du.edu/onebook/index.html (page discontinued).

University of Miami Libraries. "One Book, One U." Accessed January 20, 2020. https://culture.miami.edu/programs/one-book/index.html.

Virginia Commonwealth University. "Common Book." Accessed January 20, 2020. https://commonbook.vcu.edu/.

CHAPTER 12

Bridging the Gap between Residencies and Retention

A Case Study of the University of North Carolina at Greensboro's Diversity Resident Librarian Program and the Inception of the Library Diversity Institute

LaTesha Velez

The University of North Carolina at Greensboro (UNCG) Libraries began their Diversity Residency Program in 2008. Although a relatively new residency program, it can be considered a success with all of its residents successfully transitioning into permanent positions in libraries or LIS education.[1] Diversity residency librarian programs are time limited, post-MLIS jobs that aim to recruit and retain a more diverse professional librarian workforce. These positions are designed to attract recently graduated library professionals from marginalized backgrounds and provide them with professional work

experience.[2] Recognizing that isolation hampers many diversity residency programs and wishing to have a positive impact on residency experiences broadly, not just localized to UNCG Libraries, they did not stop with the residency program but began the Library Diversity Institute (LDI), bringing together residents from across the United States for a weekend of workshops, networking, and collegiality.[3] The primary goals of the LDI were designed around the desire to create a strong cohort experience, suggestions gleaned from a careful reading of the research surrounding diversity residency programs, and recommendations from UNCG Libraries' current and former diversity residents. This chapter is a case study detailing the best practices and lessons learned from UNCG's Diversity Resident Librarian program and two LDIs. It is written from the perspective of a former UNCG Libraries diversity resident librarian, a current member of the LDI program grant advisory and institute planning committee, and a two-time speaker at the LDI workshops. Although the institute itself was limited to residents, much of the information that went into designing the institute, the curriculum, and the knowledge that arose from the LDI is meant to be shared with interested parties such as residency program coordinators so we can build a sustainable culture of information and best practice sharing.

The term *diversity* may encompass ethnicity, gender identity, sexuality, and disability status, and one individual may embody several of those identities at once. According to the US Census Bureau Population Estimates Program, 76.3 percent of the US population is White; Hispanics make up 18.5 percent; Blacks, 13.4 percent; Asians, 5.9 percent; American Indian or Alaskan Native, 1.3 percent; and 0.2 percent identify as Native Hawaiian or other Pacific Islander.[4] According to the *2017 ALA Demographic Study*, 0.2% of ALA members identify as Hawaiian or other Pacific Islander; 1.2 percent as American Indian or Alaskan Native; 3.6 percent Asian; 3.9 percent Hispanic; and 4.4 percent, Black. The majority of ALA members who completed the survey, 86.7 percent, identify as White.[5] Of ALA members surveyed, only 2.91 percent identified as disabled, as opposed to 12.8 percent of the US population.[6] When we compare those statistics, it is clear that Hispanics, Blacks, and Asians are underrepresented in the LIS profession compared to the population, as are those who classify themselves as disabled. It was also projected in 2012 that the US population of non-Whites will outnumber Whites by 2043,[7] and updated census projections from 2017 reinforce that projection.[8]

LIS researchers have noted that the demographics of the United States are becoming more diverse while the library profession is not.[9] Jaeger and colleagues and Shorter-Gooden take that observation a step further. The former states that library professionals should be a more integrated part of the communities they serve, and the latter warns that institutions that do not diversify may not persist.[10] This mismatch between library demographics and the communities we serve may cause our patrons to overlook the library as a source of information, preferring to turn to neighbors who have more in common with them but may or may not provide the most accurate information.[11] Shorter-Gooden identifies three primary benefits of encouraging diversity in organizations: (1) that it is, quite simply, the right thing to do; (2) that as the diversity of the population increases, schools and businesses must learn how to engage a diverse workforce and serve diverse clients simply to survive; and (3) having access to diverse perspectives can help institutions be more creative and innovative, which, in turn, can help institutions better solve complex problems.[12] The American Library Association seconds those assertions on its website, saying, "By assembling the perspectives and experiences of multiple diversities—age, gender, ethnicity, physical ability, sexuality, and more—libraries can continue to innovate and improve services and respond to the needs of the nation's changing communities."[13]

One answer that has arisen to increase the representation of marginalized people in the library profession is the creation of diversity residency librarian positions. Residency programs have been in existence in some form since around 1923 when Charles C. Williamson published recommended training guidelines for post-LIS education internships. These guidelines included suggestions for rotations, which many modern-day residencies still include.[14] Libraries across the country began implementing Williamson's advice in the 1930s, and even the prestigious Library of Congress and National Library of Medicine started residencies in 1949 and 1957, respectively. The first academic library residency began at Ohio State University in 1961.[15] However, using residencies as a tool to diversify the profession is a relatively recent phenomenon, which started in 1984 with the University of Delaware's post-master's internship program.[16] Some residencies, including those that follow the principles outlined by the Association of College and Research Libraries (ACRL) Diversity Alliance, specify that residents should be of a marginalized ethnic or racial background. "Library leaders participating in the ACRL Diversity Alliance are committed to opening doors, sharing their networks, and preparing residents for success in scholarship, professional service, and leadership."[17] In 2015, Rutledge et al. used ACRL residency interest group job ads to estimate that there are approximately forty diversity residencies.[18]

Understanding the need to be part of the push for change in the profession, UNCG Libraries created its own diversity residency program. Each of UNCG's diversity resident librarians came from a marginalized racial or ethnic group. Although admittedly not always a perfect solution, well-designed residency programs can fill a need and align with the goals of some new professionals. Gerald Holmes, the residency coordinator of UNCG's Diversity Residency Program, observed that some LIS students who were members of the UNCG LIS Academic Cultural Enrichment (ACE) Scholars program had the choice between beginning a standard new librarian position or a residency position.[19] Many of them chose to accept the residency position because they felt they would get broader insight into the profession because of the rotations offered in their residencies, the increased focus on attending and presenting at conferences, the visibility of residency positions, and the focus on networking. These students saw residencies as a way to make them more competitive in future permanent jobs.[20] As a former resident, I echo those sentiments. I hoped to transition into library administration or LIS education and felt that the breadth of experience and connections I would make as a diversity resident librarian would be invaluable in either field.

Another aspect to consider is that many diversity residencies require little to no prior experience. The first UNCG diversity resident, Dr. Jason Alston, who received a scholarship to complete his degree at North Carolina Central University, remarked that "job ad after job ad for librarians requested two years of practical library experience."[21] Although he completed a three-month internship at Perry Memorial Library in Henderson, North Carolina, he was making a career change from journalism to librarianship. He did not have the prior experience that many of his NCCU LIS peers did. Alston's recognition that he had a degree but still lacked job experience caused him to question the efficacy of using LIS scholarships alone as a tool for diversifying librarianship. He astutely pointed out, "After all, if such people enroll in library schools and earn degrees without gaining experience, how can they be expected to compete with degree-earning paraprofessionals for professional jobs requiring experience?"[22] For him, a residency position became one of the few genuinely entry-level jobs he was qualified for.

Before beginning a diversity residency program, the UNCG Libraries created a Diversity Committee. The UNCG Libraries understood that part of a resident's success and well-being depended on creating a welcoming and inclusive library atmosphere. This atmosphere would also benefit other library patrons and staff. The library profession is guilty of microaggressions and even more overt aggression that may make visiting a library, working in a library, and, at times, the library profession as a whole feel unwelcoming to librarians of color and patrons alike.[23] This unwelcoming climate causes some librarians of color to leave the profession and be hesitant to recommend the profession to other people of color.[24]

Although diversity residencies take steps to diversify the library profession, they have also been plagued with persistent problems. The job titles themselves may be stigmatizing, and the temporary nature of residency programs may imply that the resident is not ready for a regular position.[25] Some residents report being treated as students or interns, having microaggressions perpetrated against them, and having the institution heap the responsibility for building or maintaining a diversity, equity, and inclusion (DEI) program on the resident's head.[26] Creating or maintaining a DEI program is a huge role and a lot to expect of a new professional, in addition to the fact that DEI work may run counter to the interests of that resident. Such stressors can affect a resident's desire to remain in their current position, librarianship as a whole, and may negatively impact their emotional wellness.[27]

The UNCG Libraries Diversity Committee set about ensuring that the UNCG library environment would be one in which a new professional from a marginalized population could flourish. It solidified the libraries' commitment to diversity by creating a diversity strategic plan. This culture of inclusion spawned projects such as creating American Sign Language (ASL) library tutorials for deaf and hard of hearing patrons and the libraries' participation in the Academic and Culture Enrichment (ACE) Scholars program. The ACE Scholars program was designed to recruit diverse students into LIS programs and provide them with scholarships, mentorship, and professional development opportunities to prepare them for professional library careers.[28]

Before the first resident began work on July 15, 2008, the UNCG University Libraries convened a planning committee comprised of UNCG librarians and LIS faculty to implement a residency program "designed to foster new librarians' professional growth while demonstrating the Libraries' commitment to diversity and investing in the future of the library profession."[29] The committee interviewed past and current resident librarians at other programs and other residency coordinators. It also researched current models of residency programs and read the available literature to glean best practices for starting a diversity resident librarian program. The culmination of this research was a planning report outlining the overall shape of the residency, such as the program's structure, the goals, resident onboarding, and mentorship.[30]

The UNCG Libraries structured its two-year residency program using the rotation model. Residents rotated among three departments during the first year of their residency, spending four months in each department. In the second year of the program, residents chose a department to specialize in for the year. Departments were chosen based on the needs of the library and the resident's goals and interests. It is important to clarify the distinction between diversity librarianship, in which the job function of the librarian includes diversity-related functions, and a diversity residency program, which is designed to recruit a more diverse workforce and may or may not require DEI work of the resident. UNCG Libraries chose to include diversity-related work as a job requirement for their diversity residency positions. After being in existence for eleven years, the residency program is continuing to evolve. The current resident, Deborah Caldwell, will be the first to have a three-year residency term.

The UNG Libraries' Diversity Residency Program can be considered a success, with every former resident securing a full-time position in librarianship or teaching. Two residents received PhDs in library and information science and serve the profession in teaching roles. The remainder secured positions in academic libraries. However, UNCG Libraries leadership understood that simply hiring a resident from an underrepresented group is insufficient to diversify the profession. When diversity residencies are offered, it is imperative to make the experience a positive one so that these residents are retained and are willing to recommend the profession to others.

One way of increasing retention and leaving diversity residents with a positive impression of librarianship is to encourage them to be members of supportive cohorts. Unfortunately, many residency programs hire only one resident at a time, and there may be little to no overlap between incoming residents and previous residents. Even when there is overlap or more than one resident is hired at a time, residents may still feel isolated. The Library Diversity Institute was created to address this isolation by bringing together residents from across the United States. In April 2018, UNCG's University Libraries, in collaboration with the ACRL Diversity Alliance, was awarded a $211,783 Institute of Museum and Library Services (IMLS) grant meant to support a pilot LDI program. The inaugural LDI was held on August 31 through September 2, 2018, in Greensboro, North Carolina. The second institute was held from August 23 through August 25, 2019, also in Greensboro. Both institutes exposed new residents to best practices in getting the most out of their residency experience and provided them with a national network of professional colleagues.

The structure of the LDI was informed by previous residency institutes held at West Virginia University and Virginia Tech. A former UNCG diversity resident librarian, Orolando Duffus, spoke at the institute at WVU. Those first institutes also recognized that residents are typically isolated in their respective institutions and wanted to bring them together and give them a cohort experience. A cohort is a group of people who share common experiences in order to build a sense of community. Around the time of the institute at WVU, UNCG Libraries joined the ACRL Diversity Alliance, again seeking that connection and support for the coordinators and administrators of the residency and for the residents themselves. Being part of those early efforts at creating a cohort of diversity residents around the United States spurred UNCG Libraries into action, so they decided to try to expand on those first efforts by bringing together even more residents. The IMLS grant funding made it possible to offer full funding for attendees, including travel and lodging. The institute was also shorter than WVU's institute and was held partially during the weekend in hopes that library administrators would be more willing to allow residents to attend if they knew residents would miss work for only two days. For both LDIs, informal activities began on Friday, with the more formal curriculum coming Saturday and Sunday, and the institute ended midday on Monday. To be sure, there was a lot to cover during such a short time frame, but methods for providing information outside of the LDI were built into the grant.

UNCG Libraries could have focused solely on implementing best practices in their own library by taking suggestions such as those offered by Hu and Patrick to increase the number of residents hired per residency program cycle to at least two.[31] They also could have ended the residency program altogether, instead focusing on inclusive hiring practices that would increase the diversity of the UNCG Libraries' full-time staff. However, understanding that funding does not always allow for either option, that grants for such funding are temporary fixes to budget issues, and hoping to provide a benefit to all residency programs, not just their own, UNCG Libraries decided to pilot an institute using the cohort model to bring together residents from across the country, thus providing a professional network and support group for all residents.

As was mentioned earlier, UNCG Libraries were part of early efforts at building a residency cohort. They also encouraged their residents to join the Residency Interest Group (RIG) e-mail discussion list. However, it was more than just the example of previous institutes that informed UNCG Libraries' decision to structure the LDI using the cohort method. Dr. Martin Halbert, dean of UNCG Libraries, is a "firm believer in cohort models."[32] During his time at Emory University, Emory began collaborating with the Council on Library and Information Resources (CLIR) to create the Frye Leadership Institute, now called the Leading Change Institute. Dr. Halbert had the opportunity to see a leadership institute being developed based on a cohort model and attend the institute as the inaugural representative from Emory. The institute was comprised of an in-depth, two-week lecture series hosted at Emory, followed by a yearlong practicum to be hosted by each participant's home institution.[33] The initial on-site, two-week lecture series provided a deep immersion into leadership concepts, but what became vitally important to Dr. Halbert during those two weeks was the experience of being part of a cohort. Dr. Halbert explained:

> The interaction of each of us in that group with the other people was… invaluable… because you can compare notes, you can compare thinking, you could give more a more well-rounded perspective on the topics of the institute by being in a cohort.[34]

When UNCG Libraries, in collaboration with the ACRL Diversity Alliance, started writing the IMLS grant proposal, Dr. Halbert's experience spurred them to look to a cohort model. The cohort institute model has been used in higher education and professional settings and seemed like an ideal fit for library residency programs. Cohort models have been linked to increased emotional well-being and retention among college and university students.[35] "Pride and enthusiasm in participating in such institutes… are… a real and observable beneficial result for attendees."[36] They have also resulted "in a positive feeling toward the subject matter and learning becomes more meaningful."[37] Some perceived weaknesses of cohort programs may even be considered additional strengths when applied to diversity resident librarian cohorts. Authors such as Barnett and Muse, and Basom, Yerkes, Norris, and Barnett report similar findings of faculty unease with the increased levels of empowerment cohort members felt.[38] However, helping diverse librarians find their voice and feel empowered to use it to shake up the profession with new ideas is precisely one of the benefits of diversifying librarianship. Many residencies either have only one resident at a time or very few in their cohort. The dates of employment for incoming and outgoing residents typically do not overlap, making it necessary to look outside of one's own institution to build a cohort of diversity resident librarians.[39]

The organizers of the LDI also looked at research on how to best structure residency programs when creating the goals and programming for the institute. Pickens and Coren articulated several strategies to help structure residency programs so that resident librarians could get the most out of them. As residents themselves at the time of authoring the article, they were in a unique position to give an insider perspective on the needs of resident librarians. The most relevant aspects of their paper in connection with LDI were their suggestions to help residents identify mentors and advocates, to implement a well-designed onboarding process, to encourage residents to articulate objectives and a vision, to dedicate time for scholarship and research, to create time for reflection, and to listen to feedback from residents.[40] The research of Dr. Jason Alston was also heavily consulted. His mixed-methods study is one of the few done to identify what themes positively and significantly correlate to a diversity resident's satisfaction with their residency program. Dr. Alston surfaced several themes that led to diverse residents' satisfaction or dissatisfaction with their residency programs.[41] Communication arose as a common element within these themes. Dr. Alston explains that it is essential to communicate with stakeholders so that everyone involved understands who the resident is, what a residency is—that is, they are professional librarians, not interns—and why the residency was established. It is also important to adequately communicate with the resident what is expected of them. A lack of preparedness or proper assessment tools can contribute to miscommunication and cause resident dissatisfaction. Residents also need guidance and support from residency coordinators, supervisors, administrators, and mentors. Allowing residents "to perform meaningful, challenging, and innovative work" can increase satisfaction.[42] Finally, Dr. Alston's research tells us that the resident's job duties should help them grow and advance in the field, ultimately making them more appealing job candidates.[43]

Thirty-eight residents attended the first LDI, and thirty-six attended the second, three of whom were alumni from the first institute. LDI organizers initially assumed attendees would primarily be residents near the beginning of their diversity residency programs, but residents in all stages of their residencies attended. This posed the challenge of making the institute curriculum meaningful to residents in all stages of their residency but produced the beneficial opportunity for residents to hear from those who had been in their positions for a little longer. The LDI curriculum was taught by experts in DEI, diversity residency studies, or both. The institute was purposely kept short and done over an extended weekend to make it more likely that institutions would be more willing to send their residents, knowing that they would not miss many workdays. The first two LDIs were in the hotel where residents were staying to mitigate the time and expense of traveling to and from venues.

After carefully reading the available research, institute organizers identified four areas of need in residency programs that they felt the LDI could address. Those areas of need were

1. Better preparation for residents
2. Professional networking opportunities for residents
3. Instilling a sense of pride and enthusiasm from participating in the institute
4. Developing a shared understanding of what diversity residencies are[44]

From these areas were distilled the goals of the institute, which were to

1. Orient new residents to the best practices in getting the most out of their residency experience
2. Provide diversity residents with a professional network of other resident colleagues nationally[45]

The first area of need, better preparation for residents, informed much of the LDI curriculum. Several workshops and presentations were designed with the goal of orienting diversity residents and providing best practices. Dr. LaTesha Velez, UNCG Libraries' second diversity resident, presented one such session. It was entitled "How Do I Know What I Don't Know?" and covered practical tips for continual learning, professional development, and relationship building. The session included a residency onboarding handbook Dr. Velez developed at the end of her residency. There was also a workshop activity designed to help residents share issues or fears and get advice and support from fellow residents. Another session designed to help prepare residents was given by Dr. Irene Owens, dean emerita of North Carolina Central University, titled "Conflict Management: Enhancing Strategies for Performance and Leadership Effectiveness." Dr. Owens's session introduced attendees to basic principles of conflict management and some of the causes of conflict. It also provided opportunities for the attendees to engage in active learning activities as well as a discussion of a strengths, weaknesses, opportunities, and threats (SWOT) self-assessment each attendee completed before the beginning of the session. "Library Diversity Residencies—Common Challenges and Best Practices," by Dr. Jason Alston, explained the most relevant findings from his doctoral research concerning success factors, best practices, and common pitfalls in diversity residencies.

The second area of need mentioned above was an opportunity to engage in professional networking. There were several get-to-know-you cohort development activities including "birds-of-a-feather" sessions, which were informal gatherings where residents interested in the same topic could divide into subgroups and engage in conversation around that topic. The birds-of-a-feather sessions began with historical perspectives on diversity residency programs, then transitioned to active group breakout discussions led by residents with LDI organizers roaming from topic to topic in case there were questions or concerns. Residents chose from topics of interest that were suggested by the LDI organizers and added to by attendees, then assembled in smaller, self-regulated groups to discuss those topics and share their expertise and experiences among themselves. Attendees learned about the demographics of their specific cohort, participated in icebreaker sessions designed to be informal and fun, and attended a welcome dinner. LDI attendees also have access to a private e-mail discussion list open solely to other LDI attendees so they can keep in touch. The list remains active, and several attendees have presented and authored articles together. The concluding LDI session also provided an opportunity for attendees to network. "Putting It All Together," led by Dr. Martin Halbert and Gerald Holmes, provided an opportunity for the residents to share observations and thoughts from the institute, as well as any future plans. The LDI presenters and keynote speaker Dr. Jon Cawthorne also participated in these networking/getting-to-know-you sessions and made themselves available as mentors and sounding boards.

The third area of need, instilling a sense of pride and enthusiasm, is a more amorphous goal. As was noted earlier, researchers have found that this sense of pride is frequently a benefit of cohort institutes, and Dr. Halbert experienced this himself after attending the Frye Institute. However, it is an outcome that does not neatly lend itself to some specific session or activity. Organizers and presenters spent most of their time in the same room with the attendees, talking, sharing, offering mentorship, and expressing our love of the profession. Keynote speakers were also carefully chosen from library professionals who could provide insight, information, and mentorship for new professionals. Dr. Cawthorne, dean of the Wayne State University Library System and School of Information Sciences, delivered the opening keynote for the first institute. Dr. Cawthorne was also the ACRL 2020–2021 president. Wanda Brown, director of Winston-Salem State University's C.G. O'Kelly Library and president of the American Library Association for the 2019–2020 term, delivered the concluding address for that same institute.

Anecdotal information from some attendees suggests that the LDI succeeded in instilling a sense of pride and enthusiasm. Several attendees from the first LDI asked to come to the second, but the sessions were designed for first-time attendees and space was limited, so alumni participation was limited to the first three requests. Returning alumni were also asked to participate in a panel session. One attendee wrote about her experience at the LDI, saying:

> I left the institute feeling empowered with tools, community, and support to tackle my goals, challenges, and even failures. My role in the academic library matters. I have a critical job to do on behalf of my cohort and community, including my ancestors who paved the way for me to access quality education and civil rights.[46]

Of course, further assessment will be vital in measuring whether the institute successfully instilled a sense of pride and enthusiasm in its participants and measuring the overall effectiveness of the LDI.

The final identified need was to foster a shared understanding of what residencies are. "A basic fact that often hampers residencies is that there is still confusion and a lack of shared understanding in academic libraries about the nature and purposes of diversity residencies."[47] Organizers understood that in order to meet that need, there would need to be communication beyond the institutes themselves. To that end, organizers are offering webinars, are publishing an open access journal, and hosted a conference that was open to all participants rather than being limited to diversity resident librarians. The inaugural Library Diversity and Residency Studies Conference was held on August 26–27, 2019. The conference focused on diversity residency programs and broader library DEI initiatives and topics. UNCG hosted the conference in collaboration with the ACRL Diversity Alliance and the Association of Southeastern Research Libraries (ASERL). It occurred directly after the second LDI to make it easier for institute attendees to also attend the conference.

The conference included interactive events, panel presentations, and keynote addresses. Several of the organizers and presenters from LDI also spoke at the conference, as did several attendees from the first LDI. Deena Hayes-Greene, founder of the nationally renowned Racial Equity Institute, gave the opening keynote address. The afternoon keynote speaker was DeEtta Jones, founder and principal of DeEtta Jones and Associates consulting team, and Dr. Cawthorne gave the closing keynote. Demand for such a conference far exceeded the estimates of conference organizers. Dr. Halbert, one of the primary conference organizers, said:

> That was wildly successful.... we were originally planning on no more than 60 people. We had to cap it at 110 or something like that because the venue wouldn't hold any more. And we were packed in that venue; we were absolutely packed. Now, that told us a lot of how much demand there is for this sort of thing.[48]

The free webinar series will include information to aid institutions in creating residency programs, advice from institutions that have hosted successful residencies, programming offered by residents themselves, and continuing professional development and education for current residents. The first issue of the *Journal of Library Diversity and Residency Studies* went live on May 13, 2020, and featured presentations, articles, and other aspects of the curriculum from the first institute. This open-access, online journal is available at https://librarydiversity. institute/ldrs/journal-archive. The editors hope to expand the journal to feature articles written by current residents, accounts from the LDIs, and other general articles designed to inform and guide library professionals interested in DEI and diversity residency programs.

Assessment was a critical component to measuring the institute's success and making improvements for the second iteration. Participants were sent an impact study after the LDI to judge what worked and what did not. The organizers of the LDI also held a meeting directly after the first institute to discuss their thoughts on strengths and weaknesses. Based on conversations between the organizers and responses to the survey, the second institute was restructured to incorporate suggested improvements. The institute is very short, so organizers tried to include as much as possible into those three days to ensure that attendees felt that they got value from their time spent at the LDI. However, our post-institute debriefing and the assessment surveys suggested there was too much structured time. Survey participants asked that organizers make room for more downtime and more opportunities for unstructured or less structured time for networking and cohort building. Organizers shaved a half-hour from several of the presentations to incorporate those suggested improvements. Some of that additional time was added to the birds-of-a-feather session, which was lengthened by a half hour. It was also used to add unstructured networking time that was scheduled directly after the birds-of-a-feather session to give attendees more time to talk if they wanted to continue discussions. We also provided more breaks during the institute.

The second institute included the same presentations from Drs. Alston, Owens, and Velez but also had a panel of prior attendees. The panel was a popular addition and was called "Perspectives on the Institute."[49] Panelists included Symphony Bruce, Natalie Hill, and Laura Tadena. They were considered "institute mentor residents" and, in addition to discussing their impressions of the institute and how it benefited them, they attended sessions and participated in activities with the current attendees. They also made themselves available for informal conversations with attendees. The keynote speakers for the second institute included Dr. Franklin Gilliam, chancellor of UNCG, and Loretta Parham, CEO and director of the Robert W. Woodruff Library of the Atlanta University Center.

Further assessment is planned to analyze the sustainability of the LDI. The sustainability analysis will include an examination of the results of the impact study to see if the LDI produced enough positive benefit to warrant continuation. If the institutes are revealed to have a positive impact, organizers must determine possible models for sustaining the LDI beyond the initial grant funding period, including identifying a revenue stream to host future institutes, choosing where to host future institutes, and deciding whether individual institutions or a professional association should host this project. There is also the possibility of incorporating the LDI as a 501(c)(3) nonprofit. Such discussions will include consulting with members of the ACRL Diversity Alliance to determine the long-term marketability of the institutes.[50]

Admittedly, the efficacy of residency programs as a tool to increase minority representation in the profession is unclear. These positions are time-limited with no guarantee that residents will secure full-time, permanent employment in the field. It is telling that "roughly thirty years later, academic librarianship is no more diverse than it was when these programs began to address the lack of diversity in librarianship."[51] The profession also needs to examine whether marginalized candidates see job ads, are asked to interview for positions, and are hired into inclusive, welcoming environments. Structural inequalities in the profession should be examined and addressed to make it attractive to diverse applicants. However, the profession must continue to try to attract the most talented and diverse workforce possible. In the future, this push may take a different form than diversity residencies, but the continued popularity of this model suggests it will persist. As a result, it is incumbent on the profession to study diversity residencies, suggest improvements, share information, and make positive improvements. The LDI was designed to do just that. It is a valuable tool for the retention and well-being of diverse librarians. The LDI provided a cohort of others to work, write, and present with or even just someone to talk to. The organizers of the LDI are in the beginning stages of ensuring the sustainability of the institute so that I can continue serving diversity residents for years to come.

Notes

1. UNC Greensboro University Libraries. "Post MLS Diversity Residency Program." Accessed November 26, 2019. https://library.uncg.edu/info/diversity/residency_program.aspx.
2. Jason Kelly Alston, "Causes of Satisfaction and Dissatisfaction for Diversity Resident Librarians—A Mixed Methods Study Using Herzberg's Motivation-Hygiene Theory" (doctoral diss., University of South Carolina, 2017), v, https://scholarcommons.sc.edu/etd/4080.
3. We also had one resident from an institution in Canada join us during the first year of the LDI.
4. US Census Bureau, "Quick Facts: United States," 2019, https://www.census.gov/quickfacts/fact/table/US/PST045219.

5.   Kathy Rosa and Kelsey Henke, *2017 ALA Demographic Study* (Chicago: American Library Association, 2017), http://www.ala.org/tools/sites/ala.org.tools/files/content/Draft%20 of%20Member%20Demographics%20Survey%2001-11-2017.pdf.

6.   L. Kraus et al., *2017 Disability Statistics Annual Report*, Rehabilitation Research and Training Center on Disability Statistics and Demographics, Institute on Disability, University of New Hampshire, 2018, https://eric.ed.gov/?id=ED583258; Rosa and Henke, *2017 ALA Demographic Study*.

7.   Kelly McElroy and Chris Diaz, "Residency Programs and Demonstrating Commitment to Diversity," in *Creating Sustainable Community: The Proceedings of the ACRL 2015 Conference, March 25–28, Portland, Oregon*, ed. Dawn M. Mueller (Chicago: Association of College and Research Libraries, 2015), 643, Faculty Publications, 46, Digital Commons@ NLU, National Louis University, https://digitalcommons.nl.edu/faculty_publications/46.

8.   US Census Bureau. "2012 National Population Projections Tables: Projected Race and Hispanic Origin." 2012. https://www.census.gov/data/tables/2012/demo/popproj/2012-summary-tables.html; US Census Bureau. "2017 National Population Projections Tables: Projected Race and Hispanic Origin." 2017. https://www.census.gov/data/tables/2017/demo/popproj/2017-summary-tables.html

9.   Denice Adkins, Christina Virden, and Charles Yier, "Learning about Diversity: The Roles of LIS Education, LIS Associations, and Lived Experience," *Library Quarterly* 85, no. 2 (April 2015): 139–49, https://doi.org/10.1086/680153; Roger Schonfeld and Liam Sweeney, *Inclusion, Diversity, and Equity: Members of the Association of Research Libraries* (New York: Ithaka S+R, August 30, 2017), https://doi.org/10.18665/sr.304524.

10. Paul T. Jaeger, Lindsay C. Sarin, and Kaitlin J. Peterson "Diversity, Inclusion, and Library and Information Science: An Ongoing Imperative (or Why We Still Desperately Need to Have Discussions about Diversity and Inclusion)," *Library Quarterly* 85, no. 2 (April 2015): 127–32, https://doi.org/10.1086/680151; Kumea Shorter-Gooden, "The Culturally Competent Organization," *Library Quarterly* 83, no. 3 (July 2013): 207–11, https://doi.org/10.1086/670695.

11. Samantha Kelly Hastings, "If Diversity Is a Natural State, Why Don't Our Libraries Mirror the Populations They Serve?" *Library Quarterly* 85, no. 2 (April 2015): 133–38, https://doi.org/10.1086/680152.

12. Shorter-Gooden, "Culturally Competent Organization."

13. American Library Association, "Diversity in Libraries," July 21, 2016, https://www.ala.org/educationcareers/libcareers/diversity.

14. Charles C. Williamson, *Training For Library Service* (Boston: Merrymount Press, 1923).

15. McElroy and Diaz, "Residency Programs."

16. McElroy and Diaz, "Residency Programs," 642.

17. Martin Halbert and Gerald V. Holmes, "Library Diversity Institutes Pilot Project" (grant proposal. University of North Carolina, Greensboro, April 18, 2018), 3.

18. Lorelei Rutledge et al., *Developing a Residency Program*, Practical Guides for Librarians, no. 63 (Lanham, MD: Rowman & Littlefield, 2019), 3.

19. Martin Halbert and Gerald V. Holmes, interview by the author with Dr. Martin Halbert, dean of university libraries and professor, and Gerald Holmes, reference librarian, diversity coordinator, and associate professor, December 16, 2019. The ACE Scholars are members of an IMLS grant–funded scholarship program designed to increase the cultural diversity of librarianship by offering scholarships to diverse students.

20. Halbert and Holmes, interview.

21. Jason Kelley Alston, "Minerva's First Born: My Experiences as UNCG's First Diversity Resident Librarian," *North Carolina Libraries* 68, no. 1 (2010): 14, https://doi.org/10.3776/ncl.v68i1.303.
22. Alston, "Minerva's First Born," 14.
23. Jaena Alabi, "Racial Microaggressions in Academic Libraries: Results of a Survey of Minority and Non-minority Librarians," *Journal of Academic Librarianship* 41, no. 1 (2015): 47–53, https://doi.org/10.1016/j.acalib.2014.10.008; Jaena Alabi, "'This Actually Happened': An Analysis of Librarians' Responses to a Survey about Racial Microaggressions," *Journal of Library Administration* 55, no. 3 (2015): 179–91, https://doi.org/10.1080/01930826.2015.1034040; Sharon Elteto, Rose M. Jackson, and Adriene Lim, "Is the Library a 'Welcoming Space'? An Urban Academic Library and Diverse Student Experiences," *portal: Libraries and the Academy* 8, no. 3 (July 18, 2008): 325–37, https://doi.org/10.1353/pla.0.0008; April Hathcock, "ALAMW: What Happened, and What Should Happen Next," *At the Intersection* (blog), January 30, 2019 https://aprilhathcock.wordpress.com/2019/01/30/alamw-what-happened-and-what-should-happen-next/.
24. Alabi, "Racial Microaggressions"; Alabi, "'This Actually Happened.'"
25. McElroy and Diaz, "Residency Programs," 644.
26. Alston, "Causes of Satisfaction and Dissatisfaction"; McElroy and Diaz, "Residency Programs."
27. Alston, "Causes of Satisfaction and Dissatisfaction"; Sylvia S. Hu and Demetria E. Patrick, "Our Experience as Minority Residents: Benefits, Drawbacks, and Suggestions," *College and Research Libraries News* 67, no. 5 (May 2006): 297–300, EBSCOhost; Halbert and Holmes, "Library Diversity Institutes Pilot Project"; McElroy and Diaz, "Residency Programs."
28. Gerald V. Holmes et al., "University Libraries Diversity Strategic Plan 2014–2019, Two-Year Update 2014–2016," University of North Carolina, Greensboro, June 28, 2016.
29. Michelle Belden et al., "Post MLS Diversity Residency Planning Report," University of North Carolina, Greensboro, December 21, 2007, 3.
30. Belden et al., "Post MLS Diversity Residency Planning Report."
31. Hu and Patrick, "Our Experience as Minority Residents," 299.
32. Halbert and Holmes, interview.
33. Leading Change Institute, "About the Leading Change Institute," Accessed January 15, 2020, https://leadingchangeinstitute.org/about/.
34. Halbert and Holmes, interview.
35. April Witteveen, "Better Together: The Cohort Model of Professional Development" *Library Journal* 140, no. 20 (2015): 42.
36. Halbert and Holmes, "Library Diversity Institutes Pilot Project," 4.
37. Witteveen, "Better Together," 42.
38. Bruce G. Barnett and Ivan D. Muse, "Cohort Groups in Educational Administration: Promises and Challenges," *Journal of School Leadership* 3, no. 4 (July 1993): 400–415; Margaret Basom et al., "Using Cohorts as a Means for Developing Transformational Leaders," *Journal of School Leadership* 6, no. 1 (1996): 99–112, https://doi.org/10.1177/105268469600600105.
39. Alston, "Causes of Satisfaction and Dissatisfaction"; Halbert and Holmes, "Library Diversity Institutes Pilot Project."
40. Chanelle Pickens and Ashleigh D. Coren, "Diversity Residency Programs: Strategies for a Collaborative Approach to Development," *Collaborative Librarianship* 9, no. 2 (2017): article 7, https://digitalcommons.du.edu/collaborativelibrarianship/vol9/iss2/7.
41. Alston, "Causes of Satisfaction and Dissatisfaction."

42. Alston, "Causes of Satisfaction and Dissatisfaction," vi.
43. Alston, "Causes of Satisfaction and Dissatisfaction."
44. Halbert and Holmes, "Library Diversity Institutes Pilot Project," 4.
45. Martin Halbert and Gerald V. Holmes, *ACRL Diversity Resident Institute Handbook 2018* (Greensboro: University of North Carolina at Greensboro Libraries, 2018), 6.
46. LaQuanda Onyemeh, "LaQuanda Onyemeh Reflects on UNCG Library Diversity Institute," ALA Spectrum Scholarship Program, September 18, 2018, http://www.ala.org/advocacy/spectrum/laquanda-onyemeh-uncg-institute.
47. Halbert and Holmes, "Library Diversity Institutes Pilot Project," 4.
48. Halbert and Holmes, interview.
49. Halbert, Martin, Gerald V. Holmes, and Deborah Caldwell. Library Diversity Resident Institute Handbook 2019. Greensboro: University of North Carolina at Greensboro Libraries, 2019.
50. Halbert and Holmes, "Library Diversity Institutes Pilot Project."
51. McElroy and Diaz, "Residency Programs," 642.

Bibliography

Adkins, Denice, Christina Virden, and Charles Yier. "Learning about Diversity: The Roles of LIS Education, LIS Associations, and Lived Experience." *Library Quarterly* 85, no. 2 (April 2015): 139–49. https://doi.org/10.1086/680153.
Alabi, Jaena. "Racial Microaggressions in Academic Libraries: Results of a Survey of Minority and Non-minority Librarians." *Journal of Academic Librarianship* 41, no. 1 (2015): 47–53. https://doi.org/10.1016/j.acalib.2014.10.008.
———. "'This Actually Happened': An Analysis of Librarians' Responses to a Survey about Racial Microaggressions." *Journal of Library Administration* 55, no. 3 (2015): 179–91. https://doi.org/10.1080/01930826.2015.1034040.
Alston, Jason Kelly. "Causes of Satisfaction and Dissatisfaction for Diversity Resident Librarians—A Mixed Methods Study Using Herzberg's Motivation-Hygiene Theory." Diss., University of South Carolina, 2017. https://scholarcommons.sc.edu/etd/4080.
———. "Minerva's First Born: My Experiences as UNCG's First Diversity Resident Librarian." *North Carolina Libraries* 68, no. 1 (2010): 14–16. https://doi.org/10.3776/ncl.v68i1.303.
American Library Association. "Diversity in Libraries." July 21, 2016. https://www.ala.org/educationcareers/libcareers/diversity.
Barnett, Bruce G., and Ivan D. Muse. "Cohort Groups in Educational Administration: Promises and Challenges." *Journal of School Leadership* 3, no. 4 (July 1993): 400–415.
Basom, Margaret, Diane Yerkes, Cynthia Norris, and Bruce Barnett. "Using Cohorts as a Means for Developing Transformational Leaders." *Journal of School Leadership* 6, no. 1 (1996): 99–112. https://doi.org/10.1177/105268469600600105.
Belden, Michelle, Stephen H. Dew, Julie Hersberger, Gerald V. Holmes, Mary M. Krautter, Daniel Nanez, William M. (Mac) Nelson, et al. "Post MLS Diversity Residency Planning Report." University of North Carolina, Greensboro, December 21, 2007.
Elteto, Sharon, Rose M. Jackson, and Adriene Lim. "Is the Library a 'Welcoming Space'? An Urban Academic Library and Diverse Student Experiences." *portal: Libraries and the Academy* 8, no. 3 (July 18, 2008): 325–37. https://doi.org/10.1353/pla.0.0008.
Halbert, Martin, and Gerald V. Holmes. *ACRL Diversity Resident Institute Handbook 2018.* Greensboro: University of North Carolina at Greensboro Libraries, 2018.

———. Interview with Dr. Martin Halbert, dean of university libraries and professor, and Gerald Holmes, reference librarian, diversity coordinator, and associate professor, December 16, 2019.

———. "Library Diversity Institutes Pilot Project." Grant proposal. University of North Carolina, Greensboro, April 18, 2018.

Halbert, Martin, Gerald V. Holmes, and Deborah Caldwell. *Library Diversity Resident Institute Handbook 2019*. Greensboro: University of North Carolina at Greensboro Libraries, 2019.

Hastings, Samantha Kelly. "If Diversity Is a Natural State, Why Don't Our Libraries Mirror the Populations They Serve?" *Library Quarterly* 85, no. 2 (April 2015): 133–38. https://doi.org/10.1086/680152.

Hathcock, April. "ALAMW: What Happened, and What Should Happen Next." *At the Intersection* (blog), January 30, 2019. https://aprilhathcock.wordpress.com/2019/01/30/alamw-what-happened-and-what-should-happen-next/.

Holmes, Gerald V., Michael Crumpton, Orolando Duffus, Liane Elias, Jackie Gaither, David Gwynn, Norman Hines, et al. "University Libraries Diversity Strategic Plan 2014–2019, Two-Year Update 2014–2016." University of North Carolina, Greensboro, June 28, 2016.

Hu, Sylvia S., and Demetria E. Patrick. "Our Experience as Minority Residents: Benefits, Drawbacks, and Suggestions." *College and Research Libraries News* 67, no. 5 (May 2006): 297–300. EBSCOhost.

Jaeger, Paul T., Lindsay C. Sarin, and Kaitlin J. Peterson. "Diversity, Inclusion, and Library and Information Science: An Ongoing Imperative (or Why We Still Desperately Need to Have Discussions about Diversity and Inclusion)." *Library Quarterly* 85, no. 2 (April 2015): 127–32. https://doi.org/10.1086/680151.

Kraus, L., E. Lauer, R. Coleman, and A. Houtenville. *2017 Disability Statistics Annual Report*. Rehabilitation Research and Training Center on Disability Statistics and Demographics, Institute on Disability, University of New Hampshire, 2018. https://eric.ed.gov/?id=ED583258.

Leading Change Institute. "About the Leading Change Institute." Accessed January 15, 2020. https://leadingchangeinstitute.org/about/.

McElroy, Kelly, and Chris Diaz. "Residency Programs and Demonstrating Commitment to Diversity." In *Creating Sustainable Community: The Proceedings of the ACRL 2015 Conference, March 25–28, Portland, Oregon*. Edited by Dawn M. Mueller, 642–47. Chicago: Association of College and Research Libraries, 2015. Faculty Publications, 46, Digital Commons@ NLU, National Louis University. https://digitalcommons.nl.edu/faculty_publications/46.

Onyemeh, LaQuanda. "LaQuanda Onyemeh Reflects on UNCG Library Diversity Institute." ALA Spectrum Scholarship Program, September 18, 2018. http://www.ala.org/advocacy/spectrum/laquanda-onyemeh-uncg-institute.

Pickens, Chanelle, and Ashleigh D. Coren. "Diversity Residency Programs: Strategies for a Collaborative Approach to Development." *Collaborative Librarianship* 9, no. 2 (2017): article 7. https://digitalcommons.du.edu/collaborativelibrarianship/vol9/iss2/7.

Rosa, Kathy, and Kelsey Henke. *2017 ALA Demographic Study*. Chicago: American Library Association, 2017. http://www.ala.org/tools/sites/ala.org.tools/files/content/Draft%20of%20Member%20Demographics%20Survey%2001-11-2017.pdf.

Rutledge, Lorelei, Jay L. Colbert, Anastasia Chiu, and Jason Kelly Alston. *Developing a Residency Program: A Practical Guide for Librarians*. Practical Guides for Librarians, no. 63. Lanham, MD: Rowman & Littlefield, 2019.

Schonfeld, Roger, and Liam Sweeney. *Inclusion, Diversity, and Equity: Members of the Association of Research Libraries*. New York: Ithaka S+R, August 30, 2017. https://doi.org/10.18665/sr.304524.

Shorter-Gooden, Kumea. "The Culturally Competent Organization." *Library Quarterly* 83, no. 3 (July 2013): 207–11. https://doi.org/10.1086/670695.

UNC Greensboro University Libraries. "Post MLS Diversity Residency Program." Accessed November 26, 2019. https://library.uncg.edu/info/diversity/residency_program.aspx.

US Census Bureau. "2012 National Population Projections Tables: Projected Race and Hispanic Origin." 2012. https://www.census.gov/data/tables/2012/demo/popproj/2012-summary-tables.html.

US Census Bureau. "2017 National Population Projections Tables: Projected Race and Hispanic Origin." 2017. https://www.census.gov/data/tables/2017/demo/popproj/2017-summary-tables.html

US Census Bureau. "Quick Facts: United States." 2019. https://www.census.gov/quickfacts/fact/table/US/PST045219.

Williamson, Charles C. *Training for Library Service: A Report Prepared for the Carnegie Corporation of New York.* Boston: Merrymount Press, 1923.

Witteveen, April. "Better Together: The Cohort Model of Professional Development" *Library Journal* 140, no. 20 (2015): 42–44.

SECTION IV
Reinforcing the Message

CHAPTER 13

Critical Analysis of ARL Member Institutions' Diversity Statements

V. Dozier, Sandra Enimil, and Adebola Fabiku

Introduction

Many people use information found on library websites to learn how an academic organization functions and to see how and what information that organization chooses to share. Websites also can demonstrate, for known and unknown constituents, how welcoming the institution may be.[1] Academic libraries convey their missions and values via their websites.[2] As a result, the websites can be an excellent place to demonstrate commitments to diversity. Definitions for diversity, equity, and inclusion (DEI) vary widely.[3] For the purposes of this chapter, the focus is on equity and inclusion regarding race, gender, national origin, ethnicity, religion, socioeconomic status, age, sexual orientation, veteran status, and physical and intellectual accessibility. Libraries can show a commitment to DEI in many ways, including through services, collection development, and recruitment of diverse employees. Commitment to DEI can be revealed via mission statements, diversity statements, visions, and values. Web pages can also share DEI-focused collections, programmatic efforts, committees, offices, and professional opportunities.[4] Diversity statements are a

fairly recent development in academic libraries.[5] It is critical for such information, if not prominent, to be easily accessible.[6] Libraries may receive guidance on DEI and what to include in statements on DEI from their parent institution, or they may receive encouragement and guidance from consortial partnerships or organizational associations.[7]

The Association of Research Libraries (ARL) is a member-driven research library consortium representing 125 public, private, and federal institutions in the United States and Canada. For many years, ARL and the library and information science (LIS) profession has espoused a desire to increase DEI in the field of librarianship. The lack of diversity in LIS is a known challenge that many have sought to rectify through a variety of efforts.[8] In March 2018, ARL's board of directors approved a new mission statement that includes a call to "promote equity and diversity" and lists "diversity, equity, and inclusion" as one of its four priorities. ARL also includes equity and diversity as the fifth and sixth guiding principles: (5) "Engage all member representatives in the work of the Association with respect, fairness, and integrity. Foster an environment of inclusion, equity, nondiscrimination, and pluralism," and (6) "Embrace diversity in all its dimensions and promote it as a vital stimulant to ARL's leadership and growth."[9] This project aims to review how ARL member institutions use DEI statements to address, among other concerns, issues within library spaces, the acknowledgment of marginalized communities, and larger social justice matters.

Workforce diversity in libraries has received lots of attention. Despite many efforts to promote DEI, the LIS profession remains largely white. Ithaka S+R's and the Mellon Foundation's 2017 Association of Research Libraries survey revealed whites comprise more than 75 percent of library employees at member libraries.[10] The consistently high percentage of whites and white women employed as library professionals persists even with the existence of diversity programs such as the American Library Association's Spectrum Scholars, ARL's Leadership and Career Development Program (LCDP), Kaleidoscope Program, Mosaic Fellowship, and multiple diversity resident positions nationwide. Some of these programs, such as Kaleidoscope, have existed in some form since the late 1990s. These programs are not targeted just at recruiting minorities at the beginning of the career ladder, but they are also aimed at recruiting minorities in middle and upper management positions. It is clear the ARL has a hand in trying to change the narrative of library staff being mostly white and building a diverse workforce that represents the people it serves.

Though ARL has a visible commitment to DEI on its website, it encourages, but does not require, to the extent that it could, similar visible commitments from all member institutions. This is evident on a web page that ARL maintains entitled "ARL Library Statements and Signs Affirming Our Core Beliefs."[11] As the title suggests, this web page is a collection of member statements and signage that affirm a DEI commitment. The list currently has thirty statements representing twenty-four institutions and ranging from 2013 to 2017. Member institutions self-report affirmations of inclusion on the page. The listed members represent approximately 19 percent of ARL's membership. Some web pages are no longer active. The content ranges from diversity statements to responses to incidents happening on their campuses or beyond.

This chapter builds on work done by a few scholars who analyzed diversity statements, initiatives, and websites at ARL and academic libraries.[12] The primary objective of this research project is to use the lens of critical discourse analysis to conduct a content analysis of the 125 ARL Libraries' existing diversity statements by answering the following research questions:[13] (1) How many ARL institutions have diversity statements, and how visible are the statements on the institution's website? (2) What are the stated goals of the statements? (3) Are the statements independent or copies of the statements of the parent institution? (4) For institutions with diversity statements, is there a connection between having a statement and also having diversity officers, diversity offices, or both? (5) Does the statement reveal anything about the institution's previous or current DEI work? The authors are also exploring whether the existence or placement of a diversity statement reveals anything about an institution's commitment to diversity, equity, and inclusion. DEI is action.[14] Do the websites of ARL member institutions display evidence of active DEI leadership and work within the library and larger campus community? This project will utilize existing literature to analyze diversity statements to determine what could be included in a good statement and will review the available statements to outline what the statements reveal about institutional commitment to DEI.

Literature Review

As diversity is now being considered "a requirement of excellence,"[15] are ARL libraries promoting that excellence by having and prominently displaying a diversity statement? Previous work on this topic provides insight into the themes, common mistakes, and what should be included when crafting diversity statements.

What Is a Diversity Statement?

Mestre sums up what a diversity statement is perfectly:

> A diversity statement (philosophical statement) sometimes originates from a mission statement. It may be included to supplement a mission statement by articulating a commitment to diversity. It may be a working definition or statement to use as one goes about trying to accomplish the initiatives related to diversity. Its intention may be to keep diversity at the forefront and may include goals.[16]

If a library does have a diversity statement, it should be available on the library's website. "Inadequate dissemination limits the effectiveness of a Diversity Statement. A Diversity Statement that is easy to find on the Library website is key because it provides clear communication to the public and keeps institutions and people accountable."[17] Having a diversity statement on the library's website conveys the library's commitment in working toward a discrimination-free workplace, that it values diversity, and that it provides an image to its visitors that all are welcome. However, many ARL libraries still do not highlight diversity statements on their websites.[18]

It is possible that many libraries do not display a diversity statement because the library believes that it does not need to have one if its parent institution has one. There is no legal incentive for an ARL library to have a diversity statement because "most academic libraries are covered by the umbrella plan of their parent institution."[19] But if the university has a diversity statement but the library lacks one, this could unintentionally communicate that the library does not have specific concerns that might be different from those of the parent institution.

Themes of Library Diversity Statements

The themes that appear the most often are the categories of diversity and the positive attributes of diversity.

Merkl's analysis of university diversity statements includes both a description of diversity statements and a categorical listing of the diverse groups.[20] Diversity statements that include listings of diverse groups "establishes who is considered diverse and, just as importantly, who is not. Therefore, it establishes who the statement can benefit and who it excludes."[21] Also, clarifying what diversity means and who is diverse helps make the diversity statement a guiding document "in order for programs, policies, and resources to be developed and evaluated as appropriate."[22]

The other main theme that emerges is diversity as a positive consequence for some members of the institution. "Examples of this identify interaction with diverse individuals as helping to encourage acceptance and respect, providing a greater understanding of cultures and perspectives, and preparing students to live in a global environment."[23] The benefits of these interactions with diverse individuals are experienced only by the non-diverse population of the institution. The problem with this is that it exploits the diverse population and conveys that their only value is in helping to diversify the educational or organizational experience of those who are not diverse.[24] While diversity should be a positive consequence, it becomes a negative consequence for the diverse population because they are being capitalized on.

The Common Mistakes in Diversity Statements

Even when an organization or institution does have a diversity statement, it may be poorly written or not relay the intended message and values of the organization. According to Carnes and colleagues, there are several common mistakes or pitfalls when crafting institutional diversity statements.[25]

The first mistake that organizations make with their diversity statements is claiming that diversity has already been reached or achieved. By stating that an organization does not discriminate, the organization has made a promise that it has already achieved equity, when, in fact, nondiscrimination is an ideal of the organization. When claims like these are made, it can increase employees' belief that they are fair, nonsexist, and nonracist individuals who do not need to do any work toward improving the culture of the organization around diversity.[26]

Some diversity statements make the mistake of being controlling. Diversity statements that emphasize that it is socially unacceptable to be racist or to discriminate are deemed as controlling and provide employees with no motivation to comply with the diversity statement. For example, statements that include wording such as "avoiding being racist" or the "obligation of being a non-racist" can have a counterintuitive effect. It makes employees feel that they are forced to obey, leaving them with no desire to work toward a non-biased institution.[27]

Some diversity statements make the mistake of being color-blind diversity statements. Statements that emphasize equity or embracing similarities fail to acknowledge the background and histories of the members of the organization. These types of statements are counterproductive to the message that the organization is trying to convey.[28]

Another major issue is "the degree to which [the diversity statement] does or does not reflect the experiences of current and potential members of the organization."[29] When a diversity statement is not backed up by action, it creates a false sense of acceptance for diverse individuals from those outside of the organization. Yet those inside the organization do not feel that diversity is reflected in their lived experience. These organizations haven't "actually [implemented] processes that can mitigate gender and race bias in organizational decision,"[30] although their statement says that they have.

Clifton asserts that some statements were more focused on the library or the university as an institution than they were focused on diversity itself. Focusing on the institution rather than diversity "can also diffuse accountability" and "there is less responsibility placed directly on the people who are able to make changes and decisions."[31] This also means that the university has the power to decide who to include and exclude. "Should University determine the benefits of interacting with diverse faculty and students as no longer valuable, the University has the power to exclude Diversity. The University is seen as the power agent whose benevolence towards Diversity can easily be removed."[32]

While some diversity statements focus on the institutions, others do not identify who exactly they are referring to. "Many of the Diversity Statements use the terms 'we' and 'our' throughout and the lack of salutation creates a situation where the reader does not know who 'we' is and whether the reader is a part of the 'we'/'our' being mentioned."[33]

What Diversity Statements Should Include

Carnes and colleagues stated that "diversity statements [should] be aspirational, emphasize autonomy, and express a value for difference."[34] Their research also "indicates that to achieve desired outcomes and minimize the risk of undesirable and unintended consequences, we must take considerable care in the language used and the messages conveyed when crafting diversity statements."[35]

Carnes and colleagues give several suggestions to writing better diversity statements. Instead of claiming that the library has already achieved diversity, it should emphasize its aspirations toward diversity. Crafting a message that relays that the library is striving toward a more diverse and nondiscriminatory climate is real and is the truth. Personal autonomy is another aspect that should be included in a diversity statement. "Incorporating messages such as 'Our faculty, staff, and students say they value diversity, enjoy relating to people from different groups, have fun meeting people from other cultures, and think issues of diversity are interesting,'"[36] promotes personal choice for the individual staff members of the library as opposed to being forced by their library administration. When people feel they have a choice, they are more motivated to embrace diversity.

Another recommendation that Carnes and colleagues make is to use multicultural language as opposed to color-blind language. Color-blind language is vague and demonstrates that there is no true understanding of diversity. Examples of color-blind language in diversity statements are those that claim that individuals do not see race or that everyone is the same and equal. This language results in people feeling that the organization is less diverse. Multicultural language augmented with a definition of diversity can be seen as less biased. This could include statements that acknowledge and embrace the differences in identities and experiences.

Lastly, once a diversity statement is written, the institution should practice what it preaches. The diversity statement should not just be displayed but should be backed by action where a process is implemented to mitigate biases in the organization.[37] That action should "permeate all aspects of the organization: hiring, firing, recruitment, retention, policies, architecture, design, location, projects, programs, promotions, celebrations, incentives, budgets, marketing, management styles, training, deadlines, strategic planning, families, meetings, performance."[38]

Methodology: Content Analysis

This study examined the websites of 125 ARL libraries and their parent institutions in North America for the existence of diversity statements. Existing diversity statements were analyzed using content analysis, sometimes referred to as textual analysis. Content analysis is a research methodology that has been used in social and behavioral sciences, library and information studies, communications, business, and other disciplines since the 1950s. White and Marsh describe content analysis as "a flexible research method that can be applied to many problems in information studies, either as a method by itself or in conjunction with other methods."[39] Content analysis also allows researchers to "make replicable and valid inferences from texts (or other meaningful matter) to the contexts of their use."[40]

This study employs a hybrid model of content analysis because both quantitative and qualitative methods are necessary to answer the proposed research questions. Quantitatively, the analysis explores whether there has been an increase in diversity statements among ARL libraries and the frequency of key terms such as *diversity, equity, inclusion, accessibility,* and so on. Qualitatively, the analysis seeks to identify themes or concepts potentially not identified or explored by previous LIS diversity statement research.[41]

The authors were particularly interested in evaluating the diversity statements based on White and Marsh's 2006 analysis of four of Beaugrande and Dressler's seven content analysis criteria: coherence, intentionality, acceptability, and informativity. White and Marsh expound on those four areas:

> The text has meaning, often established through relationships or implicature that may not be linguistically evident, and draws on frameworks within the recipient for understanding (coherence). The writer or speaker of the text intends for it to convey meaning related to his attitude and purpose (intentionality). Conversely, recipients of the message understand the text as a message; they expect it to be useful or relevant (acceptability). The text may contain new or expected information, allowing for judgments about its quality of informing (informativity).[42]

Library and information studies scholars also recognize that an academic library's website may be a patron's primary access point.[43] Thus, the existence and visibility of a library's diversity statement are key components to understanding the unit's values. Likewise, the parent institution's diversity statement and the diversity office's visibility give website users insight into the institution's values and the statement's coherence and informativity. A content analysis of the library and parent institution's diversity statements together will guide an exploration of the relationship between the library's and parent institution's statements (e.g., Are they coherent or aligned?); the statements' intentionality (e.g., What message does the statement convey?); acceptability (e.g., Is it useful or relevant to espoused values?); and informativity (e.g., Does the statement reveal any new information?).

Data Collection

From February 2019 to December 2019, the researchers used the list of ARL members' websites and collected data from two spaces:[44] library website (diversity statement and the statement's location) and parent institution (diversity statement and the name of the diversity office).[45] Throughout the data collection process, the collectors recorded observations or additional questions in the notes field. If diversity statements or a diversity office was not identified, an answer of *none*, *no answer*, or *not sure* with any relevant clarifying notes was recorded.

Challenges and Limitations

Website searches were limited to the search term *diversity* as it was assumed to be the most frequently occurring term and to provide consistency during data collection. If the diversity statement or office was not easily and clearly identifiable, the researcher used their own judgment to determine how deeply to explore the target websites.

The researchers generally agreed to follow Mestre's website usability recommendation of a maximum fifteen minutes per website (total thirty minutes per institution) and with the fewest clicks possible. Website usability studies show that users expect to find information quickly and that important, useful information will be prominent on the landing page. Thus, the data collectors strove to largely replicate the actions of a proficient or web-page-familiar user. Most existing diversity statements and diversity offices were found in less than ten minutes due to the established data collection workflow.

Data collection occurred over nearly a year from February 2019 to December 2019. While efforts were made to update any missing information before data analysis, it is possible diversity statements or diversity offices were added to websites or modified after the assigned collector visited.

Results and Analysis

Existence and Visibility of Diversity Statements

Table 13.1 details statistics regarding the number of ARL libraries with diversity statements, parent institutions with diversity statements and campus diversity offices, and combinations thereof. Results in the *yes* column are for those with identified diversity statements or diversity offices. Results in the *no* column indicate that a diversity statement or diversity office does not exist or was not clearly identified. Overall, sixty-five ARL libraries have a diversity statement, which represents 364 percent increase from the fourteen ARL libraries with a specific diversity statement in 2011.[46] Fifty ARL members were found to have a library diversity statement, a parent institution diversity statement, and a campus diversity office. According to this analysis, an ARL library is more likely to have a diversity statement if the parent institution also has a diversity statement and a campus diversity office.

TABLE 13.1

Fast stats

Condition	Yes	No
ARL w/a Diversity Statement	52% (n = 65)	48% (n = 60)
Parent Institution w/a Diversity Statement	81.6% (n = 102)	18.4% (n = 23)
Existence of Diversity Office	74.4% (n = 93)	25.6% (n = 32)
ARL + Parent w/a Diversity Statement	48.8% (n = 61)	51.2% (n = 64)
ARL + Parent + Diversity Office	40% (n = 50)	60% (n = 75)
ARL w/a Diversity Statement + Diversity Office	80% (n = 52)[47]	20% (n = 13)
Parent w/a Diversity Statement + Diversity Office	83.3% (n = 85[48])	16.7% (n = 17)
Total ARL Members = 125		

This analysis shows that existing diversity statements are typically placed in at least one of four areas on a library's website: about us, policy, strategic plan, or diversity page/diversity committee's page. None of the library diversity statements exist on the library's landing page, which serves as a primary access point for most users. Diversity statements embedded in a library's strategic plan, often a linked PDF, were the most difficult and time-consuming to locate (e.g., University of Alabama Libraries, University of California, Riverside Library, University of Pittsburgh Libraries[49]).

Frequently Occurring Words

Diversity statements were analyzed using QSR's NVivo 12's word frequency queries for the most frequently occurring stemmed words with four or more letters. Figure 13.1 represents the top ten stemmed words (e.g., *diverse* and *diversity* both count for *diversity*; *inclusion, inclusive, inclusivity,* and *inclusiveness* would count for *inclusion*, etc.).

Top 10 Frequently Occurring Stemmed Words

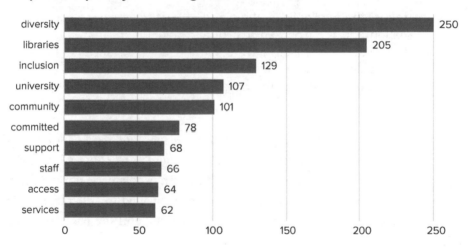

FIGURE 13.1
Top ten stemmed words—library statements

While it may not be surprising to see library statements include words like *diversity, libraries,* or *inclusion,* it is noteworthy that *access* barely cracked the top ten as it had two more counts than *services*. Upon further examination, words like *equity* ranks thirty-first, below sixteenth-ranked *respect* and twelfth-ranked *values*. If ARL libraries intend to communicate equity as a value to users, the term should appear as frequently as other DEIA (diversity, equity, inclusion, accessibility) terms.

Overall, library statements also mention historically marginalized groups less frequently than value concepts. The words *ethnicity* (#66), *race* (#70), or *nationality* (#72) are most often used in the boilerplate language pledging to welcome or serve all users regardless of ethnicity, race, nationality, and so on (e.g., University of Iowa, IUPUI, University of Kentucky, University of Maryland). According to Carnes and colleagues, this type of color-blind approach can serve to repel persons from marginalized communities who may read the statements as disingenuous.[50] Instead, diversity statements that explicitly use multicultural language and inclusive diversity definitions allow all members to identify as contributors to a diverse community.[51] Arizona State University Library's diversity statement affirms and directly quotes Arizona State University's statement:

> reflect the intellectual, ethnic and cultural diversity of our nation and the world so that our students learn from the broadest perspectives, and we engage in the advancement of knowledge with the most inclusive understanding possible of the issues we are addressing through our scholarly activities.[52]

ASU's statement includes atypical phrasing, such as *intellectual diversity* and *broadest perspectives,* to inform users of the library and university's values. Atypical phrasing can attract a user's attention; however, problematic phrasing such as *intellectual diversity* is a dog whistle to those engaged in anti-racist social justice work as a effort to circumvent ethnic, gender, and sex-based diversity efforts.

The analysis shows the word *culture* is used in a myriad of ways, from referencing the library's culture (Texas A&M), cultural heritage or norms (Arizona State University, University of California San Diego, or University of Colorado Boulder), or organizational culture (University of California Santa Barbara, University of Houston, IUPUI), or cultural competency (University of Colorado Boulder). Other libraries should consider articulating the specific use of *culture* in a phrase (e.g., cultural competency) to clearly communicate what values the library holds or actions it undertakes.

Top 10 Stemmed Words—Parent Institution Statements

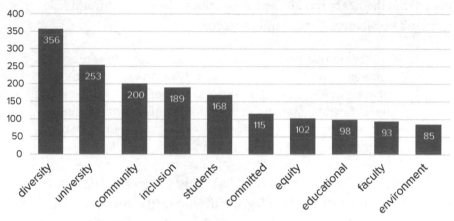

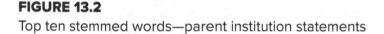

FIGURE 13.2

Top ten stemmed words—parent institution statements

Diversity Statement Goals and DEIA Work

Both the library and parent institution diversity statements use action verbs words like *strive, commit, increase, embrace, ensure, build,* and *foster* to preface intended DEIA goals (Figure 13.2). Using action verbs can indicate the organization intends to actively work toward DEIA. However, libraries and institutions should take care to avoid attaching action verbs to vague, incredibly lofty, or impossible goals, particularly using the word *all*. For example, Wayne State University Library, an ACRL Diversity Alliance member, lists as one of its library diversity goals: "Partner with all individuals within WSU to find and build meaningful relationships across diverse communities, while providing and supporting diversity initiatives that support WSU and greater Detroit.[53] Realistically, it is improbable that *all individuals within WSU* or at any other campus will embrace DEIA work. Likewise, the University of New Mexico states, "Our goal is to shape the experiences and perceptions of all individuals on campus, including all underrepresented groups—with regard to diversity, equity, inclusion, and culture, to help create a more inclusive campus."[54] While this goal sounds good and mentions marginalized groups, the word *all* indicates a lofty or improbable goal.

Some diversity statements explicitly list staff diversity goals, typically centering around themes of recruitment, professional development, and reflecting the campus's population. Carnes and colleagues state,

> If underrepresented applicants are more likely to represent themselves authentically when applying to an organization because that organization espouses egalitarian values in a public diversity statement, then the institution must ensure that the statement is backed up by real action to prevent bias and discrimination within the organization.[55]

For example, Brown University Library lists a goal to "recruit, train, and develop a diverse, dedicated, collegial staff who thrive in a continuous learning environment."[56] Wayne State University Library lists five staff goals:

- Emphasize the development and retention of a diverse staff within our hiring and professional development activities.

- Recognize that diversity of staff represents broad elements, and is not limited to racial, cultural, demographic, or cognitive categories.

- Identify, share, and implement programs and practices that support the council's mission and goals.

- Suggest ways to address problems and concerns related to collegiality and synergy.

- Seek opportunities for collaboration to create an inclusive environment that values people.[57]

Listing specific, actionable staff diversity goals in the diversity statement or on the library website is beneficial and transparent not only for current staff, but also for future candidates seeking employment.

The University of Arizona Libraries notes,

> We strive to ensure: students, scholars, and staff have equitable access to library resources; our recruitment and hiring practices are inclusive and attract candidates that reflect the diversity of our community; library employees have equal access for advancement; our collections and services reflect the breadth of human experience from many orientations.[58]

While this statement lacks measurable goals, the library's diversity page is bolstered by including specific actions undertaken by its Diversity, Social Justice, and Equity Council (DSJEC), for example, hosting implicit bias workshops. Some libraries were noted to have diversity committees or strategic plans, but the web page or strategic plan may be outdated or retired (e.g., Washington University in St. Louis Libraries, Auburn University Libraries[59]), which may indicate to users that the library no longer values this DEIA work.

Conclusion

The authors found 52 percent of ARL member institutions have DEI statements, approximately quadrupling the number from Mestre's 2011 study and the member websites featured on the ARL Library Statements web page. The statements are housed on website subpages such as About Us or Policies, not front facing on the institution's website. Usability studies show that users correlate placement to importance.[60] Thus, ARL libraries should include the diversity statement or at least a link to the statement on the library's home page. Burying diversity statements on website subpages, especially in linked strategic plan PDFs, increases the likelihood users will not see them.

The authors found ARL libraries are more likely to have a diversity statement if the parent institution also has a diversity statement and a campus diversity office. Scholars such as Carnes and colleagues and Mestre recommend that diversity statements avoid vague, color-blind, controlling, or counterproductive language. Instead, statements with specific, multicultural, autonomous, actionable, and aspirational language are more positively received and provide more transparent accountability for diversity goals. In existing library diversity statements, *diversity/diverse* is the most frequently occurring word. Words like *inclusion*, *inclusive*, *inclusiveness*, and *inclusivity* also rank highly. *Equity*, however, occurs more frequently in university statements, highlighting a key disconnect between stated institution values and library values. The analysis also reveals that libraries are more likely to mention, allude to, or affirm the university's statement—*university* is the fourth ranked most frequent word—whereas the parent institution's statement functions as the overarching statement for the entire institution. Creating a separate diversity statement allows libraries to articulate and center goals more pertinent to the library unit than general parent institution statements.

ARL libraries without a diversity statement or only post a superficial statement in their websites should consider including DEIA committees, strategic goals, and action items that communicate active DEIA work on their web pages.

Further Study

There is a gap in the literature on when ARL libraries first started creating and displaying their diversity statements. The earliest literature found centers the affirmative action statements of ARL libraries.[61] Did affirmative action statements give birth to diversity statements? Exploring the history of ARL libraries' diversity statements would be an interesting way to understand the climate of libraries and the world at that time. Was there a catalyst that prompted libraries to create diversity statements? If there was a catalyst for creation, did it change employment demographics or the perception of the commitment to diversity for users?

An assessment of the user's perspective on the diversity of the library has not been done. According to Wilson and colleagues, when "students, faculty, and staff, particularly from underrepresented groups, feel supported and engaged then they will stay."[62] A study of library users could explore whether libraries with diversity statements are seen as more welcoming to users, with diverse collections and staffing that reflects the library's commitment to diversity.

Another exploration would be to determine the authors of diversity statements of each institution. Diversity statements of institutions that deliberated with all staff members may signify that the institutions have a culture of inclusion that is expressed clearly in their diversity statements. On the other hand, including everyone in that process could result in the diversity statement being a vague document because the writer of the statement is trying to please all parties. Diversity statements written by library leadership may fall into the controlling pitfall that Carnes and colleagues noted, but could also be seen by staff members as leadership taking action and exhibiting a commitment to diversity.

Notes

1.   Here *unknown constituents* refers to persons who are not the anticipated audience of a particular academic library's website. Lori S. Mestre, "Visibility of Diversity within Association of Research Libraries Websites," *Journal of Academic Librarianship* 37, no. 2 (March 2011): 101–8, https://doi.org/10.1016/j.acalib.2011.02.001.

2. Mestre, "Visibility of Diversity," 101.
3. For the purposes of this chapter the concepts of diversity, equity, inclusion, and accessibility will be represented by the acronyms "DEI" and "DEIA."
4. Courtney L. Young, "Collection Development and Diversity on CIC Academic Library Web Sites," *Journal of Academic Librarianship* 32, no. 4 (July 2006): 370–76, https://doi.org/10.1016/j.acalib.2006.03.004.
5. Young, "Collection Development and Diversity."
6. Young, "Collection Development and Diversity," 374.
7. Young, "Collection Development and Diversity," 370.
8. Paul T. Jaeger et al., "The Virtuous Circle Revisited: Injecting Diversity, Inclusion, Rights, Justice, and Equity into LIS from Education to Advocacy," *Library Quarterly* 85, no. 2 (April 2015): 150–71, https://doi.org/10.1086/680154.
9. Association of Research Libraries, "Who We Are," accessed January 30, 2020, https://www.arl.org/who-we-are/.
10. Roger C. Schonfeld and Liam Sweeney, "Inclusion, Diversity, and Equity: Members of the Association of Research Libraries: Employee Demographics and Director Perspectives," Ithaka S+R, last updated August 30, 2017, https://doi.org/10.18665/sr.304524.
11. Association of Research Libraries, "ARL Library Statements and Signs Affirming Our Core Beliefs," accessed January 30, 2020, https://www.arl.org/resources/arl-library-statements-affirming-our-core-beliefs/.
12. Nadia Clifton, "Themes in Diversity Statements of Academic Libraries" (master's paper, University of North Carolina, 2019), https://cdr.lib.unc.edu/concern/masters_papers/jm214t77d; Mestre, "Visibility of Diversity"; Young, "Collection Development and Diversity."
13. The review period was February 2019 to December 2019.
14. Pamela Espinosa de los Monteros and Sandra Enimil, "Chapter 2: Designing a Collaborative EDI Strategy for Library Staff," in *Diversity, Equity, and Inclusion in Action: Planning, Leadership, and Programming* (Chicago, IL: American Library Association, 2020.)
15. Jeffrey Flier, "Against Diversity Statements," *Chronicle of Higher Education*, January 3, 2019, para. 1, https://www.chronicle.com/article/against-diversity-statements/.
16. Mestre, "Visibility of Diversity," 105.
17. Clifton, "Themes in Diversity Statements," 18.
18. Mestre, "Visibility of Diversity," 101.
19. Barbara B. Moran, "The Impact of Affirmative Action on Academic Libraries," *Library Trends* 34, no. 2 (Fall 1985): 201, https://eric.ed.gov/?id=EJ334698.
20. Linda A. Merkl, "Maintaining or Disrupting Inequality: Diversity Statements in the University" (PhD thesis, University of Denver, 2012), 137, https://digitalcommons.du.edu/etd/425.
21. Clifton, "Themes in Diversity Statements," 19–20.
22. Merkl, "Maintaining or Disrupting Inequality," 137–38.
23. Merkl, "Maintaining or Disrupting Inequality," 137.
24. Merkl, "Maintaining or Disrupting Inequality," 139.
25. Molly Carnes, Eve Fine, and Jennifer Sheridan, "Promises and Pitfalls of Diversity Statements: Proceed with Caution," *Academic Medicine: Journal of the Association of American Medical Colleges* 94, no. 1 (January 2019): 20–24, https://doi.org/10.1097/ACM.0000000000002388.
26. Carnes, Fine, and Sheridan, "Promises and Pitfalls of Diversity Statements," 20–21.
27. Carnes, Fine, and Sheridan, "Promises and Pitfalls of Diversity Statements," 22.
28. Carnes, Fine, and Sheridan, "Promises and Pitfalls of Diversity Statements," 22–23.

29. Carnes, Fine, and Sheridan, "Promises and Pitfalls of Diversity Statements," 23.
30. Carnes, Fine, and Sheridan, "Promises and Pitfalls of Diversity Statements," 23.
31. Clifton, "Themes in Diversity Statements," 19.
32. Merkl, "Maintaining or Disrupting Inequality," 145.
33. Merkl, "Maintaining or Disrupting Inequality," 134.
34. Carnes, Fine, and Sheridan, "Promises and Pitfalls of Diversity Statements," 20.
35. Carnes, Fine, and Sheridan, "Promises and Pitfalls of Diversity Statements," 20.
36. Carnes, Fine, and Sheridan, "Promises and Pitfalls of Diversity Statements," 22.
37. Carnes, Fine, and Sheridan, "Promises and Pitfalls of Diversity Statements," 21–23.
38. Mestre, "Visibility of Diversity," 107.
39. Marilyn Domas White and Emily E. Marsh, "Content Analysis: A Flexible Methodology," *Library Trends* 55, no. 1 (Summer 2006): 23, https://doi.org/10.1353/lib.2006.0053.
40. Klaus Krippendorff, *Content Analysis*, 2nd ed (Thousand Oaks, CA: Sage, 2004), 18.
41. Clifton, "Themes in Diversity Statements"; Mestre, "Visibility of Diversity."
42. White and Marsh, "Content Analysis," 28.
43. Mestre, "Visibility of Diversity."
44. Association of Research Libraries, "Who We Are."
45. For each library website, the assigned collector used the internal search feature to query the term *diversity*. If a diversity statement was identified, the text and corresponding web link were recorded. Next, the collector visited the parent institution's website and searched internally for the term *diversity*. Once a statement was identified, the statement's text was recorded. Then, the collector either searched the diversity results or explored the institution's website for the existence of a diversity office. Sometimes, the diversity office was easy to locate if listed on the first page of search results. In other occasions, the collector would manually search likely landing pages, such as About or Home, student affairs, the president's office, provost's office, or policy pages, for a diversity office or diversity statement. If statements were not found using internal search functions, a last resort would be to do a formal internet search using the institution name with *diversity*. All information was recorded to a shared Google spreadsheet.
46. Mestre, "Visibility of Diversity," 104.
47. 80% represents the 52 ARL libraries with a diversity statement + diversity office out of 65 ARL libraries with a diversity statement.
48. 83.3% represents the 85 parent institutions with a diversity statement + diversity office out of the 102 parent institutions with a diversity statement.
49. University of Alabama Libraries, "Strategic Plan 2017–2020," accessed January 31, 2020, https://www.lib.ua.edu/wp-content/uploads/2017/04/Strategic-Plan-11162016-FINAL.pdf; University of California, Riverside Library, "UCR Library Strategic Plan: Developed Academic Year 2014–15, Revised for 2016–2017," April 21, 2015, https://library.ucr.edu/sites/default/files/UCR%20Library%20Strategic%20Plan%202015-04-21.pdf; University of Pittsburgh, University Library System, "Goal 6 | University Library System (ULS)," accessed July 17, 2020, https://www.library.pitt.edu/goal-6 (page discontinued).
50. Carnes, Fine, and Sheridan, "Promises and Pitfalls of Diversity Statements," 22.
51. Carnes, Fine, and Sheridan, "Promises and Pitfalls of Diversity Statements," 22–23.
52. Arizona State University Library, "Commitment to Inclusion," para. 1, accessed January 30, 2020, https://lib.asu.edu/inclusion.
53. Wayne State University Libraries, "Diversity in the Library System," accessed July 17, 2020, https://library.wayne.edu/info/about/diversity/.
54. University of New Mexico, "Division for Equity and Inclusion," accessed July 17, 2020, https://diverse.unm.edu/.

55. Carnes, Fine, and Sheridan, "Promises and Pitfalls of Diversity Statements," 23.
56. Brown University Library, "Brown University Library Strategic Directions," accessed July 17, 2020, https://library.brown.edu/info/about/strategic-directions/.
57. Wayne State University Libraries, "Diversity."
58. University of Arizona Libraries, "Our Commitment to Diversity & Inclusivity," September 19, 2014, https://new.library.arizona.edu/about/diversity.
59. Rudolph Clay and Washington University in St. Louis Libraries, "Research Guides: Diversity and Inclusion," LibGuide, accessed July 17, 2020, https://libguides.wustl.edu/c.php?g=47424&p=303816; Auburn University Libraries, "Diversity," accessed July 17, 2020, https://www.lib.auburn.edu/diversity/index.php.
60. Merkl, "Maintaining or Disrupting Inequality"; Mestre, "Visibility of Diversity."
61. Moran, "Impact of Affirmative Action."
62. Jeffery L. Wilson, Katrina A. Meyer, and Larry McNeal, "Mission and Diversity Statements: What They Do and Do Not Say," *Innovative Higher Education* 37, no. 2 (2012): 138, https://doi.org/10.1007/s10755-011-9194-8.

Bibliography

Arizona State University Library. "Commitment to Inclusion." Accessed January 30, 2020. https://lib.asu.edu/inclusion.

Association of Research Libraries. "ARL Library Statements and Signs Affirming Our Core Beliefs." Accessed January 30, 2020. https://www.arl.org/resources/arl-library-statements-affirming-our-core-beliefs/.

———. "Who We Are." Accessed January 30, 2020. https://www.arl.org/who-we-are/.

Auburn University Libraries. "Inclusion." Accessed July 17, 2020. http://www.auburn.edu/inclusion/.

Brown University Library. "Brown University Library Strategic Directions." Accessed July 17, 2020. https://library.brown.edu/info/about/strategic-directions/.

Carnes, Molly, Eve Fine, and Jennifer Sheridan. "Promises and Pitfalls of Diversity Statements: Proceed with Caution." *Academic Medicine: Journal of the Association of American Medical Colleges* 94, no. 1 (January 2019): 20–24. https://doi.org/10.1097/ACM.0000000000002388.

Clifton, Nadia. "Themes in Diversity Statements of Academic Libraries." Master's paper, University of North Carolina, 2019. https://cdr.lib.unc.edu/concern/masters_papers/jm214t77d.

Espinosa de los Monteros, Pamela, and Sandra Enimil. "Chapter 2: Designing a Collaborative EDI Strategy for Library Staff." In *Diversity, Equity, and Inclusion in Action: Planning, Leadership, and Programming.* Edited by Christine Bombaro. Chicago, IL: American Library Association.

Flier, Jeffrey. "Against Diversity Statements." *Chronicle of Higher Education*, January 3, 2019. https://www.chronicle.com/article/against-diversity-statements/.

Jaeger, Paul T., Nicole A. Cooke, Cecilia Feltis, Michelle Hamiel, Fiona Jardine, and Katie Shilton. "The Virtuous Circle Revisited: Injecting Diversity, Inclusion, Rights, Justice, and Equity into LIS from Education to Advocacy." *Library Quarterly* 85, no. 2 (April 2015): 150–71. https://doi.org/10.1086/680154.

Krippendorff, Klaus. *Content Analysis: An Introduction to Its Methodology*, 2nd ed. Thousand Oaks, CA: Sage, 2004.

Merkl, Linda A. "Maintaining or Disrupting Inequality: Diversity Statements in the University." PhD thesis, University of Denver, 2012. https://digitalcommons.du.edu/etd/425.

Mestre, Lori S. "Visibility of Diversity within Association of Research Libraries Websites." *Journal of Academic Librarianship* 37, no. 2 (March 2011): 101–8. https://doi.org/10.1016/j.acalib.2011.02.001.

Moran, Barbara B. "The Impact of Affirmative Action on Academic Libraries." *Library Trends* 34, no. 2 (Fall 1985): 199–217. https://eric.ed.gov/?id=EJ334698.

Rudolph Clay and Washington University in St. Louis Libraries. "Research Guides: Diversity and Inclusion." LibGuide. Accessed July 17, 2020. https://libguides.wustl.edu/c.php?g=47424&p=303816 (page discontinued).

Schonfeld, Roger C., and Liam Sweeney. "Inclusion, Diversity, and Equity: Members of the Association of Research Libraries: Employee Demographics and Director Perspectives." Ithaka S+R, last updated August 30, 2017. https://doi.org/10.18665/sr.304524.

University of Alabama Libraries. "Strategic Plan 2017–2020." Accessed January 31, 2020. https://www.lib.ua.edu/wp-content/uploads/2017/04/Strategic-Plan-11162016-FINAL.pdf.

University of Arizona Libraries. "Our Commitment to Diversity & Inclusivity." September 19, 2014. https://new.library.arizona.edu/about/diversity.

University of California, Riverside Library. "UCR Library Strategic Plan: Developed Academic Year 2014–15, Revised for 2016–2017." April 21, 2015. https://library.ucr.edu/sites/default/files/UCR%20Library%20Strategic%20Plan%202015-04-21.pdf.

University of New Mexico. "Division for Equity and Inclusion." Accessed July 17, 2020. https://diverse.unm.edu/.

University of Pittsburgh, University Library System. "Goal 6 | University Library System (ULS)." Accessed July 17, 2020. https://www.library.pitt.edu/goal-6 (page discontinued).

Wayne State University Libraries. "Diversity in the Library System." Accessed July 17, 2020. https://library.wayne.edu/info/about/diversity/.

White, Marilyn Domas, and Emily E. Marsh. "Content Analysis: A Flexible Methodology." *Library Trends* 55, no. 1 (Summer 2006): 22–45. https://doi.org/10.1353/lib.2006.0053.

Wilson, Jeffery L., Katrina A. Meyer, and Larry McNeal. "Mission and Diversity Statements: What They Do and Do Not Say." *Innovative Higher Education* 37, no. 2 (2012): 125–39. https://doi.org/10.1007/s10755-011-9194-8.

Young, Courtney L. "Collection Development and Diversity on CIC Academic Library Web Sites." *Journal of Academic Librarianship* 32, no. 4 (July 2006): 370–76. https://doi.org/10.1016/j.acalib.2006.03.004.

SECTION V
Organizational Change

CHAPTER 14

The Making of Emory Libraries' Diversity, Equity, and Inclusion Committee

A Case Study

Saira Raza, Melissa Hackman, Hannah Rutledge, Jina DuVernay, Nik Dragovic, and Erica Bruchko

Emory Overview and Recent History

Overview of Emory University and Emory University Libraries

Emory University is a private, liberal arts research university located in the city of Atlanta, Georgia. In 2019, it had a total student enrollment of 15,451, including 8,079 undergraduates and 7,372 graduate and professional students.[1] It is divided into nine schools, four of which serve undergraduates. Among its graduate and professional schools are schools of arts and sciences, public health, business, law, theology, nursing, and medicine.[2] It is highly competitive, and in 2020 was

ranked twenty-first of the nation's national universities by *U.S. News and World Report* and was seventeenth in the size of its endowment.[3]

The Emory Libraries actively support the university's research and teaching mission.[4] Emory's collections include more than 4.2 million volumes, 83,000-plus electronic journals, 704,535 electronic books, and internationally renowned special collections.[5] It is made up of seven libraries, including the Robert W. Woodruff Library, which is home to the Stuart A. Rose Manuscript, Archives, and Rare Book Library; the Goizueta Business Library; and the Heilbrun Music and Media Library. Other libraries include the Atwood Science Commons, the Woodruff Health Sciences Library, and the Oxford College Library located on the University's Oxford Campus approximately thirty miles from Atlanta. In addition, the university maintains professional school libraries including the Pitts Theology Library and the Hugh F. MacMillan Law Library.

Diversity and Inclusion at Emory

In 2016–2017, minorities comprised 32 percent of the student body, 28 percent of faculty, and 49 percent of staff. Women constituted 58 percent of the student body, 42 percent of faculty, and 67 percent of staff. Over 65 percent of the student body received financial aid.[6] Several offices on campus support diversity, equity, and inclusion (DEI) work. While each serves a specific function, they often work together, aligned by Emory University's organizational framework and values. These include campus life organizations such as the Office of Lesbian, Gay, Bisexual and Transgender Life; the Office of Racial and Cultural Engagement; the Office of Social Justice Education; the Office of International Student Life; and the 1915 Scholars Program for first-generation students. The Center for Women, the Office of Equity and Inclusion, and the Office of Accessibility Services serve students and the larger Emory community. Prior to 2016, the libraries actively engaged with these groups and spearheaded diversity initiatives within individual units; however, it was not until dean and university librarian Yolanda Cooper issued a call for a cross-libraries working group that a formal, coordinated effort took place.[7]

Evolution and Structure of the Committee

A new chapter of diversity initiatives at Emory Libraries commenced in September 2016, when dean and university librarian Yolanda Cooper issued a call for interest and a charge for a new Diversity and Inclusion Working Group (DIWG; see figure 14.1). Cooper was motivated by the presence of similar groups at peer institutions and had been interested in chartering a group since starting at Emory in 2014. Emory Libraries' DIWG also supported major elements of the Libraries Strategic Framework, which incorporated this focus as part of Organization Development and Culture. The charge was approved by the Libraries' Cabinet—a governance group consisting of extended library stakeholders from across campus.

Cooper presented her vision, which emphasized a holistic and community-oriented perspective, as opposed to a strict focus on staff recruitment, at a kickoff meeting after sharing the charge:

> The Diversity and Inclusion Working Group is an active and on-going group composed of staff willing to develop and implement activities and programs to create and maintain a welcoming, respectful, and inclusive environment for staff and community. **The Group will assess the current state, gather information and ideas, explore initiatives at other institutions, implement activities and programs and assess to determine effectiveness.** Group activities include:
>
> - Reviewing current related activities, gathering information from stakeholders, and investigating DI activities on campus and at other institutions.
> - Implementing activities, programs/training, exhibits, etc. to build awareness, dialogue, resources and services to enhance our environment.
> - Working with Libraries Administration, Cabinet, and HR to:
>   o develop educational opportunities for staff
>   o create opportunities for programming and discussion related to DI
>   o advise on policies and resources related to diversity and inclusion and expectations related to the development of cultural competencies

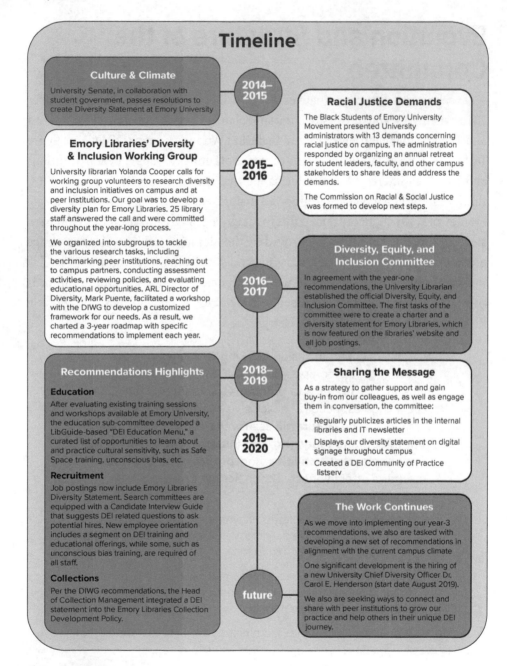

FIGURE 14.1

Time line of major committee milestones

(All figures come from Gretchen Warner et al., "Evolution of Emory Libraries' Diversity, Equity, and Inclusion Committee," poster presentation, American Library Association Annual Meeting, Washington, DC, June 20–25, 2019.)

- form partnerships with relevant groups on campus to share information and good practices
- collaborate with the Libraries departments to support and celebrate DI activities and programming[8]

Twenty library workers attended this initial meeting, with broad representation across organizational units, employee classifications, and demographics. From the beginning, the autonomy, resourcing, and support that the dean and university librarian provided were critical to this endeavor. Any employee wishing to participate was afforded the time to do so. The initial chairs self-selected from among the group, and Cooper met with them on a regular basis as a sponsor and guide. The working group was free to self-organize to achieve the goals stated in the charge and to adjust this framework as needed in the initial stages of activity.

The group's initial activities consisted mainly of introductions and information sharing to help cohere this new effort that brought together a unique and cross-functional group. The working group leadership came from cochairs who had deep interest in the group mission but limited experience in leading large organizational initiatives in academic libraries. One cochair was an alumnus of ALA and ARL diversity programs, which provided them with leadership training and connections to experts in professional organizations. The other cochair had a background in community activism through organizations such as Stand Up for Racial Justice (SURJ), which shaped the communication style and strategy of the group. Their experiences helped establish terms of engagement, a conceptual framework, broader institutional perspectives, and a network to call upon from the broader profession.

Although the open nature of our charge was empowering, it took time to develop a consensus-oriented strategy. Identifying a direction for the group was a challenge because of the many lived experiences and definitions of diversity that members brought to the committee.

We needed to develop a shared understanding and interpretation of diversity for Emory Libraries to move forward. We recognized the many different components of diversity and decided to focus on needs at the intersection of librarianship and Emory University.

The practical pathway forward was to form subgroups coinciding with the activities delineated in the charter and to start promoting the group and its new initiatives to staff with educational offerings that initially drew from existing campus and community resources, such as Emory's Office of Equity and

Inclusion training called "Creating an Environment of Courtesy and Respect," and the Center for Women's Safe Space workshop.

Research Process and Recommendations

For the first few months, the DIWG spent meeting time sharing research on peer institutions, read articles about issues and frameworks related to the scope of our work, and shared institutional knowledge about existing diversity- and inclusion-related initiatives on campus. We also shared ideas, experiences, and motivations for joining the working group and agreed on how the team would communicate with each other and make decisions. It became clear that we would need to develop a framework within which to organize the information that was being collected and transform it into meaningful recommendations. The dean and university librarian agreed to fund a half-day retreat for the DIWG with a consultant who could facilitate the ideation process and help the team organize its thoughts into a clear research plan.

Working with the dean and university librarian, the team identified some key qualities we needed in a facilitator:

- a flexible approach to facilitating in order to easily adapt to Emory Libraries' organizational culture
- clearly demonstrated experience with research libraries, including exposure to other institutions that were working on similar issues around DEI
- a holistic understanding of diversity, equity, and inclusion work, unafraid to engage in critical approaches to organizational change and centering intersectionality and social justice

Mark Puente, director of diversity and leadership programs for the Association of Research Libraries, agreed to facilitate the half-day retreat. During the four-hour workshop-style session, the working group members shared our concerns about diversity and inclusion issues at Emory Libraries and the wider Emory community. Then as a group, we organized and prioritized the various issues based on such criteria as level of urgency, feasibility, and scalability. This exercise proved to be especially helpful toward the end of the process of writing the recommendations by helping the DIWG scope the recommendations within a three-year road map. Another important outcome of the retreat was establishing reasonable expectations for the team and accepting the principle of non-closure—that there will always be problems to solve around issues of equity and inclusion. Because DEI issues are deeply personal, tackling social change can be emotionally taxing. Non-closure provides vocabulary and space for members of the DIWG to express these emotions in a constructive way and celebrates the small victories along a continual path to growth and organizational change.

Based on the priorities and issues identified in the retreat, the DIWG developed a framework for addressing DEI concerns across Emory Libraries. The core themes of the framework—*representation* and *access*—operate across the four areas of focus: *culture and climate, human resources, user services*, and *collections*.

Themes
REPRESENTATION
- Do users and staff see themselves reflected in our space, staff, and services?
- Do our policies articulate our commitment to an inclusive community?

ACCESS
- Have we considered the varying needs of different communities when it comes to using our resources and services?
- Do staff members have resources to help them navigate issues of diversity and inclusion when working with users and coworkers, and when implementing ideas?
- Do students and staff have a way to address their concerns related to diversity and inclusion in our organization?

Areas of Focus
- *Culture and climate:* our environment, our space, and the feeling we create for our users and library workers
- *Human resources:* recruitment, retention, professional development, and staff-facing policies
- *User services:* how we interact with users in person and online, and our user-facing policies
- *Collections:* how well we represent the various needs and perspectives of users in the development and management of our collections

With clearer definition of priorities, the team took inventory of the various tasks of the research process and developed subcommittees to take the lead on gathering information and insights to inform our recommendations. The subcommittees were assessment, peer benchmarking, education, and outreach.

Assessment

Two major campus-wide assessment instruments were being implemented during the 2016–2017 academic year. Library leadership felt it would be too overwhelming to develop and distribute a custom survey from the committee, so as an alternative, the DIWG was invited to design a new question for the existing biennial Emory Libraries Engagement Survey. The subcommittee worked closely with the library assessment team as well as the institutional research team to collect and analyze the results into meaningful insights.

Peer Benchmarking

The DIWG studied the diversity and inclusion work of peer academic library institutions, working from a list provided by the dean and university librarian. In addition to researching the institutions on the list, the subcommittee also compiled information from other university libraries with significant investment in diversity and inclusion activities. While the sub-committee was tasked with researching library-specific DEI initiatives, inevitably, larger institutional goals were often reflected and restated in library documentation. The following were chosen as peer institutions for the purposes of benchmarking:

- Auburn University
- Brown University
- Columbia University
- Duke University
- Indiana University–Purdue University Indianapolis
- Johns Hopkins University
- Massachusetts Institute of Technology
- Miami University
- Mississippi State University
- Northwestern University
- Notre Dame University
- Penn State University
- Rice University

- Tulane University
- University of Arkansas
- University of Chicago
- University of Georgia
- University of Illinois at Urbana-Champaign
- University of Kansas
- University of Michigan
- University of North Carolina Greensboro
- University of Oregon
- University of Pennsylvania
- University of Virginia
- University of Washington Bothell
- University of Wisconsin Madison
- Vanderbilt University
- Washington University in St. Louis

EDUCATION

The education subcommittee researched on-campus and online opportunities for trainings, workshops, and other learning tools around issues of diversity, equity, and inclusion. We coordinated and created sessions for members of the DIWG to experience and evaluate existing campus learning opportunities, such as Safe Space training. We also adapted current workshops offered on campus and customized them to the needs of library workers. For example, the education subcommittee organized a panel session made up of Emory faculty and students on working with international students and a workshop with Emory's director of social justice education on racial determination.

OUTREACH

The outreach subcommittee contacted seventy-five cultural, diversity, and ethnic-oriented student groups on campus as well as administrators from campus life, international student life, LGBT life, and so on. The subcommittee also reached out directly to students through campus events such as club activity fairs to informally talk to students about their concerns and ideas. In addition, the subcommittee spoke with individuals currently doing outreach within Emory Libraries. The purpose in reaching out was to inform community partners about the DIWG and to assess opportunities and needs for outreach on campus.

As a group, the DIWG also participated in diversity- and inclusion-related webinars offered by professional associations. We coordinated Emory Libraries' participation in the ARL SPEC survey on diversity initiatives, which provided valuable benchmarking insights. Finally, the dean and university librarian supported members of the DIWG to attend conferences related to diversity and inclusion, such as ARL's National Diversity in Libraries Conference.

Having spent the fall and spring semesters conducting research, the DIWG spent the summer months in group writing sessions, working on the final deliverable of recommendations. Upon completion, we submitted thirteen recommendations across a three-year road map, in addition to detailed reports from each subcommittee summarizing research findings.

Final Recommendations

Recommendation 1: Create and craft a formal Diversity, Equity, and Inclusion Committee and determine its formal scope and reporting structure under Library and Information Technology Services (LITS) leadership.

In 2017, the DIWG became the Diversity, Equity, and Inclusion Committee, sponsored by the dean and university librarian. The committee developed a charter, which outlined the scope and reporting structure as well as the ground rules for meetings and generally accepted principles of the committee. Those principles are as follows:

1.   Oppression is real, and discrimination is a form of oppression.
2.   There will not be closure on issues related to diversity, equity, and inclusion, but we still commit to ongoing growth and change to create a better environment for our community.

Recommendation 2: Craft clear definitions of diversity and inclusion and a diversity statement that can be referenced across initiatives, policies, and programs within Emory Libraries.

The DIWG compiled existing definitions of diversity and inclusion from various departments at Emory such as the Office of Equity and Inclusion and Campus Life. These definitions were included in the recommendations. The committee dedicated its first year to articulating a diversity statement and sharing it across organizational units for integration into their policies and literature.

Recommendation 3: Develop and implement a DEI education and training plan for Emory Libraries staff.

Continuing the work from its research, the education subcommittee compiled a DEI education menu on LibGuides, which is publicly available on the Emory Libraries website. This menu is included among the materials shared during new hire orientations.

Emory Libraries and IT Human Resources implemented recommendations to make unconscious bias training required for all employees and coordinated planning and tracking to ensure all libraries staff have an opportunity to take the in-person training offered by Emory's Office of Equity and Inclusion. They are also engaged with the DEI committee to explore ongoing diversity- and inclusion-related education.

Recommendation 4: Create a research and assessment plan to further evaluate Emory Libraries' DEI topics and pain points.

Since the inception of the DEI committee, Emory Libraries has invested in more staff to support system-wide assessment practices. Emory Libraries' assessment and user experience team communicates regularly with the DEI committee by continuing to include diversity-related questions in the biennial survey distributed to the entire Emory University community, as well as developing new instruments and assessment plans for future use across Emory Libraries.

Recommendation 5: Leverage signage, website, exhibitions, and physical space to demonstrate Emory Libraries' commitment to DEI values.

New digital signage across Emory Libraries provided an opportunity to easily share information about initiatives and events with everyone in the community across campus. The DEI committee provided content for digital signage, including a short version of the Emory Libraries diversity statement, invitations to outreach events like pronoun button making, and announcements for student diversity fellowship opportunities.

Recommendation 6: Make diversity and inclusion an integral topic in candidate searches and onboarding process.

The DEI committee created an ad hoc subcommittee to draft recommendations to HR for integrating DEI practices into the recruitment and hiring processes. These recommendations included adding the Emory Libraries diversity statement to all job postings, in addition to a more robust EEOC statement, and leveraging diversity e-mail discussion lists and publications to advertise job postings to a more diverse pool of candidates.

- Create a training program of search committee members that will develop their sensitivity to issues of diversity and inclusion.
- Provide and organize unconscious bias training.
- Explore the idea of the "search advocate," an individual with training in diversity and inclusion who speaks to these issues in a search committee, as recommended by the Office of Equity and Inclusion
- Include a statement on Emory Libraries' commitment to diversity and inclusion in job descriptions.
- Develop a list of questions related to diversity and inclusion that can be used in the interview process.
- Encourage search committees to include the topic of diversity and inclusion in candidate presentations.
- Encourage candidates to submit documentation or a statement on their engagement in diversity and inclusion issues or initiatives.
- Leverage mentoring program via Librarians Assembly to disseminate information about Emory Libraries' diversity and inclusion commitment to new hires.

Recommendation 7: Hire or designate a diversity, equity, and inclusion specialist within Emory Libraries.

The DEI committee researched roles at other academic libraries created to address issues of diversity and inclusion. Using those job descriptions as inspiration, the committee created a draft job description for such a role to be considered by the dean and university librarian and her leadership team.

Recommendation 8: Research campus outlets for reporting bias incidents and develop staff guidelines and a directory to link individuals with proper resources and support.

As the committee explored the resources available on campus for reporting biases, it became clear that this is an area for growth for our institution. Recently, the university developed new roles for an ombudsperson as well as a chief diversity officer. In light of these recent changes, we anticipate having accessible outlets for reporting bias incidents and addressing other DEI concerns in the near future.

Recommendation 9: Audit and amend library policies to align with diversity, equity, and inclusion goals.

Since members of the DEI committee represent a wide variety of units across Emory Libraries, the team was able to offer support to areas that were in the process of periodic policy reviews to offer suggestions for including the diversity statement and other DEI-related content to policies. As the committee moves into the second phase of research and recommendations, we are partnering with specific areas to create unique diversity plans for those units; for example, collection development and assessment.

Recommendation 10: Audit and amend the library website to ensure alignment with diversity, equity, and inclusion goals.

Emory Libraries underwent a web design update, which was meant to create more cohesion across the various libraries. This provided the group with a great opportunity to provide recommendations for improved content about the libraries' diversity and inclusion activities and services; for example, creating a unique page about library diversity initiatives and issues such as information about accessible and gender-neutral bathrooms and education opportunities.

Recommendation 11: Operationalize outreach to diversity and inclusion organizations on campus to optimize opportunities for collaboration.

The committee continued to work with campus life organizations to create workshops and exchange valuable information about DEI-related initiatives. For example, the DEI committee had a representative on a Social Justice Education Framework Working Group, which developed a set of recommendations for integrating social justice issues into the mainstream curriculum. The committee also has continued to participate in diversity-related student outreach events such as providing the opportunity to create pronoun buttons at student activity fairs using the button maker from the Emory Libraries TechLab makerspace.

Recommendation 12: Explore opportunities to partner with or host national professional organizations.

The dean and university librarian and library leadership team agreed to serve as a host institution for ARL's diversity fellowship program, which provided two Emory undergraduate students with paid fellowship work in Emory Libraries' digital strategy team and a stipend to attend the ARL Leadership Symposium during ALA Midwinter.

Recommendation 13: Invest in staff access and participation in the national conversation about DEI (e.g., financial support for conference travel and bringing in lecturers or experts in the field).

The dean and university librarian provided resources for at least six members of the committee to attend various conferences and sessions related to diversity, equity, and inclusion, including the Joint Council of Librarians of Color and ARL's IDEAL Conference.

Next Steps

Moving into the research and writing process for the next three-year road map and recommendations, the committee first took time to reflect on the accomplishments of the previous years. Every year, the committee cochairs delivered presentations with updates on the progress of the recommendations to the library leadership and at staff meetings. We also invited consultants, including Mark Puente, to facilitate a second day-long retreat to review and adjust the framework and organize thoughts and ideas for the next set of recommendations.

The dean and university librarian invested in library staff education in design thinking at Emory's Goizueta Business School Executive Education program. Since many of the DEI committee members attended the course, it provided helpful methodologies for approaching the research process, particularly in framing research questions by starting with "How might we… ?" and engaging in open-ended inquiry about the community's needs. The dean and university librarian also invested in some members of the committee to attend DeEtta Jones and Associates Library Management Skills Institute, which further enhanced the team's access to frameworks for understanding how to enact change in a complex and constantly evolving organization.

The process of developing and growing the DEI committee can be illustrated as an iterative process, as shown in figure 14.2. Steps 1 and 2, the environmental scan and identifying themes, are micro-processes of their own, as new information and environmental conditions reveal new themes or reprioritize existing ones. Implementation and reflection are also in conversation with each other. Putting a theoretical plan into action is a highly experimental process that requires flexibility, active listening, and humility. As Emory's community continues to elevate and prioritize diversity, equity, and inclusion initiatives, underscored in particular by the hiring of the university's first chief diversity officer, the Emory Libraries DEI committee is poised to elevate its work and impact on the community by ensuring that the diversity statement goes beyond mere words to being enacted in every facet of the library's space and operations.

1

Environmental Scan

- Context: examining institutional history and initiatives and assessing tension points
- Peer bench-marking: conducting informational interviews with university libraries and collecting resources on their efforts
- Assessment: reviewing results from libraries and university-wide climate surveys.

4

Reflection

- Assess accomplishments by revisiting road map ("map the gaps")
- Celebrate progress and forward momentum
- Prepare to repeat the process

2

Identify Themes

- Brainstorm as a working group/committee
- Refine areas of focus: prioritize based upon community needs
- Create road map: define goals and align to timeline

3

Implementation

- Build rapport with internal stakeholders (e.g. leadership, staff, HR, etc.)
- Be creative: work around barriers and regroup when challenges arise
- Distribute responsibility: utilize the expertise of individuals in small groups
- Create awareness across units within libraries

FIGURE 14.2

Iterative process for developing and implementing DEI initiatives at Emory Libraries

Practical Considerations, Challenges, and Successes

In the experience of Emory Libraries, considerations around membership structure and power dynamics were especially important and part of the learning process. Figure 14.3 exhibits the key considerations in the makeup of Emory Libraries' DEI committee as well as challenges and success factors.

Considerations for Committee Membership

Representation of **identities**

Representation of **organizational areas**

Representation of **roles/rank**

Navigating Challenges

Structures of Power
Maneuvering within existing organizational cultures

Scope
Identifying and setting boundaries

Communication
Working across silos/departments

Committee Mindset
Confronting personal biases

Success Factors

Committee Members
- Represent various organizational ideas
- Model DEI values
- Integrate DEI values into professional development goals

Leadership Champion
- Provides resources
- Helps remove obstacles
- Ties DEI work into strategic goals

HR Liaison
- Attends committee meetings
- Shares campus-wide DEI initiatives
- Implements DEI recommendations

FIGURE 14.3
Considerations, challenges, and success factors in creating a DEI committee

Committee Membership, Structure, and Function

A foundational aspect of the committee's success lay in allowing members to join voluntarily and having the support of the dean and university librarian to advocate on behalf of staff and librarians who chose to be active with the committee. All DEI committee members have historically been present because we choose to be and because we have had an interest in and see the importance of this work within the institution and Emory Libraries. It is imperative that committee members have the support of their direct supervisors and managers and are constantly aware of how we budget our time between DEI-related work and our job duties.

Members have learned together with the shared goal of improving professionally and making the institution more inclusive, equal, and diverse. Honesty and an agreement of open and safe communication have been essential. Topics related to DEI are at times uncomfortable and sensitive, so respect and trust are imperative for a successful group. Additionally, committee members hold a range of positions and ranks within the libraries, and an early agreement that committee discussions were confidential has added to the group's culture.

Emory Libraries' DEI committee has been led by cochairs who are self-nominated and elected by the committee. The work of chairing the committee is extensive and varied, so having cochairs was a requirement for the group. Responsibilities have included attending monthly meetings with the committee sponsor, organizing meeting agendas, managing the workflow of environmental scan research and implementing recommendations, and ensuring that the overall committee activities stay within the scope of the committee's charge.

Subcommittee chairs continually organize clear agendas, ensure productive use of meeting time, identify action items, and report out to the full committee at the monthly meetings. Current subcommittees include: assessment, building messaging and amenities, communications, education, outreach and engagement, peer benchmarking, professional development, and recruitment. Subcommittee members often take the lead on specific initiatives, working in tandem with the committee cochairs and other campus stakeholders and partners.

Inclusive membership from across libraries and units has brought many unexpected benefits. In addition to connecting voices across the organization, this connection of colleagues has led to new partnerships, shared best practices, and unexpected problem-solving that may not have occurred otherwise.

Challenges and Successes

EMOTIONAL LABOR: FEELING OVERWHELMED

The challenge: For at least the first year, many members struggled with the prospect of defining the concept of DEI and then having to apply it to the libraries. The key question was "What does a commitment to DEI mean for our daily work, and the bigger picture of libraries and our institution?"

The success: In the first and third years, the committee had a day-long retreat run by outside facilitators. This provided an opportunity to develop an understanding of what diversity, equity, and inclusion meant in the context of Emory Libraries; where to start and continue with the work; and then in year three, to reflect on our journey and accomplishments, and to figure out where to go moving forward.

ADMINISTRATIVE DETAILS: THE NITTY-GRITTY OF COMMUNICATION

The challenge: A committee e-mail discussion list and DEI Community of Practice (COP) e-mail discussion list were established to increase communication and sharing of relevant ideas, events, and news. Questions faced included the following: Who manages these? How does the committee communicate to all libraries and IT? Are there newsletters, e-mail discussion lists, or other avenues for communication that may provide opportunities to reach a wider audience?

The success: The committee is still exploring the most appropriate owner for the committee and COP e-mail discussion lists but is currently creating a shared calendar to ensure all committee members are aware of the regular and subcommittee meetings and any special events. For communication avenues, we reached out to our colleagues who send out weekly newsletters for their deadlines for publication, as well as their advice for other types of communications. In summary, perseverance is key to communication. Keep asking, keep exploring, and keep an eye out for new and different ways to reach people.

BOUNDARIES AND POLITICS

The challenge: While the committee has the support of the dean and university librarian and the libraries leadership team in spirit, there are still gaps in implementing DEI principles throughout the libraries. For example, who owns the process of integration? How does the committee influence policy changes and get buy-in from colleagues and leadership?

The success: The cochairs use the monthly meetings with the dean and university librarian to ensure that the work is aligned with the vision. By keeping the original charge close at hand, the committee returns to its vision frequently to ensure activities are within scope. The committee has learned over time that it is not its responsibility to do all the work; rather, the committee makes the recommendations and then empowers the appropriate department, area, or individual to act upon them. By tracking metrics for all events and communication, the committee can illustrate the value, reach, and impact of initiatives. Keeping communication open and regular with the dean and university librarian allows the committee to successfully navigate these ongoing questions of scope, transparency, and politics, as they will continue to crop up.

Moving Forward

On October 31, 2019, the committee held its second retreat. Mark Puente, Association of Research Libraries director of diversity and leadership programs, and Nikhat Ghouse, organizational development consultant and associate librarian at American University, facilitated the daylong planning session. The facilitators requested that the committee read Judith H. Katz and Frederick A. Miller's article, "Conscious Actions for Inclusion: A Common Language to Drive Uncommon Results" prior to the day of the retreat.[9] In addition to discussing the article, the facilitators highlighted Miller's Guide to Notions, Stakes, Boulders, and Tombstones model, which recommends that organizations adopt a simple, shared language in order to allow individuals to express themselves and their level of commitment on important workplace issues and initiatives. Both the article and the model helped the committee recognize our strengths and identify goals to further our mission.

The group concluded that we have several strengths, including financial support for professional development and committee members that represent varying academic disciplines and departments. Additionally, we recognized the Emory Libraries and institution as a whole's commitment to the Atlanta community. Other recognizable strengths included the fact that Emory is a multicultural, multilingual, multiethnic, and multireligious institution and the value and appreciation for different perspectives among library employees.

We developed thirteen identifiable initiatives (see Final Recommendations listed above). Each initiative was divided into sub-initiatives and assigned a projected deadline for each fiscal year. One of these initiatives centered on the management's commitment to diversity, equity, and inclusion and its ability to serve as a model for the committee, libraries, and institution. Sub-initiatives included socializing library employees' preferred pronouns and collaborating more with the Oxford campus. Another initiative proposed to have DEI integrated into teaching and learning through exhibitions and cultural competency education. Among the other initiatives were that all staff be aware of and practice DEI proficiencies and work to secure grant funding. The committee also decided to integrate DEI into the processes of accountability and performance management.

The committee also identified several opportunities to reach our goals. For instance, there are many renowned scholars affiliated with Emory who we can tap to be speakers for a variety of events and programs. In addition, the committee has the opportunity to collaborate with Emory's medical library, as well as with organizations and institutions such as the Association of Research Libraries, the Association of College and Research Libraries, and the Association of Southeastern Research Libraries.

The committee's goals and opportunities reflect our aspirations to move beyond compliance and position ourselves on campus as advocates for underrepresented people and groups. We want to take an active role in addressing issues of concern for those we represent by providing visibility of our commitment in everything that we do. In order to achieve this, the committee will need to iterate the process of collaborating with other campus groups to assist in furthering our efforts.

The committee knows that the challenge in attaining our aspirations will be in tempering any fears or concerns that leadership may have. This will have to be accomplished by gaining the trust and support of those in leadership. Although the DEI committee has received tremendous support from dean and university librarian Yolanda Cooper, we will need to garner a reputation across campus of being the advocate that we strive to be by taking advantage of every opportunity to promote the work of the committee. In doing so, we hope to gain new committee members and new groups to collaborate with.

The formation of the DEI committee created the groundwork to address the current surge of interest in anti-racism. In particular, having a strong framework, active subcommittees focused on specific topics, clearly articulated goals, and a meaningful relationship with library leadership have been key factors in preparing our organization to integrate anti-racism into all aspects of library operations.

Ideally, the committee would like to be the group that other campus organizations look to for tips and advice about DEI-related issues and concerns. As we constantly seek to stay abreast of DEI-related issues, we want to offer our knowledge to assist others to incorporate DEI within their groups. Currently, peer institutions contact us for suggestions regarding their own DEI committees. In response to the interest in Emory Libraries' organization of the committee, we have created a shareable site via LibNet: https://libnet.libraries.emory.edu/diversity. This site can be a helpful reference tool for other DEI committees. The committee strives to continue to share our work and to be DEI leaders for the Emory community and beyond.

Notes

1. Emory University, "Facts and Figures," accessed July 16, 2020, https://www.emory.edu/home/about/factsfigures/index.html.
2. The four schools that serve undergraduates are the Emory College of Arts and Sciences; Oxford College, a two-year liberal arts school; Goizueta Business School; and Nell Hodgson Woodruff School of Nursing.
3. *US News and World Report*, "Emory University," accessed July 16, 2020, https://www.usnews.com/best-colleges/emory-university-1564.
4. The Emory Libraries is a member of the Association of Research Libraries (ARL), the Coalition for Networked Information (CNI), the Center for Research Libraries (CRL), the Council on Library and Information Resources (CLIR), the Digital Library Federation (DLF), International Federation of Library Associations and Institutions (IFLA), and the Scholarly Publishing and Academic Resources Coalition (SPARC), as well as regional associations including the Association of Southeastern Research Libraries (ASERL), Georgia Library Learning Online (GALILEO), and the GETSM Consortium (a consortium of the University of Georgia, Emory, Georgia Tech, Georgia State University, and Georgia Regents University).
5. The Stuart A. Rose Manuscript, Archives, and Rare Book Library is Emory's principal repository for rare and special materials. It houses over 250,000 rare books and over 15,000 linear feet of manuscript material. The library's collections span more than 800 years of history—with particular strengths in modern literature, African American history, and the history of Georgia and the South.
6. The time frame for this case study is 2016 to the present. For additional demographic information, see Emory University, "2016–2017 Academic Profile," accessed July 16, 2020, https://web.archive.org/web/20171014155855/http://opb.emory.edu/documents/data/Emory-AcademicProfile-2016-2017.pdf.
7. From 2014 to July 2019 Yolanda Cooper served as university librarian. In 2019, Cooper was promoted to dean and university librarian.

8.   Yolanda Cooper, "Diversity and inclusion working group charge," email message to authors, September 21, 2016.
9.   Judith H. Katz and Frederick A. Miller, "Conscious Actions for Inclusion: A Common Language to Drive Uncommon Results," Kaleel Jamison Consulting Group, 2016, https://orghacking.files.wordpress.com/2018/04/47a26-consciousactionsforinclusionar.pdf.

Bibliography

Cooper, Yolanda. "Diversity and inclusion working group charge." Email message to authors. September 21, 2016.

Emory University. "Facts and Figures." Accessed July 16, 2020. https://www.emory.edu/home/about/factsfigures/index.html.

Emory University, Office of Planning and Administration. "2016–2017 Academic Profile." Accessed July 16, 2020. https://web.archive.org/web/20171014155855/http://opb.emory.edu/documents/data/Emory-AcademicProfile-2016-2017.pdf.

Katz, Judith H., and Frederick A. Miller. "Conscious Actions for Inclusion: A Common Language to Drive Uncommon Results." Kaleel Jamison Consulting Group, 2016. https://orghacking.files.wordpress.com/2018/04/47a26-consciousactionsforinclusionar.pdf.

US News and World Report. "Emory University." Accessed July 16, 2020. https://www.usnews.com/best-colleges/emory-university-1564.

Warner, Gretchen, Saira Raza, Melissa Hackman, Hannah Rutledge, Chella Vaidyanathan, Jeffery Sowder, and Erica Bruchko. "Evolution of Emory Libraries' Diversity, Equity, and Inclusion Committee." poster presentation, American Library Association Annual Meeting, Washington, DC, June 20–25, 2019.

CHAPTER 15

Framework for Change

Utilizing a University-wide Diversity Strategic Planning Process for an Academic Library

Renna Redd, Alydia Sims, and Tara Weekes

Note: This chapter is adapted and expanded from Renna Tuten Redd, Alydia Sims, and Tara Weekes, "Framework for Change: Creating a Diversity Strategic Plan within an Academic Library," *Journal of Library Administration* 60, no. 3 (2020): 263–81, https://doi.org/10.1080/01930826.2019.1698920.

Introduction

In 2017, the Clemson University administration, through the Office of Inclusion and Equity, charged each of the University's seven colleges as well as the University Libraries with creating and implementing a diversity strategic plan. The initiative was originally part of the ClemsonForward institutional strategic plan, but racially motivated incidents at the university, protests, and the resulting campus climate created a sense of urgency in the task. Utilizing a shared strategic plan framework and campus-wide resources, Clemson University Libraries (CUL) answered this charge by creating a Libraries Diversity Plan

Working Group (LDPWG), comprised of both faculty and staff. The working group conducted an inventory of current diversity, equity, and inclusion (DEI) initiatives and obtained strategic plan input, feedback, and support from all the libraries' employees. The LDPWG worked for sixteen months to create an updated libraries' mission statement, a new and robust diversity statement, and an accountable and ambitious road map to further Clemson University Libraries' DEI initiatives and impact. The LDPWG chairs then published about Clemson Libraries' diversity strategic planning process in the *Journal of Library Administration* and have adapted and expanded that article into this chapter with specific focus on collaborative work within the institution and its required framework and assessment system.[1]

Literature Review

Diversity, equity, and inclusion are founding principles of the library and information science (LIS) profession. The original 1939 adoption of the American Library Association (ALA) Bill of Rights began with the statement, "Today indications in many parts of the world point to growing intolerance, suppression of free speech, and censorship affecting the rights of minorities and individuals."[2] This statement is relevant to the current culture, and DEI-related research and efforts are still prevalent when reviewing recently published LIS scholarly literature. The literature reviewed for this project focused on best practices for developing a diversity strategic plan and how libraries can most effectively participate in a university-wide strategic planning process.

Cruz recently published a review of "the current academic literature relating to diversity initiatives in academic libraries,"[3] which revealed findings similar to the authors' research regarding numerous resources pertaining to LIS diversity-, equity-, and inclusion-related definitions, standards, competencies, and initiatives for areas of library work including user services, programming, recruitment, and climate assessment, among others. The authors, like Cruz, found few scholarly resources addressing DEI strategic planning within academic libraries.

Some of the most relevant resources regarding DEI strategic planning in academic libraries were found within LIS professional association documents. McManus wrote of the ALA's recent integration of equity, diversity, and inclusion within the organization's strategic plan,[4] and upon review of that document, the authors noted specific goals and strategies to create "a more equitable, diverse, and inclusive society."[5] Cruz also discussed the Association of College and Research Libraries (ACRL) "Plan for Excellence" update that incorporated DEI goals and objectives into its organizational strategic plan.[6]

Edwards stated there are advantages to developing a stand-alone DEI strategic plan instead of "simply incorporating diversity into a general strategic plan."[7] This assessment was found to align with the Clemson University Libraries' institutional charge and so directed the search toward more DEI-related resources. Cruz referenced the American Library Association's March 2007 Building a Diversity Plan—Strategic Planning for Diversity as one of the earliest road maps for DEI strategic planning in libraries and lists six essential elements to include in a library's diversity plan: a definition of diversity, an assessment of need, a mission or vision, goals or priorities, delegation of responsibilities, and a statement of accountability.[8] Cruz and Edwards both also pointed to the Association of Research Libraries' (ARL) *SPEC Kit 319: Diversity Plans and Programs*, which contains actual examples of academic library DEI strategic plans, as well as related statements, committee charges, programming, and recruitment activities.[9] The more recent ARL *SPEC Kit 356: Diversity and Inclusion* was located that provided more academic library DEI strategic plans and activity examples, which heavily influenced the work of the LDPWG committee.[10]

The work of the group was most informed by the discovery of Edwards's articles regarding the recent DEI strategic planning efforts of the University of Montana Mansfield Library in 2011 and 2012.[11] Edwards recounted the process of developing their academic library DEI strategic plan and discussed the importance of forming a DEI strategic planning committee with broad representation and clearly established expectations.[12] They also offered recommendations to conduct an environmental scan, including to list current library DEI initiatives for assessment purposes; to integrate existing institutional DEI plans and statements; and to ensure administrative and stakeholder feedback and support throughout the strategic planning process. Edwards also discussed their committee's success with beginning strategic planning with action item ideas and then organizing those accountable ideas into achievable goals.[13]

Aligning with Edwards's recommendation to seek and incorporate institutional resources,[14] the search was broadened to include DEI strategic planning in higher education institutions. Wilson, Leon and Williams, and LePeau, Hurtado, and Williams echoed the emphasis on administrative and institution-wide support.[15] Leon and Williams also affirmed the importance of representative

DEI strategic planning committee membership,[16] and they reference Williams's recommendation of a committee with ten to fifteen members.[17] Clemson University's assistant vice president for strategic diversity leadership also recommended Williams, Berger, and McClendon and Williams as resources for all colleges creating their diversity strategic plans.[18]

Damon A. Williams is considered an authority in the field of higher education DEI strategic planning and is cited by many other references. Williams's works often address elements for effective DEI strategic plans, and Wilson offered similar advice to include time lines for implementation, accountability measures, and designated resources to support the work.[19] Cruz echoed these recommended elements within an academic library DEI strategic plan, stating that "a well thought out diversity plan with goals, action items, and assessment measures can help libraries define their vision of diversity and lay out steps to achieve it."[20]

In addition to general strategic plan elements, Leon and Williams recommended "framing the work of the committee to address particular diversity issues on campus."[21] Building on this concept, Semeraro and Boyd offered a framework example that higher education DEI strategic plans could use to address categories including "Education and Research, Operations, Diversity and Affordability, Human Resources, Investment, Public Engagement, and Innovation."[22] McManus and Cruz also offered similar focus area frameworks for academic library DEI strategic plans.[23] McManus referenced the June 2016 *Final Report of the ALA Task Force on Equity, Diversity, and Inclusion*, which recommended efforts regarding programing, membership and participation, recruitment and retention, education, and administrative priorities and planning.[24] Cruz's literature review resulted in a framework of five areas: collections, staffing, services, programming, and culture.

There is a paucity of literature on institutional strategic planning and academic libraries in relation to equity, diversity, and inclusion. However, there is some scholarship in the area of positioning the library within the larger institutional strategic planning process. The *New Review of Academic Librarianship* created a special double issue titled "Positioning the Academic Library within the Institution: Structures and Challenges."[25] In the introduction, Appleton states that academic libraries aligning with the strategic directions of their parent institutions is imperative based on internal competition "for resource, visibility, and attention" and that "libraries need to work hard at ensuring they are visible and hold a strong position within the academy."[26] Likewise, Harland, Stewart, and

Bruce revealed "the importance of identifying the university's strategic goals, and then seeking opportunities that can support the university strategies," which, in turn, "add value or deliver impact to the university."[27]

Examples of this are described by Fister and Dempsey in the ACRL publication *New Roles for the Road Ahead: Essays Commissions for ACRL's 75th Anniversary.*[28] Fister writes that "the long-term association of libraries with academic programs is now being joined by growing connections with student life and non-curricular academic support units,"[29] while Dempsey lists practical partnerships, such as with information technology groups, learning and teaching support, publishing, research infrastructure, and research information management. However, library contributions in the area of equity, diversity, and inclusion do not make the short list.

SCONUL (Society of College, National, and University Libraries), which is based in the United Kingdom, commissioned Baker and Allden to interview executive-level university leadership to gain their perspectives on academic library leadership. The results were published in 2017 in *Leading Libraries: The View from Above*. Regarding the area of strategic alignment, "It was clear that those interviewed were keen to see those responsible for the library overtly demonstrating their engagement with and understanding of the institutional strategy."[30]

Review of recent scholarly and LIS literature provided many helpful resources and recommendations regarding the process and elements to include in Clemson University Libraries' diversity strategic planning initiative. Research was also encouraged in demonstrating that the support and framework provided by Clemson University's assistant vice president for strategic diversity leadership would ensure a comprehensive and effective plan to further the libraries' DEI efforts and impact.

Background (Climate and Context)

Clemson University is a public land-grant university established in 1889 and located in the upstate region of South Carolina. The university is comprised of seven colleges: the College of Agriculture, Forestry and Life Science; the College of Architecture, Arts and Humanities; the College of Behavioral, Social and Health Sciences; the College of Business; the College of Education; the College of Engineering, Computing and Applied Sciences; and the College of Science.

The university also oversees a statewide public service and agriculture network, a cooperative extension program, and a 17,500-acre experimental forest.

Based on demographic information located in the "Clemson University Interactive Factbook" for the current as well as previous years, Clemson University is considered a predominantly white institution (PWI). In the *Encyclopedia of African American Education*, Brown and Dancy define PWIs as

> institutions of higher learning in which Whites account for 50% or greater of the student enrollment. However, the majority of these institutions may also be understood as historically White institutions in recognition of the binarism and exclusion supported by the United States prior to 1964.[31]

Of the 18,971 undergraduate students and 2,969 graduate students at Clemson, 87.2 percent self-identify as White, and 16.6 percent self-identify as non-White. The university employs 5,392 individuals, and 79.5 percent self-identify as White, 9.4 percent identify as Black or African American, 4.9 percent identify as Asian, and 4.5 percent identify as Hispanic. Fewer than ten individuals identify as members of following groups: American Indian or Alaskan native, Native Hawaiian or Pacific Islander, nonresident alien, and multiracial. In addition, 2.2 percent are unknown.[32]

The Clemson University Libraries consist of one main library (Robert Muldrow Cooper Library); the Education Media Center and the Emery A. Gunnin Architecture Library; a Special Collections and Archives; an offsite facility that houses high-density storage and technical services offices; and a location within the Clemson University Design Center in Charleston, South Carolina. As of May 2020, the University Libraries employs eighty-four faculty and staff members. Of these, 81 percent self-identify as White, 8.3 percent as Black or African American, 3.6 percent as Asian, 3.6 percent as Hispanic, and 1.2% as two or more races. Five chose not to disclose.[33]

Clemson's profile as a public university has grown since the turn of the last century, with recognition for its programs in education, engineering, and business as well as financial value for students. In parallel, the athletic program has also gained prominence, culminating in 2016 and 2018 NCAA National College Football Championships. The geographic base for this activity is the northwest portion of South Carolina, known locally as the Upstate. The area was originally populated by the Cherokee and Chickasaw tribes before the late eighteenth century.[34] The property upon which Clemson University was built was the site of Fort Hill plantation, the home of former United States vice president and slavery advocate John C. Calhoun (1782–1850). In 1875, Calhoun's son-in-law, Thomas Greene Clemson, inherited the property and worked for the remaining thirteen years of his life to create an A&M (agricultural and mechanical) college, which opened in 1889 as Clemson College.[35] While some of the institution's history has been widely shared and lauded, the economic foundation that enabled its creation—the lives of enslaved persons and, after emancipation, prison labor—is not as widely acknowledged. Until recently, the campus did not acknowledge the people whose lives and forced labor produced the fruits the community enjoys now. To do so, the university has installed more historically accurate interpretative signage and has supported the Call My Name project by Dr. Rhondda Thomas, which documents seven generations of people of African descent in the history of the institution.[36] Many at the university and in the wider community believe that there is still significant work to be done.

On April 11, 2016, amid conversations regarding the full history of Clemson University, bananas were found hanging from a historical marker on campus acknowledging the African Americans who were enslaved at Fort Hill. Immediately after the incident, the campus climate was tense, and the university administration spoke out against it, with President James Clements stating that "this type of conduct is hurtful, disrespectful, unacceptable and will not be tolerated."[37] However, many from the campus community were unhappy with the administrative response thereafter. The students responsible for the initial act admitted their involvement on April 12 and claimed that the incident was not racially motivated;[38] they were then exonerated. The university issued a statement about its continued commitment toward a more diverse and inclusive campus community,[39] and many were concerned that the release was simply just that: a statement and not an actual plan for action to address the campus culture. This resulted in protests that included a nine-day sit-in in Sikes Hall that houses the president's offices,[40] and the birth of a Twitter hashtag #beingblackatclemson. A. D. Carson, a graduate student at the time, wrote a poem titled "See the Stripes" to draw focus to these issues. Using the university's mascot, the tiger, Carson drew a clear and compelling comparison between how this animal is unable to survive in nature without both its orange and black markings while Clemson University is focused only on the orange.[41]

Institutional Action

Inclusive Excellence in Strategic Planning

The climate of the campus, as described, may have accelerated the implementation of a university-wide inclusive excellence strategic planning process. In 2015 Clemson University created a new ten-year strategic plan, ClemsonForward, which would be implemented from 2016 to 2026. The plan prioritizes four elements: research, engagement, academic core, and living environment, and the goal of the plan is to propel the university into a national leadership position within these four areas. Living environment is defined as follows within the document:

> ClemsonForward will strengthen the sense of community and connectedness that defines the Clemson Family by enhancing diversity, improving workplace quality of life and creating an environment of inclusive excellence. ClemsonForward will further enhance student life, continue and grow high-quality athletics programs, and focus on policies, facilities and professional and leadership development opportunities to make Clemson a great place to work, study and live.[42]

The plan outlined three core strategies to implement this: increase diversity on campus among faculty, staff, and students; create and nurture a climate of inclusivity; and advance the quality of life in the workplace while rewarding performance.

The phrase *inclusive excellence* is used in the plan to help define how achievement and success do not function in a vacuum but require the inclusion of all to reach their full potential. The term is neither a creation of the authors of ClemsonForward, nor is it used exclusively by Clemson University—it was created in 2005 by the Association of American Colleges and Universities (AACU) as part of its initiative Making Excellence Inclusive.[43] Three white papers were commissioned by AACU: *Making Diversity Work on Campus: A Research-Based Perspective, Achieving Equitable Educational Outcomes with All Students: The Institution's Roles and Responsibilities,* and *Toward a Model of Inclusive Excellence and Change in Postsecondary Institutions.*[44] These briefings form a tool kit so that institutions can fully integrate the work of inclusion and equity within their core functions and forge a link between these elements and the quality of education provided. The papers assert that diversity and inclusion are not an outcome but an embedded process that, if sustained, becomes a part of the fabric of campus culture and operations.

Administration and Framework

Clemson University hired Dr. Leon Wiles, its first chief diversity officer, in 2008 so that the institution could benefit from a senior executive who oversaw equity and inclusion efforts as well as partnerships among various programs focused on diversity and inclusion among academic and student affairs programming. Wiles retired in 2015, and an announcement was made on February 10, 2016, that Lee Gill, JD, would replace him with a start date of April 18, 2016. Gill's first week at Clemson was extremely eventful given the discovery of the hanging bananas the previous week, which was followed immediately with protests and a student-led sit-in. He participated in an open forum with President Clements on his third day of work in which he said

> The challenges here over the past several days aren't just indicative to Clemson; they're happening at colleges and universities throughout the country.... Our students are challenging and looking at issues across the campus, but they are our students. We will work through this process and get to a better place.[45]

The confluence of the creation of ClemsonForward and the divisive actions of April 2016 may have accelerated Clemson University's diversity strategic planning process. In mid-2017, President Clements and chief inclusion and equity officer Lee Gill, formed the Clemson University President's Council on Diversity and Inclusion. This group was a re-formation of the Diversity Advisory Council (created in 2015) and included representatives from each of the colleges as well as the University Libraries. In December 2017, the Clemson University Office of Inclusion and Equity brought together these representatives and announced a new initiative, Strategic Planning for Inclusive Excellence. Each of Clemson University's colleges was charged to create a diversity plan to implement the goals set in ClemsonForward, and each was required to apply a framework of six strategic pillars defined in 2015 by Max Allen, vice-president and chief of staff, and Dr. Janelle Chasira, a fellow of the American Council of Education (see figure 15.1).[46]

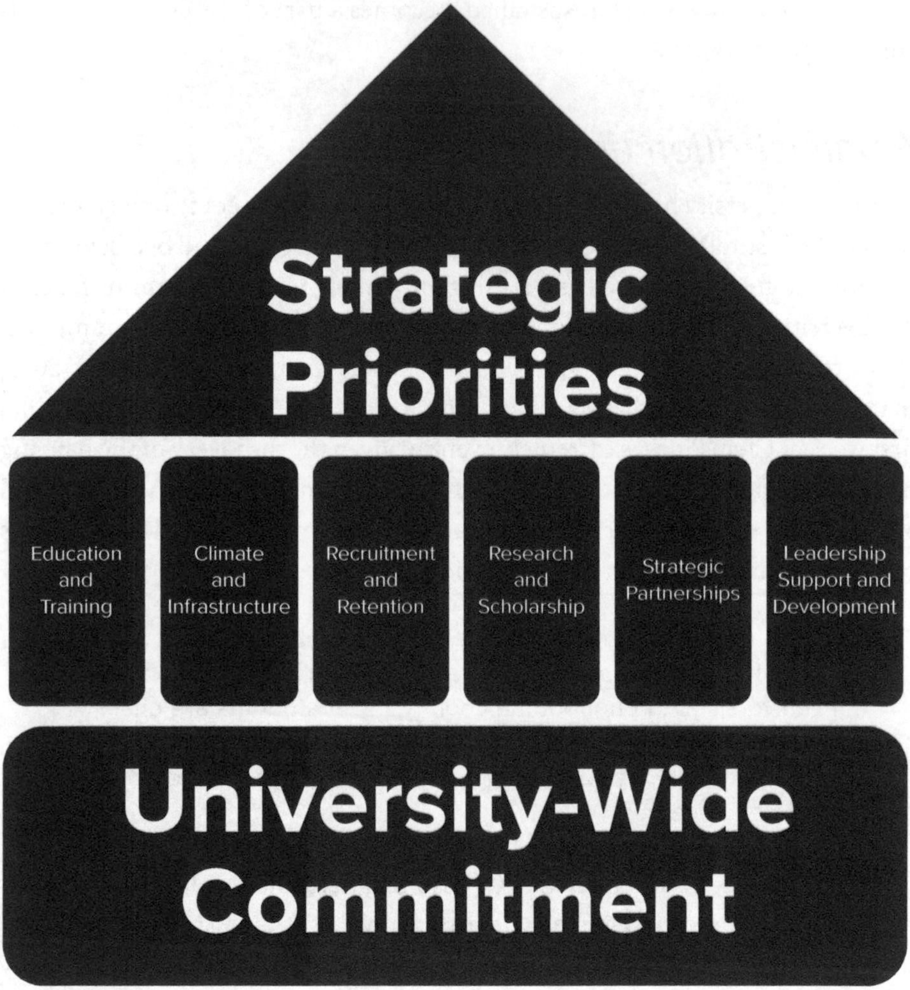

FIGURE 15.1
Renna Redd, Clemson University strategic planning pillars

- *Education and training:* education and training experiences to build cultural competencies across the organization
- *Climate and infrastructure:* creating academic and work environments that effectively support the success of all faculty, staff, and students
- *Recruitment and retention:* active and aggressive recruitment and retention of a diverse faculty, staff, and student body
- *Research and scholarship:* building and enhancing opportunities for research and scholarship in diversity fields

- *Strategic partnerships:* building and supporting strategic partnerships that respect diversity, include diverse groups, and support the advancement of diversity and inclusion for both
- *Leadership support and development:* top-down support for diversity and inclusion and the creation of a pipeline of culturally competent academic leaders

Supporting Edwards's supposition that there are advantages to developing a stand-alone DEI strategic plan,[47] the Strategic Planning for Inclusive Excellence framework for Clemson University was integral in developing a comprehensive libraries' diversity plan. Among the benefits were enhanced collaboration and the opportunity to learn about and address specific diversity, equity, and inclusion issues on campus as suggested by Leon and Williams.[48] Another result was increased accountability as the framework required step-by-step action items and assigned time lines and assessment metrics as recommended by Cruz and Wilson.[49]

Structure of Support

The importance of support at an institutional level is discussed by Wilson,[50] and support from Clemson University's administration was integral in creating comprehensive and effective plans across the university. Wilson states that implementation of a successful strategic plan should include "institutional-wide responsibility coordinated through a central command structure."[51] The creation of a new assistant vice president for strategic diversity leadership position was vital to assume responsibility of coordinating Clemson University's campus-wide strategic planning process.[52]

As part of the Clemson University diversity strategic planning process, the assistant vice president for strategic diversity leadership advocated for and communicated university support. She also met with each college dean to explain the planning process and requirements and asked that each designate a plan administrator. Wilson suggests including a "representative body of the institution within the composition of the planning committee,"[53] and the assistant vice president for strategic diversity leadership frequently met with plan administrators to discuss progress, share challenges and solution ideas, and coordinate efforts across campus. Wilson also recommends that diversity strategic plans incorporate data-driven goals, objectives, methods of measuring effectiveness, and alignment with an institution's mission and culture,[54] and these were addressed by the assistant vice president for strategic diversity leadership as well.

As plan administrators, the cochairs of the LDPWG also met with the assistant vice president for strategic diversity leadership once a month, and these meetings were vital to the process of creating the libraries' plan. Many meetings helped address adapting the diversity strategic plan requirements designed for Clemson colleges to library science work. The meetings also helped address internal LDPWG concerns and well as using language in the libraries' plan for broader understanding by others.

Clemson Libraries' Work
Working Group and Communications

In response to the institution's charge to develop a diversity strategic plan, the interim dean of the libraries sent an e-mail to all employees in January 2018 asking for volunteers to participate in a new Libraries Diversity Plan Working Group (LDPWG), the composition of which would be coordinated by the libraries' representative to the Clemson University Council on Diversity and Inclusion. Williams recommended that a diversity committee consist of ten to fifteen members,[55] so twelve individuals who expressed an interest were selected to serve on the LDPWG. Edwards stressed the importance of having a DEI strategic planning committee with broad representation,[56] so LDPWG members included both faculty and staff from a variety of units, employment classifications, and self-identities.

Edwards also discussed the need for a DEI strategic planning committee to have clearly established expectations,[57] so once the LDPWG composition was confirmed, many of the members attended a meeting with the assistant vice president for strategic diversity leadership to ensure understanding of the campus-wide initiative and framework. Later that month, the LDPWG held its first meeting, which began with members introducing themselves and sharing why they were interested in contributing to the group's efforts and the work of diversity, equity, and inclusion. This was a vital step to create a sense of personal investment in the work of the group as well as committee purpose. Next, the LDPWG discussed its charge, time line, and the framework's six strategic priority areas required by the university. The LDPWG then selected cochairs who would also act as the libraries' plan administrators.

The LDPWG then discussed how to best move forward with such a complex task. The group decided to create and implement an e-mail discussion group, a shared Google Drive folder, and a web page on Clemson University Libraries' intranet, StaffWeb, to facilitate communication within the LDPWG and with all the libraries' employees. The LDPWG utilized the StaffWeb page to record and share a time line of all its activities as well as referenced resources. The LDPWG also sent frequent e-mails and intranet announcements to the libraries' employees to provide periodic updates.

Guiding Statements

In order to communicate the libraries' value of diversity, equity, and inclusion, the group decided to create a diversity statement to direct our strategic planning process as well as all the work of Clemson University Libraries. The decision to create a dedicated diversity statement was later affirmed by the dean of the libraries when he requested that the LDPWG include an action item to publicly communicate a diversity statement. Edwards suggested integrating existing institutional DEI materials,[58] so the LDPWG decided to begin its work by reviewing current Clemson Libraries and university statements related to DEI. A review of these materials brought up the following questions:

- What is our definition of diversity? How granular do we get? Do we include things like citizenship status, socioeconomic background, and so on?
- Is there a university-level glossary of terms that we can all refer to?
- What is the Clemson University statement on diversity and inclusion? Where is it?
- What does our library service philosophy say? Does it reflect the same values?
- How do collections fall into the work of diversity and inclusion? For some, the areas that are most ripe for work are spaces and personnel.

The LDPWG also discussed that knowing what other academic libraries were doing to contribute to diversity, equity, and inclusion would be very useful. As a result, members were asked to review ARL's *SPEC Kit 356: Diversity and Inclusion* in small groups.[59] Each small group selected three to four libraries within the publication and examined the positive and negative aspects of their diversity statements and websites. Members were also tasked to read at least one academic library's diversity strategic plan. Penn State, Texas A&M, and Indiana University at Bloomington were particularly recommended for review by various LDPWG members.

The LDPWG soon held its second meeting to share what we had learned from *SPEC Kit 356*. Each member discussed aspects of other libraries' diversity statements and websites that they thought were valuable, which sparked more and deeper discussion. Some keywords and phrases noted by members of the LDPWG included

- Diversity and inclusion enable us to better serve/best serve.
- Historically aware and compassionate.
- An environment of respect and inclusion.
- Inclusion is essential to continued success.
- "Foster an internal environment with equal partnership among all employees, based on the principles and practices of courtesy, professionalism, and mutual respect."[60]

The group also discussed some key concepts to include:

- The work of diversity and inclusion is essential to continued success in our field of librarianship and for Clemson University.
- The three core values of Clemson University: integrity, honesty, respect.[61]
- The statement applies to employees, collections, spaces, services, and experiences.
- This is ongoing work; an iterative process that calls for constant review and refining of policies and procedures.

Using these notes, the LDPWG developed a draft Clemson University Libraries diversity statement with much debate and refinement in subsequent meetings. The group created the following statement:

> Clemson University Libraries seeks to best serve our community through creating a welcoming environment in which diverse ideas and perspectives come together to achieve common goals. We are committed to the practice of inclusion as it is essential to the continued success not only of Clemson University but of the library and information science profession. We embrace Clemson's core values of integrity, honesty, and respect, and add to those the ideals of compassion, dignity, and historical awareness so that Clemson Libraries'

staff, collections, spaces, and services inform the interest, information, and enlightenment of all whom we serve.[62]

The assistant vice president for strategic diversity leadership also encouraged the libraries to update their organization mission statement to better incorporate our values of diversity, equity, and inclusion. This was supported by the libraries' dean, so the LDPWG soon began our next challenge of crafting a new mission statement. As in the diversity statement development process, there was much discussion and debate concerning terminology and semantics. Eventually, the LDPWG asked the assistant vice president for strategic diversity leadership for advice about specific elements, such as listing possible individual identities—such as sexuality, race, or religion—within our statements. Instead of incorporating an exhaustive and ever-changing list, she recommended using the phrase "backgrounds, cultures, and identities," which satisfied all the LDPWG members. After incorporating her suggestions, the LDPWG agreed upon a draft:

> Clemson University Libraries embrace excellence in developing and providing innovative and inclusive collections, programs, services, and technologies that support Clemson University goals and the information needs of students, faculty, staff, and visitors. We are committed to creating a welcoming, safe, and inclusive environment for all, and we encourage the use of our facilities and services regardless of background, culture, or identity.

Feedback on the proposed mission statement update was sought from all Clemson University Libraries' employees, and we received very helpful suggestions, such as the removal of the word *regardless* and several other semantic improvements. Much of the feedback from employees, and especially senior leadership, was that the statement was too long and pulled too much focus away from the core goal of librarianship. The end product was a slight but important modification of our previous mission statement to include the terms *inclusive* and *all*. The following is our adopted revised mission statement:

> Clemson University Libraries embrace excellence in providing innovative and inclusive collections, programs, services, and technologies that support Clemson University goals and the information needs of all.

Initiatives: Past, Present, Future

Edwards recommended conducting an environmental scan that includes current library DEI initiatives.[63] An inventory of current activities was also required as part of Clemson University's institutional framework, and the LDPWG soon realized that this initial inventory would be essential in determining what to include in the libraries' diversity strategic plan as well as later for assessment purposes.

Utilizing the six strategic priority areas, the LDPWG decided to divide into subgroups to inventory current activities that the libraries had sponsored, cosponsored, or participated in within the past three to five years. The inventory was recorded in a Google Sheets document online so that everyone in the LDPWG could contribute information. The subgroups quickly realized that the task of gathering an initial inventory of previous and in-progress DEI initiatives required the input of all Clemson University Libraries' employees as the organization was involved in many DEI-related activities but these efforts had never been communicated and compiled into a comprehensive record.

Some activities were easy to identify, such as hosting a welcome reception for international students or holding a workshop on unconscious bias for library employees, but others were not as straightforward. Do we claim things we have participated in that are actually "owned" by another entity on campus, such as sponsoring a table at an event geared toward prospective Latinx students? It became evident that the libraries did a lot of ad hoc programming with different offices and groups on campus but did not have a single person who was responsible for coordinating who we worked with, communicating those collaborations to the body of library employees, or recording outcomes of these events. Likewise, identifying and assembling a list of relevant baseline assessment data required inquiries into the findings of employees throughout the libraries as well as the Office of Inclusion and Equity and other Clemson University entities.

Once the LDPWG had an idea of the kind of activities and initiatives the libraries had participated in, we determined that we should create a wish list of potential activities to implement and groups with whom to collaborate. This approach followed Edwards's recommendation to begin strategic planning with action item ideas and then organize those ideas into objectives and goals,[64] and it allowed the LDPWG to easily incorporate all of our ideas into the required institutional framework. The LDPWG also decided to invite colleagues within the libraries who serve on some of the Clemson University President's Commissions (the Commission on the Status of Women, the Commission on the Black Experience, the LGBTQ Commission, and the Commission on Latino Affairs) to participate in this exercise at their next meeting.

During that meeting, the cochairs put large Post-it Note posters labeled with each of the six strategic priority areas on the walls, and each member placed their ideas on the posters they thought the activity might support. After this, the group took time to walk around and read ideas, placing a sticker of endorsement or writing a comment next to them. The group discussed each idea, grouping similar ones, recategorizing some to more related strategic priorities, and recording additional ideas that came from these discussions. Group members took photographs of the posters so that the ideas and comments could be transcribed and recorded in their original state.

Soon after this meeting, the assistant vice president for strategic diversity leadership shared a spreadsheet with all plan administrators that enabled each college and the libraries to record goals, objectives, and action steps grouped by the framework strategic priority areas. The spreadsheet also contained fields for the estimated time frame for the completion of each objective as well as areas to identify potential partners (both internal and external to the university), existing baseline data, and the metrics needed to assess the success of each objective.

With this spreadsheet in hand, the LDPWG cochairs met to start fitting the ideas generated by the working group into the provided format. The LDPWG and President's Commissions representatives of the libraries met many times in the months after to refine goals, create measurable objectives, determine time frames, and identify any existing baseline data as well as potential partners and metrics for assessment.

Organization Input and Support

Edwards stressed the importance of obtaining administrative and stakeholder feedback and support throughout the strategic planning process[65] as demonstrated by the LDPWG workflow in figure 15.2. While the LDPWG continued to create a draft diversity strategic plan, the dean of libraries gave the cochairs the opportunity to present an overview of the project and the framework at a library all-employee meeting. The presentation included contextual information regarding the development of a diversity strategic plan across campus that involved each of Clemson University's colleges and would also expand to include divisions, such as Student Affairs, Athletics, and the Office of Inclusion and Equity. The six strategic priority areas and examples of activities that might fall under each were introduced, and members of the audience were asked to write

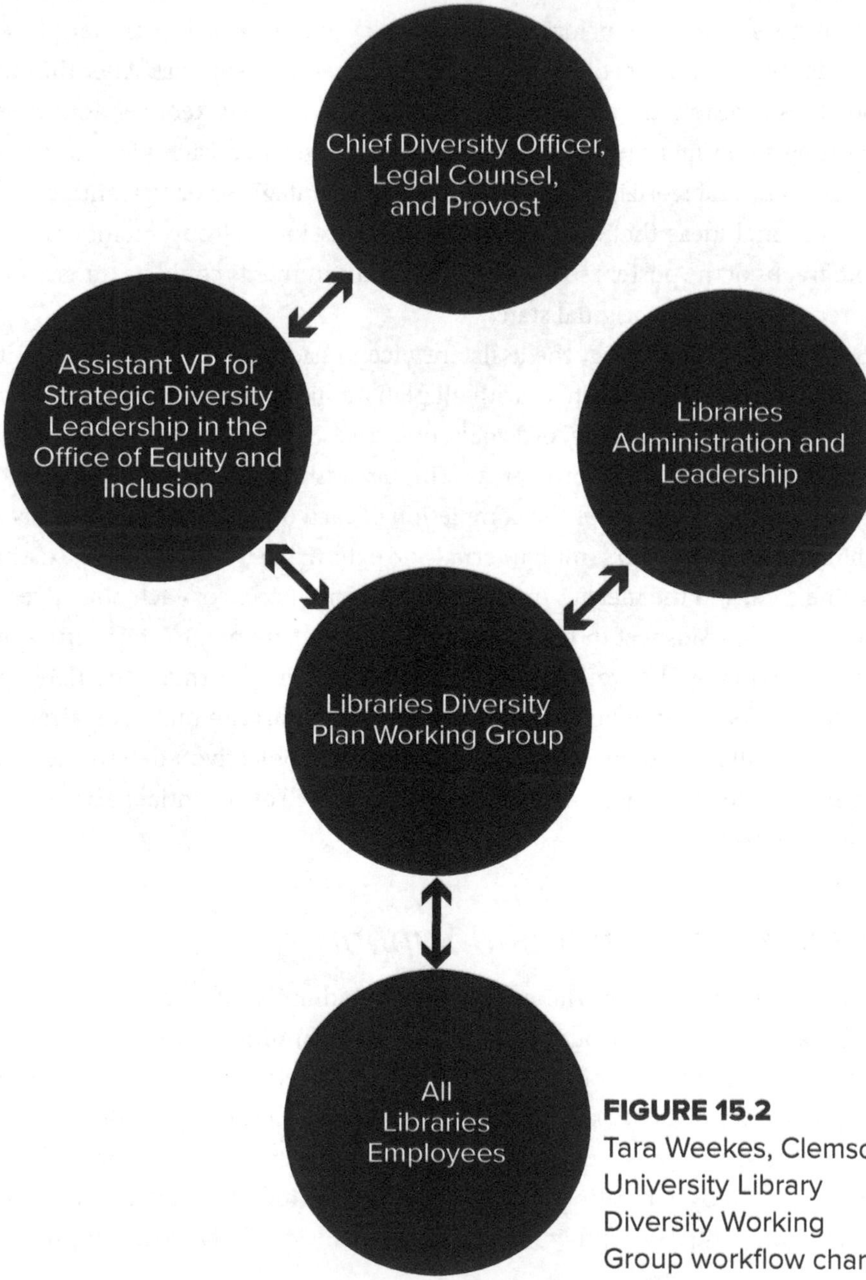

FIGURE 15.2
Tara Weekes, Clemson University Library Diversity Working Group workflow chart.

down any ideas they had on provided Post-it Notes and place those ideas on larger Post-it Note posters labeled with the strategic priority area they thought their idea might fall under, mimicking the initial LDPWG brainstorming session. The presentation concluded with a tour of the LDPWG StaffWeb page, which included a month-by-month record of the group's activities, a DEI resource list, and an option for anonymous ideas and feedback. After an extended comments period, the cochairs reviewed the activity ideas and general feedback from the libraries' employees and incorporated these things into the draft diversity strategic plan.

The LDPWG reviewed the draft and then formatted it for presentation to the dean of the libraries and the library leadership team (comprised of senior leadership) for additional input and feedback. The resulting draft was then published on the LDPWG StaffWeb page for another round of feedback from all employees. This feedback period, as well as the one after the all-employee presentation, required substantial time and effort but yielded great benefit in using an inclusive process to involve as much employee input as possible.

Outcomes

Libraries Diversity Strategic Plan

All of the LDPWG activities ultimately resulted in a Clemson University Libraries' 2019–2026 diversity strategic plan that was approved by the dean, the assistant vice president for strategic diversity leadership, and the provost of Clemson University. The following are examples of the libraries' diversity strategic plan goals for each of the six strategic priority areas with associated objectives and action steps.

CLIMATE AND INFRASTRUCTURE

Goal: Establish process of formal and continuous assessment of the Clemson Libraries' internal climate concerning diversity and inclusion.
Objective 1: Implement and utilize the Intercultural Development Inventory to periodically assess the organization's intercultural competence.[66]
Action Steps
1. January 2020–June 2020: Administer the Intercultural Development Inventory to Library Leadership Team.

2. July 2020–December 2020: Administer the Intercultural Development Inventory to all other employees.

3. January 2021–December 2026: Utilize results to develop employee trainings and workshops, and periodically readminister the Intercultural Development Inventory to assess training impact, gaps, goals, and improvement action plans.

Objective 2: Participate in and utilize a recurring Clemson University diversity and inclusion organization climate assessment.

Action Steps

1. January 2020–December 2020: Participate in Office of Inclusion, Provost, and HR diversity assessments for faculty and staff to obtain a baseline assessment of Clemson Libraries' internal climate concerning diversity and inclusion.

2. January 2021–June 2021: Analyze the resulting aggregated data and develop an action plan to address findings.

3. July 2021–December 2024: Implement action plans to address findings from the assessment.

4. January 2025–December 2026: Participate in anticipated subsequent Office of Equity and Inclusion, Provost, and HR diversity assessments for faculty and staff to obtain and conduct comparison assessment of Clemson Libraries' internal climate concerning diversity and inclusion.

Education and Training

Goal: Increase intercultural competence and inclusion training available for Clemson Libraries employees.

Objective 1: Provide Clemson Libraries employees at least two intercultural competence and inclusion training workshops each year to apply to workplace relations and public services.

Action Steps

1. January 2019–December 2020: Collaborate with campus organizations to identify, offer, and possibly adapt existing training.

2. January 2021–December 2026: Utilize the Intercultural Development Inventory results to develop, provide, and market at least two intercultural competence and inclusion training workshops each

year to apply to workplace relations and public services with periodic assessment to determine and implement improvements to curriculum and methodologies.

LEADERSHIP SUPPORT AND DEVELOPMENT

Goal: Increase communication, encouragement, and funding to support a culture of diversity and inclusion.

Objective 1: Establish, maintain, and communicate financial and work time support for all employees to participate in diversity- and inclusion-related trainings, events, conference presentations, and publications.

Action Steps

1. April 2019–December 2026: Establish and maintain financial support for all employees to participate in diversity- and inclusion-related trainings, events, conference presentations, and publications.

2. April 2019–December 2026: Establish and maintain a policy and communication method to inform employees of financial and work time support to participate in diversity- and inclusion-related trainings, events, conference presentations, and publications.

Objective 2: Develop and implement ongoing internal communications of available libraries, Clemson University, and library and information science intercultural competence and inclusion training and development opportunities, events, activities, and immersive social experiences.

Action Steps

1. April 2019–August 2019: Establish and maintain internal communication methods and procedures to promote available libraries, Clemson University, and library and information science intercultural competence and inclusion training and development opportunities, events, activities, and immersive social experiences.

2. August 2019–December 2019: Incorporate into diversity webpage.

RECRUITMENT AND RETENTION

Goal: Increase diverse representation within the Clemson Libraries workforce.

Objective 1: Assess current diverse representation of workforce and related recruitment requirements and efforts.

Action Steps

1A.   January 2020–June 2020: Compare current diverse representation demographic data within the Clemson Libraries workforce with the *2017 ALA Demographic Study* data to establish gap and goals.[67]

1B.   January 2020–June 2020: Assess existing systems of recruitment requirements and search committee training.

Objective 2: Implement improvements to recruitment and interview processes to increase diverse representation within the Clemson Libraries workforce.

Action Steps

1.   January 2019–December 2019: Establish or improve required position advertisement methods to recruit diverse faculty staff.

2.   January 2020–December 2026: Provide and require search committee diversity training for all involved in faculty, staff, and student hiring processes and require an assessment of candidate diversity, inclusion, and equity understanding during interview process.

Objective 3: Conduct an annual assessment of diverse representation within the Clemson Libraries workforce to establish goals and implement improvements.

Action Steps: July 2021–December 2026: Annually determine and record current diverse representation statistics within the Clemson Libraries workforce and compare figures with *2017 ALA Demographic Study* to establish goals and implement improvements.

RESEARCH AND SCHOLARSHIP

Goal: Increase Clemson Libraries' hosting, marketing, and participation in events and displays to showcase university scholarship pertaining to diversity and inclusion.

Objective 1: Host and market at least two events each year to showcase university diversity- and inclusion-related scholarship.

Action Steps: January 2019–December 2026: Identify and increase outreach efforts to develop event and marketing collaborative partnerships with university researchers and practitioners involved in diversity- and inclusion-related scholarship.

Objective 2: Create and market at least two displays each year to showcase university diversity- and inclusion-related research or Clemson Libraries resources.

Action Steps: January 2019–December 2026: Identify and increase outreach efforts to develop display and marketing collaborative partnerships with diversity- and inclusion-related university researchers, practitioners, and librarians.

Objective 3: Encourage and support Clemson Libraries' employees to present and publish research and activities pertaining to diversity and inclusion.

Action Steps

1. January 2019–December 2026: Identify and communicate opportunities to present at conferences and publish in publications pertaining to diversity and inclusion.

2. January 2019–December 2026: Providing funding support for presenters and publishers.

STRATEGIC PARTNERSHIPS

Goal: Increase diverse representation on the University Library Advisory Committee.

Objective 1: Reestablish and increase diverse representation on the University Library Advisory Committee.

Action Steps

1. January 2019–December 2019: Convene existing University Library Advisory Committee.

2. January 2020–December 2020: Assess and improve composition and bylaws to encourage diverse representation of faculty and staff.

3. January 2020–December 2026: Conduct outreach to encourage diverse faculty and staff representation.

Initiatives on Campus

During the last three years, Clemson University efforts and programs have developed substantially and new initiatives have taken root in conjunction with the growth of the Office of Inclusion and Equity. The university has merged multiple program areas on campus doing DEI work and created a single administrative office to share the responsibility of the Office of Access and Equity, the Charles H. Houston Center for the Study of the Black Experience in Education, the College Preparation and Outreach Program, and the Gantt Multicultural Center, among others.

New initiatives have been developed by this group that dovetail with some of the goals and objectives set in the libraries' diversity strategic plan. In the area of education and training, a director of diversity education and training was hired by the university to create a program of courses and resources. Among these programs is the Strategic Inclusive Excellence Certificate Program that offers three levels of completion. To complete the basic program, participants must take three core single-day courses focused on inclusive excellence in higher education and then select three elective courses from a set of offerings. The electives include such topics as ageism, indigeneity, and first-generation students in higher education. The second level of completion involves taking the aforementioned courses and completing a multiweek series of group dialogues. The third and highest level of achievement includes the courses, the dialogue series, and the completion of a theory-to-action project.

The Office of Inclusion and Equity now oversees what were once referred to as the President's Commissions, which are committees created by the president of the university to look at the status and well-being of specific groups on campus. These are the Commission on Accessibility, the Commission on the Black Experience, the Commission on Latino Affairs, the LGBTQ Commission, the Commission on the Status of Women, and the Veterans Commission. Previously, the commissions had no overarching reporting structure or fiscal umbrella to provide support for their work. With the expansion of the Office of Inclusion and Equity, these groups now have administrative and financial support so that they can continue to explore how each of these groups functions on campus. Some of these explorations involve programming, such as lectures, festivals, and forums, and can work hand-in-hand with the diversity strategic plans being developed.

The university committed to the purchase of an institutional assessment software called Campus Labs at the same time that groups were writing their diversity strategic plans. The assistant vice president for strategic diversity leadership was one of the first administrators allowed to use the new software so that she could create a template that aligned with the six strategic priority areas, including areas to record related goals, objectives, action items, baseline data, metrics, time lines, partners, and results. Within this system, links could be created between the libraries' diversity strategic plan and the ClemsonForward institutional strategic plan. Links could also be made between different colleges' strategic plans so that partnerships could be explored and then further documented. Required use of this university assessment system greatly enhanced campus-wide collaboration and essential accountability of the diversity strategic plans.

Other campus-wide initiatives are currently in development and support the objectives laid out in the plans, such as the mentoring task force developed by the provost's office. The university received a multiyear National Science Foundation ADVANCE grant to promote gender equality in STEM fields. Mentoring has risen as one of the top strategic initiatives from this grant program, and university administration is laying groundwork to develop a faculty mentoring program that addresses the needs of multiple underrepresented groups on campus.

Challenges
Leadership Turnover

It is vital that we, the authors, are transparent about the challenges we encountered during the creation and implementation of the libraries' diversity strategic plan. The first challenge in the creation of the plan was a rapid turnover of library administrators. Former University Libraries' dean Maggie Farrell was the initial champion of the libraries' participation in campus equity initiatives. She appointed a designated representative to the Council on Diversity and Inclusion and led the libraries in being a sponsor of the first annual Clemson University Men of Color National Summit.

After Farrell's departure in 2017, an interim dean, Joyce Garnett, was chosen to lead the University Libraries while a search for a new dean was conducted. During this period all representatives to the Council on Diversity and Inclusion were called together and charged with creating diversity strategic plans for each college and the libraries. With Dean Garnett's support, the Library Diversity Plan Working Group was formed and began its work investigating what other university libraries were doing and what tools were available to aid the work of inclusion in libraries. The ARL ClimateQUAL survey instrument was an early discovery, and the group recommended its implementation to the interim dean so that the libraries could establish a baseline of data and compare it with other participating institutions. It was also thought that this fresh data would be an extremely useful asset to have in hand as a new, permanent dean of the libraries began their tenure at Clemson University.

The vacancy of the position of dean of the libraries did allow the LDPWG to include questions to candidates regarding their commitment to DEI, the answers to which were shared with all library employees so that they could give appropriate feedback. In August 2018, Christopher N. Cox began as the dean of the University Libraries, and one of his earliest meetings was with the Library Diversity Plan Working Group to find out what progress had been made and to establish priorities for the group. In this meeting, Dean Cox stressed the idea of starting the conversation around diversity, equity, and inclusion within the libraries immediately in order to broaden the base of consensus so that the concept of a new diversity plan would not be a surprise to all employees. He expressed a desire for the libraries to be seen as a campus leader in the area of DEI.

Administrative Support

A crucial challenge faced by the LDPWG was obtaining administrative support for fiscal and human resources to carry out the work proposed in the plan. Clemson University Libraries' diversity strategic planning process was initiated and supported by the university administration and the assistant vice president for strategic diversity leadership. Financial support by the university at large to support these diversity strategic plans has been spoken of, but commitments are verbal and anything official in terms of allocations has yet to be put to paper.

Likewise, plan approval and monetary support from the libraries' administration has been difficult to obtain due to turnover of the dean position during this process. Strategic planning work, diversity plan time lines, and budgeted organization funds have been delayed as a result. Other colleges within the university are currently moving forward with plans to hire personnel in the form of associate deans or, in the instance of one college, a program coordinator to oversee the new slate of work that comes with the implementation of a diversity strategic plan; there has yet to be any discussion of a full-time position, however, to oversee these duties within the libraries. A standing Libraries Diversity Committee with six members was formed to start implementation. Given the amount of work to be done, the variety of initiatives, and its status as a new group, the committee is overburdened and has a limited range of influence. In recent efforts to share the workload and add more perspectives, the committee's size was increased and a student advisory member was added.

Group Dynamics

The LDPWG also experienced challenges with inclusion and involvement while it was functioning. The LDPWG started with twelve members representative of diverse units, positions, classifications, and identities. While this group size provided multiple perspectives during discussions, it also often hindered reaching consensus for meeting times and during discussions. The working group later expanded to include the libraries' President's Commission members which contributed valuable input but also made it more difficult to coordinate meetings and agreements. In consideration of the LDPWG expansion and our original charge time line, the cochairs decided to ask members to reevaluate their work commitments and their ability to contribute to biweekly meetings for the remaining months of work. This resulted in several LDPWG members declining to continue membership with the working group and with improvements to the LDPWG work processes after a reduction in number. The LDPWG also discussed the need for student input into the diversity strategic planning process, but the idea of adding even more people to the LDPWG as well as the institutional time line for the tasks presented obstacles for student inclusion, and it was decided to ensure student representation on a future diversity committee and advisory boards.

Fitting in the Framework

The framework's six strategic priority areas were instrumental in ensuring and organizing a comprehensive plan, but some of the recommended activities were not in the purview of the libraries, such as diverse course offerings or direct recruitment of underrepresented students to the university. Infusing the libraries' work into the requirements of that framework was difficult at times, and the LDPWG often had to seek input, adaptation, and approval of diversity strategic plan items and assessments that better aligned with our work as library and information science professionals. To help address and articulate these challenges, consulting similar frameworks tailored to academic library DEI strategic plans is recommended. Cruz recommended a particularly helpful framework that addresses collections, staffing, services, programming, and culture.[68]

Conclusion

Developing Clemson University Libraries' diversity strategic plan required substantial time, effort, and involvement. We now have clear goals, action items, and accountability to continue moving our organization and Clemson University toward being more diverse, inclusive, and equitable, but there were and are many obstacles to overcome. Agreeing on methods and language to communicate our value of DEI, obtaining an initial inventory and assessment, working within a required framework, and ensuring inclusion as well as administrative support throughout the process all presented challenges, but these impediments were ultimately beneficial to creating a sustainable strategic plan.

Beyond the work within the University Libraries, working on the plan has given us the opportunity to develop relationships with colleagues on campus with whom we would not have interacted before. Early in the process, the Office of Inclusion and Equity asked the libraries to create a tool that identifies information resources in the area of DEI within higher education, and we were able to work with faculty within the College of Education to create an extensive list. Also, the work and value of the library as a concept has been communicated to many who reviewed the plan on campus, including the provost, the chief diversity officer, and university legal counsel. Although the library is considered part of the university college structure, the organization structure is closer to that of the divisions and areas of support service that are being asked to develop their own plans during phase 2 of the university's initiative-—we now have the opportunity to work with more colleagues and share our experiences adapting our plan to a framework more focused on academics than support services. Since the completion of the libraries' plan, one of the cochairs has been tapped to serve on the College of Education's committee to complete its plan.

Overall, Clemson University Libraries' diversity strategic planning has resulted in numerous tangible products and goals that will guide our DEI impact going forward. The libraries' administration and the assistant vice president for strategic diversity leadership have praised the LDPWG's efforts and acknowledged the plan's ambitiousness; both have also committed to ensuring there is proper and sustainable funding. The final solicitation of feedback from all Clemson University Libraries employees confirms the success of our work, as one respondent wrote: "All in all, beautifully and thoughtfully constructed plan! So proud of y'all and proud to be a part of a library system that is committing itself to diversity."

Response from LDWPG state and national scholarship activities has also been positive and served as affirmation. Our eighteen months of work has resulted in a robust strategic plan to improve Clemson University Libraries' diversity, equity, and inclusion initiatives and impact, and we have now established a standing Diversity Committee to implement and oversee the plan with organization and institutional support and accountability.

Afterword

At the time of the final review of this chapter, the United States is experiencing a transformative time regarding racism in the aftermath of the murders of George Floyd, Breonna Taylor, and many others. Clemson University has responded to these events like many colleges and universities, and the impetus for change created by the 2016 events and protests has been revived. The university has now renamed what was the Calhoun Honors College to be the Clemson Honors College due to the known proslavery stance of John C. Calhoun. There is also an active request to the state legislature to restore the original building name of what is currently known as Tillman Hall. The structure had been renamed in the 1950s to honor Benjamin Tillman, a white supremacist politician who served as governor and later United States senator in the late nineteenth and early twentieth centuries. The university was also the site of a Black Lives Matter march led by student athletes and attended by an estimated 3,000 people.[69]

Clemson University Libraries has further committed to work in the area of diversity, equity, and inclusion. The first step was to release the following anti-racism statement:

> Dear community members,
>
> Clemson Libraries continues to advocate for a more diverse, inclusive and equitable society. With heavy hearts, we extend our support and gratitude to those fighting for equal rights and criminal justice reform as a result of the many African-American lives that have been devastated due to the criminalization of people of color.
>
> We recognize that information and access are not neutral, particularly for systematically disenfranchised communities. Our goal is to dismantle institutional barriers to information in

an effort to enhance the library experience of all those who use our resources. To that extent, we are committed to holding constructive conversations on racial equity throughout Clemson Libraries and advocating for conscientious training for all Libraries employees on issues of bias, social responsibility, and the role of academic libraries in supporting social change. Knowing that actions speak louder than words, a specific list of actions we intend to undertake over the next year is being developed.

We hope that through continued commitment to addressing injustice, we can make the Libraries a welcoming and safe refuge for all.

Respectfully,

Dean Christopher Cox, the Libraries Leadership Team, and the Libraries Diversity Committee[70]

Adapting the libraries' diversity strategic plan, our libraries' dean, leadership team, and diversity committee have also created and committed to a list of action steps for the current fiscal year and beyond:

FY21

1. Host library-wide conversations about race and racism.
2. Explore the inclusion of DEI goals in annual employee evaluations to ensure that all employees understand the role that diversity, equity, and inclusion play in their positions.
3. Develop and implement diversity and inclusion training and development opportunities for library leadership team members and unit leaders, employee supervisors, and student supervisors.
4. Conduct a collection analysis to determine gaps in the collection related to critical studies in diversity, including race, religion, and sexuality.
5. Seek diverse representation on library advisory groups.
6. Visibly demonstrate our commitment to DEI through our web presence, social media, and marketing and communication efforts.

FY22 and Beyond

1. Hire a permanent diversity coordinator to lead our DEI efforts. This individual would serve as a member of the libraries' leadership team and lead the libraries' diversity committee.

2. Develop recruitment and retention programs to expand the number of staff and faculty from underrepresented groups in our organization and support their ongoing growth and success.

3. Rejuvenate our Diversity Fellows program, hiring at least one diversity fellow annually to help the progression of individuals from different backgrounds in our profession.

4. Enter into agreements with library and information science programs such as the one at the University of South Carolina to develop internships and assistantships for students of color.

5. Explore the inclusion of DEI goals in annual employee evaluations to ensure that all employees understand the role that diversity, equity, and inclusion play in their positions.

6. Develop and implement diversity and inclusion training and development opportunities for library leadership team members and unit leaders, employee supervisors, and student supervisors.

7. Establish an organizational climate where discrimination and oppression are not tolerated and incidents are actively addressed.

8. Actively invest in the development of collections related to diversity.

9. Coordinate displays, social media campaigns, blogs and website postings, campus or public events, and so on to highlight historical or modern views related to diversity and inclusion in LIS or South Carolina history.

10. Encourage and support Clemson Libraries' employees to present and publish research pertaining to diversity and inclusion through communication of opportunities and financial support.

11. Collaborate with the Multicultural Center, campus commissions, and other entities across campus that are taking concrete actions to demonstrate commitment to DEI. Engage in conversations about DEI among Oconee, Pickens, and Anderson Libraries (OPAL)

members and actively participate in initiatives as part of library organizations and societies.

12. Establish ourselves as a leader in this area both at Clemson and within the profession[71]

We are excited about these and other changes that have been made and look forward to continuing on a more equitable, inclusive, and diverse path forward for Clemson Libraries and our university.

Acknowledgments

The authors of this paper would like to thank the Libraries Diversity Plan Working Group: Rodger Bishop, Lisa Bodenheimer, Brenda Burk, Robin Chambers, Jan Comfort, Lita Davis, Lili Klar, Nashieli Marcano, Josh Morgan, Ed Rock, Suzanne Rook-Schilf, and Derek Wilmott. We would also like to thank Altheia Richardson for her guidance, and Christopher Cox for his support. We also thank Cierra Townson and Jenessa McElfresh for their feedback.

Notes

1. Renna Tuten Redd, Alydia Sims, and Tara Weekes, "Framework for Change: Creating a Diversity Strategic Plan within an Academic Library," *Journal of Library Administration* 60, no. 3 (2020): 263–81, https://doi.org/10.1080/01930826.2019.1698920.
2. Louise S. Robbins, *v* (Westport, CT: Greenwood Press, 1997), 13.
3. Alice M. Cruz, "Intentional Integration of Diversity Ideals in Academic Libraries: A Literature Review," *Journal of Academic Librarianship* 45, no. 3 (May 2019): 220, https://doi.org/10.1016/j.acalib.2019.02.011.
4. Alesia McManus, "Thoughts on Equity, Diversity, and Inclusion in Reference and User Services," From the President of RUSA, *Reference and User Services Quarterly* 56, no. 4 (2017): 226–27, https://journals.ala.org/index.php/rusq/article/view/6348/8318.
5. American Library Association, "American Library Association Strategic Directions," 2017, p. 6, http://www.ala.org/aboutala/sites/ala.org.aboutala/files/content/governance/StrategicPlan/Strategic%20Directions%202017_Update.pdf.
6. Cruz, "Intentional Integration"; Association of College and Research Libraries, "ACRL Plan for Excellence," 2011, rev. November 2019, http://www.ala.org/acrl/aboutacrl/strategicplan/stratplan.
7. Julie Biando Edwards, "Developing and Implementing a Diversity Plan at Your Academic Library," *Library Leadership and Management* 30, no. 2 (2015): 1, https://journals.tdl.org/llm/index.php/llm/article/view/7129.
8. Cruz, "Intentional Integration";

9. Cruz, "Intentional Integration"; Edwards, "Developing and Implementing"; Julie Biando Edwards, "Diversity Plans for Academic Libraries: An Example from the University of Montana," *Library Leadership and Management* 29, no. 2 (2015). https://journals.tdl.org/llm/index.php/llm/article/view/7110; Charlene Maxey-Harris and Toni Anaya, *SPEC Kit 319: Diversity Plans and Programs* (Washington, DC: Association of Research Libraries, 2010), https://publications.arl.org/Diversity-Plans-and-Programs-SPEC-Kit-319/.

10. Charlene Maxey-Harris and Toni Anaya, *SPEC Kit 356: Diversity and Inclusion* (Washington, DC: Association of Research Libraries, 2017), https://publications.arl.org/Diversity-Inclusion-SPEC-Kit-356/.

11. Edwards, "Developing and Implementing"; Edwards, "Diversity Plans."

12. Edwards, "Developing and Implementing."

13. Edwards, "Diversity Plans."

14. Edwards, "Developing and Implementing."

15. Jeffrey L. Wilson, "Presidential Plans: New College Presidents and Diversity Efforts," *Planning for Higher Education Journal* 44, no. 1 (October–December 2015): 76+, Gale Academic OneFile, document no. A449344847; Jeffrey L. Wilson, "Public Institution Governing Boards: The Invisible Key Factor in Diversity Planning Efforts in Higher Education," Planning for Higher Education Journal 44, no. 4 (2016): 58+, Gale Academic OneFile, document no. A471001702; Raul A. Leon and Damon A. Williams, "Contingencies for Success: Examining Diversity Committees in Higher Education," *Innovative Higher Education* 41, no. 5 (2016): 395–410, https://doi.org/10.1007/s10755-016-9357-8; Lucy A. LePeau, Sarah Socorro Hurtado, and Latosha Williams, "Institutionalizing Diversity Agendas: Presidents' Councils for Diversity as Mechanisms for Strategic Change," *Journal of Student Affairs Research and Practice* 56, no. 2 (2019): 123–37, https://doi.org/10.1080/19496591.2018.1490306.

16. Leon and Williams, "Contingencies."

17. Damon A. Williams, *Strategic Diversity Leadership* (Sterling, VA: Stylus, 2013).

18. Damon A. Williams, Joseph B. Berger, and Shederick A. McClendon, *Toward a Model of Inclusive Excellence and Change in Postsecondary Institutions*, white paper (Washington, DC: Association of American Colleges and Universities, 2005), https://www.aacu.org/sites/default/files/files/mei/williams_et_al.pdf; Damon A. Williams, "Achieving Inclusive Excellence: Strategies for Creating Real and Sustainable Change in Quality and Diversity," *About Campus* 12, no. 1 (January–February 2007): 8–14, https://doi.org/10.1002/abc.198.

19. Wilson, "Presidential Plans."

20. Cruz, "Intentional Integration," 220.

21. Leon and Williams, "Contingencies," 397.

22. Elizabeth Semeraro and Neil M. Boyd, "An Empirical Assessment of Administration and Planning Activity and Their Impact on the Realization of Sustainability-Related Initiatives and Programs in Higher Education," *International Journal of Sustainability in Higher Education* 18, no. 7 (2017): 1311, https://doi.org/10.1108/IJSHE-03-2016-0047.

23. McManus, "Thoughts on Equity"; Cruz, "Intentional Integration."

24. American Library Association, *Final Report of the ALA Task Force on Equity, Diversity, and Inclusion* (Chicago: American Library Association, June 2016), https://www.ala.org/aboutala/sites/ala.org.aboutala/files/content/TFEDIFinalReport_ALA_CONNECT.pdf.

25. Leo Appleton, "Positioning the Academic Library within the Institution: Structures and Challenges," *New Review of Academic Librarianship* 28, no. 3–4 (2018): 209–16, https://doi.org/10.1080/13614533.2019.15820708.

26. Appleton, "Positioning," p. 209, 215

27. Fiona Harland, Glenn Stewart, and Christine Bruce, "Aligning Library and University Strategic Directions: A Constructivist Grounded Theory Study of Academic Library Leadership in Australia and the U.S.A.," *New Review of Academic Librarianship* 28, no. 3–4 (2018): p. 272-, https://doi.org/10.1080/13614533.2018.1498797.

28. Barbara Fister, "Libraries as Catalysts for On-Campus Collaboration," in Steven Bell, Lorcan Dempsey, and Barbara Fister, *New Roles for the Road Ahead: Essays Commissioned for ACRL's 75th Anniversary*, ed. Nancy Allen (Chicago: Association of College and Research Libraries, 2015), 46–49, https://www.ala.org/acrl/sites/ala.org.acrl/files/content/publications/whitepapers/new_roles_75th.pdf; Lorcan Dempsey, "Intra-institutional Boundaries: New Contexts of Collaboration on Campus," in Steven Bell, Lorcan Dempsey, and Barbara Fister, *New Roles for the Road Ahead: Essays Commissioned for ACRL's 75th Anniversary*, ed. Nancy Allen (Chicago: Association of College and Research Libraries, 2015), 80–82, https://www.ala.org/acrl/sites/ala.org.acrl/files/content/publications/whitepapers/new_roles_75th.pdf.

29. Fister, "Libraries as Catalysts," p. 57.

30. David Baker and Alison Allden, *Leading Libraries* (London: SCONUL, 2017), p. 30, https://www.sconul.ac.uk/sites/default/files/documents/LL%20View%20from%20above.pdf.

31. M. Christopher Brown II and T. Elon Dancy II, "Predominantly White Institutions," in *Encyclopedia of African American Education*, ed. Kofi Lomotey (Thousand Oaks, CA: Sage, 2010), 524-526.

32. Clemson University, Office of Institutional Research, "Clemson University Interactive Factbook," Clemson University Interactive Factbook | Clemson University, South Carolina, 2018, accessed June 15, 2019, https://www.clemson.edu/institutional-effectiveness/oir/factbook/.

33. Clemson University, Office of Institutional Research, "Interactive Factbook."

34   Wagner, John R., "Native Americans of Upstate South Carolina." Clemson University,." 2005. Accessed on January 23, 2020. https://web.archive.org/web/20200709164442/https://cecas.clemson.edu/geolk12/scstudies/files/NativeAmericanFinal%20-%20Copy.pdf.

35. Clemson University, "Select Dates in Clemson's History," 2020, https://www.clemson.edu/about/history/notable-dates.html.

36. Rhondda Thomas, Call My Name website, accessed October 16, 2020, http://www.callmyname.org/.

37. Nathaniel Cary, "Emails: Students Claimed Clemson Banana Incident Not Racist," Greenville News Online, June 3, 2016, https://www.greenvilleonline.com/story/news/education/2016/06/03/emails-students-claimed-clemson-banana-incident-not-racist/85291820/.

38. Almeda Jacks, "Message to Campus from VP of Student Affairs Almeda Jacks Regarding Campus Incident/Meeting," *Inside Clemson*, Clemson Blogs, April 12, 2016, https://blogs.clemson.edu/inside-clemson/inside-news/message-to-campus-from-vp-of-student-affairs-almeda-jacks-regarding-campus-incidentmeeting/.

39. James P. Clements, "Campus Message from President Clements Regarding University Diversity and Inclusion Programs," *Inside Clemson*, Clemson Blogs, April 14, 2016, https://blogs.clemson.edu/inside-clemson/inside-news/campus-message-from-president-clements-regarding-university-diversity-and-inclusion-programs/.

40. Matt Vasilogambros, "Five Arrested in Clemson University Racism Protests," *Atlantic*, April 15, 2016, https://www.theatlantic.com/national/archive/2016/04/clemson-university-arrests/478455/

41. A. D. Carson, "See the Stripes," See Stripes, AyDeeTheGreat.com, accessed January 25, 2020, https://web.archive.org/save/https://aydeethegreat.com/see-the-stripes/see-stripes/.

42. Clemson University, *ClemsonForward Strategic Plan* (Clemson, SC: Clemson University, 2016), 5, https://www.clemson.edu/provost/strategic-plan.

43. Association of American Colleges and Universities, "Making Excellence Inclusive," accessed January 23, 2020, https://www.aacu.org/making-excellence-inclusive.

44. Jeffrey F. Milem, Mitchell J. Chang, and Anthony Lising Antonio, *Making Diversity Work on Campus*, white paper (Washington, DC: Association of American Colleges and Universities, 2005), https://www.aacu.org/sites/default/files/files/mei/MakingDiversityWork.pdf; Georgia L. Bauman et al., *Achieving Equitable Educational Outcomes with All Students*, white paper (Washington, DC: Association of American Colleges and Universities, 2005), https://www.aacu.org/sites/default/files/files/mei/bauman_et_al.pdf; Williams, Berger, and McClendon, *Toward a Model of Inclusive Excellence*.

45. Lee Gill, quoted in Michael Eads, "Clemson University Staff, Faculty Defend Sikes Sit-In," *Anderson Independent*, April 20, 2016, https://www.independentmail.com/story/news/local/2016/04/20/clemson-university-staff-faculty-defend-sikes-sitin/88633628/.

46. Max Allen and Dr. Janelle Chasira, Strategic Priorities Chart—Figure 1, 2015.

47. Edwards, "Developing and Implementing."

48. Leon and Williams, "Contingencies."

49. Cruz, "Intentional Integration"; Wilson, "Presidential Plans."

50. Wilson, "Presidential Plans."

51. Wilson, "Presidential Plans," 17.

52. Wilson, "Presidential Plans."

53. Wilson, "Presidential Plans," 17.

54. Wilson, "Presidential Plans."

55. Williams, *Strategic Diversity Leadership*.

56. Edwards, "Developing and Implementing."

57. Edwards, "Developing and Implementing."

58. Edwards, "Developing and Implementing."

59. Maxey Harris and Anaya, *SPEC Kit 356*.

60. University of Florida, "George A. Smathers Library, Strategic Directions," October 2014, accessed August 15, 2019, https://web.archive.org/web/20200709165211/https://cms.uflib.ufl.edu/portals/communications/Strategic-directions-complete.pdf

61. Clemson University, *Clemson University Student Code of Conduct*, accessed August 13, 2019, https://web.archive.org/web/20200410221816/http://www.clemson.edu/studentaffairs/student-handbook/code-of-conduct/student_code_of_conduct.pdf.

62. Clemson University Libraries, "Statement on Race and Social Equity," Clemson Libraries News, June 24, 2020, https://web.archive.org/web/20200716140509/https://libraries.clemson.edu/news/2020/06/24/statement-on-race-and-social-equity/. Page content changed.

63. Edwards, "Developing and Implementing."

64. Edwards, "Developing and Implementing."

65. Edwards, "Developing and Implementing."

66. Intercultural Development Inventory website, May 21, 2019, https://idiinventory.com/.

67. Clemson Libraries' Diversity Plan Working Group recognized that the *2017 ALA Demographic Study* numbers are not ideal, and this strategic plan action step in no way seeks to normalize them. However, they are aspirational from our current library organization demographics, and they are one of the few benchmarks available aside from state demographic data, which was also discussed as a potential benchmark. Since this is our organization's first diversity strategic plan, the LDPWG decided upon an initial goal to first meet and then improve upon these numbers in comparison with other individuals reflected in the library and information science profession.

68. Cruz, "Intentional Integration."
69. Barrett Sallee, "Clemson QB Trevor Lawrence, Other Tigers Players to Lead Black Lives Matter Protest," June 11, 2020, CBS Sports Digital, https://www.cbssports.com/college-football/news/clemson-qb-trevor-lawrence-other-tigers-players-to-lead-black-lives-matter-protest/.
70. Clemson University Libraries, "Statement on Race and Social Equity," Clemson Libraries News, June 24, 2020, https://web.archive.org/web/20200716140509/https://libraries.clemson.edu/news/2020/06/24/statement-on-race-and-social-equity/.
71. Cox, Christopher. Libraries Diversity Initiatives/Actions. Email, 2020.

Bibliography

Allen, Max, Dr. Janelle Chasira. "Strategic Priorities Chart—Figure 1." Lecture, 2015

American Library Association. "American Library Association Strategic Directions." 2017. https://www.ala.org/aboutala/sites/ala.org.aboutala/files/content/governance/StrategicPlan/Strategic%20Directions%202017_Update.pdf.

———. Final Report of the ALA Task Force on Equity, Diversity, and Inclusion. Chicago: American Library Association, June 2016. https://www.ala.org/aboutala/sites/ala.org.aboutala/files/content/TFEDIFinalReport_ALA_CONNECT.pdf.

———. "Member Demographics Study." Accessed December 16, 2019. https://www.ala.org/tools/research/initiatives/membershipsurveys.

Appleton, Leo. "Positioning the Academic Library within the Institution: Structures and Challenges." New Review of Academic Librarianship 24, no. 3–4 (2018): 209–16. https://doi.org/10.1080/13614533.2019.1582078.

Association of American Colleges and Universities. "Making Excellence Inclusive." Accessed January 23, 2020. https://www.aacu.org/making-excellence-inclusive.

Association of College and Research Libraries. "ACRL Plan for Excellence." 2011, rev. November 2019. https://www.ala.org/acrl/aboutacrl/strategicplan/stratplan.

Baker, David, and Alison Allden. Leading Libraries: The View from Above. London: SCONUL, 2017. https://www.sconul.ac.uk/sites/default/files/documents/LL%20View%20from%20above.pdf.

Barrett Sallee, B., June 11, 2020, "Clemson QB Trevor Lawrence, Other Tigers Players to Lead Black Lives Matter Protest," June 11, 2020, CBS Sports Digital, accessed July 16, 2020, from https://web.archive.org/web/20200716135708/https://www.cbssports.com/college-football/news/clemson-qb-trevor-lawrence-other-tigers-players-to-lead-black-lives-matter-protest/.

Bauman, Georgia L., Leticia Tomas Bustillos, Estela Mara Bensimon, M. Christopher Brown II, and RoSusan D. Bartee. Achieving Equitable Educational Outcomes with All Students: The Institution's Roles and Responsibilities. White paper. Washington, DC: Association of American Colleges and Universities, 2005. https://www.aacu.org/sites/default/files/files/mei/bauman_et_al.pdf.

Carson, A. D. "See the Stripes." See Stripes, AyDeeTheGreat.com. Accessed January 25, 2020. https://web.archive.org/save/https://aydeethegreat.com/see-the-stripes/see-stripes/.

Cary, Nathaniel. "Clemson Investigating Defaced Sign." The State, April 12, 2016. accessed July 9, 2020. https://web.archive.org/web/20200709171447/https://www.thestate.com/news/state/article71290177.html.

———. "Emails: Students Claimed Clemson Banana Incident Not Racist." Greenville News Online, June 3, 2016. https://www.greenvilleonline.com/story/news/education/2016/06/03/emails-students-claimed-clemson-banana-incident-not-racist/85291820/.

Clements, James P. "Campus Message from President Clements Regarding University Diversity and Inclusion Programs." *Inside Clemson*, Clemson Blogs, April 14, 2016. https://blogs.clemson.edu/inside-clemson/inside-news/campus-message-from-president-clements-regarding-university-diversity-and-inclusion-programs/.

Clemson University. *ClemsonForward Strategic Plan*. Clemson, SC: Clemson University, 2016. https://www.clemson.edu/provost/strategic-plan.

———. *Clemson University Student Code of Conduct*. Accessed August 13, 2019. https://web.archive.org/web/20200410221816/http://www.clemson.edu/studentaffairs/student-handbook/code-of-conduct/student_code_of_conduct.pdf.

———. "Select Dates in Clemson's History." 2020. https://www.clemson.edu/about/history/notable-dates.html.

Clemson University Libraries. "Statement on Race and Social Equity." Clemson Libraries News, June 24, 2020. https://web.archive.org/web/20200716140509/https://libraries.clemson.edu/news/2020/06/24/statement-on-race-and-social-equity/.

Clemson University, Office of Institutional Research. "Clemson University Interactive Factbook." Accessed June 15, 2019. https://www.clemson.edu/institutional-effectiveness/oir/factbook/.

Cruz, Alice M. "Intentional Integration of Diversity Ideals in Academic Libraries: A Literature Review." *Journal of Academic Librarianship* 45, no. 3 (May 2019): 220–27. https://doi.org/10.1016/j.acalib.2019.02.011.

Dempsey, Lorcan. "Intra-institutional Boundaries: New Contexts of Collaboration on Campus." In Steven Bell, Lorcan Dempsey, and Barbara Fister, *New Roles for the Road Ahead: Essays Commissioned for ACRL's 75th Anniversary*. Edited by Nancy Allen, 80–82. Chicago: Association of College and Research Libraries, 2015. https://www.ala.org/acrl/sites/ala.org.acrl/files/content/publications/whitepapers/new_roles_75th.pdf.

Eads, Michael. "Clemson University Staff, Faculty Defend Sikes Sit-In." *Anderson Independent*, April 20, 2016. https://www.independentmail.com/story/news/local/2016/04/20/clemson-university-staff-faculty-defend-sikes-sitin/88633628/.

Edwards, Julie Biando. "Developing and Implementing a Diversity Plan at Your Academic Library." *Library Leadership and Management* 30, no. 2 (2015). https://journals.tdl.org/llm/index.php/llm/article/view/7129.

———. "Diversity Plans for Academic Libraries: An Example from the University of Montana." *Library Leadership and Management* 29, no. 2 (2015).

Fister, Barbara. "Libraries as Catalysts for On-Campus Collaboration." In Steven Bell, Lorcan Dempsey, and Barbara Fister, *New Roles for the Road Ahead: Essays Commissioned for ACRL's 75th Anniversary*. Edited by Nancy Allen, 46–49. Chicago: Association of College and Research Libraries, 2015. https://www.ala.org/acrl/sites/ala.org.acrl/files/content/publications/whitepapers/new_roles_75th.pdf.

Harland, Fiona, Glenn Stewart, and Christine Bruce. "Aligning Library and University Strategic Directions: A Constructivist Grounded Theory Study of Academic Library Leadership in Australia and the U.S.A." *New Review of Academic Librarianship* 28, no. 3–4 (2018): 263–85. https://doi.org/10.1080/13614533.2018.1498797.

Intercultural Development Inventory website. May 21, 2019. https://idiinventory.com/.

Jacks, Almeda. "Message to Campus from VP of Student Affairs Almeda Jacks Regarding Campus Incident/Meeting." *Inside Clemson*, Clemson Blogs, April 12, 2016. https://blogs.clemson.edu/inside-clemson/inside-news/message-to-campus-from-vp-of-student-affairs-almeda-jacks-regarding-campus-incidentmeeting/.

Jones-Wilson, Faustine C. *Encyclopedia of African-American Education*. Westport, CT: Greenwood Press, 1996.

Leon, Raul A., and Damon A. Williams. "Contingencies for Success: Examining Diversity Committees in Higher Education." *Innovative Higher Education* 41, no. 5 (2016): 395–410. https://doi.org/10.1007/s10755-016-9357-8.

LePeau, Lucy A., Sarah Socorro Hurtado, and Latosha Williams. "Institutionalizing Diversity Agendas: Presidents' Councils for Diversity as Mechanisms for Strategic Change." *Journal of Student Affairs Research and Practice*. 56, no. 2 (2019): 123–37. https://doi.org/10.1080/1949 6591.2018.1490306.

Lomotey, Kofi, ed. *Encyclopedia of African American Education.* Thousand Oaks, CA: Sage, 2010.

Maxey-Harris, Charlene, and Toni Anaya. *SPEC Kit 319: Diversity Plans and Programs.* Washington, DC: Association of Research Libraries, 2010. https://publications.arl.org/ Diversity-Plans-and-Programs-SPEC-Kit-319/.

———. *SPEC Kit 356: Diversity and Inclusion.* Washington, DC: Association of Research Libraries, 2017. https://publications.arl.org/Diversity-Inclusion-SPEC-Kit-356/.

McManus, Alesia. "Thoughts on Equity, Diversity, and Inclusion in Reference and User Services." From the President of RUSA. *Reference and User Services Quarterly* 56, no. 4 (2017): 226–27. https://journals.ala.org/index.php/rusq/article/view/6348/8318.

Milem, Jeffrey F., Mitchell J. Chang, and Anthony Lising Antonio. *Making Diversity Work on Campus: A Research-Based Perspective.* White paper. Washington, DC: Association of American Colleges and Universities, 2005. https://www.aacu.org/sites/default/files/files/mei/ MakingDiversityWork.pdf.

Redd, Renna Tuten, Alydia Sims, and Tara Weekes. "Framework for Change: Creating a Diversity Strategic Plan within an Academic Library." *Journal of Library Administration* 60, no. 3 (2020): 263–81. https://doi.org/10.1080/01930826.2019.1698920.

Robbins, Louise S. *Censorship and the American Library: The American Library Association's Response to Threats to Intellectual Freedom, 1939–1969.* Westport, CT: Greenwood Press,1997.

Sallee, Barrett. "Clemson QB Trevor Lawrence, Other Tigers Players to Lead Black Lives Matter Protest." June 11, 2020. CBS Sports Digital. https://www.cbssports.com/college-football/ news/clemson-qb-trevor-lawrence-other-tigers-players-to-lead-black-lives-matter-protest/.

Semeraro, Elizabeth, and Neil M. Boyd. "An Empirical Assessment of Administration and Planning Activity and Their Impact on the Realization of Sustainability-Related Initiatives and Programs in Higher Education." *International Journal of Sustainability in Higher Education* 18, no. 7 (2017), 1311–30. https://doi.org/10.1108/IJSHE-03-2016-0047.

Thomas, Rhondda. Call My Name website. Accessed October 15, 2020. http://www.callmyname. org/.

University of Florida. "George A. Smathers Library, Strategic Directions." October 2014. Accessed August 15, 2019. https://web.archive.org/web/20200709165211/https://cms.uflib. ufl.edu/portals/communications/Strategic-directions-complete.pdf.

Vasilogambros, Matt. "Five Arrested in Clemson University Racism Protests." *Atlantic.* April 15, 2016. https://www.theatlantic.com/national/archive/2016/04/ clemson-university-arrests/478455/.

Wagner, John R., "Native Americans of Upstate South Carolina." Clemson University,." 2005. Accessed on January 23, 2020. https://cecas.clemson.edu/geolk12/scstudies/files/NativeAmericanFinal%20-%20Copy.pdf, Tara, Clemson University Library Diversity Working Group workflow chart, 2017.

Williams, Damon A. "Achieving Inclusive Excellence: Strategies for Creating Real and Sustainable Change in Quality and Diversity." *About Campus* 12, no. 1 (January–February 2007): 8–14. https://doi.org/10.1002/abc.198.

———. *Strategic Diversity Leadership: Activating Change and Transformation in Higher Education*. Sterling, VA: Stylus, 2013.

Williams, Damon A., Joseph B. Berger, and Shederick A. McClendon. *Toward a Model of Inclusive Excellence and Change in Postsecondary Institutions*. White paper. Washington, DC: Association of American Colleges and Universities, 2005. https://www.aacu.org/sites/default/files/files/mei/williams_et_al.pdf.

———. "Presidential Plans: New College Presidents and Diversity Efforts." *Planning for Higher Education Journal* 44, no. 1 (October–December 2015): 76+. Gale Academic OneFile, document no. A449344847.

———. "Public Institution Governing Boards: The Invisible Key Factor in Diversity Planning Efforts in Higher Education." *Planning for Higher Education Journal* 44, no. 4 (2016): 58+. Gale Academic OneFile, document no. A471001702.

CHAPTER 16

An Introductory Indigenous Cultural Competency Training Program in the Academic Environment

Camille Callison and Lyle Ford

Over the last decade, we have seen substantive work relating to Indigenous people (First Nations, Métis, and Inuit), knowledge, and information held in cultural memory institutions of Canada. In 2015, the Truth and Reconciliation Commission (TRC) of Canada delivered its report on Indian Residential Schools and produced the ninety-four Calls to Action, providing the catalyst for change.[1] First introduced in 1876, the Indian Act is Canadian legislation that attempted to control all aspects of the lives of those considered "Indians."[2] Among other paternalistic policies were prohibitions on holding potlatches, sundances, or traditional ceremonies until 1951.[3] Libraries, archives, traditional knowledge, language repositories, and cultural memory institutions play a central role in the preservation of Indigenous knowledge by gathering written records, recorded

oral knowledge, and languages, as well as digitized Indigenous knowledge, history, culture, and language. These collections have become very important in reclamation and intergenerational transfer of Indigenous knowledges, languages, and culture. Therefore, those working in libraries, archives, and other cultural memory institutions need to understand:

- Indigenous peoples' worldview
- the validity and dynamic nature of oral traditions
- Canadian history of colonization, decolonization attempts, and Indigenous self-determination and re-empowerment

The University of Manitoba Libraries embarked on the creation, development, and implementation of Indigenous Cultural Competency Training (ICCT). This is a thirteen-week blended learning program developed specifically for the University of Manitoba Libraries (UML). We combined online training, a weekly workshop building relationships with the Indigenous community in Migizii Agamik Circle Room (an Indigenous sacred space), and experiential, land-based education with three goals, namely,

1. exposing library staff to an Indigenous worldview holistically;
2. teaching Canadian history from an Indigenous perspective; and
3. allowing libraries faculty and staff to form relationships with the UM Indigenous community.

The critical component of the ICCT is creating relationships with Indigenous faculty, staff, and students and those working with Indigenous communities. The ICCT is founded upon the guiding principles of respect, reverence, reciprocity, and relationship described in the seminal work by Kirkness and Barnhardt in "First Nations and Higher Education" in 1991.[4]

Background

Indigenous peoples' (First Nations, Métis, and Inuit) rights and title as the original peoples in this land now known as Canada are specifically entrenched in the Canadian Constitution.[5] Education about Indigenous peoples and their worldviews needs to be addressed and taught about separately from other much-needed equity, diversity, and inclusion education for those who work in libraries. The training came about as a partial response to the TRC's ninety-four Calls to Action. In 2008, the TRC of Canada was established as part of the Indian

Residential Schools Settlement Agreement. The TRC was to learn what happened in residential schools and to tell Canadians the truth about what happened.

For more than 100 years, Canada's Aboriginal policy tried to eliminate Aboriginal governments; ignore Aboriginal rights; end the Treaties; and, through assimilation, cause Aboriginal people to cease to exist as legal, social, cultural, religious, and racial entities in Canada. The residential schools were central to this policy, which is best described as "cultural genocide":[6]

> Cultural genocide is the destruction of structures and prac-
> tices that allow the group to continue as a group. States that
> engage in cultural genocide set out to destroy the political
> and social institutions of the targeted group. Land is seized,
> and populations are forcibly transferred and their movement is
> restricted. Languages are banned. Spiritual leaders and prac-
> tices are persecuted and forbidden, and objects of spiritual
> value are confiscated and destroyed. Families are disrupted
> to prevent the transmission of cultural values and identity from
> one generation to the next.[7]

The TRC engaged in years of listening to survivor stories and gathered them together, and in 2015, the TRC concluded its work by publishing its report, the ninety-four Calls to Action. The ninety-four Calls for Action task Indigenous and non-Indigenous Canadians to come together in an effort to help repair the damage created by residential schools and to move toward reconciliation. The TRC saw reconciliation as an ongoing individual and collective process that requires participation from all those affected by the residential school experience. This includes First Nations, Inuit, and Métis former students, their families, communities, religious groups, former Indian Residential School employees, government, and the people of Canada.

In June 2016, the Canadian Federation of Library Associations (CFLA-FCAB) was founded to become the national voice for libraries in Canada. One of the first things the CFLA-FCAB did was to include an Indigenous representative on the board of directors (a first for Canada) and to make truth and reconciliation a top priority of the newly formed association. The Indigenous representative formed a national committee to make recommendations for Canadian libraries. The *CFLA-FCAB Truth and Reconciliation Committee Report and Recommendations: A Response to the TRC Recommendations by the Canadian Federation of Library Associations/Fédération canadienne des associations de bibliothèques*

(CFLA-FCAB), made a number of recommendations to Canadian libraries.[8] One recommendation was "Encourage libraries, archives and cultural memory institutions to implement the Truth and Reconciliation Commission of Canada 94 Calls to Action, several of which have been identified as having a direct impact on libraries and archives."[9]

The CFLA-FCAB *Truth and Reconciliation Committee Report* includes ten overarching recommendations to achieve its mandate of promoting initiatives to all types of libraries to advance reconciliation by supporting the Truth and Reconciliation Commission (TRC) Calls to Action and to promote collaboration on these issues across Canadian library, archives, and cultural memory communities. This CFLA-FCAB report identifies which TRC Calls to Action libraries can and should respond to, advises on "decolonizing libraries and spaces through culturally appropriate interior design, signage, and territorial acknowledgment in collaboration with stakeholders; enhancing opportunities for Indigenous information professionals through appropriate pedagogy, recruitment, and training; and respecting the Indigenous cultural concept of copyright."[10] The report lists training as one of its ten recommendations:

> 7. Enhance opportunities for Indigenous library, archival and information professionals as well as the inclusion of Indigenous epistemologies in the Canadian library and archives profession through culturally appropriate pedagogy, recruitment practices, professional and continuing education and cross-cultural training in collaboration with local Indigenous stakeholders and partners.[11]

The University of Manitoba Libraries (UML) endorsed the *CFLA-FCAB Truth and Reconciliation Committee Report and Recommendations* in July 2018. Planning went ahead to investigate how to implement the ninety-four Calls to Action. One outcome of the planning process was the Indigenous Cultural Competency Training (ICCT), a blended learning program integrating online learning, in-person dialogues, and land-based education. It is comprised of Indigenous Canada, a twelve-lesson massive open online course (MOOC) developed by the University of Alberta's Faculty of Native Studies that explores Indigenous histories and contemporary issues from an Indigenous perspective; weekly in-person gatherings known as Meaningful Dialogues; and culminating with a land-based, experiential learning opportunity of a Cultural Immersion Day at the Turtle Lodge International Centre for Indigenous Education and Wellness, a sacred lodge of the Anishinabe Peoples, situated in Sagkeeng First Nation on the southern tip of Lake Winnipeg.

The ICCT program was constituted in part to fulfill the TRC's fifty-seventh call to action, which calls upon Canadian federal, provincial, territorial, and municipal governments to provide education to public servants on the history of Aboriginal peoples. As defined by the TRC, reconciliation is

> about establishing and maintaining a mutually respectful relationship between Aboriginal and non-Aboriginal peoples in this country. In order for that to happen, there has to be awareness of the past, acknowledgement of the harm that has been inflicted, atonement for the causes, and action to change behavior.[12]

The University of Manitoba Libraries are information hubs on campus and often operate as a space for dialogue, education, and programs with Indigenous and non-Indigenous community members. Therefore, librarians, staff, and others that work in libraries were in a position to advance reconciliation efforts to support the TRC Calls to Action at the University of Manitoba.

We aligned our work with the University of Manitoba strategic plan, *Taking Our Place*.[13] The following points were identified with reference to four of the plan's strategic priorities in our planning. First, we focused on the "Inspiring Minds" priority of ensuring that UML faculty and staff understand the importance and contributions of Indigenous peoples and to make sure that undergraduate and graduate students have an outstanding educational experience by providing educational opportunities for academic staff members to ensure they can incorporate Indigenous knowledge in their areas of practice. We also aimed to address the priority of "Driving Discovery and Insight" by fostering the inclusion of Indigenous perspectives in research, scholarly work, and other creative activities and by supporting the advancement of Indigenous research and scholarship. Finally, we planned to link to the priority of "Creating Pathways to Indigenous Achievement," as the final report on the strategic plan says,

> By incorporating Indigenous perspectives into our learning, discovery and engagement programs, the University will help to transform the lives of both Indigenous and non-Indigenous peoples and communities, and make Manitoba and Canada a

> better place to live. Through the sharing of Indigenous knowl-
> edge, cultures and traditions across our campuses, we will
> build a stronger foundation for students, staff and the wider
> community.[14]

This also aligns with the UML's strategic direction of "Building Community That Creates an Outstanding Learning and Working Environment." The ICCT exemplified fostering a greater understanding of Indigenous knowledge, cultures, and traditions by widening opportunities for students, faculty, and staff to learn about Indigenous perspectives (e.g., through courses/new curricula, service learning, research projects, workshops, lectures, events, etc.).

The UML ICCT consisted of an introduction to the Indigenous worldviews from the UM Elders and Cultural Advisor before beginning the Indigenous Canada MOOC of twelve modules over twelve weeks. "At the core of the ICCT is relationship-building facilitated by weekly Meaningful Dialogues, led by Indigenous Elders, leaders, traditional teachers, faculty, and staff at the University of Manitoba. Participants gather in the Migizii Agamik (Bald Eagle Lodge) Circle Room—an Indigenous sacred space—to discuss the week's module, listen to teachings or hear about the journey of an invited guest, and participate in ceremonies and sharing circles. Migizii Agamik generously allows the libraries to use the Circle Room, which was a suggestion from Elder Norman Meade."[15] This promoted relationships between the UM Indigenous community and the libraries. The Indigenous and non-Indigenous faculty and staff came from across the UM community and were extremely generous with their time. ICCT culminated with a one-day cross-cultural immersion at Turtle Lodge, which involved the participants travelling in groups of twenty-five to Sagkeeng First Nation to spend the day with Elders and Traditional teachers.

ICCT was co-facilitated by Camille Callison and Lyle Ford in the Anishnaabe tradition of having both male and female leaders. We went to UM Elder Norman Meade and Cultural Advisor Carl Stone, who gave us valuable advice and instruction before commencing the training. The Indigenous Student Centre director, Christine Cyr, also provided direction and led a traditional healing circle and "letting go ceremony," which occurred within the sacred circle and included a sacred fire, creating a safe space for sharing and support.

Program Highlights

Challenges

The main challenge was in finding speakers among the Indigenous faculty and staff. Indigenous faculty and staff were enthusiastic and willing, but they are already overburdened, busy with hectic schedules, and bearing heavy burdens in the work of reconciliation.

Important Lessons

1. The co-facilitators felt that Elder Norman Meade's advice to hold the training in Migizii Agamik Circle Room, a sacred space on the UM campus, really situated the ICCT in a meaningful and powerful way. The participants also commented on how coming to this space prepared them for the teaching and dialogue that followed.

2. The emotional and spiritual labour for the co-facilitators was not taken into account when planning the program. It is not like teaching a university class; there is a toll taken when sharing deeply and making personal connections in a spiritual setting.

3. It is important that the necessary time be given for the co-facilitators to prepare for the training as there is shopping to do for the cultural materials, food to order, and speakers, Elders, or invited guests who can be sent letters of invitation and e-mails only *after* asking them personally with tobacco in accordance with cultural protocols.

4. On the day of training, there should be no other duties or meetings planned for co-facilitators so there is time for preparation. Additionally, co-facilitators should be given time for a rest day after the Turtle Lodge Cultural Immersion Day. The Elders and Cultural Advisor both mentioned this is an important consideration for doing this type of work.

5. The success in finding Indigenous faculty and staff willing to come and be part of the ICCT program was possible only because of the relationship developed and trust built over seven years of embedded Indigenous library services.

6. It was equally important that there be both male and female co-facilitators to respect the local Indigenous traditions and that the co-facilitators be culturally and spiritually knowledgeable to facilitate the cultural protocols, respect, reciprocity, and day of cultural immersion.

7. During the winter session, there was a buildup to the letting go ceremony and cultural immersion day that worked very well.

8. The spring/summer session started with the letting go ceremony and cultural immersion day, which was a bit too heavy for participants at the beginning. In future, the co-facilitators would not recommend this timeline but would recommend the original timeline used in winter session.

9. It is extremely important to give the invited speakers an honorarium. This emphasizes to library staff that reciprocity is a key component of creating relationships with Indigenous people and community.

10. Food is a necessary and important part of Indigenous gatherings and conversations. Therefore, it was a crucial component of the ICCT Meaningful Dialogues.

Recommendations from ICCT Co-facilitators after the Pilot Project

1. Indigenous Cultural Competency Training (ICCT) has been successful in every aspect and has become a model for other cross-cultural training on UM campus. It is highly recommended that UML continue this program.

2. It is important to have a male and female co-facilitator since this is a culturally based tradition specific to the Indigenous territory the course is taking place on.

3. Peer mentoring could be considered for future sessions so other libraries faculty and staff can become more active allies. It is important to continue this work with libraries faculty and staff since cultural competency is not a box to be checked off but requires work over a period of time to become culturally fluent.

Components of the ICCT Program

ROLES AND RESPONSIBILITIES

- *Champion for the project:* Lisa O'Hara, Vice Provost and University Librarian
- *Oversight for the project* Christine Shaw, Associate University Librarian, Contract Services (External Agreements) and Staff Administration
- *Proposal development, logistics, co-facilitator, and curriculum development and implementation:* Camille Callison, Learning and Organizational Development Librarian
- *Co-facilitator and curriculum development and implementation:* Lyle Ford, Liaison Librarian for Classics; English, Theatre, Film and Media, and Native Studies

RELEASE TIME FOR STAFF ATTENDING

In order to complete the course, librarians and library staff needed to be released from other duties for three hours per week for twelve weeks and for one full day for the cultural immersion at Turtle Lodge. Staff completed the coursework independently and then met weekly for two-hour Meaningful Dialogues with other librarians and staff members taking the training. At the conclusion of the online Indigenous Canada MOOC training and the Meaningful Dialogues, all librarians and staff who completed both components were invited to attend a Cultural Immersion Day at Turtle Lodge and be given a certificate of completion then.

TRAINING AND MODULES

The Indigenous Canada MOOC formed the basis of the UML Indigenous Cultural Competency Training pilot project. The Indigenous Canada MOOC is meant to be completed over twelve weeks, taking approximately three to five hours a week. In addition, there were twelve in-person weekly sessions and a one-day cross-cultural immersion at Turtle Lodge.

- The Indigenous Canada MOOC is organized into twelve modules over twelve weeks.
- Training was online with weekly Meaningful Dialogues in which the participants met together to discuss the week's module and spend time

with an Indigenous Elder or Traditional Teacher to discuss the module's subject matter.

- Participants concluded the training with a Cultural Immersion Day at Turtle Lodge.

INDIGENOUS CANADA MOOC MODULES

The following section is taken from the Indigenous Canada course description at https://www.coursera.org/learn/indigenous-canada.[16]

Training sessions are comprised of both activities and lectures touching upon the following subjects:

Week 1—Worldview
In this introductory module, students learn the significance of stories and storytelling in Indigenous societies. We explore history that comes from Indigenous worldviews, this includes worldviews from the Inuit, Nehiyawak, Kanien:keha'ka and Tlingit peoples.

Week 2—Fur Trade
This module discusses pre-contact trading systems between Indigenous peoples of North America with a focus on the geographical region of Canada. We examine the chronological events of contact with Europeans and the events leading up to, and during the fur trade. This module also explores the long lasting social, political and economic ramifications of the fur trade on Indigenous peoples.

Week 3—Trick or Treaty
Examines Indigenous and settler perspectives of treaty making. Discusses the variation of treaties in Canada and the unique circumstances surrounding these events. Outlines the temporal and geographical history of the numbered treaties (beginning on the east) and ends with a discussion of the historical events and policies leading up to Métis scrip.

Week 4—New Rules, New Game
This lesson begins with a discussion about what is distinctive in Indigenous legal traditions. Explores impacts of policies put in place as British North America attempted to solidify itself

geographically and socially. Examines the ways in which the Indian Act contributed to assimilation.

Week 5—"Killing the Indian in the Child"

Outlines characteristics of teaching and learning in Indigenous communities and discusses how relationships were critical in teaching and learning. Traces the development and implementation of the Residential school system in the period after Confederation. Discusses intergenerational impact of Residential school system and the creation of the Truth and Reconciliation Commission.

Week 6—A Modern Indian?

This lesson examines the burgeoning resistance of Indigenous leaders and the formation of Indigenous-led organizations as the Canadian government employed strategies to encourage assimilation of Aboriginal peoples and communities into mainstream society, specifically relating to urbanization.

Week 7—Red Power

In this lesson students will learn about key characteristics of a few different Indigenous political structures and the impacts of colonialism on these structures (e.g., Indian Act, Red Power/AIM, White Paper, Red Paper-Citizens Plus). Concepts explored include self-government, self-determination, and Indigenous resurgence.

Week 8—Sovereign Lands

Utilizing contemporary and traditional examples, this lesson connects Indigenous worldviews and traditional ecological knowledge. As well, this lesson traces the historical impacts of settlement. Discusses key concepts of case law associated with Aboriginal title, rights to land and resources. List the on-going threats to Indigenous lands and how these threats and challenges are being addressed.

Week 9—Indigenous Women

Exploring Indigenous concepts of gender, and the traditional roles and responsibilities, this lesson then moves into an examination of how colonization can be characterized as a gendered project. Identifies some concrete examples of the impact of colonialism on Indigenous women.

Week 10—Indigenous in the City

Looking critically at the statement: "Cities are the place where Aboriginal culture goes to die", this lesson explores sites of urban Aboriginal agency/active participation, urban Aboriginal governance practices, and urban reserves.

Week 11—Current Social Movements

What is an Indigenous concept of community? How do Indigenous people form communities traditionally and today? This module will explain how social and environmental activism can mobilize and create communities. This module identifies key moments such as the Oka Crisis, Idle No More and Missing and Murdered Indigenous Women and Girls are grassroots resistance movements.

Week 12—'Living' Traditions: Expressions in Pop Culture and Art

Finally, we will explore how geographical location, trading networks and partnerships have influenced Indigenous art in the past. As well, we will examine contemporary iterations of Indigenous art and explore some of the artistic responses of Indigenous artists, musicians, and writers to the impacts of colonialism.

TRAINING COMMITMENTS (PER INTAKE)

The participants signed a training commitment to commit to completing the online training, participating in the weekly sessions, and attending the Cultural Immersion Day at Turtle Lodge. The University of Manitoba Libraries paid for the certification of completion ($70) for each participation and for honoraria, as well as tobacco, cloth, and yarn to make tobacco ties for each invited guest who spoke at the sessions. The libraries also funded the Cultural Immersion Day at Turtle Lodge and transportation to and from Turtle Lodge. The composition of the groups taking part is shown in table 16.1.

TURTLE LODGE—CULTURAL IMMERSION DAY

Winter and spring/summer session participants attended the Cultural Immersion Day, and UML invited the Faculty of Arts' Summer Institute on Indigenizing Curriculum to attend with us. The day started by meeting at 7:30 a.m. at the University of Manitoba, with the buses leaving at 8 a.m. Participants were given a box breakfast as they traveled to Turtle Lodge, located on Sagkeeng First Nation, which was approximately a two-hour drive. When the buses arrived, there was a sacred fire lit outside and participants were welcomed by the Turtle Lodge Coordinator Sabina Ijaz to the lodge, where respected Manitoba Elders and Knowledge Keepers from this traditional territory were waiting for the group. These respected Elders and Knowledge Keepers are fluent in their original languages; strongly connected to the ceremonies, traditions, and teachings; and have been identified internally within the communities as respected Elders and representatives of the Nations in this area. Elders and Knowledge Keepers shared with a group, interspersed with the drum group and singers gifting the attendees with ceremonial songs. There was a traditional feast catered locally by the community, and participants were given tobacco ties during the event to be burned later in the sacred fire. The participants also gave the Elders, Knowledge Keepers, Singers, and Drum group the tobacco prepared for this occasion. There ICCT participants were all given a copy of the *Turtle Lodge Central House of Knowledge Cultural Guide* created especially for ICCT participant by Turtle Lodge. The buses departed at 3 p.m., arriving back at UM by 5 p.m.

TABLE 16.1
Staff participant composition

	Librarians	Support Staff	Total
Inaugural Winter Session	10	15	25
Spring/Summer Session	7	14	21

ASSESSMENT

The assessment instrument (in the appendix) was a series of multiple-choice questions with room for narrative at the bottom. The assessment was of the entire training effort from beginning to end. Highlights of the survey were the following:

> Participants indicated that the online course content presented information that was mostly new to them, with two participants indicating that it was all new to them.
>
> The participants overwhelmingly enjoyed all the speakers, food, and cultural immersion day at Turtle Lodge, with only one set of invited speakers receiving a "Somewhat enjoyed" rating.

After completing the online content, most participants felt more comfortable learning about, discussing, and interacting with Indigenous cultures.

Similarly, after completing the in-person discussions, most participants felt more comfortable learning about, discussing, and interacting with Indigenous cultures.

PARTICIPANTS' COMMENTS FROM THE FIRST TRAINING SESSION

"Thoroughly enjoyable from an intellectual and spiritual perspective. I am not exaggerating when I say that the course was transformative and I'm grateful to Camille, Lyle and UML for providing the opportunity. I would highly recommend to other staff."

"The online course did several things well, including providing a huge amount of content succinctly. However, I didn't find it to be engaging. I think this part of the program could be improved. Otherwise, this was such a positive experience. The speakers have been outstanding, and I feel that my mind has been widened. Thanks for providing this opportunity and moving the Libraries forward in our journey to Reconciliation."

"The MOOC was a really strong base. The weekly discussions were excellent and furthered the learning. Turtle Lodge was the perfect ending. The whole program was exceptional, probably the best training I've had. It has made me a better person."

"Percy Lezard and Justin Rasmussen were the most interesting and challenging talk. It is too bad this course had to end and we will go just go back to same old same old."

"Fantastic!!!"

"Thank you very much for an amazing opportunity! Turtle Lodge is wonderful and mind opening."

"Fantastic! Thank you for the opportunity and to all the facilitators and speakers for their time and wisdom."

"Thank you for providing me with this incredible learning experience and chance to connect with the Indigenous culture and community, as well as with my colleagues!"

"'Enjoyed' does not capture how incredibly valuable this entire experience has been. It's been the most incredible learning experience! Thank you! Meduh! Miigwetch!"

"Excellent—I also enjoyed the weeks without speakers to discuss and reflect."

"I am so very grateful to have been given the opportunity to participate. Thank You!"

"It was excellent! Thanks!"

Conclusion

As Callison stated during her keynote for the American Indian Library Association President's Program on June 25, 2020, librarians and other academics "now recognize a critical need to encourage rethinking protocols around the sharing, teaching and intergenerational transfer of knowledge and embedding Indigenous epistemologies."[17] It is critical that this be voiced by Indigenous peoples and honoured by relationships that refine and adapt cultural memory praxis by integrating Indigenous worldviews.

An unspoken but intimately understood responsibility of Indigenous librarians, archivists, and cultural memory and heritage professionals is to unsettle, disrupt, and sometimes dismantle existing frameworks and pedagogy to examine how to respectfully engage with other cultural memory professionals and academics who work with Indigenous communities and their knowledge.

> The task for Indigenous academics has been to affirm and activate the holistic paradigm of Indigenous knowledge to reveal the wealth and richness of Indigenous languages, worldviews, teaching and experiences, all of which have been systematically excluded from contemporary education institutions and from Eurocentric knowledge systems.[18]

For many participants, this is their first introduction to looking at history and culture through a decolonizing and anti-racist lens. Indigenous ways of knowing and historical understandings exemplify the interconnectedness of the natural world and may have the answer to many of the crucial issues we face as a global community today. In both the online course and the weekly Meaningful Dialogue sessions, the participants were encouraged to think critically about education, economic and social justice, anti-racism strategies, and basic human decency for all peoples. The introduction to an Indigenous worldview of historical and contemporary understandings of Indigenous lived experiences in North America provoked a conversation and dialogue. Many of the ICCT participants said that their experience was transformative and pivotal in their increased understanding of and empathy for Indigenous peoples in the Americas.

Providing space for this critical conversation about Indigenous peoples, who are underrepresented in this profession, opens the door for further much-needed conversation about other underrepresented groups and populations. This increases awareness of issues of diversity, equity, and inclusion in the library, information and archival profession, and community. Over 80 percent of UML librarians and staff completed or partially completed the ICCT training in person. In order to strengthen the libraries' commitment to the program, participation in the ICCT was an expectation of all library staff and is incorporated into annual performance reviews. The remainder partially completed with the final cohort online due to COVID-19 restrictions on in-person instructions. The final component of cultural immersion at Turtle Lodge will resume when in-person gatherings are permitted again.

The University of Manitoba Libraries is committed to professional and continuing education of its faculty and staff on Indigenous history, significant events, and matters of importance today as relates to Indigenous (First Nations, Métis, and Inuit) peoples of Canada and providing this education in collaboration with Indigenous Elders, people, stakeholders, and partners. Although the ICCT program was developed to create relationships and facilitate cross-cultural understanding with Indigenous communities, this program can be adapted to achieve these goals with Black, ethnically diverse, LGBTIQ2S (lesbian, gay, bisexual, trans, intersex, and questioning, two-spirited), and other marginalized communities, which in part could answer the call for cultural inclusion and equity. Libraries are information hubs and often operate as safe spaces in which there are opportunities for dialogue, education, and programs. Therefore, librarians and library staff are in key positions to advance reconciliation and implement the TRC Calls to Action. We hope that the introduction to Indigenous worldviews through the online course, the weekly sessions, and cultural experiences on the land will assist in relationship building and increased education for librarians and library staff.

Appendix

INDIGENOUS CULTURAL COMPETENCY TRAINING FEEDBACK

April 17, 2019

1. Did the online course content present information you were unfamiliar with?

   O Didn't learn anything   O Somewhat   O No opinion
   O Most of it was new   O It was all new

MEANINGFUL DIALOGUES SPEAKERS

2. Norman Meade
   O Didn't enjoy at all O Didn't enjoy O No opinion
   O Somewhat enjoyed O Enjoyed

3. Carl Stone
   O Didn't enjoy at all O Didn't enjoy O No opinion
   O Somewhat enjoyed O Enjoyed

4. Fred Shore
   O Didn't enjoy at all O Didn't enjoy O No opinion
   O Somewhat enjoyed O Enjoyed

5. Cary Miller/Vanessa Lillie
   O Didn't enjoy at all O Didn't enjoy O No opinion
   O Somewhat enjoyed O Enjoyed

6. Ry Moran
   O Didn't enjoy at all O Didn't enjoy O No opinion
   O Somewhat enjoyed O Enjoyed

7. Nigaan Sinclair
   O Didn't enjoy at all O Didn't enjoy O No opinion
   O Somewhat enjoyed O Enjoyed

8. Chris Trott
   O Didn't enjoy at all O Didn't enjoy O No opinion
   O Somewhat enjoyed O Enjoyed

9. Cary Miller/Adele Perry
   O Didn't enjoy at all O Didn't enjoy O No opinion
   O Somewhat enjoyed O Enjoyed

10. Adele Perry
    O Didn't enjoy at all O Didn't enjoy O No opinion
    O Somewhat enjoyed O Enjoyed

11. Justin Rasmussen/Percy Lezard
    O Didn't enjoy at all O Didn't enjoy O No opinion
    O Somewhat enjoyed O Enjoyed

12. Christine Cyr/Ruth Shead
    O Didn't enjoy at all O Didn't enjoy O No opinion
    O Somewhat enjoyed O Enjoyed

13. After completing the online content, did you feel more comfortable learning about/discussing/interacting with Indigenous cultures?
    O No O A bit O No opinion O Mostly O Yes

14. After completing the in-person discussions, did you feel more comfortable learning about/discussing/interacting with Indigenous cultures?
    O No O A bit O No opinion O Mostly O Yes

15. Did you feel the food and amenities provided for the training program were appropriate?
    O Need Improvements O Neutral O Fair O Good O Excellent

16. Facilitators. How did they do in leading discussion?
    O Didn't enjoy at all O Didn't enjoy O No opinion
    O Somewhat enjoyed O Enjoyed

17. Turtle Lodge. How did you enjoy the cultural immersion day?
    O Didn't enjoy at all O Didn't enjoy O No opinion
    O Somewhat enjoyed O Enjoyed

18. Any further comments you would like to make

Notes

1. Truth and Reconciliation Commission of Canada, *Calls to Action* (Ottawa: Truth and Reconciliation Commission of Canada, 2015), https://nctr.ca/assets/reports/Calls_to_Action_English2.pdf (page discontinued). The Truth and Reconciliation Commission of Canada that ran between 2008 to 2015 related to Indian Residential Schools active in Canada from approximately 1831 to 1996. For more information, the reports from the TRC are held at the National Centre for Truth and Reconciliation, "Reports," https://nctr.ca/reports2.php.
2. Indian Act, RSC 1985, c I-5, accessed February 8, 2021, https://canlii.ca/t/5439p.
3. For more information see Bob Joseph, *21 Things You May Not Know about the Indian Act: Helping Canadians Make Reconciliation with Indigenous Peoples a Reality* (Port Coquitlam, BC, Canada: Indigenous Relations Press, 2018).
4. Verna J. Kirkness and Ray Barnhardt, "First Nations and Higher Education: The Four R's—Respect, Relevance, Reciprocity, Responsibility," *Journal of American Indian Education* 30, no. 3 (May 1991): 1–15, https://www.jstor.org/stable/24397980.
5. Constitution Act, 1982, Schedule B to the Canada Act 1982 (UK), 1982, c 11, Section 35, accessed February 8, 2021, https://canlii.ca/t/ldsx.
6. Truth and Reconciliation Commission of Canada, *Honouring the Truth, Reconciling for the Future* (Ottawa: Truth and Reconciliation Commission of Canada, 2015), http://www.trc.ca/assets/pdf/Honouring_the_Truth_Reconciling_for_the_Future_July_23_2015.pdf.
7. Truth and Reconciliation Commission of Canada, *What We Have Learned* (Ottawa: Truth and Reconciliation Commission of Canada, 2015), 5, https://publications.gc.ca/collections/collection_2015/trc/IR4-6-2015-eng.pdf.
8. Canadian Federation of Library Associations, *Truth and Reconciliation Committee Report and Recommendations* (Canadian Federation of Library Associations, 2016), http://cfla-fcab.ca/wp-content/uploads/2017/04/Truth-and-Reconciliation-Committee-Report-and-Recommendations.pdf
9. Canadian Federation of Library Associations, *Truth and Reconciliation Committee Report and Recommendations*, 6.
10. Dankowski, Terra, American Libraries, *Decolonizing Knowledge: Libraries can aid Truth and Reconciliation by Restoring Indigenous Cultural Memory*, June 25, 2020, https://americanlibrariesmagazine.org/blogs/the-scoop/decolonizing-knowledge/
11. (CFLA-FCAB Truth and Reconciliation Committee Report and Recommendations: A Response to the TRC Recommendations by the Canadian Federation of Library Associations / Fédération canadienne des associations de bibliothèques (CFLA-FCAB), 2016, http://cfla-fcab.ca/wp-content/uploads/2017/04/Truth-and-Reconciliation-Committee-Report-and-Recommendations.pdf)
12. Truth and Reconciliation Commission of Canada, *Honouring the Truth*, 6–7.
13. University of Manitoba, *Taking Our Place: University of Manitoba Strategic Plan 2015–2020: Final Report* http://umanitoba.ca/admin/president/strategic_plan.
14. University of Manitoba, *Taking Our Place*, 39.
15. Camille Callison, Lyle Ford and Christine Shaw. "University of Manitoba Libraries Staff Build Indigenous Cultural Competency." Accessed July 27, 2020. https://www.arl.org/university-of-manitoba-libraries-staff-build-indigenous-cultural-competency.
16. Paul L. Gareau, "Indigenous Canada," offered by the University of Alberta, Coursera, https://www.coursera.org/learn/indigenous-canada.
17. Camille Callison, "Honouring and Respecting Relationship: Rethinking Library Praxis" (keynote address, American Indian Library Association President's Program, ALA Annual Conference, held online, June 25,2020).

18.   Marie Battiste. "Indigenous knowledge and pedagogy in First Nation education: A literature review with recommendations." 2002, 4.

Bibliography

Battiste, Marie. *Indigenous knowledge and pedagogy in First Nation education: A literature review with recommendations.* Apamumek Institute, 2002. Accessed July 27, 2020. https://www.afn.ca/uploads/files/education/24._2002_oct_marie_battiste_indigenousknowledgeandpedagogy_lit_review_for_min_working_group.pdf.

Callison, Camille. "Honouring and Respecting Relationships: Rethinking Library Praxis." Keynote address, American Indian Library Association President's Program, ALA Annual Conference, held online, June 25,2020.

Callison, Camille, Lyle Ford and Christine Shaw. "University of Manitoba Libraries Staff Build Indigenous Cultural Competency." Accessed July 27, 2020. https://www.arl.org/university-of-manitoba-libraries-staff-build-indigenous-cultural-competency.

Canadian Federation of Library Associations (CFLA-FCAB). *Truth and Reconciliation Committee Report and Recommendations: A Response to the TRC Recommendations by the Canadian Federation of Library Associations.* Canadian Federation of Library Associations, 2017. Accessed July 27, 2020. http://cfla-fcab.ca/wp-content/uploads/2018/10/Truth-and-Reconciliation-Committee-Report-and-Recommendations-ISBN1.pdf.

Constitution Act, 1982, Schedule B to the Canada Act 1982 (UK), 1982, c 11, Section 35. Accessed on February 8, 2021. https://canlii.ca/t/ldsx.

Dankowski, Terra. "Decolonizing Knowledge: Libraries Can Aid Truth and Reconciliation by Restoring Indigenous Cultural Memory." *The Scoop* (blog), *American Libraries*, June 25, 2020. https://americanlibrariesmagazine.org/blogs/the-scoop/decolonizing-knowledge/.

Gareau, Paul L. "Indigenous Canada." Offered by the University of Alberta. Coursera. https://www.coursera.org/learn/indigenous-canada.

Indian Act, RSC 1985, c I-5. Accessed February 8, 2021. https://canlii.ca/t/5439p.

Joseph, Bob. *21 Things You May Not Know about the Indian Act: Helping Canadians Make Reconciliation with Indigenous Peoples a Reality.* Port Coquitlam, BC, Canada: Indigenous Relations Press, 2018.

Kirkness, Verna J., and Ray Barnhardt. "First Nations and Higher Education: The Four R's—Respect, Relevance, Reciprocity, Responsibility." *Journal of American Indian Education* 30, no. 3 (May 1991): 1–15. https://www.jstor.org/stable/24397980.

National Centre for Truth and Reconciliation. "Reports." https://nctr.ca/reports2.php.

Truth and Reconciliation Commission of Canada. *Calls to Action.* Truth and Reconciliation Commission of Canada, 2015. https://nctr.ca/assets/reports/Calls_to_Action_English2.pdf (page discontinued).

———. *Honouring the Truth, Reconciling for the Future: Summary of the Final Report of the Truth and Reconciliation Commission of Canada.* Truth and Reconciliation Commission of Canada, 2015. http://www.trc.ca/assets/pdf/Honouring_the_Truth_Reconciling_for_the_Future_July_23_2015.pdf.

———. *What We Have Learned: Principles of Truth and Reconciliation.* Ottawa: Truth and Reconciliation Commission of Canada, 2015. https://publications.gc.ca/collections/collection_2015/trc/IR4-6-2015-eng.pdf.

University of Manitoba. *Taking Our Place: University of Manitoba Strategic Plan 2015–2020: Final Report.* http://umanitoba.ca/admin/president/strategic_plan.

CHAPTER 17

Journeying to Accountability

Labor and Responses of Settler Knowledge Institutions to Indigenous Communities and Issues

Oy Lein "Jace" Harrison, Jamie Lee Morin, Desmond Wong, and May Chan

Introduction

Librarianship as a profession is often complicit in the reinforcing of settler colonialism. Settler colonialism is the process in which settlers, people who benefit from the displacement, theft, and erasure of Indigenous peoples as beneficiaries of the settler state, replace Indigenous peoples.[1] As library staff working within the University of Toronto, a settler institution in what is now Canada, we are learning about our responsibilities and obligations toward the Indigenous Nations of this Land.[2] In this chapter, we will discuss Canadian institutions' response to the Truth and Reconciliation Commission (TRC) of Canada's ninety-four Calls to Action and final report, which concluded that "residential schools were a key component of a Canadian government policy of cultural genocide."[3] The release of the TRC report was a turning point for Canadian institutions, which highlighted the fact that many were ignoring or underserving Indigenous patrons.

Many initiatives were proposed and approved without proper relationship building, consultation, and accountability. The effect of this fever pitch toward TRC activities was a reproduction of colonial relationships and power over the needs of Indigenous patrons. Without meaningful action based on community relationships and accountability, there cannot be legitimate change. We note that the responsibility of learning and relationship building in reconciliation should be settler labor, as Indigenous people have been the communities affected by settler colonialism.

Through this chapter, we hope to share our experiences and specific examples of building cultural competency and awareness through professional development toward organizational change in the library system. First, we will discuss the context in which the University of Toronto Libraries exist, their organizational history, and their fundamental links to settler colonialism as a settler colonial institution. Next, we will discuss organizational changes and Canadian national movements, inspired and spurred by the Truth and Reconciliation Commission of Canada. While building authentic relationships necessarily began with a couple of library staff initially, the work required to realize meaningful reconciliation cannot be done by a few individuals at the workplace. To start this work in a culturally appropriate way, we need to build deep and meaningful relationships with Elders, Knowledge Keepers, and Indigenous community members. Through this relational work, we found that Indigenous Research Methods, Indigenous Languages, and cultural competency for settlers was at the heart of moving forward with the right relationship. Developing cultural competency has involved taking both a deliberate and an organic approach to hiring and staff engagement as part of the scaffolding process. Without prescribing solutions, this chapter will detail the approaches taken thus far, which include a series of generative conversations among individuals and teams, and the outcomes of these conversations.

Finally, as part of a large-scale environmental scan, we interviewed thirty-eight institutions, specifically in the realm of libraries, archives, and museums. These results provide a comparative look at how cultural heritage institutions across Canada are engaging and moving toward better relationships with Indigenous peoples. It is not our intention to use comparisons between institutions in a consumptive or competitive manner, but rather to take stock and survey the state of Indigenous relations in cultural heritage institutions five years after the release of the TRC's findings. We seek to understand how our institutions have acclimated in an environment where Indigenous patrons continue to find their voices and demand more of us. Libraries are now servicing patrons through an active rise in Indigenous political and activist movements: movements such as Standing Rock; Idle No More; the Missing and Murdered Indigenous Women, Girls and Two Spirit Inquiry; Wet'suwet'en Blockades; and more. Outside of Canada and the United States, Indigenous peoples continue to advocate for the stewardship of their Lands, waters, and sacred spaces in New Zealand, Australia, Hawai'i, Taiwan, Ecuador, Japan, and beyond. The time has come for libraries to position themselves in solidarity with or in opposition to these futurities. Indeed, the need for continued relevance to the communities we serve demands that we become more educated and less resistant to ways of thinking, knowing, and being that are outside of traditional library practice.

In the spirit of revisioning our ways of knowing (epistemologies) and ways of being (ontologies), we want to dedicate the following space to our positionality and presencing in relation to Indigenous Nations and our relationship to the Land that we are on.

Oy Lein Jace Harrison is a Black, Chinese, and Jamaican woman. Her maternal grandparents emigrated from Canton, China, and her father from St. Andrew, Jamaica. Jace uses the intersectionality of Black and Indigenous oppression to understand the ongoing impacts of colonization. She is still learning what it means to be an active accomplice and what it means to stand in solidarity with Indigenous communities. She believes that Black and Indigenous futures live in unity.

Jamie Lee Morin is a Métis woman raised in the city. Her community is modernly based in the Ottawa Valley. As a white-passing, urban-raised Indigenous woman, she recognizes her privilege and tries to bring in more Indigenous folx whenever possible. She is thankful for the active allies she works with, as they help to push for further implementations of the TRC Calls to Action in library practice. She is still learning what it means to stand in solidarity and active allyship with Black and other Persons of Colour communities. She believes that without truths, there cannot be meaningful reconciliation.

May Chan is a second-generation Chinese-Canadian settler, whose parents grew up in colonial Hong Kong and eventually immigrated to Canada. Her experience of and pride in being Canadian is shaped by her immigrant roots. She did not reflect on the impact of colonialism and colonizing processes such as immigration on the Indigenous peoples of Turtle Island until her faith and professional communities began to respond to the TRC Calls to Action. Given her privileges as a settler and a manager for a large academic library, she continues to grapple with the tension between being complicit in colonial oppression and being active in supporting reconciliation.

Desmond Wong is a Chinese-Canadian settler and a member of the Hong Kong diaspora who traces his ancestry back through Hong Kong and China. His homelands, Hong Kong, were a British colony until 1997, and as a result, he has grown up with an embodied understanding of colonialism and colonial trauma. With that in mind, he works in solidarity with Indigenous Nations to disrupt settler colonial processes in library practice and to reaffirm Indigenous sovereignties and nationhoods through library work. Desmond understands that his community, that of the Hong Kong diaspora, will need to work toward a futurity in solidarity with Black, Indigenous, and other communities of colour.

The University of Toronto Libraries Context

The University of Toronto Libraries (UTL) is situated on Mississauga of the Credit River First Nation territory. This Land, which is now known as Toronto, continues to be the home of many Indigenous people and has been traditionally stewarded by the Wendat and the Seneca. For thousands of years, Toronto was known as Tsi Tkarón:to, which means the place where the trees are standing in the water in Kanien'kehà:ka (Mohawk Language).[4] As in many library systems, a few dedicated librarians had cultivated long-standing and meaningful relationships with Indigenous communities throughout their careers. The Centre for Indigenous Studies was founded in 1994, along with Indigenous Student Services through First Nations House. In addition, the University of Toronto's Ontario Institute for Studies in Education has hosted the Indigenous Education Network since 1989, making it one of the oldest Indigenous student- and education-focused organizations in North America. While collections work and instruction were ongoing, there was a general lack of awareness of the importance of widespread cultural competency and relationship-building work with Indigenous users for library staff. Working with Indigenous peoples was seen as a largely specialized library focus that many colleagues did not consider part of their obligations or duties. As will be later discussed, the dawning awareness that work with Indigenous users needed to be a priority for all library staff was a cosmic shift in significance, with this increasing consciousness brought forward by the Truth and Reconciliation Commission of Canada.

In 2015, the TRC released its Final Report along with an executive summary containing ninety-four Calls to Action. These ninety-four Calls to Action were meant to inspire action and reflection and were divided into two parts—legacy (1 to 42) and reconciliation (43 to 94).[5] The Truth and Reconciliation Commission was a commission investigating the legacy and lasting damage of the Indian Residential School System. From approximately 1830 to 1996, Indigenous children were forcibly removed from their families and communities in order to be "educated" in Residential Schools. The goal of the Residential School System was, as shared by a contemporary of the system, "to kill the Indian in the child"[6]—in other words, to systematically attack Indigenous Nations through the erasure of cultural connections, Indigenous languages, and community knowledge-sharing practices. A similar system was in place in the United States, known as the American Indian Boarding Schools. The University of Toronto, being one of the preeminent contemporary postsecondary education institutions, contributed significantly to the development and expansion of the assimilationist policies and systematic erasure of Residential Schools. Many of the teachers, administrators, and clergy affiliated with Residential Schools were trained at the University of Toronto. In addition, there are definitive connections between researchers at the University of Toronto and unethical practices and experimentations on Indigenous communities and especially students in Residential Schools.[7] With this legacy in mind, it is imperative that as a settler institution, the University of Toronto reckon with its past and commit to move forward in a place of cultural humility and toward a better relationship.

Commitment toward learning about Indigenous issues and building relationships that center Indigenous voices was of chief concern. In Canada, there have been several commissions and public inquiries into the oppressive structures that continue to affect Indigenous people. Notably, in 1996, the Royal Commission on Aboriginal Peoples released its final report, with recommendations on how the government of Canada should move forward in its relationships with Indigenous Nations. These included provisions for intergovernmental relationships and sovereignty, as well as social, cultural, and health reforms. While the Royal Commission on Aboriginal Peoples set out a twenty-year timeline to implement change, as of 2016, Indigenous peoples continue to wait for the crucial changes proposed by the commission.[8] In a similar vein, while the TRC ignited significant public discourse on Indigenous peoples and the need for settlers to learn more about Indigenous cultures and histories, there has been a lack of commitment on the part of the Canadian government to implement significant changes. In "Calls to Action Accountability: A Status Update on Reconciliation," Eva Jewell and Ian Mosby on behalf of the Yellowhead Institute remind us that of the ninety-four Calls to Action, only ten were completed as of 2019. The report states that at this rate of completion (2.25 Calls per year), it will take thirty-eight additional years to fully enact the changes of the Truth and Reconciliation Commission.[9] In the context of the University of Toronto Libraries, there were public acknowledgments of Truth and Reconciliation, as well as a commitment to move forward with accountability with Indigenous students, faculty, and staff. While these desires are genuine, given the neoliberal environment of the academic library, it is crucial that there be library workers committed to advancing these issues with clarity and holding this library system to account.

The goal of this work is moving toward relational accountability. In *Research Is Ceremony*, Shawn Wilson tells us that relational accountability as "the methodology needs to be based in a community context (be relational) and has to demonstrate respect, reciprocity, and responsibility (be accountable as it is put into action)."[10] While there was some interest from University of Toronto library staff in learning about Indigenous issues, there is a growing awareness that in order to move toward relational accountability, ongoing, sustained relationships need to be built as a foundation for working with Indigenous patrons. This will require continued commitment at all levels and in all sectors of the library system.

Cultural Competencies

In order to move toward relational accountability with Indigenous patrons, there first needed to be widespread knowledge of Indigenous histories, issues, and cultures. Later in this chapter, we will discuss a specific resource for cultural competency development in the form of a tool kit. However, in this section, we want to examine some of the ways in which, with the guidance of Elders, Knowledge Keepers, and Indigenous Faculty, opportunities to learn about Indigenous cultures were created for library staff. As the library staff is mostly comprised of non-Indigenous people (and none of the organizers of these events was Indigenous), it was of utmost importance that we follow the guidance of community members. At this juncture, it is important to note that our approach to relationship building with Indigenous folx must be reciprocal in nature. Indigenous people are consulted but rarely in an act of good faith. Verna J. Kirkness and Ray Barnhardt remind us that in order to be reciprocal in the context of higher education, "the emphasis is on making teaching and learning two-way processes, in which the give-and-take between faculty and students opens up new levels of understanding for everyone."[11] It was important to us to consistently center the question of how our work was going to positively impact or benefit Indigenous patrons using library services. For too long, labor and advocacy for Indigenous people has been exploitative and unilateral. In approaching Indigenous community members, we wanted to ensure that our intention was to work together with them, following the lead of community leaders.

In order to better understand the needs of Indigenous patrons, first we needed to understand the histories and systems of oppression experienced by Indigenous peoples in the Nation State of Canada. Here, we hesitate to call this history Indigenous history. Rather, the histories that we were engaging with are the history of colonialism and white possession. It is inappropriate to include Indigenous peoples in this history, though the history of dispossession certainly has ongoing effects on Indigenous communities. As Elders and community members repeatedly reminded us, Indigenous Nations have their own histories, spanning millennia, that do not include settlers. Instead, what we wanted to learn was how legal and social institutions systemically dispossessed Indigenous peoples of their Lands and Sovereignties in order to profit from settler colonial erasure. To that end, it was recommended that we bring the KAIROS Blanket Exercise as a learning exercise.[12] The Blanket Exercise is a simulated experience detailing the policies and institutions that systematically dispossess Indigenous Nations from their Lands. Using blankets as a metaphor for Land and the decreasing access to Land, participants learn about assimilationist policies and institutions such as the Indian Residential School System, the Sixties Scoop, and the Reserve System. Critiques of the Blanket Exercise note that it continues to center the experiences and agency of predominantly white settlers. Being aware of this critique going into the Blanket Exercise, we ensured that the facilitator of the exercise was a Mohawk woman and invited an Anishinaabe Elder to provide additional context and perspectives.

As part of a series of professional development opportunities funded by a grant intended for innovation from the chief librarian, we approached Elders and Indigenous Student Services on campus to initiate a process of learning. These consultations encouraged us to run events focused on Indigenous Research, Local Indigenous Knowledges, and the legacy of the Indian Residential School System. Elders reminded us that Indigenous Knowledges have been cast as subjective and not valuable to the academic process of knowledge creation. In *Indigenous Methodologies: Characteristics, Conversations, and Contexts*, Margaret Kovach reminds us that "colonial interruptions of Indigenous culture continue, and there is no way to address tribal epistemologies and Indigenous research frameworks without considering these relations."[13] In order to address this process, we invited an Anishinaabe Knowledge Keeper, who was also a PhD student at the university, to share teachings through their epistemology as an Anishinaabe Two-Spirit person. These teachings bridged Indigenous Knowledge that has been shared on the Lands where the library now stands for millennia. It was imperative to bring Indigenous Knowledge through traditional means of oral dissemination, thus refusing and disrupting colonial occupations of knowledge sharing and dissemination.

In bringing Elders, Knowledge Keepers, community members, and faculty into library spaces, we intended to disrupt the regular functioning of the library in order to reflect on our services, programs, and collections. Within the academy and academic libraries, Western academic practices are presented as the default, and often the barriers that this creates for other epistemologies and ontologies become invisible to library workers. Improvements to our institutions for Indigenous patrons can come only through thoughtful, relationally accountable work with Indigenous communities. Within the name of the Truth and Reconciliation Commission, there is a reminder that before our institutions can reconcile with Indigenous Nations, there must first be a pursuit of truth.

The Beginnings of Engaging UTL Staff Systemically

Since the release of the Calls to Action, UTL has introduced a number of reconciliation initiatives in response to the TRC. These efforts include creating an Indigenous outreach librarian position, adjusting collection development and access to collections, and adopting a revised classification schedule for law resources to support Indigenous users more effectively. However, these reconciliation initiatives were supported by at most a handful of staff working in disparate units across the library ecosystem, a complex network of both centralized and decentralized libraries and library services. The active work of reconciliation and relationship building with Indigenous communities and library users often fell on the same few individuals.

One issue increasingly reported by library users to public services staff was the library's use of the subject heading "Indians of North America," a vestige of colonialism, similar to that of "East Indians," to describe resources about Indigenous peoples in North America in the library catalog.[14] Desmond, the Indigenous outreach librarian, whose position was newly created in 2016, having fielded enough of these concerns, approached May, the head of metadata services for central libraries, to explore ways to change cataloging practices at UTL. The initial conversations revealed the need to expand the work of reconciliation to the wider library community deliberately and systemically.

Given the pressure to be efficient and make resources accessible to library users as soon as possible, libraries around the world depend upon each other to create and share standardized records to be readily used. Many standards are involved in dictating how resources are described. "Indians of North America" comes from the Library of Congress Subject Headings (LCSH), a thesaurus widely used by Anglo-American libraries. Because the Library of Congress officially serves the United States Congress and because the United States does not share the same reconciliation mandate as Canada, changing terminology pertaining to Indigenous peoples has not been a priority for the Library of Congress.

Developing, adopting, and maintaining a more localized subject heading standard is costly in terms of human resources, but users of Canadian libraries are increasingly expecting educational institutions to support reconciliation through respectful terminology. The need to use more respectful metadata practices is recognized by the Canadian library community as a pressing social justice issue.[15] At the same time, the challenge of making the changes expected while upholding the value of making resources accessible as quickly as possible is a barrier to considering a way forward. This tension resides between the need for change and the challenge in how to make the change palpably felt at UTL given its organizational complexities.

In the spring of 2018, an opportunity arose for Desmond and May to hire a student intern from the Faculty of Information (iSchool) as a research assistant to help with the work of addressing metadata practices. The TALint program, a partnership between the iSchool and UTL, is an internship program designed to enrich the education of iSchool students through workplace-integrated learning and develop future library leaders.[16] In 2018, this partnership began dedicating a TALint position specifically to Indigenous students as a concrete way to increase inclusion, diversity, and equity in the library profession, respond to the TRC, and build on existing commitments to support Indigenous students, such as the Grace Buller Indigenous Student Scholarship. This initiative resulted in the opportunity to hire not one, but two research assistants to help with addressing metadata practices.

Jamie, the successful candidate for the Indigenous student internship, was given the liberty to choose a project submitted to the TALint program. Although one might assume that she would be an ideal candidate for the research assistant position, this approach was deliberately taken to avoid unduly imposing the burden of reconciliation work on Indigenous persons.[17] However, Jamie did end up expressing interest in the position, which satisfied staffing the research project as originally conceived. When May and Desmond were asked whether there was enough work for two research assistant positions, they took the opportunity to expand the scope of work; they envisioned the potential for decolonial praxis, through relationality, in having a settler and a person with Indigenous roots inform each other in their work.[18] They believed that authentic, meaningful reconciliation is generative and realized through mutual learning.

When Jace interviewed for the position, she demonstrated awareness and sensitivity toward building relationships of trust with Indigenous communities. She chose to disclose how intersectionality impacted her worldview, citing that her background as Jamaican-Chinese gave her some ability to authentically empathize with what it means to be oppressed.[19] While all the candidates for the position were very strong, both May and Desmond saw the value of Jace's willingness to be vulnerable; they felt this would be a key ingredient to forming relational accountability, both in working with Jamie and also in connecting with settler and Indigenous communities external of the University of Toronto.

With the two research assistants, Desmond and May expanded the research project to include (1) an environmental scan, and (2) a cultural competency tool kit. Jamie took on the work to develop a cultural competency tool kit after confirming with Desmond that this work aligned with her professional interests.[20] The environmental scan project was assigned to Jace.

In the next section, we will present the results of the environmental scan and the process of writing and creating the tool kit as a responsive intervention.

Methodology

Forty-eight librarians and archivists, representing thirty-eight institutions across Canada, participated in the environmental scan study. Data was collected through semi-structured interviews that were conducted over the phone, through web conferencing, and in person. Interviewees were professionals working at academic, public, and school libraries or archives. In most cases, the head of metadata/cataloging or the Indigenous liaison librarian was contacted, as these positions were the most likely to be working on Indigenous initiatives. Many of these professionals were only just beginning to critically assess the coloniality of their institutions, while others had been working with Indigenous communities for decades. Participants were not asked to share their race, gender, or ethnicity, although this information was often offered as a way of positioning themselves within the reconciliation process. Out of those who self-identified, 94 percent were settlers (the vast majority of whom were white or white-passing), and 6 percent were Indigenous. Four librarians declined the invitation to interview because they felt that either they or their institution had been inactive in Indigenous initiatives. Others asserted that their library had not made any changes or did not plan to make any changes now or in the near future.

Each interview was guided by an interview form containing open-ended questions segmented as follows: Personnel, Policy and Institutional Backing, Cataloging Practices, Classification, Language, Cultural Competency, and Community Consultation. Field notes were recorded and organized using these seven categories and transcribed, and themes were determined from the data.

Findings and Results

The TRC's Calls to Action call upon post-secondary institutions to (1) support the integration of "Indigenous knowledge and teaching methods into classrooms," (2) support the revitalization of Indigenous languages through the creation of "university and college degree and diploma programs in Aboriginal languages" and (3) support the "teaching of Aboriginal languages as credit courses."[21] As caretakers of knowledge and history, librarians and archivists have played and continue to play an important role in their institution's journey toward these goals and supporting new faculty and curricula. Those libraries that are actively engaged in the reconciliatory process are reexamining the content of their

Indigenous collections, issues surrounding material access and how materials are organized, among other things. For example, the TRC has called upon law programs to create compulsory courses examining Indigenous issues.[22] And, in response, many of the law libraries that were interviewed are allocating more funding to Indigenous projects and initiatives and have prioritized expansion and diversification of their Indigenous collections.

It is important to acknowledge that these changes did not come about solely from the release of the TRC Calls to Action. Criticisms from faculty, students, and staff regarding the library's misrepresentation and underrepresentation of Indigenous knowledge ensued long before the TRC's release. Librarians have long struggled to get management and library staff to prioritize Indigenous access and are consistently met with barriers in a colonial system. These initiatives have been labelled as personal projects that lack adequate funding, commitment, and time. The enormous burden of reconciliatory labor has often fallen on the shoulders of a handful of professionals or an individual within the library. The results of this study show that the biggest barrier by far is the persistent apathy in our peers.

Building Cultural Literacy

When implementing cultural literacy-building programs, librarians often received pushback from staff who felt that Indigenous issues were not a part of their job description or were not directly relevant to their position. Almost every librarian that was interviewed said that their colleagues displayed unconscious incompetence. The same professionals that purported being very knowledgeable on Indigenous issues (both in and outside the library), and consequently did not require cultural competency training, were in actuality ignorant to the systemic racism found in our libraries and the challenges faced by Indigenous patrons. The realization that there is space to improve through cultural competency is a difficult reality to accept. As librarians, we have a belief, and to a certain extent perceived knowledge, that we are knowledgeable enough to assist others, or at least able to find out what we do not already know. The theory of four competency levels by Broadwell demonstrates the ideal journey of going from not recognizing the needed knowledge, to recognition, understanding, unconscious implementation, and maintenance of that knowledge.[23] For centuries, disinformation concerning Indigenous Peoples and their experiences has been directed to the non-Indigenous populations of North America. This is especially true in the Canadian education system, where the types of knowledge being disseminated are mandated by a governing body. In recognition of this gap, it is up to the librarian to find ways of bridging this knowledge gap.

Understanding Indigenous ways of knowing is vital to implementing Indigenous worldviews into a library. In "Imagining: Creating Spaces for Indigenous Ontologies," Marisa Elena Duarte and Miranda Belarde-Lewis write that "understanding how colonialism works can help those in the field of knowledge organization appreciate the power dynamics embedded in the marginalization of Native American and Indigenous Peoples materials."[24] They stress that it is important to develop an understanding of the ongoing processes of colonization so that we can see the oppressive role that our profession, practices, and standards play in the larger political context. While understanding the differences between Indigenous and Western knowledge management is important, it is also vital that we understand the principles, values, and ontologies from which these systems are derived. Studying Indigenous knowledge management solely in comparison to its Western counterpart centres colonial knowledge systems. Many of the librarians that were interviewed are moving beyond the confines of literature and scholarship that are limited to the context of the library and its institution. Librarians are attending Indigenous-organized events on and off-campus, or, travelling directly to Indigenous communities with whom they have relations. In the discussion of this finding, we want to make clear that we are not condemning focusing solely on Indigenous issues within a library context, but rather suggesting that one should form a critical lens when considering one's role as a settler. That is, there is multiplicity when pursuing reconciliation, as we are learning about how we perpetuate oppressive structures through not only our practices as librarians, but also as individuals.

While feeling shame about this knowledge gap is valid, an unacceptable response to shame and discomfort is inaction. The culpability of disinformation is not the responsibility of librarians, but it is a professional obligation to unlearn and consult Indigenous communities and Knowledges.

In our study, many forms of cultural competency and professional development exercises were suggested and examples implemented. Examples of cultural literacy–building programs that have been, or are currently being, implemented in libraries across Canada are as follows:

- mandatory ethics training for all library and university staff and faculty
- attending Indigenous-run or -organized events on campus or in the community

- film and documentary screenings
- participating in a massive open online course, Indigenous Canada, screened for library staff and open to the public
- trauma counselors for Indigenous Peoples engaging with sensitive materials
- Indigenous-focused Wikimedia presentations and Wikipedia-edit-a-thons
- Indigenous guest lecturers (in and outside the GLAM [galleries, libraries, archives, and museums] professions, community members)
- workshops on colonization and Indigenous education (e.g., KAIROS Blanket Exercise)
- engaging with Indigenous faculty and staff (e.g., collaborating on reading courses, seminars on how to use the library for Indigenous students)
- Indigenous Cultural Competency Training for management and staff (e.g., Ontario Federation of Indigenous Friendship Centres program, History of Indigenous Peoples' Network)
- OCAP (ownership, control, access, possession) training for professionals helping the academic community with research projects
- increasing educational resources for faculty through subject guides and other digital resources (e.g., basic terminology, an overview of major issues, atlases)
- reading groups surrounding the TRC and Canadian Federation of Library Associations' response report, *Truth and Reconciliation Report and Recommendations*.

Whether or not managers participated in this training, largely determined whether Indigenous issues were considered in the department's strategic planning. This was also true for the chief librarian and the library as a whole. All library staff should be participating in cultural literacy–building programming because reconciliation is a holistic process. Cultural change cannot occur when only one department is being critical in isolation.

Scaffolding Institutional Knowledge and Cultural Competency
This Knowledge Is Necessary

Indigenous knowledges and inclusivity are incredibly important and valid to all aspects of librarianship. This is arguably even more necessary "especially

because more Aboriginal faculty are conducting research and producing scholarly literature that incorporates an Indigenous world view and Indigenous
methodologies."[25] Since Deborah Lee's article in 2008, the need to work with
Indigenous communities and materials has increased dramatically, especially in
response to the TRC's Calls to Action. Interest in working with Indigenous folx
and Indigenous materials has expanded beyond Indigenous communities and
into the mainstream. Seeking and building knowledge about Indigenous issues
will benefit not only library patrons, but also librarianship practice. By collectively increasing knowledge on culturally appropriate content for the library
and within library materials through professional development and appropriate
metadata, librarians can only increase satisfaction "to a job well done in terms
of academic learning and community-building."[26] For a long time, this labor has
fallen on Indigenous librarians and their allies. However, as we have stated, there
is a need for solidarity and the growing awareness that this is labor that needs to
be shared, and it is incumbent on settler library workers to dismantle systems
created to marginalize Indigenous peoples. Thus, it is crucial in librarianship to
have non-Indigenous librarians gain experience and eventually develop a certain
degree of familiarity with working with and discussing Indigenous knowledges
and issues, especially where they concern topics of cultural appropriation and
cultural protection.[27]

Indigenous librarianship and solidarity action are already practiced and
reflected by critical library workers across many institutions. As seen by our
continuing discussion of results of the environmental scan, many practitioners
already take the active practice of librarianship and frame it within "Indigenous
approaches to knowledge, theory, and methodology."[28] It "is rooted in long-standing and established practices that Indigenous peoples employ to create, trans-
mit, and preserve knowledge.... These practices maintain Indigenous cultural
and social systems and provide protocols for ownership and appropriate use of
community knowledge."[29] This form differs slightly from traditional librarianship, but Indigenous librarianship is more holistic and relational. Despite the
growing bodies within this community sharing practices of relationality and
accountability, it takes time not only "to make [our] presence known," but also
"to convince the faculty that [Indigenous-specific approaches to] bibliographic
instruction or information literacy sessions are or will be beneficial to their
students."[30] These librarians in particular take on the labor of raising awareness
on the necessity of working with and for Indigenous patrons in a meaningful and

accountable manner through organizing workshops, writing academic papers, or making conference presentations.[31] In doing this, they raise awareness of the need for the profession as a whole to become adept in working and connecting with Indigenous patrons.[32]

Responsibility of Knowledge Seeking

It is important to note that the onus of professional and personal development is always on the individual. The weight of conferring this knowledge does not reside on the shoulders of Indigenous Peoples. It is also not the responsibility of Indigenous Peoples to constantly lead in knowledge sharing, as it is quite frankly exhausting, especially when consistently done as one of the only Indigenous people in a workplace. This is one of many factors that may lead to burnout and a reduction in Indigenous employment in your knowledge-keeping organization.

Most librarians have begun their Indigenous metadata projects by conducting a literature review of scholarship on Indigenous issues within a library and archival context. This includes an exploration of Canadian resources, as well as resources from the US, Australia, and New Zealand—all of which have colonial structures similar to Canada. Case studies and projects conducted by the Manitoba Archival Information Network (MAIN) and UBC's Xwi7xwa Library were seen as primary sources of sound Indigenous metadata practices.

Space

Libraries are attempting to create more physical and ontological Indigenous spaces within the institution. Physically, libraries are including culturally relevant artwork, cultural belongings, posters, and Indigenous language signage in library spaces. They are also creating offices for Elders and safe spaces for smudging and other ceremonial practices. Spatial organization is being made more reflective of Indigenous beliefs and values. For example, one library was designed to reflect the region's northern landscape, its rolling bookcases reflecting the rolling tundra. Other libraries are creating more space for collaboration with peers through group study rooms and seating areas—creating a collectivist culture to counter the Western individualism present in so many library spaces. Part of increasing Indigenous space also comes with reflecting on how the library could be made more relevant to Indigenous patrons. There is a focus on how the Indigenous collection could be made more diverse in terms of its subject matter and author-ship. Fundamentally, the creation of more physically Indigenous space has lead to more ontological spaces for Indigenous Peoples. Language speakers need to be consulted when making signage, Indigenous architects are working to design new entryways and foyers, and paintings are purchased from Indigenous artists.

Within librarianship, space is both a physical and an ontological phenomenon. For example, recognizing that the field of librarianship is a predominantly white space, libraries are also creating programs to alleviate barriers for Indigenous Peoples seeking to enter the profession. This has been realized by way of schol-arships, as well as cooperative and internship programs. While many of these programs are successful, some received few or no applicants. This may be because there are a limited number of library schools in the country, or because there is minimal Indigenous enrollment in library schools. It could need to reconsider how to reimagine library schools and curricula into places where Indigenous Peoples feel comfortable entering. It is difficult to work in a space that does not reflect Indigenous Peoples or kinship ties.

Many of the librarians that were interviewed recognized the need for more Indigenous Peoples in the galleries, libraries, archives, and museums (GLAM) professions. Several interviewees stated that they are "hoping to get more Indig-enous Peoples into this space. In particular, an Indigenous liaison librarian." But, many later added that, once more Indigenous Peoples are ushered into library spaces, "Then they [the Indigenous librarian] could work on these [Indigenous] projects." This assumes that Indigenous library professionals want to, and should be, the ones working on Indigenous projects; they are labelled as "the Indigenous librarian" and are forced into the role of Indigenous spokesperson. Indigenous professionals become siloed and isolated. Some librarians suggested that this isolation is also evident in Indigenous internship programs proposing that a resolution may be found in connecting Indigenous interns across institutions through a national program—alleviating some of these negative experiences.

Relationship Building

With consistent cuts in funding and personnel in libraries across Canada, the labor cost of reconciliation responses was a major concern. To disperse said labor, many librarians have reached out to other professionals in the region, and across the country, seeking consultation and the opportunity to collaborate on projects. For example, many public and college libraries have smaller staff models and have heavily leaned on university libraries for cataloging and development of metadata. In comparison, many of the larger university libraries have adopted and employed the labelling and classification strategies found in smaller libraries, who have more room to experiment due to greater collection manageability. For many libraries, collaboration was not only ideal but necessary as their collections are a part of a shared catalog. In a shared cataloging system the burden of labor can be dispersed across institutional barriers. In most cases, this gives librarians who may find themselves working alone on these projects the opportunity to find allies at their sibling institution. However, in other cases, an increase in the number of stakeholders means competing priorities. In this model, every institution would need to comply with changes made to the catalog for the sake of interoperability and a consistent vocabulary.

Like librarians at the University of Toronto Libraries, other librarians are conducting their own investigations and assessing the actions and strategies of their peers. Smaller libraries are looking to larger institutions for best practices, as they do not have the resource capacity to conduct this research themselves. But, larger libraries also seem to lack the capacity because the sheer size of the institution has employees wearing several hats. Acknowledging the importance of relationality and shared responsibility, many libraries are forming working groups across their province or nationally. In Toronto, Ontario, Ryerson, and York University have formed a working group for libraries, archives, and museums in the Greater Toronto Area (GTA) and beyond. This followed a series of symposiums entitled Decolonizing Description that began in the fall of 2016. Similar groups have formed in the western and prairie provinces and are comprised of mostly settlers. Many interviewees have criticized these groups: while it is important to begin having critical discussions about the coloniality of the library, we should also be taking the necessary actions to dismantle it. This is a shared criticism of the many symposia and conferences that have taken place across Canada. How can we take the theory and criticisms that we discuss in academic conversations and transform them into collaborative practice? Changes that are made in isolation, whether in a single department or within a single institution in the region, will have limited impact. Issues faced by Indigenous patrons are not the result of one particular department, but the holistic experience of a colonial institution. Librarians need to reflect on how they might be able to make small changes in their workflows. The dismantling of the library systems of suppression and marginalization of Indigenous knowledge systems will not be carried out by a single institution, but is instead the responsibility of all Canadian libraries.

Outside of metadata, librarians are seeking guidance on how to consult and engage with the Indigenous community and often expressed that they experienced difficulty when attempting to form a relationship with the community on campus or in the region. When discussing consultation, a recurring theme was fear. Many librarians feared that any contact would further contribute to the consultation fatigue that many communities have and are currently experiencing. Others admitted they are embarrassed and ashamed to show the community just how prejudiced and racist their catalogs really are. And many simply stated that they just don't know what to say. For those who did reach out to their respective communities, responses varied. Some librarians did not receive a response, and any further attempts at contact ceased. We must be mindful that Indigenous Nations are still living with the ongoing impacts of colonization and oppression. Many librarians were focused on obtaining the knowledge, understanding, or, context that they need to feed library initiatives and were less concerned with what Indigenous patrons needed. Or, the relationship-building needed to understand the changing educational and informational needs of Indigenous communities.

Barriers

Most institutions began Indigenous metadata initiatives by identifying the number of problematic terms that appear in their catalog. This was important in gauging the extent of the problem and determining resources needed to create a sustainable project: funding, other resources, labor, and the proper revision of departmental workflows needed to sustain a long-term project. Arguably, these projects are not just long-term, but become active, permanent components of the library workflow—until changes are made at a national and international level. Librarians have used the Manitoba Archival Information Network (MAIN) ontology as a starting point because it suggests alternative terminology specific to problematic subject headings identified in LCSH. It is important to note, however, that the MAIN ontology was developed for *MAIN* and the specific materials that it houses. As Bone states, "some changes were made only to terms affecting Manitoba peoples specifically. Applying these changes to all the individual peoples in the Americas, or even just to those in North America, would have been far too labour-intensive."[33] Acknowledging the limitations of MAIN, some librarians are combining this list with the product of other vocabulary projects at Xwi7xwa and Union of British Columbia Indian Chiefs (UBCIC) Resource Centre in order to expand their vocabulary's scope. In June 2019, the Canadian Federation of Library Associations Indigenous Matters Committee released its own ontology of Nation and Community names, which is currently under consultation. Similar to MAIN, these lists have their limitations in scope and should not be used to homogenize Indigenous nations. These projects have undergone consultation processes based on relationship building with Indigenous communities in their respective regions and cannot always be applied to similar terminology in the catalog. We must also keep in mind that the terminology used in these ontologies is are living documents and will be subject to change because identities and naming practices within communities are dynamic and likely to shift. It is for this reason that many librarians are advocating for the creation of a national "living" thesaurus. However, the sheer magnitude of this work has led to some inaction.

Many librarians viewed these projects as free labor, arguing that they will wait for larger institutions and associations like UBCIC, MAIN, Xwi7xwa, and CFLA's Indigenous Matters Committee to continue consulting and building ontologies so that libraries may slowly add them to their catalog as they are released. The intention behind this discussion is not to discourage implementing best practices and the product of successful projects into our libraries, but rather to remind us that this should not replace the need for relationship building between libraries and their Indigenous patrons. Librarians are also using this internal scan to determine the breadth of their Indigenous materials, including subject materials and represented mediums, and identifying gaps in the collection: that is, the variety of subjects and mediums that are represented. Correspondence with collection development colleagues determines whether there are gaps that need to be filled.

At this point, institutions are addressing broader Library of Congress Subject Headings, primarily "Indians of North America" and so on because they are easier to change than terminology that is deeply impacted by structure. Thus, most institutions have changed "Indians of North America" to "Indigenous peoples—North America." Depending on their library services platform, librarians are monitoring incoming records that contain these subject headings and updating the records as they appear. Throughout the scan, all of these changes were described as "patchwork" until Library and Archives Canada agrees to update the Canadian Subject Heading List or there is a lobby for changes to the Library of Congress Subject Headings.

Instructional Scaffolding

We recognize that beginning the journey of learning and working in solidarity with Indigenous communities is daunting, especially given the role that disinformation and lack of appropriate cultural knowledge can play. This is an inherently disorienting process, as library workers work through a centuries-long system that intentionally erases and invisibilizes Indigenous presence from these Lands. It is important, however, to take time to identify problematic assumptions, misinformation, and culturally inappropriate materials. From there, consider the institutional responses and responses from your colleagues. How is the institution being responsive and relational to issues affecting Indigenous communities? At the heart of these matters is the question of how the work done in libraries and other settler institutions directly benefits Indigenous patrons. A guiding method to increasing knowledge and active practice is instructional scaffolding. Derived from Vygotsky's theory on the zone of proximal development, instructional scaffolding is designed to build up from previously gained knowledge, "but with support to get to that next stage or level" of understanding needed.[34] In the following section, we will discuss the cultural competency tool kit, which is our response as an intervention as a scaffolding tool to build awareness and knowledge on basic Indigenous issues. We recognize that gaining this knowledge as a librarian will benefit not only librarians and Indigenous community members, but also patrons at large. Incorporating Indigenous epistemologies into the library makes for a higher elevation of social justice within librarianship, thus bringing Indigenous issues into conversation with library principles such as access, diversity, education and lifelong learning, service, and social responsibility.[35]

In this way, instructional scaffolding also increases relational accountability between local Indigenous communities and non-Indigenous communities, both within the library and beyond. It means being responsive and having the ability to locate and name problematic materials held within collections and being able to listen to communities and implement changes requested by Indigenous patrons concerning problematic materials and access issues.[36] As library workers, we have a responsibility to increase the visibility of Indigenous knowledges within the library, whether by having an exhibit on Indigenous authors or artists, or by having posters or photographs of high profile Indigenous community members.[37]

Indigenous Library Service Tool Kit as Intervention

Development

In order to combat disinformation and lack of knowledge on Indigenous peoples at a library system level, a tool kit was envisioned as a form of interventional knowledge building concerning Indigenous issues and ways of being and their implications in libraries. This tool kit is specifically focused on non-Indigenous librarians in order to guide them in their journey from conscious incompetence to conscious competence. The tool kit was developed with a mixed-methods approach, combining lived experiences from colleagues, empathy mapping for learning journeys (an element of user experience design), engagement with local Indigenous communities, and extensive online research examining similar tool kits. This was done in tandem with the environmental scan, which informed how other institutions were intervening in cultural competency.

Walk-Through

The tool kit begins with the University of Toronto's Land Acknowledgements. The University of Toronto comprises three campuses, one urban and two suburban, that are part of different territories and treaties, which are in turn reflected by shifting Land Acknowledgements. In the tool kit, there are discussions on the significance of the Land Acknowledgement—especially that it must be invoked with meaning. Land Acknowledgements began as a practice of radical presencing for Indigenous Nations, recognizing ongoing stewardship and resistance in the face of settler colonial violence. However, we note that with the spreading of this practice, especially across postsecondary institutions, this process has become rote and meaningless. We encourage action, relationship, and accountability beyond Land Acknowledgement statements.

After the Land Acknowledgements, there is an overview of considerations when encountering Indigenous patrons and materials, especially materials about

Indigenous peoples, cultures, ways of life, and beyond. We challenge readers on considerations of authorship and authenticity (Are the authors Indigenous or non-Indigenous? What are their relationships with Indigenous Nations?), the content's contribution to the field (What does this material contribute to our knowledge on Indigenous Peoples? Where and from whom did this Knowledge originate?), its description and access (How is it described? Where is it placed?), and level of accessibility to library patrons (Should it have unmediated or mediated access? Is it appropriate for circulation?). This tool kit is an information source. The answers to some of these questions can arise through basic searches, but others cannot be so easily located. This tool kit was created with the hopes that in responding to these questions, more questions will arise. The correct sources of information in Indigenous matters are varied and require research outside of typical bibliographic or electronic media. For instance, responses to the questions above would depend on the local Indigenous community's research needs. While there are books in the University of Toronto Libraries collection that were used as tools for Christianization and ultimately colonization, such as *Rand's Micmac Dictionary from Phonographic Word-Lists* by Reverend Silas Tertius Rand and *Kekichemanitomenahn gahbemahjeinnunuk Jesus Christ: otoashke wawweendummahgawin* (an Anishininaabemowin translation of the Bible's New Testament), they were created with the intent of communicating with and colonizing Indigenous peoples. Speaking to the resistance of Indigenous communities, these materials are now integral tools to revitalize Indigenous Languages, in this case Mi'kmaq and Anishinaabemowin. Other records created by non-Indigenous peoples, such as those describing genocidal and assimilationist tactics undertaken by colonial governments, should be examined more rigorously to determine whether they help community research or harm the community. Regardless, decisions should likely be made for how mediated their access should be.

The tool kit also provides some basic introductory information on Indigenous topics, such as what is appropriate or inappropriate phrasing and terminology concerning Indigenous peoples. For example, while *powwow* is appropriate for the Indigenous social gathering, it is inappropriate to use for a team meeting. Other examples of naming include the need for specificity in referring to a Nation or community rather than use of a pan-Indigenous moniker. This section especially is informed from Jamie Lee's experiences working in the field, from discussions over many years with Indigenous community members, and from researching Indigenous Knowledge and other tool kits. The tool kit ends with a call for responsibility of knowledge. It includes a list of resources to assist with scaffolding knowledges into librarianship practices through various forms of media, from academic articles to podcasts.

Conclusion and Moving Toward

The work of doing the environmental scan and developing a cultural competency tool kit was gradually introduced to various stakeholder communities. Initial attempts to engage the UTL cataloging community through group discussion with the idea of "decolonizing description" were met with mixed reactions. The barrier to action was primarily centered around consequences of becoming more inefficient due to moving away from a shared infrastructure of international cataloging standards. While staff at first were more concerned about inefficiency than the negative impact of cataloging practices on Indigenous users at UTL, they eventually began to distinguish the will to make changes from the challenge of making changes after the progress of the environmental scan and tool kit development were presented to them at a subsequent meeting. Eventually, they came to be convinced of the need to revise cataloging practices, which was a remarkable shift in attitude as a group. Figuring out how to make the changes sustainably is the next step to action. This work has been temporarily put on hold due to a migration to a new library services platform. The technology of this platform will affect how our system designs a solution. So as not to lose the momentum of will, we are planning small-scale pilot linked-data projects independent of mainstream cataloging workflows to expose Indigenous collections using emergent technologies and standards respectful toward Indigenous peoples.

In addition to presenting to the UTL cataloging community, there have been opportunities to present this work to library administration and senior managers to begin seeding the idea that reconciliation needs to be supported in all aspects of library work, by all staff. One recent indication of effective engagement is seeing the University of Toronto Archives and Records Management Services respond to the environmental scan, resulting in further connection for guidance to make accessible a collection of interest to Indigenous students and faculty using culturally appropriate metadata practices. This type of interest and movement toward thoughtful planning from within UTL is exactly the type of outcome one could hope for from the process and product of the research projects. As we close this chapter, we reflect that this work is ongoing. The work highlighted in this chapter is primarily for settler library staff, with the main objective being capacity building and cultural competency so that as a library system and library staff, we can have the historical and contemporary knowledge to engage meaningfully with Indigenous community members and users. While consultation and relationality continue to be at the heart of our work, we are reminded that we are still working toward an engagement that collectively, radically asserts a future of Indigenous participation and presencing within our institution. Thus, we conceptualize that this work is working toward that futurity rather than the futurity work itself, which would present as forward-facing. It is our hope that this work inspires other library workers to take on the mantle of Indigenous relational work so that our institutions can locally build right, dynamic relationships with the Indigenous Nations whose Lands we continue to occupy.

Notes

1.   Patrick Wolfe, "Settler Colonialism and the Elimination of the Native," *Journal of Genocide Research* 8, no. 4 (2006), 387.
2.   Throughout this chapter, words such as Indigenous, Land, and Elder are capitalized, following the recommendations of Greg Younging, who states in *Elements of Indigenous Style*, "It is a deliberate decision that redresses mainstream society's history of regarding Indigenous Peoples as having no legitimate national identities; governmental, social, spiritual, or religious institutions; or collective rights." Gregory Younging, *Elements of Indigenous Style,* Indigenous Collection, Edmonton, Alberta: Brush Education, 2018, 77.
3.   Truth and Reconciliation Commission of Canada, ed., *Canada's Residential Schools,* McGill-Queen's Native and Northern Series 80–86 (Montreal: published for the Truth and Reconciliation Commission of Canada by McGill-Queen's University Press, 2015), vii.
4.   Ryan DeCaire, "Wall Text," *Indigenous Language Spots,* Hart House at University of Toronto, Ontario, exhibited October 25–November 4, 2018.
5.   Susana Mas, "Truth and Reconciliation Offers 94 'Calls to Action,'" CBC News, December 15, 2015, https://www.cbc.ca/news/politics/truth-and-reconciliation-94-calls-to-action-1.3362258.
6.   Truth and Reconciliation Commission of Canada, *Canada's Residential Schools,* 12.
7.   Ian Mosby, "Administering Colonial Science: Nutrition Research and Human Biomedical Experimentation in Aboriginal Communities and Residential Schools, 1942–1952," *Histoire Sociale/Social History* 46, no. 91 (2013): 157.
8.   Martha Troian, "20 Years Since Royal Commission on Aboriginal Peoples, Still Waiting for Change," CBC News, March 3, 2016, https://www.cbc.ca/news/indigenous/20-year-anniversary-of-rcap-report-1.3469759.
9.   Eva Jewell and Ian Mosby, "Calls to Action Accountability: A Status Update on Reconciliation," Yellowhead Institute, December 17, 2019, https://yellowheadinstitute.org/2019/12/17/calls-to-action-accountability-a-status-update-on-reconciliation.

10. Shawn Wilson, *Research Is Ceremony* (Halifax, NS: Fernwood, 2008), 99.
11. Verna J. Kirkness and Ray Barnhardt, "First Nations and Higher Education: The Four R's—Respect, Relevance, Reciprocity, Responsibility," *Journal of American Indian Education* 30, no. 3 (1991): 11.
12. KAIROS Blanket Exercise Community, "History of the Blanket Exercise," accessed January 10, 2020, https://www.kairosblanketexercise.org/about.
13. Margaret Kovach, *Indigenous Methodologies* (Toronto: University of Toronto Press, 2009), 76.
14. Paromita Biswas, "Rooted in the Past: Use of 'East Indians' in Library of Congress Subject Headings," *Cataloging and Classification Quarterly* 56, no. 1 (2018): 5, https://doi.org/10.1080/01639374.2017.1386253.
15. Ashley Edwards, "Unsettling the Future by Uncovering the Past: Decolonizing Academic Libraries and Librarianship." *Partnership: The Canadian Journal of Library and Information Practice and Research* 14, no. 1 (May 2019): 8, https://doi.org/10.21083/partnership.v14i1.5161.
16. Julie Hannaford and Siobhan Stevenson, "TALint at the University of Toronto: Bridging the Gap between iSchool and Academic Librarianship" (paper, IFLA WLIC 2017, Wrocław, Poland, August 21, 2017), http://library.ifla.org/1641.
17. Royal Canadian Geographical Society, "The Road to Reconciliation," in *Indigenous Peoples Atlas of Canada*, created in conjunction with Inuit Tapiriit Kanatami, the Assembly of First Nations, the Métis National Council, the National Centre for Truth and Reconciliation, and Indspire, accessed January 28, 2020, https://indigenouspeoplesatlasofcanada.ca/article/the-road-to-reconciliation.
18. Walter D. Mignolo and Catherine E. Walsh, *On Decoloniality* (Durham, NC: Duke University Press, 2018), 100–101.
19. Kimberle Crenshaw, "Demarginalizing the Intersection of Race and Sex: A Black Feminist Critique of Antidiscrimination Doctrine, Feminist Theory and Antiracist Politics," *University of Chicago Legal Forum* 1989, no. 1 (1989): article 8, p. 166, https://chicagounbound.uchicago.edu/uclf/vol1989/iss1/8.
20. Anne Carr-Wiggin et al., "Raising Indigenous Librarians: A Canadian Internship Story" (paper, IFLA WLIC 2017, Wrocław, Poland, August 22, 2017), http://library.ifla.org/1765.
21. Truth and Reconciliation Commission of Canada, *Canada's Residential Schools*, 2.
22. Truth and Reconciliation Commission of Canada, *Canada's Residential Schools*, 3.
23. Martin M. Broadwell, "Teaching for Learning XVI," *Gospel Guardian* 20 no. 41 (1969): 1–3a.
24. Marisa Elena Duarte and Miranda Belarde-Lewis, "Imagining: Creating Spaces for Indigenous Ontologies," *Cataloging and Classification Quarterly* 53, no. 5–6 (2015): 694, https://doi.org/10.1080/01639374.2015.1018396.
25. Deborah Lee, "Indigenous Knowledges and the University Library," *Canadian Journal of Native Education* 31, no. 1 (2008): 149, http://hdl.handle.net/10388/293.
26. Lee, "Indigenous Knowledges," 150.
27. Lee, "Indigenous Knowledges," 152–53.
28. Kathleen Burns et al., "Indigenous Librarianship," in *Encyclopedia of Library and Information Science*, 4th ed. Ed. John D. McDonald and Michael Levine-Clark (Boca Raton, FL: CRC Press, 2018), 2031, https://doi.org/10.1081/E-ELIS4-120044735.
29. Burns et al., "Indigenous Librarianship," 2031.
30. Lee, "Indigenous Knowledges," 150.
31. Lee, "Indigenous Knowledges," 152–53.
32. Lee, "Indigenous Knowledges," 152–53.

33. Christine Bone and Brett Lougheed, "Library of Congress Subject Headings Related to Indigenous Peoples: Changing LCSH for Use in a Canadian Archival Context," *Cataloging and Classification Quarterly* 56, no. 1 (2018): 90. https://doi.org/10.1080/01639374.2017.1382641.
34. Dawn Castagno-Dysart, Bryan Matera, and Joel Traver, "The Importance of Instructional Scaffolding," *Teacher Magazine*, April 23, 2019, https://www.teachermagazine.com.au/articles/the-importance-of-instructional-scaffolding.
35. American Library Association, "Core Values of Librarianship," January 2019, http://www.ala.org/advocacy/intfreedom/corevalues.
36. Julie Blair and Desmond Wong, "Moving the Circle: Indigenous Solidarity for Canadian Libraries," *Partnership: The Canadian Journal of Library and Information Practice and Research* 12, no. 2 (2017): 3, https://doi.org/10.21083/partnership.v12i2.3781.
37. Lee, "Indigenous Knowledges," 152.

Bibliography

American Library Association. "Core Values of Librarianship." January 2019. http://www.ala.org/advocacy/intfreedom/corevalues.

Biswas, Paromita. "Rooted in the Past: Use of 'East Indians' in Library of Congress Subject Headings." *Cataloging and Classification Quarterly* 56, no. 1 (2018): 1–18. https://doi.org/10.1080/01639374.2017.1386253.

Blair, Julie, and Desmond Wong. "Moving in the Circle: Indigenous Solidarity for Canadian Libraries." *Partnership: The Canadian Journal of Library and Information Practice and Research* 12, no. 2 (2017). https://doi.org/10.21083/partnership.v12i2.3781.

Bone, Christine, and Brett Lougheed. "Library of Congress Subject Headings Related to Indigenous Peoples: Changing LCSH for Use in a Canadian Archival Context." *Cataloging and Classification Quarterly* 56, no. 1 (2018): 83–95. https://doi.org/10.1080/01639374.2017.1382641.

Broadwell, Martin M. "Teaching for Learning XVI." *Gospel Guardian* 20, no. 41 (1969): 1–3a.

Burns, Kathleen, Ann Doyle, Gene Joseph, and Allison Krebs. "Indigenous Librarianship." In *Encyclopedia of Library and Information Sciences*, 4th ed. Edited by John D. McDonald and Michael Levine-Clark. Boca Raton, FL: CRC Press, 2018. https://doi.org/10.1081/E-ELIS4-120044735.

Carr-Wiggin, Anne, Tanya Ball, Kayla Lar-Son, and Lorisia MacLeod. "Raising Indigenous Librarians: A Canadian Internship Story." Paper presented at IFLA WLIC 2017, Wrocław, Poland, August 22, 2017. http://library.ifla.org/1765.

Castagno-Dysart, Dawn, Bryan Matera, and Joel Traver. "The Importance of Instructional Scaffolding," *Teacher Magazine*, April 23, 2019. https://www.teachermagazine.com.au/articles/the-importance-of-instructional-scaffolding.

Crenshaw, Kimberle. "Demarginalizing the Intersection of Race and Sex: A Black Feminist Critique of Antidiscrimination Doctrine, Feminist Theory and Antiracist Politics." *University of Chicago Legal Forum* 1989, no. 1 (1989): article 8. https://chicagounbound.uchicago.edu/uclf/vol1989/iss1/8.

DeCaire, Ryan. "Wall Text." *Indigenous Language Spots*. Exhibited October 25–November 4, 2018. Hart House at University of Toronto, Ontario.

Duarte, Marisa Elena, and Miranda Belarde-Lewis. "Imagining: Creating Spaces for Indigenous Ontologies." *Cataloging and Classification Quarterly* 53, no. 5–6 (2015): 677–702. https://doi.org/10.1080/01639374.2015.1018396.

Edwards, Ashley. "Unsettling the Future by Uncovering the Past: Decolonizing Academic Libraries and Librarianship." *Partnership: The Canadian Journal of Library and Information Practice and Research* 14, no. 1 (May 2019): 1–12. https://doi.org/10.21083/partnership.v14i1.5161.

Hannaford, Julie, and Siobhan Stevenson. "TALint at the University of Toronto: Bridging the Gap between iSchool and Academic Librarianship." Paper presented at IFLA WLIC 2017, Wrocław, Poland, August 21, 2017. http://library.ifla.org/1641.

Jewell, Eva, and Ian Mosby. "Calls to Action Accountability: A Status Update on Reconciliation." Yellowhead Institute, December 17, 2019. https://yellowheadinstitute.org/2019/12/17/calls-to-action-accountability-a-status-update-on-reconciliation.

KAIROS Blanket Exercise Community. "History of the Blanket Exercise." Accessed January 10, 2020. https://www.kairosblanketexercise.org/about.

Kirkness, Verna J., and Ray Barnhardt. "First Nations and Higher Education: The Four R's—Respect, Relevance, Reciprocity, Responsibility." *Journal of American Indian Education* 30, no. 3 (1991): 1–15.

Kovach, Margaret. *Indigenous Methodologies: Characteristics, Conversations and Contexts.* Toronto: University of Toronto Press, 2009.

Lee, Deborah. "Indigenous Knowledges and the University Library." *Canadian Journal of Native Education* 31, no. 1 (2008): 149–63. http://hdl.handle.net/10388/293.

Mas, Susana. "Truth and Reconciliation Offers 94 'Calls to Action.'" CBC News, December 15, 2015. https://www.cbc.ca/news/politics/truth-and-reconciliation-94-calls-to-action-1.3362258.

Mignolo, Walter, and Catherine E. Walsh. *On Decoloniality: Concepts, Analytics, Praxis.* Durham, NC: Duke University Press, 2018.

Mosby, Ian. "Administering Colonial Science: Nutrition Research and Human Biomedical Experimentation in Aboriginal Communities and Residential Schools, 1942–1952." *Histoire Sociale/Social History* 46, no. 91 (2013): 145–72.

Royal Canadian Geographical Society. "The Road to Reconciliation." In *Indigenous Peoples Atlas of Canada.* Created in conjunction with Inuit Tapiriit Kanatami, the Assembly of First Nations, the Métis National Council, the National Centre for Truth and Reconciliation, and Indspire. Accessed January 28, 2020. https://indigenouspeoplesatlasofcanada.ca/article/the-road-to-reconciliation.

Troian, Martha. "20 Years Since Royal Commission on Aboriginal Peoples, Still Waiting for Change." CBC News, March 3, 2016. https://www.cbc.ca/news/indigenous/20-year-anniversary-of-rcap-report-1.3469759.

Truth and Reconciliation Commission of Canada, ed. *Canada's Residential Schools: The Final Report of the Truth and Reconciliation Commission of Canada,* McGill-Queen's Native and Northern Series 80–86. Montreal: published for the Truth and Reconciliation Commission of Canada by McGill-Queen's University Press, 2015.

Wilson, Shawn. *Research Is Ceremony: Indigenous Research Methods.* Halifax, NS: Fernwood, 2008.

Wolfe, Patrick. "Settler Colonialism and the Elimination of the Native." *Journal of Genocide Research* 8, no. 4 (2006): 387–409.

Younging, Gregory. *Elements of Indigenous Style: A Guide for Writing by and about Indigenous Peoples.* Indigenous Collection. Edmonton, Alberta: Brush Education, 2018.

SECTION VI

Assessment

CHAPTER 18

Assessing DEI Efforts in Academic Libraries

More Than a Body Count

Kawanna Bright

Introduction

In libraries, discussions of diversity, equity, and inclusion (DEI) often center on the library and information science (LIS) field's struggles to recruit and retain librarians of color. The lack of diversity or the inability to increase the number of librarians of color has been well documented.[1] For libraries, especially academic libraries, this intense focus on the race and ethnicity of their employees may lead to the overemphasis on human resources as a way to assess or measure how well a library is doing in terms of its diversity efforts. As noted by a recent annotated bibliography of diversity initiatives in academic libraries, the main focus tends to be the diversity of the workforce.[2] If you have hired a librarian of color, then you have reached all of your DEI goals.[3]

But DEI encompasses more than having a diverse workforce. As outlined by the Association of College and Research Libraries (ACRL) "Diversity Standards," DEI also includes cultural awareness, cross-cultural knowledge, organizational and professional values, collection, program, and service development, service delivery, language diversity, and organizational dynamics.[4] Even if a library has identified other factors to use as an indication of its DEI efforts, how to assess the success of work in those areas can be a difficult and daunting task and not

something widely covered in the literature.[5] Assessment in academic libraries, in general, is problematic in terms of knowing what to assess, how to assess it, and who has the ability.[6] Adding in the additional layer of DEI means introducing a new hurdle in the assessment process, especially when the process should include reviewing all of the library's policies, services, and practices.[7]

Pre-existing means of assessing diversity in libraries are often limited in scope, as they try to focus on one aspect of DEI. These assessment tools may assess an organization's DEI climate, like ClimateQUAL, or DEI in collections,[8] but most do not offer a way to assess multiple aspects of DEI throughout the organization. Tools designed for organizations in general and not just libraries or information centers also exist but may be too broad for service-oriented organizations like libraries. For a complete DEI evaluation, multiple tools would be recommended, making the assessment of DEI both time-consuming and potentially expensive, as many commercial assessment products require a financial investment. In an effort to offer a more holistic method of assessing DEI within academic libraries, the author set out to create a single assessment instrument that would encompass multiple aspects of DEI. The results of those efforts led to the creation of the Diversity, Equity, and Inclusion Self-Assessment Audit (DEISAA).

This chapter offers a brief overview of efforts to assess DEI in academic libraries, describes the creation of the DEISAA, shares the results of an initial piloting of the audit in a variety of academic libraries, and introduces an updated assessment instrument based on the results of the pilot study. The goal of this chapter is to offer libraries insight into the struggles that exist when attempting to assess DEI, but also showcase viable options for completing these assessments in a logical and useful way. Additionally, this chapter offers a snapshot of the updated DEI assessment instrument that libraries may be interested in investigating further.

Assessing DEI in Academic Libraries

The library and information science (LIS) literature supports the idea that assessment is key to the overall success of libraries in meeting their goals and objectives and showing their value.[9] In 2010, the ACRL released *The Value of Academic Libraries,* a report that detailed the twenty-two different ways that academic libraries could show their value, all tied directly to assessment and assessment practices.[10] However, it should be noted that the only mention of DEI within the ACRL report was the listing of "diversity/global learning" as a high-impact educational practice in one of the twenty-two items.[11] This appears to be the norm for any assessment article that is not specifically geared toward DEI work. But does this absence imply that DEI efforts are not as important or do not require assessment? It is more likely that the absence of DEI within these broad guidelines is indicative of how nuanced assessment of DEI efforts is, and that special attention should be given to DEI assessment practices.

Moving beyond Demographics

The suggestion that academic libraries use means of determining their success with DEI other than counting the number of employees they have from different racial and ethnic groups is not made to discount the importance of having a diverse workforce. Indeed, research indicates that "numerical representation (i.e., having a critical mass of people from different groups represented) is a crucial cue for signaling inclusion."[12] However, there is a danger in relying solely on numerical representation as the marker for successful DEI work within libraries, especially given the issues with retention of librarians of color. For many academic libraries, there is a revolving door of diverse librarians moving into and out of the institution, giving the impression of continuous diversity but not acknowledging specific issues with retaining diverse librarians.[13] These issues typically hint at broader concerns, those that include the culture of the organization and how to assess that culture.[14]

Standardized DEI Assessment Practices

While a few standardized library assessment instruments and approaches have been created,[15] there are few standardized assessment instruments specifically for assessing DEI in libraries. Most instruments that can be found in the literature are focused on climate assessment and are often homegrown.[16] These climate assessment instruments can offer libraries a snapshot of issues related to workplace diversity but are not holistic in nature.[17] Researchers have developed and shared frameworks as the first step of creating more all-inclusive assessment instruments,[18] though these efforts do not appear to have gone beyond the framework stage. One example of this was a detailed Diversity Assessment Model designed to help libraries with the assessment of their DEI efforts beyond counting employees and focusing on more than race and gender.[19] Development of the model relied on a survey to collect the data, but there is no evidence that anything was officially created from the model or utilized by other libraries.[20]

The best-known and most used standardized instrument for assessing aspects of diversity is the Association of Research Libraries' (ARL's) ClimateQUAL. As described by ARL, ClimateQUAL "is an assessment of library staff perceptions concerning (a) their library's commitment to the principles of diversity, (b) organizational policies and procedures, and (c) staff attitudes."[21] As its title indicates, ClimateQUAL focuses on the climate of the library and relies on the perception of those working in the library to identify issues and concerns with DEI within the organization.[22] One of the positive aspects of ClimateQUAL is that it involves employees, utilizing direct feedback and employee involvement in the process of assessing DEI in the organization.[23] What ClimateQUAL offers most academic libraries is a starting point for both understanding and improving DEI in their organization, with the added benefit of supporting work with patrons. It also offers a continuous push for DEI assessment, helping libraries move beyond single DEI snapshots.

While ClimateQUAL is a beneficial method of assessment, it has limitations, including a very long assessment instrument (~150 questions) and limited detailed analysis for smaller libraries where less diversity exists among employees.[24] Some potential barriers to the use of ClimateQUAL include a requirement that libraries register to use the instrument only during set times, a fairly substantial cost, and a requirement of a minimum of fifty employees.[25] The cost in and of itself may be enough to deter some libraries, as the money needed to support diversity initiatives is often beyond the means of most academic libraries.[26] The limitations and potential barriers of ClimateQUAL are indicative of a need for other means of assessing DEI in academic libraries.

The Diversity, Equity, and Inclusion Self-Assessment Audit (DEISAA)

In the summer of 2017, a personalized diversity audit was developed by the author as part of a consultation with a medical library.[27] The goal of the instrument was to offer the library a way to determine both how engaged the library was in DEI efforts and how much progress it was making toward those efforts. As the library was at a level of "little to no DEI efforts" at the start of the consultation, the instrument would serve to set the baseline for all future assessment of DEI work.

Consultation Audit Development

The development of the consultation audit followed a standardized instrument creation process that included an organizational needs analysis, research to identify supporting frameworks, creation of items or statements for the instrument, determining a rating system, expert review, cognitive interviews, and an initial pilot by the requesting library.[28] The expert review, cognitive interviews, and pilot all led to small adjustments in the audit, including removal of some items, rewording of other items, and a grouping of remaining items into a new structure based on a version of the Galbraith Star Model.[29] The addition of the Galbraith Star Model introduced Organization Development (OD) principles into the audit, emphasizing the importance of looking at the whole organization as part of the DEI assessment process.

Organization Development (OD) in Audit Development

The decision to align the consultation audit's organization with the Galbraith Star Model came at the suggestion of an expert interviewer who specializes in OD as well as DEI work. As they reviewed the audit for content, their expertise identified a pattern "that aligned with the existing structure of the Galbraith Star Model."[30] While not a model specific to DEI, the Galbraith Star Model is a diagnostic tool that could be layered over the audit.[31] The Star Model features a five-pointed star and an additional environmental or external factor that surrounds the star, offering six categories that were used to organize the consultation audit's statements: Strategy, Structure, Processes, Rewards, People, and External Environment.[32] The restructured audit offered a clearer view of the issues that the organization was facing in terms of its DEI efforts.

Creation of the DEISAA

While the consultation audit was successfully applied to the requesting library, initially there was no intention of expanding its availability to other libraries. However, a presentation at the 2018 ARL Symposium for Strategic Leadership in Diversity, Equity, and Inclusion introduced the audit to a wider audience, with a number of academic libraries expressing interest in applying it to their organizations. The level of interest indicated a need for a tool that could be applied broadly to multiple types of academic libraries. With this in mind, the initial audit was adapted to remove aspects that were specific to the medical library and to include aspects that might resonate more widely with other types of academic libraries. This version of the audit was renamed the Diversity, Equity, and Inclusion Self-Assessment Audit (DEISAA). Of the ten academic libraries that expressed interest in the DEISAA, eight were able to participate in a pilot that took place during the fall of 2018.

Results of the DEISAA Pilot: Positive Outcomes

Completion of interviews with the pilot participants revealed a number of positive aspects of the DEISAA. Similar to other survey instruments that ask participants about services, many libraries found that they were not engaged with DEI in some areas and now wanted to consider adding those initiatives to their work. This appears to be related to a phenomenon known as mere measurement effect found in consumer behavior studies, where simply completing a survey about a product or service can increase the likelihood of someone buying or using the service in the future.[33] This idea has been suggested in library use and satisfaction surveys where asking students or faculty about their use of library services often revealed that respondents were unaware of the services, but more likely to try them because of the survey.[34] In this way, the DEISAA, like other surveys, served as an educational tool of possible DEI work the libraries could undertake.[35]

Results of the DEISAA Pilot: Issues with a Single DEI Assessment Tool

While the DEISAA pilot proved to be beneficial on many levels for the libraries that participated, the process also revealed issues with the assessment instrument. Some of the issues were instrument-based (wording of some statements and the need for clarifying examples).[36] But other issues were more nuanced and individualized, often to the institution or to the persons completing the audit. These issues included questions of who has responsibility for leading and tracking DEI efforts, the influence of personal experience, position in the organization, and negative impact of the scoring system.

Who Has Responsibility?

One issue identified during the pilot was the question of who has responsibility for DEI efforts in the library and thus would likely have responsibility for completing the audit. For the pilot, participating libraries were directed to have at least two people complete the audit, with the intention of using statistical analysis to determine the validity and reliability of the instrument.[37] Despite these instructions, some of the piloting libraries took a different approach—with one library having their two participants complete the audit together and another using the entire diversity committee. These varied approaches to completing the audit helped to reveal useful information about the feasibility of using the audit in different settings.

For all piloting libraries, the question of responsibility for DEI efforts and audit completion led to discussions about who would be the best person to complete the audit. For some of the piloting libraries, it was difficult to identify just one person working on DEI efforts, as the work was often dispersed throughout the library. Additionally, one participant raised the question of whether the involvement needed to be formalized: "Some might include the informal thoughts and actions of a single library employee, others might only include a formal, well documented effort." This suggestion aligns with the results of a survey conducted by Koury, Semenza, and Shropshire, which indicated responsibility for DEI initiatives often varies and can include those in high levels of leadership or designated committees, but that often many different people in the library were "leaders even if not necessarily charged with responsibility for diversity and inclusion initiatives."[38] Other discussions in the literature of diversity initiatives in academic libraries echoed these findings, indicating how the work could be done by everyone from public services librarians to administrators.[39]

This wide range of people involved in DEI initiatives means that knowledge of the initiatives is not always kept with one or two people. This proved to be the case with the audit, as some respondents reported struggling to respond to some statements as they were not directly involved with the work. Comments of "I wasn't sure of the answer" or "I'm not sure about this" were common, along with acknowledgment of not even knowing where to look for the information: "I'm not actually sure what our policies consist of, or where to find them!" The pilot also showed that institutions that collaborated most widely (such as using the diversity committee to complete the audit), reported feeling more comfortable and confident in their findings. Those that relied mostly on the two identified completers often found themselves struggling to respond to some of the statements due to lack of knowledge.

In response to this issue, the initial suggestion for any future use of the audit is to encourage libraries to identify multiple people to complete the audit, working as a team to rate statements based on their collective knowledge and reaching out to others who might have more information. This process would include either having individuals complete the audit separately and then meeting to discuss items where there was disagreement or completing the audit in a group setting, where statements are discussed as a group and a final rating decided. Either option would help to alleviate the issue of having one or two individuals attempt to complete the audit when they may have limited knowledge of all the organization's DEI efforts. However, questions of group dynamics would also have to be considered, as pointed out by one participant who suggested this approach.

While having the viewpoint of employees from different levels in the library is clearly important for the successful completion of DEI assessment, the distance between their perceptions of progress could be problematic. Whose perspective will be dominant in the final analysis of the initiative? Will the lower-ranked employee defer to the rankings of the higher-ranked employee even if they disagree? As research indicates, status and power do impact levels of participation in group decision-making situations, even if on the surface everyone is seen as equal.[40] Considering the suggestion that respondents work together to determine final rankings for audit statements where initial disagreement is seen, there are valid concerns for how representative the audit's scores would truly be.

Influence of Personal Experience

One of the most striking findings from the pilot study was the influence of personal experience on audit results. In development of the audit, every effort was made to create statements that could be responded to easily and without interpretation. However, the success of these efforts seemed to depend on personal factors, such as whether respondents had prior positive or negative experiences with DEI at their institutions. As one respondent commented after completing the audit, "I wonder if others in my library would agree with the score from my assessment. I'm not sure if that is a reflection of the instrument, my place in the organization, or my own views about DEI outcomes." Another respondent indicated in a follow-up interview that they realized after completing the audit that their responses were framed by negative experiences with DEI at their home institution. Previous efforts had not received support from the institution, so they considered all efforts to be at a lower level in terms of progress than what was likely the reality.

This lack of trust in the organization clearly impacted whether respondents saw the library's current DEI efforts as being successful or not. Based on research into how success of DEI initiatives is determined, this result may not be a surprise, as evaluation of success for DEI efforts appears to be influenced by levels of trust in the organization and a positive organizational climate.[41] This research also suggested that how success of DEI efforts is measured will be impacted by an individual's experiences and perceptions,[42] and that how they define success will be an internally focused process.[43] This insight impacts the usefulness of an assessment instrument, as changes would need to be made to take into account the impact and influence of personal perception.

In response to this issue, how the different statements in the audit are worded would need to be assessed. While attempts to eliminate the possibility of subjective responses were made, additional analysis of the wording is clearly needed to further remove even the appearance of subjectivity.[44] Research in assessment development has shown that utilizing statements that are fact-based can help to reduce the impact of subjectivity bias,[45] thus improving overall performance of an assessment instrument. The DEISAA's statements could be specifically reviewed for factualness and adjustments made accordingly.

Organizational Position

One final interesting finding from the pilot study was the difference in how those who were in administrative positions responded to statements, compared to how those in lower level positions responded. A few of the piloting libraries had the dean or director of the library complete the audit as one of the respondents. The second respondent was often a librarian who did not necessarily have administrative duties, but often worked with assessment in the library. When interviewing these respondents, it was found that administrators tended to have a more positive view of DEI efforts in the library, especially in terms of the progress being made. Nonadministrative librarians tended to have a more negative view of DEI efforts, also especially in relation to progress being made.

Negative Impact of Audit Scoring System

The DEISAA scoring system was designed to offer libraries a way to understand where they stood in terms of DEI efforts and what they needed to do to make progress toward their DEI goals. Respondents were able to rate statements on a scale from 0 to 4, where 0 indicated work and progress were nonexistent and 4 indicated an expert and evolving level of work (figure 18.1). Not surprisingly, many libraries were at either a nonexistent or novice/initiating level for many items on the audit, resulting in a lower overall total. As is often seen with any

FIGURE 18.1

Original DEISAA rating guidelines for status and progress.

Status		Progress	
Non-Existent	Not in place or not considered **Does not describe Library at all**	**Non-Existent**	Not considered/Not started/No longer engaged in **No progress**
Novice	Library is considering, but nothing in place yet **Describes Library only partially**	**Initiating**	Work on outcome has just started **Some progress**
Intermediate	Library has implemented recently but no data available for evaluation **Describes Library somewhat**	**Improving**	Work on outcome is continuing; Outcome is being assessed for impact **Good progress**
Advanced	Library is actively engaged in this outcome, data available but impact has not been evaluated **Describes Library Well**	**Stable**	Work on outcome is completed; Outcome continuously assessed for impact and need for changes **Exceptional progress**
Expert	Library is fully engaged in this outcome and impact has been evaluated **Describes Library exactly**	**Evolving**	Work on outcome is evolving to further improve impact **Extensive progress**

type of scoring system, low scores were often interpreted negatively or seen as not representative. As one respondent commented, "I think the scores here turned out a bit low compared to how I think we measure up."

While many of the libraries in the pilot acknowledged that they had work to do toward their DEI efforts, they were often still surprised at the audit scoring placing them at a lower overall status, indicating that they had a lot of work to do toward full engagement with DEI. However, what is difficult to determine from a single pilot is whether the lower scores were a reflection of the actual work being done by the libraries or a reflection of limitations with the audit instrument itself. In some cases, there was a clear absence of work being done; in others there was acknowledged lowering of scores based on subjectivity. Where do these libraries really stand on the DEISAA? Likely somewhere in the middle, though additional piloting and assessment of the instrument would be needed to ascertain this.

Impact of Identified Issues on Audit Usefulness

Identifying issues with any assessment instrument is part of the process of instrument development. The next logical step is to determine what changes need to be made to improve the instrument. However, in the case of the DEISAA, the issues identified indicated a need to reconsider the usefulness of the audit as a one-stop assessment tool. Any assessment tool that can be overly influenced by the subjectivity of the respondent cannot be considered to have a high level of validity or reliability.[46] With this in mind, the logical solution is to create an updated instrument with changes made to address the identified issues. As a first step, a second version of the DEISAA (see appendix) was created to address some of the issues identified in the pilot. However, to fully address all of the issues, a new instrument is needed. The development of that new instrument, The Diversity, Equity, and Inclusion Library Inventory and Audit will be described next.

The Diversity, Equity, and Inclusion Library Inventory and Audit (DEILIA): A Proposed Solution

While only one pilot was completed for the DEISAA, it was clear that in its current form, the assessment instrument does not meet the needs of most academic libraries. Relying on the pilot feedback, the audit will be altered to add an inventory feature. The decision to add an inventory to the auditing instrument arose during interviews with piloting participants, as it was noted that the library did not have a clear view of all of its DEI efforts. This made it difficult for the library to determine its level of effort or its progress, as participants were often unaware of those efforts. The addition of the inventory will allow libraries to first focus on identifying and articulating their DEI efforts before moving on to assessing those efforts.

Instrument Structure

While the updated instrument (DEILIA) follows a similar structure to that found in the original audit, the overall structure will shift to accommodate the addition of the inventory, as well as updating the wording of all statements, recategorizing items to better reflect library work, and removing the scoring interpretation aspects of the instrument. The scoring interpretation will be replaced with guidelines to assist libraries in moving forward after completion of the instrument.[47]

Indicating Status of DEI Initiatives: The Inventory

One aspect of the original audit that many found confusing was the distinction between the status of an initiative and the progress toward that initiative. The update removes the confusing status rating section and replaces it with the inventory, where the library can record examples of the work being done that aligns with or best fits under each initiative or statement. For example, the statement "The Library has collected relevant DEI related data for use in assessing the status of DEI within the organization" from the original audit would be reworded to "Data collected for use in assessing DEI within the organization." The responding library would then list the sources of data that have been collected for the purpose of assessment. To aid in this process, the instrument would offer different categories of potential data that could be collected.

Identifying Level of Effort

The only rating aspect of the instrument that will remain is the ability to determine progress or level of work with different DEI initiatives, though it will be

FIGURE 18.2

Original and suggested progress scoring for audit

Original Progress Scoring	Suggested Levels of Effort*
Non-Existent: Not considered/Not started/ No longer engaged in **(No Progress)**	**Level 0:** No efforts are currently being put into this activity. This activity has not been identified as one of interest for the library.
Initiating: Work on outcome has just started **(Some Progress)**	**Level 1:** This activity has been identified as one of interest for the library but no concrete work has been directed towards this activity. Being identified as an area of interest indicates that the activity is on the library's radar as one that could be implemented in the future. The library is discussing the activity and determining the feasibility of future implementation.
Improving: Work on outcome is continuing; Outcome is being assessed for impact **Good Progress)**	**Level 2:** This activity has been identified as one of interest and steps have been taken to implement the activity into the work of the Library. Taking steps to implement an activity means that specific resources (personnel, space, financial, etc.) have been identified with plans to apply those resources to the implementation and support of the activity.
Stable: Work on outcome is completed; Outcome continuously assessed for impact and need for changes **(Exceptional Progress)**	**Level 3:** This activity has been fully implemented into the work and processes of the library. Full implementation indicates that resources (personnel, space, financial, etc.) have been directed into the activity, with plans to continue the work into the future. Means of assessing the impact or success of the activity have been identified and will be applied.
Evolving: Work on outcome is evolving to further improve impact **(Extensive Progress).**	**Level 4:** This activity is viewed as essential for the DEI work of the library and has been fully integrated into the work and processes of the library. Continuous resources (personnel, space, financial, etc.) have been directed into the activity, with plans for continuous support. Means of assessing the impact or success of the activity are in place; The activity has been in place long enough (minimum 1 year) for an initial level of impact or success to be determined.
	N/A: Not applicable to this library.

*These labels are still under consideration and are subject to change.

relabeled as Level of Effort. This step is important for allowing a library to determine how much effort it wants or needs to focus on specific DEI initiatives. The original instrument asked participants to rate progress on a five-point scale (Non-Existent, Initiating, Improving, Stable, and Evolving). While the five-point scale was useful, the categorizations were not always clear. The updated instrument will feature a five-point scale with categorizations that are much easier to use (see figure 18.2). Like other tools and at the request of piloting libraries, an N/A option will also be provided. This will likely be particularly useful for smaller libraries, as those in the pilot indicated that their institution addressed some aspects of DEI assessment on their behalf, but that they did not have any control or input in these processes. As one respondent noted when asked about DEI within tenure and promotion, "This is a campus-level responsibility and not within the purview of a college/small institution library."

Item Recategorization

The original instrument relied on an organizational design framework called the Galbraith Star Model to provide a categorical structure for the items found in the instrument. While this structure was a natural fit for the audit form, it did not provide a clear way to categorize the service areas of most academic libraries. For example, within the original audit, a final section for external efforts was created to include all interactions with the community and users. However, many of these items might better fit under a different category, such as Outreach or Community Engagement. The updated audit plus inventory will keep most of the categories created by the Star Model, but will also offer expanded categorization that aligns with the services offered by academic libraries.

Wording of Statements

In order to ensure that an inventory of items can be created, all statements in the original audit will need to be updated. This process will include making statements more factual in nature to avoid the influence of subjectivity. In addition to wording changes, examples will be added to serve as guidelines for respondents as they identify items for the inventory. These wording changes will be especially beneficial for avoiding the potentially double-barreled items, where respondents were asked to rate multiple items in one statement. For example, the statement "DEI are explicitly addressed in the Library's mission, vision, and values statement" was difficult for some libraries to rate, as the answer would shift for the mission or the vision, and they might not have a values statement. For the updated instrument, a broader category will be presented that will allow libraries to indicate whether DEI is being addressed within each of these items individually.

Guidelines

Upon completion of the instrument, libraries will not be presented with a score for their DEI efforts. Instead, the library will be able to view its activities individually, review the level of effort assigned, and make a decision for future directions based on that information. The library will also be presented with guidelines for how to proceed with its DEI work based on the level of effort it currently has and the level it hopes to attain. In the original instrument, the scoring aspects left libraries feeling as if they had failed a test and, without a separate report developed by the author, no sense of what the results really meant or what to do with them. The guidelines that will accompany the updated instrument will allow libraries to determine their next steps with DEI work on their own.

Conclusion

As seen throughout the process of creating the DEISAA and the DEILIA, assessing DEI in academic libraries is not an easy task. Indeed, the large-scale changes driving the creation of the DEILIA are indicative of just how difficult the task has been and will likely remain. However, efforts like DEILIA, in combination with ClimateQUAL and homegrown climate assessment products, are all necessary for libraries that are serious about understanding and assessing their DEI work. The information presented here about the DEILIA is only a rough framework, and additional development and testing will be needed to determine if it can become a go-to DEI assessment instrument for academic libraries. But even as just a framework, the DEILIA has the potential to impact academic libraries in a positive way, much as the DEISAA did during the pilot, simply by asking libraries to think more holistically about their DEI efforts. As the DEISAA showed, DEI should not be a separate part of a library organization, and assessing DEI requires much more than a body count.

Appendix

DIVERSITY, EQUITY, INCLUSION AUDIT, V. 2*

Completing the Audit

Ranking Activities/Items

Please rank the following activities/items related to DEI efforts that may take place in the library. You will be ranking the activities/items based on the library's level of effort toward that particular activity or item. This effort is an indication of where the library currently stands in terms of engagement with an activity/item. The ranking options range from "nonexistent," which indicates that the library is not addressing or not considering the activity/item, to "expert," which indicates full engagement with the activity/item.

Use the following information to determine the best ranking for each activity/item:

- **Nonexistent (0)**: The activity/item is not in place or not currently being considered by the library.
- **Novice (1)**: The library is considering this activity/item, but nothing concrete is in place yet.
- **Intermediate (2)**: The library has implemented (or started) the activity/item recently, but no data is available yet for evaluation.
- **Advanced (3)**: The library is actively engaged in this activity/item, and data is available if needed to evaluate the impact of the activity/item.
- **Expert (4)**: The library is fully engaged in this activity/item; data is available and has been used to evaluate the impact of the activity/item.
- **N/A**: The activity/item does not apply to the library.

Strategy

	0	1	2	3	4	N/A	Notes
DEI are explicitly addressed in the library's strategic plan.							
DEI are explicitly addressed in the library's mission statement.							
DEI are explicitly addressed in the library's vision statement.							

	0	1	2	3	4	N/A	Notes
DEI are explicitly addressed in the library's values statement.							
DEI are explicitly addressed in the library's internal policies (e.g., hiring, promotion, etc.)							
A DEI plan of action has been developed.							
Library has defined what it means by DEI.							
Library has created a diversity statement/ stance.							

Structure

	0	1	2	3	4	N/A	Notes
The library's administration employs a decision-making process that explicitly includes DEI.							
The library's administration is committed to assessing the library's DEI efforts.							
The library's administration is dedicated to addressing the library's DEI needs.							
The library has established clear internal channels to communicate DEI efforts to all library employees.							
The library has established clear internal channels for all employees to communicate about DEI efforts.							
The library's leadership has acknowledged the importance of DEI to the success of the library (as evidenced by actions such as inclusion of DEI in the library's mission, vision, and values statements)							
The library works with its employees from underrepresented groups to support its DEI efforts.							
The library has established financial resources within the budget to support DEI efforts (e.g., training/learning opportunities, communications/outreach efforts, programs/services, and collection development).							

Processes

	0	1	2	3	4	N/A	Notes
The library collects DEI-related data as part of organizational assessment.							
The library has taken actions that have resulted in an increase in internal DEI training/learning opportunities.							
The library has taken actions that have resulted in an increase in internal DEI programs/services.							
The library has reviewed its collection development processes for DEI elements.							
The library has reviewed its collection development policies for DEI elements.							
The library has identified gaps in DEI programming, services, or training available to library employees.							
The library has established method(s) for collecting employee feedback related to DEI education/training needs.							
The library has established methods for collecting employee feedback about the library's DEI efforts.							

Rewards

	0	1	2	3	4	N/A	Notes
The library has completed a salary equity study.							
The library has policies in place for equitably supporting employee professional development.							
The library has policies in place to support an equitable tenure process (if applicable).							
The library has policies in place to support equitable salary raises.							
The library has policies in place to support equitable awarding of employee bonuses that are in addition to salary raises.							
The library acknowledges employees' internal DEI efforts.							

	0	1	2	3	4	N/A	Notes
The library acknowledges employees' external DEI efforts.							

People

	0	1	2	3	4	N/A	Notes
The library utilizes employee demographic data for assessing **representation** of historically underrepresented groups among its employees.							
The library utilizes employee demographic data for assessing **retention** of historically underrepresented groups among its employees.							
The library has assessed the climate of the organization.							
The library has developed strategies to increase employee diversity.							
The library has implemented strategies to increase employee diversity.							
The library has created DEI indicators for use in annual assessment of all employees.							
The library has integrated DEI indicators into the annual assessment of all employees.							
The library offers all employees opportunities to engage in DEI education/training.							
The library requires all employees to participate in DEI education/training annually.							
The library supports employees' ability to participate in external DEI education/training (i.e., approval, time off, financially).							

External DEI Efforts

	0	1	2	3	4	N/A	Notes
The library has established collaborative partnerships with campus departments to advance DEI at the institution.							
The library has assessed the demographic profile of its external community: faculty, staff, students, and the public.							

	0	1	2	3	4	N/A	Notes
The library has conducted an external community climate assessment (community defined by library).							
The library has identified the gaps in DEI programming offered to the external community.							
The library has identified the gaps in DEI services offered to the external community.							
The library has assessed its collection DEI strength relevant to the external community's needs.							
The library has a targeted community outreach plan to promote the library's DEI efforts to its stakeholders.							
The library has a communication plan to promote the library's DEI efforts to its communities.							
The library has clear external channels of communication about DEI efforts for the communities it serves.							
Library's employees contribute to the advancement of DEI within their profession.							

* Those interested in using version 1 or version 2 of the DEISAA can request access to the online version of both instruments by contacting the author.

Notes

1. Jaena Alabi, "From Hostile to Inclusive: Strategies for Improving the Racial Climate of Academic Libraries," *Library Trends* 67, no. 1 (Summer 2018): 132, https://doi.org/10.1353/lib.2018.0029; Kimberley Bugg, "The Perceptions of People of Color in Academic Libraries Concerning the Relationship between Retention and Advancement as Middle Managers," *Journal of Library Administration* 56, no. 4 (2016): 429, https://doi.org/10.1080/01930826.2015.1105076; Kyung-Sun Kim and Sei-Ching Joanna Sin, "Increasing Ethnic Diversity in LIS: Strategies Suggested by Librarians of Color," *Library Quarterly* 78, no. 2 (April 2008): 154, https://doi.org/10.1086/528887; Janice Y. Kung, K-Lee Fraser, and Dee Winn, "Diversity Initiatives to Recruit and Retain Academic Librarians: A Systematic Review," *College and Research Libraries* 81, no. 1 (January 2020): 97, https://doi.org/10.5860/crl.81.1.96; Teresa Y. Neely and Lorna Peterson, "Achieving Racial and Ethnic Diversity

among Academic and Research Libraries: The Recruitment, Retention, and Advancement of Librarians of Color—A White Paper," *College and Research Libraries News* 68, no. 9 (October 2007): 562–65.

2. Jenny Lynne Semenza, Regina Koury, and Sandra Shropshire, "Diversity at Work in Academic Libraries 2010–2015: An Annotated Bibliography," *Collection Building* 36, no. 3 (2017): 89, https://doi.org/10.1108/CB-12-2016-0038.

3. Tarida Anantachai et al., "Establishing a Communal Network for Professional Advancement among Librarians of Color," in *Where are All the Librarians of Color? The Experiences of People of Color in Academia*, ed. Rebecca Hankins and Miguel Juárez (Sacramento: Library Juice Press, 2016), 39; Isabel Espinal, Tonia Sutherland, and Charlotte Roh, "A Holistic Approach for Inclusive Librarianship: Decentering Whiteness in Our Profession," *Library Trends* 67, no. 1 (Summer 2018): 148, https://doi.org/10.1353/lib.2018.0030.

4. Association of College and Research Libraries, "Diversity Standards: Cultural Competency for Academic Libraries (2012)," accessed January 8, 2020, http://www.ala.org/acrl/standards/diversity.

5. Semenza, Koury, and Shropshire, "Diversity at Work," 90.

6. Joseph R. Matthews, *Library Assessment in Higher Education*, 2nd ed. (Santa Barbara, CA: Libraries Unlimited, 2015), 2–3.

7. Alabi, "From Hostile to Inclusive," 142.

8. Association of Research Libraries, "What Is ClimateQUAL®?" accessed January 13, 2020, https://www.climatequal.org/home; Matthew P. Ciszek and Courtney L. Young, "Diversity Collection Assessment in Large Academic Libraries," *Collection Building* 29, no. 4 (2010): 154–61, https://doi.org/10.1108/01604951011088899.

9. Simone Clunie and Darlene Ann Parrish, "How Assessment Websites of Academic Libraries Convey Information and Show Value," *Performance Measurement and Metrics* 19, no. 3 (2018): 205, https://doi.org/10.1108/PMM-12-2017-0061; Gregory Arnold Smith, Howard Dale Tryon, and Lori Beth Snyder, "Developing an Academic Library Assessment Plan: A Case Study," *Performance Measurements and Metrics* 16, no. 1 (2015): 55, https://doi.org/10.1108/PMM-12-2014-0045; Agnes Tatarka et al., "Library Assessment Plans: Four Case Studies," *Performance Measurement and Metrics* 11, no. 2 (2010): 200, https://doi.org/10.1108/14678041011064106.

10. Megan Oakleaf, *The Value of Academic Libraries* (Chicago: Association of College and Research Libraries, 2010), 12–17, http://www.ala.org/acrl/sites/ala.org.acrl/files/content/issues/value/val_report.pdf.

11. Oakleaf, *Value of Academic Libraries*, 120.

12. Tiffany N. Brannon et al., "From Backlash to Inclusion for all: Instituting Diversity Efforts to Maximize Benefits across Group Lines," *Social Issues and Policy Review* 12, no. 1 (2018): 71.

13. Espinal, Sutherland, and Roh, "Holistic Approach," 148.

14. Jennifer Brown et al., "We Here: Speaking Our Truth," *Library Trends* 67, no. 1 (Summer 2018): 169, https://muse.jhu.edu/article/706994.

15. LibQUAL and Balanced Scorecard are the most often referred to in the literature. Sarah M. Passonneau, "Library Assessment Activities: Using ISO 11620 to Review the Assessment Data of Academic Libraries in North America," *Performance Measurement and Metrics* 14, no. 3 (2013): 177, https://doi.org/10.1108/PMM-05-2013-0015.

16. Paula M. Smith, "Beyond Diversity: Moving towards Inclusive Work Environments," in *Workplace Culture in Academic Libraries: The Early 21st Century*, ed. Kelly Blessinger and Paul Hrycaj (Witney, UK: Elsevier Science & Technology, 2013), 105.

17. Paula M. Smith, "Culturally Conscious Organizations: A Conceptual Framework," *portal: Libraries and the Academy* 8, no. 2 (2008): 145.
18. Johnnieque B. (Johnnie) Love, "The Assessment of Diversity Initiatives in Academic Libraries," *Journal of Library Administration* 33, no. 1–2 (2001): 80, https://doi.org/10.1300/J111v33n01_07; Smith, "Culturally Conscious Organizations," 145.
19. Love, "Assessment of Diversity Initiatives," 85.
20. A search of SCOPUS and Google Scholar revealed seven and twenty-two citations (respectively) of Love's article. A review of those articles did not indicate widespread application of the survey instrument used by Love.
21. Association of Research Libraries, "What is ClimateQUAL®?"
22. Association of Research Libraries, "What is ClimateQUAL®?"
23. Association of Research Libraries, "What is ClimateQUAL®?"
24. Association of Research Libraries, "About: What is ClimateQUAL®," accessed January 16, 2020, https://www.climatequal.org/about.
25. ARL does not list the cost of ClimateQUAL® on its website, but a recent press release used to recruit libraries to use the instrument indicated a cost of $5,000; Shaneka Morris, "Register for ClimateQUAL 2018 to Assess Your Library's Climate for Diversity and Inclusion," Association of Research Libraries, accessed January 16, 2020, https://www.arl.org/news/register-for-climatequal-2018-to-assess-your-librarys-climate-for-diversity-and-inclusion/.
26. Regina Koury, Jenny Lynne Semenza, and Sandra Shropshire, "A Survey of Diversity and Inclusiveness Initiatives at Carnegie Doctoral Research Institutions Libraries," *Library Management* 40, no. 1/2 (2019): 27, https://doi.org/10.1108/LM-10-2017-0117.
27. Additional information about the initial audit development can be found in Kawanna Bright and Nikhat Ghouse, "Taking AIM: Integrating Organization Development into the Creation of a Diversity, Equity, and Inclusion Audit," in *Proceedings of the 2018 Library Assessment Conference: Building Effective, Sustainable, Practical Assessment*, ed. Sue Baughman, Steve Hiller, Katie Monroe, and Angela Pappaldaro (Washington, DC: Association of Research Libraries, 2018), 589–99.
28. The process offered by DeVellis was followed for creation of the audit; Robert F. DeVellis, *Scale Development* (Los Angeles: Sage, 2012). Many aspects of the audit's structure and questions were drawn from a social inclusion audit created by the Canadian Urban Libraries Council; Canadian Urban Libraries Council, "Social Inclusion Audit," accessed January 16, 2002, http://www.siatoolkit.com/#axzz5ExeirtRa.
29. Jay R. Galbraith, "The Star Model™," accessed January 16, 2020, http://www.jaygalbraith.com/images/pdfs/StarModel.pdf.
30. Bright and Ghouse, "Taking AIM," 591.
31. Bright and Ghouse, "Taking AIM," 591.
32. Donald L. Anderson, *Organization Development* (Los Angeles: SAGE, 2017), 304.
33. Sharad Borle et al., "The Impact of Survey Participation on Subsequent Customer Behavior: An Empirical Investigation," *Marketing Science* 26, no. 5 (September–October 2007): 721, https://www.jstor.org/stable/40057091; Vicki G. Morwitz, Eric Johnson, and David Schmittlein, "Does Measuring Intent Change Behavior?" *Journal of Consumer Research* 20, no. 1 (June 1993): 46, https://www.jstor.org/stable/2489199.
34. Laura L. Haines et al., "Information-Seeking Behavior of Basic Science Researchers: Implications for Library Services," *Journal of the Medical Library Association* 98, no. 1 (2010): 78; Jonathan Miller, "A Method for Evaluating Library Liaison Activities in Small Academic Libraries," *Journal of Library Administration* 54, no. 6 (2014): 490, https://doi.org/10.1080/01930826.2014.953387; Michele R. Tennant and Tara Tobin Cataldo, "Development and

Assessment of Specialized Liaison Librarians Services," *Medical Reference Services Quarterly* 21, no. 2 (2002): 33, https://doi.org/10.1300/J115v21n02_03.

35. Audrey F. Bancroft et al., "A Forward-Looking Library Use Survey: WSU Libraries in the 21st Century," *Journal of Academic Librarianship* 24, no. 3 (1998): 222.

36. Bright and Ghouse, "Taking AIM," 592–93.

37. Of the libraries that did use at least two separate participants, most did not show a high level of agreement between raters for the different items on the audit, supporting the idea that the instrument allows for subjectivity; Bright and Ghouse, "Taking AIM," 593–94.

38. Koury, Semenza, and Shropshire, "Survey of Diversity," 28.

39. Melissa Mallon, "Diversity, Equity, and Inclusion," *Public Services Quarterly* 15, no. 4 (2019): 320, https://doi.org/10.1080/15228959.2019.1664360; Sarah Leadley, "Reflections on Diversity and Organizational Development," *Reference and User Services Quarterly* 54, no. 4 (Summer 2015): 6.

40. Karin Hansson et al., "Reputation, Inequality and Meeting Techniques to Support Collaboration: Visualising User Hierarchy to Support Collaboration," *Computational and Mathematical Organization Theory* 20, no. 2 (2014): 157–58. https://doi.org/10.1007/s10588-013-9165-y.

41. Keri L. Heitner, Amy E. Kahn, and Kenneth C. Sherman, "Building Consensus on Defining Success of Diversity Work in Organizations," *Consulting Psychology Journal: Practice and Research* 65, no. 1 (2013): 65.

42. This implies a level of subjectivity due to individual differences, often found in the development of other workplace assessment tools. See Tom D. Taber and Elisabeth Taylor, "A Review and Evaluation of the Psychometric Properties of the Job Diagnostic Survey," *Personnel Psychology* 43, no. 3 (Autumn, 1990): 494, ProQuest.

43. Heitner, Kahn, and Sherman, "Building Consensus," 67.

44. Love, "Assessment of Diversity Initiatives," 90–91.

45. Isabell Schneider, Martin Mädler, and Jessica Lang, "Comparability of Self-Ratings and Observer Ratings in Occupational Psychosocial Risk Assessments: Is There Agreement?" *BioMed Research International* 2019: 2, https://pubmed.ncbi.nlm.nih.gov/31309118/.

46. Subjectivity bias is common in any assessment that involves self-rating. The DEISAA adds an interesting layer of having subjectivity bias impact self-ratings of the organization.

47. The updated structure of the instrument is very similar to the Diversity and Inclusion Charter created by the Peel Region in Canada. While this instrument was found after redesign of the audit, the structures of the two instruments are very similar, indicating similar methods applied to creating an instrument for similar topics. Regional Diversity Roundtable of Peel, "Achieving the Vision of an Inclusive Peel Region: A Diversity, Equity, and Inclusion Organizational Self-Assessment Tool," Diversity and Inclusion Charter of Peel, accessed January 16, 2020, https://docplayer.net/59092439-Achieving-the-vision-of-an-inclusive-peel-region-a-diversity-equity-and-inclusion-organizational-self-assessment-tool.html.

Bibliography

Alabi, Jaena. "From Hostile to Inclusive: Strategies for Improving the Racial Climate of Academic Libraries." *Library Trends* 67, no. 1 (Summer 2018): 131–46. https://doi.org/10.1353/lib.2018.0029.

Anantachai, Tarida, Latrice Booker, Althea Lazzaro, and Martha Parker. "Establishing a Communal Network for Professional Advancement among Librarians of Color." In *Where are All the Librarians of Color? The Experiences of People of Color in Academia.* Edited by Rebecca Hankins and Miguel Juárez, 31–54. Sacramento: Library Juice Press, 2016.

Anderson, Donald L. *Organization Development: The Process of Leading Organizational Change.* Los Angeles: SAGE, 2017.

Association of College and Research Libraries. "Diversity Standards: Cultural Competency for Academic Libraries (2012)." Accessed January 8, 2020. https://www.ala.org/acrl/standards/diversity.

Association of Research Libraries. "About: What Is ClimateQUAL®." Accessed January 16, 2020. https://www.climatequal.org/about.

———. "What Is ClimateQUAL®?" Accessed January 13, 2020. https://www.climatequal.org/home.

Bancroft, Audrey F., Vicki F. Croft, Robert Speth, and Dretha M. Phillips. "A Forward-Looking Library Use Survey: WSU Libraries in the 21st Century." *Journal of Academic Librarianship* 24, no. 3 (1998): 216–24.

Borle, Sharad, Utpal M. Dholakia, Siddharth S. Singh, and Robert A. Westbrook. "The Impact of Survey Participation on Subsequent Customer Behavior: An Empirical Investigation." *Marketing Science* 26, no. 5 (September–October 2007): 711–26. https://www.jstor.org/stable/40057091.

Brannon, Tiffany N., Evelyn R. Carter, Lisel Alice Murdock-Perriera, and Gerald D. Higginbotham. "From Backlash to Inclusion for All: Instituting Diversity Efforts to Maximize Benefits across Group Lines." *Social Issues and Policy Review* 12, no. 1 (2018): 57–90.

Bright, Kawanna, and Nikhat Ghouse. "Taking AIM: Integrating Organization Development into the Creation of a Diversity, Equity, and Inclusion Audit." In *Proceedings of the 2018 Library Assessment Conference: Building Effective, Sustainable, Practical Assessment.* Edited by Sue Baughman, Steve Hiller, Katie Monroe, and Angela Pappaldaro, 589–99. Washington, DC: Association of Research Libraries, 2018.

Brown, Jennifer, Jennifer A. Ferretti, Sofia Leung, and Marisa Méndez-Brady. "We Here: Speaking Our Truth." *Library Trends* 67, no. 1 (Summer 2018): 163–81. https://muse.jhu.edu/article/706994.

Bugg, Kimberley. "The Perceptions of People of Color in Academic Libraries Concerning the Relationship between Retention and Advancement as Middle Managers." *Journal of Library Administration* 56, no. 4 (2016): 428–43. https://doi.org/10.1080/01930826.2015.1105076.

Canadian Urban Libraries Council. "Social Inclusion Audit." Accessed January 16, 2002. http://www.siatoolkit.com/#axzz5ExeirtRa.

Ciszek, Matthew P., and Courtney L. Young. "Diversity Collection Assessment in Large Academic Libraries." *Collection Building* 29, no. 4 (2010): 154–61. https://doi.org/10.1108/01604951011088899.

Clunie, Simone, and Darlene Ann Parrish. "How Assessment Websites of Academic Libraries Convey Information and Show Value." *Performance Measurement and Metrics* 19, no. 3 (2018): 203–12. https://doi.org/10.1108/PMM-12-2017-0061.

DeVellis, Robert F. *Scale Development: Theory and Applications.* Los Angeles: Sage, 2012.

Espinal, Isabel, Tonia Sutherland, and Charlotte Roh. "A Holistic Approach for Inclusive Librarianship: Decentering Whiteness in Our Profession." *Library Trends* 67, no. 1 (Summer 2018): 147–62. https://doi.org/10.1353/lib.2018.0030.

Galbraith, Jay R. "The Star Model™." Accessed January 16, 2020. http://www.jaygalbraith.com/images/pdfs/StarModel.pdf.

Haines, Laura L., Jeanene Light, Donna O'Malley, and Frances A. Delwiche. "Information-Seeking Behavior of Basic Science Researchers: Implications for Library Services." *Journal of the Medical Library Association* 98, no. 1 (2010): 73–81.

Hansson, Karin, Petter Karlström, Aron Larsson, and Harko Verhagen. "Reputation, Inequality and Meeting Techniques: Visualising User Hierarchy to Support Collaboration." *Computational and Mathematical Organization Theory* 20, no. 2 (2014): 155–75. https://doi.org/10.1007/s10588-013-9165-y.

Heitner, Keri L., Amy E. Kahn, and Kenneth C. Sherman. "Building Consensus on Defining Success of Diversity Work in Organizations." *Consulting Psychology Journal: Practice and Research* 65, no. 1 (2013): 58–73.

Kim, Kyung-Sun, and Sei-Ching Joanna Sin. "Increasing Ethnic Diversity in LIS: Strategies Suggested by Librarians of Color." *Library Quarterly* 78, no. 2 (April 2008): 153–77. https://doi.org/10.1086/528887.

Koury, Regins, Jenny Lynne Semenza, and Sandra Shropshire. "A Survey of Diversity and Inclusiveness Initiatives at Carnegie Doctoral Research Institutions Libraries." *Library Management* 40, no. 1/2 (2019): 23–33. https://doi.org/10.1108/LM-10-2017-0117.

Kung, Janice Y., K-Lee Fraser, and Dee Winn. "Diversity Initiatives to Recruit and Retain Academic Librarians: A Systematic Review." *College and Research Libraries* 81, no. 1 (January 2020): 96–108. https://doi.org/10.5860/crl.81.1.96.

Leadley, Sarah. "Reflections on Diversity and Organizational Development." *Reference and User Services Quarterly* 54, no. 4 (Summer 2015): 6–10.

Love, Johnnieque B. (Johnnie). "The Assessment of Diversity Initiatives in Academic Libraries." *Journal of Library Administration* 33, no. 1–2 (2001): 73–103. https://doi.org/10.1300/J111v33n01_07.

Mallon, Melissa. "Diversity, Equity, and Inclusion." *Public Services Quarterly* 15, no. 4 (2019): 319–25. https://doi.org/10.1080/15228959.2019.1664360.

Matthews, Joseph R. *Library Assessment in Higher Education*, 2nd ed. Santa Barbara, CA: Libraries Unlimited, 2015.

Miller, Jonathan, "A Method for Evaluating Library Liaison Activities in Small Academic Libraries," *Journal of Library Administration* 54, no. 6 (2014): 483–500. https://doi.org/10.1080/01930826.2014.953387.

Morris, Shaneka. "Register for ClimateQUAL 2018 to Assess Your Library's Climate for Diversity and Inclusion." Association of Research Libraries. Accessed January 16, 2020. https://www.arl.org/news/register-for-climatequal-2018-to-assess-your-librarys-climate-for-diversity-and-inclusion/.

Morwitz, Vicki G., Eric Johnson, and David Schmittlein. "Does Measuring Intent Change Behavior?" *Journal of Consumer Research* 20, no. 1 (June 1993): 46–61. https://www.jstor.org/stable/2489199.

Neely, Teresa Y., and Lorna Peterson. "Achieving Racial and Ethnic Diversity among Academic and Research Libraries: The Recruitment, Retention, and Advancement of Librarians of Color—A White Paper." *College and Research Libraries News* 68, no. 9 (October 2007): 562–65.

Oakleaf, Megan. *The Value of Academic Libraries: A Comprehensive Research Review and Report.* Chicago: Association of College and Research Libraries, 2010. http://www.ala.org/acrl/sites/ala.org.acrl/files/content/issues/value/val_report.pdf.

Passonneau, Sarah M. "Library Assessment Activities: Using ISO 11620 to Review the Assessment Data of Academic Libraries in North America." *Performance Measurement and Metrics* 14, no. 3 (2013): 175–96. https://doi.org/10.1108/PMM-05-2013-0015.

Regional Diversity Roundtable of Peel. "Achieving the Vision of an Inclusive Peel Region: A Diversity, Equity, and Inclusion Organizational Self-Assessment Tool." Diversity and Inclusion Charter of Peel. Accessed January 16, 2020. https://docplayer.

net/59092439-Achieving-the-vision-of-an-inclusive-peel-region-a-diversity-equity-and-inclusion-organizational-self-assessment-tool.html.

Schneider, Isabell, Martin Mädler, and Jessica Lang. "Comparability of Self-Ratings and Observer Ratings in Occupational Psychosocial Risk Assessments: Is There Agreement?" *BioMed Research International* 2019: 1–10. https://pubmed.ncbi.nlm.nih.gov/31309118/.

Semenza, Jenny Lynne, Regina Koury, and Sandra Shropshire. "Diversity at Work in Academic Libraries 2010–2015: An Annotated Bibliography." *Collection Building* 36, no. 3 (2017): 89–95. https://doi.org/10.1108/CB-12-2016-0038.

Smith, Gregory Arnold, Howard Dale Tryon, and Lori Beth Snyder. "Developing an Academic Library Assessment Plan: A Case Study." *Performance Measurements and Metrics* 16, no. 1 (2015): 48–61. https://doi.org/10.1108/PMM-12-2014-0045.

Smith, Paula M. "Beyond Diversity: Moving towards Inclusive Work Environments." In *Workplace Culture in Academic Libraries: The Early 21st Century*. Edited by Kelly Blessinger and Paul Hrycaj, 99–110. Witney, UK: Elsevier Science & Technology, 2013.

———. "Culturally Conscious Organizations: A Conceptual Framework." *portal: Libraries and the Academy* 8, no. 2 (2018): 141–55.

Taber, Tom D., and Elisabeth Taylor. "A Review and Evaluation of the Psychometric Properties of the Job Diagnostic Survey." *Personnel Psychology* 43, no. 3 (Autumn 1990): 467–500. ProQuest.

Tatarka, Agnes, Kay Chapa, Xin Li, and Jennifer Rutner. "Library Assessment Plans: Four Case Studies." *Performance Measurements and Metrics* 11, no. 2 (2010): 199–210. https://doi.org/10.1108/14678041011064106.

Tennant, Michele R., and Tara Tobin Cataldo. "Development and Assessment of Specialized Liaison Librarians Services." *Medical Reference Services Quarterly* 21, no. 2 (2002): 21–37. https://doi.org/10.1300/J115v21n02_03.

CHAPTER 19

Diversity, Equity, and Inclusion Plans and Programs in ARL Libraries

Toni Anaya and Charlene Maxey Harris

Introduction

Over the last seven years, the Association of Research Libraries (ARL) published two SPEC Kits related to diversity and inclusion: *SPEC Kit 319: Diversity Plans and Programs* and *SPEC Kit 356: Diversity and Inclusion.*[1] Prior to 2019, ARL would generally publish six surveys each year, providing access to survey responses and documentation from member institutions on issues related to the ever-changing challenges faced by research libraries.[2] ARL worked with the authors to develop and design the survey, distributed it to the member libraries, and published the results. Library administrators or a representative completed the surveys within the designated time frame. The final publication contains an executive summary, survey results, examples of representative documents, and selected resources. Prior to these two publications, diversity, equity, and inclusion (DEI) efforts in this group of academic libraries had not been well documented from the administrative perspective. Results from ARL *SPEC Kits 319* and *356* provide a picture of how ARL libraries are managing and responding to the changing diversity landscape.

Just as the definitions of DEI change to reflect the needs of society, the strategies and tactics evolve to address the overall goals of the libraries and universities. Over the last ten years, the variety of identities that fall under the diversity umbrella have expanded to include issues beyond race and ethnicity. Issues of gender, sexual orientation, age, political beliefs, ability, language, national origin, and religious beliefs all now have a place in how diversity is defined. This chapter will examine and compare how diversity and inclusion activities have evolved at ARL libraries, as well as identifying trends and changes in managing diversity issues and issues and challenges faced by these institutions. Between 2010 and 2017, libraries reported that their activities and efforts were influenced by the political environment and recent social justice movements. These snapshots in time provided insight into the growing advocacy role of libraries on the campus and in the community.

ARL Libraries: Diversity in Practice

In the 2010 survey, forty-nine research libraries completed the survey, compared to sixty-eight of the 124 ARL member libraries that completed the survey in 2017. There were several questions that were the same on both surveys, allowing for direct comparison. In general, the questions centered on diversity plan development, including the responsible parties involved with the implementation, scope, time frame, and assessment of the plan. Outlined in the plans were programs that support an inclusive work environment, recruitment and retention strategies and tactics for underrepresented librarians and staff, and assessment and evaluative tools.

New questions that were added to the 2017 survey asked about funding strategies in order to understand how these programs were sustained and supported in the organization. Libraries were also asked to describe how their DEI efforts had changed over the last five years. The responses to this question provided a wealth of information about specific initiatives and partnerships with campus departments and communities, as well as issues and barriers that libraries were grappling with. These narratives provided rich insight about how libraries are embracing the changes.

Diversity Plans

Library diversity plans vary by institution but should be based in a strategic framework addressing the library's underlying beliefs, central diversity values, vision of diversity, mission, diversity goals, and strategies. The plans should be driven by climate assessment, include a time line for review, and include meaningful goals, objectives, and strategies.[3] *SPEC Kit 319: Diversity Plans and Programs* provided responding libraries descriptions of these plans, which might include a statement of diversity values or goals, a description of strategies for recruiting ethnically and culturally diverse staff to the library and retaining them once they are hired, an outline of programs that promote ethnic and cultural sensitivity in the workplace, results from a work climate assessment, and other similar elements. A diversity plan might be a stand-alone document or part of a broader document, such as a library strategic plan on an institution-wide diversity plan.[4] In both surveys, thirty-six libraries had a diversity plan that was described as having a statement about diversity with values, goals, and strategies. Diversity/Inclusion plans were present in thirty-six (53 percent) of the responding institutions in 2017; in 2010, the thirty-six libraries accounted for 73 percent of the respondents. Questions added in 2017 sought to determine who is responsible for implementing the plan, the length of the plan, and the connection to the campus strategies. A deeper dive into the results revealed some of the factors that contribute to sustainable and productive programs. Although there were the same number of libraries with diversity and inclusion plans, there were triple the number of positions (e.g., multicultural or diversity librarians; diversity officers) dedicated to diversity efforts in 2017. Additionally, respondents were asked to summarize how DEI efforts changed in the previous five years. Responses were encouraging. Libraries had aligned with the campus DEI framework and had been incorporated into the strategic planning process. Libraries partnered with campus departments to provide diversity education, training, and professional development opportunities. The combined result of the campus and library efforts expanded the array of activities that had not been available previously. It was also reported that library task forces and committees were organized focusing on increased efforts to recruit more diverse applicant pools.

Universities, many with DEI administrative leadership positions, established or revised their definitions for diversity, expanding them to encompass inclusion and equity issues. Other strategies mentioned included the creation of statements defining inclusive excellence within colleges and departments, the addition of language in job positions that requests the applicant to provide support of DEI, and implementation of surveys for assessing workplace climate. The average life span of plans was between three and five years before review and revision. In both surveys, diversity plans at some libraries were stand-alone library documents, some were included as part of the strategic plans, and others were part of a larger campus initiative. Research library DEI plans in action encompassed programs that promote an inclusive work environment, recruitment and retention strategies, and evaluation and assessment tools and outcomes.

Library programming on racial and ethnic diversity, sexual orientation, physical abilities, and gender and age discrimination appeared in both surveys. It was evident that the political issues influenced and impacted newer topics within the seven-year span. Social justice topics were more common in 2017, as well as training on implicit bias and microaggressions. There were a number of training opportunities provided by the campus, community, national, and state library associations, including ACRL, ALA, and ARL, and DEI consultants (e.g., DeEtta Jones).

Recruitment

One of the most effective ways of developing a more diverse workplace is to increase the diversity of applicant pools. This is the goal of a variety of recruitment programs on the national level from ALA and ACRL, yet challenges still exist in attracting diverse applicant pools. Measures need to be taken to increase the number of LIS students from diverse backgrounds and to develop culturally inclusive teaching and learning environments within these programs. Eighty percent of libraries that completed the survey in 2010 and 2017 have incorporated recruitment strategies to attract racially and ethnically diverse candidates. Successful strategies that were identified from both reports included the following:

- targeted job ads to participants in diversity and inclusion library programs
- support and participation of ARL initiatives programs
- offering a post-LIS residency program for underrepresented groups
- training search committee members on how to attract a diverse applicant pool
- partnering with professional, local, or student organizations to aid in the recruitment of diverse individuals

Although recruitment practices have evolved and more libraries are utilizing these strategies, they are not always successful, and demonstrating sustainable change has proven challenging. In the most recent survey, only 53 percent of libraries felt their strategies led to pools that were more inclusive.[5] Comments in both studies indicated that barriers to recruitment of a diverse workforce include geographic location of the university and the lack of racial and ethnic diversity in the workplace, lack of diverse candidates, and state political climate.[6] Comments from responding libraries in 2017 also showed frustration about the lack of demographic data available from university equity and compliance offices with search committees during the application process, which made it challenging to determine if application pools were more diverse.

Retention

In 2010, only four libraries reported having a program that is specifically intended to help underrepresented librarians attain advancement. In 2017, the scope of this question was expanded to collect retention strategies for all staff members working in the library, not only individuals with the title of librarian. Forty-eight libraries responded yes when asked if they employed retention strategies and programs. Respondents identified the most successful strategies to be leadership development and training opportunities, mentoring programs, and diversity residency programs. One tactic that was noted on the list of potential options was supporting membership in or engagement with campus affinity groups (e.g., African American faculty staff caucus). One comment which stood out was this:

> Having a diverse staff helps to retain a diverse staff. Individuals from underrepresented groups are not isolated or alone when there is broader diversity throughout the library and campus. Providing opportunities such as affinity groups and diversity committees for those who wish to connect or contribute in that way. Ensuring that supervisors and managers are welcoming, inclusive, and respectful.[7]

Assessment

Assessment of DEI initiatives and programs continues to be a challenge for research libraries. Fewer than 25 percent of respondents in both surveys had a way to measure the success of efforts to recruit a diverse workforce. Beyond just looking at the number of librarians and staff, climate surveys and exit interviews are a couple of ways libraries are learning about diverse librarians' experiences. In 2017, nearly 70 percent of libraries had surveyed their work climate, and another 12 percent were planning to. When asked about who developed the climate survey, libraries responded that they developed their own or used a campus survey. Additional research is needed to evaluate how libraries are using these assessment tools and how those efforts are impacting DEI efforts.

Discussion: The Changing Diversity Landscape

New in 2017 was the question about how libraries had responded to social justice movements. The seven years between reports saw a series of protests on immigration, Black Lives Matter, and the Dakota Access Pipeline in the United States, which marked a shift in how the definition of DEI ignited a newly revived era of social justice movements.

Among 2017 respondents, thirty-eight (64 percent) reported changes in senior campus administrators, and thirty-four (58 percent) reported new leadership on campus. These were characterized as factors that prompted changes in diversity and inclusion activities. These new leaders supported and invested in making DEI a priority in their institution's mission. Part of this mission is changing workplace climate to attract individuals who will commit to an inclusive and engaging campus. In libraries, DEI priorities have centered on recruitment and retention and programming. Efforts on analyzing collections, developing teaching resources, and partnering with campus and community groups are also on the rise. As one respondent shared, "Diversity and inclusion is woven into the fabric of all we do."[8] Involvement in and reaction to social justice movements was described in fifty-two comments.[9] In answer to a related question asking libraries to comment on the impact of recent social justice movements, seven out of thirty-three reported that these movements have not impacted or affected DEI plans and programs. Others shared they accelerated and increased awareness of the role of the library of these activities. One comment noted social justice issues expanded the scope of their diversity efforts to also include activities on equity and inclusion. Libraries reported hosting exhibits on social justice movements, issuing statements of support, and becoming involved in and backing campus initiatives, as well as encouraging and supporting staff and faculty involvement in local events.[10]

National library leadership programs provided mentoring fellowships that also embraced diversity and inclusion.[11] Programs like Harvard's Contemporary Challenges in Library Leadership: Building Community, Leading Change and the ARL Leadership Fellows built into their syllabi how to manage trends and introduced strategies to prepare for the changing demographics of the workplace. Early participants from diversity leadership programs such as the ARL Leadership Career and Development Program, the ALA Diversity Leadership Institutes, and the Gates Millennium Scholars program were now moving into administrative positions. Examples include Elaine Westbrooks, vice provost of university libraries and university librarian, University of North Carolina at Chapel Hill; Trevor Dawes, vice provost for libraries and museums and May Morris university librarian, University of Delaware; Adriene Lim, dean of university libraries, University of Maryland; and Janice Simmons-Welburn, dean of libraries, Marquette University, to name a few.

Many of these new administrators were ARL alumni, who waited patiently for their opportunity to lead, developing skills in emotional intelligence, assessment, change management, and cultural competencies, which greatly impacted their leadership style and how they lived out DEI. Members of these alumni groups, to which authors Anaya and Maxey-Harris belong, developed close relationships with fellow participants through committee membership and ARL networking opportunities. Alumni mentored each other or were supervised by fellow alumni and followed common research interests, creating a network of library leaders focused on increasing diversity in the profession. Alumni created affinity groups and support systems, which resulted in changes in their approach and desire to look for new innovative ways to influence and connect with faculty on their campuses. Incidentally, based on the comments from the 2017 survey, as these leaders were hired into university librarian and associate university librarian positions, commitments to DEI were rejuvenated. They recommitted to DEI projects (e.g., ACRL Diversity Alliance) and had success in shifting the workplace culture to assess needs and bring about different outcomes. Many of these leaders were receptive to supporting attendance and participation in leadership academies or programs that embraced the changing environment and prepared not only themselves but their libraries to understand the impact of recruiting and retaining librarians from marginalized groups.

Anecdotally, unlike their predecessors, these new diverse leaders often participated in and shared similar leadership development training. They encouraged their librarians and staff to be culturally responsive when providing instruction, developing collections, and serving their faculty, students, staff, and communities. When asked to share strategies used or developed to promote inclusive workplaces, respondents to the 2017 survey included specific examples demonstrating how their library promoted this work.[12] This work ranged from training on implicit bias and microaggressions for staff to hosting DEI events and exhibits, supporting and encouraging DEI research, creating committees focused on DEI, and including diversity statements in evaluations, job descriptions, and strategic plans.[13] There is a gap in the literature on the impact of this more diverse leadership cohort and their management style. Librarians were encouraged and supported by these new leaders to develop research agendas focused on diversity and equity issues that explored issues such as microaggressions, critical pedagogy, and information literacy, furthering the study of the field with trainings and publications delivered by a new class of developing leaders well versed in issues related to diversity, equity, and inclusion. Their efforts have yet to be documented.

Conclusion: The Path Forward

In 2017, while the *Diversity and Inclusion* SPEC kit was under development, Ithaka S+R released a research study commissioned by the Andrew Mellon Foundation that gathered and analyzed the demographics of library staff in academic libraries and the perspectives of library leadership about diversity, equity, and inclusion in their library and the library community.[14] This study was unique because it asked academic deans and directors or their representatives for elusive insider information to serve as a baseline. Response rate for this survey was fairly similar to that of *Diversity and Inclusion*, with 56 responding ARL libraries' data gathered in June 2016. It provided a snapshot of the barriers library directors face when attempting to achieve an appropriate level of diversity in their library. The concerns shared in the Ithaka survey mirrored those in the 2010 and 2017 SPEC kits. Based on the data and the survey, the results revealed a glass ceiling for underrepresented librarians working in senior administrative positions. Not only are there advancement issues for underrepresented librarians in administrative positions, it is becoming increasingly apparent that retention of members of these populations persistently remains low, especially for academic librarians who are African American or Latinx.[15] More effort must be made and more study be done in order to not only recruit but also *retain and promote* members of these groups.

The effort to create effective methods to gauge developments in an area where perception is often influenced by unconscious bias is hard work. It takes a deep understanding of the issues and factors that influence how success is defined in relation to ideas that do not easily lend themselves to assessment. Future research in this area can begin to identify common characteristics in the ARL members that participated in and responded to SPEC kit surveys around DEI issues. These institutions have shared how they have consistently been involved in DEI efforts over the years, and research can be done to assess whether those efforts have contributed to success in promoting and supporting diversity, equity, and inclusion. An important factor that must be explored is the evaluation of the leadership team to determine where and how different priorities have taken place in relation to staffing, financial investment, research collections and data, and the work climate. Examples of how leaders have effected change would provide a road map for others in deciding whether to implement or avoid similar strategies.

The library must serve as the principal building on campus where one can truly experience and benefit from the centrality of an institution's intellectual community and where diversity in all of its forms is welcomed and celebrated.[16] Research libraries must begin not only to take a hard look at their leadership, workforce, and policies, but also to make efforts to understand how their users perceive these efforts. Studies must begin to focus on the library as a whole: from how welcome and supported students, faculty, and staff feel when using the library and its services to the library's commitment to fostering access to diverse voices found in print and digital collections, as well as the commitment to employing a diverse group of individuals who come together to represent and reflect not only their users but also the values of the institution.

Notes

1. Charlene Maxey-Harris and Toni Anaya, *SPEC Kit 319: Diversity Plans and Programs* (Washington, DC: Association of Research Libraries, 2010); Toni Anaya and Charlene Maxey-Harris, *SPEC Kit 356: Diversity and Inclusion* (Washington, DC: Association of Research Libraries, 2017).
2. Association of Research Libraries, "SPEC Kits," https://publications.arl.org/SPEC_Kits.

3.   James F. Williams, "Managing Diversity: Library Management in Light of the Dismantling of Affirmative Action," *Journal of Library Administration* 27, no. 1–2 (1999): 27–48.
4.   Maxey-Harris and Anaya, *Diversity Plans and Programs*, 18.
5.   Anaya and Maxey-Harris, *Diversity and Inclusion*, 4.
6.   Ali Rizvi, Nicole L. Cvetnic, and Sohail. A. McClatchy, "Understanding HB2: North Carolina's Newest Law Solidifies State's Role in Defining Discrimination," *Charlotte Observer*, March 6, 2020, https://www.charlotteobserver.com/news/politics-government/article68401147.html.
7.   Anaya and Maxey-Harris, *Diversity and Inclusion*, 40.
8.   Anaya and Maxey-Harris, *Diversity and Inclusion*, 6.
9.   Anaya and Maxey-Harris, *Diversity and Inclusion*, 51.
10.   Anaya and Maxey-Harris, *Diversity and Inclusion*, 53.
11.   Linda C. Smith, "From Foundation to Federal Funding: The Impact of Grants on Education for Library and Information Science," *Advances in Librarianship* 31 (2008): 141–65.
12.   Anaya and Maxey-Harris, *Diversity and Inclusion*, 20.
13.   Anaya and Maxey-Harris, *Diversity and Inclusion*, 30
14.   Roger Schonfeld and Liam Sweeney, *Inclusion, Diversity, and Equity* (New York: Ithaka S+R, August 30, 2017), https://doi.org/10.18665/sr.304524.
15.   Ione T. Damasco and Dracine Hodges, "Tenure and Promotion Experiences of Academic Librarians of Color," *College and Research Libraries* 73, no. 3 (2012): 280.
16.   Geoffrey T. Freeman, "The Library as Place: Changes in Learning Patterns, Collections, Technology, and Use," in *Library as Place: Rethinking Roles, Rethinking Space* (Washington, DC: Council on Library and Information Resources, 2005), 2.

Bibliography

Anaya, Toni, and Charlene Maxey-Harris. *SPEC Kit 356: Diversity and Inclusion*. Washington, DC: Association of Research Libraries, 2017.

Association of Research Libraries. "SPEC Kits." https://publications.arl.org/SPEC_Kits.

Damasco, Ione T., and Dracine Hodges. "Tenure and Promotion Experiences of Academic Librarians of Color." *College and Research Libraries* 73, no. 3 (2012): 279–301.

Freeman, Geoffrey T. "The Library as Place: Changes in Learning Patterns, Collections, Technology, and Use." In *Library as Place: Rethinking Roles, Rethinking Space*, 1–9. Washington, DC: Council on Library and Information Resources, February 2005.

Maxey-Harris, Charlene, and Toni Anaya. *SPEC Kit 319: Diversity Plans and Programs*. Washington: DC: Association of Research Libraries, 2010.

Rizvi, Ali, Nicole L. Cvetnic, and Sohail A. McClatchy. "Understanding HB2: North Carolina's Newest Law Solidifies State's Role in Defining Discrimination." *Charlotte Observer*, March 6, 2020, https://www.charlotteobserver.com/news/politics-government/article68401147.html.

Schonfeld, Roger, and Liam Sweeney. *Inclusion, Diversity, and Equity: Members of the Association of Research Libraries: Employee Demographics and Director Perspectives*. New York: Ithaka S+R, August 30, 2017. https://doi.org/10.18665/sr.304524.

Smith, Linda C. "From Foundation to Federal Funding: The Impact of Grants on Education for Library and Information Science." *Advances in Librarianship* 31 (2008): 141–65.

Williams, James F. "Managing Diversity: Library Management in Light of the Dismantling of Affirmative Action." *Journal of Library Administration* 27, no. 1–2 (1999): 27–48.

Afterword

While working on this book, we encountered other intriguing writings that also offered practical approaches to diversity, equity, and inclusion in libraries. We also found ourselves asking more questions that we hope other library researchers will someday answer. This afterword is by no means a comprehensive overview of DEI initiatives in libraries. Although recommendations are summarized here, the articles all deserve a fuller reading.

A survey of the literature by Kung, Fraser, and Winn identifies the categories of the most frequent interventions mentioned in the library literature: internships/residencies, mentorship programs, professional development, recruitment, and surveys.[1] Kung, Fraser, and Winn conclude that "despite the fact that academic librarians have been concerned about the lack of diversity within the field since the 1920s, the number of diverse librarians in the profession remains low to this day."[2] They recommend that any program with the goal of diversifying the profession include a clear statement of program goals and an assessment component. These programs should also take into account intersectional identity rather than a single dimension of identity and should also target mid- to late-career librarians.

> However, there remains a large gap in these interventions between diverse librarians' entrance into the field and whether they are encouraged to stay. There is limited commitment to supporting and retaining mid- to late-career diverse librarians, many of whom face barriers when striving to advance their careers beyond entry-level positions.[3]

A white paper by Neely and Peterson recommends a "comprehensive, collaborative recruitment and public awareness campaign for recruitment purposes."[4] They also recommend that ACRL develop a research agenda "that addresses the lack of membership data for decision-making and goal setting."[5] Their recommendations include identification of best practices for recruitment "accompanied by sound empirical evidence with results,"[6] realistic goals for assessment and analysis, more reliable data, more research about retention.

According to Neely and Peterson, the literature on retention is "weak,"[7] but strategies mentioned include orientations and welcomes, programming that addresses work culture, opportunities for professional development, a positive environment, compensations and rewards, good management, and recognition of work-life balance needs. Some ideas from their literature review for supporting advancement include mentoring, shadowing library leaders, proactive nominations for awards and recognition, job rotations, participation in fellowships and institutes, job rotations, and better data on library leaders of color and tracking available leadership pools of minority candidates. Damasco and Hodges also recommend mentoring programs, which should include an assessment component, and ensuring the librarians of color develop successful grant writing skills.[8] "Library administrators should also emphasize the value of the work of library faculty of color who engage with and provide service to communities of color served by their institutions."[9]

It would appear that directors of ARL libraries need a better understanding of what constitutes diversity, equity, and inclusion and the factors that have allowed the profession to remain mostly white, including structural issues within the profession itself. Two Ithaka S+R reports surveyed directors of libraries that are members of the Association of Research Libraries.[10] The 2017 report finds that library directors were more likely to consider their own library more equitable than other libraries, that directors of more homogenous libraries saw their libraries as more equitable than the overall library community, and that "they do so by a larger margin than the more diverse institutions. We observe a similar pattern with regards to inclusivity."[11] These library directors recognize the lack of racial and ethnic diversity among their staff as a problem, but they perceive it as related to external factors (limited applicants from diverse backgrounds, geographic locations) and not internal factors (implicit bias or markers of inclusiveness in the library culture). The 2021 report notes that "most library directors did not expect that employees of color would be disproportionately affected by cuts due to COVID-19. However, job types with relatively greater percentages of employees of color were more impacted by recent furloughs and role eliminations."[12]

Neely and Peterson, among others, recommend looking at the strategies used by other fields to recruit a more diverse workforce.[13] Kim and Sin also recommended that

> investigating approaches used in other professional fields
> might also offer some insight on successful strategies.
> Pre-college bridge programs used for recruiting minorities
> in engineering and nursing; partnerships among research
> universities, colleges and community colleges used for devel-
> oping systematic recruitment programs in psychology, and
> early intervention programs and nationwide campaigns used
> for improving the public's image of the professions in nursing
> and other healthcare fields[14]

are among the strategies included.

Alburo, Bradshaw, Santiago, Smith, and Vinopal looked at corporate diversity initiatives for ideas.[15] Target Corporation makes diversity a central tenet; its extensive diversity plan includes recruiting directly from the communities it wishes to hire from, affirmative steps to achieve parity between diverse and non-diverse team members in turnover, in workplace experiences, and in diversity at mid- to upper-staffing levels. It also conducts regular pay audits and launched extensive training programs. The MetLife insurance company created a program to attract recent college graduates by "demonstrating to them before they were hired why working at MetLife would be beneficial to them and their careers."[16] Coca Cola launched a comprehensive mentoring program, and T-Mobile worked to maintain and continually assess a climate of inclusivity, using assessment tools developed by marginalized communities. Alburo and colleagues draw many actionable conclusions from these examples that libraries should consider.

What other professional fields do people of color enter?[17] What can we learn from the fields that are successful in attracting people of color? Two other fields dominated by women, nursing and social work, are more racially and ethnically diverse, at least at first glance;[18] why do these fields succeed where the library world has failed?

The demographic problem of the library field begins with the demographics of library school students.[19] It would be interesting to look at which fields are successful in attracting postgraduate students of color and why.[20] In some fields—for instance, law—the student body is more diverse than the population of practicing attorneys, which may mean that in time the profession will become more diverse.[21] Meanwhile, what can other LIS programs learn from Knowledge River, a library and information science program focusing specifically on Latino and Native American perspectives?[22]

Kim and Sin asked librarians of color for their suggestions on increasing ethnic diversity in library schools.[23] Their suggestions included financial aid; ethnic diversity of faculty; role models; presence of faculty and staff of color in the recruitment process; opportunities for students of color to work in LIS-related fields or with LIS faculty, graduate students or librarians; advertising; presence of alumni of color in the recruitment process; availability of career services/job placement in the LIS school; and active solicitation and personal contacts by the LIS school. Many of these strategies were also listed in their survey of library literature. Additional strategies suggested in the literature: creative delivery of classes, sensitivity to diversity and anti-racism, diversity in the curriculum, and internship placements that entail working with minority communities.

It will surprise no one that Kim and Sin, along with Steffen and Lietzau, among others, suggest that the low salary of librarians is a barrier to recruiting;[24] they cite fields with higher salaries (e.g., lawyers and engineers) as more successful in recruiting ethnic minorities. The negative image of librarians, cited by both articles, is another obstacle. Clearly, as a field, we need some creative new ideas to address both of these fundamental issues.

The cost of an MLIS is undoubtedly a barrier to people of color considering the library field. Espinal, Hathcock, and Rios make a radical yet simple proposal: every academic library with an annual budget above $500,000 should take salary savings from retirements and sponsor two new people of color each year to attain their MLIS.[25] They estimate that this would increase the number of librarians of color by over 3,000 per year; if we added large public library systems, we could support even more new librarians. As the authors point out, salary savings are often redirected to support technology and innovation. Why not use them to support the strategic goal of increasing and enhancing diversity, inclusion, and equity?

In 2011, Brett Bonfield asked the question "Is the United States training too many librarians or too few?"[26]—an excellent question, though a hard one to answer, given limited availability and inaccuracy of the data—a project for our professional organizations and research entities. What kind of employment situation are we asking new librarians to enter?

According to Michael Kelley, "African Americans and Hispanics are some of the strongest supporters of libraries, and yet they continue to be thinly represented among the ranks of librarians."[27] Why don't people of color want to go into the field? The coeditors of this book speculated among ourselves that the general public doesn't know what librarians do, but in fact the teaching profession has similarly lopsided demographics,[28] and most Americans have had direct experience with teachers.

Although it isn't practical to survey all college graduates to ask why they don't consider librarianship, there is one population we can ask: library assistants. In 2005, Keith Curry Lance wrote that the demographics of library assistants were much closer to those of the general American population (this was based on 2000 census data, so the data needs updating).[29] Steffen and Lietzau interviewed Colorado library assistants about the factors that discouraged them from pursuing a career in librarianship: pay, negative stereotypes, limited job opportunities.[30] Lance, and Kim and Sin, and Kelley are among those who recommend recruiting and supporting library assistants as a way to diversify the profession.[31]

For many writers, these strategies are not enough without a critical reexamination of the profession itself.

> Critical librarianship offers a framework for thinking about our work that asks how library structures came to be and what ideologies underpin them. Viewing librarianship through this frame allows us to imagine new and better worlds on our way to making them.[32]

April Hathcock writes:

> Reading through the onerous application process, the realization hit me: our diversity programs do not work because they are themselves coded to promote whiteness as the norm in the profession and unduly burden those individuals they are most intended to help.[33]

The standard requirements of application form, résumé, essay, transcripts, and letters of support from faculty or employer

> assumes that applicants are situated in positions of white, middle-class, cisgender normativity that allow for the temporal, financial, and educational privilege that fulfilling these criteria would require.... Reworking application processes to accommodate applicants with different backgrounds and experiences in no way requires lowering standards.[34]

Hathcock suggests allowing applicants to submit letters of recommendation from members of the community or an acquaintance familiar with their qualifications, as well as teaching new librarians "how to navigate effectively the white system that we have. We also need to teach these new librarians how to dismantle whiteness' stranglehold on the profession."[35] She recommends that librarians of color seek out the mentorship groups, social media spaces, and relevant library organizations that exist to support diverse library workers. And she exhorts all librarians to find ways to make change—serving on ALA diversity-related committees, taking part in formal and informal mentoring programs—librarians with privilege should speak up on behalf of those without privilege.

Michelle Gohr also recommends "dismantling the current system of accreditation for librarians by accounting for different combinations of skills and education."[36] This includes revising job descriptions, hiring practices, and communication styles that are exclusionary to marginalized populations. White allies are urged to "critically unpack the anxieties, apprehension, and defensiveness"[37] they may feel about these changes and to understand that these feelings are rooted in privilege.

Jennifer Vinopal brings together ideas of actions that library leaders must take to "make our organizations and our profession inclusive, open to difference, and diverse."[38] They include raising awareness of implicit bias, including diversity initiatives in the library's strategic plan, and providing time and support for staff to accomplish them; creating a stand-alone diversity plan; collecting data; recruiting job candidates from among the communities you wish to include; devising targeted mentoring and professional development strategies; and offering paid internships. She also lists some areas that require further research: better data on diversity; effective organizational processes that might help "push an organization toward a better understanding of privilege and discrimination";[39] why staff from underrepresented groups are leaving the profession; and leadership styles and methods that can help leadership "promote awareness of bias and discrimination and… develop actions to address them."[40]

Brown, Ferretti, Leung, and Mendez-Brady write that

> a common misconception about our failures to diversity librarianship is that there is nothing wrong with the profession.... Framing the library as "inherently good," or within contexts such as centers of "democracy" and "neutrality," conceals covert structural forms of racial exclusion that protect white interests.[41]

They demonstrate that the incorporation of critical race theory into the LIS curriculum is essential: "When we fail to take into account the lived experiences of those we provide service to, we not only fail our patrons and communities but also uphold whiteness—through the standardized exclusion of people of color."[42]

They note that "diversity programs and initiatives make the profession *appear* more diverse without actually tackling the systemic issues underlying librarianship, which we believe is the work of the... institution."[43] Although mentorship is key to retention, "white centered mentorship opportunities often have the unintended consequence of pushing librarians of color to assimilate into the whiteness of librarianship, alienating those at the margins even further."[44] One of the coauthors of the article created a Facebook group called We Here, "designed as a space for librarians of color to reach out."[45] This group now sponsors a community school, book reviews, and other support systems for library workers of color, while also working to "recognize, discuss, and intervene in systemic social issues that have plagued these professions both currently and historically."[46]

These voices, and those of the contributors to this book, are among the many to challenge us to reflect even more deeply about how diversity, equity, and inclusion will continue to be addressed within the academic library workforce. We invite academic librarians and affiliated stakeholders to engage with emerging solutions and work together to build a more inclusive and productive future.

Notes

1. Janice Y. Kung, K-Lee Fraser, and Dee Winn, "Diversity Initiatives to Recruit and Retain Academic Librarians: A Systematic Review," *College and Research Libraries* 81, no. 1 (2020): 96–108, https://crl.acrl.org/index.php/crl/article/view/17484/32063.
2. Kung, Fraser, and Winn, "Diversity Initiatives," 104.
3. Kung, Fraser, and Winn, "Diversity Initiatives," 103.
4. Teresa Y. Neely and Lorna Peterson, "Achieving Racial and Ethnic Diversity among Academic and Research Librarians: The Recruitment, Retention, and Advancement of Librarians of Color—A White Paper," *College and Research Libraries News* 68, no. 9 (2007): 563, https://crln.acrl.org/index.php/crlnews/article/view/7869/7869.563.
5. Neely and Peterson, "Achieving Racial and Ethnic Diversity," 564.
6. Neely and Peterson, "Achieving Racial and Ethnic Diversity," 564.
7. Neely and Peterson, "Achieving Racial and Ethnic Diversity," 564.
8. Ione T. Damasco and Dracine Hodges, "Tenure and Promotion Experiences of Academic Librarians of Color," *College and Research Libraries* 73, no. 3 (2012): 279–301, https://crl.acrl.org/index.php/crl/article/view/16231/17677.
9. Damasco and Hodges, "Tenure and Promotion Experiences," 300.
10. Roger C. Schonfeld and Liam Sweeney, *Inclusion, Diversity and Equity* (New York: Ithaka S+R, August 30, 2017), https://sr.ithaka.org/publications/

inclusion-diversity-and-equity-arl/; Jennifer K. Frederick and Christine Wolff-Eisen-berg, *National Movements for Racial Justice and Academic Library Leadership* (New York: Ithaka S+R, March 17, 2021), https://sr.ithaka.org/publications/national-movements-for-racial-justice-and-academic-library-leadership/.

11. Schonfeld and Sweeny, *Inclusion, Diversity and Equity*, 27.
12. Frederick and Wolff-Eisenberg, *National Movements for Racial Justice*, 2.
13. Neely and Peterson, "Achieving Racial and Ethnic Diversity."
14. Kyung-Sun Kim and Sei-Ching Joanna Sin, "Increasing Ethnic Diversity in LIS: Strategies Suggested by Librarians of Color," *Library Quarterly* 78, no. 2 (2008): 156, https://doi.org/10.1086/528887.
15. Jane Alburo et al., "Looking beyond Libraries for Inclusive Recruitment and Retention Practices: Four Successful Approaches," in *Critical Librarianship*, ed. Samantha Schmehl Hines and David Ketchum (Bingley, UK: Emerald Publishing, 2020), 85–109.
16. Alburo et al., "Looking beyond Libraries," 93.
17. US Bureau of Labor Statistics, "Labor Force Statistics from the Current Population Survey," 2020, https://www.bls.gov/cps/cpsaat11.htm.
18. US Bureau of Labor Statistics, "Labor Force Statistics."
19. National Center for Education Statistics, "Table 323.30. Master's Degrees Conferred by Postsecondary Institutions, by Race/Ethnicity and Field of Study: 2017–18 and 2018–19," *Digest of Education Statistics*, Institute of Education Science, US Department of Education, 2020, https://nces.ed.gov/programs/digest/d20/tables/dt20_323.30.asp.
20. National Center for Education Statistics, "Master's Degrees Conferred."
21. American Bar Association, *ABA Profile of the Legal Profession 2020* (Chicago: American Bar Association, 2020), 36, 58, https://www.americanbar.org/content/dam/aba/administrative/news/2020/07/potlp2020.pdf.
22. Patricia Montiel-Overall and Sandra Littletree, "Knowledge River: A Case Study of a Library and Information Science Program Focusing on Latino and Native American Perspectives," *Library Trends* 59, no. 1–2 (June 2010): 67–87, http://hdl.handle.net/2142/18722.
23. Kim and Sin, "Increasing Ethnic Diversity."
24. Nicolle Steffen and Zeth Lietzau, "Retirement, Retention, and Recruitment in Colorado Libraries: The 3Rs Study Revisited," *Library Trends* 58, no. 2 (2009): 179–91, https://muse.jhu.edu/article/375514. Thanks to Bernadette Lopez Fitzsimmons and Kanu A. Nagra for alerting us to this study.
25. Isabel Espinal, April M. Hathcock, and Mario Rios, "Dewhitening Librarianship: A Policy Proposal for Libraries," in *Knowledge Justice: Disrupting Library and Information Studies through Critical Race Theory,* ed. Sofia Y. Leung and Jorge R. López-McKnight (Cambridge, MA: MIT Press, 2021), 223–40, https://direct.mit.edu/books/edited-volume/5114/Knowledge-JusticeDisrupting-Library-and.
26. Brett Bonfield, "Is the United States Training Too Many Librarians or Too Few? (Part 1)," *In the Library with the Lead Pipe*, September 21, 2011, https://www.inthelibrarywiththe-leadpipe.org/2011/is-the-united-states-training-too-many-librarians-or-too-few-part-1/.
27. Michael Kelley, "Diversity Never Happens: The Story of Minority Hiring Doesn't Seem to Change Much," editorial, *Library Journal*, February 20, 2013, https://www.libraryjournal.com/?detailStory=diversity-never-happens-the-story-of-minority-hiring-doesnt-seem-to-change-much.
28. US Bureau of Labor Statistics, "Labor Force Statistics."
29. Keith Curry Lance, "Racial and Ethnic Diversity of U.S. Library Workers," *American Libraries* 36, no. 5 (May 2005): 41–43, EBSCOhost.

30. Steffen and Lietzau, "Retirement, Retention, and Recruitment"; Kim and Sin, "Increasing Ethnic Diversity."
31. Lance, "Racial and Ethnic Diversity"; Kim and Sin, "Increasing Ethnic Diversity"; Kelley, "Diversity Never Happens."
32. Emily Drabinski, "What Is Critical about Critical Librarianship?" abstract, accepted manuscript, CUNY Academic Works, City University of New York, 2019, https://academicworks.cuny.edu/gc_pubs/537/.
33. April Hathcock, "White Librarianship in Blackface: Diversity Initiatives in LIS," *In the Library with the Lead Pipe,* October 7, 2015, https://www.inthelibrarywiththeleadpipe.org/2015/lis-diversity/.
34. Hathcock, "White Librarianship in Blackface."
35. Hathcock, "White Librarianship in Blackface."
36. Michelle Gohr, "Ethnic and Racial Diversity in Libraries: How White Allies Can Support Arguments for Decolonization," *Journal of Radical Librarianship* 3 (2017): 53, https://core.ac.uk/download/pdf/150799786.pdf.
37. Gohr, "Ethnic and Racial Diversity," 53.
38. Jennifer Vinopal, "The Quest for Diversity in Library Staffing: From Awareness to Action," *In the Library with the Lead Pipe,* January 13, 2016, https://www.inthelibrarywiththeleadpipe.org/2016/quest-for-diversity/.
39. Vinopal, "Quest for Diversity."
40. Vinopal, "Quest for Diversity."
41. Jennifer Brown et al., "We Here: Speaking Our Truth," *Library Trends* 67 no. 1, (2018): 4-5, https://doi.org/10.1353/lib.2018.0031.
42. Brown et al., "Speaking Our Truth," 6.
43. Brown et al., "Speaking Our Truth," 169.
44. Brown et al., "Speaking Our Truth," 173–74.
45. Brown et al., "Speaking Our Truth," 176.
46. We Here website, "About Us," https://www.wehere.space/about.

Bibliography

Alburo, Jade, Agnes K. Bradshaw, Ariana E. Santiago, Bonnie Smith and Jennifer Vinopal. "Looking beyond Libraries for Inclusive Recruitment and Retention Practices: Four Successful Approaches." In *Critical Librarianship.* Edited by Samantha Schmehl Hines and David Ketchum, 85–109. Bingley, UK: Emerald Publishing, 2020.

American Bar Association. *ABA Profile of the Legal Profession 2020.* Chicago: American Bar Association, 2020. https://www.americanbar.org/content/dam/aba/administrative/news/2020/07/potlp2020.pdf.

ALISE. *Summary Report: Trends and Key Indicators in Library and Information Science.* Westford, MA: ALISE, 2020. https://www.alise.org/statistical-report.

Bonfield, Brett. "Is the United States Training Too Many Librarians or Too Few? (Part 1)." *In the Library with the Lead Pipe,* September 21, 2011. https://www.inthelibrarywiththeleadpipe.org/2011/is-the-united-states-training-too-many-librarians-or-too-few-part-1/.

Brown, Jennifer, Jennifer A. Ferretti, Sofia Leung, and Marisa Mendez-Brady. "We Here: Speaking Our Truth." *Library Trends* 67 no. 1, (2018): 163–81. https://doi.org/10.1353/lib.2018.0031.

Damasco, Ione T., and Dracine Hodges. "Tenure and Promotion Experiences of Academic
    Librarians of Color." *College and Research Libraries* 73, no. 3 (2012): 279–301. https://crl.acrl.
    org/index.php/crl/article/view/16231/17677.
Drabinski, Emily. "What Is Critical about Critical Librarianship?" Accepted manuscript. CUNY
    Academic Works, City University of New York, 2019. https://academicworks.cuny.edu/
    gc_pubs/537/.
Espinal, Isabel, April M. Hathcock, and Mario Rios. "Dewhitening Librarianship: A Policy
    Proposal for Libraries." In *Knowledge Justice: Disrupting Library and Information Stud-
    ies through Critical Race Theory*. Edited by Sofia Y. Leung and Jorge R. López-McK-
    night, 223–40. Cambridge, MA: MIT Press, 2021. https://direct.mit.edu/books/
    edited-volume/5114/Knowledge-JusticeDisrupting-Library-and.
Frederick, Jennifer K., and Christine Wolff-Eisenberg. *National Movements for Racial
    Justice and Academic Library Leadership: Results from the Ithaka S+R US Library
    Survey 2020*. New York: Ithaka S+R, March 17, 2021. https://sr.ithaka.org/publications/
    national-movements-for-racial-justice-and-academic-library-leadership/.
Gohr, Michelle. "Ethnic and Racial Diversity in Libraries: How White Allies Can Support Argu-
    ments for Decolonization." *Journal of Radical Librarianship* 3 (2017): 42–58. https://core.
    ac.uk/download/pdf/150799786.pdf.
Hathcock, April. "White Librarianship in Blackface: Diversity Initiatives in LIS." *In the Library
    with the Lead Pipe*, October 7, 2015. https://www.inthelibrarywiththeleadpipe.org/2015/
    lis-diversity/.
Kelley, Michael. "Diversity Never Happens: The Story of Minority Hiring Doesn't
    Seem to Change Much." Editorial. *Library Journal*, February 20, 2013. https://www.
    libraryjournal.com/?detailStory=diversity-never-happens-the-story-of-minority-hir-
    ing-doesnt-seem-to-change-much.
Kim, Kyung-Sun, and Sei-Ching Joanna Sin. "Increasing Ethnic Diversity in LIS: Strategies
    Suggested by Librarians of Color." *Library Quarterly* 78, no. 2 (2008): 153–77. https://doi.
    org/10.1086/528887.
Kung, Janice Y., K-Lee Fraser, and Dee Winn. "Diversity Initiatives to Recruit and Retain
    Academic Librarians: A Systematic Review." *College and Research Libraries* 81, no. 1 (2020):
    96–108. https://crl.acrl.org/index.php/crl/article/view/17484/32063.
Lance, Keith Curry. "Racial and Ethnic Diversity of U.S. Library Workers." *American Libraries*
    36, no. 5 (May 2005): 41–43. EBSCOhost.
Montiel-Overall, Patricia, and Sandra Littletree. "Knowledge River: A Case Study of a Library
    and Information Science Program Focusing on Latino and Native American Perspectives."
    Library Trends 59, no. 1–2 (June 2010): 67–87. http://hdl.handle.net/2142/18722.
National Center for Education Statistics. "Table 323.30. Master's Degrees Conferred by Post-
    secondary Institutions, by Race/Ethnicity and Field of Study: 2017–18 and 2018–19." *Digest
    of Education Statistics*. Institute of Education Science, US Department of Education, 2020.
    https://nces.ed.gov/programs/digest/d20/tables/dt20_323.30.asp.
Neely, Teresa Y., and Lorna Peterson. "Achieving Racial and Ethnic Diversity among Academic
    and Research Librarians: The Recruitment, Retention, and Advancement of Librarians
    of Color—A White Paper." *College and Research Libraries News* 68, no. 9 (2007): 562–65.
    https://crln.acrl.org/index.php/crlnews/article/view/7869/7869.
Schonfeld, Roger C., and Liam Sweeney. *Inclusion, Diversity and Equity: Members of
    the Association of Research Libraries: Employee Demographics and Director Perspec-
    tives*. New York: Ithaka S+R, August 30, 2017. https://sr.ithaka.org/publications/
    inclusion-diversity-and-equity-arl/.

Steffen, Nicolle, and Zeth Lietzau. "Retirement, Retention, and Recruitment in Colorado Libraries: The 3Rs Study Revisited." *Library Trends* 58, no. 2 (2009): 179–91. https://muse.jhu.edu/article/375514.

US Bureau of Labor Statistics. "Labor Force Statistics from the Current Population Survey." 2020. https://www.bls.gov/cps/cpsaat11.htm.

Vinopal, Jennifer. "The Quest for Diversity in Library Staffing: From Awareness to Action." *In the Library with the Lead Pipe*, January 13, 2016. https://www.inthelibrarywiththeleadpipe.org/2016/quest-for-diversity/.

We Here website. "About Us." https://www.wehere.space/about.

Biographies

Toni Anaya (she/her/hers) is associate professor and coordinator of user experience at the University of Nebraska–Lincoln Libraries. In this capacity, she provides leadership and oversees the unit charged with communication, public relations, staff development, and user-centered design of library online resources and spaces. Toni also serves as the librarian for the Institute of Ethnic Studies, department of Global Studies, and department of Modern Languages and Literatures. Her current area of research is exploring the recruitment, retention, and leadership development of people of color in the library profession and student success of first-generation and nontraditional students. Elected in 2020, she is a director-at-large of the Association of Research Libraries (ACRL) board of directors.

Scott Ayotte (he/him/his) joined the Haworth Human Resources team in Holland, Michigan as the Manager of Global Diversity, Equity, and Inclusion in 2021. Scott is responsible for leading company-wide diversity, equity, and inclusion strategies, programs, and initiatives that enhance the company's diversity across supplier, designer, dealer, and member populations. In his role, he partners with leaders across the company to identify priorities, develop and enhance the company's DEI strategy, and fosters a globally diverse and inclusively equitable environment. His primary areas of expertise include inclusive talent acquisition, organizational development, talent management, and strategic planning. He has presented on the regional and national level to private and nonprofit organizations on topics relating to innovative talent acquisition, generational diversity and succession planning, leadership development, and healthcare HR management.

Scott is a graduate of Grand Valley State University with a Bachelor of Business Administration in Economics. He earned his Doctor of Jurisprudence from Western Michigan University Cooley Law School, focusing on constitutional and civil rights law.

Kelsa Bartley (she/her/hers) is the education and outreach librarian in the Learning, Research and Clinical Information Services department at the Louis Calder Memorial Library, University of Miami Miller School of Medicine. Her role includes providing education, research services and support, in addition to outreach and promotion of library services and resources. Her interests include diversity, equity, and inclusion in libraries; library marketing and outreach; social media and mobile technology for health information promotion; and library instruction and instructional design. Kelsa graduated with her master of science in information degree from Florida State University in December 2018.

Sarah Beaubien is the associate university librarian, academic at the McLaughlin Library, University of Guelph. In this capacity, she provides leadership and oversight for access services, collections & content, learning & curriculum services, and the library's participation in the quality assurance process.

Sarah earned her MLS from Indiana University. She serves on the executive committee for Reveal Digital and as an advisory board member for Next Generation Library Publishing, a collaborative initiative involving Educopia, California Digital Library, LYRASIS, Confederation of Open Access Repositories (COAR), and Longleaf Services.

Annie Bélanger has been the dean of university libraries at Grand Valley State University since June 2017. In this capacity, she provides strategic leadership for the libraries and their related programmatic areas, leads strategic planning efforts, oversees IDEA efforts, and sponsors GVSU's ACRL Diversity Alliance Diversity Residency program. She is a Grand Valley State University Inclusion Advocate.

Annie is currently a board member of the Midwest Collaborative for Library Services, serving as the chair of the Ownership Linkage Board Committee. She was the chair for the Michigan Academic Libraries Association's Inclusion, Diversity, Equity and Accessibility Taskforce. She is a board member for the Disability Associates of Kent County. Annie is Québéçoise, disabled, and a native French speaker. She received her master's in library and information sciences from Western University in Canada. She is an Association of Research Libraries Leadership Fellow.

Melanie Bopp is the head of access services at George Mason University, having moved recently from Northeastern University, where she worked as an access services librarian. In both positions, she has handled a variety of customer service and information provision challenges, working to create that link between user and information. Melanie received her MLIS from Louisiana State University in 2011. Her primary interests in fifteen years of access services has been both customer service and the student worker experience.

Dr. **Kawanna Bright** is an assistant professor of library science at East Carolina University, where she teaches courses in library administration and management, services to diverse populations, academic librarianship, and collection development. Dr. Bright earned her doctorate in research methods and statistics from the University of Denver in 2018 and her MLIS from the University of Washington iSchool in 2003. Prior to earning her doctorate, Dr. Bright worked as an academic librarian specializing in public services. Her research focuses on assessment in libraries; diversity, equity, and inclusion (DEI) in libraries; the application of research methodology to the study of library and information science; and the importance of the liaison librarianship role in academic libraries.

Erica Bruchko (she/her/hers) is the librarian for African American studies and US history at the Emory University Libraries. She holds a PhD and MA in history from Emory University and a BA in history and anthropology from the University of South Carolina, Columbia. She has served on Emory University Libraries' Diversity, Equity, and Inclusion Committee since 2016, as a past chair of the Outreach subcommittee, and as a member of the Professional Development subcommittee.

Tatiana Bryant (she/her/hers) is the research librarian for digital humanities, history, and African American studies at University of California Irvine Libraries. She holds an MPA in international public and nonprofit administration, management, and policy from New York University, an MSLIS from Pratt Institute, and a BA in history from Hampton University. She has been a SPARC/OpenCon Berlin fellow and a Digital Native American and Indigenous Studies Fellow through the National Endowment for the Humanities Office of Digital Humanities Institute. She teaches courses on Black digital humanities, and her research includes studies on gender identity and performance in library work as well as perceptions of open access publishing among faculty who identify as Black, Indigenous, or people of color.

Kimberley Bugg, PhD is the associate library director at AUC Woodruff Library in Atlanta, Georgia. Previously, she was the chief of the researcher and reference services at the Library of Congress. Her research interests include organizational culture and library employee health and wellness. She holds a PhD in library science from Simmons College in Boston.

Jonathan Cain (he/him/his) is the associate university librarian for research and learning at Columbia University. He is passionate about making libraries and information centers more collaborative, equitable, and inclusive for learners and knowledge workers.

He holds an MSLIS from Pratt Institute, an MA in Africana studies from New York University, and a BS in anthropology from the College of Charleston. He is a 2020–2021 ARL Leadership and Career Development Program Fellow. Cain believes libraries play a prominent role in higher education and society. His research centers on understanding and interrogating the inequity in data and technology cultures and the role of libraries as organizations for the public good, privacy in education, and social justice and equity.

Camille Callison (she, her) is a member of the Tahltan Nation, and was the Indigenous Strategies Librarian at the University of Manitoba. She is now the University Librarian at the University of the Fraser Valley and is working toward a PhD in anthropology. She is a passionate cultural activist who served as the chair of the Indigenous Matters Section and as a member of the Cultural Heritage Advisory Committee, now the chair of Professional Division H for the International Federation of Library Association. She is a board member of the Canadian Research Knowledge Network and a working group member of the IEEE P2890 Recommended Practice for Provenance of Indigenous Peoples' Data. She is committed to creating meaningful change in cultural memory professions and has served locally, nationally, and internationally to advance matters related to Indigenous peoples as well as equity, diversity, and inclusivity.

May Chan (she/her) is a second-generation Chinese-Canadian settler, whose parents grew up in colonial Hong Kong and eventually immigrated to Canada.

Her experience as a Canadian is shaped by her immigrant roots and has only begun in recent years reflecting on the impact of colonial processes such as immigration on Indigenous peoples. Given her privileges as a settler and as Head of Metadata Services at University of Toronto Libraries, she continues to grapple with the tension between being complicit in colonial oppression and being active in supporting reconciliation.

Meghan Cook (she/her/hers) is a Postdoctoral Fellow at Purdue Northwest's Center for Faculty Excellence. She worked as a coordinator of library operations at the University of South Florida Libraries. Her main role was the subject expert for the School of Geosciences Research Platform Team. Her job was to support the graduate students and faculty in the School of Geosciences with their research and scholarly needs. She graduated in spring 2021 with her PhD in geology from the USF School of Geosciences, specializing in geoscience education. Her dissertation work focused on ways to positively impact diversity, equity, and inclusion in the geosciences by understanding the affective impact of field trips on students. Meghan also taught earth science/geology at nearby community and state colleges and is in pursuit of a MLIS degree.

Melissa DeSantis (she/her/hers) is the director of the Strauss Health Sciences Library at the University of Colorado Anschutz Medical Campus. Her research interests include diversity, equity, and inclusion in libraries; developing library staff; and the relationships between academic health sciences libraries and affiliated health care systems. Melissa earned her MLIS from UCLA.

Vanjury "V" Dozier is an education librarian and assistant professor at the University of San Diego, in San Diego, California. She is the embedded librarian to the School of Leadership and Educational Sciences (SOLES), where she facilitates library instruction sessions and research support workshops and consultations, and curates a resource collection designed to support SOLES's interdisciplinary teaching and research needs, with an emphasis on needs of BIPOC and other underrepresented faculty, staff, and students. V's research interests include critical librarianship and pedagogy, the experiences of BIPOC and other marginalized populations in academic libraries, and graphic novels and comics in educational settings. She earned degrees from Tuskegee University (BA—English), Duke University (MAT—secondary English education), and the University of Alabama (MLIS). In addition to serving as a member of local, regional, and national library committees and organizations, V is a dedicated member of Zeta Phi Beta Sorority, Incorporated.

Nik Dragovic (he/him/his) is a product manager with Emory Libraries' Digital Product Strategy unit and also serves as subject selector for LGBTQ studies and library science. He joined the Diversity and Inclusion Working Group at its inception.

Jina DuVernay (she/her/hers) is the collection development archivist for African American collections at the Stuart A. Rose Manuscript, Archives, and Rare Book Library at Emory University, where she curates acquisitions for the African American collecting area. She holds an MLIS from the University of Alabama and is a member of the Emory Libraries DEI Professional Development sub-committee. DuVernay, a 2018 ALA Emerging Leader and 2018–2020 BCALA board member, serves on a number of professional committees, including the ALA Committee on Diversity.

Sandra Aya Enimil (she/her) is the copyright librarian and contracting specialist at Yale University Library. At Yale, Sandra is the chair of the License Review Team and provides consultation on licenses of all types for the library. Sandra also provides information and resources on using copyrighted materials and assists creators in protecting their own copyright. Sandra collaborates with individuals and departments within the library and across campus. She has given numerous presentations on various aspects of copyright. Prior to this role, she was the copyright services librarian at Ohio State University Libraries. Sandra is committed to diversity, equity, and inclusion (DEI) and is interested in the intersection of DEI and intellectual property. Sandra earned her law and MSLIS degrees from the University of Illinois at Urbana-Champaign. Sandra has BAs in political science and psychology from the University of Michigan and an MA in international relations from the University of Ghana.

Adebola Fabiku is the department head, access services at North Carolina State University Libraries in Raleigh, North Carolina. In this role, she provides leadership and management for the Access Services department, which connects users with experts, collections, technology, and spaces. The department is comprised of the Ask Us and Resource Sharing services. She is passionate about researching and utilizing various methods to advocate, retain, and motivate BIPOC library staff and student workers. She enjoys planning events for student workers, such as pizza and cupcake crawls, as well as Zumba Fridays in the ILL office. Adebola currently serves as the chair-elect of ALA's RUSA (Reference and User Services Association) STARS (Sharing and Transforming Access to Resources Section) executive committee.

Adebola obtained her MSLIS from the University of Illinois at Urbana-Champaign as well as a BS in journalism from the same institution.

Lyle Ford (he/him) is Métis and is the Indigenous Strategies Librarian, and a liaison librarian at the University of Manitoba, with responsibility for Native studies. He is a past member of the Canadian Federation of Library Associations' Indigenous Matters Committee and is a current member of the Indigenous Connect Committee at the University of Manitoba. A librarian since 1995, he strives to bring Indigenous matters forward in library planning and activities.

Elizabeth Galoozis (she/her) is head of information literacy and student engagement at the Claremont Colleges Library. Her research interests include critical information literacy, feminist pedagogy, and identity in the library workplace. Her work has appeared in *Library Quarterly, In the Library with the Lead Pipe*, Library Juice Press, and at ACRL and LOEX conferences.

Melissa Hackman (she/her/hers) is the librarian for sociology, African studies, and development studies at the Emory University Libraries. She holds a PhD in anthropology from the University of California, Santa Cruz, a master of theological studies from Harvard Divinity School, and a BA from Temple University in women's studies. She is a member of the Emory Libraries DEI Committee and is the chair of the Emory Libraries DEI Committee's Professional Development subcommittee.

Ryan Harris (he/him/his) is head of research and instructional services for the J. Murrey Atkins Library, University of North Carolina, Charlotte. He has served in this role since 2017. His research interests include strategic planning and development of mission, vision values, systematic reviews, and design thinking in librarianship. He earned his MLIS from Louisiana State University.

Oy Lein Jace Harrison (she/her) is a Black, Chinese, and Jamaican woman who works and lives on the traditional territories of the Seneca, the Huron-Wendat and Mississauga of the Credit First Nation. As both a Black woman and a person of colour, Oy Lein has a complex relationship with the land and does not identify as a settler. Her ancestors' bodies were stolen and coerced from their Indigenous lands to build the violent, anti-Black, settler-colonial structures that continue to oppress her communities. In her efforts to live in right relationship with Indigenous lands, and the Indigenous Nations that are their caretakers, Oy Lein uses the intention of her name as a guiding principle: Oy Lein, meaning precious love, and Jace, meaning created. Oy Lein seeks to create the love that she holds precious in her communities for other racialized and oppressed communities. She currently works as an Impact Analyst for the Indigenous Innovation Initiative at Grand Challenges Canada.

Don Jason (he/him/his) serves as the health informationist for the University of Cincinnati's (UC) Donald C. Harrison Health Sciences Library. Prior to his time at UC, Don completed the National Library of Medicine's Associate Fellowship Program. Don earned two graduate degrees from Kent State University. These degrees are an MLIS and an MS in information architecture knowledge management with a focus in health informatics. His research interests include pedagogy and learning outcomes for clinical care staff as well as diversity, equity, and inclusion in libraries.

Latanya Jenkins (she/her) was the government information and African American studies librarian at Temple University Libraries. Ms. Jenkins received her master of science in library science and information science from Drexel University and her BA in anthropology and English from Franklin and Marshall College. Ms. Jenkins's many awards, presentations, and service to the field include the Margaret T. Lane/Virginia F. Saunders Memorial Research Award from the Government Documents Round Table for the coauthored book *Government Information Essentials* (2019); Temple University Library Information Literacy Cross-Team grants for 2016 and 2020; work at the Diversity and Outreach Fair at the American Library Association Annual Conference (2012); ALA Emerging Leader (2008); and "Project to Recruit the Next Generation of Librarians Wrap-up Talk" at the University of Notre Dame (2007).

Shannon Jones (she/her/hers) is director of libraries and professor for the Medical University of South Carolina, where she has worked since 2014. Shannon is the coeditor of *Diversity and Inclusion in Libraries: A Call to Action and Strategies*. Her research interests include staff recruitment, retention, and reward; diversity, equity, and inclusion in libraries; and leadership in academic health sciences libraries. She earned her MLS from North Carolina Central University and an MEd in adult learning from Virginia Commonwealth University. She is currently pursuing an EdD in educational leadership at Charleston Southern University.

Katherine Kapsidelis (she/her/hers) is a research and instruction librarian at the University of California, Los Angeles, where she supports undergraduate teaching and learning. Previously, she taught primary source literacy workshops that emphasized a hands-on approach to learning about rare books and archival materials at the University of Southern California. Katherine holds an MSIS from the University of Texas at Austin.

Corliss Lee (she/her/hers) is the American cultures librarian at the UC Berkeley Library as well as the liaison to the American studies, college writing, and ethnic studies departments and a member of the Instruction Services division. Her interests include diversity, equity, and inclusion in libraries; disinformation literacy; and empowering undergraduates through information literacy. She is a two-time graduate of UC Berkeley (BA, English, and MLIS). Corliss was awarded the Distinguished Librarian Award by the Librarians Association of the University of California, Berkeley, in 2020.

Barbara Lewis (she/her/hers) is digital learning librarian at the University of South Florida Tampa Library and the library liaison to the departments of anthropology, communication, history, humanities and cultural studies, women's and gender studies, and world languages and the Zimmerman School of Advertising and Mass Communications at the University of South Florida. In addition to research and instruction activities, she works to inform and educate students and faculty about the many digital and multimedia options available to complement, supplement, or replace analog course assignments with the goal of helping students develop digital and media literacy and skills of value to future employers.

Kenneth D. Litwak (he/him/his) is the reference and instructional services librarian for Gateway Seminary Library in Ontario, California. His interests include diversity, equity, and inclusion in academic libraries, especially for librarians with disabilities; accessibility; instruction; instructional design; collection development; and library marketing.

Kenneth's MLIS is from San José State University (2009). He currently serves in the Diversity, Equity, and Inclusion committee of the American Theological Library Association and has participated in programming for the Diversity in Academic Libraries interest group of California Academic and Research Libraries.

Brian Lym has been an academic library leader in New York and California. He has served as dean of libraries and chief librarian at Hunter College, dean of university libraries at Adelphi University, and director of library services at Napa Valley College. His career began as a student library employee at the University of California, Berkeley, where he earned his MLIS, MS (wildland resource science), and BA (humanities) degrees. Having retired from academic librarianship, Brian is supporting and advancing inclusivity, equity, and diversity efforts in the Sonoma County Library system where he serves as an adult services librarian.

Charlene Maxey-Harris (she/her/hers) is associate professor and associate dean for collections and resource management at the University of Nebraska–Lincoln Libraries. Formerly, as the diversity librarian, she developed and managed diversity initiatives over the last fifteen years at the University of Nebraska, improving work climate to be more welcoming and inclusive to all individuals, but especially to underrepresented groups, and increased diversity of the faculty. Ms. Maxey-Harris chairs the Libraries Diversity Committee and was past chair of the Nebraska Library Association Diversity Committee. Her research focuses on diversity and multicultural issues in academic libraries and library instruction for first-generation college students. In 2017 and 2010, Maxey-Harris compiled a study of diversity plans and programs in academic libraries, published by the Association of Research Libraries. In addition, she is a graduate of the ARL Leadership and Career Development Program 2012.

Jamie Lee Morin (she/her/hers) is Métis and currently is a Digital Content Lead at Toronto Public Library. She acknowledges her privilege as a white-passing

Indigenous woman, and endeavours to use her privilege to help create more spaces for Indigenous communities and other communities in solidarity. She does this in her current role by amplifying Indigenous voices and worldviews represented in various formats on the library's website.

Saira Raza (she/her/hers) is a business librarian at Emory University's Goizueta Business Library. She holds an MSLS from University of North Texas, an MPS in Africana studies from Cornell University, and a BA in international studies from Wells College. She has served as a cochair of Emory Libraries DEI Committee since its start as a working group in 2016, witnessing the committee's sustained growth over the years to nearly thirty highly engaged volunteer members. Prior to working at Emory, Saira worked as a business librarian at Lehman Brothers (now Barclays) and King and Spalding. Saira's interests are in decolonizing libraries and educating future leaders to harness the power of good research skills to make informed, ethical, and equitable decisions.

Renna Tuten Redd (she/her/hers) is the interlibrary loan librarian at Clemson University Libraries, where she oversees a team of five who perform all document delivery and resource sharing duties. She holds an MLS from the University of South Carolina, an MA in Southern studies from the University of Mississippi, and a BA in art history from the University of Georgia. She has served as cochair of the Clemson University Libraries Diversity Plan Working Group, which created a diversity strategic plan for the libraries, and has acted as liaison to the Clemson University President's Council on Diversity and Inclusion.

Dede Rios (she/her/hers) is the director of optometric and clinical library services at the University of the Incarnate Word, Rosenberg School of Optometry, and has served as a director since 2014. Her research interests include leadership in higher education; diversity, equity, and inclusion; student engagement; and scholarly communication. She earned her MS in library science from the University of North Texas and a PhD in education with a specialization in leadership for higher education from Capella University.

Hannah Rutledge (she/her/hers) is the director of the Biomedical Library at the University of Pennsylvania. Previously, she served as the head of clinical informationist services at Emory University Libraries and was active in its DEI committee from inception through May 2020. She served as co-chair and was a member of the Education and Professional Development subcommittees. Her research interests include the history of libraries, history of medicine, information behavior and access, leadership, health inequities, and diversity, equity, and inclusion in all areas of life. She earned her PhD in information science and MLIS from the University of North Texas and a BA in forensic anthropology from Millsaps College in Jackson, Mississippi.

Kenneth Schlesinger has served as chief librarian at Lehman College since 2007. Previously he was director of media services at LaGuardia Community College and worked in the archival collections of Thirteen/WNET public television and Time Inc. He was board president of Independent Media Arts Preservation and served as president of the Theatre Library Association. In 2018, the Theatre Library Association honored him with the Louis Rachow Performing Arts Librarianship Distinguished Service Award. He received two Fulbright Senior Specialist Grants to contribute to international library projects: international copyright and strategic planning in Vietnam in 2005, and designing a library and archival strategic plan for the Steve Biko Centre in South Africa in 2011. Mr. Schlesinger has an MLS from Pratt Institute's School of Information, an MFA in dramaturgy and dramatic criticism from Yale School of Drama, and a BA in dramatic art from University of California, Berkeley.

Alydia Sims (she/her/hers), MAED, is the library manager of the Standards Management and Assessment team in Clemson University Libraries' Technical Services unit. She has served on the CU Library Diversity Working Group and Diversity Committee. She is also an IDI, LLC, Qualified Administrator (Intercultural Development Inventory). In these roles, she produces and maintains name authority control records and cataloging policies and procedures for the university library system and promotes DEI initiatives at the library. She is co-leader of Clemson University Libraries' participation in Leading the Charge: Advancing the Recruitment, Retention and Inclusion of People of Color within the Library and Information Science Field.

Sally Stieglitz, JD, MSLS (she/her/hers), is communications and Outreach oordinator, liaison to academic, hospital, and special libraries, at Long Island Library Resources Council (LILRC) in Bellport, New York. Previous positions included digital learning and instruction librarian, Adelphi University Libraries, and visiting assistant librarian, Stony Brook University Libraries. Her scholarship has appeared in *Issues in Science and Technology Librarianship, Journal of the Medical Library Association, RBM: A Journal of Rare Books, Manuscripts, and Cultural Heritage,* and *Engaged Scholar Journal: Community-Engaged Research, Teaching, and Learning.*

Professor **Elizabeth L. Sweet** (she/her/ella) focuses on planning theory and qualitative research methodologies, and teaches in the departments of urban planning and community development and Africana studies at the University of Massachusetts Boston. She engages in collaborative community economic development, specifically the links between economies, violence, and identities. Using feminist, anti-racist, and decolonial frameworks, her work in US Native, Black, Latino, and Latin American communities has led to long-term collaborations and inclusive projects that push the boundaries of planning theory and methods while at the same time provides practical planning interventions. She has proposed the use of body-map storytelling and community mapping as innovative ways to cocreate data and strategies with communities on a wide range of issues and urban problems. Sweet has also been very active in promoting diversity, equity, and inclusion within universities through organizing events and student recruitment and publishing both research and teaching articles on the same.

Tomaro Taylor is head of special collections at the University of South Florida Libraries Tampa. Tomaro's research interests include ethnography, documentation, special collections and archives management, and popular culture in the United States. A librarian and certified archivist, Tomaro has master's degrees in library and information science and American studies.

Matt Torrence (he/him/his) serves as the librarian for the Geosciences and Marine Science Research Platform Teams at the University of South Florida Libraries in Tampa. Along with the rest of the library professionals and subject specialists, he provides information expertise to students and faculty, with a special focus on the research, impact, and metrics needs of the clients in a range of topics related to the sciences. He works extensively in evaluating the resource requirements of these and other subject areas to enhance and improve library collections and services. His research focuses on public services, faculty and library collaboration, and research services to an academic library community.

Amy Tureen (she/her/hers) is the head, library liaison program, at the University of Nevada, Las Vegas, where she oversees a large, diverse team based in three different libraries. She is passionate about making libraries more inclusive spaces for both students and employees and has worked extensively to change and adapt hiring processes to make the employee search process more equitable. Her research focuses on the many intersections of wellness, diversity, and leadership. Amy holds an MLIS from Drexel University, an MA in gender in cultural studies from Simmons University (then College), and a BA from Scripps College in English literature.

LaTesha Velez (she/her/hers) is an assistant professor in the University of North Carolina, Greensboro, LIS department. After working in libraries off and on since 1994, Dr. Velez is now focused on teaching new professionals to thrive in a growingly diverse and globalized field. She received her doctorate from the University of Illinois at Urbana-Champaign iSchool. Dr. Velez's research critically examines and contextualizes information in society and the role of information institutions in society. Her research interests include EDI issues in LIS, critical LIS history, and critical examinations of information in society.

Dr. **Michele A. L. Villagran** (she/her/hers) is an accomplished educator, innovative speaker, entrepreneur, consultant, cultural intelligence, and diversity and inclusion expert with over twenty-seven years of experience in the public and private sectors. She is an assistant professor with the San José State University School of Information and serves as CEO of CulturalCo, LLC. Dr. Villagran's research focuses on diversity and social justice in library and information science and cultural intelligence phenomena within libraries.

Dr. Villagran earned her doctorate of education in organizational leadership, with her dissertation focusing on cultural intelligence, in 2015 with Pepperdine University. She also completed her master of dispute resolution degree and certificate of dispute resolution with Pepperdine. At the University of North Texas, Dr. Villagran completed her MLS degree in legal informatics and her MBA in strategic management.

Tara Weekes (she/her/hers) is the library manager of Clemson University's Education Media Center and Digital Media Learning Lab. She earned her MLIS degree from Valdosta State University in 2017 and also has a master's degree in human resources received from Western Carolina University in 2010. Much of her professional career has been in contribution to equity, diversity, inclusion, and anti-racism efforts, including serving as a founding member of Western Carolina University's Council on Diversity and Inclusion and as co-chair of Clemson University Libraries' Diversity Plan Working Group as well as Clemson University's College of Education Community and Diversity Committee. She was also part of the inaugural cohort to earn Clemson University's Strategic Inclusive Excellence Certificate and has published and presented about her EDI work in the *Journal of Library Administration* and at various national, regional, and state conferences, including ACRL, SELA, SCLA, and SC LIBRIS.

Desmond Wong (he/him) is the outreach librarian at the University of Toronto Libraries. He is a Chinese settler who lives and works on the Lands of the Mississauga of the Credit River First Nation, and the Wendat, Haudenosaunee, and Anishinaabe Nations. As a librarian, he is committed to justice on these Lands for Black and Indigenous peoples and fights in solidarity for the recognition of Indigenous Nationhood, Sovereignties, and stewardship in the occupying Settler Colonial state. He believes in a librarianship practice of solidarity, rooted in an ethic of care, towards transformation, coalition building, and collective liberation.